Language in Education

Morgan

The Open University
Faculty of Educational Studies

The following members of the Language and Learning
Course Team were responsible for the compilation of this reader:

A. Cashdan (Chairman)

G. M. Esland

Elizabeth Grugeon

A. E. Harris

V. J. Lee

J. Oates

D. C. Stringer

Other members of the Course Team include:

Christine Gravell

W. Prescott

G. Pritchard

D. M. Seligman

Editors: *A. Cashdan and Elizabeth Grugeon*

Language in Education
A source book

Prepared by the
Language and Learning Course Team
at the Open University

Routledge & Kegan Paul
London, Boston and Henley

First published 1972
by Routledge & Kegan Paul Ltd
39 Store Street
London WC1E 7DD,
Broadway House, Newtown Road
Henley-on-Thames
Oxon RG9 1EN and
9 Park Street,
Boston, Mass. 02108, U.S.A.
Reprinted 1974, 1975, 1977 and 1979
Printed in Great Britain by
Lowe & Brydone Printers Ltd,
Thetford, Norfolk

ISBN 0 7100 7430 1 (c)
ISBN 0 7100 7431 X (p)

Contents

Acknowledgments

The Open University and the publishers would like to thank the following for permission to reproduce copyright material. All possible care has been taken to trace ownership of the selections included and to make full acknowledgment for their use.

Reading

1　© Heinemann Educational Books Ltd, 1968.

2　© 1961, The Aristotelian Society.

3　© R. H. Robins, 1971.

4/5　© Randolph Quirk and Longman, 1968.

6　© Linguistic Circle of New York Inc., 1959.

7　Reproduced by permission of the American Anthropological Association.

8　Copyright © 1963 by the Estate of C. Wright Mills. Reprinted by permission of Oxford University Press, Inc.

9　Copyright © 1966 by Peter L. Berger and Thomas Luckmann. Reprinted by permission of Doubleday & Company Inc. and The Penguin Press.

10　Copyright © 1959 by The Free Press, A Corporation.

11　Reproduced by permission of the American Anthropological Association.

12　Reprinted by permission of *Social Research*.

13　© Mouton Publishers, 1968.

14　By permission of the Editors of the *Educational Review*.

15　© Routledge & Kegan Paul, 1971.

16　Reprinted by permission of the *Journal of Curriculum Studies*, Collins, and the author.

17　© Methuen & Co. Ltd, 1967.

18　Copyright © Communications/Research/Machines Inc., 1969.

19　Copyright © 1964 by the President and Fellows of Harvard College.

20　© *Science Journal*, 1966.

21　© Linguistic Circle of New York, 1959.

22　Copyright © 1969 by Oxford University Press, Inc. Reprinted by permission.

23　Copyright 1946 by the American Psychological Association and reproduced by permission.

24　Copyright © 1965 The Society for Research in Child Development, Inc.

25　Copyright © 1969 The Society for Research in Child Development, Inc.

26　Copyright © 1970 by the President and Fellows of Harvard College.

27　Copyright 1969 Georgetown University Press, Washington D.C.

28　This article first appeared in *New Society*, the weekly review of the social sciences, 128 Long Acre, London W.C.2.

29　By permission of the Clarendon Press, Oxford.

30　By permission of the *Journal of the History of Ideas*.

31　By permission of the author and the Royal Institute of Philosophy.

32　By permission of the author and Cambridge University Press.

33　By permission of the Editors of the *Educational Review*.

Introduction

This book of readings has been compiled for the use of Open University students following the second level course *Language and Learning* in the Faculty of Educational Studies. As such, it does not stand on its own. Open University students will also be reading prescribed texts (a list of which is given at the end of this book) and following a guided course of study and activity, including radio and television components and the analysis of specially collected language samples.

Nevertheless, in producing this source book we have kept in mind a much larger group of readers who are interested in language in the educational context. Language is a field in which academic interest has increased enormously in the last few years—and that from a multiplicity of different disciplinary standpoints. So it is not surprising that there are many useful collections of readings available already, including, for example, those edited by Oldfield and Marshall (1968), John Lyons (1970) and Pier Paolo Giglioli (1972). Most such collections, however, look at language through the eyes of a particular discipline, be it psychology, linguistics, or sociology. In our case, we are considering language as an applied problem area in a particular context and draw for our purpose on what seems most relevant and usable from all these disciplines and others besides.

Our central concern is with language and learning. We want to examine the uses of language and its limitations as a tool for learning. What sort of tool is it, how is it acquired, how are its meanings determined by the social context and how does the user himself affect its meanings? How is communication affected by the varieties of language found in a community, by the differing statuses and relationships of speakers, and whose language (if anyone's) may properly be considered inadequate? How is language study relevant to the development of mature judgment and proper communication in value areas and in considering (and producing) literature? And what philosophical questions are raised by our whole study of language?

To consider questions such as these we have brought together a course team which includes people with backgrounds in relevant areas of philosophy, psychology, sociology and linguistics, all of whom have in addition more applied experience in school and higher educational teaching. But we have not chosen to use this fund of expertise to produce a fused-together consensual course—or book. Rather, we have chosen to compare and contrast, to bring out our differences in approach and perspective and to offer them for mutual examination. The course which has resulted is one which has been as stimulating and demanding an experience for its constructors as we hope it will prove for its students.

It will be obvious, then, that the readings included in this book have been selected on a number of criteria. These include their representativeness and accessibility in terms of the main discipline areas involved in the course, their relevance to learning and education generally as well as their suitability for the students we have in mind, taking particular account of the length and level of the *Language and Learning* course.

The readings have been chosen, then, as appropriate starting points for undergraduates who are not specialists in any of the relevant areas, but who have a developed and informed interest in education and are prepared to look carefully at language from a variety of perspectives and levels ranging from the inductive and highly applied to the experimental and the purely theoretical. We have included, wherever relevant, extracts from the major thinkers and experimenters in the different fields and have tried to present extracts which are long enough to allow the writer to speak for himself and develop his own argument with the absolute minimum of editorial intervention between him and the reader.

With one or two exceptions, the order of the Reader sections follows that of the Open University course, in a sequence which we would justify pedagogically rather than in terms of a strict conceptual ordering, though there is inevitably something of this also.

We start with two papers by philosophers with an interest in language. John Wilson raises some deceptively simple questions which have considerable relevance to many later sections and Ryle and Findlay grapple with the problems of language usage. It seemed logical to place these papers at the beginning of the book, though in fact Open University students will be asked to consider them after they have worked through most of the course, and can then make use of the philosophical papers in asking further questions about the material they have been studying. Many other readers may like to consider following this alternative order.

Section I is concerned with the linguist's approach, with looking at language systems and their use in social life. So its emphasis is not highly theoretical. From Robins' paper onwards we are examining language as a human activity and not simply as a codified scheme of noises. Section II, though more theoretical, takes us from the social use of language right into the heart of the sociological perspective. The sociologist's contribution is twofold. He insists on seeing language as both a mediator of the social system to the individual and as a means of preserving and publicising human knowledge. In Section III we examine a specific question of concern to psychologists, sociologists and linguists—perhaps the psycholinguistic contribution is the dominant one, as Bernstein suggests—are there different language codes, how are they learned and employed and how far may they truly be claimed to be distinct from each other?

Section IV, though short, is of particularly central significance in the Reader. It picks up many of the sociologist's concepts and concerns and applies them in the classroom, while looking forward at the same time to the psychological approach which constitutes Section V. Here we look first at language acquisition and employment, starting from Chomsky's analysis and then moving to the classic studies of Brown and Bellugi. Language in thinking is here examined, first from the Soviet point of view then via the Geneva school to Bruner's work, which many see as the best synthesis yet achieved in this field.

Section VI is frankly controversial; hence the question mark in its title. We start with two expositions of the psychological view and then challenge these from a sociological standpoint. But although language may well be crucial in learning, not even the psychologist would claim that a breakthrough in language teaching would solve even all of our educational problems. So the section closes with Bernstein's paper in which he raises the broader questions of social policy and planning.

In Section VII the readings selected provide a theoretical basis for the examination of the development of moral, political and aesthetic judgment and of both the inhibiting and facilitating roles which language can play in these contexts. Similarly, Section VIII examines the language of literature and in particular the role of the onlooker, as a background to the whole question of literature study and personal expression in school and college.

Finally, it seems worth pointing out that though this is a collection of readings on language in a wide variety of contexts, language does not always occupy the centre of the stage for each of the writers. For in considering language we are always raising questions which, however they permeate the topic, have also an independent existence: questions which range from the philosopher's preoccupations with meaning or the psychologist's with early learning to the much larger issues of the structure and control of our whole social system.

Asher Cashdan

References

Language, ed. R. C. Oldfield and J. C. Marshall, Penguin (1968).
New Horizons in Linguistics, ed. John Lyons, Penguin (1970).

Language and Social Context, ed. Pier Paolo Giglioli, Penguin (1972).

1   Language and society

John Wilson

One significant difference—perhaps ultimately the most significant—between man and the other animals is that man is psychologically and sociologically more flexible than they. This mental flexibility can be expressed in various ways. We can say that animals are tied down to a comparatively rigid system of behaviour-patterns and instincts and responses to stimuli, whereas man has free choice and intelligence; or we can say that animals are unconscious of what they are doing, whereas man is conscious and aware; or we can say that animals use only their natural resources, whereas man is capable of using tools. But one of the most illuminating ways of putting the point is to say that man alone is capable of controlling his environment and himself by means of language-techniques.

A language, in the strict sense, is an artificial and consciously-organized method of control by the use of symbols or conventions, which involves the notion of meaning. The behaviour of animals satisfies some of these criteria, but not all: thus beavers control their environment artificially, but not by the use of symbols, and rooks communicate (in some sense) to each other by making various sounds, but this is not a consciously-organized language. None of the actions or signs of animals have meaning in the sense that they are consciously agreed and understood as symbols; and this, we might say, is why the so-called languages of animals are inflexible, or not really languages at all.

Without going too deeply into the matter, we can see that there are various senses of 'meaning', as of 'communications', which do not satisfy these conditions. Thus, if a man licks his lips, it is correct to say that this 'means' he is hungry; dark clouds 'mean', or are signs of, rain; a handshake 'means' that someone wants to be friends; a husband's bad temper over the breakfast table may 'mean' lack of sexual satisfaction on the previous night; and so forth. None of these, however, are agreed and artificial symbols, consciously used, and none of them are cases of communi-

Source: John Wilson, *Philosophy*, Heinemann (1968), 96–106.

cation in this narrow sense. Thus, to take a further example, a kiss may be a communication in the sense that the people who kiss react on each other in certain ways, have certain feelings and intentions, etc., and also no doubt in the sense that they both 'share the same feeling' (though it is not clear what this means exactly). But a kiss need not be a communication in the narrow sense, for it may not be used or understood as a symbol; it may be just a kiss.

The whole point of having a language, of course, is precisely that it *is* artificial and can therefore give us more control than less flexible natural methods. This becomes most obvious if we consider, say, trying to solve a problem about measuring water by pouring it into different jugs of different capacities. Here the 'natural' method is to deal directly with actual jugs and actual water; but this is cumbersome and tedious, and the artificial method of using pencil and paper and playing around with figures is more efficient. Here we use, in a simple or advanced form, a *notation*, and the importance of notation in mathematics is well known. Again, we could consider the invention and development of maps. Like every other language, maps act as an artificial intermediary between ourselves and the real world; they are one method of reducing the real world to manageable proportions, of extracting and identifying certain features of the real world, inventing artificial signs for them and representing them in a convenient form. The more informative and useful the map, the more artificial and the less naturalistic it tends to be; dragons and cherubs puffing their cheeks tend to disappear, to be replaced by the artificialities of contour lines and conventional signs of other sorts. We can think also of the greater degree of abstraction reached by advanced as against primitive languages, and of modern physics as against Newtonian physics; in both these cases the language becomes less like a simple representation of the outside world, in terms of objects we can picture, and more like a set of useful symbols, no one of which necessarily 'stands for' a 'thing' in the world, in the sense in which proper names 'stand for' the things or people to which they refer.

The usefulness of increased artificiality is apparent in at least two different ways. First, it allows greater discrimination and a higher degree of specification. Thus, if we remove the cheek-puffing cherubs, we leave room for symbols indicating the strength, duration and direction of winds; and by inventing artificial signs like ¼ or ¾ we allow ourselves to specify more than we can specify by the use of whole numbers alone. Secondly, it allows increased possibility of generalization and classification: thus by moving from arithmetic to algebra, from 1, 2 and 3 to x, y and z, we can generalize about numbers more freely, and by inventing words like 'object' and 'symmetry' we can say things that we could not otherwise say, not at least without considerable difficulty. Increased control over our environment, or new and creative thinking, is not only always accompanied by a new terminology; in an important sense the discovery of a new terminology is part of the invention and the increased control. Anyone who invents something or discovers something thereby makes sense, as it were, of a part of our environment which did not make sense before: he identifies its features, names them, maps them, turns them from meaninglessness into language. He brings them under conscious control, enables us to keep tabs on them.

Any improvement of control is thus an improvement in consciousness, and any improvement in consciousness is an improvement in language. The process of thinking is itself linguistic or symbolic; it is a scaled-down version of acting or doing something, in which we move small quantities of energy around on a map in order to see the probable outcome of various courses of action. Many psychologists have put this by saying that our thinking should be rational or realistic rather than 'autistic' (self-centred) or magical, and this is to say that the symbols and meaning of our thoughts should connect closely with reality, and not be merely the magical projections of our own unconscious fears and desires. If we are masters of our own symbols, using them artificially to suit our own convenience, we act freely; if we become dominated or bewitched by them, we act and think compulsively. The processes of philosophical or psychological analysis, and to a great extent of other ways of thinking also, are designed to free us from bewitchment; to make what is unconscious conscious; to give us a clearly-understood language in which to solve our problems. Thus a neurotic problem in psycho-analysis, or a problem in philosophy, is precisely a problem whose chief difficulty consists in our own unawareness of what we are saying, in a lack of self-consciousness about language. The neurotic *says* things, but plainly he does not (in one sense) *mean* them; there is a fatal gap between the language he uses consciously and the unconscious features of his personality which he is unable to identify and express in linguistic form, and his cure consists precisely in giving him a language which will enable him to incorporate those features into his conscious mind and hence to handle them in whatever way he chooses. It is a matter of getting the unconscious features to *own up*, as it were. So too in philosophical problems: by linguistic analysis we have to bring whatever is at the back of our minds to the front, so as to bring it under the conscious control of a language.

We could put this point another way by saying that we exercise control over ourselves and our environment in so far as *we* give meaning to features in the world, rather than simply allowing these features to 'mean' things to us—or as we ought rather to say, allowing them to act on us as inevitable stimuli. Animals do not handle reality at all; they merely react to it. Men can handle it, but only by the medium of language. Belief in features of the environment or of ourselves that have some kind of independent or magical power or existence—such as belief in fairies or demons, in metaphysical or moral absolutes ('Truth', 'Beauty', etc.) which are supposed to have independent existence, and many others—can thus be regarded as a failure of language. In these cases there is a sense in which *we* give meaning to these features: that is, we invest them with magical properties and powers. But this is an unconsciously-inspired process: the features act upon our unconscious minds, which in turn project parts of themselves upon the features. Thus we make our gods, our lovers and even some objects in the physical world in the image of our own minds. We do not *choose* meanings for them, in the same sense that we choose, for instance, that a certain stone shall be the corner-stone of a building. Stones—unless you are still in the stage of primitive religion—are not magic: they do not mean things on their own account.

Greater control and consciousness mean greater flexibility and greater freedom. We have achieved a large measure of this flexibility and freedom in the case of the physical world; we have divested it of magic and evolved the language of scientific method to deal with it. But in the case of the inner psychological world—the world of politics, religion, and personal relationship—we are still slaves. Our actions, feelings and talk are compulsive and without conscious meaning; we serve them rather than vice versa. Thus we lament the lack of freedom in modern states, and the lack of co-operation and fellow-feeling in modern society; we lament the lack of understanding between human individuals, the tragedies of failure in communication, the apparent or real conflicts of desires between various parties, and so on. Rather than pin our faith on whatever miracle-working spirit happens to be fashionable, we need to evolve languages for these unsatisfactory situations. It at once becomes obvious that the development of a language involves a practical and down-to-earth attitude, together with a great deal of hard work. We need to regard it as essentially like determining the rules for a game or the rules of procedure in a law-court. To get good results—to play the game enjoyably, to dispense justice fairly—we do not need any very exciting qualities of personality. We need only to experiment sensibly in making up the rules of procedure, and learn them properly, and abide by them; after that, the course of the game or the trial is largely settled for us.

To imagine perfect languages to deal with every human situation is, of course, utopian. But we can make a start. At present we do little more than outline certain qualities which we think useful in solving human problems; thus we could include honesty and truthfulness, being able to express oneself, talking over a situation, and so forth. It is possible to think of methods of formalizing these qualities, of arranging the situation so that it is as easy as possible for people to use them. To take a common example, it is well known that on many committees honesty does not flourish, because many of the members are waiting in fear to see what other members think: a junior member does not wish to advance an opinion against his boss, other members may not wish to appear revolutionary or unorthodox to their fellows, and so on. In this situation it is useless to try and persuade the members to be honest and outspoken, to give their real opinions, or to forget that they are in a particular social situation. The whole point is to try to replace an existing language with a new one. The existing language of many committees is well known. The individual members speak (as it were) with a public voice, through a mask donned for the benefit of the group and their own public images: their private voice, often used in the lobby, is unheard in the committee-room. People are often unwilling to assume personal responsibility, and often committees reach decisions that no individual member, at least in his private role, would himself have reached. This is, then, an inefficient language. Now suppose we extend the principle of the secret ballot—itself a first-rate 'linguistic' invention for dealing with political situations. Suppose we devise machinery whereby each member can record his views and opinions, as well as his votes, anonymously—on a tape-recorder which makes no differentiation between the different speaking-voices of individuals, for instance; no doubt a cumbersome device, but one which would eliminate the dangers outlined above. Such an invention would produce a more efficient language.

This hints at the most important feature of a language dealing with human situations—the degree of objectivity or 'externalization'. Everybody knows that in such situations people interrupt other people, lose their tempers and shout, contradict themselves, misunderstand each other and so forth. Now imagine a series of devices and a formalized ritual designed to reduce this to a minimum. Imagine, for instance, a device through which each party spoke which went dead if his voice were raised above a certain volume or pitch; imagine that only one of these devices could operate at a time, only after the previously-used device had been switched off by the party who spoke last; imagine that the ritual included playing the whole conversation back through a recorder, giving people the chance to emend or alter what they wanted, and also—more important—the ability to hear their own words externalized by the recorder. Imagine further that the session could not be broken up before a certain time, and could thus be free from the sort of emotional interruptions that often interrupt such efforts, such as somebody walking out of the room in tears.

Naturally this is only one language-ritual, and would not be appropriate for the whole range of individual communication or understanding. We need to know a number of factors which the above language would disallow: thus, anger, rage, fear of someone else, and so on are all real factors which must be expressed somehow if they are to be dealt with. This points to the second important feature of a language—that it should be flexible enough to include all that we want in a particular situation. We need not confine ourselves to one language, however; indeed a good deal of our present difficulty is that we attempt to deal with an almost infinite number of human and social contexts in what appears to us to be—and in one sense is—only a single language. We use the same words for rational discussion, for bullying, educating, exhorting, praying, threatening, making love and countless other purposes. What we require is a number of different language-rituals to cover the variety of situations; and one of the most important matters is that it must be clear to everybody when a person is using one language-ritual and when he is using another. The inner intentions of human beings are hard to verify even for themselves, and this makes it all the more essential to establish, by social usage, what a person is doing—what sort of game he is playing—at any one time.

The existence of a greater number of conventions, however, would in itself make a great many human situations easier, just as conventions in bidding in the game of bridge, by their mere existence and recognition, allow the players to express a variety of meanings and intentions. It now becomes apparent that one considerable difficulty is going to consist of learning and teaching the language. It is easy to recognize when you want to tell your partner that you have no spade, or four certain tricks in hearts, but not so easy to recognize *what* you want to express about your own feelings or the behaviour of other people. Phrases like 'I am angry' or 'I am hurt', admittedly, are slightly less crude than a threatening gesture or a flood of tears, but they still cover a great multitude of varied feelings. We feel tempted here to talk about self-awareness and perceptiveness; we need to be able to feel and distinguish between, say, anger at someone else for thwarting us, and anger at ourselves for being unable to meet a particular situation. But, as with the young child learning the simple language of material objects, the existence of an already-established language goes a long way towards helping the individual actually to make the distinctions about his own feelings. Thus, given (say) three different words for 'anger', with carefully specified meanings, it would not be hard for any normal individual to distinguish the feelings within himself to which the three words were intended to apply. It is plain that a similar sophistication of language in reference to words like 'love', 'attractive', 'friendship', and 'fear', to name but a few, would be of immense value.

We are entitled to expect far-reaching changes in our general attitude to ourselves and other people as a result of new language-techniques. There are many features of our behaviour which we take for granted, but which are nevertheless compulsive, and which would disappear as a result of greater control. Thus we are accustomed to regard our 'natural' likes and dislikes, desires and aversions, loves and hates as unchangeable parts of our nature. One man is powerfully attracted by tall, willowy blondes; another hates anyone else sleeping with his wife; another is frightened of cats; another dislikes bananas; another is addicted to cigarettes; another dislikes jazz; another has a penchant for high-powered cars. Some of these, it will be noticed, are commonly regarded as 'normal' features, others as unusual, others again as signs of mental illness. But this sort of classification is nearly always done only by reference to a particular society; and it is in any case irrelevant to the question of free or compelled behaviour. All of them are cases where men are under the influence of magical symbols. To one man tall, willowy blondes 'mean' something in a language which he does not understand, the pseudo-language of his own unconscious mind; to another his wife is symbolically a possession, something which he alone can or should use; to another cats symbolize something frightening, and so on.

There may of course be different levels of awareness, different levels of language, in any case of compulsive choosing. Thus it is possible for someone to like high-powered and glossy cars without being aware that they are status-symbols; it is possible for him to be aware that they are status-symbols and be aware of why he is influenced by status-symbols; and so on. We require a different language to cater for all these cases. At present we try to make do with a single language, which operates moderately well for the object-world of physical reality, but which begins to come apart at the seams when we talk even about shallow sociological factors such as 'status', 'class' and 'communication' in a simple sense, and which fails almost totally if we want to take a look at and control the factors dealt with by depth-psychology, such as the origins of the need for status or of sexual choices. Given such languages, languages which will map out the most

basic factors of our personality and subject them to the scrutiny of our consciousness, our will, our intentions and our reason, we may hope for infinitely greater flexibility of behaviour. No longer will certain types of women, certain foodstuffs, certain physical objects or certain behaviour-patterns come to seem compulsively preferable or compulsively intolerable. We should be able, as the psychologists keep telling us, to 'accept reality' for more fully what it is, for we should then have reduced more of it to linguistic form.

We do possess some languages for mapping our unconscious minds, besides the language of psycho-analysis. They are the languages of the various art-forms. As a method of control they are hopelessly incapable; indeed, in so far as the conventional signs used by them are rarely agreed or consciously understood (though they are artificial), it is perhaps strictly incorrect to call them languages, in our restricted sense, at all. In general they are stimuli, which move us, often profoundly; but there are some agreed conventions which can, by common consent as it were, affect us in certain ways, evoke certain types of feelings and enable us to put them on the map. Thus the use of a minor key in music, or a certain type of sentimental story, or certain emotive symbols in poetry, can by common consent evoke certain specific feelings or moods. As used in art-forms, of course, these forms are not so much symbolic of certain feelings as evocative of them—though they are artificially evocative. Their chief function as language, from our point of view, is that they do at least enable us to *identify* and face feelings which we might otherwise not identify and face, or at any rate not so clearly. Some degree of externalization has been achieved.

Moreover, they do something to bridge the horrifying gulf between the language of psycho-analysis and the wholly non-linguistic and uncritically-experienced feelings of everyday life. As has often been noticed, the difficulty with psycho-analytic language is that its statements are systematically difficult to prove; not in the sense that it is hard to collect evidence, but in the sense that the meaning of the statements is unclear. There is a gulf between the word 'want', say, in a statement like, 'Every boy wants to kill his father', and any conscious experience of wanting in the average person. In order to bring their points home in an effective way, psycho-analysts have to refer to case-histories, novels, plays and so forth—to a language or a pseudo-language which, though it does nothing to explain or even perhaps (in a strict sense) describe, can nevertheless evoke more subtly and specifically than the crude terminology of psycho-analysis.

2 Use, usage and meaning

Gilbert Ryle and J. N. Findlay

In 1932 Mr (now Sir) Alan H. Gardiner published *The Theory of Speech and Language* (Clarendon Press). A central theme of his book was what, with some acknowledged verbal artificiality, he labelled the distinction between 'Language' and 'Speech'. I shall draw, develop and apply this distinction in my own way.

A language, such as the French language, is a stock, fund or deposit of words, constructions, intonations, *cliché* phrases and so on. 'Speech', on the other hand, or 'discourse' can be conscripted to denote the activity or rather the clan of activities of saying things, saying them in French, it may be, or English or some other language. A stock of language-pieces is not a lot of activities, but the fairly lasting wherewithal to conduct them; somewhat as a stock of coins is not a momentary transaction or set of momentary transactions of buying, lending, investing, etc., but is the lasting wherewithal to conduct such transactions. Roughly, as Capital stands to Trade, so Language stands to Speech.

A Language is something to be known, and we get to know it by learning it. We learn it partly by being taught it, and partly by picking it up. For any given part of a language, a learner may not yet have learned that part; or he may have learned it and not forgotten it, or he may have learned it and forgotten it, or he may have half-learned it; or he may have half-forgotten it. A Language is a corpus of teachable things. It is not, of course, a static corpus until it is a dead language. Nor would two teachers of it always agree whether something should be taught as a part of that language. Is French literary style to be taught by teachers of the French Language or by teachers of French Literature? Just when does an acceptable turn of phrase become an idiom? How old can a neologism be? What about slang?

Saying something in a language involves but does not reduce to knowing the requisite pieces of that

Source: *Proceedings of the Aristotelian Society* (1961), supp. vol. 35, 223–42.

language. The speaker is here and now employing what he had previously acquired and still possesses. He is now in the act of operating with things of which he has, perhaps for years, been the possessor. The words, constructions, intonations, etc., that he employs in saying what he says in these words, constructions, etc., is not another part of that language. It is a momentary operation *with* parts of that language, just as the buying or lending that I do with part of my capital is not itself a part of that capital, but a momentary operation with a part of it. That, indeed, is what my capital is for, namely, to enable me to make purchases, benefactions, loans, etc., with parts of it whenever I wish to do so. It is a set of moderately permanent possibilities of making particular momentary transactions.

If I say something in French, then, even though what I say has never been said before, I do not thereby enlarge the French language, i.e., increase the amount to be learned by a student of the French language. The fact that he does not know what I said does not entail that there is a bit of the French language that he has still to learn. Dicta made in French are not parts of the French language. They are things done with parts of the French language. You might utilize the same parts in saying something identical with or quite different from what I said. Your act of saying it is not mine, and neither is a part of the fund on which we both draw. But dicta can notoriously fossilize into *clichés*. '*Je ne sais quoi*' can now be used as a noun; and '*Rest and be Thankful*' can be a proper name.

We are tempted to treat the relation between sentences and words as akin to the relation between faggots and sticks. But this is entirely wrong. Words, constructions, etc., are the atoms of a Language; sentences are the units of Speech. Words, constructions, etc., are what we have to learn in mastering a language; sentences are what we produce when we say things. Words have histories; sentences do not, though their authors do. I must have learned the words that I utter when I say something with them. I need not, and, with reservations, cannot have learned the sentence that I come out with when I say something. It is something that I compose, not something that I have acquired. I am its author, not its employer. Sentences are not things of which I have a stock or fund. Nor are my buyings and lendings things of which I have a hoard or purseful.

In daily life we do not often mention as such the sentences that people produce. We speak instead of their allegations, complaints, promises, verdicts, requests, witticisms, confessions and commands. It is, in the main, people like grammarians, compositors, translators, amanuenses and editors who need to refer to the things that people say as 'sentences', since they are *ex officio* concerned with such matters as page-space, punctuation, syntax, plagiarization, and so on. None the less, what they are interested in are instances of someone, actual or imagined, alleging, complaining, warning, joking, etc., though their special concern is with the punctuation of them and not with their humorousness; with their length and not with their truth; with their moods and tenses and not with their relevance or rudeness.

When Caesar said '*Veni; vidi; vici*', he said three things, though he used only three Latin words. Then is '*Vici*' a word or a sentence? The queerness of this disjunctive question is revealing. What Caesar produced, orally or in writing, on a certain day, was a laconic sentence, if a sentence is an instance of someone saying something. In this instance Caesar said something which was true. But he said it using only one Latin word, a word which had long been there for anyone to use anywhen in saying all sorts of considerably different things. The word was not true, or, of course, false either. Caesar boasted '*Vici*', but the dictionary's explanation of the verb '*Vici*' need say nothing about Caesar boasting. What it describes was, perhaps, also used by, *inter alios*, some concussed gladiator asking anxiously '*Vici?*'. The boast '*vici*' was a different sentence from the question '*vici?*', though the authors of both used the same Latin word, of which neither was the inventor. The word '*vici*' was there, in their common fund, to be employed, misemployed or left unemployed by anyone anywhen. The boast '*vici*' and the query '*vici?*' were two momentary speech-acts in which this one word was utilized for saying different things. Our question 'Is "*vici*" a word or a sentence?' was queer because its subject was ambiguous. Was it about a speech-episode, like a boast or a query, or was it about an inflected Latin verb? It was queer also because '. . . a word or a sentence?' was a disjunction between predicates of quite different categories, on a par with '. . . a bat or a stroke?'

Is the interrogative sentence '*vici?*' a part of the Latin language? Well, would a student still have some Latin to learn who had never met it? Surely not. What he had learned is enough to enable him to construe it if he should ever meet it. What he construes are employments of Latin words, constructions, etc.; what he

must know in order to construe or understand these employments, are the Latin words, inflections, constructions, etc. He must know the word in order to understand the one-word boast or question; but that knowing is not this understanding; what he had long since known is not what he has just understood or misunderstood. As we employ coins to make loans, but do not employ lendings, so we employ words, etc., in order to say things, but we do not employ the sayings of things—or misemploy them or leave them unemployed either. Dictions and dicta belong to different categories. So do roads and journeys; so do gallows and executions.

Sometimes a person tries to say something and fails through ignorance of the language. Perhaps he stops short because he does not know or cannot think of the required words or constructions. Perhaps he does not stop, but produces the wrong word or construction, thinking it to be the right one, and so commits a solecism. Perhaps his failure is of lesser magnitude; he says something unidiomatically or ungrammatically; or he gets the wrong intonation or he mispronounces. Such failures show that he has not completely mastered, say, the French language. In the extended sense of 'rule' in which a rule is anything against which faults are adjudged to be at fault, solecisms, mispronunciations, malapropisms, and unidiomatic and ungrammatical constructions are breaches of the rules of, e.g., the French language. For our purposes we do not need to consider the sources or the status of rules of this kind, or the authorities whose censures our French instructor dreads. Solecisms are in general philosophically uninteresting. Nor, for obvious reasons, do we often commit solecisms, save when young, ill-schooled, abroad or out of our intellectual depth.

The reproof 'You cannot say that and speak good French' is generically different from the reproof 'You cannot say that without absurdity'. The latter is not a comment on the quality of the speaker's French, since it could be true though the speaker had spoken in flawless French, or had not been speaking in French at all, but in English or Greek instead. The comment, if true, would be true of what was said whatever language it was said in, and whether it was said in barbarous or impeccable French or English. A mispronunciation or a wrong gender may be a bit of faulty French, but a self-contradiction is not a fault-in-French. Cicero's *non sequiturs* were not lapses from good Latin into bad Latin. His carelessness or incompetence was not linguistic carelessness or incompetence, if we tether the adjective 'linguistic' to the noun 'Language' as this is here being contrasted with 'Speech'.

There is an enormous variety of disparate kinds of faults that we can find or claim to find with things that people say. I can complain, justly or else unjustly, that what you said was tactless, irrelevant, repetitious, false, inaccurate, insubordinate, trite, fallacious, ill-timed, blasphemous, malicious, vapid, uninformative, over-informative, prejudiced, pedantic, obscure, prudish, provocative, self-contradictory, tautologous, circular or nonsensical and so on indefinitely. Some of these epithets can be appropriate also to behaviour which is not speech-behaviour; some of them cannot. Not one of them could be asserted or denied of any item in an English or French dictionary or Grammar. I can stigmatize what you said with any one of these epithets without even hinting that what you said was faulty in its French or whatever other language you said it in. I grumble at your dictum but not at your mastery of the language that it was made in. There are countless heterogeneous disciplines and corrections which are meant to train people not to commit these Speech-faults. Not one of them belongs to the relatively homogeneous discipline of teaching say, the French language. Speech-faults are not to be equated with Language-faults. Nothing need be wrong with the paints, brushes and canvas with which a portrait is bungled. Painting badly is not a pot of bad paint.

Logicians and philosophers are, *ex officio*, much concerned with kinds of things that people say or might be tempted to say. Only where there can be fallacies can there be valid inferences, namely in arguments; and only where there can be absurdities can there be non-absurdities, namely in dicta. We are presented with *aporiai* (difficulties) not by the telescope or the trawling-net, but by passages in books or by ripostes in debates. A fallacy or an impossible consequence may indeed have to be presented to us in French or English, etc. But it does not follow from this that what is wrong with it is anything faulty in the French or English in which it is presented. It was no part of the business of our French or English instructors to teach us that if most men wear coats and most men wear waistcoats it does not follow that most men wear both. This is a different sort of lesson and one which we cannot begin until we have already learned to use without solecism 'most', 'and', 'if', etc. There are no French implications or non-implications, so though '*p*' may be said in French and '*q*' may be said in French, it is nonsense to say '*q* does not follow from *p* in the best French'. Similarly, what is impossible in 'The Cheshire Cat vanished, leaving only her grin behind her' is not any piece of intolerably barbarous English. Carroll's wording of the impossible story could not be improved, and the impossibility of his narrated incident survives translation into any language into which it can be translated. Something was amusingly wrong with what he said, but not with what he said it in.

I have a special reason for harking on this point that what someone says may be fallacious or absurd without being in any measure solecistic; i.e. that some Speech-faults, including some of those which matter to logicians and philosophers, are not and do not carry with them any Language-faults. Some philosophers, oblivious of the distinction between Language and Speech, or between having words, etc., to say things with and saying things with them, give to sentences the kind of treatment that they give to words, and, in particular, assimilate their accounts of what a sentence means to their accounts of what a word means. Equat-

ing the notion of the meaning of a word with the notion of the use of that word, they go on without apparent qualms to talking as if the meaning of a sentence could equally well be spoken of as the use of that sentence. We hear, for example, that nonsensical English sentences are sentences that have no use in English; as if sentences could *be* solecisms. Should we expect to hear that a certain argument is henceforth to contain an Undistributed Middle in BBC English?

My last sentence but three, say, is not something with which I once learned how to say things. It *is* my saying something. Nor is an execution something erected to hang people on. It *is* the hanging of somebody. Part of what we learn, in learning the words of a language, is indeed how to employ them. But the act of exercising this acquired competence, i.e., the saying something with them is not in its turn an acquired wherewithal to say things. It neither has nor lacks a use, or, therefore, a use in English.

The famous saying: 'Don't ask for the meaning; ask for the use', might have been and I hope was a piece of advice to philosophers, and not to lexicographers or translators. It advised philosophers, I hope, when wrestling with some *aporia*, to switch their attention from the trouble-giving words in their dormancy as language-pieces or dictionary-items to their utilizations in the actual sayings of things; from their general promises when on the shelf to their particular performances when at work; from their permanent purchasing-power while in the bank to the concrete marketing done yesterday morning with them; in short, from these words *qua* units of a Language to live sentences in which they are being actively employed.

More than this; the famous saying, in association with the idea of Rules of Use, could and I think should have been intended to advise philosophers, when surveying the kinds of live dicta that are or might be made with these trouble-giving words, to consider especially some of the kinds of non-solecistic Speech-faults against which the producer of such live dicta ought to take precautions, e.g., what sorts of dicta could not be significantly made with them, and why; what patterns of argument pivoting on these live dicta would be fallacious, and why; what kinds of verification-procedures would be impertinent, and why; to what kinds of questions such live dicta would be irrelevant, and why; and so on. To be clear about the 'how' of the employment of something we need to be clear also about its 'how not to', and about the reasons for both.

Early in this century Husserl and later Wittgenstein used the illuminating metaphors of 'logical syntax' and 'logical grammar'. Somewhat as, say, indicative verbs used instead of subjunctive verbs render some would-be Latin sentences bad Latin, so certain category-skids and logical howlers render dicta, said in no matter which tongue, nonsensical or absurd. A so-called Rule of Logical Syntax is what a nonsensical dictum is in breach of. But the analogy must not be pressed very far. The rules of Latin syntax are part of what we must learn if we are to be able to produce or construe Latin dicta. They are parts of the equipment to be employed by someone if he is to say either sensible or silly things in decent Latin. The Rules of Logical Syntax, on the other hand, belong not to a Language or to Languages, but to Speech. A person who says something senseless or illogical betrays not ignorance but silliness, muddle-headedness or, in some of the interesting cases, over-cleverness. We find fault not with his schooling in years gone by but with his thinking here and now. He has not forgotten or misremembered any of his lessons; he has operated unwarily or over-ingeniously in his execution of his momentary task. In retrospect he will reproach not his teachers, but himself; and he will reproach himself not for never having known something but for not having been thinking what he was saying yesterday.

The vogue of using 'Language' and 'linguistic' ambivalently both for dictions and for dicta, i.e., both for the words, etc., that we say things in and for what we say in them, helps to blind us to the wholesale inappropriateness of the epithets which fit pieces of language to the sayings of things with those pieces; and to the wholesale and heterogeneous inappropriatenesses of the variegated epithets which fit things said to the language-pieces and language-patterns that they are said in.

It remains true that philosophers and logicians do have to talk about talk or, to put it in a more Victorian way, to discourse about discourse. But it is not true that they are *ex officio* concerned with what language-teachers are *ex officio* concerned with.

(2) J. N. Findlay

I am in great agreement with what I regard as the substantial points in Professor Ryle's paper. His definition of language I think rather arbitrarily narrow: for him it is a 'stock, fund or deposit of words, constructions, *cliché* phrases and so on'. I should have thought it would be wrong not to include in a language the various syntactical and other *rules* which restrict our employment of the capital of expressions mentioned by Professor Ryle, though perhaps I am wrong in thinking he meant to exclude them. That adjectives must agree with the gender of their substantives in certain cases would certainly be held to be part of the French language, as it is not part of the English. There is also, I think, a further arbitrariness in excluding sentences from *language*, and in making them the units of *speech* which are produced when we say things. I think we can and should distinguish between the sentence *Je ne sais quoi* as a mere possibility permitted by the French language, and the same sentence as used or produced by someone to say something. I can in fact see no good reason why one should not have a narrower and wider conception of a language. On the narrower conception, a language includes a vocabulary and rules, whereas on the wider conception it includes also *all* the possible sentences that could be framed out

of the vocabulary in accordance with the rules. In this sense French or English would include all the permissible sentences that could be framed in it, whether anyone ever uttered or wrote or thought them or not. If this conception of a language makes it absurdly wide, the conception of it as a vocabulary plus rules makes it unduly narrow. Certainly, however, I think we want to distinguish between a sentence as a grammatically permissible word-combination, and the utterance or writing down or silent thinking of that sentence by someone on some occasion to make an allegation, raise a query, express a doubt, etc., etc., and in the latter case I find a language of *use* or *employment* more natural than Professor Ryle's language of *production*. I think therefore that Professor Ryle is legislating rather vexatiously in forbidding us to speak of sentences as parts of language, or to say that such sentences can be *used* by speakers. I do not, however, think that this vexatious piece of legislation is in the forefront of Professor Ryle's intentions.

What Professor Ryle is mainly concerned to do seems to me to be to distinguish between grammatical faults in the use of words in constructing sentences, and faults in what may be called 'logical syntax' or 'logical grammar', which involve the use of words to construct perfectly grammatical sentences, but which none the less violate a deeper set of rules, the rules of sense, the rules of logic, the rules regulating the mutual relations of categories, etc., etc. With all this I am deeply in agreement, because it involves precisely the recognition that different sorts of words, as it were, make different sorts of abstract *cuts* in their subject-matter, or help to execute different sorts of abstract *cuts*—some, as Aristotle might say, tell us *what* things are, others *how* they are, others *how many* they are, others *conjoin*, others *emphasize*, others *bracket*, etc., etc.—and that in making such quite different types of cross-section they become subject to the relations necessarily obtaining among such cross-sections, so that some verbal combinations which are smooth and pretty grammatically none the less make hideous nonsense. Professor Ryle, it seems to me, is here suggesting that it is the relations of different sorts of *meanings* to one another which determine the depth-grammar of words, and that these meanings and their relations are matters that must be *independently* considered if we are to study logical as well as grammatical syntax. If this suggestion is not implicit in his words, perhaps he will explain what sort of abuse of words it is that is logical or depth-grammatical as opposed to merely surface-grammatical abuse. Incidentally, I feel in the contexts invoked by Ryle that it is doubly tempting to talk of the *use* and *abuse* of grammatical sentences. The sentence is there, a fully-fashioned grammatical entity, and it is its use to express a categorically possible combination of meanings which is at times possible and legitimate, whereas at other times there is really only an abuse.

Having expressed my agreement and disagreement with Ryle, I may perhaps allow myself to dwell a little on the famous dictum which he quotes and which has dominated philosophical discussion for the past twenty years: 'Don't ask for the meaning: ask for the use.' I wish to make against it the not often raised objection that the use for which it bids us ask, is of all things the most obscure, the most veiled in philosophical mists, the most remote from detailed determination or application, in the wide range of philosophical concepts. There is, I think, a use of 'use' which is humdrum and ordinary, but in which a study of the use of expressions is of only limited philosophical importance and interest. There is also a use of 'use' characteristic of the later writings of Wittgenstein which is utterly remote from the humdrum and ordinary, and which has won its way into the acceptance of philosophers largely because it has *seemed* to have the clearness and the straightforwardness of the ordinary use. We are all proof against the glozing deceits of words like 'substance', 'being', 'nothingness', 'consciousness', etc., etc.: we at once see that some occasions of their employment are really only abuses—but we are not yet proof against the fascinations exerted by the singular abuses of so ordinary a term as 'use'. When these abuses are exposed, the whole attitude represented by the slogan quoted by Ryle reveals itself as completely without significant basis, which unfortunately puts an end to all but a limited emphasis on 'use' and 'usage' by philosophers. Since the suggestion that use and usage—in some acceptable sense—*are* philosophically very important, certainly underlies Ryle's paper, I need not apologize for irrelevance in proceeding to demolish this suggestion.

The reason why it is absurd to tell us *not* to attend to the meaning of expressions but to concentrate on their use, is perfectly simple: it is that the notion of use, as it ordinarily exists and is used, presupposes the notion of meaning (in its central and paradigmatic sense), and that it cannot therefore be used to elucidate the latter, and much less to replace or to do duty for it. The notion of use is a *wider* notion than the paradigmatic notion of meaning: it covers many *other* things beside the meaning of an expression, but the meaning-function in its paradigmatic sense is certainly *one* of the things it covers, and it is not possible to give a clear account of use without presupposing this function. What I am saying is simply that we cannot fully say, in a great many cases, how an expression is used, without saying what sort of things it is intended to refer to, or to bring to mind, and just how, or in what angle or light, it purports to refer to them, or to bring them to mind. And in cases where it would be wrong and absurd to say that an expression *independently* brought something to mind, or presented it in a certain light, it would none the less be uncontestably right to say that it *helped* to do such things in some definite manner, so that what was brought to mind would be *different*, or *differently presented*, if the expression were not part of our total utterance. Thus if I make use of the word 'dragon' in a large number of contexts, I use it to refer to a human being or beings,

generally mature and female, and I use it also to represent such a human being or beings as being restrictive, uncompromising and somewhat terrifying. And if I *apply* the term in a certain context I see that to which I apply it in the light connoted by my words. And if I use the words 'such a' before uttering the word 'dragon', these words certainly help to suggest that what I am describing is *very* restrictive, *very* uncompromising and *very* terrifying, i.e., they contribute to the force of my description without playing an independent part of it. In saying what the use of my expressions is, I therefore have to say what, in the ordinary diction of logicians, they denote and connote, what their precise reference is or what their general scope, or how they contribute to connotation or denotation, and it is not thought possible to say how many expressions are *used*, without bringing in such connotative and denotative particulars.

The notion of use of course goes far *beyond* that of connotation and denotation, and it is one of the extremely important discoveries of modern semantics that there are *some* expressions whose use, in certain contexts, is *not* to connote or denote anything, nor even to help to do either, but to do such things as give voice to feelings and wishes, evoke certain attitudes in others, or *perform* certain formal social acts, e.g., promises, which have certain definite social consequences, etc., etc. That *not* all expressions, on all occasions of their *use*, perform the functions of reference or characterization, or assist in such performance, is certainly a discovery not to be underestimated, which has cleared the deck of much tangled tackle and many stumbling-blocks. But this kind of *non*-referential, *non*-connotative use is parasitic upon a connotative, referential one, and could hardly exist without it. It is one of Wittgenstein's more irresponsible fancies that there could be a language composed *only* of commands, or *only* of curses, or *only* of greetings. The concept of use also certainly covers all the hidden *implications* and *suggestions* which attach to the writing or utterance of a word or a sentence, but which are not strictly part of what it means or says: thus when I say 'He did not commit this murder' I may use this sentence to imply that he committed certain other murders, that I absolutely believe him to be no murderer, that we live under laws forbidding the taking of life, etc., etc. But all such implications and suggestions are likewise dependent upon the function of directly connoting or denoting something, and are in fact an extension of the same. Use also obviously covers the mere requirements of accidence and syntax, though these, as Ryle has shown, are mere instrumentalities in the task of significant diction.

What is implicit, however, in the slogan 'Don't ask for the meaning: ask for the use' is not that use covers much *more* than the connotative and denotative functions of language, but that it somehow resumes and completely explains the latter, that we can completely see around and see through talk about the reference and connotation of expressions by taking note of the way people operate with such expressions, how they combine them with other expressions to form sentences, and the varying *circumstances* in which producing such sentences is reckoned appropriate or fully justifiable. This study of verbal manoeuvres, and of appropriate and justifying circumstances, must not, however, be confined to the single instant of utterance: it must point *backwards* to the all-important situations in which use was *learnt* or *taught*, and it must point *forwards* to the innumerable situations in which the utterance in question will again be found *appropriate*, or will be found to be more and more abundantly *justified*. The study of use therefore includes a genealogy and a prognosis of the most indefinite and complex kind, much more extensive than any that occurs in a merely grammatical or philological study. In another respect, however, the slogan gives 'use' an extraordinarily restricted interpretation. The operations involved in use are not to be operations conducted privately in anyone's head, or at least such operations can only be brought into consideration in so far as they can be narrowly tied up with other non-private operations, and the *circumstances* in which such operations are conducted must all be circumstances belonging to what may be called the common public environment, circumstances in which bricks are being assembled into buildings, apples taken from drawers and handed over to customers, railway-signals altered, or hunting expeditions conducted. The sort of change which is a mere change in perspective or in conscious 'light' is *not* among the circumstances mentionable in describing use.

And there is yet another most extraordinary restriction placed upon our account of the *circumstances* in which a word is correctly used: we must not employ the word or its equivalent to explain those circumstances. We must not, e.g., say, that when a man is confronted by three apples in a drawer, or by an apple and another apple and yet another apple, he is then justified in employing the word 'three' in connexion with such apples. The word 'three' may be employed in describing the circumstances justifying countless *other* sorts of utterance, but not the circumstances justifying its *own* employment. In the same way we must never say that it is when a man is confronted by a red object, or has learnt to discriminate its colour, that he is justified in calling it 'red'. Such accounts are held to be wholly trivial and unilluminating, and are moreover held to suggest various deep philosophical fallacies: the belief that meanings exist 'out there' in the things we deal with *before* we find the appropriate words to 'pick them out', or that they exist 'in the mind' or the understanding before we find words to express them. Whatever we suggest by our accounts of use, we must never suggest that there are *pre-existent meanings*. Words enjoy meaning and reference in and by our use of them, and our use cannot be explained in terms of any meaning that antedates the use of words. And since understanding and thinking are defined in terms of the

operation with signs, we must never speak as if we could understand or think anything before we dispose of appropriate verbal expressions and have been taught to employ them. The programme of this extreme 'utilitarianism'—as one may perhaps call the use-doctrine—is impressive: it resembles nothing so much as the brave empiricist programme of Locke and Hume, in which no idea was to be admitted into the charmed circle of thought and knowledge without producing a genealogy purer than any required by the Nuremberg laws, exhibiting a proper origin in sensation and reflection, and a derivation from these by approved processes. But, like that brave programme, it faces the crucial objection that it cannot be carried out completely, and that no comprehensive account of use and usage can be given which does not contain some members of impure origin. That the brave programme was hopeless Wittgenstein himself perhaps obscurely realized, when he wrongly said of the *Brown Book*, the most profound and wonderful of his writings, that it was *nichts wert* (worthless). But if success, rather than stimulus and provocation, is the criterion of philosophical value, his judgement was entirely justified.

I need not range far nor cite many instances to make plain the totally unilluminating, indeed deeply obfuscating character of attempts to give a complete account of the use of expressions in terms of merely public operations and circumstances. The very conception of a *rule*, central to the 'utilitarianism' in question, abounds in difficulty. For we are expressly told that to follow a rule is not necessarily to be guided by a spoken or written formula, since each such formula admits of interpretation in terms of another formula, and this in terms of another, and so on indefinitely. Nor is the following of a rule to be identified with any sort of inner personal understanding of that rule which can guide one's subsequent performance, since to hold this would be to accept pre-existent meanings resident in the queer medium of the mind. Nor can the following of a rule be identified with one's actual performance up to a point, since this is always compatible with an infinity of rules. In the end it would seem that following a rule must be an ineffable sort of affair: it must be something that can be accomplished in one's *doing* (in this case, speaking), but not effectively spoken *about*. It is something that one can know how *to do* without being able to know how what one does is done. The conception of a linguistic rule has, in fact, all the irretrievable obscurity of the structural resemblance constitutive of meaning in the *Tractatus*, which cannot be expressed but only *shown*. If it is at least *possible* that a rule should at times be understood or grasped in thought, we can understand what it is like to follow it without thought, but if grasping is a function of following, the whole activity of following dissolves in mystery. I do not myself know how it differs from the most arbitrary irregularity except that it mysteriously *feels* right at every stage, and that others, standing at my side, mysteriously agree in such feelings. And if it is hard to throw light on the following of rules in terms of outward circumstances and performances, how much harder it is to say in what lies conformity to an *open* rule, one which is to be applied over and over *indefinitely*. While the *thought* expressed by the phrase 'and so on indefinitely' is most absolutely simple and easy to entertain, it is a thought *logically* impossible to evince adequately in one's performance. Much has been written, from the standpoint of the use-doctrine, about the difference between closed and open games, but the discussion ends up with very much what it started from, that it is a difference in the *spirit* with which the respective games are played. A man, e.g. using an open arithmetic simply has a system or general rule for constructing numerals *indefinitely*. That a spirit is operative in this case I should not care to deny, but that it consorts well with the use-doctrine, or establishes its superiority, I cannot conceive.

Similar difficulties confront us if we consider the use-account of the use of descriptive adjectives like those of colour. We are forbidden to talk of prior colour-differences in objects, or prior colour-discriminations in persons, as this would involve the grave error of positing pre-existent meanings. We are introduced to imaginary tribal activities which involve the picturesque carrying about of charts of colour samples and their comparison with, or imposition on objects, but these it would seem explain little or nothing, since the charts are dispensable and admit moreover of a wrong use. From the use of charts the tribe progresses to the use of colour samples carried somehow in the mind's eye, and ultimately to the mere unhesitant pronouncement, after sufficient training, of certain colour-words in the presence of certain objects. With this pronouncement others as unhesitatingly agree. From the Scylla of holding that 'blue' stands for a discriminable blueness in objects, or expresses an awareness of blueness in one's mind, one proceeds to the Charybdis of saying that those things are blue which we and others agree, and have been trained, to call so. It is plain, of course, that one must have ultimates somewhere, and it is plain also that there are different possibilities of colour-discrimination corresponding to different possibilities of usage: what is *not* plain is why one should prefer such a strange, secondary ultimate as a *use* to the more obvious, understandable ultimates of discriminating thoughts in the mind, or discriminable features in things.

The most superb example of the problem-increasing character of the use-semantics is, however, to be found in its treatment of cases where men use expressions without obvious reference to any palpable feature of the public environment, when they give voice, e.g., to recollections or anticipations, or describe their personal feelings or impressions, or report their fantasies or their dreams. Here the course is followed of attempting to account for such uses by supposing men to be such as *spontaneously* to want to use expressions taught in certain contexts in contexts

where their normal justification is absent, and that these non-normal needs, so strangely universal among us, constitute the basis for a new *secondary* set of linguistic usages, where the sole fact that we agree in feeling certain linguistic urges is the sole criterion of their correctness. Thus children perhaps spontaneously run over the names of objects recently presented to them, or can be encouraged to do so without difficulty: meaning can then be given to the *past tense*, and they can learn to say that they *had* a ball, a stick, a rattle, etc. To 'refer to the past' is merely to learn to employ the past tense in such circumstances, an account as amusingly free in presupposing pastness and temporal passage in the *circumstances* of the learning, as it is firm in denying any non-verbal *understanding* of them. Men then spontaneously begin to use the past tense where there is no such recent provocation: we then give a use to talk about 'remembering', particularly if others agree in such spontaneous inclinations. The reference to the past in memory is therefore not the ultimate, mysterious thing that Husserl, Broad and others have supposed it to be: it merely reflects the strange tendency of men to talk preteritively beyond the limits of recency, and the further linkage of this fact with the readings of instruments, the reports of others, and many other observed matters. It may now happen that men waking from sleep spontaneously talk in the past tense *as if* recalling happenings which no one remembers, and which do not fit in with the observable contemporary state, or with the memory-inclinations of others. The concept of 'dreaming' now makes its *debut* to take care of these extraordinary performances. Malcolm, the admirable exponent of a preposterous analysis, admits[1] that on it dream-language is very odd: it is *as if* one is faithfully recalling something, but one cannot explain this fact by saying that one *did* experience what one is disposed to report, since this would involve an unintelligible hypothesis, one excluded by the guiding assumptions of the doctrine of use. What these queernesses surely show is the profound mistakenness somewhere of these guiding assumptions. To make use of a gnostic principle used by Moore in other contexts: we *know* certain facts about meaning much more absolutely than we can be sure of the premises, or the inferential rules, of semantic arguments designed either to establish them, or to explain them away. Obviously we cannot make straight sense of many linguistic usages without postulating just those pre-existent understandings (not confined to matters in the public forefront) and the possibility of communicating such understandings to others, which it is the whole aim of the use-doctrine to exclude.

The use-doctrine may further be objected to for its profoundly circular, question-begging character. This is a point ably made by Mr. Gellner in a book[2] where some of the most profound criticisms of the use-doctrine and its consequences lie hidden under a somewhat popular exterior. To have seen an unacceptable, unargued naturalism behind Wittgenstein's brilliant façade of exposition, is no mean insight. By describing the functioning of linguistic expression exclusively in public and social terms, we at once *go too far* in assuming such approaches to be wholly justified and clear, and we also *do not go far enough* in refusing to recognize aspects of language not fitting an approach of this sort, or in 'proving' them to be misguided or senseless. These two lines of objection really coincide, since it is by turning away from aspects of language it cannot readily accommodate that the use-doctrine is unable to see its own difficulties and obscurities. The use-theorists have dwelt much on the profound subtlety of ordinary language, but they have been far from recognizing *how* subtle it actually is. For it not only uses expressions to point to, or to throw light on, ordinary objects, but it also uses them *reflexly*, in the manner studied in Husserl's *Logische Untersuchungen*, to point to or throw light on its own *meanings*, thereby setting up an order of objects as clear-edged and partial as its normal objects are fuzzy and full, and as delicate in their abstraction as they are indispensable for the higher flights of thought. That a phrase like 'the third door on the right' can be used both straightforwardly to refer to a door, and reflexly to refer to its own meaning, is a truth plain to babes, but occasioning headaches to the semantically over-wise and prudent. Ordinary speech further, provides us with an instrument for communicating with others about matters public and common, which is also an instrument for purely personal use, in which different observations, different views, different judgements provide much the same complementary parallax, and the same corrective or confirmatory testing as in the interpersonal case. But not only is it thus double in its use, it also manages to incorporate the personal in the public use, and the public in the personal, in a regress pursuable as far as even we choose. Thus we all understand other people's first-person talk by analogy with our own, and its imperfect public intelligibility is also perfectly and publicly intelligible, since everyone makes just such first-person statements in his own case. The manner in which we smoothly swing over from another man's perfectly understood use of the first-person pronoun 'I', and replace it with 'he' in reporting the content of his statement, and expect the other man to do the same in regard to us, as well as the children's games in which these proprieties are amusingly violated: all these show an understanding of the antithesis of contrasted privacies, and of their overcoming in a wider publicity, of which the use-semantics betrays no inkling. In the same manner, ordinary speech has in it the germs of what may be called the Cartesian or the Lockean inversion, the reversal of the ordinary approach from outward things to the mind, into an approach to outer things from the facts of our subjective life. Though the language in which we talk of and to ourselves—the best subject-matter and audience —may have had its *source* in contexts of public ostensibility, it can, by a profitable ingratitude, use the personal language thus painfully acquired to cast doubt upon, or to throw light on, its own origin. We may illuminate our understanding and knowledge of public matters in terms of just those personal experiences and pre-existent understandings which talk about public matters first renders possible. And this personal Cartesian or Lockean story can then achieve the widest publicity, since to have back rooms continuous with those opening on the public square is the most universal, most inescapable of predicaments. It is no doubt by a creative transformation that the rumour of the square penetrates backwards, and is re-echoed in the small back rooms, and it is likewise by a creative transformation that these transformed echoes rejoin the rumour of the square. All this, however, unquestionably happens, and it is the task of a philosophical semantics to make sense of it, and not to declare it unintelligible.

Nothing that has been said in the foregoing is meant to reflect on the painstaking, detailed study of linguistic usage, or the actual manner of its teaching, if used to show how we actually come to mean what we undoubtedly do mean, or to throw light on the complexity and subtlety of our meanings, or to show how we come to be misled into supposing we mean what really conflicts with the 'depth-grammar' of our meanings. Our criticisms are only of a radical use-theory carried to extremes, which constructs fables as to how we might have been taught the meanings of words in order to buttress *a priori* doctrines as to what we *must* or *cannot* mean. If anyone thinks such doctrines archaic and superseded, and so not requiring rebuttal, he is wide of the truth. Wittgenstein's accounts of language-games are so arresting, so novel, so subtle in their detailed development, so daring in their frank embrace of the unplausible, so imbued with intellectual seriousness and earnestness, and so great, finally, in their aesthetic appeal, that it is hard to see through them or around them. They fascinate the philosopher in the same way that Wittgenstein claimed that philosophers were fascinated by the forms of ordinary language, and against such fascination determined steps are necessary. The steps I have taken in this paper may not have been sufficiently subtle, and may have involved certain misunderstandings of detail: I shall hope, at least, to have incited others to do better.

All this should not, of course, be taken as reflecting on the philosophical greatness of Wittgenstein. Wittgenstein is the author of three wholly differing accounts of meaning, all of which merit entire rejection: meaning is *not* repudiation of structure, it is *not* verification or verifiability, it is plainly *not* what he meant by 'use'. It is not these things, though it is of course intimately connected with them all, but it will be best illuminated by construing further the old humdrum notions of connotation and denotation, and by seeking painfully to throw light on the 'thought behind our words', for which, on account of the peculiar categories it involves, it would seem that no adequate surrogate has been, or can be, offered. It is, I surmise, in the 'intentional nature of thought' that the true solution of the problems of meaning is to be found. But by formulating these three inadequate accounts, Wittgenstein has given the semantic problem the central place it deserves in philosophy, and has contributed vastly to its solution. Through his inability to account satisfactorily for certain linguistic performances, he has indicated the precise nodes where language makes its various creative leaps and has thereby given philosophical semantics its opportunity and its task. Moreover, each of Wittgenstein's frequent rhetorical questions is such that, if answered in the sense *not* intended by the question, it will lead to an illuminating result: they are practically all arrows which, if read in the reverse direction, point unerringly to some truth. A philosophy of meaning so valuably wrong does not differ profoundly from one that is systematically right.

Notes

1 N. Malcolm, *Dreaming* (London: Routledge & Kegan Paul 1959).

2 E. Gellner, *Words and Things* (London: Gollancz 1959 and Penguin 1968).

Section I Language as system and language as behaviour

Our everyday use of the word 'language' is ambiguous. Consider these two sentences, for example:

1 English is a difficult language for foreigners to learn.
2 The language those children were using at the bus stop last night was shocking.

In the first case we are talking about language as a system of rules which English speakers have mastered for producing and understanding an indefinitely large number of utterances. We are not talking about any specific utterances. In the second case, however, we are talking about a certain use of the language system; we are making a value judgment about the linguistic behaviour of certain people. Thus, language can be studied from (at least) two points of view, as a system for the coding of meaning or as a form of behaviour. The articles in this section reflect these two ways of viewing language.

In conceiving of a language as a system, we abstract from speech behaviour only those characteristics which give us insight into its structural properties. Ultimately, the search may be for structural properties common to all languages. A major preoccupation of modern linguistics is to develop theories and descriptive categories which allow of the explicit description of the structural properties of all languages. The Robins article gives a brief account of the categories of linguistics. These are being drawn upon increasingly in psychological and sociological studies of language behaviour where accurate linguistic analysis is needed.

To speak is a social act. Speech is primarily a form of social interaction and is central to every human society. In studying language as behaviour, therefore, we concentrate as much on the speakers and the social relationships which hold between them at any given time as on their use of language. We try to relate different ways of using language to different types of user and different patterns of social interaction.

At first sight, Quirk's article seems to have little connection with interaction patterns. But a reading of the article shows that Standard English is used for communication in national and international networks. Thus a definition of Standard English excludes those varieties of language such as dialect and slang which are typically used in smaller networks of interaction. The tendency of a group of people who regularly interact in some way to develop their own variety of language is well illustrated in Quirk's second article. The existence of jargons reflects social differentiation, usually according to occupation. These occupational varieties of English can claim to be Standard English by virtue of their widespread usage throughout the English-speaking world. At the same time they reflect a specialization of social rôles to which not all speakers of English, even the most educated, have access.

The tendency of all language to become differentiated in use is further illustrated by the classic case of diglossia where a society recognizes two (or more) distinct varieties of language for communication. The two varieties complement each other; they are used for different purposes. The 'high' language is used as the language of religion, education and other aspects of high culture. The 'low' vernacular language is used in everyday affairs, for example at home or among friends. Ferguson's article is valuable in two ways. Firstly, it draws attention to the symbolic value of language. Different varieties of language may enjoy different prestige in a community; this springs from their association with patterns of social interaction which are differently valued within a culture. For the English speaker this article may throw light on why Standard English and certain accents of English enjoy high prestige, why dialects may be thought uncouth or quaint, and why certain types of language are considered bad or incorrect. The article is valuable secondly because it separates three distinct, though related, aspects of the study of language behaviour—the description of the varieties used within a community, the investigation of the social relationships with which each is regularly associated, and the symbolic

15

value they acquire for members of a community as a consequence.

Gumperz' article directs attention more closely to the study of speech in different situations. From his description of two very different speech communities— one in India, the other in Norway—he is able to develop a conceptual framework which allows of the more precise study of speech as part of the social process in any community. The value of studying multilingual speech communities lies in the fact that the object of study—the differential use of speech in different situations—is more open to view than it is in monolingual communities, where the boundaries between different language varieties are more fluid.

English speakers who live in monolingual communities may thus gain a clearer insight into their own speech habits.

The general phenomenon of language, then, can be studied both as a system and as behaviour. In studying a language system we abstract speech from its social context and concentrate on its structural properties, that is, on the finite resources of which we can make infinite use. In studying language behaviour we concentrate on the variety of ways in which language is used and we attempt to look at speech as part of a social process.

David Stringer

3 The structure of language

R. H. Robins

Introduction

Linguistics is quite simply the scientific study of human language in all its manifestations and uses, near and far, present and past, without restriction on time, place, or culture. In this respect linguistics is different from language study, since this latter term is ordinarily used to refer to the study of a particular language, say Latin, French, or German, as a means to reading its literature in the original, or for purposes of written or spoken communication with its speakers in the case of a living language. The linguist, in the sense of the student of linguistics, studies languages, his own and foreign languages, as examples of mankind's faculty of language, to learn more about the way language works and how it may best be described and analysed. An American linguist has put this well: 'Linguistic scientists are engaged in developing a sound body of scientific observations, facts, and systematic theory about language in general and languages in particular.'[1]

In one way language is too familiar to us all; every normal human being has thoroughly mastered one language in childhood without knowing much about the process, and in areas and in social situations that require and facilitate it many persons of no more than average intelligence and application have a fluent command of two or even more different languages. Just because language is universal and so much taken for granted as part of our lives, its problems and perplexities, but also its incredible fascination to those who take the trouble to examine it for its own sake, often pass unnoticed among otherwise sensitive and percipient persons.

Linguistics as a subject of learning happens to be very much in the news today. Since the Second World War it has more than kept pace with the general expansion of university education over almost the whole world, and one of its ablest and most stimulat-

Source: *Linguistics at Large*, ed. N. Minnis, Gollancz (1971), 13–32.

ing scholars, Noam Chomsky, known both for the far-reaching changes he has brought about in almost all aspects of linguistic studies and for his public championing of certain political causes, has been accorded the status of one of the thousand makers of the twentieth century in a recent Sunday newspaper magazine series.

Though as a recognized independent subject linguistics is fairly new, linguistic speculation and the analysis of languages have occupied men's minds from the earliest days of civilization in a number of different cultures. In the history of European civilization linguistic thought, like thought in so many other areas, began in Ancient Greece, under the cover-all title of 'philosophy' (philosophía). Pre-Socratic philosophers discussed language, and one of the Socratic dialogues of Plato, the *Cratylus*, is devoted to language. The observations of Plato, Aristotle, and the Stoics on language appear as part of their general exposition of the theory of knowledge and of the principles of logic, though it is to the Stoics that we much attribute the recognition of a specific branch of study relating to the form and function of human speech.

Under the influence of Alexandrian literary criticism, linguistic studies developed some degree of independence in later antiquity, but subsequently other factors promoted close contacts between philosophers and grammarians. This was notably the case with the 'speculative grammars' of the later Middle Ages, when scholastic metaphysics and Priscian's Latin grammar (itself a product of Alexandrian literary scholarship) were fused together in a remarkable synthesis of logic, metaphysics, and grammatical theory.[2]

Thereafter empiricism and rationalism made their contributions to the linguistic thinking of Europe in and after the Renaissance; but in addition Europeans were now learning not only about languages spoken outside Europe, but also about the work of linguists in other parts of the world. China, the Jews and the Arabs, and the Sanskrit phoneticians and grammarians of Ancient India have all contributed to our present-day achievements in linguistic science. In particular the excellence of the Indian work and the knowledge gained from it of the Sanskrit language vitally stimulated European linguistics in the early nineteenth century. Sir William Jones, the two Schlegels, Wilhelm von Humboldt, Jakob Grimm, Schleicher, Whitney, Brugmann, and de Saussure are just a few of those who at the end of the eighteenth century and throughout the nineteenth laid the foundations on which we today are still building.

Speech

We do well to examine language primarily and principally from the starting point of speech. One is used in literate civilizations like our own to think of languages as systems of writing with a pronunciation; it is better to think of them as systems of oral communication that may in some way be represented in writing. Every normal person speaks, but in many language areas those who can write are few, and everywhere speaking and hearing occupy far more time than writing and reading. Speech is a skill acquired by a child before writing, and in the span of human history writing is very much a newcomer, perhaps three to four thousand years old, while speech is probably coeval with homo sapiens. We may say that it is the conditions of speaking and listening rather than those of writing and reading that have determined the development of language in general and of each particular language. Moreover (and this is one of the more valuable incidental lessons of linguistic studies) the orderliness, complexity, and efficiency of the languages of illiterate peoples, whose cultures are labelled primitive by outside observers, are not inferior (or superior) in quality or degree; nor indeed are the languages of such peoples markedly different in form from languages long studied and familiar as the literate vehicles of world-wide civilizations.

Speaking is essentially making and responding to certain sets of noises by means of which we co-operate in living in and understanding our common world and in regulating our relations with one another therein; the more portentous definition of speech as the expression and communication of thought may be taken as covering a relatively small part of this more general and humdrum activity. The material of speech, sounds emitted from the vocal tract, is limited, but its range and application, nothing less than the entire furniture of earth and heaven and all our doings therein, is unlimited. Yet speaking is only a by-product, an exploitation of waste; with few exceptions, that do not alter the general picture, speaking is simply the noisy interference with expiratory, used, air as it passes up from the lungs through and over the various organs of speech: glottis, tongue, palate, teeth, lip, nasal passage, etc. Breathing out, expiration, is a biologically essential process of ridding the lungs of air charged with carbon dioxide. The energy expended

in additionally interfering with it to make a noise, that is, to speak, is minute. In the light of the place taken by language (i.e. by speech) in human life as we know it, one may challenge anyone to name any other use of a spent material that comes anywhere near it in power and significance. Moreover the organs of speech, as they are called, the tongue, the teeth, and so on, are not primarily organs used in speaking, in the way that, for example, the lungs are the organs of breathing and the stomach the organ of digestion; they are organs performing a number of functions in the economy of the human body, and speaking, noisily and purposively interfering with spent breath, is just one function superimposed on them.

Yet this wonderful and complex activity is learned by any normal child in his or her early years. In childhood we master the pronunciation and the grammar of our native, our first or only, language, and its basic vocabulary; grammar and pronunciation are more or less exhaustively acquired for the spoken language in childhood (except in cases of rapid language change, personal dialect replacement, or the like), but our vocabulary goes on changing and enlarging itself all our lives; we learn new words and new uses of old words almost every day, fitting them in to our established pronunciation patterns and grammatical rules.

Form and meaning

We have, then, two sides to language: form and meaning. We can use a range of noises in socially shared patterns to achieve some purpose. Form and meaning are thus in part related as means to end, and both are the proper objects of linguistic science. While other disciplines, such as philosophy, psychology, and literary criticism, all concern themselves with language and with meaning, they do not, rightly from their points of view, hold the whole of language central in their focus of attention, but they are concerned primarily with the place of language in their own fields of inquiry. Some linguists have been almost frightened away from the study of the meaning side of language, because it seems so full of pitfalls and so much less tangible than the forms themselves. One should try to keep both form and meaning within the discipline of linguistics, but one can more easily start with form because it is more readily observable; its field is delimited (sounds and written marks), while that of meaning, if not actually infinite, is certainly unlimited in range. Meaning has in the past been confused with reference or denotation, one aspect of language use, the association of many words, but not of all, in languages with identifiable individual things, persons, processes, and states of affairs, or with classes of them. Too often reference has been universalized by the hypothetizing of 'ideas' as the other end of a binary relation between the word and its meaning, though it may be hard to say just what an idea in such a use is except (circularly) that it is the supposed meaning of the word in question. It is probably better to regard meanings as the ways in which words, and types of sentence construction (statement, question, etc.) are used in different situations, or part of the rules for their use, rules known performatively by speakers, acquired by children and second language learners, and made explicit by linguists, especially in their rôle as makers of dictionaries. Referential or denotative use is part of the use to which many words are put, but it is not to be equated with the whole of meaning.

The linguist, then, starts from linguistic form, or from linguistic forms, which he assumes to be meaningful, for that is the main criterion of language as contrasted with babbling or scribbling. But form is not the same as all the sounds spoken or all the symbols written in a language. In studying a language the linguist is not just collecting utterances on tape or on paper and stopping there. Understanding a language means making abstractions from the material, to which the multiplicity of actual utterance can be referred and by which it can be explained. The child does this unconsciously as he learns his language; the linguist does it consciously and makes his work explicit. It involves two things, discovering the relevant facts and framing abstractions to cover them, and stating these in such a way as to make this acquired knowledge available to all comers. Work with languages that do not possess a writing system has taught us a great deal about the techniques of discovery and of statement, essentially speeding up and ordering the work of the language learner anywhere.

Linguistic form, the product of the abstraction process that the linguist applies to his material, covers a familiar field: pronunciation, grammar, and vocabulary, though it deals with this field somewhat differently from traditional pedagogy. In many respects the linguist's abstractions correspond with the intuitions of native speakers themselves on the working of their language. His abstractions fall into general and particular, phonetics, phonology, and grammar on the one hand, and lexicon or vocabulary on the other, the provinces of the grammar book (in its widest sense) and the dictionary respectively. All of this may be considered from two points of view, that of a language as it operates at any one time as a means of communication and without reference to its past or its future, and that of a language as a continuing system that evolves through time, though its speakers are largely unaware of the process. Both these points of view, descriptive linguistics and historical linguistics, as they are called, are equally important in the understanding of human language. At present most attention seems to be devoted to descriptive linguistics; in the nineteenth century the historical point of view predominated, largely under the influence of the discovery of the genetic relations linking Sanskrit with the classical and with most of the modern languages of Europe in the Indo-European family. In England this field of study was often designated 'comparative philology', and the term is still in use.

Phonetics and phonology

If, in line with what was said earlier, we consider language primarily in its spoken form, we see that a double set of abstractions can be made from speech: the virtually infinite number of phonetic differences in people's speech can be assigned to limited sets of units with rules of combination and sequence, and the limitless word stock of a language (limitless because it can always be added to by borrowing or by new creations) can be assigned to limited sets of classes that exhibit limited sets of categories controlling their occurrence in constructions or sentence structures.

The abstractions involved in linguistic form can best be illustrated in the first place at the level of phonology. Phonetics and phonology cover the field rather loosely called 'pronunciation' in many textbooks of foreign languages. An abstraction at this level is indeed unconsciously made or assumed whenever we speak of 'the English language', 'the German language', and so on, with reference to speakers of the standard dialect (or to any other dialect, though in the context of foreign language learning and teaching, the standard dialect is usually taken without comment to represent 'the language'). Every person's speech is different from everyone else's; we can distinguish voices over very imperfect channels like telephones; the voices of several speakers of the same age, sex, and locality can be kept distinct throughout a radio play or discussion, though we may never have heard any of the speakers before; and we can recognize the voices of our friends from behind closed doors. Every different feature of these different voices, like every other audible aspect of speech, is the product of slightly different shapes, positions, and movements of the vocal organs, resulting in different configurations of the sound waves and in their different impact through the ears on the auditory perceptual centres of the brain of the hearer.

But in listening to what is said, to the message as opposed to recognizing who is talking (and we often do not care, as when we are shopping, travelling, listening to news broadcasts, and the like), we push all this aside and concentrate on certain differences only. The total number of differences which the vocal organs are capable of making and the auditory mechanism is capable of receiving may be virtually limitless (at least one knows as yet no way of setting limits, which probably vary with each individual); but in the ordinary use of our language, or of any language, we seize on distinctive differences, not just any differences. These distinctive differences can largely be located in segments, and this is the basis of alphabetic writing, just one more legacy of Ancient Greek genius. An alphabet does not cover the representation in writing of all and only the distinctive differences in the spoken words of a language; hence the notorious difficulties of English spelling, though most orthographies have similar weaknesses from this point of view; and in all languages there are some non-segmental features, such as stress in English (compare *import* as a noun and as a verb in pronunciation) and intonation, which also can and should be analysed in terms of limited sets of distinctive differences.

For these reasons phonological transcriptions have been devised, partly as the result of years of attempted 'spelling reforms'. A phonetic transcription represents as far as it can every perceptible difference in what is said; a phonological transcription only employs separate symbols for those segments and other elements that are distinctively different in the language for which it is constructed. In the English word *pin* there are only three such units. *Pin* is minimally distinct from *bin*, from *pen*, and from *pit*. Other audible differences, such as loudness and pitch, do not alter the word you recognize. But such features may be distinctive in the words of other languages; in north Chinese *pin* said on a level tone and *pin* said on a rising tone are different words. Phonetic differences are indefinitely divisible, but the phonological form of a language recognizes only discrete distinctions. I can say the words *pin* and *bin* in all sorts of ways, with more or with less initial aspiration, with heavier or lighter vibration of the vocal cords in the *b*, etc., but as long as·you assume that I am talking English you will try to assign what I say to one or the other of the two words. You may think that I am teasing, that I am a bit drunk, that I am a foreigner or a speaker of an unfamiliar dialect, but you will always seek to impose on what I say the pattern of distinctive segments and other elements that you have come to recognize for the English language. *Pin*, *bin*, *pen*, and *pit* can differ distinctively at three places only, and there only by the substitution of limited sets of consonants and vowels.

Certain marginal aspects of language are not like this. If I speak softly you will understand that I am being confidential, intimate, or perhaps reassuring; if I shout you assume that I am angry or excited, and the louder I shout the angrier you think I am. We are all familiar with arguments in which each party gets more and more worked up and shouts louder and louder. There are no distinctive jumps here from one unit of loudness to another, but a continuous scale interpreted as such by speaker and hearer. This sort of scalar characteristic of the marginal aspects of speech is found also in non-linguistic ejaculations like screams, but it is not found with the central and specifically linguistic component of the speech signal.

Differences that are not distinctive of one unit from another in a particular language are either ruled out by correct (i.e. a native speaker's) pronunciation, or are irrelevant to the form of the utterance, as are differences in personal voice quality, or are conditioned by the position of the sound unit in relation to neighbouring sounds. Languages differ in their allocation of distinctiveness. English /k/ (the set of sounds heard initially in words like *keep*, *cut* and *card*) is articulated with a more forward part of the tongue before /i:/, a vowel articulated in the front of the mouth, as in *keep* (/ki:p/), and with a part of the tongue further back before /u:/, a vowel articulated in

the back of the mouth, as in *cool* (/ku:l/). These two sorts of /k/ sound are not of themselves distinctive in English, and cannot alone distinguish one word from another; they belong therefore to the same distinctive unit, or phoneme, as such units are technically called. In southern English /k/ sounds are aspirated (pronounced with a little puff of air) initially, as in *kin*; after an /s/ this is not the case; in *skin* the /k/ is unaspirated, but in view of the different environments in which these two varieties of /k/ sounds occur they are not distinctive, and they are assigned to the same phoneme. But in other languages, where they can stand in the same environment in minimal contrast, an aspirated and an unaspirated *k* sound can constitute separate phonemes, as in Hindi, where /k/ and /kʰ/ distinguish the two words /kana/, one-eyed, and /kʰana/, to eat. We saw that in Chinese the pitch, or tone, of a syllable can by itself distinguish one word from another, and in Chinese one must recognize tone phonemes, varying in their number from four in the north to eight or nine in some varieties of Cantonese in the south.

Thus for each language there are found a limited number of distinctive units, or phonemes, that carry the messages and represent the phonological form of the language. In this connection it is necessary to recognize the various dialects of a language as separate languages as far as their phonological form is concerned. The limited number of phonemes may vary a little as between one description and another according to the precise method used by the linguist, but the principle is the same; from the virtually limitless stock of possible phonetic differences a strictly limited set of phonemes may be abstracted, and it is these that constitute the phonological form of the language and are the bearers of its messages.

Phonemes are limited in number, varying between around fifteen and fifty for different languages. But these limited numbers may be resolved into combinations of even fewer distinctive features. English /p/, /t/, and /k/ differ by their place of articulation only, being bilabial, alveolar, and velar, respectively; they share the features of voicelessness (non-vibration of the vocal cords) and the feature of plosion (complete stoppage of air followed by sudden release). /p/ and /b/, /t/ and /d/, and /k/ and /g/ (as in *get* and *gate*) differ only in respect of voicelessness versus voice (vibration of the vocal cords) in each pair. /m/, /n/, and /ŋ/ (spelled *ng*, as in *sing*) share the three articulatory positions of /p/ and /b/, /t/ and /d/, and /k/ and /g/, respectively, and differ from them only in being nasally released, the air passing out through the nose while they are being articulated. So in this section of English phonology nine distinctive units, nine phonemes, are the product of just six distinctive features, three of place of articulation, and three of manner of articulation; and each of these features, and of all the others likewise involved in the phonological form of any language, depends for its production on the particular configuration of the vocal tract at the time of articulation.

Control over such configurations and recognition of the features resulting from them are part of what is familiarly known as learning a language.

Phonological form involves more than the recognition of the phonemes and distinctive features of a language. Consonant and vowel phonemes occur sequentially in syllables, and the possibilities of syllable structure vary greatly from one language to another. In English /h/ cannot occur finally (the letter *h* when final usually indicates a long vowel, not aspiration, as in *hurrah*), and /ŋ/ cannot occur initially in a word. They can in Malay, as in *tengah* (/tŋah/), 'middle', and *ngaran* (/ŋaran/), 'name', words which English speakers find difficult to pronounce, although they contain no non-English consonants, but just non-English arrangements of them. English and German permit far more clustering of consonants before and after a vowel than many languages do; word forms like *strengths* and *sprichst* would be quite impossible in Italian and still more outlandish in Fijian or Hawaiian, where no syllable is closed with a consonant at all (all syllables being open, like English *he* and *to*). In English voiced and voiceless consonants are distinctive initially and finally in words (*pit, bit, cup, cub*), but in German this distinction does not operate finally: *Deich* and *Teich* contrast, but *Bad* and *bat*, though different words and different spellings, are pronounced exactly alike.

Only the main outlines of phonological analysis have been sketched here, but this may be enough to make clear the difference between the gross phonetic repertoire employed by a language and the phonological form of that language. The phoneme theory and phonological theory generally is full of controversies, some of them quite radical, which are not even touched on here. In the study of an unwritten language a phonemic analysis is the prerequisite for a usable transcription, and a subconscious apperception of phonemic principles underlay the Greek adaptation of the Phoenician syllabary to the form of an alphabet.

Phonological form depends not on absolutes, but on contrastive entities defined by their relations with one another in structures within the phonological system of the language. This is why linguistics is frequently called 'structural' and why we speak so often of 'linguistic systems'. System and structure, internal organization, are being opposed to mere aggregations of independent entities, and form is being opposed to substance. One can illustrate how different functions may determine form differently, though the brute facts of substance are the same; in English /b/ contrasts in the bilabial consonants with voiceless /p/ and nasal /m/, and its form and designation is 'voiced bilabial plosive', nothing else being distinctively involved; but in Hindi a phonetically identical consonant sound contrasts with /pʰ/ (voiceless aspirated) and /bʰ/ (voiced aspirate) as well as with /p/ and /m/, and it is in consequence designated in Hindi phonology as a 'voiced unaspirated bilabial plosive', entering into a different set of immediately contrastive relations.

Grammar

The concept of form in language, which has been explained and illustrated through phonology, is equally valid and essential in grammar, and the distinction of phonetics and phonology gives us only half the picture. Grammar involves a separate level of analysis and description and is no less systematic and structured. Grammatical form is indeed probably the more familiar in the guise of traditional grammar, since both phonetics and phonology have traditionally lain too much under the misleading heading of 'the pronunciation of the letters'.

Grammar is less dependent on the phonetic substance itself than is phonology; therefore the grammar of a written language (e.g. written English) is similar to, but not the same as, the grammar of a spoken language (e.g. spoken English), and we can study the grammar of a dead language, like Latin or Ancient Greek, without knowing all we would like to about its phonetics (and what we do know is happily ignored by most teachers and students of these languages). In the European grammatical tradition the system of word classes, or 'arts of speech', is long established and familiar, and with it the sets of grammatical categories (case, number, tense, person, gender, etc.) that are assigned to the classes and define their membership.

The concept of the word class is a sound one in principle as well as in practice, but the word as a formal unit in grammar cannot be taken for granted, however obvious a sort of unit it appears to us who are familiar with dictionaries and with printed spaces between orthographic words. Formally it must be defined in some way. Very practically, in a newly discovered language where shall we write our spaces in transcribed sentences? We do not hear a pause between most words in connected speech (*a loan* and *alone* are exact homophones), and meanings are a poor guide. *The house* is two words in English, but its translation *huset* is one word in Norwegian; *multiracial* and *consisting of several races* mean much the same, but the former is one word and the latter comprises four words. But what we do find in all languages, written and unwritten, is that sentences consist of sequences of smaller stretches which occur again and again, and which exhibit an internal stability and cohesion together with an external mobility in relation to other such stretches in sentences. *Indefensibility* and *interdenominationalism* keep their syllables in the same order and they cannot be split up by the insertion of other words, but they can appear at almost any point in a sentence. Of course there are marginal cases; it is not easy to decide firmly one way or the other on the status of the unemphatic pronouns in French, which are traditionally written with spaces when they occur before the verb and are hyphenated when they follow it. But the principle is clear, and techniques have been devised for applying it to the grammatical analysis of unwritten languages as well as for checking it against the orthographic practice of written ones.

The importance of the word as a formal grammatical unit is partly that on it rests the distinction between morphology, the study of word structure, and syntax, the study of sentence structure, a traditional division within grammar, which despite, or perhaps because of, a good deal of reexamination is still a useful part of the linguist's descriptive apparatus. What is important to reverse is the too frequent attitude that treats morphology as the prime or central part of grammar and syntax as its appendix; from this attitude spring absurd judgments such as 'English has less grammar than Latin', or 'languages like Chinese have no grammar'. The burden of sentence construction and sentence interpretation may be differently divided between word form variation and the grouping and order of words, and languages like Chinese have little of what corresponds to morphological structure in languages like English and German, but no language just strings its words together, and Chinese syntax can be stated systematically (indeed it must be so stated) no less than the syntax of English or Latin, or of any other language. If anything syntax is the heart and soul of language, with morphology a means of marking syntactic relations employed to varying degrees in different languages.

The phonological form and the grammatical form of a language are interrelated but distinct, and one may approach them from either direction, phonology first or grammar first; and on this there is no lack of controversy. The essential point is that phonology alone does not tell us all we need to know about the sentences of a language, and patterns and structural constraints depending on considerations other than those of phonology force themselves on our attention. *The horse are sleeping* and *the horses is sleeping* are as pronounceable as *the horse is sleeping* and *the horses are sleeping*, but only the last pair is acceptable in standard English. *Horse horses, dog dogs, cat cats*, and *penny pence* are grammatically associated, whereas *fen fence, hen hence*, and *Len lens* are not; and the phonologically very unlike pairs *foot feet, hand hands, mouse mice*, and *rat rats* are grammatically equivalent, and so are *bake baked* and *take took*.

A manifest fact of language is that grammar is more obviously related to meaning than phonology is; the meaning of categories like singular and plural and of their representations in word forms (*cat cat-s*, etc.) is fairly clear, whereas meaning can scarcely be said directly to attach to phonological entities as such, except perhaps for intonation tunes and the use of emphatic stress or the like. Once more it must be admitted that on the exact relationship between grammar and meaning and on the place that meaning should occupy in grammatical analysis there is still a great deal of unresolved argument. Traditional names of grammatical classes and categories are often semantic in origin; *Nennwort, dative case, past tense* are obvious examples. But such names or labels are

not necessarily, or even properly, complete definitions; 'giving to', however widely interpreted, can hardly cover all the uses of the dative case in Greek, Latin, and German, uses that in fact are somewhat different in each of these languages; and the term *accusative case*, though now devoid of extragrammatical meaning and probably owing its origin to an ancient mistranslation, has survived quite happily. Grammatical number is fairly congruent with singularity and plurality, but gender, which is no less important in several well-known languages as a mark of concord and of syntactic structure, is notoriously out of line as regards animacy and sex differentiation. The relations between grammatical categories and meanings are of great significance in understanding the ways in which languages work, but one can only be on safe ground in working from the forms, which are usually fairly definite, to the meanings, which are much less so, rather than the other way round. A field of grain is a collective, one or many as you may choose to look at it, but *oats* is plural (*the oats are growing well*) and *wheat* is singular (*the wheat is growing well*); *sunset* is a noun in English, but it would be hard to say whether a sunset is definitely a thing, the usual correlate of nouns, or a process, one of the usual correlates of verbs. It is all very well, and rather charming, to say that in German the compounds of *Mut* are masculine or feminine according to whether the characteristic referred to is masculine or feminine: *Demut*, 'humility', and *Anmut*, 'grace', are feminine, but *Freimut*, 'frankness', and *Übermut*, 'arrogance' are masculine.[3] What about *Schwermut*, 'sadness'? Is it a masculine characteristic or a feminine one, or neither? But formally we know at once that it is a feminine noun, because a native speaker will put the feminine form of the article in front of it (*die Schwermut*). The forms are there, the meanings are the uses to which the forms are put in discourse.

The logical structure of a proposition and the syntactic structure of a sentence are two different things, though they do, in fact, often correspond with one another; traditional grammar did not really get this distinction clear. But when this has been said, it must be stressed that it remains the ultimate aim of grammatical analysis and description to be able to account formally for every semantic distinction that is carried by the grammatical structure of sentences, as against their lexical content. This aim is now in the forefront of the attention of many present-day linguists, who are developing important insights into the semantic potentialities of grammatical structures.

The elements of grammatical form belong in systems and make up structures. The dative case (or, equivalently, the dative forms of nouns, pronouns, adjectives, etc.) cannot be defined in isolation and identified as the same in different languages. There is certainly some correspondence of use, and therefore some translation equivalence, between the Greek, Latin, and German datives; but the grammatical function and status of each must be different, because in Greek it is a member of a five term system of cases, in Latin it is a member of a six term system, and in German of a four term system. The Greek and German datives are involved in constructions with prepositions, but the Latin dative does not construct directly with any preposition. Sets of relations like these between the members of grammatical classes and between the constituents of grammatical structures or constructions are what constitute the grammatical form of a language.

Lexicon

In considering phonology and grammar we have stressed that the elements of language are not to be considered as aggregated isolates but as interrelated members of systems and structures. This applies also to the lexical aspect of language. We are familiar with the standard equipment of the language learner, the grammar book, which includes some account of the phonology, and the dictionary. The lexical description of a language, the task of the dictionary, does not cover other material than that which is dealt with by phonetics, phonology, and grammar, but it deals with it from a different point of view. In grammar and phonology we are concerned with what is common to a large and often open-ended number of items: sentence structures, word classes, grammatical categories, syllable structures, phonemes, etc. In the dictionary we are dealing with each word separately, individually focusing attention on what distinguishes it from all other words in the language.[4] Naïvely one feels that the main province of the dictionary is meaning, the meaning of each word listed, whether the dictionary be unilingual or bilingual; and this is true, just because the meaning of a word, the rules for its use in relation to some aspect or part of the world and of human life therein, must be stated individually. No two words are precisely alike in meaning, absolute synonyms, in all circumstances, and consequently the dictionary must deal with each word in turn. But this does not exhaust its function; grammatical irregularities (like *took* as the past tense of *take* and *men* as the plural of *man*) must also be noted just for their being irregular, outside the general rules for the formations of the word class concerned, and so idiosyncratic to the particular word itself. As Henry Sweet put it, grammar deals with the general facts of a language, lexicology with the special facts.[5]

Because grammar and phonology are concerned with general features and with classes and the lexicon comprises individual words as separate entities, the lexicon of a language is much more flexible and readily changeable and shows more variation between persons speaking the same dialect of a single language. Probably few persons possess exactly the same word stock at any one time, although, of course, all the commoner words they use will be most likely to be shared. Changes in grammar and in phonology are long term affairs, normally noticeable only over spans of hundreds of years; such changes seriously affect mutual intelligibility, in time producing different languages from a common source, as happened with the development of colloquial Latin into the present day Romance languages. But words can be borrowed from other languages or created anew, and then assigned to existing grammatical classes with no difficulty; consider the great number of technological newcomers in English since the end of the war and the rapid rise and evanescence of the slangs and jargons of advertisers, self-conscious teenagers, and others, all within the abiding framework of English grammatical and phonological form. We have ordinarily mastered the pronunciation and the grammar of our native language by mid-childhood; inevitably we have to go on learning new words and new ranges of meaning for existing words all our lives.

Though the lexicon of a language is flexible and personally variable, being composed of individual words as individuals, it is still structured, though more loosely than grammar or phonology, and we can legitimately speak of lexical form and lexical structure, and languages differ in their lexical form as they do in other aspects of linguistic form. Vocabulary is indefinitely extensible through the acquisition of loan words and the invention of neologisms, but at any one time the word stock available to a speaker and his hearers is finite. On the other hand the furniture of earth and heaven is infinite, or at least we have no way of asserting an inventory of its components or of the different ways in which it may be considered and examined. This is what the early nineteenth-century philosopher and linguist, Wilhelm von Humboldt, meant when he said that a language makes infinite use of finite resources.[6] We claim to be able to talk about anything and everything, and we can do this because word meanings are not fixed individual relationships between word and thing aggregated into a lexical heap, like so many labels tied to suitcases in a luggage store; word meanings are in part a function of the total number of words and wordlike phrases available for use in a language at a given time. In a sense a sort of 'Parkinson's law' applies in vocabulary; the meanings of words expand or contract to fill the available semantic space. We can distinguish as many things as we can name, and we can class them in as many ways as we can use a common term to refer to them. A familiar example of this is in the field of colour recognition.[7] The range of humanly discriminable hues, if not infinite, far exceeds the colour word vocabulary of any known language, and it is well known that different languages make their primary cuts in the colour spectrum at different places; a single colour word in one language has to be translated by two or perhaps more colour words in another language and vice versa. In the learning process it is doubtful if a child learns the main colour words in his language separately (in English, *red*, *green*, *blue*, *yellow*, etc.); each one occupies the place it does in the colour spectrum by virtue of the co-presence of the rest of the colour vocabulary. When we need to be more precise than is normally necessary we subdivide the main terms or invent new ones or press other words into technical service: *blush-pink*, *bice green*, *eau-de-nil*, *cream*, etc. The more words there are in a given range the more restricted and exact the function or meaning of each one is. One of the main reasons for the precision of quantitative arithmetical statement as compared with qualitative statement is the infinite extensibility of quantitative terms on the basis of a very small basic lexical stock. According to the degree of exactness required there is always a further term between any two prior terms; thus between 11 and 12 there is $11\frac{1}{2}$ or $11\cdot5$, between 11 and $11\frac{1}{2}$ ($11\cdot5$) there is $11\frac{1}{4}$ ($11\cdot25$), between 11 and $11\frac{1}{4}$ ($11\cdot25$) there is $11\frac{1}{8}$ ($11\cdot125$), and so on indefinitely.

Colour terms are a convenient illustration of the way in which the individual words of a language acquire and are credited with their meanings through their systematic relations with one another in the total vocabulary of the language at any one time and in any one style. If in different styles and in different contexts the system changes, so will the meaning of each word within it, as the words readjust their mutually exhaustive coverage of the whole relevant field of human perception or judgment. If candidates in an examination are graded 'good', 'fair', 'poor', and 'fail', then 'good' is very good indeed and highly commendable; but if a different system of grading is employed over the same field: 'excellent', 'very good', 'good', and 'fail', then 'good' is much lower in rating and less a matter of rejoicing for the candidates so designated. 'A good hotel' means a good hotel generally, but we all know the grading system used by some travel agents: 'first class', 'superior', and 'good', and we may do well to avoid those labelled 'good'.

Conclusion

We have, then, the circumscribed but probably unlimited range of actually different vocal sounds, and we have the unbounded and infinite range of the universe of experience. Our social life depends on our use of language, and in language form and structure are imposed in phonology, grammar, and lexicon on these vocal sounds; and through their use form and structure are imposed on our environment, creating indeed what we call our common world. Many traditions treat language as a sacred thing; they are justified in so doing, for it is language that gives order and significance to primal chaos.

Notes

1 J. B. Carroll, *The study of language* (Cambridge, Mass.: M.I.T. 1953), 2.
2 Cf. George Steiner's outline of the rhetorical approach to language in classical antiquity, in N. Minnis, ed., *Linguistics at Large* (Gollancz 1971), 115–16.
3 P. G. Wilson, *Teach yourself German grammar* (London: E.U.P. 1950), 38.
4 The problem of how the lexicographer verifies the precise meaning of words is discussed by Randolph Quirk in *Linguistics at Large*, 298–310.
5 H. Sweet, *Collected papers* (Oxford 1913), 31.
6 'Sie (sc. die Sprache) muss daher von endlichen Mitteln einen unendlichen Gebrauch machen.'
W. Von Humboldt, *Ueber die Verschiedenheit des menschlichen Sprachbaues* (Berlin 1836, reprinted Darmstadt 1949), 103.
7 See also Stephen Ullmann in *Linguistics at Large*, 83–4 and Claire and W. M. S. Russell, ibid., 166.

4 What is standard English?

Randolph Quirk

All the various kinds of English (determined by differences in occupation, place, education and the like) display their variety in terms of the three dimensions of language: vocabulary, grammar, and transmission. Let us examine how this works out in the following examples of English by present-day writers.

1 Dickie: I'm on Mother's side. The old boy's so doddery now he can hardly finish the course at all. I timed him today. It took him seventy-five seconds dead from a flying start to reach the pulpit, and then he needed the hip coming round the bend . . .
  Arthur: Doddery though Mr Jackson may seem now, I very much doubt if he failed in his pass mods when he was at Oxford.

2 Tonight the wind gnaws
  with teeth of glass,
  the jackdaw shivers
  in caged branches of iron,
  the stars have talons.

3 'What's the matter with your hand?'
  'I seem to have the most boring *thing*,' Vera replied. 'So unattractive.'
  'If it isn't better in the morning, we'll run you in to angel Dr Wingfield in the village. An absolute pie-man, charges two dollars a visit, and looks, I promise you, like Santa Claus.'
  'Heaven,' Vera declared.

4 Nah Jooab's middlin' thick like, bur 'e'd a 'ad to be a deeal thicker net ta know ut ther wer summat wrang t'way ut shoo wer preychin' on, an' so 'e late paper tummle ontut' flooar an 'e sez, 'What the heck 'as to agate on, lass? Is ther summat up or summat?' An' that didnt mend

matters one iota. All it did wer ta start 'er off ageean.
  'Just 'ark at 'im,' shoo sez. ''Ere's me, as thrang as Throp's wife when shoo 'ung 'ersen wit' dishcleyat, an' theer's 'im cahrd uv 'is backside! Coint see a job ut ther is ta do! Wodnt dreeam o' doin' it if 'e cud . . .'
  'Nay!' bust in Jooab. 'Ahm nooan takkin' that quietly. Thers monny a one war ner me an' full weel tha knows it.'

5 At the end of the first act we went out with all the other jerks for a cigarette. What a deal that was. You never saw so many phonies in all your life, everybody smoking their ears off and talking about the play so that everybody could hear and know how sharp they were. Some dopey movie actor was standing near us, having a cigarette. I don't know his name, but he always plays the part of a guy in a war movie that gets yellow before it's time to go over the top. He was with some gorgeous blonde, and the two of them were trying to be very blasé and all, like as if they didn't even know people were looking at him.

6 I met ayont the cairney
  A lass wi' tousie hair
  Singin' till a bairnie
  That was nae langer there.

  Wunds and walds to swing
  Dinna sing sae sweet.
  The licht that bends owre a' thing
  Is less ta'en up wi't.

7 A thrush on the lawn kept looking with its small round eye. Then he would make a dive to see if a worm was there. When he had eaten, he flew away but came back quickly, landing gracefully with a little curtsey. He stood

Source: Randolph Quirk, *The Use of English*, 2nd ed., Longmans (1968), 84–100.

listening. He hopped once, twice, three times....
Then listened again. He repeated this several
times before he got his worm.

8 'Well,' says Ma, 'I kind o' had my face fixed
fer chicken, but I guess we c'n manage.
Here, Lump, you run down to Perkins'
grocery and fetch up a few cans salmon an' any
other vittle ye might think tech the spot.'
    'Not me,' Lump says, 'Jedge tole me ef I got
caught swipin' any more stuff out'n stores, he'd
send me to state's prison sure 'nough.'
    'That so, young Mister High-an'-Mighty!'
snaps Pa Jukes. 'Well, lemme tell you one
thing, you young whippersnapper, ef state's
prison's good enough fer yer brother Timmy,
it's plenty good enough fer you.'

9 My own nostalgia has risen in the memory of
a camp by a rushing stream at the bottom of a
gorge where the sun shines but a few hours
each day. There the smoke of the camp was
redolent with the scent of burning gum leaves;
there was the splash of a lizard taking to the
water, the twittering of birds in the trees, the
laugh of the kookaburra, the call of the thrush,
the crack of the coach-whip bird. The mimicry of
the lyre bird echoed across the gully, while
wonga pigeons and satin bower birds fed on
berries in the neighbouring brush.

There are big differences between these nine passages.
Some of the language we can 'place' at once. We can
say that one is Scots; that another is a northern
English dialect (even if we cannot be more precise);
that another is to be 'placed' socially rather than
regionally—a conversation between two rather fashionable people; that another is an American dialect; that
another is American but is not so much dialectal as
racy and slangy. The sources of the passages are
here listed in random order, and you can probably
pair off each passage with its source quite easily:

Christmas Landscape, a poem by Laurie Lee;
The Face of Australia, by C. F. Laseron;
The Catcher in the Rye, by J. D. Salinger;
The Winslow Boy, by T. Rattigan;
'Runnin' Repairs', by G. Vine, in the *Transactions of
the Yorkshire Dialect Society*;
Empty Vessel, a poem by Hugh MacDiarmid;
Child's essay quoted by M. Langdon, in *Let the
Children Write*;
The Pattern of Perfection, by Nancy Hale;
'The Jukes Family', by Frank Sullivan, in the *New
Yorker*.

Let us consider first the differences in the *transmission* aspect. If we look at passages 1 and 3, we can find
no sign of any difference in this respect, yet if we heard
the four characters speaking, we would at once notice
a sharp difference between on the one hand Arthur
and Dickie (educated British), and on the other hand

Vera and her companion (educated Americans). A
difference in the primary kind of English transmission
(pronunciation) does not necessitate a difference in the
secondary kind (spelling), and in fact does not *usually*
entail a difference. Thus passages 2, 5, 7, and 9 also
use a spelling which is completely neutral as to pronunciation, though two of them are written by English
people, one by an American, and one by an Australian.
This kind of spelling is called English *orthography*, a
word which means the *right* way of spelling.

Here, then, is the first sight of Standard English—a
standard way of writing the language, which is
accepted (with some slight variations) all over the
world as the 'right way' to spell, no matter what the
English it represents sounds like. Indeed, unless we
have had special training in phonetics so that we can
recognize sounds and write them in phonetic script, we
have no other means of writing English than in terms
of the conventions of English orthography. If, for
example, we write *thought* as *thort*, we are not
departing from the principles of English orthography:
we are merely replacing one set of possibilities by
another—instead of the *-ough-* as in *bought, ought,
nought, thought*, we have the *-or-* of *port, sort, short,
fort*. In other words, the spelling *thort* would not
suggest the sound of the word 'thought' to a French-
man or a Russian, but only to someone who knows
English orthography. That English orthography has a
clear systematic basis is shown by the following witty
note by Mr K. Clements in the *Daily Telegraph* (28
Sept. 1955), correcting a writer who had used the
spelling 'gawmless': '"gawmless" is awften spelt
"gormless" by Nawtherners. Orful, isn't it?'

The dominance of orthography over any more direct
representation of pronunciation is also illustrated—
paradoxically enough—in the eighth passage by the
departures from orthography. The writer uses a number of non-standard spellings such as *fer, o', tole,
jedge*, and these are enough for us to be able to give the
writing a context of place and culture. If our experience of the dialect is great enough, we are then able to
supply a dialect pronunciation to the whole passage,
despite the fact that no attempt has been made to
show this pronunciaion in the spelling. For instance,
young, enough, brother, grocery, stores and many other
words are given in the ordinary orthography which is
'neutral' as to pronunciation.

Similarly, although the fourth passage shows a
much more persistent attempt to show pronunciation
in the spelling (and we find it far harder to read in
consequence), there is still a fundamental connexion
with orthography. Indeed, here too there are many
words given in the standard spelling, as for example
thicker, know, gaped, stopped, matters, wife. We must
also notice that although some of the non-standard
spellings in both 4 and 8 indicate dialectal pronunciation (*jedge* in 8 and *takkin'* in 4, for example),
many of them indicate ordinary and universal pronunciation: *sez* in 4 and *c'n* ('we c'n manage') in 8. In
cases of this kind, the convention seems to be that the

non-standard spelling suggests a lack of formal education by implying an ignorance of orthography.

On the other hand, in passage 5 we have a convention of a different kind. In Scots, there has actually developed a partially independent orthography; basically, of course, it is identical with the English orthography used the world over, but there are regular deviations which are widely known among Scotsmen. A Scot will have a 'right' spelling for his form of 'so', 'light' and many other words, whereas a Yorkshireman usually will not.

To a much lesser extent, American usage has developed a separate orthography (*theater*, *leveled*, *defense*, etc), but differences between British and American practice are so slight that we may reasonably regard both these main branches of English as using a single orthography. It is interesting to notice that passages 1, 2, 3, and 5 do not happen to show a single divergence in orthography, although two are British and two American. This may be the point also for us to remember that there is some scope for variation in spelling *within* both the American and British habits: for instance, *judgment* and *judgement*, *connection* and *connexion*, *tyre* and *tire* (the latter being the usual American spelling but sufficiently common in Britain to be given precedence in the *Concise Oxford Dictionary*), *programme* and *program* (the latter again being the chief American spelling but not uncommon in Britain also, especially in the computational sense), and a few others.

On the whole, then, variations in spelling are small, and we may say that in this mode of transmission we have a fairly clear and consistent 'standard'. But in the primary mode of transmission—pronunciation—the situation is very different. Indeed, the chief advantage of our *un*phonetic orthography lies precisely in the fact that it does not carry with it a commitment to a particular area's pronunciation. It is 'neutral' to the vast differences that can be *heard* in the varieties of English, and so it can be understood wherever English is spoken—however English is spoken.

There are great impediments to the general use of a standard in pronunciation comparable to that existing in spelling. One is the fact that pronunciation (the *primary* form of transmission, we remember) is learnt 'naturally' and unconsciously, whereas orthography is learnt deliberately and consciously. Large numbers of us, in fact, remain throughout our lives quite unconscious of what our speech sounds like when we speak, and it often comes as a shock when we first hear a recording of ourselves. It is not a voice we recognize at once, whereas our own handwriting is something that we almost always know. We begin the 'natural' learning of pronunciation long before we start learning to read or write, and in our early years we go on unconsciously imitating and practising the pronunciation of those around us for many more hours per day than we ever have to spend learning even our difficult English spelling. It is 'natural', therefore, that our speech-sounds should be those of our immediate circle; after all, as we have seen, speech operates as a means of holding a community together and to give a sense of 'belonging'. We learn quite early to recognize a 'stranger', someone who speaks with an accent of a different community—perhaps only a few miles away. And quite often, even if we don't habitually speak with our original local dialect, we may feel the need to retreat into it on occasion— as into our own home, when we want to be particularly private and personal, or when we want to declare our basic loyalties.

'Why do you speak Yorkshire?' she said softly.

'That! That's non Yorkshire, that's Derby.'

He looked back at her with that faint distant grin.

'Derby, then! Why do you speak Derby? You spoke natural English at first.'

'Did Ah though? An' canna Ah change if Ah'm a mind to 't? Nay, nat, let me talk Derby if it suits me. If yo'n nowt against it.'

'It sounds a little affected,' said Hilda.

'Ay, 'appen so! An' up i' Tevershall yo'd sound affected' . . .

'Still!' she said, as she took a little cheese. 'It would be more natural if you spoke to us in normal English, not in vernacular.'

He looked at her, feeling her devil of a will.

'Would it?' he said in the normal English.

'Would it? Would anything that was said between you and me be quite natural . . .?'

(D. H. Lawrence, *Lady Chatterley's Lover*.)

As Lawrence implies here, it seems quite natural in most societies for people to recognize two distinct degrees of community: the immediate, local, and familiar community on the one hand; and on the other, a wider and less familiar community to which one also belongs and beyond which begins the foreign world proper. Linguistically, these two degrees are marked by a local dialect and a speech-form which is not specifically regional and which may have an additional prestige. It is to this latter, wider form of English that Hilda is referring when she speaks of 'normal' English as opposed to the 'vernacular'.

Most of us have an image of such a normal or standard English in pronunciation, and very commonly in Great Britain this is 'Received Pronunciation', often associated with the public schools, Oxford, and the BBC. Indeed, a pronunciation within this range has great prestige throughout the world, and for English taught as a foreign language it is more usually the ideal than any other pronunciation. At the same time, it must be remembered that, so far as the English-speaking countries are concerned, this 'Received Pronunciation' approaches the status of a 'standard' almost only in England: educated Scots, Irishmen, Americans, Australians, and others have their own, different images of a standard form of English.

Even in England it is difficult to speak of a standard in pronunciation. For one thing, pronunciation is infinitely variable, so that even given the will to adopt a single pronunciation, it would be difficult to achieve. The word *dance* may be pronounced in a dozen ways even by people who do not think of themselves as dialect speakers: there is no sure way of any two people saying the same word with precisely the same sound. In this respect, pronunciation much more closely resembles handwriting than spelling. In spelling, there are absolute distinctions which can be learnt and imitated with complete precision: one can know at once whether a word is spelt in a 'standard' way or not. But two persons' handwriting and pronunciation may both be perfectly intelligible, yet have obvious differences without our being able to say which is 'better' or more 'standard'.

Moreover, while the easy and quick communications of modern times have mixed up and levelled dialectal distinctions to a great extent, and encouraged the spread of a 'neutral', 'normal' pronunciation, the accompanying sociological changes have reduced the prestige of Received Pronunciation. When Mr Robert Graves returned to Oxford in October 1961 to take up the Professorship of Poetry, *The Times* reported him as saying, 'Only the ordinary accent of the undergraduate has changed. In my day you very seldom heard anything but Oxford English; now there is a lot of north country and so on. In 1920 it was prophesied that the Oxford accent would overcome all others. But the regional speech proved stronger. A good thing.'

We have seen, then, that while there can be said to be *orthography*, a standard spelling, we can scarcely speak of an *orthoepy*—which would be the corresponding word for a universally recognized 'right pronunciation', if we had such a thing. It has long since ceased to be educationally fashionable to teach 'the art of right speaking and pronouncing English' (Simon Daines, *Orthoepia Anglicana*, 1640). We shall leave at this point the transmission side of English.

Although pronunciation is an obvious and immediately noticeable way in which two kinds of English may differ, it is not of course the only way. If we look back at the nine passages which open this chapter, we shall see that they differ very sharply in *vocabulary*. This is perhaps most noticeable in the specifically regional words in passages 4 and 6 (*thrang* and *cairney*, for example) which mark the passages as Yorkshire and Scots. In passage 5, words like *jerks*, *phonies*, *movie*, *guy* mark the passage regionally as American, but also stylistically— within American English—as *colloquial*. That is to say, 'movie' is *merely* American; 'jerk' is *additionally* slang, and as such is largely restricted to familiar, uninhibited, colloquial speech. Vocabulary can also show stylistic stratification without carrying any regional mark. In the American passage 5, we have *yellow* in the sense of 'cowardly' and in the Yorkshire speech of passage 4 we have *gaped* in the sense of 'stared'. Both are characteristic of the colloquial style, but in this style they can be used wherever English is spoken. Lexical differences of still another kind are to be found in the ninth passage. Words like *kookaburra* and *wonga pigeon* are part of the regional usage of Australia only because they represent things in the specifically Australian environment. Thus they mark Australian English very differently from the way in which words like *cairney* mark Scots or *thrang* the English of Yorkshire.

Most of the words we have considered so far proclaim their regional or stylistic status in isolation: *bairnie* is recognizably Scots and *kookaburra* Australian, *movie* American and *doddery* colloquial. But when *yellow* and *gaped* were mentioned in the preceding paragraph, a special note had to be added stating the sense in which each had been used. These words are not colloquial in themselves but only when they are used in a particular way. It is in fact usual to find that the status of a word is to be decided only from the way it is used on a particular occasion. There is nothing colloquial or slangy or American or British about 'old', 'boy', 'jerk' ('the car stopped with a jerk'), 'angel', 'smoking', 'ears'—so far as the words themselves are concerned. But when *angel* is used to describe a doctor it is colloquial, and when people are said to be 'smoking their ears off' this is slang; when a parson is referred to as an 'old boy', these words are being used in a way that is recognizably colloquial (and chiefly British); and when *jerk* is used in the sense of 'odd person', it is both slang and American.

It will be noticed that we are distinguishing between 'colloquial' (also called 'informal' and 'familiar') and 'slang'. There is, of course, some overlap; that is to say, it is unusual to find slang outside colloquial speech. But describing a usage as 'colloquial' means only that it tends not to be used on formal occasions though perfectly polite and acceptable in informal conversation. A slang usage, on the other hand, is not generally introduced into informal conversation unless the speakers are on very intimate terms: slang embraces precisely those racy, daring and (at their best) fairly new expressions that have not been accepted by the majority of us as 'standard English'.[1] This is not to deny that the majority of us can keenly appreciate the wit, vividness or purely bizarre quality that slang may have. It has been described as the ordinary man's poetry, and it is true that the imagery involved in slang is not so very different from that in poetry. On the one hand, we may call a girl a 'heart-throb' or speak of an arduous task that 'creased' us; on the other hand, we have a poetic image like 'the wind gnaws with teeth of glass' in passage 2. The following discussion is interesting in this connexion:

'But'—here Rosamond's face broke into a smile which suddenly revealed two dimples. She herself thought unfavourably of those dimples and smiled little in general society. 'But I shall not marry any Middlemarch young man.'

'So it seems, my love, for you have as good as refused the pick of them; and if there's better to be had, I'm sure there's no girl better deserves it.'

'Excuse me, mamma—I wish you would not say, "the pick of them".'

'Why, what else are they?'

'I mean, mamma, it is rather a vulgar expression.'

'Very likely, my dear; I never was a good speaker. What should I say?'

'The best of them.'

'Why, that seems just as plain and common. If I had had time to think, I should have said, "the most superior young men". But with your education you must know.'

'What must Rosy know, mother?' said Mr Fred, who had slid in unobserved through the half-open door while the ladies were bending over their work, and now going up to the fire stood with his back towards it, warming the soles of his slippers.

'Whether it's right to say "superior young men",' said Mrs Vincy, ringing the bell.

'Oh, there are so many superior teas and sugars now. Superior is getting to be shopkeepers' slang.'

'Are you beginning to dislike slang, then?' said Rosamond, with mild gravity.

'Only the wrong sort. All choice of words is slang. It marks a class.'

'There is correct English: that is not slang.'

'I beg your pardon: correct English is the slang of prigs who write history and essays. And the strongest slang of all is the slang of poets.'

'You will say anything, Fred, to gain your point.'

'Well, tell me whether it is slang or poetry to call an ox a *leg-plaiter*.'

'Of course, you can call it poetry if you like.'

'Aha, Miss Rosy, you don't know Homer from slang. I shall invent a new game; I shall write bits of slang and poetry on slips, and give them to you separate.'

Middlemarch, Bk. I, Ch. xi.

When we noted a little earlier that many words were not in themselves to be given restrictive labels such as 'American' or 'colloquial' but only in particular usages, this was equivalent to saying that there was some kind of neutral usage. Fred may claim, for the sake of argument, that 'correct English is the slang of prigs who write history and essays', but even he would not be able to identify the 'prigs' for whom words like 'thrush', 'lawn', 'round' in passage 7 were slang. And of course this applies equally to the majority of the words in the majority of the passages quoted in this chapter. Even those passages which have the most obvious stylistic marks of one kind or another contain for the most part perfectly ordinary words used in perfectly ordinary ways—as they might appear in private conversation, in a sermon, or in a history book. Words of which this can be said are clearly 'Standard English'. Some people would agree with Fred Vincy to the extent of calling highly technical jargon a sort of slang. In general, we can say that there is far greater agreement in the English-speaking world about standard vocabulary than about standard pronunciation, though with vocabulary too the image of 'standardness' varies to some extent as between the major communities (particularly Britain and America), and even as between individuals.

Finally, let us look at *grammar* in relation to the various kinds of English presented in the nine passages. In number 4, we find numerous features which—although they may seem expected and ordinary in the context of Yorkshire dialect—would be very surprising, and possibly incomprehensible, in any of the other passages. For example, 'shoo wer preychin' on', begins with two features of purely regional grammar: *shoo* is a northern dialect form of 'she', and in the same area *wer* is often used for standard English 'was'. On the other hand, '*e sez* (which differs from Standard English grammatically in having a present tense form instead of a past) cannot be said to represent specifically Yorkshire dialect grammar. Any of us has experience enough to be aware that 'he says' or 'says he' can be heard *anywhere* in this usage, on the lips of people who have had little education. It is not dialectal so much as uneducated or (to use another common term) 'sub-standard' grammar.

In passage 8, *out'n* for Standard English 'out of' is a feature of dialect grammar in the southern states of America, but *Not me*, used by the same speaker, is neither dialectal nor sub-standard but *colloquial* grammar, used everywhere. And of course the same applies to features like the contracted forms of negatives and verbs (such as *won't, isn't, we'll*) which are to be found in passages 1, 3, 4, 5 and 8. These are colloquial grammatical forms which occur in everyone's speech except sometimes when we are being very formal; they are usually avoided in print—except in representations of spoken English. This is why we find the contractions in passage 1, for instance, but not in 7 or 9. Another feature of colloquial grammar which would be avoided in careful, formal writing is to have the plural pronoun *they* referring to an indefinite pronoun like *everybody*: 'everybody smoking their ears off' in passage 5 is in harmony with the rest of the colloquial features in these informal reminiscences.

Grammatical differences between colloquial English and formal, 'literary' English can be further seen in comparing passage 9 with most of the others. For example, we have 'the sun shines but a few hours'—a form of expression uncommon in colloquial English where we would more usually find 'the sun only shines a few hours' or (from a somewhat more careful speaker) 'the sun shines only a few hours'. We may also notice the formal grammatical patterning in passage 9: 'there was the splash of a lizard taking to the water, the twittering of birds in the trees'—two complex nominal groups with close correspondence of form: *splash* balanced against *twittering*, *lizard* against *birds*, and *taking to the water* against *in the trees*. This pair is followed by a list of three further items expressed with identical grammatical structure: 'the laugh of the kookaburra, the call of the thrush, the crack of the coach-whip bird'. Careful balancing of this kind is a characteristic of some kinds of formal, literary English. By contrast, the writer of passage 3 (equally carefully, of course) imitates the careless ease of the informal grammar found in light conversation: 'So unattractive.' 'An absolute pie-man, charges two dollars a visit.'

As we see from these nine passages, the greater part of English grammar is common to all dialects, educational levels and styles: such grammar is clearly within the range of what can be called standard English. But we see also that there are some grammatical features which distinguish one dialect from another within Great Britain, or which distinguish British from American usage, or which distinguish formal from colloquial and colloquial from uneducated usage. There is one other thing that is important for us to see. The major regional distinctions (between British and American usage in particular) do not over-ride others. That is to say, passages 1 and 3 (although British and American) have features in common, because they are both colloquial, and are together in contrast with passage 9—not, of course, because this is Australian in origin, but because it is formal.

It is reasonable to make the term 'Standard English' cover not only the grammar that is common to *all* kinds of English but also the grammar used in the speech and writing of educated people: in other words, we should exclude grammar which is peculiar to dialectal or uneducated use. In effect, this means the usage of the 'wider community' which we discussed earlier in this chapter, the usage that bears least restrictive (such as regional) mark, the usage that has widest acceptability. Since, however, one of the marks of the 'educated' is that they use this kind of English, we are undoubtedly involved in some circularity here as has long been recognized. As an American scholar put it in the late nineteenth century: 'If pressed to say definitely what good American English is, I should say, it is the English of those who are believed by the greater number of Americans to know what good English is' (R. O. Williams, *Our Dictionaries*). To learn

what determines that belief, we should be led to inquire into the workings of that delicate structure, society itself. But Williams's statement reminds us afresh that there are standards, not *a* standard. In grammar, as with vocabulary and transmission, the image of a standard varies to some degree along with the limits of the 'wider communities': in British English, *I have gotten* is dialectal and hence non-standard, but in American English the same form has the status of standard grammar.

Standard English is, as Lawrence's Hilda put it, 'normal English'; that kind of English which draws least attention to itself over the widest area and through the widest range of usage. As we have seen, this norm is a complex function of vocabulary, grammar, and transmission, most clearly established in one of the means of transmission (spelling), and least clearly established in the other means of transmission (pronunciation). This latter point draws attention to one important factor in the notion of a standard: it is particularly associated with English in a *written* form, and we find that there are sharper restrictions in every way upon the English that is written (and especially *printed*) than upon English that is spoken. In fact, the standards of Standard English are determined and preserved, to no small extent, by the great printing houses.

We have seen that Standard English is basically an ideal, a mode of expression that we seek when we wish to communicate beyond our immediate community with members of the wider community of the nation as a whole, or with members of the still wider community, English-speakers as a whole. As an ideal, it cannot be perfectly realized, and we must expect that members of different 'wider communities' (Britain, America, Nigeria, for example) may produce different realizations. In fact, however, the remarkable thing is the very high degree of unanimity, the small amount of divergence. Any of us can read a newspaper printed in Leeds or San Francisco or Delhi without difficulty and often even without realizing that there are differences at all.

Note

1 See further the useful and entertaining account of this subject in Eric Partridge, *Slang Today and Yesterday* (4th ed., London: Routledge & Kegan Paul 1967).

5 Looking at English in use
Randolph Quirk

Rather more than a century ago, Thomas Wade started off on the road to becoming one of the outstanding Chinese scholars of his time. He sought out the best-qualified man he could find and said, 'Please teach me Chinese.' We may imagine his dismay at the reply: 'Which Chinese is it you want to learn, sir? There is the Chinese of the ancient Classics, the Chinese of official documents, the Chinese used in writing letters, and there is the spoken Chinese, of which there are many dialects. Now which Chinese is it that you want to learn?'

Now, of course, Chinese is a notoriously extreme case, but as we have seen, the situation with English is certainly analogous. We are all aware of the distinctiveness of the regional dialects, but we less generally acknowledge the comparable distinctiveness—both in spoken and written English—of other kinds of 'dialect' which are comparably self-consistent and (with a different concept of speech 'community') comparably justified. The incomplete recognition of these makes us too liable to join in the intolerant and ill-informed tirades upon jargon—a wholly pejorative word often applied to a perfectly respectable 'trade dialect' which has its own rules and the users of which have their own rights. We become susceptible also to the great deal of nonsense which is written about incorrectness and impropriety of expression, insisting mistakenly that a given form is either 'correct' or 'incorrect' in all styles and circumstances.

We have seen that the word 'English'—like 'Chinese' —is an abstraction, conveniently summarizing a wide range of different, partly self-contained forms of communication. Only the individual forms themselves have an 'actual existence' as English, but they all have enough in common to justify the application of the generic term 'English' to all of them. One may compare the word 'dog'. Everyone can tell the difference between a dog and a cat, but there is an immense

Source: Randolph Quirk, *The Use of English*, 2nd ed., Longmans (1968), 163–82.

range of animals which share the designation 'dog', and one cannot point to one dog that has all the features present in all dogs: there is no actual embodiment of 'dogginess'. Nor can we say (if the analogy may be pressed a little further) that one dog is 'doggier' than another: a feature that is 'correct' in one variety of dog is 'incorrect' in another.

So it is with English, and in the article entitled 'What is standard English?' (pp. 25–30) we attempted to show something of the total range of English, and singled out from that range some features and forms which we said could be called 'Standard English'. The object now is to look at the corresponding range that exists within educated usage itself and especially at the forms of English that characterize the various *uses* of Standard English. No attempt can be made, however, to discuss all the varieties even within this relatively narrow band which is loosely called 'Standard'. But it is worth emphasizing that the few, very distinctive varieties exemplified in this chapter could easily have come from the lips and pens of people who, for ordinary purposes, would seem to be using as uniform a type of English as it is possible to find. The distinctive features revealed are no less real for that, and may be all the more noteworthy.

Let us consider first an example of religious English, written within the past few years:

1 Eternal God, Who dost call all men into unity
  with Thy Son, Jesus Christ our Lord, we pray
  Thee to pour Thy spirit upon the students of
  all nations, that they may consecrate themselves
  to Thy service; that being joined together by
  their common faith and obedience, they may
  come more perfectly to love and understand
  one another, that the world may know that
  Thou didst send Thy Son to be the Saviour
  and the Lord of all men; through the same
  Jesus Christ our Lord Who with Thee and the
  Holy Spirit liveth and reigneth one God world

without end. Amen. (Prayer published for the
Universal Day of Prayer for Students,
15 February 1953.)

Even the opening two words embody a construction
which is almost entirely restricted to religious usage—
adjective plus noun in direct address. One may
compare the epistolary formula, 'Dear (Sir)', and
beyond that there is little except some colloquial
expressions like 'old man'. We notice that in religious
English the noun in direct address may be postmodified by a relative clause, a feature which is a
common and living one in this kind of English but
virtually unknown outside it.

Perhaps the most obvious characteristic is the use
of the distinctive second person pronoun and the
equally distinctive second and third person singular
verb forms. What is more, the pronoun has separate
subject and object forms, a feature absent from the
usual second person pronoun: something more is
involved than a straightforward one-for-one correspondence such as we find between *lives* and *liveth*;
you corresponds to *thou* or *thee* according to rules
which do not affect you. Such special pronoun and
verb forms are all but absent from other varieties of
Standard English, though some continue to crop up
in poetry from time to time. And some, of course,
continue to flourish in several regional dialects. Of
them all perhaps the third person inflexion in *-eth* is the
most restricted. About two hundred years ago, the
grammarian John Ash tells us that the termination is
'used in the *grave* and *formal* Style; but *s* . . . in the
free and *familiar* Style'. From this time there has been
a severe limiting of the functions grave enough to
require the *-eth* forms and a corresponding extension
of the occasions on which *-s* would not sound to flip-
pant. Even today, however, the special pronoun and
verb forms are not merely optional in religious usage;
if we were to repeat the last part of the prayer,
replacing *Thee* by *You*, and *liveth and reigneth* by *lives
and reigns*, it would sound to most people intolerably
impertinent and irreverent, perhaps even profane. It is
a matter of common observation that forms which are
thoroughly to be expected in one variety of English
give us a sensation of shock when they are introduced
into a variety in which they are not expected.

There are several other features that one might
mention even in this short passage. There is the special
use of *through* in 'through . . . Jesus Christ' which we
nevertheless accept so readily in religious discourse.
And there are lexical words which, if not actually
confined to religious use (*saviour, consecrate, amen*),
are used in other kinds of English chiefly when it is
desirable to convey the echo or suggestion of devotion, piety or high seriousness. But we must turn our
attention to other varieties.

The English of laws and regulations is an easy butt,
and passages like the following can be cited as almost
beyond the reach of ridicule and derision:

2 In the Nuts (Unground) (Other than

Groundnuts) Order, the expression nuts shall
have reference to such nuts, other than
groundnuts, as would, but for this Amending
Order, not qualify as nuts (Unground) (Other
than Groundnuts) by reason of their being nuts
(Unground). (Quoted in the *Daily Telegraph*,
3 April 1956.)

For the purposes of this Part of this Schedule
a person over pensionable age, not being an
insured person, shall be treated as an
employed person if he would be an insured
person were he under pensionable age and
would be an employed person were he an
insured person.
(National Insurance Act, 1964, 1st Schedule,
Part II.)

Yet even this style of writing has its justification
undiminished by the fact that some specimens of
writing in this style may be bad or unnecessarily clumsy.
Any of us with the smallest experience of drawing up
regulations even for a small society or club must find
it easy to sympathize with the lawyer.

Contrary to popular belief, there are few lawyers
who contrive obscurity to make a mystery of their
profession: they regret it, as much as we, that a
contract is difficult to understand—and indeed
impossible if it is heard instead of being studied
visually. The sad fact is that regulations and deeds
have to be drawn up with one's eye steadily on the
potential cheat, not on the majority of us who merely
want to know as simply as possible what our liabilities
or rights are. To this extent, the style of legal English,
too, then, is obligatory and not optional. As the late
Lord Justice Birkett has said (*The Magic of Words*,
English Association, 1953), 'the lawyer . . . must
resolutely eschew the words that have colour, and
content himself with the "hereinbefores" and "afore-
saids" in order to achieve precision.' He does not
actively wish to write obscurely, nor does he wish to
omit the commas which would make his document so
much easier to read. But a very 'light' punctuation is
part of the tradition of statute composition, in
deference to such principles as 'Punctuation is no part
of the English language' and 'Words should stand by
their own strength'. There has thus been a feeling that
if a statute requires punctuation to make it clear, then
the wording must to that extent be deficient and
perhaps dangerously ambiguous. On pp. 366ff of
D. Mellinkoff's valuable study of legal language,[1]
the reader will find a useful discussion of this point.

Here is an example of quite ordinary legal English:

3 Whereas the Insured described in the Schedule
has by the proposal the date of which is
specified in the Schedule which proposal and
declaration the Insured has agreed shall be the
basis of this Contract and be held as
incorporated herein applied to The ——
Assurance Company Limited (hereinafter

called 'the Company') for insurance against the contingencies hereinafter specified Now this Policy witnesseth that in consideration of the Insured paying to the Company for this Insurance the First Premium specified in the Schedule the Company hereby agrees (subject to the conditions contained herein or endorsed or otherwise expressed hereon which conditions shall so far as the nature of them respectively will permit be deemed to be conditions precedent to the right of the Insured to recover hereunder) that in the event of any of the said contingencies happening. . . . (Preamble to a current Insurance Policy.)

The suffixed prepositions (as in *hereunder*) are well in evidence, and we see a good deal of the 'continuous chain' type of grammatical expression that has also been mentioned. Both are in fact long-standing characteristics of legal expression. In the eighteenth century, Shaftesbury writes of the suffixed preposition as being a feature of the 'complicated periods' which 'are so curiously strung, or hook'd on, one to another, after the long-spun manner of the bar'. What is called the 'hook'd on' manner can be seen in the compound reference expressions like 'which conditions' and 'the said contingencies', both making the reference back more precise and unambiguous (if clumsier) than an ordinary relative clause in the first case or an article without 'said' in the second. As a wit has said (*The Times*, 20 April 1963), a lawyer 'has a hereditament in his speech'.

The fact that we still have these characteristics 250 years later shows that legal language is very traditional. It is also, of course, formulaic. Thus *witnesseth* in this passage does not indicate a general use of *-eth* forms as in religious English (*agrees* also occurs in the passage); the archaic *witnesseth* stands in a set piece (additionally marked typographically in the original) dividing the preamble from the main undertaking. The way in which such a fixed formula can stand apart from ordinary linguistic structure reminds us of similar phenomena in (for example) proverbs.

The language of officialdom, which has some affinities with that of the Law, is worth a separate mention, though its features have been the object of much widely read criticism in the past thirty years, from the Fowlers to Sir Alan Herbert and Sir Ernest Gowers. One characteristic is the use of words and phrases that we condemn with the value-judgment 'pompous'. This generally means that words have been chosen which have as little popular echo as possible, since the composing official is afraid—and often with good reason—of being accused by superiors or the public of lacking a proper command of 'dignified', remote, impersonal English. The story is told of how Canning included the phrase 'He died poor' in the text of a monument to Pitt; an official was scandalized by this, feeling that it was grossly deficient in dignity, and he proposed instead of Canning's words, 'He expired

in indigent circumstances'. Smile as we may, we must all have felt similar pressures and inhibitions at some time, even in drafting something simple to put up on a noticeboard. Official English has become a little less obtrusive in recent years, and here is a typical example of it:

4 The symbol † against a subscriber's entry in the Directory denotes that the telephone number is withheld from publication at the subscriber's request and the Post Office is not authorized to supply it to enquirers. The names and addresses of such subscribers are, however, shown in the Directory in cases where frequent enquiries are received by the Post Office for the exchange number, with a view to saving members of the public the trouble of fruitless enquiry. (*London Telephone Directory*, 1955.)

Even here, we may note the phrases 'in cases where' (reminding us of Quiller-Couch's devastating criticism)[2] and 'with a view to', not to mention the rather formidable 'authorized'. We notice also the impersonal style: the writer did not put 'We show the names and addresses', as he might have *said* if he had been explaining the system to an inquirer orally, but 'The names and addresses . . . are . . . shown'. Such a use of the passive (and it occurs a little earlier, too, in 'the . . . number is withheld') was attacked not long ago in a speech at Nottingham, which was reported in the *Guardian* beneath the headline. 'Too Much of the Passive Voice in Local Government' (4 September 1956). The speaker, Mr Derek Senior, had said: 'Half the dilatoriness, the passing of the bucks, the shirking of responsibility, the lazymindedness, and the want of initiative . . . could be eradicated overnight by the simple expedient of forbidding the use of the passive voice in any official document.' This is no doubt a little optimistic, but we can see what is in Mr Senior's mind.

There are similarities to both legal and official usage in the English of industry and commerce, but here we run deeply into the much-discussed, much-misunderstood question of 'jargon'. Let us take the following passage:

5 The programme has included the replacement of existing coke ovens, a new material handling terminal, a sinter plant, the redesign and enlargement of the Company's eight fixed open hearth steel melting furnaces, the installation of two Bessemer converters and a mixer and blower to raise the potential of the melting shop, the installation of a combined slabbing, blooming and continuous billet mill and construction of a new basic refractory brick works at Jarrow.

The five per cent. redeemable Debenture Stock 1975/85 was created by resolution of the Directors and will be constituted and secured by a trust deed charging the undertaking and all the property and assets of the Company present and future (including any uncalled capital) by way of a first floating charge. The stock will be redeemable by a cumulative sinking fund calculated to redeem by annual operation not less than half of the stock at par by 30th September, 1985. (Public Notice of the Consett Iron and Steel Company, December 1955.)

At 'melting shops' and 'floating charges' and 'sinking funds' many may throw up well-bred hands in horror, but though this be jargon, yet there is method in it. Indeed, since the word 'jargon' carried such overtones of disapproval, it would be best to reserve it for recurrent slipshod pomposities as distinct from technical expressions like 'sinter plant' which are admirably clear to those who understand these things, and which are therefore completely legitimate. One frequently hears writing like this condemned because it is incomprehensible, but criticism on this score is often grossly unjust: if we do not understand the *processes* of a given context of activity and situation, we cannot expect to understand the labels for those processes, however they are 'addressed', so to speak. Replacing the terms *sinter plant* or *sinking fund* by something comprehensible to all would involve replacing them with manuals of instruction in metallurgy and finance respectively.

We find the same problem with modern scientific usage, which is particularly fertile in producing expressions totally obscure to the general public:

6 Neuraminic acid in the form of its alkali-stable methoxy derivative was first isolated by Klenk from gangliosides and more recently from bovine sub-maxillary gland mucin and from a urine muco-protein, its composition being $C_{11}H_{21}NO_9$ or perhaps $C_{10}H_{19}NO_8$. This substance has no reducing power, but is ninhydrin-positive. Sialic acid and the methoxy derivative of neuraminic acid are characterized by the purple colour they give on heating with Ehrlich's *p*-dimethylaminobenzaldehyde reagent even without alkali pretreatment (direct Ehrlich reaction), by the violet colour they produce on treatment with Bial's orcinel reagent and by the considerable humin formation on heating with dilute mineral acid . . . Neuraminic acid may be regarded as an aldol type of condensation product of 2-amino-2-deoxy-hexose with pyruvic acid, the aldol type of linkage rendering recovery of the amino sugar by acid treatment impossible. (Letter in *Nature*, November 1955.)

But quite apart from the *lexical* problems confronting us in these industrial and scientific passages, there is a prominent *grammatical* feature that has been subjected to a good deal of criticism. Thus, in place of what we find in passage 5, 'eight fixed open hearth steel melting furnaces', many critics of this style would prefer to see something like 'eight furnaces, of a fixed type with open hearth, for the melting of steel'. Similarly in place of 'bovine sub-maxillary gland mucin' in passage 6 they would prefer a rephrasing to 'mucin from the sub-maxillary gland of cattle': they would prefer to see more 'postmodified nominal groups' and fewer of the heavily 'premodified' ones.

Premodification was roundly condemned by Dr John Baker of Oxford (himself a scientist) in the number of *Nature* from which passage 6 was taken. As a matter of taste, of course, it must remain an open question, though obviously protagonists of the style will rightly advance its brevity on the credit side. But Dr Baker's objection seems to derive its vigour from his conviction that the habit of premodification is reaching Britain from the United States, where in turn it springs from the usage of the many German-born scientists now working in American laboratories. This seems rather dubious, since the premodification of nouns by nouns was a common feature of English before Germans studied science or America was discovered. Heavy modifications in this manner are very frequent in the most commonplace and least scientific English. We not only have 'refreshment room' and 'railway station' but also 'railway station refreshment room', which few would prefer to see broken down into 'room for refreshments at the station of that kind of way which consists of rails'.

Of course, we should always do well to remember that the excessive use of any stylistic device, be it never so genuinely native and natural, can become a serious source of irritation. Some of the varieties of English used in journalism bear this out only too well. In the last resort, the determiners of any linguistic form are mainly habit and fashion, however much we may like to believe there is some useful purpose justifying it. Probably, therefore, it is to these two that outstanding peculiarities in journalistic writing owe their persistence rather than to the demands of brevity and other factors sometimes offered as excuses. One such peculiarity is a piling up of adjectives and relative clauses, even though the information so conveyed is frequently not properly relevant to the rest of the sentence. Consider the following:

7 . . . this dark, slimly built young chemistry student from New South Wales is England-bound next April. A Sydney colleague tells me that the modest, 17-year-old Craig—who celebrated his recent double century against the South Africans by week-ending at his local Youth Club camp—is considered a certainty for the England tour. Craig, who has been handling a bat since he was eight, celebrated his entry into first-class cricket with a streamlined 91 against South Australia at the belligerent age of 16. His tally to date is 654 runs in 13 first-class innings—twice not out. Complementary to his cricket, Craig was

planning to have started a pharmacy course at Sydney University next March. (*Evening Standard*, January 1953.)

Apparently, the Sydney colleague did not say simply that 'Craig is considered a certainty for the England tour' but that '*the modest 17-year-old* Craig is considered a certainty for the England tour', which surely very few people would in fact be heard saying. And in the middle, the writer has interposed (presumably from other sources) the lengthy relative clause about 'week-ending' at the camp, which neither helps to identify Craig nor concerns the certainty of his 'England tour'. Craig's age, of course, is fair material here, but often age and other 'personal angles' dominate a journalistic sentence with less justification. Take the following, for example:

8 Mr John William Allaway, a 46-year-old plumber, his wife, Florence, aged 32, and their 15-year-old son, John, escaped unhurt in their nightclothes after fire broke out at their 200-year-old home, Rose Hill Cottage at Gallows Hill, Kings Langley, Herts. (ibid)

Notice first the special journalistic function of the indefinite article—'a 46-year-old plumber': it conveys the information that Mr Allaway has not been in the news before (otherwise he would be 'the well-known 46-year-old plumber' or at any rate *the* something). It is the more noteworthy, therefore, that in this single sentence about a man we have not heard of, we are given not only *his* age but also that of his house and of its every occupant.

Now, this heavy modification of nouns leads to another fairly widespread feature in journalese. In the *Daily Mail*, July 1958, we find: 'Her 35-year-old Etonian husband, grandson of a millionaire steel-master, said . . .' Here is a rhythm which is atypical in English structure, the heavy qualification of the subject (normally the first noun) of a sentence; in general, the English balance is found by making such heavy modifications to a noun after the main verb (normally the object or complement). And so there develops a tendency to inversion, illustrated in the same column, same 'story', in the *Daily Mail*; a paragraph begins: 'Said the new owner, 31-year-old Mrs Sheena Simmons, wife of a retired auctioneer from Bourne End . . .' We may compare the following piece from the *Daily Express*, August 1958: 'Presiding at the victims' funeral service will be rugged Army chaplain Captain Robin Roe, ex-Ireland international Rugby player, who was one of the first on the scene of the disaster.'

The stylistic traits shown here are widely current in an extreme form in some American journalistic writing, particularly that associated with *Time*. They were amusingly pilloried in 1937 by the late Wolcott Gibbs in *A Bed of Neuroses*; his by no means unfair parody includes the following:

Sad-eyed last month was nimble, middle-sized

Life-President Clair Maxwell as he told newshawks of the sale of the 53-year-old gagmag to *Time*. . . . Behind this latest, most incomprehensible Timenterprise looms, as usual, ambitious, gimlet-eyed, Baby Tycoon Henry Robinson Luce. . . . Once to interviewer who said, 'I hope I'm not disturbing you,' snapped Luce, 'Well, you are.'

It would seem that writers in this style have reconciled a passion for piling adjectives on to the subject of a sentence with the English rhythmic pattern which requires heavily modified nouns to follow the verb; it has been done by reversing the normal English word-order with such results as 'Presiding . . . will be rugged Army chaplain Captain Robin Roe' and 'Sad-eyed last month was nimble, middle-sized *Life*-President Clair Maxwell'.

Not all writing in journalism is 'journalistic' in the sense that it necessarily embodies features found in the passages quoted here. That is to say, we define the features of this style only on positive grounds: they characterize journalistic writing in that they rarely occur outside it. A corresponding caveat is equally required when we come to consider 'literary' English; there are as many varieties of English in literature as there are outside it, to the extent that literature imitates life. When 'literary' is applied to style, therefore, the term is usually rather unfairly restricted to a *belles lettres* sense, referring to linguistic features which, although not having of necessity to be used in literary writing, are fairly rare in other kinds of usage. Let us consider the three following passages in this connexion:

9 It has given me pain to have to relate this incident. To suppress it indefinitely would be impossible. Besides, the Australian people have a right to know what happened and why. On the other hand, it must be remembered that, apart from the limitations of their rigid party system, the Australian Governments had little reason to feel confidence at this time in British direction of the war, and that the risks their troops had run when the Desert Flank was broken, and also in the Greek campaign, weighed heavily upon them. (W. S. Churchill, *The Grand Alliance*, 1950.)

10 That a great many people in this country are but dimly aware of what the banishment of the artist has cost them is certainly true. The tidal wave of ugliness has swept away all but a few of the older, finer things which provided a salutary comparison.

Nor have many manufacturers perceived that the artist-craftsman of yesterday, who has been put out of business by their machines, might at least be replaced by the industrial designer of today, who could show them how to bring seemliness and beauty into the products of the machine. (Gordon Russell, in the *Observer*, February 1953.)

11 Although the power to communicate with others is no longer regarded as a characteristically human achievement, for which no other animal possesses the capacity, the habit of speaking in different languages is peculiar to Man. Thus there has arisen a situation which is biologically unique—the existence of a species in which some individuals are unable to understand the words and meanings of some other individuals. (T. Savory, *The Art of Translation*, 1957.)

If one had to say in three words how these passages differed from the varieties previously discussed, one might reasonably choose 'precision with elegance'. The writer seeks the *mot juste* from a fairly large vocabulary and embeds it in an elegant pattern of word-order and clause interrelationship. Thus in the second paragraph of the Russell passage, one recognizes the precision of *perceived* (a word uncommon except in 'literary' usage) and the elegant network in which it appears; this opens with an inversion preceded by *nor* (again, a literary connective when used after positive statements) and proceeds to a pretty balance of 'yesterday' plus relative clause against 'today' plus relative clause.

Some other features in these passages which have a literary flavour may be mentioned briefly. As already stated, the typical and unremarkable English utterance has a light subject followed by the verb with the heavily modified parts then following; this pattern applies also to the disposition of subordinate clauses: they generally follow a part of the sentence which can be seen as in some way nuclear, thus conforming with the broad underlying pattern of having the main fabric of a structure take shape before the qualifications are added. The opening of the Savory passage illustrates how differently this matter can be treated in literary English: a concessive clause and a relative clause (one of an uncolloquial type) precede the nuclear part which even so begins with a 'heavy' subject. The second sentence of the Churchill passage and the first of the Russell one have as subjects a non-finite and a finite verb clause respectively; in spoken English, both would probably have had 'it' as the subject ('It would be impossible . . .' and 'It is certainly true . . .'). Churchill's last sentence has a noun clause interrupted by a lengthy parenthetic phrase, and a parallel noun clause whose subject is followed by a relative clause, a temporal clause and a parenthetic phrase before the verb, reserved in the majestic Ciceronian manner, makes its appearance.

Although in the criticism of a piece of literary English one may sometimes have occasion to draw attention to the flavours of religious, journalistic, scientific, or even legal style which the author has introduced, it is more usual to find oneself weighing the style against that of *colloquial* usage: 'literary' chiefly operates in contrast with 'colloquial'. Let us therefore turn to the features which characterize conversational usage, and consider first of all the following passage:

12 I often pop an odd paper in here. Do look at this! A bell-ringer's outing to Skegness, before the war, in one of those charabancs with a hood and, I should think by the look of our hair, no mica side curtains that buttoned and split half your nails! Would you remember those, dear? This is the most likely spot in the house. I know I put the recipe in just such a hidey-hole. The bicarb goes with the warm milk. Take a look at that! Got up by a crank uncle of mine. He had eccentric ideas on breathing. One long in, and two short out, I think he advocated, or am I thinking of Morse? (*Punch*, February 1953.)

At once one notices words which would not appear in a prayer or a law or in Mr Savory's book on translation: 'pop', 'hidey-hole', 'bicarb'. And there is colloquial syntax too: an expanded form of the imperative with *do* ('Do look at this'), the indefinite *you* ('split half your nails'), the special use of *would* ('Would you remember those, dear?'). A noun clause introduced without *that* ('I know I put') is also usually colloquial; compare Churchill's 'it must be remembered *that*' and Russell's 'perceived *that*'. Two verb expressions may also be mentioned as commoner in colloquial than in other varieties of English. The first is the 'phrasal verb' as it is usually called, illustrated in '*Got up* by a crank uncle'; one may compare 'put up with' meaning 'tolerate' and 'take in' meaning 'device'. Secondly, there is the feature illustrated by 'Take a look at that'—in other words, the use of a copula-type verb plus noun in place of a fully 'lexical' verb; other common examples are 'have a swim' for *swim*, 'have a smoke', 'have a try', 'take a bath'. It may be recalled that one of the outstanding characteristics of C. K. Ogden's system of Basic English is the replacement of practically all our verbs by nouns preceded by one of a small number of 'operators': instead of 'a war to end war', Basic has 'a war to put an end to war'.

But the piece of spoken English quoted above was never spoken: it is a writer's imaginative attempt to capture the style of spoken English, and although it captures certain aspects of that style very well, one must not leave the impression that spoken English is typically and only this. The writer here is using literary conventions (punctuation marks, for instance) to convey one type of frivolous talk, and the conventions of writing cannot express such features as intonation, stress, tempo and rhythm which belong specifically to *speech*. Moreover, a great deal of spoken English is concerned with topics as serious as those which occupy the writers of 'literary' English. In the following passage, we have a transcript of a piece of serious conversation, recorded from life. The dashes indicate pauses; 'er' and 'um' give conventional expression to voiced pauses:

13 You see um the the um the chief lecturer there is is er um—he is the main lecturer though really he has one or two subordinates but he is the— he gives the lectures the main lectures—there are seminars as well and discussions following upon those but the main lectures are given by him— and he tries—to maintain—um a balance I mean he talks so far he's talked about I missed the last one um unfortunately but he's talked— er and given various sides he's given what he called the er the religious—um aspects of philosophy those who have—a religious point of view who believe in values you know er existing outside the human community—and then what he calls—the—the the secular point of view or the transsecular I think oh no secular point of view—opposed to the transsecular which embodies religious and er the other—er mystical er um approaches I suppose. (Part of a conversation, transcribed from a recording.)

If we are struck by the clumsiness of expression and the inelegant hesitations, we must remember that the conventional orthography used for the transcription has no means of showing those features like intonation which were mentioned above, and which are described in Supplement I. Because of the features which belong *only* to speech, the conversation itself did not sound unduly clumsy. It was in fact fairly representative of the talk we hear around us every day. It serves to emphasize the art which the novelist has to cultivate in order to make his dialogue seem natural *and yet* readable.

There are numerous varieties of English that have not been illustrated here. It is important to realize, after all, that conversation itself can take place on many different subjects and that these subjects will influence the selection of linguistic forms in speech somewhat as we have seen them doing in the written language. And there are some spoken varieties, even among educated people, that we rarely find represented in writing. Mothers and fathers (or at any rate aunts and grannies) are still liable to address a baby with some such verbiage as:

Will the baby-boodlum havums teeny-weeny drinkum-winkum now? Will he then! There now! Mummy wipum baby's mouffy.

Even this kind of 'specialized' language has its traditional characteristics. In his book on English grammar, the pioneer chemist, Joseph Priestley, noted in 1768 that in addressing very young children 'we sometimes use the third person singular instead of the second; as *will he* or *she* do it'.

It is hoped that enough of the varieties of English have been discussed to bring out the extent to which they have characteristic linguistic features. Whether or not we need to be proficient in *producing* all these varieties in our own usage, it is surely useful to be able to *recognize* them and to cultivate a sympathetic, urbane reaction to them. Each has a good deal of interest for the objective student of English and their degree of internal consistency should make us look with a critical eye on any handbook which would seem to suggest that there is a single set of Standard English forms which are 'right' for all occasions.

Notes

1 *The Language of the Law*, Boston 1963.
2 In his fifth lecture *On the Art of Writing*, Cambridge 1916.

6 Diglossia
C. A. Ferguson

In many speech communities two or more varieties of the same language are used by some speakers under different conditions. Perhaps the most familiar example is the standard language and regional dialect as used, say, in Italian or Persian, where many speakers speak their local dialect at home or among family or friends of the same dialect area but use the standard language in communicating with speakers of other dialects or on public occasions. There are, however, quite different examples of the use of two varieties of a language in the same speech community. In Baghdad the Christian Arabs speak a 'Christian Arabic' dialect when talking among themselves but speak the general Baghdad dialect, 'Muslim Arabic', when talking in a mixed group. In recent years there has been a renewed interest in studying the development and characteristics of standardized languages (see especially Kloss, 1952, with its valuable introduction on standardization in general), and it is in following this line of interest that the present study seeks to examine carefully one particular kind of standardization where two varieties of a language exist side by side throughout the community, with each having a definite role to play. The term 'diglossia' is introduced here, modeled on the French *diglossie*, which has been applied to this situation, since there seems to be no word in regular use for this in English; other languages of Europe generally use the word for 'bilingualism' in this special sense as well. (The terms 'language', 'dialect', and 'variety' are used here without precise definition. It is hoped that they occur sufficiently in accordance with established usage to be unambiguous for the present purpose. The term 'superposed variety' is also used here without definition; it means that the variety in question is not the primary, 'native' variety for the speakers in question but may be learned in addition to this. Finally, no attempt is made in this paper to examine the analogous situation where two distinct (related or unrelated) languages are used side by side

Source: *Word* (1959), **15**, 325–40.

throughout a speech community, each with a clearly defined role.)

It is likely that this particular situation in speech communities is very widespread, although it is rarely mentioned, let alone satisfactorily described. A full explanation of it can be of considerable help in dealing with problems in linguistic description, in historical linguistics, and in language typology. The present study should be regarded as preliminary in that much more assembling of descriptive and historical data is required; its purpose is to characterize diglossia by picking out four speech communities and their languages (hereafter called the defining languages) which clearly belong in this category, and describing features shared by them which seem relevent to the classification. The defining languages selected are Arabic, Modern Greek, Swiss German, Haitian Creole. (See the references at the end of this Reading.)

Before proceeding to the description it must be pointed out that diglossia is not assumed to be a stage which occurs always and only at a certain point in some kind of evolution, e.g., in the standardization process. Diglossia may develop from various origins and eventuate in different language situations. Of the four defining languages, Arabic diglossia seems to reach as far back as our knowledge of Arabic goes, and the superposed 'Classical' language has remained relatively stable, while Greek diglossia has roots going back many centuries, but it became fully developed only at the beginning of the nineteenth century with the renaissance of Greek literature and the creation of a literary language based in large part on previous forms of literary Greek. Swiss German diglossia developed as a result of long religious and political isolation from the centers of German linguistic standardization, while Haitian Creole arose from a creolization of a pidgin French, with standard French later coming to play the role of the superposed variety. Some speculation on the possibilities of development will, however, be given at the end of the paper.

For convenience of reference the superposed variety in diglossias will be called the H ('high') variety or simply H, and the regional dialects will be called L ('low') varieties or, collectively, simply L. All the defining languages have names for H and L, and these are listed in the accompanying table.

ARABIC

H is called	L is called
Classical (= H) *'al-fuṣḥā*	*'al-ᶜāmmiyyah,* *'ad-dārij*
Egyptian (= L) *'il faṣīḥ,* *'in-nahawi*	*'il-ᶜammiyya*

SW GERMAN

Stand. German *Schriftsprache* (= H)	[*Schweizer*] *Dialekt,* *Schweizerdeutsch*
Swiss (= L) *Hoochtüütsch*	*Schwyzertüütsch*

H. CREOLE

French (= H) *français*	*créole*

GREEK

H and L *katharévusa*	*dhimotikí*

It is instructive to note the problems involved in citing words of these languages in a consistent and accurate manner. First, should the words be listed in their H form or in their L form, or in both? Second, if words are cited in their L form, what kind of L should be chosen? In Greek and in Haitian Creole, it seems clear that the ordinary conversational language of the educated people of Athens and Port-au-Prince respectively should be selected. For Arabic and for Swiss German the choice must be arbitrary, and the ordinary conversational language of educated people of Cairo and of Zürich city will be used here. Third, what kind of spelling should be used to represent L? Since there is in no case a generally accepted orthography for L, some kind of phonemic or quasi-phonemic transcription would seem appropriate. The following choices were made. For Haitian Creole, the McConnell–Laubach spelling was selected, since it is approximately phonemic and is typographically simple. For Greek, the transcription was adopted from the manual *Spoken Greek* (Kahane *et al.*, 1945), since this is intended to be phonemic; a transliteration of the Greek spelling seems less satisfactory not only because the spelling is variable but also because it is highly etymologizing in nature and quite unphonemic. For Swiss German, the spelling backed by Dieth (1938), which, though it fails to indicate all the phonemic contrasts and in some cases may indicate allophones, is fairly consistent and seems to be a sensible systematization, without serious modification, of the spelling conventions most generally used in writing Swiss German dialect material. Arabic, like Greek, uses a non-Roman alphabet, but transliteration is even less feasible than for Greek, partly again because of the variability of the spelling, but even more because in writing Egyptian colloquial Arabic many vowels are not indicated at all and others are often indicated ambiguously; the transcription chosen here sticks closely to the traditional

systems of Semitists, being a modification for Egyptian of the scheme used by Al-Toma (1957).

The fourth problem is how to represent H. For Swiss German and Haitian Creole standard German and French orthography respectively can be used even though this hides certain resemblances between the sounds of H and L in both cases. For Greek either the usual spelling in Greek letters could be used or a transliteration, but since a knowledge of Modern Greek pronunciation is less widespread than a knowledge of German and French pronunciation, the masking effect of the orthography is more serious in the Greek case, and we use the phonemic transcription instead. Arabic is the most serious problem. The two most obvious choices are (1) a transliteration of Arabic spelling (with the unwritten vowels supplied by the transcriber) or (2) a phonemic transcription of the Arabic as it would be read by a speaker of Cairo Arabic. Solution (1) has been adopted, again in accordance with Al-Toma's procedure.

Function

One of the most important features of diglossia is the specialization of function for H and L. In one set of situations only H is appropriate and in another only L, with the two sets overlapping only very slightly. As an illustration, a sample listing of possible situations is given, with indication of the variety normally used:

	H	L
Sermon in church or mosque	x	
Instructions to servants, waiters, workmen, clerks		x
Personal letter	x	
Speech in Parliament, political speech	x	
University lecture	x	
Conversation with family, friends, colleagues		x
News broadcast	x	
Radio 'soap opera'		x
Newspaper editorial, news story, caption on picture	x	
Caption on political cartoon		x
Poetry	x	
Folk literature		x

The importance of using the right variety in the right situation can hardly be overestimated. An outsider who learns to speak fluent, accurate L and then uses it in a formal speech is an object of ridicule. A member of the speech community who uses H in a purely conversational situation or in an informal activity like shopping is equally an object of ridicule. In all the defining languages it is typical behaviour to have someone read aloud from a newspaper written in H and then proceed to discuss the contents in L. In all the defining languages it is typical behaviour to listen to a formal speech in H and then discuss it, often with the speaker himself, in L.

(The situation in formal education is often more

complicated than is indicated here. In the Arab world, for example, formal university lectures are given in H, but drills, explanation, and section meetings may be in large part conducted in L, especially in the natural sciences as opposed to the humanities. Although the teachers' use of L in secondary schools is forbidden by law in some Arab countries, often a considerable part of the teachers' time is taken up with explaining in L the meaning of material in H which has been presented in books or lectures.)

The last two situations on the list call for comment. In all the defining languages some poetry is composed in L, and a small handful of poets compose in both, but the status of the two kinds of poetry is very different, and for the speech community as a whole it is only the poetry in H that is felt to be 'real' poetry. (Modern Greek does not quite fit this description. Poetry in L is the major production and H verse is generally felt to be artificial.) On the other hand, in every one of the defining languages certain proverbs, politeness formulas, and the like are in H even when cited in ordinary conversation by illiterates. It has been estimated that as much as one-fifth of the proverbs in the active repertory of Arab villagers are in H (*Journal of the American Oriental Society*, 1955, vol. 75, pp. 124ff.).

Prestige

In all the defining languages the speakers regard H as superior to L in a number of respects. Sometimes the feeling is so strong that H alone is regarded as real and L is reported 'not to exist'. Speakers of Arabic, for example, may say (in L) that so-and-so doesn't know Arabic. This normally means he doesn't know H, although he may be a fluent, effective speaker of L. If a non-speaker of Arabic asks an educated Arab for help in learning to speak Arabic the Arab will normally try to teach him H forms, insisting that these are the only ones to use. Very often, educated Arabs will maintain that they never use L at all, in spite of the fact that direct observation shows that they use it constantly in all ordinary conversation. Similarly, educated speakers of Haitian Creole frequently deny its existence, insisting that they always speak French. This attitude cannot be called a deliberate attempt to deceive the questioner, but seems almost a self-deception. When the speaker in question is replying in good faith, it is often possible to break through these attitudes by asking such questions as what kind of language he uses in speaking to his children, to servants or to his mother. The very revealing reply is usually something like: 'Oh, but they wouldn't understand [the H form, whatever it is called].'

Even where the feeling of the reality and superiority of H is not so strong, there is usually a belief that H is somehow more beautiful, more logical, better able to express important thoughts, and the like. And this belief is held also by speakers whose command of H is quite limited. To those Americans who would like to evaluate speech in terms of effectiveness of communication it comes as a shock to discover that many speakers of a language involved in diglossia characteristically prefer to hear a political speech or an expository lecture or a recitation of poetry in H even though it may be less intelligible to them than it would be in L.

In some cases the superiority of H is connected with religion. In Greek the language of the New Testament is felt to be essentially the same as the *katharévusa*, and the appearance of a translation of the New Testament in *dhimotiki* was the occasion for serious rioting in Greece in 1903. Speakers of Haitian Creole are generally accustomed to a French version of the Bible, and even when the Church uses Creole for catechisms and the like, it resorts to a highly Gallicized spelling. For Arabic, H is the language of the Qur'an and as such is widely believed to constitute the actual words of God and even to be outside the limits of space and time, i.e. to have existed 'before' time began with the creation of the world.

Literary heritage

In every one of the defining languages there is a sizeable body of written literature in H which is held in high esteem by the speech community, and contemporary literary production in H by members of the community is felt to be part of this otherwise existing literature. The body of literature may either have been produced long ago in the past history of the community or be in continuous production in another speech community in which H serves as the standard variety of the language. When the body of literature represents a long time span (as in Arabic or Greek) contemporary writers—and readers—tend to regard it as a legitimate practice to utilize words, phrases, or constructions which may have been current only at one period of the literary history and are not in widespread use at the present time. Thus it may be good journalistic usage in writing editorials, or good literary taste in composing poetry, to employ a complicated Classical Greek participial construction or a rare twelfth-century Arabic expression which it can be assumed the average educated reader will not understand without research on his part. One effect of such usage is appreciation on the part of some readers: 'So-and-so really knows his Greek [or Arabic]', or 'So-and-so's editorial today, or latest poem, is very good Greek [or Arabic].'

Acquisition

Among speakers of the four defining languages adults use L in speaking to children and children use L in speaking to one another. As a result, L is learned by children in what may be regarded as the 'normal' way of learning one's mother tongue. H may be heard by children from time to time, but the actual learning of H is chiefly accomplished by the means of formal education, whether this be traditional Qur'anic schools, modern government schools, or private tutors.

This difference in method of acquisition is very

important. The speaker is at home in L to a degree he almost never achieves in H. The grammatical structure of L is learned without explicit discussion of grammatical concepts; the grammar of H is learned in terms of 'rules' and norms to be imitated.

It seems unlikely that any change toward full utilization of H could take place without a radical change in this pattern of acquisition. For example, those Arabs who ardently desire to have L replaced by H for all functions can hardly expect this to happen if they are unwilling to speak H to their children. (It has been very plausibly suggested that there are psychological implications following from this linguistic duality. This certainly deserves careful experimental investigation. On this point, see the highly controversial article which seems to me to contain some important kernels of truth along with much which cannot be supported—Shouby (1951).)

Standardization

In all the defining languages there is a strong tradition of grammatical study of the H form of the language. There are grammars, dictionaries, treatises on pronunciation, style, and so on. There is an established norm for pronunciation, grammar, and vocabulary which allows variation only within certain limits. The orthography is well established and has little variation. By contrast, descriptive and normative studies of the L form are either non-existent or relatively recent and slight in quantity. Often they have been carried out first or chiefly by scholars OUTSIDE the speech community and are written in other languages. There is no settled orthography and there is wide variation in pronunciation, grammar, and vocabulary.

In the case of relatively small speech communities with a single important center of communication (e.g., Greece, Haiti) a kind of standard L may arise which speakers of other dialects imitate and which tends to spread like any standard variety except that it remains limited to the functions for which L is appropriate.

In speech communities which have no single most important center of communication a number of regional L's may arise. In the Arabic speech community, for example, there is no standard L corresponding to educated Athenian *dhimotiki*, but regional standards exist in various areas. The Arabic of Cairo, for example, serves as a standard L for Egypt, and educated individuals from Upper Egypt must learn not only H but also, for conversational purposes, an approximation to Cairo L. In the Swiss German speech community there is no single standard, and even the term 'regional standard' seems inappropriate, but in several cases the L of a city or town has a strong effect on the surrounding rural L.

Stability

It might be supposed that diglossia is highly unstable, tending to change into a more stable language situation. This is not so. Diglossia typically persists at least several centuries, and evidence in some cases seems to show that it can last well over a thousand years. The communicative tensions which arise in the diglossia situation may be resolved by the use of relatively uncodified, unstable, intermediate forms of the language (Greek *mikti*, Arabic *al-lugah al-wusṭā*, Haitian *créole de salon*) and repeated borrowing of vocabulary items from H to L.

In Arabic, for example, a kind of spoken Arabic much used in certain semi-formal or cross-dialectal situations has a highly classical vocabulary with few or no inflectional endings, with certain features of classical syntax, but with a fundamentally colloquial base in morphology and syntax, and a generous admixture of colloquial vocabulary. In Greek a kind of mixed language has become appropriate for a large part of the press.

The borrowing of lexical items from H to L is clearly analogous (or for the periods when actual diglossia was in effect in these languages, identical) with the learned borrowings from Latin to Romance languages or the Sanskrit *tatsamas* in Middle and New Indo-Aryan. (The exact nature of this borrowing process deserves careful investigation, especially for the important 'filter effect' of the pronunciation and grammar of H occurring in those forms of middle language which often serve as the connecting link by which the loans are introduced into the 'pure' L.)

Grammar

One of the most striking differences between H and L in the defining languages is in the grammatical structure: H has grammatical categories not present in L and has an inflectional system of nouns and verbs which is much reduced or totally absent in L. For example, Classical Arabic has three cases in the noun, marked by endings; colloquial dialects have none. Standard German has four cases in the noun and two non-periphrastic indicative tenses in the verb; Swiss German has three cases in the noun and only one simple indicative tense. *Katharévusa* has four cases, *dhimotiki* three. French has gender and number in the noun, Creole has neither. Also, in every one of the defining languages there seem to be several striking differences of word order as well as a thorough-going set of differences in the use of introductory and connective particles. It is certainly safe to say that in diglossia *there are always extensive differences between the grammatical structures of H and L*. This is true not only for the four defining languages, but also for every other case of diglossia examined by the author.

For the defining languages it may be possible to make a further statement about grammatical differences. It is always risky to hazard generalizations about grammatical complexity, but it may be worthwhile to attempt to formulate a statement applicable to the four defining languages even if it should turn out to be invalid for other instances of diglossia (cf. Greenberg, 1954).

There is probably fairly wide agreement among linguists that the grammatical structure of language A is 'simpler' than that of B if, other things being equal,

1 the morphophonemics of A is simpler, i.e. morphemes have fewer alternants, alternation is more regular, automatic (e.g., Turkish *-lar~-ler* is simpler than the English plural markers);

2 there are fewer obligatory categories marked by morphemes or concord (e.g., Persian with no gender distinctions in the pronoun is simpler than Egyptian Arabic with masculine-feminine distinction in the second and third persons singular);

3 paradigms are more symmetrical (e.g., a language with all declensions having the same number of case distinctions is simpler than one in which there is variation);

4 concord and rection are stricter (e.g., prepositions all take the same case rather than different cases).

If this understanding of grammatical simplicity is accepted, then we may note that in at least three of the defining languages, the grammatical structure of any given L variety is simpler than that of its corresponding H. This seems incontrovertibly true for Arabic, Greek, and Haitian Creole; a full analysis of standard German and Swiss German might show this not to be true in that diglossic situation in view of the extensive morphophonemics of Swiss.

Lexicon

Generally speaking, the bulk of the vocabulary of H and L is shared, of course with variations in form and with differences of use and meaning. It is hardly surprising, however, that H should include in its total lexicon technical terms and learned expressions which have no regular L equivalents, since the subjects involved are rarely if ever discussed in pure L. Also, it is not surprising that the L varieties should include in their total lexicons popular expressions and the names of very homely objects or objects of very localized distribution which have no regular H equivalents, since the subjects involved are rarely if ever discussed in pure H. But *a striking feature of diglossia is the existence of many paired items, one H one L, referring to fairly common concepts frequently used in both H and L, where the range of meaning of the two items is roughly the same, and the use of one or the other immediately stamps the utterance or written sequence as H or L.* For example, in Arabic the H word for 'see' is *ra'ā*, the L word is *šāf*. The word *ra'ā* never occurs in ordinary conversation and *šāf* is not used in normal written Arabic. If for some reason a remark in which *šāf* was used is quoted in the press, it is replaced by *ra'ā* in the written quotation. In Greek the H word for 'wine' is *ínos*, the L word is *krasí*. The menu will have *ínos* written on it, but the diner will ask the waiter for *krasí*. The nearest American English parallels are such cases as *illumination ~ light*, *purchase ~ buy*, or *children ~ kids*, but in these cases both words may be

written and both may be used in ordinary conversation: the gap is not so great as for the corresponding doublets in diglossia. Also, the formal-informal dimension in languages like English is a continuum in which the boundary between the two items in different pairs may not come at the same point, e.g., *illumination*, *purchase*, and *children* are not fully parallel in their formal-informal range of usage.

A dozen or so examples of lexical doublets from three of the same languages are given below. For each language two nouns, a verb, and two particles are given.

GREEK

H		L
íkos	house	*spíti*
ídhor	water	*neró*
éteke	gave birth	*eyénise*
alá	but	*má*

ARABIC

ḥiδā'un	shoe	*gazma*
'anfun	nose	*munaxīr*
δahaba	went	*rāḥ*
mā	what	*'ēh*
'al'āna	now	*dilwa'ti*

CREOLE

homme, gens	person, people	*moun* (not connected with *monde*)
âne	donkey	*bourik*
donner	give	*bay*
beaucoup	much, a lot	*âpil*
maintenant	now	*kou-n-yé-a*

It would be possible to present such a list of doublets for Swiss German (e.g., *nachdem ≅ no* 'after', *jemand ≅ öpper* 'someone', etc.), but this would give a false picture. In Swiss German the phonological differences between H and L are very great and the normal form of lexical pairing is regular cognation (*klein ≅ chly* 'small', etc.).

Phonology

It may seem difficult to offer any generalization on the relationships between the phonology of H and L in diglossia in view of the diversity of data. H and L phonologies may be quite close, as in Greek; moderately different, as in Arabic or Haitian Creole; or strikingly divergent, as in Swiss German. Closer examination, however, shows two statements to be justified. (Perhaps these will turn out to be unnecessary when the preceding features are stated so precisely that the statements about phonology can be deduced directly from them.)

1 *The sound systems of H and L constitute a single phonological structure of which the L phonology is the basic system and the divergent features of H phonology are either a subsystem or a parasystem.* Given the mixed forms mentioned above and the corresponding difficulty of identifying a given word in a given

utterance as being definitely H or definitely L, it seems necessary to assume that the speaker has a single inventory of distinctive oppositions for the whole H–L complex and that there is extensive interference in both directions in terms of the distribution of phonemes in specific lexical items. (For details on certain aspects of this phonological interference in Arabic, cf. Ferguson, 1957.)

2 *If 'pure' H items have phonemes not found in 'pure' L items, L phonemes frequently substitute for these in oral use of H and regularly replace them in tatsamas.* For example, French has a high front rounded vowel phoneme /ü/; 'pure' Haitian Creole has no such phoneme. Educated speakers of Creole use this vowel in *tatsamas* such as *Luk* (/lük/ for the Gospel of St Luke), while they, like uneducated speakers, may sometimes use /i/ for it when speaking French. On the other hand /i/ is the regular vowel in such *tatsamas* in Creole as *linèt* 'glasses'.

In cases where H represents in large part an earlier stage of L, it is possible that a three-way correspondence will appear. For example, Syrian and Egyptian Arabic frequently use /s/ for /q/ in oral use of Classical Arabic, and have /s/ in *tatsamas*, but have /t/ in words regularly descended from earlier Arabic not borrowed from the Classical. (See Ferguson, 1957.)

Now that the characteristic features of diglossia have been outlined it is feasible to attempt a fuller definition. DIGLOSSIA *is a relatively stable language situation in which, in addition to the primary dialects of the language (which may include a standard or regional standards), there is a very divergent, highly codified (often grammatically more complex) superposed variety, the vehicle of a large and respected body of written literature, either of an earlier period or in another speech community, which is learned largely by formal education and is used for most written and formal spoken purposes but is not used by any sector of the community for ordinary conversation.*

With the characterization of diglossia completed we may turn to a brief consideration of three additional questions: How does diglossia differ from the familiar situation of a standard language with regional dialects? How widespread is the phenomenon of diglossia in space, time, and linguistic families? Under what circumstances does diglossia come into being and into what language situations is it likely to develop?

The precise role of the standard variety (or varieties) of a language *vis-à-vis* regional or social dialects differs from one speech community to another, and some instances of this relation may be close to diglossia or perhaps even better considered as diglossia. As characterized here, diglossia differs from the more widespread standard-with-dialects in that no segment of the speech community in diglossia regularly uses H as a medium of ordinary conversation, and any attempt to do so is felt to be either pedantic and artificial (Arabic, Greek) or else in some sense disloyal to the community (Swiss German, Creole). In

the more usual standard-with-dialects situation the standard is often similar to the variety of a certain region or social group (e.g., Tehran Persian, Calcutta Bengali) which is used in ordinary conversation more or less naturally by members of the group and as a superposed variety by others.

Diglossia is apparently not limited to any geographical region or language family. (All clearly documented instances known to me are in literate communities, but it seems at least possible that a somewhat similar situation could exist in a non-literate community where a body of oral literature could play the same role as the body of written literature in the examples cited.) Three examples of diglossia from other times and places may be cited as illustrations of the utility of the concept. First, consider Tamil. As used by the millions of members of the Tamil speech community in India today, it fits the definition exactly. There is a literary Tamil as H used for writing and certain kinds of formal speaking and a standard colloquial as L (as well as local L dialects) used in ordinary conversation. There is a body of literature in H going back many centuries which is highly regarded by Tamil speakers today. H has prestige, L does not. H is always superposed, L is learned naturally, whether as primary or as a superposed standard colloquial. There are striking grammatical differences and some phonological differences between the two varieties. (There is apparently no good description available of the precise relations of the two varieties of Tamil; an account of some of the structural differences is given by Pillai (1960). Incidentally, it may be noted that Tamil diglossia seems to go back many centuries, since the language of early literature contrasts sharply with the language of early inscriptions, which probably reflect the spoken language of the time.) The situation is only slightly complicated by the presence of Sanskrit and English for certain functions of H; the same kind of complication exists in parts of the Arab world where French, English, or a liturgical language such as Syriac or Coptic has certain H-like functions.

Second, we may mention Latin and the emergent Romance languages during a period of some centuries in various parts of Europe. The vernacular was used in ordinary conversation but Latin for writing or certain kinds of formal speech. Latin was the language of the Church and its literature, Latin had the prestige, there were striking grammatical differences between the two varieties in each area, etc.

Third, Chinese should be cited because it probably represents diglossia on the largest scale of any attested instance. (An excellent, brief description of the complex Chinese situation is available in the introduction to Chao (1947, pp. 1–17).) The *weu-li* corresponds to H, while Mandarin colloquial is a standard L; there are also regional L varieties so different as to deserve the label 'separate languages' even more than the Arabic dialects, and at least as much as the emergent Romance languages in the Latin example. Chinese, however, like modern Greek, seems to be developing away from diglossia toward a standard-with-dialects in that the standard L or a mixed variety is coming to be used in writing for more and more purposes, i.e. it is becoming a true standard.

Diglossia is likely to come into being when the following three conditions hold in a given speech community: (1) There is a sizeable body of literature in a language closely related to (or even identical with) the natural language of the community, and this literature embodies, whether as source (e.g., divine revelation) or reinforcement, some of the fundamental values of the community. (2) Literacy in the community is limited to a small elite. (3) A suitable period of time, of the order of several centuries, passes from the establishment of (1) and (2). It can probably be shown that this combination of circumstances has occurred hundreds of times in the past and has generally resulted in diglossia. Dozens of examples exist today, and it is likely that examples will occur in the future.

Diglossia seems to be accepted and not regarded as a 'problem' by the community in which it is in force, until certain trends appear in the community. These include trends toward (1) more widespread literacy (whether for economic, ideological or other reasons), (2) broader communication among different regional and social segments of the community (e.g., for economic, administrative, military, or ideological reasons), (3) desire for a full-fledged standard 'national' language as an attribute of autonomy or of sovereignty.

When these trends appear, leaders in the community begin to call for unification of the language, and for that matter, actual trends toward unification begin to take place. These individuals tend to support either the adoption of H or of one form of L as the standard, less often the adoption of a modified H or L, a 'mixed' variety of some kind. The arguments explicitly advanced seem remarkably the same from one instance of diglossia to another.

The proponents of H argue that H must be adopted because it connects the community with its glorious past or with the world community and because it is a naturally unifying factor as opposed to the divisive nature of the L dialects. In addition to these two fundamentally sound arguments there are usually pleas based on the beliefs of the community in the superiority of H; that it is more beautiful, more expressive, more logical, that it has divine sanction, or whatever their specific beliefs may be. When these latter arguments are examined objectively their validity is often quite limited, but their importance is still very great because they reflect widely held attitudes within the community.

The proponents of L argue that some variety of L must be adopted because it is closer to the real thinking and feeling of the people; it eases the educational problem since people have already acquired a basic knowledge of it in early childhood; and it is a more effective instrument of communication at all levels. In addition to these fundamentally sound arguments there is often great emphasis given to points of lesser importance such as the vividness of metaphor in the colloquial, the fact that other 'modern nations' write very much as they speak, and so on.

The proponents of both sides or even of the mixed language seem to show the conviction—although this may not be explicitly stated—that a standard language can simply be legislated into place in a community. Often the trends which will be decisive in the development of a standard language are already at work and have little to do with the argumentation of the spokesmen for the various viewpoints.

A brief and superficial glance at the outcome of diglossia in the past and a consideration of present trends suggests that there are only a few general kinds of development likely to take place. First, we must remind ourselves that the situation may remain stable for long periods of time. But if the trends mentioned above do appear and become strong, change may take place. Second, H can succeed in establishing itself as a standard only if it is already serving as a standard language in some other community and the diglossia community, for reasons linguistic and non-linguistic, tends to merge with the other community. Otherwise H fades away and becomes a learned or liturgical language studied only by scholars or specialists and not used actively in the community. Some form of L or a mixed variety becomes standard.

Third, if there is a single communication center in the whole speech community, or if there are several such centers all in one dialect area, the L variety of the center(s) will be the basis of the new standard, whether relatively pure L or considerably mixed with H. If there are several such centers in different dialect areas with no one center paramount, then it is likely that several L varieties will become standard as separate languages.

A tentative prognosis for the four defining languages over the next two centuries (i.e. to about AD 2150) may be hazarded:

SWISS GERMAN: Relative stability.

ARABIC: Slow development toward several standard languages, each based on an L variety with heavy admixture of H vocabulary. Three seem likely: Maghrebi (based on Rabat or Tunis?), Egyptian (based on Cairo), Eastern (based on Baghdad?); unexpected politico-economic developments might add Syrian (based on Damascus?), Sudanese (based on Omdurman-Khartoum), or others.

HAITIAN CREOLE: Slow development toward unified standard based on L of Port-au-Prince.

GREEK: Full development to unified standard based on L of Athens plus heavy admixture of H vocabulary.

This paper concludes with an appeal for further study of this phenomenon and related ones. Descriptive linguists in their understandable zeal to describe the internal structure of the language they are studying often fail to provide even the most elementary data about the socio-cultural setting in which the language functions. Also, descriptivists usually prefer detailed descriptions of 'pure' dialects or standard languages rather than the careful study of the mixed, intermediate forms often in wider use. Study of such matters as diglossia is of clear value in understanding processes of linguistic change and presents interesting challenges to some of the assumptions of synchronic linguistics. Outside linguistics proper it promises material of great interest to social scientists in general, especially if a general frame of reference can be worked out for analysis of the use of one or more varieties of language within a speech community. Perhaps the collection of data and more profound study will drastically modify the impressionistic remarks of this paper, but if this is so the paper will have had the virtue of stimulating investigation and thought.

References on the four defining languages

The judgments of this paper are based primarily on the author's personal experience, but documentation for the four defining languages is available, and the following references may be consulted for further details. Most of the studies listed here take a strong stand in favour of greater use of the more colloquial variety since it is generally writers of this opinion who want to describe the facts. This bias can, however, be ignored by the reader who simply wants to discover the basic facts of the situation.

Modern Greek

Hatzidakis, G. N. (1905). *Die Sprachfrage in Griechenland*. Chatzedaka, Athens.

Kahane, H., Kahane, R. and Ward, R. L. (1945). *Spoken Greek*. Washington.

Krumbacher, K. (1902). *Das Problem der modernen griechischen Schriftsprache*. Munich.

Pernot, H. (1898). *Grammaire Grecque Moderne*. Paris, vii–xxxi.

Psichari, J. (1928). Un pays qui ne veut pas sa langue. *Mercure de France*, 1 October, 63–121. Also in Psichari, *Quelques travaux.* . . . Paris, 1930, vol. I, 1283–337.

Steinmetz, A. (1936). Schrift und Volksprache in Griechenland. Deutsche Akademie (Munich), *Mitteilungen*, 370–9.

Swiss German

Dieth, E. (1938). *Schwyzertütsch Dialäkschrift*. Zurich.

Greyerz, O. von (1933). Vom Wert und Wesen unserer Mundart. *Sprache, Dichtung, Heimat*. Berne, 226–47.

Kloss, H. (1952). *Die Entwicklung neuer germanischer Kultursprachen von 1800 bis 1950*. Pohl, Munich.

Schmid, K. (1936). 'Fur unser Schweizerdeutsch'. *Die Schweiz: ein nationales Jarhbuch 1936*. Basle, 65–79.

Senn, A. (1935). Das Verhältnis von Mundart und Schriftsprache in der deutschen Schweiz. *Journal of English and German Philology*, vol. 34, 42–58.

Arabic

Al-Toma, S. J. (1957). The teaching of Classical Arabic to speakers of the colloquial in Iraq: a study of the problem of linguistic duality. Doctoral dissertation, Harvard University.

Chejne, A. (1958). The role of Arabic in present-day Arab society. *The Islamic Literature*, vol. 10. no 4, 15–54.

Lecerf, J. (1932). *Littérature Dialectale et renaissance arabe moderne* (Damascus, 1932–3), 1–14; *Majallat al-majmaᶜ al-ᶜilmī al-ᶜarabī* (Dimashq), vol. 32, no 1 ᶜAdad xāṣṣ bilmuꞌ tamar al-ꞌawwal lilmajāmiᶜ al-lugawiyyah al-ᶜilmiyyah al-ᶜarabiyyah (Damascus, January 1957).

Marçais, W. (1930–1). Three articles, *L'Enseignement Public*, vol. 97, 401–9; vol. 105, 20–39, 120–33.

Haitian Creole

Comhaire-Sylvain, S. (1936). *Le Créole haitien*. Wetteren and Port-au-Prince.

Hall, R. A., Jr. (1953). *Haitian Creole*. Menasha, Wis.

McConnell, H. O., and Swan, E. (1945). *You Can Learn Creole*. Port-au-Prince.

Other references

Chao, Y. R. (1947). *Cantonese Primer*. Harvard University Press.

Ferguson, C. A. (1957). Two problems in Arabic phonology. *Word*, vol. 13, 460–78.

Greenberg, J. H. (1954). A quantitative approach to the morphological typology of language, in R. Spencer (ed.), *Method and Perspective in Anthropology*. University of Minnesota Press, 192–220.

Pillai, M. (1960). Tamil—literary and colloquial, in C. A. Ferguson and J. J. Gumperz (eds.), *Linguistic Diversity in South Asia*. Indiana University Research Center in Anthropology, Folklore and Linguistics: Publication 13, 27–42.

Shouby, E. (1951). The influence of the Arabic language on the psychology of the Arabs. *Middle East Journal*, vol. 5, 284–302.

7 Linguistic and social interaction in two communities[1]

John J. Gumperz

The universe of sociolinguistic analysis

Sociolinguistics has been described as the study of verbal behaviour in terms of the social characteristics of speakers, their cultural background, and the ecological properties of the environment in which they interact (Hymes 1962; Ervin-Tripp 1964). In this paper we will explore some of the formal aspects of this relationship. We will examine the language usage of specific groups and attempt to relate it to linguistically distinct dialects and styles on the one hand and variables employed in the study of social interaction on the other.

The raw material for our study is the distribution of linguistic forms in everyday speech. As is usual in descriptive analysis, these forms are first described in terms of their own internal patterning at the various strata (phonemic, morphemic, etc.) of linguistic structure (Lamb 1964; Gleason 1964). Ultimately, however, the results of this analysis will have to be related to social categories. This condition imposes some important restrictions on the way in which data are gathered. Since social interaction always takes place within particular groups, linguistic source data will have to be made commensurable with such groups. We therefore choose as our universe of analysis a speech community: any human aggregate characterized by regular and frequent interaction over a significant span of time and set off from other such aggregates by differences in the frequency of interaction. Within this socially defined universe forms are selected for study primarily in terms of who uses them and when, regardless of purely grammatical similarities and differences. If two grammatically distinct alternatives are employed within the same population, both will have to be included. On the other hand, in cases where socially significant differences in behaviour are signaled by grammatically minor lexical or phone-

Source: *The Ethnography of Communication*, ed. John J. Gumperz and Dell Hymes (*American Anthropologist* special publication), 66 (6), part 2 (1964), 137–53.

mic correlates, the latter cannot be omitted from consideration.

Verbal repertoires

Procedures such as these enable us to isolate the verbal repertoire, the totality of linguistic forms regularly employed in the course of socially significant interaction. Since spoken communication of all kinds is describable by a finite set of rules which underlie the formation of all possible sentences, verbal repertoires must have structure. The structure of verbal repertoires, however, differs from ordinary descriptive grammars. It includes a much greater number of alternants, reflecting contextual and social differences in speech. Linguistic interaction, as Bernstein (1964) has pointed out, can be most fruitfully viewed as a process of decision making, in which speakers select from a range of possible expressions. The verbal repertoire then contains all the accepted ways of formulating messages. It provides the weapons of everyday communication. Speakers choose among this arsenal in accordance with the meanings they wish to convey.

Grammatical and social restraints on language choice

Ultimately it is the individual who makes the decision, but his freedom to select is always subject both to grammatical and social restraints. Grammatical restraints relate to the intelligibility of sentences; social restraints relate to their acceptability. In expressing his opinion about the weather, Smith might say, 'It looks as if it isn't going to rain today,' or 'It looks like it ain't gonna rain today.' Both messages have similar referents and, in comparison to ungrammatical sentences like 'Its look it like gonna ain't rain today,' are equally likely to be understood. Since linguistic analysis deals with grammatical restraints on language choice, alternations such as the above are not considered part of the linguistic structure. If they are listed at all they are relegated to the realm of free variation. What then can be the reason for their persistence and what is their function in the overall communication process?

If the choice among them were completely a matter of individual freedom, the connotations of his message would be idiosyncratic to the speaker and this would result in misunderstanding. The power of selection is therefore limited by commonly agreed-on conventions which serve to categorize speech forms as informal, technical, vulgar, literary, humorous, etc. To be sure, such conventions are subject to considerably greater variations than grammatical restraints, but wherever they are well established, the style of a message also gives advance information about its content. When we hear, 'Mr President, Ladies and Gentlemen,' we suspect that we are in for something like a formal address or a political speech. We can turn on the radio and recognize a news broadcast without actually understanding the words that are being spoken. In listening to someone talking on the telephone, we can make a good guess as to whether he is talking to a friend or taking care of routine business. The more we know about a particular society, the more efficiently we can communicate in it. Speech styles provide advance information about the nature of messages and speed up communication in somewhat the same way that titles and tables of contents help in reading a book. The social etiquette of language choice is learned along with grammatical rules and once internalized it becomes a part of our linguistic equipment. Conversely, stylistic choice becomes a problem when we are away from our accustomed social surroundings. Expressions which are customary in our own group might quite easily offend our interlocutor and jeopardize our mutual relationship by mislabeling messages.

When regarded from this point of view, social restraints on language choice are an important component of the relationship between signs and their meanings. Every message must conform to the grammatical restraints of the verbal repertoire but it is always interpreted in accordance with social restraints. As Bernstein (1964) says, 'Between language and speech there is social structure.' This connection must be statable in terms of regular rules allocating particular sets of forms to particular kinds of interaction. These rules should allow us to predict which of the several possible alternative realizations of messages is most likely to be employed in any instance.

Social relationships and social occasions

Our discussion of social interaction will employ the term social relationship to refer to regular patterns or types of interaction. Every society has a finite number of such relationships. They are abstracted from everyday behavior in somewhat the same way that linguistic forms are derived from language texts. Some common examples are: The father-son relationship,

salesman-customer relationship, husband-wife relationship, etc. All such types of interaction are carried on by individuals, but in analyzing social relationships we think of participants not as persons but as occupants of statuses defined in terms of rights and obligations. An individual occupies a number of such statuses. He may be a father, an employer, a passenger on a public conveyance, a member of a club, etc. Each is associated with fairly well-defined norms of behavior. Any one social relationship focuses on one of these while others remain suspended.

As Goffman (1963) has shown, social acts always form part of broader social settings—more or less closely defined behavioral routines which are regarded as separate in a society. Our usual round of activities is segmented into a number of such routines: we eat breakfast, travel to the office, participate in meetings, go out on dates, etc. Social occasions limit the participants and more importantly limit the kinds of social relationships that may be brought into play. They are in turn divisible into subroutines, encounters, or speech events (Goffman 1964; Hymes 1961). On our way to work we may first turn to our neighbor and then strike up a conversation with a stranger. During a meeting we may step aside with one or two participants to talk about a side issue. While generally related to broader social settings, encounters more narrowly restrict the selection of social relationships and thus bear a somewhat closer relation to modes of acting and speaking.

Let us now examine some common variants such as 'dine—eat,' 'house—mansion,' 'talk—lecture,' or even 'going—goin'.' All such sets refer to broadly similar classes of objects and activities. They share some attributes, but differ in other more specific features. Dining and eating both indicate consumption of food, but the former tends to imply more elaborate menus and more rigidly defined etiquette than the latter. Similarly mansions are more spacious and better furnished than houses. Beyond this, however, the difference in referents also carries some important implications about the social positions of the actors concerned. Not everyone can 'dine.' Certainly not two laborers during a dinner break, no matter how well prepared the food they consume and how good their table manners. To use dine in their case might be appropriate in jest, but not in normal conversation.

Alternation of this type may thus be viewed from two perspectives. In the realm of semantics it selects among subclasses of referents. In the sphere of social interaction it reflects the positions actors wish to assume relative to each other, i.e., the quality of their relationship. Whenever a set of linguistic forms is interchangeable within the same frame without significant change in meaning, it is this second aspect which becomes most important. In the course of any one encounter mutual relationships are constantly defined and redefined in accordance with the speaker's ultimate aim. But each encounter sets bounds to this type of variation. Social restraints on language choice express the norms defining such bounds. If he violates these, an actor risks misunderstanding.

Co-occurrence restrictions

Aside from their purely social aspects, restraints on language choice have one other important set of characteristics. This concerns the linguistic relationship among the constituents of a statement. An alternant once chosen sets limits to what can follow within the same utterance. In the example of alternation given above, the form 'ain't' must be followed by 'gonna'; similarly, 'as if' in the first example requires a following 'isn't going to.'

Speech events differ in the rigidity with which such co-occurrence restrictions apply. In some cases (e.g., public ceremonies, religious rituals, etc.) modes of speaking are narrowly prescribed; in others (e.g. conversations among personal friends, party chitchat, etc.) there may be scope for a wide range of alternate sequences. Regardless of particular instances, however, discourse of all types always shows some form of co-occurrence restrictions. From the point of view of linguistic structure, it is important to note that co-occurrence restrictions apply, not to any particular segment within an utterance, but always to the utterance as a whole. The informal ending '-in' in items such as 'going' could hardly appear with learned verbs like 'purchase.' Substitution of a learned alternant for a colloquial word also requires elimination of colloquial pronunciations. Co-occurrence rules affect all linguistic strata (Joos 1960). They simultaneously condition the morphological and phonological realizations of messages. This property enables us to segment verbal repertoires into distinct speech varieties. A verbal repertoire then is not simply composed of linguistic forms. It is always a *set of varieties*, each with its own internal grammatical structure.

A survey of the literature on bilingualism and dialectal variation from the point of view of language choice shows that linguistic interaction in all communities involves alternation among distinct varieties. But this is not to say that the same or similar connotational meanings are realized through grammatically equivalent choices in all cases. In an American community, the substitution of 'goin' ' for 'going' may signal a switch from formality to informality (Fischer 1958): in France, on the other hand, like ends may be accomplished by selecting *tu* rather than *vous* (Brown and Gilman 1960). In Java, the rules of linguistic etiquette may require alternate use of High Javanese, Low Javanese, and local dialect forms (Geertz 1961). Whenever several languages or dialects appear regularly as weapons of language choice, they form a behavioral whole, regardless of grammatical distinctness, and must be considered constituent varieties of the same verbal repertoire.

Compartmentalized and fluid repertoires

The concept of the verbal repertoire allows us to deal with speech communities of all types. Monolingual and multilingual repertoires can be analyzed within the same general framework. They differ in internal grammatical diversity and more importantly in the co-occurrence rules. In multilingual repertoires, co-occurrence rules tend to be more rigid. Verbal behavior seems to be neatly divided among a series of compartments: choice of an initial form commits the speaker to a particular line of approach. The monolingual repertoires, on the other hand, show a greater degree of flexibility. Different types of verbal behavior seem to shade off into one another.

Allocation of speech varieties to social relationships, co-occurrence rules, and internal language distance provide the structural criteria for the analysis of speech behavior. As indices, these are independent of particular languages and cultures. They form a general framework for the study of speech communities of all types in terms which are commensurable with the anthropologist's social structure.

Social organization in Khalapur[2]

The data for our analysis are drawn from Khalapur, an agricultural village about 80 miles north of Delhi, India, in the Gangetic *doab* (the plain between the Ganges and Jumna rivers), and Hemnesberget (Hemnes), a small commercial settlement in the Rana fjord of Northern Norway just south of the Arctic circle.

The Gangetic *doab* is one of the most fertile and densely settled regions of northwestern India. Since the turn of the century, it has developed into a major sugar-producing region. With its population of about 3,000 Khalapur is somewhat larger than most neighboring villages, but its economy and social organization are typically rural. The main Delhi railroad and a major highway pass within three miles of Kalapur; and two industrial sugar mills six miles away employing several hundred persons consume most of the village cane crop. Until recently, the village remained quite separate from the interurban communication network. There are many signs that this isolation is beginning to break down. Community development is showing its effect and a recently established intercollege (junior college) provides instruction up to the college sophomore level to students from many surrounding localities. Paved roads have recently been constructed, and a regular *tonga* service (horse-drawn taxi) now connects with the railroad.

Khalapur inhabitants are divided by profound differences in ritual status, wealth, political power, occupation, and education, affecting every aspect of daily interaction. In the ritual sphere, 31 distinct castes or extended kin groups are recognized. Ninety per cent of these are Hindu, and ten per cent are Muslim. Each is set off from its neighbors by differences in marriage patterns and ritual practices. Castes may be ranked along the usual ritual prestige scale with Brahmans, Rajputs (Warrior-landholders), and merchants at the top, and untouchable Chamars (landless laborers) and Sweepers at the bottom.

Distribution of wealth and political power shows only partial agreement with this ranking. Rajputs are the dominant caste. They constitute more than 40% of the population and own 90% of the land. All others, including Brahmans, are dependent on them for their subsistence. But Rajputs are in turn sectioned off by residence patterns into seven neighborhoods. Political and economic control in each neighborhood is held by a few wealthy families. As a result of their wealth, political power, and education, these families have become an aristocracy set off from their poorer Rajput neighbors, whose holdings are small compared to theirs. These latter are often tenants and may be economically no better off than the bulk of the lower caste population. Wealthy families often maintain friendlier relations with powerful merchants or artisans and with other land-holding castes from neighboring villages than with their poorer caste brothers.

The new intercollege and the resulting increase in educational opportunities have added another dimension to the ritual and socio-economic distinctions. Education is now within the reach of all groups. The majority of students still come from the Rajputs and upper castes, but now both the poor and the wealthy have access to schooling. Many lower caste persons have obtained government or commercial employment and have become the equals of the influential Rajput families in education and general sophistication.

Although the recent changes in technology and education have begun to loosen the rigidity of inter-group separation, social stratification is still an integral part of the village value system and is symbolized in a variety of ways in dress, posture, and everyday demeanor. Untouchable women are readily recognizable by their *lahnga* (skirts) and their silver jewelry. Educated men tend to wear Western type shirts and pajamas or khaki trousers, while the ordinary farmer wears the traditional kurta and dhoti, which may be made of mill cloth or of material grown and woven within the village. Others oriented towards Congress Party politics are beginning to replace their locally made cloth with the homespun material produced in the Gandhi centers and sold through the local Congress organization stores.

Whenever two or more people sit together on the cots which serve for most seating, rigid seating rules are observed. If all are members of one caste, the oldest person sits at the head of the cot (which has a special name); others sit next in order of prestige ranking. If a Brahman is present he will be offered the head seat. Lower caste persons and sometimes also poor Rajputs will sit on the floor and untouchables at a slight distance from the group. Wealthy merchants or artisans or other distinguished visitors however may find a seat on a special cot. Similar patterns apply also to seating at a feast where the upper castes tend to sit together in an order determined partly by ritual

status and partly by wealth whereas the poorer lower castes sit aside in their own separate place. Only caste brothers may smoke from the same hookah (water-pipe) and they do so in order of rank. Special pipes may be kept for respected guests from other castes.

In speaking, each caste is designated by a special caste title and each person by a term of reference which usually reflects his caste affiliation or his occupation. Relatively strict rules of deference seem to apply to interaction with everyone except one's closest friends and one's family members. Since the term 'friend' may be synonymous with 'relative', the two groups tend to overlap. So great is the guardedness which governs interaction that even an age mate from an adjoining neighborhood is accorded respect behavior and is addressed by his title rather than by his family name.

Khalapur verbal repertoire[3]

Local speech and standard language

Intra-village communication in Khalapur is carried on primarily in the local dialect (Grierson 1916). The official standard language, however, is Hindi and villagers list themselves as speakers of Hindi for census purposes. The standard is learned either in elementary school, through residence in cities or through outside contacts. Educated persons, village leaders, businessmen, and all those who deal regularly with urbanites speak it. In village interaction Hindi symbolizes the new status relationships created by the increasing involvement of villagers in state politics, modern commerce, village development, and state education. Norms call for the use of Hindi in contacts with representatives of the post-independence élite, as well as in the classroom and on the lecture platform. Those individuals who do not speak Hindi modify their speech with appropriate loan words when the social occasion demands. Purely local relationships, on the other hand, always require the dialect and everyone, including highly educated villagers, uses it to symbolize participation in these relationships.

The dialect and standard Hindi define the linguistic bounds of the verbal repertoire. A portion of the grammatical characteristics of this repertoire is, common to all speech varieties. There is, for example, a common core of phonemes which are realized the same pronunciations regardless of which style is spoken. Similarly the basic grammatical categories of noun and verb inflection are shared. But we also find a significant number of differences and these constitute the inventory of structural variants from which speakers select in accordance with situational and co-occurrence restraints. Some examples of these are given below.

On the level of phonology, tne dialect shows a special set of contrasts between retroflex and non-retroflex /n/ and /n/ and /l/ and /l/ and between retroflex flap /r/ and retroflex stop /d/, as well as a special set of diphthongs consisting of vowels followed by a short up glide: /ūi/ /āi/ /ōi/. The Hindi distinction between alveolar /s/ and palatal /š/ is lacking. Another dialect feature is the frequency of medial double consonants in words such as dialect (K) *loṭṭa* 'jug' *vs.* Hindi (H) *loṭa*. Word pairs resulting from this difference in phonemic distribution are frequently mentioned in popular stereotypes of dialect speech. Morphological differences are most frequent in the phonological realization of shared morphemic categories, i.e., in inflectional endings. The dialect lacks a feminine plural suffix, e.g., (K) *bhæ̃s* 'female buffaloes,' (H) *bhæ̃sē*. The plural oblique case suffix is (K) o and (H) ō, e.g., (K) *bhæ̃so-ka* 'of the female buffaloes' (H) *bhæsō-ka*. Dialect verbs have the infinitive suffix *-n* and the past participle ending *-ya* in place of Hindi ending *-na* and past participle *-a*, e.g., (K) *bolan*, 'to speak' (H) *bolna*, (K) *bolya* 'spoke' (H) *bola*. There are syntactical differences in the use of inflected subjunctive forms, e.g., (K) *bolæ* 'he speaks' when Hindi calls for a complex construction of present participle plus auxiliary, e.g., (H) *bolta hæ* 'he speaks.' Striking differences occur in the system of function words, i.e. grammatically important pronouns, adverbs of place and manner, conjunctions, post-positions (corresponding to prepositions in English), e.g.:

Dialect	Hindi	English
o	wo or wah	he
wa	wo or wah	she
mhara	həmara	our
-lo	-tak	until
-tæ	-se	from
ib	əb	now
inghæ	yəhā	here
təlae	nice	below
kyukkər	kæsa	how
kətek	kitna	how much

Additional speech varieties

The Khalapur repertoire is subdivided into several additional speech varieties with somewhat more limited occurrence. In a previous study, several minority subdialects were described which reflect the social isolation of the three local untouchable groups (Gumperz 1958). These groups are segregated residentially, wear special clothing and ornaments, and are in many ways culturally distinct. Here we will deal with superposed variants (i.e., variants occurring within a single population) in the speech of the majority of Rajputs and touchable castes. Members of these groups distinguish between two forms of the vernacular: *moṭi boli* and *saf boli*. The former is used primarily within the family circle, with children and with close relatives as well as with animals and untouchable servants. It symbolizes the informality that attends these relationships. *Saf boli*, on the other hand, reflects the guardedness of the relationships outside the immediate friendship group and the

respect towards elders. *Moṭi boli* contains the greatest number of purely local features. Among its phonetic characteristics are: a special high allophone [Ɨ] of the phoneme /ə/ occurring before /i/ in the next syllable; a pronounced pitch glide on the vowel preceding the medial voiced aspirate in words such as *pīdha* 'steel'; a very pronounced up glide in the phonetic realization of diphthongs /ūi/ /ai/ /oi/. Morphologically this style shows greater frequency of deviant function words of the type listed in the dialect column above. In *saf boli*, on the other hand, the above phonetic features are closer to standard Hindi and dialect function words such as *kətek* and *kyukkər* tend to be replaced by their Hindi equivalents.

Yet another speech variety characterizes interaction of villagers with merchants in the local bazaar, wandering performers, and priests—the traditional fringe groups of rural India. This regional speech variety is grammatically intermediate between the local vernacular and Hindi. In pronunciation it shows no diphthongs of the type /ui/ but retains the retroflex/nonretroflex nasal and lateral distinction. In grammar the Hindi-like present tense construction is employed and Hindi function words prevail. There are furthermore three varieties of what is ordinarily called Hindi. Before independence Urdu served as a medium of instruction and some of the elder village residents still employ Urdu forms (Gumperz 1960) in interaction with strangers. Such usages have a distinctly old-fashioned flavor. Village Hindi itself has a conversational and an oratorical style. The latter is characterized by a large number of Sanskrit loan words which affect both the lexicon and the system of functors (e.g., conversational *aur* 'and', oratorical *tətha* 'and'), and by initial and final consonant clusters in words such as *krišna* 'name of the God,' *gram* 'village' (conversational *gãw*). In phonology this style shows many special initial and final consonant clusters. The oratorical style, as its name implies, serves as the norm for public lectures and for some classroom lectures. It is used on such social occasions even though the audience often does not understand the Sanskrit expressions. Intelligibility is achieved by interspersing such lectures with explanatory passages in conversational Hindi or in the regional dialect.

Social organization in Hemnesberget[4]

Hemnesberget (or Hemnes), is a commercial settlement of about 1,300 inhabitants in the Rana Fjord of Northern Norway. Until the 19th century, the Rana area, located in one of the most sparsely settled regions in Europe, was directly controlled by a small aristocracy of merchants, landowners, and government officials who controlled the land and monopolized the trading rights. Vast differences in wealth and education separated them from the majority of the population, who were their tenants, fishermen, and estate laborers. In the late 19th century, trade monopolies were abolished and land turned over to settlers. The region is now one of small farmers, who earn their livlihood through dairying, lumbering, fishing, and boatbuilding.

Government-sponsored economic development during the last three decades has turned the Rana area into an important iron and steel producing center. The area of Mo-i-Rana at the head of the fjord has grown from about 1,000 inhabitants in the 1920s to almost 20,000 in 1960, largely through immigration from southern Norway and Trondheim. The city reflects this growth in its several department stores, hotels, restaurants, and cinemas. A railroad from Trondheim to Mo-i-Rana and on to Bodø was recently completed, and the road system is steadily improving. But Hemnes remains relatively unaffected by these developments. Although regular once-a-day boat service to Mo and two daily buses to the nearby railroad station are available, and a few people commute to Mo by private auto or motorcycle, for the bulk of local residents, life centers in and around Hemnes. They form their friendships primarily with other local inhabitants. Our interviews showed that events in Mo-i-Rana or even in neighboring small towns are only of marginal interest to them.

With the disappearance of the earlier aristocratic upper classes, the bulk of the inhabitants now stem from similar social backgrounds. The social system shows a fluidity of class structure quite similar to that described by Barnes for Southern Norway (1954). Extremes of poverty and wealth are absent. Occupationally the residents fall into four groups: artisans and workers, small shopkeepers and farmers, large merchants, and officials. These differences in occupation carry with them some real distinctions in authority. Yet for all but a few individuals who tend to identify with the older aristocratic classes, the local value system tends to minimize such distinctions, the usual way of expressing this sentiment being, 'we are all equal here in Hemnes.'

Hemnesberget verbal repertoire

The internal social homogeneity of Hemnes is reflected in the somewhat lessened compartmentalization of the verbal repertoire. Inhabitants speak both a local dialect, Ranamål (R), and a standard. The former is the native tongue and the chief medium of intra-village communication. But whereas the Khalapur vernacular is divided into several linguistically distinct subdialects and superposed speech varieties, the Hemnes variety shows only minor distinctions relating to residence patterns and generational discrepancies rather than rigid social cleavages.

The Hemnes standard is Bokmål (B) (or Riksmål as it used to be called), one of the two officially recognized literary languages in Norway (Haugen 1959). Bokmål is universally accepted throughout Northern Norway, while the other literary language, Nynorsk (formerly Landsmål), is more current in central and western coastal districts. Children learn the standard

in school and in church and through regular exposure to radio broadcasts. Since education is universal and Hemnes residents are highly literate, Bokmål can be said to be somewhat more firmly established in Hemnes than Hindi in Khalapur.

In spite of their familiarity with Bokmål, villagers take considerable pride in the dialect as a vehicle for spoken discourse. Unlike its Khalapur equivalent, Ranamål is not simply an in-group tongue, regarded as out of place in urban contexts and not worthy of serious scholarly attention. Hemnes residents consider their local speech suitable for oral interaction both in their home surroundings and outside. Although they may often employ Bokmål in their dealings in the city they insist on their right to use the dialect, to show, as they put it 'that we are not ashamed of our origin.' Local norms thus confine Bokmål to a very limited number of social relationships, relating to literature, church, and some types of interaction with nonlocals.

Grammatical differences

Some of the more important grammatical distinctions between Bokmål (B) and Ranamål (R) are listed below. The dialect has a series of alveolar palatalized consonants /tj dj nj lj/ which contrast with their nonpalatalized counterparts. Some differences in the distribution of vowels phonemes are frequent correspondences between (B) /i/ and (R) /e/ and (B) /e/ and (R) /æ/, e.g., *men/mæn* 'but' and *til/tel* 'to, towards.' As in Khalapur, broader grammatical categories are shared and distinctions occur primarily in the phonological realizations of particular allomorphs. Thus the plural suffix with nouns like *hæst* 'horse' is (B) -er and (R) -a. The present tense for the verb 'to come' is (R) *çaem* and (B) *komer*. Other important differences affect commonly employed function words:

Bokmål	Ranamål	English
dere	dɔk	you (plural)
han	hanj	he
vem	kem	who
wa	ke	what
vordan	ke . . . lesn	how
til	tel	towards
fra	ifrɔ	from
mellom	imelja	in between

Linguistic characteristics of Khalapur and Hemnes repertoires

Comparison of our two verbal repertoires with respect to the internal linguistic distinctions among constituent varieties brings out some interesting points of similarity. Ultimately verbal repertoires are socially defined concepts, but it would seem from our study and from other work along similar lines (Gumperz 1964) that they also have certain linguistic characteristics which set them off from verbal repertoires in other societies. These characteristics stem from the fact that internal differences tend to be localized in specific strata of structure. We have already suggested that there is considerable overlap in our two verbal repertoires. In terms of the stratificational model of language structure proposed by Lamb (1964), this overlap tends to be greatest in the sememic (semantic categories) and lexemic (grammatical categories) strata and in phonetics. Major form classes and inflectional categories as well as word order rules seem almost identical within our two repertoires. In the realm of phonology, the totality of distinct segments can be divided into two sets: a common core, i.e., a set of obligatory distinctions which everyone in the community makes, and a set of optional distinctions. The phonetic realizations of alternants in constituent varieties vary only with respect to the optional distinctions and not with respect to the obligatory distinctions. Thus in (K) *kətek* and (H) *kitna*, 'how much', the allophones of /k/ and /t/ are the same in each case and (K) /ə/ is phonetically the same as (H) /ə/ in *həmara* 'our'. Hemnes also, (B) *til* and (R) *tel* 'to' share the same realizations of initial /t/ and the /e/ of *tel* is the same as the /e/ in (B) *vem* 'who'. Similar instances of phonetic overlap were also noted by Ferguson (1959).

Aside from optional distinctions in phonology, linguistic differences among constituent varieties seem to be concentrated largely in what Lamb (1964) calls the morphemic stratum (the phonological realizations of lexemic categories). It would seem that wherever alternation among linguistic variants by the same populations creates grammatical overlap, this overlap provides the structural basis for the isolation of verbal repertoires.

Speech variation and social relationships in Khalapur and Hemnes

The fact that verbal repertoires in both communities are compartmentalized has some important social implications. From the point of view of local populations it means that many of the activities that individuals might be called on to engage in require considerable linguistic as well as technical skill. To talk to a government official, or to deal with a local merchant, a Khalapur villager must control distinct rules of linguistic etiquette. He must be able to manipulate not one, but several grammatical systems. In all societies there are certain specialized activities which require special vocabularies. Scientific and legal discourse as well as communication among artisans would be difficult without carefully defined technical vocabularies. Furthermore, oral and written communications require different types of syntax. But phonemic and morphophonemic differences of the type found in our study are hardly related to the nature of the activities they symbolize. They constitute cultural restraints imposed upon interaction above

and beyond what can be justified on purely technical grounds and are thus ritual in the sense in which this word is used by Leach (1954: 10).

Ritual barriers to interaction affect different spheres of activity in our two communities. In Hemnes they apply only to a limited number of scholarly, literary, administrative, and religious relationships, while the bulk of intra-village communication reflects the lack of rigidly defined stratification within the community. In Khalapur, on the other hand, ritual barriers affect every aspect of community life. They are part of the elaborate rules of etiquette which are also evident in dress, seating, and smoking, and seem to mirror the guardedness which attends the bulk of interpersonal relations. In contrast to Hemnes, Khalapur village life is not a single whole, but rather a broad grouping of sets of distinct relationships signaled by differences in linguistic and other modes of behavior. The details of this grouping are in themselves of interest, since they provide interesting insights into social structure. Thus servants as well as junior kin may be addressed in *moṭi boli*. The two statuses seems to share some common characteristics. Similarly religious, political, and educational activities all require the oratorical style and are thus regarded as related. The difference between Hindi and the regional dialect suggests a status distinction between two types of non-locals: traditional merchants and itinerants and modern businessmen and government officials. More detailed analysis of this type should furnish fruitful insights into native status definitions.

Linguistic interaction in Khalapur and Hemnes

Our discussion of verbal repertoires so far has dealt only with normative aspects of language choice. We have described the constituent speech varieties in terms of the social relationships they normally symbolize. Behavior in actual encounters, however, is not always predictable on the basis of these associations alone. Just as individual words may be used in meanings which are different from their primary referents, so also speech styles need not always signal the exact social relationships with which they are associated. Thus speakers may employ the word 'fox' either in its primary meaning to designate an animal or to refer to a human being to whom they wish to assign some of the connotations of 'foxiness'. Similarly some aspects of formal lecture style can be introduced into informal discussions to convey some of the connotations of formality for the sake of emphasis.

This use of superposed variation constitutes a different dimension of linguistic behavior. We account for it by distinguishing two types of interaction: transactional and personal. Transactional interaction centers about limited socially defined goals, i.e., a religious service, a petition, a job interview, etc. Participants in such interaction in a sense suspend their individuality in order to act out the rights and obligations of relevant statuses. Hence their linguistic and other modes of behavior must be predictable from the social definition of these statuses.

In personal interaction, on the other hand, participants act as individuals, rather than for the sake of specific social tasks. This behavior predominates in periods of relaxation among friends, and within peer groups. It is also common in scholarly discussions where the subject is more important than the social characteristics of participants. It gives scope to all facets of experiences, and individuals may resort to changes in speech style in order to underscore particular meanings. Personal switching is associated with differences in emphasis and in topic, and thus contrasts with transactional switching, which correlates with such alterations in the formal characteristics of encounters as changes in participants or in their relative statuses.

The linguistic effect of personal switching is a loosening of co-occurrence restrictions. Forms which would not appear together in transactional encounters may now co-occur. Some social restraints on language choice of course always remain. Strictures on obscenity and other types of taboos are rarely violated no matter how free the dialogue. Baby talk is not appropriate in most discussion among adults.

It is important to note that personal switching achieves its effect in non-transactional encounters because there exists a regular association between choice of linguistic form and social relationships in transactional encounters. It is this latter association which gives rise to relevant differences in connotation. Stylistic alternation which remains confined to transactional encounters need not necessarily lead to linguistic change, since the differences between variants are reinforced by nonlinguistic correlates. When switching occurs in personal encounters, on the other hand, situational reinforcement is lacking and hence there is a greater likelihood of change. Both types of linguistic alternation therefore must be taken into account in sociolinguistic study.

The balance of personal and interactional switching varies both from community to community and from subgroup to subgroup within the same population. An individual's expertise in manipulating speech varieties is a function of his position within the social system. In Khalapur, poorer Rajputs and members of the lower castes who spend their days in physical labor and interact primarily within the immediate kin group tend to use *moṭi boli*. They sound ill at ease when required to switch to *saf boli* and have a tendency to revert to *moṭi boli* when they become agitated. Their knowledge of the regional speech and of standard Hindi furthermore is limited to a few stereotyped phrases which they tend to intersperse with *moṭi boli* forms. Wealthier Rajputs, merchants and artisans, those who held clerical positions, and especially political leaders, show the greatest skill in switching. Intergroup differences in linguistic expertise are somewhat smaller in Hemnes but there are nevertheless many farmers and local artisans who show less skill in spoken Norwegian than those who are called upon to use it regularly.

In Khalapur only *moṭi boli* and *saf boli* alternate in personal switching. Hindi and regional speech occur exclusively in transactional interaction. Our field observations furthermore show personal switching primarily in gatherings of politically more active Rajputs who are not necessarily close kin. Here *saf boli* is the usual form of speech while *moṭi boli* is used in joking and quarreling. Although there seems to be some correlation between linguistic expertise and personal switching in Khalapur, the connection is probabilistic rather than causal, since not all speakers who are highly adept at stylistic manipulation engage in the latter.

Personal switching was the object of a special study in Hemnesberget, reported in greater detail elsewhere (Gumperz 1964; Blom 1964). Linguistic data were collected through tape recorded informal discussions with groups of two types; members of purely local 'closed' friendship networks (Barnes 1954) and members of 'open' networks. The former included individuals whose significant social relationships were confined to Hemnes. The latter were made up of university students, a clerk in a local office, and others who maintained relationships both with Hemnes residents and with the urban elite.

All groups were exposed to topical stimulae ranging from local issues such as fishing, personal relationships in Hemnes, etc., to superlocal issues such as city life, government investment, national politics, etc. It was found that local groups tended not to switch from the dialect to standard Norwegian except in transactional encounters (i.e., when talking to the anthropologist observers). Internal discussion within the group was carried on entirely in the dialect regardless of topic. Open network groups on the other hand engaged both in transactional and in personal switching. They tended to use a high proportion of standard Norwegian forms both when talking to the observers and in their own internal discussion dealing with supralocal topics.

In our field interviews we were unable to determine any differences in attitude toward language use among these groups. Members of both groups adhered to the prevalent norms which call for dialect forms in all types of oral interaction. In fact, when tapes of open network group discussions were played back to one participant, she expressed surprise and stated she had not realized that she had been using Bokmål forms.

Our data seem to indicate that intergroup distinctions in linguistic behavior are attributable to the different ways in which participants of open and closed network groups in Hemnes society define their mutual relationships. All members of open network groups share in a much broader range of experiences than those who belong to closed networks. They regard each other as students, literati, or part of the politically conscious national elite as well as friends and fellow Hemnes residents. Hence they feel compelled to symbolize these additional relationships through stylistic shifts when the discussion demands it.

In assessing the effect of personal switching for linguistic change we take into account both the specific varieties which are affected as well as the position of the group within the local social system. In the case of Khalapur we might predict that *moṭī bolī* is on its way out since the behavior of upper class Rajputs who use it in personal switching is being increasingly imitated by others. The prevalence of personal switching among open network groups in Hemnes however is not necessarily an indication that the local dialect is about to be replaced by standard Norwegian. Open network groups such as we studied are relatively marginal in the community as a whole. Their members will probably find employment elsewhere and pass out of the community. Any radical shift in the verbal repertoire such as changeover from a compartmentalized to a fluid structure (which the loss of the local dialect would imply) should, if our analysis is correct, also require a restructuring of social relationships within the majority group.

Conclusion

Our comparison of verbal behavior in Khalapur and Hemnes is intended to be suggestive rather than definitive. Nevertheless we hope that the information we present demonstrates the fruitfulness of the verbal repertoire as a sociolinguistic concept. We have stated that a verbal repertoire is definable both in linguistic and social terms. As a linguistic entity it bridges the gap between grammatical systems and human groups. The common view that language stands apart from social phenomena, which is held by anthropologists of many persuasions (Sapir 1921: 228; Radcliffe-Brown 1957: 143; Nadel 1951: 89), would seem to be valid only if we confine our analysis to single homogeneous systems abstracted from the totality of communicative behavior. If, however, we follow the procedure suggested in this paper and consider the linguistic resources of human groups to be divisible into a series of analytically distinct speech varieties, showing various degrees of grammatical overlap and allocated to different social relationships, then the connection between linguistic and social facts is readily established. It is the language distance between these varieties rather than the internal phonological or morphological structure of specific varieties which most readily reflects the social environment. Since language distances can be studied through contrastive linguistic analysis independently of extralinguistic phenomena, their measurement provides a valuable index for the study of society.

Social restraints on language choice, on the other hand, are also a part of social structure. They are thus susceptible to analysis in terms of generalized relational variables which apply to interaction in all human groups. The study of particular sets of grammatical systems and cultural norms in terms of these variables enables us to treat linguistic behavior as a form of social behavior, and linguistic change as a special case of social change.

Notes

1 The study of verbal behaviour in Hemnesberget was sponsored by the Institute of Sociology, University of Oslo, Norway, and was carried out in cooperation with Jan-Petter Blom. Thanks are due to the latter, to Sverre Holm, Professor of Sociology, University of Oslo, and to Dr. Hallfrid Christiansen for assistance in the project. The author's stay in Norway was made possible by a grant from the National Science Foundation.

2 For more detailed ethnographic data on Khalapur, see Hitchcock and Minturn (1963).

3 A detailed analysis of Khalapur phonology is given in Gumperz (1958b). Our phonetic transcription here differs slightly from the above. The vowels ə, i, and u are short; vowels i̇, ū, e, o, æ, ɔ, and a are long. For discussion of the various subvarieties of Hindi in the Hindi language area, see Gumperz (1960).

4 Ethnographic data cited is based largely on the work of Jan-Petter Blom (1964), although the author takes full responsibility for the interpretation presented here. In local usage the term Hemnes refers to both the town and the entire region, while Hemnesberget is the name of the town proper. In the present paper the two terms are sometimes used interchangeably.

References

Bernstein, Basil (1964). Elaborated and restricted codes: their social origins and some consequences. *The Ethnography of Communication*, ed. J. J. Gumperz and Dell Hymes (*American Anthropologist* special publication), 66 (6), part 2, 55–60.

Blom, Jan-Petter (1964). Friendship networks in Hemnes. Unpublished.

Brown, R. W. and Gilman, A. (1960). The pronouns of power and solidarity. In *Style and Language*. Thomas Sebeok, ed. New York: Technology Press of Massachusetts Institute of Technology.

Ervin-Tripp, Susan (1964). An analysis of the interaction of language, topic, and listener. *The Ethnography of Communication*, ed. J. J. Gumperz and Dell Hymes (*American Anthropologist* spec. pub.), 66, (6) part 2, 86–102.

Ferguson, Charles A. (1959). Diglossia. *Word* 15, 325–40.

Fischer, John L. (1958). Social influences in the choice of a linguistic variant. *Word* 14, 47–56.

Geertz, Hildred (1963). *The Javanese Family*. New York: Free Press.

Gleason, H. S. (1964). *The organization of language*.

Georgetown University Monographs in Linguistics and Language Teaching.

Goffman, Erving (1963). *Behaviour in public places.* New York: Free Press.

Gumperz, John J. (1958a). Dialect differences and social stratification in a North Indian village. *American Anthropologist* 60, 668–81.

Gumperz, John J. (1958b). Phonological differences in three Hindi village dialects. *Language* 34, 212–24.

Gumperz, John J. (1960). Formal and informal standards in the Hindi regional language area (with C. M. Naim), in *Linguistic diversity in South Asia.* C. A. Ferguson and J. J. Gumperz, eds. Indiana University Research Center, Bloomington, Indiana.

Gumperz, John J. (1964). On the ethnology of linguistic change. UCLA Conference on Sociolinguistics, May 1964.

Hitchcock, John T. and Leigh, Minturn (1963). The Rajputs of Khalapur, in *Six cultures: Studies in child rearing.* Beatrice B. Whiting, ed. New York: John Wiley.

Hymes, Dell (1962). The ethnography of speaking, in *Anthropology and human behaviour.* T. Gladwin and W. D. Sturtevant, eds. Washington, D. C.; Anthropological Society of Washington, 15–33.

Joos, Martin (1960). *The isolation of styles.* Report of the 10th Annual Round Table Meeting on Linguistics and Language Studies. R. S. Harrell, ed. Georgetown University.

Lamb, Sidney M. (1964). The sememic approach to structural semantics. *American Anthropologist* 66 (3), part 2, 57–78.

Leach, E. R. (1954). *Political systems of highland Burma.* Cambridge, Mass: Harvard University Press.

Nadel, S. F. (1951). *The foundations of social anthropology.* Chicago: Free Press.

Radcliffe-Brown, A. R. (1957). *A natural science of society.* Chicago: Free Press.

Sapir, Edward (1921). *Language.* New York: Harcourt, Brace.

Section II Language and social reality

The readings in this section have been chosen for their relevance to the sociological study of language. Common to all of them is a view of language as a major cultural phenomenon in human societies and, therefore, an important regulator of individual consciousness and social action.

It is clear from the papers selected that the sociologist's interest in language is usually part of a much wider concern with the problems of culture and social order in a society. Through the various forms of analysis he uses, he attempts to reveal and to explain systematically what is often implicit and taken for granted in human relationships. This has frequently been done through the examination of the beliefs which prevail in a given society and the structural conditions under which they arise. Only during the last decade, however, have sociologists seriously begun to appreciate the significance of language for the study of social behaviour. For each of the writers included here, the understanding of the use of language is an essential key to understanding not only the processes and structures of communication in society, but also important aspects of personal identity and social status. By examining the meanings, knowledge and intentions which are conveyed through language and its accompanying sign systems (gesture, physical movement, etc.), the sociologist has a powerful means of apprehending the social realities of those whom he studies.

The theoretical ideas which are represented in this selection of readings draw on three major perspectives in sociology. These are the Weberian perspective on society as a network of meanings, the Meadian perspective of symbolic interactionism with its emphasis on the social nature of the self, and the phenomenological analysis of Alfred Schutz on the social structuring of reality.[1]

Each of the readings is concerned in different ways with the *dialectic* nature of language. One of the fundamental themes which runs through them is that language exists both as subjectivity and as objectivity. As subjectivity, it structures an individual's intentions and thought processes; as objectivity it preserves and makes public vast systems of knowledge in human societies.

The mediation of the external culture into internal consciousness comes about through social interaction. Through his sensory perceptions and his possession of memory, man is able to constitute in his mind the meanings which are communicated to him by others. The sharing of a language is, in fact, the chief means by which the objective world becomes represented in consciousness as a subjective world. Thus, we learn to attach names to objects, to understand causality and relatedness, we develop a sense of reflexiveness with our environment, and we learn to abstract and generalize. In addition, language provides us with a system of interpretation which is activated in all new experience. On the basis of prior knowledge, we formulate intention, plan and programme actions, and hypothesize their consequences. In short, we are continually engaged in constructing our reality. This reality is however, a social and not simply an inner 'psychological' reality. Although these are all in a sense internal processes, the categories in which an individual conducts his internal dialogue are all derived from his culture, and have been made available to him by others. By the same token, through his vocal expression, an individual is able to externalize, or objectify his thought, thus making it available for the interpretations of others. In this way, man is both a product and a producer of his culture. The possession of language gives him a range of controls over phenomena, but he is in turn controlled by his language.[2]

The contents of subjective knowledge are, therefore, products of a particular culture and are generated in specific social settings. This brings us to another important idea contained in the readings: that knowledge, and, therefore, language, is socially distributed.

Much of the language variation between communities is a result of their different histories, leading to differences of culture. People born into them inherit different sets of meanings, conflicting standards and relevances, different life styles, and so on. The patterns of behaviour which evolve are inevitably expressed in different linguistic usage. One of the interests of the sociologist lies in tracing these differences—both within and between communities—and in analysing their social consequences. It then becomes possible to examine such questions as the formation of certain cultures as socially dominant and the existence of socially-favoured types of verbal expression. It is also possible to consider particular areas of specialist knowledge and language—for example, various professional languages—and the kinds of control which are developed by their exponents in dealing with clients. This latter type of analysis, for example, is particularly fruitful in examining the classroom relationships between teachers and pupils.

Each of the readings, while sharing a similar view of language and social relationships, provides a different set of insights for the study of human learning.

Mills' main concern is with developing a sociological theory of mind. He begins by criticizing the prevalence in the social sciences of individualistic theories which separate man from his social context and represent his thought as the result of inner processes alone. He recommends the importance of developing theories which relate mental processes to the collective life which produces a society's culture. 'What is needed', he argues, 'is a concept of mind which incorporates social processes as intrinsic to mental operations.'

This concern leads Mills to consider the importance of language as both a cultural and a mental phenomenon. He suggests that an individual's thought and language arise out of the residues of meaning which have become institutionalized in a society. Thus, 'A thinker's social and political "rationale" is exhibited in his choice and use of words. Vocabularies socially canalize thought.' From this viewpoint, it is possible to understand social relationships in terms of the different vocabularies which are used by various groups of people in a society and the 'different names of meaning and value' which they embody. Social and political conflict, therefore, become analysable in terms of the legitimacy of one set of meanings in relation to another.

Berger and Luckmann, in their extract, develop a similar view of language and its relationship to thought and culture. Their main concern is with the instrumentality of language in the construction of social reality. They suggest that because it is integral with the development of identity, language continually proclaims and validates the reality of everyday life. Not only are its categories taken for granted, but so fundamental are they to daily life that human relationships are inconceivable without them.

Like Mills, Berger and Luckmann touch on the social processes through which certain kinds of knowledge and language are diffused within society. Particularly significant are the structural factors which promote an individual's access to certain kinds of knowledge and exclude him from others. Social status and the authority of some individuals to define or defeat the realities of others are closely related to the social use of language.

The reading from Strauss considers the importance of language in the various processes of labelling and classification which prevail in a society. One of his central arguments is that objects take on the meanings which are assigned to them in social interaction: they do not have intrinsic meaning. Language 'maps out' the salient characteristics of the objective world. Thus, when people describe the behaviour of others or the features of an object, they formulate their descriptions through socially relevant categories. The problematic nature of this activity for the development of the self and for relationships with others is the subject of this chapter.

Goffman's concern is to remind us that communication is structured by the social situations in which it occurs, and that the understandings which the participants have about their situations are crucial for the kinds of self-expression they use. He is critical of studies of language which fail to take account of the situated nature of language use. He also points out that in addition to verbal language there are numerous non-verbal cues which people depend on for receiving and conveying meaning.

Finally, Kellner's paper provides a summary of the main problems and developments in the sociology of language. For him, the importance of studying language as a social phenomenon is that it can extend our knowledge both of human relationships and of the nature of man's consciousness and identity.

Geoffrey Esland

Notes

1 More detailed discussion of these intellectual traditions and their application to education can be found in the Open University Second Level course in Educational Studies, *School and Society*.

2 For a detailed treatment of this aspect of language and its importance in maintaining individual conceptions of reality see P. L. Berger and H. Kellner, Marriage and the construction of reality, reprinted in *School and Society: A Sociological Reader*, 23–31. Routledge & Kegan Paul in association with the Open University Press 1971.

8 Language, logic and culture

C. Wright Mills

Problems of a sociology of knowledge arise when certain conceptions and findings of the cultural sciences are confronted by theories of knowing and methodology. Awareness of the social and economic factors operative in the reflective process has arisen within American sociology as peripheral notations on specific researches and as implicit in psychology when sociologically approached.[1] However, the relevant sociological materials, particularly as they bear on the nature of mind and language, are as yet unexploited by those interested in sociological theories of knowledge and in the cultural careers of ideas.

Sociologies of knowledge have found elaborate statement in other contexts[2], but American social scientists have not assimilated or developed theories adequate to carry on historical reconstructions of thought from a cultural standpoint, nor have they attempted systematically to state the implications of such an attempt for methodology and theories of reflection.[3] Despite this lack of postulational framework and empirical hypotheses, assumed and unanalyzed 'answers' to certain theoretical questions are operative in the minds of many sociologists. It is the business of the theorist to articulate such assumptions as precise hypotheses and to examine them critically.

There are two viewpoints from which the social determination of mentality and ideas may be regarded. These are *historical* and *socio-psychological*. Without a formulation of mind which permits social determinants a role in reflection, assertions on the larger historical level carry less intellectual weight. A theory of mind is needed which conceives social factors as intrinsic to mentality. We may view the problems of a sociology of knowledge on a historical level; but we must also view our generic hypothesis on the socio-psychological level.

One chief defect of extant sociologies of knowledge is that they lack understanding and clear-cut formulations of the *terms* with which they would connect mind and other societal factors. This deficiency is, in turn, rooted in a failure to recognize the psychological problems arising from the acceptance of the generic hypothesis.

Sidney Hook has recently contended that it is not difficult to point out 'historical relations' of 'rationalism' with 'conservatism'; 'empiricism' with 'liberalistic' political orientations.[4] It is not difficult to impute historical relations, but what exactly is a historical relation? Although doctrines, like other complexes in culture, have a sort of existence apart from any one or two biological organisms, we must admit that ultimately reflection (a process whereby beliefs come to be doubted, discarded, or reformulated) has its seat in a minded organism and is a symbolic performance by it. Perhaps any one individual does not seriously dent a given system of belief. Perhaps in the long historical trends of belief, the drift of thought is, as Lecky believed,[5] determined more by minute changes effected by hundreds of thinkers than by a dozen 'great' ones. Nevertheless, we must ask for the *modus operandi* of these rejections, reformulations, and acceptances. The rounding out of a systematic sociological theory of knowledge involves our handling that question in socio-psychological categories. Granted that changes in culture influence trends in intellectual work and belief we must ask *how* such influences are exerted. That is a question to be answered by a social psychology, a psychology which studies the impact of social structures and objects, of class biases, and technological changes upon the mind of an organism.

Strictly speaking, the psychological is not 'the personal'. The individual is not the point of departure for contemporary social psychology; the 'mental' is not understood apart from definitely social items. At present, the sociology of knowledge needs a more adequate psychological base than has been given it.

Source: *Power, Politics and People, The Collected Essays of C. Wright Mills*, ed. I. L. Horowitz. New York: Oxford University Press (1963), 423–38.

Many sociologists of knowledge disregard psychological considerations as 'irrelevant to a sociological setting' of intellectual patterns. The socio-psychological 'aspect of the problem is either altogether disregarded or is disguised in terms which baffle empirical investigation.'[6] We find this deficiency exhibited by Marxists. From psychological and epistemological standpoints, such general terms as are used by Marxists to relate 'ideas' and societal factors (e.g., 'reflect,' 'mold,' 'determine,' 'penetrate') are not incisive; question-begging, they hide inadequate analysis. Marxists have not translated their connective terms into sound and unambiguous psychological categories.[7] Much criticism of their numerous attempts at ideological analysis are ground in the implicit assumption, on the part of both Marxists and their critics, of traditional, individualistic theories of mind. What is needed is a concept of mind which incorporates social processes as intrinsic to mental operations.

This lack of psychological formulation is by no means confined to Marxism. More sophisticated sociologies of knowledge contain the same deficiency. Mannheim, e.g., covers up his psychological inadequacy with a vague and unanalyzed 'collective unconsciousness.'[8] The psychological difficulties attendant upon such a conception are evidently not recognized.

Even if we grant that 'thought' in some manner involves social processes, the thought is, nevertheless, a lingual performance of an individual thinker. We cannot 'functionalize' reflection in social terms by postulating a 'collective subject;'[9] nor can we avoid the fact that there is no 'group mind' by conveniently using implicit conceptions of 'collective subjects.' We can socially functionalize a given thinker's production only when we have made explicit, and systematically applied, a sound hypothesis of the specific socio-psychic mechanisms by which cultural determinants are operative. Without a thorough-going social theory of mind, there is real danger that research in the sociology of knowledge may become a set of mere historical enumerations and a calling of names. Only with such construction can we gain a clear and dynamic conception of the relations imputed between a thinker and his social context. Until we build a set of theoretically substantial hypotheses of socio-psychological nature, our research is likely to remain frustrated and our larger theoretical claims feeble. I wish to advance two such hypotheses.

The first is derived from the social statement of mind presented by G. H. Mead.[10] It is his concept of the 'generalized other' which, with certain modification and extension, we may employ to show how societal processes enter as determinants into reflection.[11] The generalized other is the internalized audience with which the thinker converses: a focalized and abstracted organization of attitudes of those implicated in the social field of behavior and experience. The structure and contents of selected and subsequently selective social experiences imported into mind constitute the generalized other with which the thinker converses and which is socially limited and limiting.[12]

Thinking follows the pattern of conversation. It is a give and take. It is an interplay of meanings. The audience conditions the talker; the other conditions the thinker and the outcome of their interaction is a function of both interactants. From the standpoint of the thinker, the socialization of his thought is coincidental with its revision. The social and intellectual habits and character of the audience, as elements in this interaction, condition the statement of the thinker and the fixation of beliefs evolving from that interplay. Thought is not an interaction as between two impenetrable atoms; it is conversational and dynamic; i.e. the elements involved interpenetrate and modify the existence and status of one another. Imported into mind, this symbolic interplay constitutes the structure of mentality.

It is in conversing with this internalized organization of collective attitudes that ideas are logically, i.e., implicitly, 'tested.' Here they meet recalcitrance and rejection, reformulation and acceptance. Reasoning, as C. S. Peirce has indicated,[13] involves deliberate approval of one's reasoning. One operates logically (applies standardized critiques) upon propositions and arguments (his own included) from the standpoint of a generalized other. It is from this socially constituted viewpoint that one approves or disapproves of given arguments as logical or illogical, valid or invalid.

No individual can be logical unless there be agreement among the members of his universe of discourse as to the validity of some general conception of good reasoning. Deliberate logical approval is based upon comparison of the argument approved with some common idea of how good argument should appear. The 'laws of logic' impose a restriction upon assertion and argument. They are the rules we must follow if we would socialize our thought.[14] They are not arrived at intuitively, nor are they *given* 'innate within the mind.' They are not to be 'taken as formulating generic characters of existences outside of inquiry or the traits of all possible being.' Rather, the principles of logic are 'the rules by means of which the meanings of our terms are explicated . . . the principles of logic are . . . conventional without being arbitrary . . . they are shaped and selected by the instrumental character of discourse, by the goals of inquiry and discourse.'[15]

There is evidence that the so-called laws of proof may be merely the conventional abstract rules governing what are accepted as valid conversational extensions. What we call illogicality is similar to immorality in that both are deviations from norms. We know that such thought-ways change.[16] Arguments which in the discourse of one group or epoch are accepted as valid, in other times and conversations are not so received.[17] That which was long meditated upon is now brushed aside as illogical. Problems set by one logic are, with a change in interests, outgrown, not solved.[18] The rules of the game change with a shift in interests, and we must accept the dominant rules if we would make an impress upon the profile of thought. Our logical apparatus is formulated by the rebuffs and approvals received from the audiences of our thought. When we converse with ourselves in thought, a generalized other as the carrier of a socially derived logical apparatus restricts and governs the directions of that thought. Although not always the ultimate critique, logical rules serve as an ultimatum for most ideas. Often on this basis are selected out those ideas which will not be spoken, but forgotten; those that will not be experimentally applied, but discarded as incipient hypotheses. In general, conformity to current principles of logic is a necessary condition for the acceptance and diffusion of ideas. This is true because principles of logic are the abstracted statements of social rules derived from the dominant diffusion patterns of ideas. In attempting to implement the socialization of our interests and thought, we acquire and utilize a socially derived logical apparatus. Within the inner forum of reflection, the generalized other functions as a socially derived mechanism through which logical evaluation operates.

Social habits are not only overt and social actions which recur,—they leave residues, 'apperceptive masses,' which conform to dominant and recurring activities and are built by them. In human communities, such dominant fields of behavior have implications in terms of systems of value. The interest-evaluative implication of a social structure has been termed its ethos.[19] Dominant activities (e.g., occupations) determine and sustain modes of satisfaction, mark definitions of value preference; embodied in language, they make perception discriminatory. The stuff of ideas is not merely sensory experiences, but meanings which have back of them collective habits.

When a system of social actions actually 'breaks down' in 'social conflict,' *some* thinkers call this a 'social problem,' but not all 'conflicts' of all groups are termed problematic by all thinkers. 'Social problems' are not universally recognized as problematic, as occasions for thought: there is no '*the* economic problem.' The 'direction' of organized social action which sustains specific values conditions what constitutes a problem. The value-interest implications of a social structure are the guiding threads along which problems emerge. Problems are relative to an ethos.[20]

The thinker does not often play an immediate active role in large social strata or institutional frames, and hence, does not build through direct action a generic pattern of habit and value which would constitute a selective detector of 'problems,' a background of mind. Nevertheless, there are two other modes by which he may come to be influenced by such residues. He may intentionally identify himself with an ethos[21] rooted in a structure of social habits, thus vicariously participating in and articulating a particular social segment's interests, or, if his thought is appreciatively diffused, members of his audience will possess mental characteristics built by direct social action. It is often through such audiences that a thinker is culturally claimed, because, when his doctrine and his *further* thought gravitate toward a responsive audience it means that he has responded (whether he is at first aware of it or not) to 'problems' defined by the activities and values of his audience. A reflective response to a social environment, assimilated by its members, is always related to the 'needs' of that particular environment. Defined operationally (externally and behaviorally), that environment is the largely unreflective behavior patterns of a specific set of groups, e.g., a class, or a set of institutions. Viewed internally, as a function or field of mind, we have contended for this environment's influence on thought, because such specific fields of social behavior develop and sustain organized sets of attitudes; when internalized, these constitute a thinker's generalized other which functions as that with and against which he carries on his internal conversation. It is by virtue of this essentially social structure of mind that sociological factors influence the fixation not only of the evaluative but also of the intellectual. On the one hand, the generalized other is an element involved in the functioning and conditioning of the outcome of the reflective processes; it is the seat of a logical apparatus; on the other hand, it is constituted by the organized attitudinal implicates of cultural forms, by institutional ethos, and by the behavior of economic classes.

When confronted with a system of thought, or the reasoned assertions of a thinker, our sociological perspective toward knowledge attempts to 'locate' a set of determinants within contemporaneous fields of societal values. We try to locate the thinker with reference to his assimilated portion of culture, to delineate the cultural influences in his thought and the influences (if any) of his thought upon cultural changes.

In an attempt to outline approaches to this problem, we now take another angle of departure from which we cast a hypothesis and a methodology. We might conceive the following set of remarks as a formulation of another socio-psychological 'mechanism' connecting thinking with societal patterns. We construct it from a conjunction of the social dimensions of language with the fundamental role of language in thought. By approaching the interrelatedness of sociality and reflection, our perspective enables us to view as a 'unit' matters which have traditionally been handled on three levels of theory. Between them are two 'gaps' which we 'fill.' First, we consider the nature of language and meaning in terms of social behavior. Second, we consider the nature of reflection in terms of meaning and language.

From a concept of language as an 'expression of antecedent ideas,' the psychologists have gravitated toward a functional conception of language as a mediator of human behavior. From the isolated grammatical and philological field ethnologists have moved to the social-behavioral setting of linguistic materials.[22] Given additional cogency by their convergence, both these movements proceed toward the notion that the meanings of symbols are defined and redefined by socially co-ordinated actions. The function of words is the mediation of social behavior, and their meanings are dependent upon this social and behavioral function. Semantical changes are surrogates and foci of cultural conflicts and group behavior. Because language functions in the organization and control of behavior patterns, these patterns are determinants of the meanings in a language. Words carry meanings by virtue of dominant interpretations placed upon them by social behavior. Interpretations or meanings spring from the habitual modes of behavior which pivot upon symbols. Such social patterns of behavior constitute the meanings of the symbols. Nonlinguistic behaviors are guided or manipulated by linguistic materials, and language is the ubiquitous string in the web of patterned human behavior.

We can view language functionally as a system of social control. A symbol, a recurrent language form, gains its status as a symbol, an event with meaning, because it produces a similar response from both the utterer and the hearer.[23] Communication must set up common modes of response in order to be communication; the meaning of language is the common social behavior evoked by it. Symbols are the 'directing pivots' of social behaviors. They are also the indispensable condition of human mentality. The meanings of words are formed and sustained by the interactions of human collectivities, and thought is the manipulation of such meanings. Mind is the interplay of the organism with social situations mediated by symbols. The patterns of social behavior with their 'cultural drifts', values, and political orientations extend a control over thought by means of language. It is only by utilizing the symbols common to his group that a thinker can think and communicate. Language, socially built and maintained, embodies implicit exhortations and social evaluations.[24] By acquiring the categories of a language, we acquire the structured 'ways' of a group, and along with the language, the value-implicates of those 'ways.' Our behavior and perception, our logic and thought, come within the control of a system of language. Along with language, we acquire a set of social norms and values. A vocabulary is not merely a string of words; immanent within it are societal textures—institutional and political coordinates. Back of a vocabulary lie sets of collective action.

No thinker utilizes the total vocabulary afforded by his societal context nor is he limited to it. We acquire the systematic vocabularies of intellectual traditions built by other thinkers from diverse cultures. We build an intellectual orientation by gathering for ourselves a dictionary of interrelated terms. As we 'grow' intellectually, we selectively build new linguistic habits. Like other habits, linguistic or conceptual ones are built on previous residues. Prior linguistic and conceptual accomplishments are conditions for the aquisition of new habits of thought, new meanings. Thinking is the selection and manipulation of available symbolic material.

We may 'locate' a thinker among political and social coordinates by ascertaining what words his functioning vocabulary contains and what nuances of meaning and value they embody. In studying vocabularies, we detect implicit evaluations and the collective patterns behind them,—'cues' for social behavior. A thinker's social and political 'rationale' is exhibited in his choice and use of words. Vocabularies socially canalize thought.

We must recognize the priority of a system of meanings to a thinker. Thinking influences language very little, but thought, as Malinowski has indicated, 'having to borrow from (social) action its tool, is largely influenced thereby.'[25] No thinker can assign arbitrary meanings to his terms and be understood. Meaning is antecedently *given*; it is a collective 'creation'. In manipulating a set of socially given symbols, thought is itself manipulated. Symbols are impersonal and imperative determinants of thought because they manifest collective purposes and evaluations. New nuances of meaning which a thinker may give to words are, of course, socially significant in themselves;[26] but such 'new' meanings must in their definition draw upon the meanings and organization of collectively established words in order that they may be understood, and they are conditioned thereby; and so is the acceptance and/or rejection of them by others.

Here, again, the thinker is 'circumscribed' by his audience, because, in order to communicate, to be understood, he must 'give' symbols such meanings that they call out the same responses in his audience as they do in himself. The process of 'externalizing' his thought in language is thus, by virtue of the commonness essential to meaning, under the control of the audience. Socialization is accompanied by revision of meaning. Seldom do identical interpretations obtain. Writings get reinterpreted as they are diffused across audiences with different nuances of meanings. We call the tendency to telescope (by variations of interpretation) the meaning of concepts into a given set of social habits, ethnocentrism of meanings.[27] Functionally, i.e., as far as communication obtains, the reader is a factor determining what the thinker writes.

A symbol has a different meaning when interpreted by persons actualizing different cultures or strata within a culture. In facing problems incident to a translation from Chinese to English, I. A. Richards got 'the impression that an unwritten and unelucidatable *tradition* accompanies and directs their interpretation', and that 'this tradition is *by no means uniform*.'[28] We hold that this *tradition* which is *by no means uniform* is the linguistic reflex of the socially controlled behaviors from which a scholar is derived, which he 'lives' (behaviorally and/or vicariously), or which constitutes the audience of his thought, or all three. These 'esoteric determinants of meaning are the logical interpretants,'[29] residues derived from the meaningful behavior of such constellations.

A block in social actions, e.g., a class conflict, carries a reflex back into our communicative medium and hence into our thought. We then talk past one another. We interpret the 'same' symbol differently. Because the coordinated social actions sustaining the meaning of a given symbol have broken down, the symbol does not call out the same response in members of one group that it does in another, and there is no genuine communication.

Richards detects in the Chinese thinking of Mencius' period a strong *dependence of conception upon social purpose*. Mencius' thought on man was governed by a social purpose, the 'enforcement of a schema of conduct.' The concepts which he utilized were good servants of the accepted moral and social order. The success of Richards' study leads us to consider tenable the hypothesis that *conceptions* and distinctions, including those of our philosophic and social jargon, are such as to 'hide' factors from us in the interests of social purposes woven through various cultural patterns.

Different traditions of · thinking have different distinctions in their vocabularies, and these differences are related to differences in other spheres of their respective cultural setting. The distinctions in Chinese thinking are quite different from those in Western thought. The Chinese, for example, did not set the subject over against the object, and hence had no 'problem of knowledge.' Nor did Chinese thought of this period separate psychology and physics into two separate studies. Richards suggests:

> The problems which for any one tradition are obtrusive—especially the more insoluble of them, and thus, it may seem, the more 'important'— may often have arisen as a result of accident— grammatical or social. (Op. cit., 3–5)

The manner in which 'lack' of distinctions in a language limits thought and the formulation of problems is aptly illustrated by Richards' analysis of the Chinese word for 'aged.' There is no distinction between age in the chronological sense and the sense of an ethical pattern toward those who are old. Consequently, Mencius cannot separate in his thinking a man's age and the reverence that is due him because of it. Here is a direct connection of a *mos*,

embodied in language, with a limitation of thinking. Thinkers of Mencius' period do not 'discuss or treat as open to discussion the rightness of paying respect to age as age.'[30] Their language would not allow a definition of the problem. The employment of one word for both chronological age and the honorable pattern of behavior toward old persons reflects and preserves the unquestioned appropriateness of the reverential conduct better than any separate terms could. Agreement with the *mos* or institution was evoked by the very mentioning of the symbol around which it was organized and which defined it in behavior. Chinese thinking on this head is thus seen to operate within an unquestioned limit set by the language itself.

What if this *mos*, reverence to old age, were to change radically? What if shortage of young men for warriors in a long series of wars forces the group to shift its respect to 'young warrior' roles? What would then happen to the old concept now carrying dual meaning? It would become ambiguous and eventually, split. Newly sanctioned social habits force new meanings and changes in old meanings. A distinction would be drawn which was not existent in Mencius' thinking. Problems would result from the competing meanings where before an unquestioned belief had reigned. Thus is reflection related in terms of meanings to areas of conflicts and drifts within social orders.[31]

It is a necessary consequence of any unaccustomed perspective that matters traditionally viewed disjunctively, be considered conjunctively. I have presented certain coordinates for a sociological approach to reflection and knowledge, viewing conjointly sociality and mind, language and social habit, the noetic and the cultural. Such contexts may be said to operate as determinants in thought in the sense that given social textures there will be present certain various and limited materials for assimilation; or, in the sense that thinkers programmatically identify themselves with an order of interests. I have analyzed the matter more deeply (1) by instituting the socio-psychological problem of the *modus operandi* of such determinations, and (2) by advancing and partially elaborating as hypotheses two connective mechanisms. It should be apparent that these formulations also provide research leads equipping attempts at concrete reconstructions of intellectual patterns from a cultural standpoint.

Notes

1 Cf. L. Wirth's preface to Karl Mannheim's *Ideology and Utopia*, xxi (New York 1936; Routledge paperback).

2 The German *Wissenssoziologie* and the French sociological theories of knowledge. For a reasonably adequate bibliography of the German materials, see Wirth-Shils' translation of Mannheim, op. cit., 281 ff. For French, see reviews and monographs in *L'Année Sociologique*, vols. I-XII.

3 Cf. however, H. Becker's brief, substantive presenta-

tions scattered through his and H. E. Barnes' *Social Thought from Lore to Science* (New York 1938).

4 *Social Frontier*, vol. VI, no. 32, Feb. 1938.

5 *History of the Rise and Influence of Rationalism in Europe* (1919 edition), vol. I, 15–16; vol. II, 100–1.

6 Hans Speier, The Social Determination of Ideas, gives a brief indication of the need for handling the problems of a sociology of knowledge on a psychological level. *Social Research*, May 1938.

7 K. Marx, *Capital*, vol. I, 25, 84–5, and Introduction to

Critique of Political Economy. V. Lenin, *Materialism and Empirio-Criticism*, 300. Engels, *Feuerbach*, 73, 96, 177. Also, M. M. Bober, *Marx's Interpretation of History*, 298. More recently, see Pannecoek's psychologically feeble attempt to relate 'thought' and social factors in *Science and Society*, vol. I, Summer 1937, 445. For positive contributions of Marxism to the sociology of knowledge, cf. Mannheim, op. cit., 51, 66–7, 69, 110, 112, 248, 278.

8 Op. cit., 28, 30–48.

9 Cf. von Schelting's review of Mannheim's *Ideology and Utopia*, *Amer. Sociol. Rev.*, Feb. 1936, 665.

10 *Mind, Self, and Society* (Chicago 1934). Also see bibliography of Mead's articles.

11 Op. cit., 155 ff.

12 My conception of the generalized other differs from Mead's in one respect crucial to its usage in the sociology of knowledge: I do not believe (as Mead does, op. cit., 154) that the generalized other incorporates 'the whole society,' but rather that it stands for selected societal segments. Mead's statements regarding this point are, I believe, functions of an inadequate theory of society and of certain democratic persuasions. These are not, however, logically necessary to the general outline of his social theory of mind.

13 *Collected Papers of Charles Peirce*, vol. II, 108 (Cambridge, Mass. 1934).

14 Jean Piaget's experiments on children substantiate such a viewpoint. Cf. *The Language and Thought of the Child* (New York 1926; Routledge & Kegan Paul, rev. ed. 1959); *The Judgement and Reasoning in the Child* (New York 1928; Routledge & Kegan Paul 1969); For Durkheim's view of the rise of logical categories from social forms, see his and Mauss' monograph in *L'Année Sociologique*, vol. VI, Paris 1903, 1–72; also M. Granet's Durkheimian analysis of non-Aristotelian Chinese categories, in *La Pensée Chinoise* (Paris 1934).

15 Ernest Nagel, Some Theses in the Philosophy of Logic, *Phil. of Sci.*, Jan. 1938, 49–50. Nagel notes 'a marked tendency' in pure logic towards the view 'that the subject matter of logic is discourse.' The linguistic view of logic I believe eminently sound, but with a growing recognition of the social and behavioral character of language, it needs to be set within a social context. From another angle, I should ask of Nagel that some order be found among these 'shifts' in the 'goals of inquiry and discourse' which shape and select the principles of logic. Such an attempt would require a sociological implementation. An attempt to isolate the social determinants of 'goals of inquiry and discourse' would not only be in line with the program of the sociology of knowledge but, if successful, would strengthen Nagel's thesis that the principles of logic are 'conventional without being arbitrary.'

16 Bogoslovsky in his *Technique of Controversy* (New York, 1928), has shown that, e.g., John Dewey's writings reveal grave logical fallacies if judged by the rules of classical logic. He attempts to delineate a new set of logical principles based on an analysis of Dewey's actual modes of thought. Bogoslovsky is tabulating new rules that have come into being. No logician can 'make up' a system of logic. Like coins, they are genuine by virtue of their dominant currency.

17 Cf. Lecky, op. cit., vol. II, 100–1, etc. Also Sumner's *Folkways*, 33, 174–5, 193–5, 225.

18 Cf. Dewey's article in *Creative Intelligence*, 3 (New York 1917).

19 Cf. H. Speier's usage of ethos, op. cit., 196.

20 Cf. T. Parson's presentation of Max Weber's notion of *Wertbeziehung* ('relevance to value'), as a methodological concern, *i.e.*, as an organizing principle within empirical research, *The Structure of Social Action*, 593, 601 ff. (New York 1938).

21 This 'special pleading' is the most usual 'connection' imputed—often it is considered exhaustive. (E.g., S. Hook: *Marxist Quarterly*, vol. I, 454). Undoubtedly many social doctrines are definitively affected by their originator's or publicist's interest in intentionally aiding or hindering the perpetuation of a social movement or institution; but I would not confine the connection between thought and other cultural items to a thinker's conscious 'interest' or the conscious utilization of a doctrine as a 'social forensic' by any professional talker. If this were the only connection to be ascertained, then our generic hypothesis would be seriously weakened. We should have to impute to the thinker the attributes of the 'economic man,' i.e., knowing what are his social interests and thinking accordingly. Moreover, the connection stated merely in terms of 'interest' begs the major question; it tells us nothing as to exactly *how* such 'social interests' climb into thinking, and this is what we must explain. Without such an explanation, the imputation of interest connotes that the relationship occurs 'rationally,' within the mind of the thinker, within his conscious intellectual and social intentions. If the sociology of knowledge is to be psychologically limited to this economic man theory of the thinker, we had all better reduce our expectations of it, both as theory and as an integrating viewpoint for cultural reconstruction of intellectual history.

22 For an excellent summary of these movements' literature, see E. Esper's article 'Language' in *Handbook for Social Psychology*, ed. Carl Murchison (Worcester, Mass. 1934). See his comments on Grace DeLaguna and B. Malinowski.

23 Cf. Mead, op. cit., sec. II.

24 K. Burke puts it thus: 'Speech takes its shape from the fact that it is used by people acting together. It is an adjunct of action—and thus naturally contains the elements of exhortation and threat which stimulate action and give it direction. It thus tends naturally towards the use of implicit moral weightings: the names for things and operations smuggle in connotations of good and bad—a noun tends to carry with it a kind of invisible adjective, and, a verb an invisible adverb.' *Permanence and Change*, 243–4. Cf. also Marcel Granet, op. cit., for discussion of the heavy value-dimension in Chinese vocabularies and syntax.

25 The Problem of Meaning in Primitive Languages, op. cit., 498.

26 Cf. Karl Mannheim, op. cit., 74.

27 E.g., approached with this 'lead' in mind, the 'diffusion pattern' of the Bible exhibits one reason for its continuance: its language is capable of being 'strained' (reinterpreted) through the purposes and orientations implicitly contained in the languages of a great variety of cultural segments and milieux.

28 *Mencius on the Mind*, 33 (New York 1932; Routledge & Kegan Paul 1964).

29 The incipient theory of meaning found in C. S. Peirce is compatible with the sociological slant on meaning. I

find in his work an added support for a belief in an intrinsic, controlling relation of social habits to reflection through meaning. For Peirce, 'the ultimate meaning (logical interpretant) of a concept is a habit change.' (*Collected Papers*, vol. V, paragraph 476.) Habits are, of course, socially acquired and transmitted.

30 I. A. Richards, op. cit., 55–6.

31 I am indebted to C. E. Ayres for indicating the similar instance involved in the rise of the concept 'capital.' Since Aristotle, it was agreed that money is obviously sterile. Hence, for 'money' and 'wealth,' the substitution of the equivocal 'capital' *as a factor in production*. The 'capitalist fallacy' may be regarded as a continuation of the 'mercantilist fallacy' which pivoted around the fluid concept 'wealth.' It is significant that 'capital' emerged in the period and milieu in which book-keeping underwent its great development. The ambivalence of 'capital' represents in a business culture a confusion of bookkeeping entries with things, machines. As in Mencius' period, no one debated the differences between *pecuniary* and *physical* capital. I am not implying that the classicists' dual usage was deliberately cultivated as special pleading.

9 Language and knowledge in everyday life

Peter L. Berger and Thomas Luckmann

Human expressivity is capable of objectivation, that is, it manifests itself in products of human activity that are available both to their producers and to other men as elements of a common world. Such objectivations serve as more or less enduring indices of the subjective processes of their producers, allowing their availability to extend beyond the face-to-face situation in which they can be directly apprehended. For instance, a subjective attitude of anger is directly expressed in the face-to-face situation by a variety of bodily indices—facial mien, general stance of the body, specific movements of arms and feet, and so on. These indices are continuously available in the face-to-face situation, which is precisely why it affords me the optimal situation for gaining access to another's subjectivity. The same indices are incapable of surviving beyond the vivid present of the face-to-face situation. Anger, however, can be objectivated by means of a weapon. Say, I have had an altercation with another man, who has given me ample expressive evidence of his anger against me. That night I wake up with a knife embedded in the wall above my bed. The knife *qua* object expresses my adversary's anger. It affords me access to his subjectivity even though I was sleeping when he threw it and never saw him because he fled after his near-hit. Indeed, if I leave the object where it is, I can look at it again the following morning, and again it expresses to me the anger of the man who threw it. What is more, other men can come and look at it and arrive at the same conclusion. In other words, the knife in my wall has become an objectively available constituent of the reality I share with my adversary and with other men. Presumably, this knife was not produced for the exclusive purpose of being thrown *at me*. But it expresses a subjective intention of violence, whether motivated by anger or by utilitarian considerations, such as killing for food. The weapon *qua* object in the real world continues to express a general inten-

Source: P. L. Berger and T. Luckmann, *The Social Construction of Reality*, Allen Lane, The Penguin Press (1966), 49–61.

tion to commit violence that is recognizable by anyone who knows what a weapon is. The weapon, then, is both a human product and an objectivation of human subjectivity.

The reality of everyday life is not only filled with objectivations; it is only possible because of them. I am constantly surrounded by objects that 'proclaim' the subjective intentions of my fellowmen, although I may sometimes have difficulty being quite sure just what it is that a particular object is 'proclaiming', especially if it was produced by men whom I have not known well or at all in face-to-face situations. Every ethnologist or archaeologist will readily testify to such difficulties, but the very fact that he *can* overcome them and reconstruct from an artifact the subjective intentions of men whose society may have been extinct for millennia is eloquent proof of the enduring power of human objectivations.

A special but crucially important case of objectivation is signification, that is, the human production of signs. A sign may be distinguished from other objectivations by its explicit intention to serve as an index of subjective meaning. To be sure, all objectivations are susceptible of utilization as signs, even though they were not originally produced with this intention. For instance, a weapon may have been originally produced for the purpose of hunting animals, but may then (say, in ceremonial usage) become a sign for aggressiveness and violence in general. But there are certain objectivations originally and explicitly intended to serve as signs. For instance, instead of throwing a knife at me (an act that was presumably intended to kill me, but that might conceivably have been intended merely to signify this possibility), my adversary could have painted a black X-mark on my door, a sign, let us assume, that we are now officially in a state of enmity. Such a sign, which has no purpose beyond indicating the subjective meaning of the one who made it, is also objectively available in the common reality he and I share with other men. I recognize its meaning, as do other men, and indeed it is available to its producer as an object-ive 'reminder' of his original intention in making it. It will be clear from the above that there is a good deal of fluidity between the instrumental and the significa-tory uses of certain objectivations. The special case of magic, in which there is a very interesting merging of these two uses, need not concern us here.

Signs are clustered in a number of systems. Thus there are systems of gesticulatory signs, of patterned bodily movements, of various sets of material artifacts, and so on. Signs and sign systems are objectivations in the sense of being objectively available beyond the expression of subjective intentions 'here and now'. This 'detachability' from the immediate expressions of subjectivity also pertains to signs that require the mediating presence of the body. Thus performing a dance that signifies aggressive intent is an altogether different thing from snarling or clenching fists in an outburst of anger. The latter acts express my subject-ivity 'here and now', while the former can be quite detached from this subjectivity—I may not be angry or aggressive at all at this point but merely taking part in the dance because I am paid to do so on behalf of someone else who *is* angry. In other words, the dance can be detached from the subjectivity of the dancer in a way in which the snarling *cannot* from the snarler. Both dancing and snarling are manifestations of bodily expressivity, but only the former has the character of an objectively available sign. Signs and sign systems are all characterized by 'detachability', but they can be differentiated in terms of the degree to which they may be detached from face-to-face situations. Thus a dance is evidently less detached than a material artifact signifying the same subjective meaning.

Language, which may be defined here as a system of vocal signs, is the most important sign system of human society. Its foundation is, of course, in the intrinsic capacity of the human organism for vocal expressivity, but we can begin to speak of language only when vocal expressions have become capable of detachment from the immediate 'here and now' of subjective states. It is not yet language if I snarl, grunt, howl or hiss, although these vocal expressions are capable of becoming linguistic in so far as they are integrated into an objectively available sign system. The common objectivations of everyday life are maintained prim-arily by linguistic signification. Everyday life is, above all, life with and by means of the language I share with my fellowmen. An understanding of language is thus essential for any understanding of the reality of everyday life.

Language has its origins in the face-to-face situa-tion, but can be readily detached from it. This is not only because I can shout in the dark or across a distance, speak on the telephone or via the radio, or convey linguistic signification by means of writing (the latter constituting, as it were, a sign system of the second degree). The detachment of language lies much more basically in its capacity to communicate meanings that are not direct expressions of subjectivity 'here and now'. It shares this capacity with other sign systems, but its immense variety and complexity make it much more readily detachable from the face-to-face situation that any other (for example, a system of gesticulations). I can speak about innumerable matters that are not present at all in the face-to-face situation, including matters I never have and never will exper-ience directly. In this way, language is capable of becoming the objective repository of vast accumula-tions of meaning and experience, which it can then preserve in time and transmit to following generations.

In the face-to-face situation language possesses an inherent quality of reciprocity that distinguishes it from any other sign system. The ongoing production of vocal signs in conversation can be sensitively syn-chronized with the ongoing subjective intentions of the conversants. I speak as I think; so does my partner in the conversation. Both of us hear what each says at virtually the same instant, which makes possible a continuous, synchronized, reciprocal access to our two subjectivities, an intersubjective closeness in the face-to-face situation that no other sign system can duplicate. What is more, I hear *myself* as I speak; my own subjective meanings are made objectively and continuously available to me and *ipso facto* become 'more real' to me. Another way of putting this is to recall the previous point about my 'better knowledge' of the other as against my knowledge of myself in the face-to-face situation. This apparently paradoxical fact has been previously explained by the massive, continuous and prereflective availability of the other's being in the face-to-face situation, as against the requirement of reflection for the availability of my own. Now, however, as I objectivate my own being by means of language, my own being becomes massively and continuously available to myself at the same time that it is so available to him, and I can spontaneously respond to it without the 'interruption' of deliberate reflection. It can, therefore, be said that language makes 'more real' my subjectivity not only to my conversation partner but also to myself. This capacity of language to crystallize and stabilize for me my own subjectivity is retained (albeit with modifications) as language is detached from the face-to-face situation. This very important character-istic of language is well caught in the saying that men must talk about themselves until they know themselves.

Language originates in and has its primary reference to everyday life; it refers above all to the reality I experience in wide-awake consciousness, which is dominated by the pragmatic motive (that is, the cluster of meanings directly pertaining to present or future actions) and which I share with others in a taken-for-granted manner. Although language can also be employed to refer to other realities, which will be discussed further in a moment, it even then retains its rootage in the common-sense reality of everyday life. As a sign system, language has the quality of objectivity. I encounter language as a facticity external to myself and it is coercive in its effect on me. Language forces me into its patterns. I cannot use the rules of German syntax when I speak English; I cannot use words invented by my three-year-old son if I want to communicate outside the family; I must take into account prevailing standards of proper speech for various occasions, even if I would prefer my private 'improper' ones. Language provides me with a ready-made possibility for the ongoing objectification of my unfolding experience. Put differently, language is pliantly expansive so as to allow me to objectify a great variety of experiences coming my way in the course of my life. Language also typifies experiences, allowing me to subsume them under broad categories in terms of which they have meaning not only to myself but also to my fellowmen. As it typifies, it also anonymizes experiences, for the typified experience can, in principle, be duplicated by anyone falling into the category in question. For instance, I have a quarrel with my mother-in-law. This concrete and subjectively unique experience is typified linguistically under the category of 'mother-in-law trouble'. In this typification it makes sense to myself, to others, and, presumably, to my mother-in-law. The same typification, however, entails anonymity. Not only I but *anyone* (more accurately, anyone in the category of son-in-law) can have 'mother-in-law troubles'. In this way, my biographical experiences are ongoingly subsumed under general orders of meaning that are both objectively and subjectively real.

Because of its capacity to transcend the 'here and now', language bridges different zones within the reality of everyday life and integrates them into a meaningful whole. The transcendences have spatial, temporal and social dimensions. Through language I can transcend the gap between my manipulatory zone and that of the other; I can synchronize my biographical time sequence with his; and I can converse with him about individuals and collectivities with whom we are not at present in face-to-face interaction. As a result of these transcendences language is capable of 'making present' a variety of objects that are spatially, temporally and socially absent from the 'here and now'. *Ipso facto* a vast accumulation of experiences and meanings can become objectified in the 'here and now'. Put simply, through language an entire world can be actualized at any moment. This transcending and integrating power of language is retained when I am not actually conversing with another. Through linguistic objectification, even when 'talking to myself' in solitary thought, an entire world can be appresented to me at any moment. As far as social relations are concerned, language 'makes present' for me not only fellowmen who are physically absent at the moment, but fellowmen in the remembered or reconstructed past, as well as fellowmen projected as imaginary figures into the future. All these 'presences' can be highly meaningful, of course, in the ongoing reality of everyday life.

Moreover, language is capable of transcending the reality of everyday life altogether. It can refer to experiences pertaining to finite provinces of meaning, and it can span discrete spheres of reality. For instance, I can interpret 'the meaning' of a dream by integrating it linguistically within the order of everyday life. Such integration transposes the discrete reality of the dream into the reality of everyday life by making it an enclave within the latter. The dream is now meaningful in terms of the reality of everyday life rather than of its own discrete reality. Enclaves produced by such transposition belong, in a sense, to both spheres of reality. They are 'located' in one reality, but 'refer' to another.

Any significative theme that thus spans spheres of reality may be defined as a symbol, and the linguistic mode by which such transcendence is achieved may be called symbolic language. On the level of symbolism, then, linguistic signification attains the maximum detachment from the 'here and now' of everyday life, and language soars into regions that are not only *de facto* but *a priori* unavailable to everyday experience. Language now constructs immense edifices of symbolic representations that appear to tower over the reality of everyday life like gigantic presences from another world. Religion, philosophy, art, and science are the historically most important symbol systems of this kind. To name these is already to say that, despite the maximal detachment from everyday experience that the construction of these systems requires, they can be of very great importance indeed for the reality of everyday life. Language is capable not only of constructing symbols that are highly abstracted from everyday experience, but also of 'bringing back' these symbols and appresenting them as objectively real elements in everyday life. In this manner, symbolism and symbolic language become essential constituents of the reality of everyday life and of the common-sense apprehension of this reality. I live in a world of signs *and* symbols every day.

Language builds up semantic fields or zones of meaning that are linguistically circumscribed. Vocabulary, grammar and syntax are geared to the organization of these semantic fields. Thus language builds up classification schemes to differentiate objects by 'gender' (a quite different matter from sex, of course) or by number; forms to make statements of action as against statements of being; modes of indicating degrees of social intimacy, and so on. For example, in languages that distinguish intimate and formal discourse by means of pronouns (such as *tu* and *vous* in French, or *du* and *Sie* in German) this distinction marks the coordinates of a semantic field that could be called the zone of intimacy. Here lies the world of *tutoiement* or of *Bruderschaft*, with a rich collection of meanings that are continually available to me for the ordering of my social experience. Such a semantic field, of course, also exists for the English speaker, though it is more circumscribed linguistically. Or, to take another example, the sum of linguistic objectifications pertaining to my occupation constitutes another semantic field, which meaningfully orders all the routine events I encounter in my daily work. Within the semantic fields thus built up it is possible for both biographical and historical experience to be objectified, retained and accumulated. The accumulation, of course, is selective, with the semantic fields determining what will be retained and what 'forgotten' of the total experience of both the individual and the society. By virtue of this accumulation a social stock of knowledge is constituted, which is transmitted from generation to generation and which is available to the individual in everyday life. I live in the common-sense world of everyday life equipped with specific bodies of knowledge. What is more, I know that others share at least part of this knowledge, and they know that I know this. My interaction with others in everyday life is, therefore, constantly affected by our common participation in the available social stock of knowledge.

The social stock of knowledge includes knowledge of my situation and its limits. For instance, I know that I am poor and that, therefore, I cannot expect to live in a fashionable suburb. This knowledge is, of course, shared both by those who are poor themselves and those who are in a more privileged situation. Participation in the social stock of knowledge thus permits the 'location' of individuals in society and the 'handling' of them in the appropriate manner. This is not possible for one who does not participate in this knowledge, such as a foreigner, who may not recognize me as poor at all, perhaps because the criteria of poverty are quite different in his society—how can I be poor, when I wear shoes and do not seem to be hungry?

Since everyday life is dominated by the pragmatic motive, recipe knowledge, that is, knowledge limited to pragmatic competence in routine performances, occupies a prominent place in the social stock of knowledge. For example, I use the telephone every day for specific pragmatic purposes of my own. I know how to do this. I also know what to do if my telephone fails to function—which does not mean that I know how to repair it, but that I know whom to call on for assistance. My knowledge of the telephone also includes broader information on the system of telephonic communication—for instance, I know that some people have unlisted numbers, that under special circumstances I can get a simultaneous hook-up with two long-distance parties, that I must figure on the time difference if I want to call up somebody in Hong Kong, and so forth. All of this telephonic lore is recipe knowledge since it does not concern anything except what I have to know for my present and possible future pragmatic purposes. I am not interested in *why* the telephone works this way, in the enormous body of scientific and engineering knowledge that makes it possible to construct telephones. Nor am I interested in uses of the telephone that lie outside my purposes, say in combination with short-wave radio for the purpose of marine communication. Similarly, I have recipe knowledge of the workings of human relationships. For example, I know what I must do to apply for a passport. All I am interested in is getting the passport at the end of a certain waiting period. I do not care, and do not know, how my application is processed in government offices, by whom and after what steps approval is given, who puts which stamp in the document. I am not making a study of government bureaucracy—I just want to go on a vacation abroad. My interest in the hidden workings of the passport-getting procedure will be aroused only if I fail to get my passport in the end. At that point, very much as I call on a telephone-repair expert after my telephone has broken down, I call on an expert in passport-getting—a lawyer, say, or my Congressman, or the American Civil Liberties Union. *Mutatis mutandis*, a large part of the social stock of knowledge consists of recipes for the mastery of routine problems. Typically, I have little interest in going beyond this pragmatically necessary knowledge as long as the problems can indeed be mastered thereby.

The social stock of knowledge differentiates reality by degrees of familiarity. It provides complex and detailed information concerning those sectors of everyday life with which I must frequently deal. It provides much more general and imprecise information on remoter sectors. Thus my knowledge of my own occupation and its world is very rich and specific, while I have only very sketchy knowledge of the occupational worlds of others. The social stock of knowledge further supplies me with the typificatory schemes required for the major routines of everyday life, not only the typifications of others that have been discussed before, but typifications of all sorts of events and experiences, both social and natural. Thus I live in a world of relatives, fellow-workers and recognizable public functionaries. In this world, consequently, I experience family gatherings, professional meetings and encounters with the traffic police. The natural 'backdrop' of these events is also typified within the stock of knowledge. My world is structured in terms of routines applying in good or bad weather, in the hay-fever season and in situations when a speck of dirt gets caught under my eyelid. 'I know what to do' with regard to all these others and all these events within my everyday life. By presenting itself to me as an integrated whole the social stock of knowledge also provides me with the means to integrate discrete elements of my own knowledge. In other words, 'what everybody knows' has its own logic, and the same logic can be applied to order various things that I know. For example, I know that my friend Henry is an Englishman, and I know that he is always very punctual in keeping appointments. Since 'everybody knows' that punctuality is an English trait, I can now integrate these two elements of my knowledge of Henry into a typification that is meaningful in terms of the social stock of knowledge.

The validity of my knowledge of everyday life is taken for granted by myself and by others until further notice, that is, until a problem arises that cannot be solved in terms of it. As long as my knowledge works satisfactorily, I am generally ready to suspend doubts about it. In certain attitudes detached from everyday reality—telling a joke, at the theatre or in church, or engaging in philosophical speculation—I may perhaps doubt elements of it. But these doubts are 'not to be taken seriously'. For instance, as a businessman I know that it pays to be inconsiderate of others. I may laugh at a joke in which this maxim leads to failure, I may be moved by an actor or a preacher extolling the virtues of consideration and I may concede in a philosophical mood that all social relations should be governed by the Golden Rule. Having laughed, having been moved and having philosophized, I return to the 'serious' world of business, once more recognize the logic of its maxims, and act accordingly. Only when my maxims fail 'to deliver the goods' in the world to which they are intended to apply are they likely to become problematic to me 'in earnest'.

Although the social stock of knowledge appresents the everyday world in an integrated manner, differentiated according to zones of familiarity and remoteness, it leaves the totality of that world opaque. Put differently, the reality of everyday life always appears as a zone of lucidity behind which there is a background of darkness. As some zones of reality are illuminated, others are adumbrated. I cannot know everything there is to know about this reality. Even if, for instance, I am a seemingly all-powerful despot in my family, and know this, I cannot know all the factors that go into the continuing success of my despotism. I know that my orders are always obeyed, but I cannot be sure of all the steps and all the motives that lie between the issuance and the execution of my orders. There are always things that go on 'behind my back'. This is true *a fortiori* when social relationships more complex than those of the family are involved—and explains, incidentally, why despots are endemically nervous. My knowledge of everyday life as the quality of an instrument that cuts a path through a forest and, as it does so, projects a narrow cone of light on what lies just ahead and immediately around; on all sides of the path there continues to be darkness. This image pertains even more, of course, to the multiple realities in which everyday life is continually transcended. This latter statement can be paraphrased, poetically if not exhaustively, by saying that the reality of everyday life is overcast by the penumbras of our dreams.

My knowledge of everyday life is structured in terms of relevances. Some of these are determined by immediate pragmatic interests of mine, others by my general situation in society. It is irrelevant to me how my wife goes about cooking my favourite goulash as long as it turns out the way I like it. It is irrelevant to me that the stock of a company is falling, if I do not own such stock; or that Catholics are modernizing their doctrine, if I am an atheist; or that it is now possible to fly non-stop to Africa, if I do not want to go there. However, my relevance structures intersect with the relevance structures of others at many points, as a result of which we have 'interesting' things to say to each other. An important element of my knowledge of everyday life is the knowledge of the relevance structures of others. Thus I 'know better' than to tell my doctor about my investment problems, my lawyer about my ulcer pains, or my accountant about my quest for religious truth. The basic relevance structures referring to everyday life are presented to me readymade by the social stock of knowledge itself. I know that 'woman talk' is irrelevant to me as a man, that 'idle speculation' is irrelevant to me as a man of action, and so forth. Finally, the social stock of knowledge as a whole has its own relevance structure. Thus, in terms of the stock of knowledge objectivated in American society, it is irrelevant to study the movements of the stars to predict the stock market, but it is relevant to study an individual's slips of the tongue to find out about his sex life, and so on. Conversely, in other societies, astrology may be highly relevant for economics, speech analysis quite irrelevant for erotic curiosity, and so on.

One final point should be made here about the social distribution of knowledge. I encounter knowledge in everyday life as socially distributed, that is, as possessed differently by different individuals and types of individuals. I do not share my knowledge equally with all my fellowmen, and there may be some knowledge that I share with no one. I share my professional expertise with colleagues, but not with my family, and I may share with nobody my knowledge of how to cheat at cards. The social distribution of knowledge of certain elements of everyday reality can become highly complex and even confusing to the outsider. I not only do not possess the knowledge supposedly required to cure me of a physical ailment, I may even lack the knowledge of which one of a bewildering variety of medical specialists claims jurisdiction over what ails me. In such cases, I require not only the advice of experts, but the prior advice of experts on experts. The social distribution of knowledge thus begins with the simple fact that I do not know everything known to my fellowmen, and vice versa, and culminates in exceedingly complex and esoteric systems of expertise. Knowledge of *how* the socially available stock of knowledge is distributed, at least in outline, is an important element of that same stock of knowledge. In everyday life I know, at least roughly, what I can hide from whom, whom I can turn to for information on what I do not know, and generally which types of individuals may be expected to have which types of knowledge.

10 Language and identity

Anselm L. Strauss

Central to any discussion of identity is language. The word 'central' is used advisedly. Language is ofttimes construed as just one more kind of behavior—encompassing speaking, reading, writing, and hearing—within a long listing of other kinds of behavior. An important and recurring theme of this essay is that a proper theoretical account of men's identities and action must put men's linguistics into the heart of the discussion.

Names

Consider, as a beginning, that *distinctive appelation by which a person is known*: his name. A name can be very revealing, both of its donor and its owner; if we are observant we shall find it speaks volumes. First generation Jewish immigrants to this country were called by old-fashioned names resounding with rich historical overtones, names like Isaac, Benjamin, Abraham, Hannah, and Ruth; but the children of their children are hardly ever named after such Biblical models, since as their styles of life change so have their ideals and aspirations. The children's names represent this change if not as precisely, at least as surely, as pink litmus signifies acid. Any name is a container; poured into it are the conscious or unwitting evaluations of the namer. Sometimes this is obvious, as when post-civil war Negroes named their children after the Great Emancipator; sometimes the position of the namer has to be sought and one's inference buttressed by other evidence.

If the name reveals the judgments of the namer, what of the person who receives it? How does he react to this attempt to fix his identity in some way, beforehand. There is a range here running from relative indifference to violent rejection or prideful acceptance. There is the name that announces its bearer to be the third of

a line of famous personages, destined not to be the last to do it honor. Probably more common in this country are those names over which children have blushed and been ashamed as their teachers stuttered over pronunciation, these names often later to be shortened, discarded, or relegated to alphabetized shorthand. The point is not whether or not a man can be wholly indifferent to his name but that an extensive range of reaction can be evoked by his imaginings of what he must look like to certain audiences if he bears the name that he does.

The names that are adopted voluntarily reveal even more tellingly the indissoluble tie between name and self-image. The changing of names marks a rite of passage. It means such things as that the person wants to have the kind of name he thinks represents him as a person, does not want any longer to be the kind of person that his previous name signified. The commonest and perhaps least emotionally charged instance of name-changing occurs when a bride takes over her husband's last name and so signifies her changed status. Suppose the wife of an American male were to insist that he change his last name to hers! The phenomenon of 'passing' is often marked by name-changing: you disguise who you were or are in order to appear what you wish to be. Benny Ginsburgh may become Basil Gainsborough to express—not necessarily passing and secrecy—but only mobility aspirations. Secrecy sometimes gets mingled with personality transition, as when revolutionists adopt new names and thus seek to bury publicly their pasts; but the new names also mark passage to new self-images. Conversion, religious or otherwise, is often marked by a complete change of name, that act signifying the person's new status in the eyes of God, the world, and himself—marking status and setting a seal upon it.

Less complete changes of status are commonly marked by the partial qualifications of name through the addition of a title, as if to say 'this man is now a member of the Senate, so let us accord him his due

Source: A. L. Strauss, *Mirrors and Masks: The Search for Identity*, The Free Press (1959), 15–25.

and address him as Senator.' There are some names, like titles, that have to be earned; having earned them, one tells himself that this is what he is and that other poeple think so too or they would not so address him. Some Indian tribes, for instance, recognized a warrior's major achievement in battle by sanctioning an entire change of name. Americans use a similar device in applying nicknames to express earned status, and by them, can denote a change in status.

Naming as an act of placement

The philosophers, John Dewey and Arthur Bentley, in *Knowing and the Known*, have argued that to name is to know, and that the extent of knowing is dependent upon the extent of the naming. By this they do not mean to suggest anything magical about the act of naming, but to make that act central to any human's cognition of his world. This view informs much of the discussion that will follow.

Suppose a mother wishes her very young child to pay attention to an object. She moves his body so that his eyes focus somewhere near the object and then she points toward it. But when he is at an age when he can respond to a word, she will hope to attract his attention more efficiently to something by naming it. This is what is called 'ostensive definition,' meaning an indication of an object without any description whatever; it is the simplest kind of identification. The first identifications are singular; they indicate particular objects. But the child soon learns that certain objects can be called by the same word, albeit his groupings are frequently amusing and seem incorrect to his elders. At first parents often bow to the child's peculiar classification of objects, in order to keep peace in the family, but in the end they win the game, for the youngster must eventually conform to more conventional, if less colorful, lexicology.

To name, then, is not only to indicate; it is to identify an object as some kind of object. An act of identification requires that the thing referred to be placed within a category. Borrowing from the language of logic, we may say that any particular object that is referred to is a member of a general class, a representative of that class. An orange is a member of a class called oranges; but note that this class itself receives its placement, or definition, only by virtue of its relationships with other classes. These relationships are of quite a systematic sort. Thus oranges may be defined in relation to such classes as fruits, foods, tropical growths, tree products, and moderately priced objects. Defining any class, then, means relating it to systematically associated classes. 'To tell what a thing is, you place it in terms of something else. This idea of locating, or placing, is implicit in our very word for definition itself: to *define*, or *determine* a thing, is to mark its boundaries.'[1]

It should be noted, however, that any particular object can be named, and thus located, in countless ways. The naming sets it within a context of quite differently related classes. The nature or essence of an object does not reside mysteriously within an object itself but is dependent upon how it is defined by the namer. An object which looks so much like an orange —in fact which really is an orange—can also be a member of an infinite number of other classes. If it is in its nature to be an orange, it is also in its nature to be other things. In the case of an orange, we may choose to view it within different contexts for other equally legitimate purposes. It may thus be viewed as a spherical object, with rough, warm-colored skin, suitable for catching and casting lights, hence eminently definable as a model for a beginning art student. Essentially it is just that. This is only to repeat a point made earlier that to name or designate is always to do this from some point of view. From a single identical perspective, otherwise seemingly different things can be classed together. Justification lies in the perspective, not in the things. If you do not agree with your neighbor's classification, this may only signify that you have a somewhat or wholly different basis for drawing symbolic circles around things.

The way in which things are classed together reveals, graphically as well as symbolically, the perspectives of the classifier. For instance, an anthropologist (Robert Pehrson) studying the Laplanders recently discovered that a single word is used to encompass both 'people' and 'reindeer.' The life of the Laplander revolves around activities having to do with reindeer. Is a reindeer a human or is a human a reindeer? The question is senseless; the people and reindeer are identified, they go together, and the very fact of their identification in terminology gives the anthropologist one of his best clues to the Laplander's ordering of the world and its objects.

Any group of people that has any permanence develops a 'special language,' a lingo or jargon, which represents its way of identifying those objects important for group action. Waitresses classify types of customers and other workers in the restaurant, give shorthand names to foods, and have special signs and gestures standing for important activities. So do criminals; and even ministers are not immune from the necessity of classifying their clientele and colleagues, otherwise how could they organize activity in an orderly and sensible manner?

The propensity for certain categories invented by any group to be slanderous, to partake of epithet, derogation and innuendo, has been bemoaned by liberals, debunkers, teachers, and all others who have wished to set others' classifications straight. Since groups inevitably are in conflict over issues—otherwise they would not be different groups—and since events inevitably come to be viewed differently by those who are looking up or down opposite ends of the gun, it is useless to talk of trying to eradicate from the human mind the tendency to stereotype, to designate nastily, and to oversimplify. This is not to say that humans are brutish, but that they are thoroughly human. Animals do not namecall, neither do they possess or assign identities in the elaborate sense in which we are discussing identity.

Classification and the direction of action

This necessity for any group to develop a common or shared terminology leads to an important consideration: the direction of activity depends upon the particular ways that objects are classified. This can be simply illustrated. Not so long ago, children used to be fed large quantities of spinach according to the syllogism that spinach contained iron and that iron was needed for building bones. Now it appears that excessive consumption of spinach reduces body calcium and therefore is bad for the bones. Spinach is thus reclassified and only if you wish to reduce calcium content should you overindulge. The renaming of any object, then, amounts to a reassessment of your relation to it, and *ipso facto* your behavior becomes changed along the line of your reassessment. In any event it is the definition of what the object 'is' that allows action to occur with reference to what it is taken to be. Mark Twain tells how as an apprentice pilot he mistook a wind reef (not dangerous) for a bluff reef (deadly dangerous) and, to the hilarity of his boss who 'properly' read the signs, performed miraculous feats of foolishness to avoid the murderous pseudo-bluff.

The naming of an object provides a directive for action, as if the object were forthrightly to announce, 'You say I am this, then act in the appropriate way toward me.' Conversely, if the actor feels he does not know what the object is, then with regard to it his action is blocked. Suppose that in the dark he reached for a glass of milk, raised it to his lips, recoiled at the strange taste, and stood immobilized until he was able to label the taste as tomato juice. Energy for action was there, but was temporarily unharnessed, immobilized, until naming occurred. Of course, in this example the moment of immobilization would be fleeting, since as soon as one set about to discover what the taste was he would be acting toward something belonging to the category of 'unidentified liquid, whose nature is to be discovered.' A person need not be certain that he knows what an object is in order to organize a line of action toward it—he merely has to be willing to take a chance on his judgment.

Classification and evaluation

An act of classification not only directs overt action, but arouses a set of expectations toward the object thus classified. A chair ought to hold anyone who sits on it, not turn into a piano or a cat, and a buzzing housefly should not piteously ask us not to swat her, saying she is a fairy in disguise. We are surprised only if our expectations are unfulfilled, as when a presumed salesman in a department store assures us that he is just an ordinary shopper like ourselves, or when milk turns out to be strongly spiked with rum. When we classify, our expectations necessarily face both past and future. Expectations have to do with consequential relations between ourselves and the object. However, expectations rest also upon remembrances of past experiences with objects resembling—we believe—the one currently before us.

Since this is so, classifications not only carry our anticipations but also those values that were experienced when we encountered the things, persons, or events now classified. For example, the Japanese have a food called 'tofu' which is a soy-bean product. Let us imagine that the first time we meet tofu it is served cold with soy sauce over it and that it strikes us as unpalatable. Tofu is for us an indifferent food, and if at some future time we should see tofu or hear the word our images would likely be of the indifferent experience we had with a whitish jellied object covered with brown sauce. But suppose that some time later we are treated to a delicious soup in which there are pieces of a mushy substance. 'What is that good stuff in the soup?' we ask, and are surprised to find it is cooked tofu. Now we revise our evaluation: tofu in soup, good; tofu uncooked, not so good. This substance, as used by the Japanese, appears in several guises, so yet more surprises may be in store for us. The range of our experience with tofu is both what we know of it and how we value it. The wider grows this range, the better we know the object—what it can do and what can be done with it—and likewise the more extensive become our judgments of its capacities and qualities. It would appear that classification, knowledge and value are inseparable.

There are several more lessons suggested by the illustration. One is that values attributed to any object —like 'good' or 'hateful'—really are not 'in' the object. In having an experience one does not put value into it like water into a kettle. Value is not an element; it has to do with a relation between the object and the person who has experiences with the object. This is just another way of stating that the 'essence' or 'nature' of the object resides not in the object but in the relation between it and the namer. Value as a relation is easily seen in conjunction with such an adjective as 'useful'—useful for whom, under what conditions, for which of his purposes? Precisely the same is true whether the object is a thing or an event, and whether the value is 'useful' or, say, 'sinful.' Sinfulness is not fixed in the event, a quality of it within the eye of God. An act is sinful to particular definers when perceived as committed under certain circumstances by persons of specified identities.

Since values are not in objects but are evaluations of objects, it follows that persons must do their own experiencing in order to do their own evaluating. This does not mean that I cannot teach you the meaning of something prior to your direct experience of it. I can say that the dust rises off the city streets in a certain country and constantly hangs so heavy in the air that it is hard to breathe. You have experienced similar conditions, so readily understand. But when you are introduced to a new terminology, the best you can do is draw upon possibly analogous experiences, and these may or may not lead to accurate conceptions. To experience, hence to evaluate, a Balinese trance as do the Balinese probably cannot even be approximated by an American. Everyone has at some time been introduced to new terms representing new ways of looking at objects, as when entering upon a new job. Such occupational terms cannot be fully grasped, the objects and events be perceived as others perceive them, until we have undergone similar experiences ourselves. Of course an articulate informant drawing colorfully and accurately upon whatever is similar in his and your experiences can bring you to closer comprehension and appreciation; hence the great usefulness of some novels and biographies. But no amount of description in advance, if the shift in perspective called for is radical, will teach you how yourself will finally evaluate. You yourself must do, suffer, and undergo—to use John Dewey's terms.[2]

As people 'undergo,' their evaluations change. Values are not eternal. Expectations cannot always be fulfilled. Things change; so do we. 'Good things change and vanish not only with changes in the environing medium but with changes in ourselves.'[3] Even without direct new experience something novel may be learned about an object—such as one might learn something new about life in prison, or as when a college student studies about geological strata and rainfall and so comes into somewhat different relationships with rocks, rain, and water. As long as learning continues, revision of concepts continues; and as long as revision takes place, reorganization of behavior takes place.

The naming or identifying of things is then, a continual problem, never really over and done with. By 'continual' I do not mean 'continuous'—one can lie in a hammock contentedly watching the moon rise and raising no questions about it, the world, or oneself. Nevertheless, some portion of one's classificatory terminology, the symbolic screen through which the world is ordered and organized, is constantly under strain—or just has been—or will be. George H. Mead (who asserted that classifications are really hypotheses) would say it necessarily must be, from the very nature of action which brings in its train the reconstruction of past experience and the arising of new objects.[4]

Notes

1 Kenneth Burke, *A Grammar of Motives* (New York: Prentice-Hall 1945), 24.

2 John Dewey, *Reconstruction in Philosophy* (New York: Henry Holt 1920), 86.

3 John Dewey, *Experience and Nature* (Chicago: Open Court 1925), 399.

4 George H. Mead, *Mind, Self and Society* (University of Chicago Press 1934).

11   The neglected situation

Erving Goffman

It hardly seems possible to name a social variable that doesn't show up and have its little systematic effect upon speech behavior: age, sex, class, caste, country of origin, generation, region, schooling; cultural cognitive assumptions; bilingualism, and so forth. Each year new social determinants of speech behavior are reported. (It should be said that each year new psychological variables are also tied in with speech.)

Alongside this correlational drive to bring in ever new social attributes as determinants of speech behavior, there has been another drive, just as active, to add to the range of properties discoverable in speech behavior itself, these additions having varied relations to the now classic phonetic, phonemic, morphemic and syntactical structuring of language. It is thus that new semantic, expressive paralinguistic and kinesic features of behavior involving speech have been isolated, providing us with a new bagful of indicators to do something correlational with.

I'm sure these two currents of analysis—the correlational and the indicative—could churn on for ever (and probably will), a case of scholarly coexistence. However, a possible source of trouble might be pointed out. At certain points these two modes of analysis seem to get unpleasantly close together, forcing us to examine the land that separates them—and this in turn may lead us to feel that something important has been neglected.

Take the second-mentioned current of analysis first —the uncovering of new properties or indicators in speech behavior. That aspect of a discourse that can be clearly transferred through writing to paper has been long dealt with; it is the greasy parts of speech that are now increasingly considered. A wagging tongue (at certain levels of analysis) proves to be only one part of a complex human act whose meaning must also be sought in the movement of the eyebrows and hand. However, once we are willing to consider these gestural, nonwritable behaviors associated with speaking, two grave embarrassments face us. First, while the substratum of a gesture derives from the maker's body, the form of the gesture can be intimately determined by the microecological orbit in which the speaker finds himself. To describe the gesture, let alone uncover its meaning, we might then have to introduce the human and material setting in which the gesture is made. For example, there must be a sense in which the loudness of a statement can only be assessed by knowing first how distant the speaker is from his recipient. The individual gestures with the immediate environment, not only with his body, and so we must introduce this environment in some systematic way. Secondly, the gestures the individual employs as part of speaking are much like the ones he employs when he wants to make it perfectly clear that he certainly isn't going to be drawn into a conversation at that juncture. At certain levels of analysis, then, the study of behavior while speaking and the study of behavior of those who are present to each other but not engaged in talk cannot be analytically separated. The study of one teasingly draws us into the study of the other. Persons like Ray Birdwhistell and Edward Hall have built a bridge from speaking to social conduct, and once you cross the bridge, you become too busy to turn back.

Turn now from the study of newly uncovered properties or indicators in speech to the first-mentioned study of newly uncovered social correlates of speech. Here we will find even greater embarrassment. For increasingly there is work on a particularly subversive type of social correlate of speech that is called 'situational'. Is the speaker talking to same or opposite sex, subordinate or superordinate, one listener or many, someone right there or on the phone; is he reading a script or talking spontaneously; is the occasion formal or informal, routine or emergency? Note that it is not the attributes of social structure that

Source: *The Ethnography of Communication*, ed. John J. Gumperz and Dell Hymes (*American Anthropologist* special publication), 66 (6), part 2 (1964), 133–6.

are here considered, such as age and sex, but rather the value placed on these attributes as they are acknowledged in the situation current and at hand.

And so we have the following problem: a student interested in the properties of speech may find himself having to look at the physical setting in which the speaker performs his gestures, simply because you cannot describe a gesture fully without reference to the extra-bodily environment in which it occurs. And someone interested in the linguistic correlates of social structure may find that he must attend to the social occasion when someone of given social attributes makes his appearance before others. Both kinds of student must therefore look at what we vaguely call the social situation. And that is what has been neglected.

At present the idea of the social situation is handled in the most happy-go-lucky way. For example, if one is dealing with the language of respect, then social situations become occasions when persons of relevant status relationships are present before each other, and a typology of social situations is drawn directly and simply from chi-squaredom: high-low, low-high and equals. And the same could be said for other attributes of the social structure. An implication is that social situations do not have properties and a structure of their own, but merely mark, as it were, the geometric intersection of actors making talk and actors bearing particular social attributes.

I do not think this opportunistic approach to social situations is always valid. Your social situation is not your country cousin. It can be argued that social situations, at least in our society, constitute a reality *sui generis* as He used to say, and therefore need and warrant analysis in their own right, much like that accorded other basic forms of social organization. And it can be further argued that this sphere of activity is of special importance for those interested in the ethnography of speaking, for where but in social situations does speaking go on?

So let us face what we have been offhand about: social situations. I would define a social situation as an environment of mutual monitoring possibilities, anywhere within which an individual will find himself accessible to the naked senses of all others who are 'present', and similarly find them accessible to him. According to this definition, a social situation arises whenever two or more individuals find themselves in one another's immediate presence, and it lasts until the next-to-last person leaves. Those in a given situation may be referred to aggregatively as a *gathering*, however divided, or mute and distant, or only momentarily present, the participants in the gathering appear to be. Cultural rules establish how individuals are to conduct themselves by virtue of being in a gathering, and these rules for commingling, when adhered to, socially organize the behavior of those in the situation.[1]

Although participation in a gathering always entails constraint and organization, there are special social arrangements of all or some of those present which entail additional and greater structuring of conduct. For it is possible for two or more persons in a social situation to jointly ratify one another as authorized co-sustainers of a single, albeit moving, focus of visual and cognitive attention. These ventures in joint orientation might be called *encounters* or face engagements. A preferential mutual openness to all manner of communication is involved. A physical coming together is typically also involved, an ecological huddle wherein participants orient to one another and away from those who are present in the situation but not officially in the encounter. There are clear rules for the initiation and termination of encounters, the entrance and departure of particular participants, the demands that an encounter can make upon its sustainers, and the decorum of space and sound it must observe relative to excluded participants in the situation. A given social gathering of course may contain no encounter, merely unengaged participants bound by unfocused interaction; it may contain one encounter which itself contains all the persons in the situation—a favoured arrangement for sexual interaction; it may contain an accessible encounter, one that must proceed in the presence of unengaged participants or other encounters.

Card games, ballroom couplings, surgical teams in operation, and fist fights provide examples of encounters; all illustrate the social organization of shared current orientation, and all involve an organized interplay of acts of some kind. I want to suggest that when speaking occurs it does so within this kind of social arrangement; of course what is organized therein is not plays or steps or procedures or blows, but turns at talking. Note then that the natural home of speech is one in which speech is not always present.

I am suggesting that the act of speaking must always be referred to the state of talk that is sustained through the particular turn at talking, and that this state of talk involves a circle of others ratified as co-participants. (Such a phenomenon as talking to oneself, or talking to unratified recipients as in the case of collusive communication, or telephone talk, must first be seen as a departure from the norm, else its structure and significance will be lost.) Talk is socially organized, not merely in terms of who speaks to whom in what language, but as a little system of mutually ratified and ritually governed face-to-face action, a social encounter. Once a state of talk has been ratified, cues must be available for requesting the floor and giving it up, for informing the speaker as to the stability of the focus of attention he is receiving. Intimate collaboration must be sustained to ensure that one turn at talking neither overlaps the previous one too much, nor wants for inoffensive conversational supply, for someone's turn must always and exclusively be in progress. If persons are present in the social situation but not ratified as participants in the encounter, then sound level and physical spacing will have to be managed to show respect for these accessible others while not showing suspicion of them.

Utterances do of course submit to linguistic

constraints (as do meanings), but at each moment they must do a further job, and it is this job that keeps talk participants busy. Utterances must be presented with an overlay of functional gestures—gestures which prop up states of talk, police them, and keep these little systems of activity going. Sounds are used in this gestural work because sounds, in spoken encounters, happen to be handy; but everything else at hand is systematically used too. Thus many of the properties of talk will have to be seen as alternatives to, or functional equivalents of, extra-linguistic acts, as when, for example, a participant signals his imminent departure from a conversational encounter by changing his posture, or redirecting his perceivable attention, or altering the intonation contour of his last statement.

At one level of analysis, then, the study of writable statements and the study of speaking are different things. At one level of analysis the study of turns at talking and things said during one's turn are part of the study of face-to-face interaction. Face-to-face interaction has its own regulations; it has its own processes and its own structure, and these don't seem to be intrinsically linguistic in character, however often expressed through a linguistic medium.

Note

1 I have attempted to present this argument in detail in *Behavior in Public Places* (Collier-Macmillan 1963).

12   On the sociolinguistic perspective of the communicative situation

Hansfried Kellner[1]

The social phenomena of communication can be approached from many sides. Within the sociolinguistic perspective a central question is the relation of language and cognition with respect to the manifold social and linguistic dimensions in communicative events, which, of course, are always social events, located in specific contexts.

This problem has profoundly troubled cultural anthropologists for a long time. It became obvious to them quite early that they could not understand an alien culture if they approached it with preconceived ideas derived from their own. Instead, in one way or another, they had to 'go native'—that is, they had to make the effort to understand the alien culture in its own terms. In doing this they almost invariably encountered peculiar relations between the language and its culture, relations which frequently differed greatly from those taken for granted in the anthropologists' own culture. On the other hand, 'going native' was not enough. If they were to make cross-cultural generalizations they had to detach themselves from any single case and to search for broader generalizations. Sociologists, who traditionally have been mainly concerned with their own cultures, did not usually confront this problem. In the actual practice of sociology it is particularly two developments that have forced sociologists to face the problem: one, the accumulation of data on stratification and subcultures, which has made evident the linguistic differentiations even within a single society. Second, on a more existential level, sociologists have been informed (by C. Wright Mills,[2] some years ago, and recently by radical critics of academic sociology) that the cognitive and linguistic universe in which professional sociologists operate has itself a highly specific class location.

Almost anyone familiar with academic life in Western Europe or America in recent years has experienced meetings of students, professors, or administrators characterized by a veritable Babel or

Source: *Social Research* (1970), 37 (1), 71–87.

confusion of tongues. Each group, and different factions within each group, not only have disagreed on particular issues, but have seemed to speak mutually incomprehensible languages. In such situations the problematic of the relation between language, cognition, and social group becomes dramatically visible. A term like 'academic freedom,' for example, means, something entirely different to an elderly humanities professor and a student radical. These differences in linguistic usage are attached to vastly different cognitive styles. Also (and both elderly professors and radical students have an aversion to facing this fact), linguistic and cognitive differences are closely related to very concrete, in some cases even economic, group interests. This example suggests that language is determined by social factors. It is equally important, however, to understand how social processes are themselves dependent upon language. Language is not only an instrument for legitimating particular social interests, but has also a dynamic of its own which can in turn engender social processes. In sociology itself there are different theoretical schemes, each with its highly peculiar language, for the interpretation of social situations. For instance, it is possible to analyze any number of social situations in terms of conflict theory and in this analysis to apply to them the peculiar language of conflict theory. What can happen, however, is that the sociologist who uses this linguistic and cognitive style not only perceives conflict in situations which others interpret differently, but that he actually *produces* conflict in situations where it was empirically absent before his particular theoretical interpretations entered the scene. In other words, linguistic and cognitive styles can operate as self-fulfilling prophecies in actual social life.

These examples illustrate the relationship of the sociolinguistic problematic to very common occurrences in everyday social life. Any sustained consideration of the problematic, however, leads on into far-reaching theoretical considerations. It seems to me that such theoretical considerations will, in the broadest sense, have to be made within a framework of the sociology of knowledge. More precisely, the sociology of language will have to be extended into a sociology of knowledge.

One of the major problems we face is this: how and to what degree is the use of language in concrete acts of speech determined by the linguistic structure of a given language? And how, on the other hand, is it determined by social factors of communication which are relatively independent of the linguistic structure? It is my opinion that this kind of approach must concern itself with the social as well as the psychological structure and mechanisms of conversation in everyday face-to-face encounters. This becomes obvious when we consider—a common-place of any social psychology—that not only the primary process of language acquisition but also the primary socialization into the patterns of social perception takes place within processes of verbal communication.

I would think, however, that this question particularly refers to the structures and mechanisms of everyday conversation in face-to-face encounters, as these have been institutionally defined.[3] It is in everyday conversation that there occur the primary processes of language acquisition and thus also the process of socialization establishes the patterns of social perception. It is in everyday conversation that the meaning content of the social world is continuously communicated and this, again and again, intersubjectively confirmed and validated. Only on the basis of this process of validation is it possible for the individual to acquire a stable basis for his taken-for-granted interpretations of social life, the loss of which would constitute for him a grave threat of anomie. Beyond this the continuous conversation of everyday life also contains those processes which lead to the reinterpretations and redefinitions of the individual's universe of meanings. As a rule, such reinterpretations and redefinitions take place through the medium of the same type of social validation, and thus lead to new taken-for-granted patterns of experience.

It will be clear from the preceding discussion that the analysis of processes of communication from the perspective of a sociology of knowledge points to the general relationship of language and cognition and thus, I think, to a question of semantics. Such a semantic analysis must attempt two things: first, to comprehend the social patterns for interpretation and experience as these are objectivated in the sign system of language; second, to relate the structure of this semantic field to the social situation in which the language is used. In other words, what is required here is not semantic analysis in a formal linguistic sense, but rather an analysis of the dynamic processes of semantic fields as expressed in concrete social situations, especially in face-to-face communication.

What especially must be answered here is the previously mentioned question of the relationship between the formal intrinsic structure of language and the patterns of experience as displayed in the social communication process, these two being understood as discrete entities. Put differently, we have here two variables—linguistic structure and the social psychological processes of cognition operative in the processes of communication; the question is how these two variables relate to each other. In the literature of linguistics an answer to this question may be found in opposing conceptions of linguistic determinism and linguistic instrumentalism. A flat linguistic instrumentalism which conceives of the function of language in terms of expressing experiences and thoughts—both of which have been derived more or less independently of language—is no longer viable in the face of modern research. However, the various arguments advanced in the discussion of linguistic determinism are still open.

One of the best-known and most far-reaching formulations of language determinism is presented by the so-called hypothesis of 'linguistic relativity' associated with Sapir and Whorf.[4] This hypothesis maintains that the individual experience of reality (and thereby, in a mediate mode, social reality as such) is functionally dependent upon the language and linguistic behavior of a given society. The verification of this hypothesis, however, comes up against virtually unsurmountable methodological difficulties.[5] This is the case, almost regardless of whether this hypothesis is taken up in more rigid or less rigid fashion; i.e., whether particular experiences are seen as being directly molded in particular linguistic expressions or whether language is seen as a guiding pattern for experience. For both approaches there is the problem of how to distinguish linguistically determined and linguistically undetermined cognitive moments. This would be necessary for any empirical verification of either approach. However, because of the logical construction of the hypothesis, this is hardly possible.

Nevertheless, examination of the extensive literature pertinent to the question of linguistic determinism permits us to make some indirect conclusions. It seems to me that critical consideration of the results of recent research[6] on the relation of language and cognition makes it very difficult to maintain the notions of determinism associated with Sapir and Whorf. One is then rather inclined to the view that a particular language (be it the language of a culture, sub-culture, or social group) maps out the world for the individual in different degrees of intensity and typicality. In other words, language functions so as to filter and mediate cognitive processes; it does not causally determine them. Aspects of reality are not perceived in a certain way *only* because a certain linguistic system is superimposed upon them. Rather, language affects perception in connection with the specific problems posed for individuals or for groups by their social action.[7] To mention two frequently cited examples, the linguistic complexity with which Eskimos approach snow and Arabs deal with camels illustrates this point. Only because 'snow' is highly relevant to the activity of Eskimos and 'camels' to that of desert Arabs have these groups developed highly differentiated terminologies referring to these experiences. One can say, therefore, with some assurance that a linguistic sign system *per se* does not determine cognitive processes. Rather, it does so only in connection with its use in activity, which is co-determined both by the social biography of the actor and by the social structures within which his actions take place. In other words, a linguistic sign system is always used within sociologically specific relevance structures. On the basis of such considerations a strict linguistic determinism, in the sense of a one-to-one determination of cognitive elements by linguistic features, has to be equally rejected as the conception of linguistic instrumentalism.

A more viable course would be to start out with a stricter differentiation between language as an 'external' sign system and the acts of language usage. Such differentiation, of course, does not put in question a systematic relationship between the two. It is possible in this connection to make use, though with modifications, of some of the notions developed by Chomsky in his 'linguistics of transformational grammar.'[8] The 'external' sign system of language is given to the individual as a program of linguistic rules. This program is the necessary, although not sufficient, condition for the individual's understanding and use of language. The individual is only more or less competent in his performance of the program. His linguistic articulations realize the program to a limited degree only, most of the time abbreviating and transforming it. The actual linguistic behavior of the individual refers only in part to the 'external' sign system that presents him with the rules of language. In an important way, it is also determined by social factors that are relatively independent of the linguistic system. What is more, if the linguistic system is to be realized in speech this requires a steady input of social communications. These serve as mediating processes that carry both the rules of the linguistic system as well as the social factors that are relatively independent of the former. These social factors constitute, as it were, a second system of rules. They correspond to the forms of behavior that are institutionalized in the society in question and acquired in the social biography of individuals.[9] These rules govern the socially learned strategies of communicative behavior. Goffman's analyses of *Behavior in Public Places*[10] provide a large quantity of empirical indications of this process.

For example, the two participants in a minor traffic accident in America will carry on a conversation that is highly predictable to some extent on both systemic levels. On the level of linguistic system as such, not only do they both speak English, but their conversation converges on a predefined and very limited range of topics, which are dealt with in linguistically stylized forms: 'May I have your driver's license?,' 'Let me take down your registration number,' 'With whom are you insured?,' and so on. On the level of the 'second system', there are equally predictable stylizations, such as the repression of violent instincts, forms of politeness and, if necessary, offers to get medical assistance or to provide transportation to a garage. We can easily imagine a comparable incident in an exotic country (or, for that matter, in a non-middle class sub-culture in America) in which one or both systematizations are either different or absent. Thus, rudimentary and non-verbal forms of communication will have to be resorted to if the participants do not speak each other's 'language'. Predictability on the level of the 'second system' might still hold—after all, one can be polite, either in English or without words, to someone who is muttering away in Rumanian. The reverse may also occur. In that case one might even find, for instance, that the other participant in the collision, while speaking perfect English, regards the pulling of a knife as an appropriate response to the situation.

The focus of research in the sociology of language has always been the relationship of language disposition and use to variables of social structure, such as social strata, sub-cultures, or role complexes, as these are effective as models for interaction in the social life of individuals. The observations or measurements of the co-variations between linguistic peculiarities of this language disposition and usage and sociological groupings of users are not enough. Such empirical data then only become decidedly theoretically relevant—especially also within a sociology of knowledge perspective—if they can be related to the concrete communicative contexts, that is, to the actual situation of linguistic interaction as understood both by the participants and the observer. In sum, the effect of language on cognition is made manifest via its role in acts of speech and in social communication. Its study, however, I think points centrally to the analysis of the dynamic processes of semantic structures as expressed in concrete social situations.

The semantic problem in social communication is rooted in the primary significance of action-oriented language used as against the purely formal sign system of language. Structural linguistics, of course, deals mostly with the latter. Any sociology of language will have to deny the adequacy of this approach for the study of language. Interestingly enough, it is not only sociologists, but increasingly linguists who take this position.[11]

The semantic problem[12] of communication, I think, must be approached from two directions. First, it must be approached, as it were, from the 'outside', that is, via the relation between the objective, 'external' sign system of language and the 'objective' social-structural and institutional factors which predefine the contexts of communication. Second, it must be approached from the 'inside', that is, via the subjective structure which the individual brings to the communicative situation by virtue of his subjective meanings, motives, and even idiosyncracies. These two approaches together form the necessary frame within which the semantic aspects of language and communication can be fully grasped.

Language use takes place in socially determined contexts of action. It is at least partially determined by them. The actor selects from the total 'program' which the objectively available language provides those particular elements that are relevant and functional in terms of his activity. But, on the other hand, the objective structures of language themselves contain sedimentations of activity.[13] Put simply, they did not fall from heaven, but originated in a history of social actions. There can never be a communicative situation in which the totality of the sign system of language is activated. There is always a process of selection from the objectively available 'total program' in terms of the problem at hand. The problem itself, however, (regardless of all individual qualifications) is usually pre-defined by society, as is the range of answers. Both problem and answers are surrounded by semantic fields (i.e., by relations of meaning structures), to which the individual has become habituated.

For example, the etiquette expected at a formal reception (or for that matter on an occasion in which a scholarly paper is presented) entails processes of selection that are of virtually ritualistic rigidity. In such situations, whatever might be the subjective meanings and intentions of the participants, the objectively given rules can usually be relied upon to provide a stable background for whatever is going on. Our attention is usually captured by the little dramas that are produced by the dynamics of the immediate situation. This makes it difficult for us to see how stylized the overall process really is. Thus, individuals might wish to use a formal reception or a scholarly gathering for political purposes. They may be thinking of nothing else at the time. With a little detachment, however, one is able to observe that the pre-defined ceremony, with all its wealth of semantic and behavioral elements, proceeds virtually undisturbed despite the frantic subjectivities that might be present. As far as language is concerned, while it may serve as the vehicle of the political games carried on behind the scene, each participant is forced to express himself in the terms that are socially pre-defined as appropriate to the occasion. The innocent bystander, not being able to decode what is actually going on, can live through the whole ceremony without noticing a thing.

As previously mentioned, the sign system of language itself already contains patterns for action in an objectivated form. Thus, the objectively given language mediates experience and triggers action. Only because language carries meaning in this way, can social interaction based on communication take place.

If, however, we were to understand the dynamics of communication and language use as being determined predominantly by the objectively given, 'external' factors that we have discussed, then what we would have would be merely a modification in terms of

sociology of the linguistic determinism which is associated with the work of Sapir and Whorf. We would then have a rather one-sided determination of the communicative processes by the objective system of language as well as by the objectively given social structure. Both would be understood as controlling, if not coercive, determinants of action in what could be called a Durkheimian modification of the Sapir-Whorf theory. Examples of this may not only be found in the work of Durkheim himself, but also in that of his followers, notably A. Meillet, M. Mauss, and M. Halbwachs.[14] The exaggeration of objectivity that this entails can also be found, though in a different form, in contemporary linguistic structuralism and in its sociological applications as exemplified by the work of Lévi-Strauss.[15] If I may stretch the point a bit, in such a view the individual actor is seen as locked in a cage of imposed linguistic and social structures. His experience and thought are nearly perfectly conditioned by these structures. In the extreme, the individual may even be seen as comparable to a computer: he can perform only in strict accordance with the way in which he has been programmed.[16]

This one-sided approach or distortion can be avoided, however, by always keeping in mind the dialectical relation between 'inner' and 'outer' processes, that is, the objectively given and the subjectively intended communicative situation.[17]

In trying to grasp 'inner' aspects of the events in a communicative situation, the conceptions on the experiential processes developed within the field of phenomenological research are especially helpful. In particular, we can make use of the phenomenologically as well as sociologically oriented concepts of A. Schutz.[18] I would imagine that these—including his work in the sociology of language itself—are sufficiently familiar to make it unnecessary to elaborate upon them here at any length.[19] However, the main features of the argumentation as to the 'inner' dimensions of communication may be outlined in a summarized fashion as follows.

As Schutz, among others, has pointed out, the social sciences, if they are not to misconstrue their data, have always to give proper consideration to the Weberian postulate of the interpretation of the social world in terms of the 'subjective meaning' of the social actor.[20] For, the world presents itself to the individual fundamentally, as a subjective texture of meanings. He carries these meanings into the concrete situation of his actions and by means of them he comes to understand and project his bearings in it. While, of course, the core of most of these meanings has by way of the individual's socialization been socially derived, and is thus 'objectively' provided by the social structure, the individual, nevertheless, has to actualize these meanings subjectively in the social situation. He has to 'thematize' them in his mental and conscious activities, in order to grasp and determine the state of affairs in question.

It is this process of thematization[21] of meaning

which is at the core of the problematic of the 'inner' aspects of the communicative situation. It is basic for two related reasons: First, if *rapport* in the communicative situation is to be brought about, it is necessary that the communicators thematize meaning-constructs subjectively in a sufficiently like manner. That is, they have to converge upon an intersubjective 'definition of the situation' in terms of their experiences and interpretations in order to make their communication an effective one. Second, if this is to be accomplished, the participants by necessity have to be 'attuned' to one another attentionally. Each has to 'take the role of the other', as it were, and thematize the schemes of meaning in terms of the (imputed) perspectives of the other partners in the situation.

It is obvious that the characterization of these two aspects of thematization is fully valid only in the limiting case of an ideal communicative context. Most concrete situations of communication, of course, deviate from this ideal in varying modes and to different degrees. This may be caused by such things as diverging purposes and motives of communication, conflicting problems at hand, differing repertoires of knowledge and modes of experience, membership in distinct social groups, absence of interest and attention, personal idiosyncrasies and pathologies, etc. What is more, a good deal of these and other possible causes are, of course, not only social in origin, but usually also imply typical social habitudes with specific social distributions. While to the student of communication all these manifestations are of particular interest and are frequently at the center of his work, it proves necessary to employ the ideal of a communicative context as defined above as an at least implicit measure, against which the 'inner' aspects of the concrete forms of communication can be made apparent.

It is evident that the social structure of language is intimately connected with these processes. It is connected with them both in the mode of an 'external' system of signs and significations as well as in the sense of a foil against which the 'inner' aspects of a communicative event become transparent. As far as the external dimension is concerned, the general problematic has been described before and need not be commented upon again here. It may suffice to recall that with regard to this dimension the process of selection of schemes of meaning in communication is basically determined through the relation between the semantic structure as objectified in language and the objective social-structural factors which predefine the contexts and strategies of communication. As far as the 'inner' dimension is concerned, however, it is necessary to point out that this process of selection is *not* co-extensive with the process of thematization of meaning as used here (though there exists an intrinsic relationship between these two). Thematization of affinitive horizons of meaning as it is involved in a communicative rapport (at least in its ideal form), does not rest *as such* on a commonly pre-given and shared system of linguistic significations. In other words, an equivalent language disposition and usage by two or more individuals does not furnish them automatically with a mutual understanding of their given context.[22] This rather depends on first establishing the rapport on the basis of a 'reciprocity of perspectives'[23] in terms of an intersubjective intentionality, or, as G. H. Mead has put it, in terms of 'the taking of the role of the other', [24] before language comes to play its important mediating function in these processes. It does not causally yield and determine them.

The mediating function of language in these processes, however, must be seen again in two perspectives. On the one hand, as has been shown, language facilitates communication because it embodies objectified patterns of social actions and schemes of interpretations and in this way mediates the thematization of meaning, as it were, from the 'outside'. On the other hand language mediates thematization also from the 'inside', i.e., via processes taking place in experience. This form of mediation, however, is neither built up directly on the basis of language as an 'external' sign system, nor immediately on the basis of its usage in verbal speech, but rather on the basis of a process which has been aptly called 'inner speech' by L. Vygotsky.[25]

In a rather abbreviated sense 'inner speech' can be understood as a form of an 'inner conversation'[26] of significations, by means of which the individual subjectively orders both his reflective as well as his spontaneous cogitations. The specific course, however, which the inner conversation is taking at a given instance, is tantamount to the process of thematization of meaning occurring at this point. Yet, *which* meaning constructs are thematized is dependent on the configuration and weight of the factors that are entering into the forum of inner conversation and are qualifying its course in turn. Both linguistic factors and linguistically relatively independent factors, are involved here. Next to the sociolinguistic input originating in the objective definitions of the 'external' communicative situation, the most important factors to be mentioned here are the effectivity of the inter-subjective role-taking process and the subjective relevance structure and stock of knowledge which the individual carries into the situation. The concrete dynamics of a communicative situation are primarily determined by the interplay of these elements.

The previous example of a social gathering in which a scholarly paper is presented and discussed, may be used again as an illustration of the above argumentation. While this communicative setting follows almost standardized rules of procedures in terms of the 'external' sociolinguistic dimensions and shows in its 'outer' semantic patterns even a certain amount of predictability, it shows at the same time that its 'inner' aspects are stratified along manifold subjective layers. I, for instance, who present this paper, have already drafted this manuscript not only with respect to the scientific subject matter dealt with here, but also in terms of various expectations I hypothetically imputed to be typically given in the audience. In assuming, for example, that not everybody in the audience is very familiar with the sociolinguistic framework, I tried to stay on a generally understandable level of semantic wording. At the same time, however, because I know that highly competent scholars in this particular field are also present, I attempted through the same wording to signify to them the competence of my argumentation. In general, by virtue of distinct systems of relevances this paper also involves distinct subjective references. On the other side, the actual meanings that the presentation of this paper may convey to the audience may also differ from person to person in terms of the manifold subjective references under which this communicative event can be attended. If, for instance, someone were to thematize my presentation solely in terms of possible cues relating to the psychic structure of my personality, a 'reciprocity of perspectives' could hardly seem to have been given. Perhaps this illustration, which could be extended almost endlessly, will illustrate that the rather abstract considerations of this paper are directly relevant to the understanding of numerous situations of social life.

In conclusion I would contend that the emerging field of research in the sociology of language is one of the most exciting enterprises in which sociologists can engage. The problems are very complex and the data so far collected are not of the kind to permit full theoretical integration. The task of theoretical integration is difficult because sociolinguists will not only have to engage in continuous interdisciplinary discussion (especially with linguists, phenomenologists in the technical philosophical sense, psychologists and cultural anthropologists), but will also have to revise their own theories of social action so as to do justice to the dimension of language and knowledge.

Notes

1 This is a revised version of a paper presented before the Graduate Faculty of Political and Social Science, New School for Social Research, October 1969.

2 Cf. C. Wright Mills, Situated actions and vocabularies of motive, *American Sociological Review*, 5 (1940).

3 Peter L. Berger and Thomas Luckmann, *The Social Construction of Reality* (Allen Lane The Penguin Press 1966), especially chs. II and III; also Peter L. Berger and Hansfried Kellner, Marriage and the construction of reality, *Diogenes*, 46 (1964), reprinted in *School and Society*, Routledge & Kegan Paul and The Open University 1971, 23–31.

4 The linguistic system and reasoning of Sapir and Whorf are best outlined in Edward Sapir, *Language: An Introduction to the Study of Speech* (New York: Harcourt, Brace 1921) and Benjamin Lee Whorf, *Language, Thought and Reality*, J. B. Carroll (ed.) (Cambridge, Mass.: MIT Press 1956).

5 For a discussion of some of the methodological difficulties of the Sapir-Whorf hypotheses, cf. Harry Hoijer (ed.), *Language in Culture: Conference on the Inter-relations of Language and Other Aspects of Culture* (University of Chicago Press 1954).

6 There exist now quite a few valuable readers in the field of the sociology of language, which provide a general view on research done in the field. To mention just four: Joshua A. Fishman (ed.), *Readings in the Sociology of Language* (The Hague: Mouton 1968); William Bright (ed.), *Sociolinguistics: Proceedings of the UCLA Sociolinguistics Conference, 1964* (The Hague: Mouton 1966); Dell Hymes (ed.), *Language in Culture and Society: A Reader in Linguistics and Anthropology* (New York: Harper & Row 1964); John J. Gumperz and Dell Hymes (eds.), The ethnography of communication, *American Anthropologist*, special publication (1964). In the German literature two lengthy reviews of research in the field of the sociology of language have been particularly helpful to me in this context: cf. Thomas Luckmann, Soziologie der Sprache, in Rene König (Hrsg.), *Handbuch der Empirischen Sozialforschung*, II. Band, (Stuttgart: Enke 1969); and Ulrich Oevermann, Schichtenspezifische Formen des Sprachverhaltens und ihr Einfluss auf die kognitiven Prozesse, in H. Roth (Hrsg.), *Begabung und Lernen*, (Stuttgart: Klett 1968).

7 The intrinsic relation between the organization of experience and the problematics arising in action has of course been a central theorem of pragmatistic philosophy and psychology for a long time. By way of a semiotics developed within this tradition, notably by George H. Mead and Charles Morris, it has fruitfully influenced theories in the emerging fields of socio- and psycholinguistics.

8 Cf. in particular, Noam Chomsky, *Aspects of the Theory of Syntax* (Cambridge, Mass.: MIT Press 1965). Chomsky's general outlook on language is in some of its dimensions akin to the perspectives of Schutz. Clearly, this could not be discussed here.

9 For an excellent presentation of this problematic, see, Ulrich Oevermann, op. cit.; cf. also Basil Bernstein, Elaborated and restricted codes: their origins and some consequences in John J. Gumperz and Dell Hymes (eds.), *American Anthropologist*, special publication, op. cit.

10 Erving Goffman, *Behavior in Public Places* (Collier-Macmillan 1963).

11 Again, Noam Chomsky stands out most prominently here.

12 It is needless to say that—quite in accordance with modern socio- and pyscholinguistics—in such a study of semantic structures, considerable attention is given also to the concomitant role of syntactic relations.

13 Cf. Alfred Schutz, *Collected Papers, Vol I* (The Hague: Nijhoff 1962), especially Part II; also, Thomas Luckmann, op. cit.

14 Cf. especially, Emile Durkheim, *The Elementary Forms of the Religious Life* (New York: Free Press 1965); Antoine Meillet, Comment les mots changent de sens. *Année Sociologique*, 10 (1905–6); Emile Durkheim and Marcel Mauss, De quelques formes primitives de classification. Contribution à l'étude des représentations collectives, *Année Sociologique*, 6 (1901–2); Maurice Halbwachs, *Les cadres sociaux de la mémoire* (Paris: PUF 1925).

15 Cf. especially, Claude Lévi-Strauss, *La Pensée sauvage* (Paris: Plon 1962).

16 The use of cybernetic models, be it by linguists or social scientists, may be useful for limited purposes, but becomes seriously distortive for the over-all interpretation of linguistic behaviour. One can put this in Marxist terms by saying that such treatment of sociolinguistic reality is reification.

17 I suspect, however, that a full correction of the distortions of linguistic determinism in all its forms could only be made, if at all, on the basis of a philosophical anthropology closely concerned with a critical examination of empirical research on all its levels.

18 Alfred Schutz, *Collected Papers*: vol. 3, op. cit.

19 In the same way I do not elaborate upon A. Gurwitsch's theory of the field of consciousness, which provides also much of the foundation for the description of the experiential processes that underlie our problem. Cf. Aron Gurwitsch, *The Field of Consciousness* (Pittsburgh: Duquesne University Press 1964).

20 Cf. Schutz, vol. 1, op. cit., especially Part I.

21 For a closer discussion of this concept, cf. Gurwitsch, op. cit., and Berger and Kellner, op. cit.

22 This has been assumed at times in behaviouristically oriented theories of semiotics; for example, cf. Morris, op. cit.

23 For the concept of the 'reciprocity of perspectives', cf. Schutz, vol. 1, op. cit.

24 George H. Mead, *Mind, Self and Society* (University of Chicago Press 1934).

25 Lew S. Vygotsky, *Thought and Language* (Cambridge, Mass.: MIT Press 1962). The highly complicated relationship between 'inner' and 'outer' speech could not be discussed here.

26 G. H. Mead's concept of the 'inner conversation of gestures' can be understood as closely connected to this subject matter.

Section III Social relationships and language codes

We turn in this section to consider one particular aspect of language, that of linguistic codes in the context of social relationships. The first reading is a report by Robinson of the work of the Sociological Research Unit at the London Institute of Education where much of the most significant recent work in this field has been carried out. After a very brief statement of some of the important considerations about language, and of Bernstein's theory of elaborated and restricted codes, Robinson considers the aims of the Sociological Research Unit, and the main areas which are proving fruitful. There follows a section on the nature of the data and procedures, which consists of a brief description of the main sample used, the information sought in two maternal interviews, and the three types of child data so far collected.

The results obtained up to the time the article was written are listed under the three headings: data from the first maternal interview, the attitudes of mothers, and the reported behaviour of mothers. A brief evaluative statement concludes this section which is followed by a section on children's language. This comprises the results so far reported, and is concerned with the differences between working-class and middle-class children, largely in terms of the restricted and elaborated codes. This section too is closed with a short evaluative statement.

The final section concerns a language programme which was designed to allow restricted code users to switch to an elaborated code. After a description of the programme, and the results obtained, the paper ends with a brief overview. An appendix gives some details of the Sociological Research Unit, of some of the problems encountered and how they were resolved.

The second and third articles are more specific discussions of the theory, although they present very different sides of the same coin. The Coulthard reading is a review of the theory of elaborated and restricted codes some eleven years after it was first mooted by Bernstein. The Bernstein article is a refine-ment and development of the theory, or, more accurately, a recent refinement and development in the long series of papers which Bernstein has produced on this topic. Generally speaking, the Bernstein article is, as might be expected, a more favourable account of the theory, whereas much of the Coulthard article is concerned with adversely criticizing the theory.

Indeed, Coulthard suggests that the theory of the codes as it now stands in its linguistic expression is likely to be dropped altogether, although it is worth remembering that the Bernstein article was published later than Coulthard's. The reasons Coulthard offers for this suggestion are that no effective teaching programme has been devised to transform a restricted code user into an elaborated code user, and that Lawton's suggestion that language varies very much according to situation raises very grave doubts as to the practical application of Bernstein's theory. He even argues that it may be impossible to devise a teaching programme, as the theory itself does not recognize *degrees* of elaboration and restriction.

One of the major points that Coulthard stresses is that there is not one theory of elaborated and restricted codes, but three theories. By this he means that Bernstein uses a sociological, a psychological and a linguistic definition of the theory, although it is probably fair to say that Bernstein concentrates on the sociological definition. Even so, Coulthard emphasizes that Bernstein stresses different definitions in different articles. Much of the article is taken up with examples of faults in empirical design in Bernstein's experimental work, and Coulthard cites examples of Bernstein's sometimes confusing and unhappy choice of words. He also considers the development of the theory after its initial statement, and some of the work of investigators who have used Bernstein's concepts.

Bernstein's article starts with a brief overview of the theoretical background of his theory of elaborated and restricted codes, followed by a brief summary of previous work in the behavioural sciences which inspired it. Here he is basically interested in the relationship between speech forms and social relationships. His general standpoint is that speech both realizes and controls social relationships. In this article, a major interest lies in the relationship between speech and socialization which Bernstein sees as the way in which the child learns his social identity, and the way in which the child responds to it. He is very interested in the contexts of socialization, but, in this article, limits himself to socialization within the family. It is evident that here Bernstein is most concerned with a sociological definition of the codes, and stresses that social class is of fundamental importance in its influence upon language performance. He points out, for example, that socialization guides a child towards either universalistic or particularistic meanings.

Bernstein stresses the influence of role in the relationship between the social structure and language, and points to four contexts of socialization, the regulative, instructional, imaginative and interpersonal, as being of particular significance in this context.

Victor Lee

13 Social factors and language development in primary school children

W. P. Robinson[1]

Source: *Education in Europe* ed. M. A. Matthijssen and C. E. Vervoort, Mouton, The Hague-Paris-La Haye (1968), 51–66.

Introduction

At a psychological level we may agree that the language we command affects our capacity for communication both with ourselves and with other people. When material to be comprehended or learned is presented verbally, or when verbal answers are required, the language we have available constrains our verbal and non-verbal behaviour. Experimental results support the view that our language influences our habitual manner of perceiving and thinking. These results do not entail that we are unable to make perceptual discriminations beyond our normal usage of language; that our experience cannot transcend our language. This is shown simply but dramatically by the fact that, although we all start life without a language, almost all of us manage to acquire at least one. However, our present and future abilities to acquire and use many types of knowledge and understanding do depend upon our ability to understand and produce appropriate language.

That this might have considerable sociological significance was highlighted by Bernstein's transposition and elaboration of the Sapir-Whorf hypothesis to the sociological level of analysis (1961a, 1961b). He has argued that within a single speech community there may exist broadly-based social differences in language. In its simplest form his argument is that while the middle class has access to both an 'elaborated' and a 'restricted' code, the working class, especially its lower stratum, is generally confined to a 'restricted' code. These two codes have different linguistic structures and functions. For Bernstein, this 'restricted' code has a predominantly social function serving to maintain or change the nature of an immediate role relationship: it defines the type of bond existing between persons in a face-to-face situation. The 'elaborated' code is a vehicle for the communication of

all manner of information about the physical and social world. Linguistically the 'elaborated' code lends itself to an exploitation of the full range of grammatical and lexical possibilities in the language, whereas the 'restricted' code has a simpler, uncomplicated grammar, with fewer completed structures, a lesser use of subordination, less complex verbal and adverbial group-structures, a narrower lexical range and a greater incidence of tags which will check upon the listener's agreement. This code will contain a high incidence of clichés. A fuller specification can only be made in the light of data as yet uncollected or unprocessed, but one additional important point that has emerged from a consideration of data concerns the contextual features of the codes, viz. the relationship between what is said and the non-verbal events being discussed. The 'elaborated' code will be firmly anchored to the external world: its essence requires that it change and grow as a function of new understanding of this world. For the 'restricted' code such correspondence is unnecessary. You can say 'Good morning' when it is raining. If this is so, the latent functions of the code render its manifest content relatively less important. Hence not only are its grammar and lexis relatively unsuited to generally accepted educational objectives, but its semantics is also directed towards other ends. We could demand more information about these codes and we could embark upon a critical evaluation. To date we have preferred to use the ideas as guides to research. The socially-oriented 'restricted' code and the everything-oriented 'elaborated' code are conceived as ideal types rather than discrete entities. It would be rash to demand too precise an operationalization too soon.

Up to 1965 small-scale studies in England (see Robinson and Rackstraw (1967) for a bibliography) had found social class differences over and above those attributable to or confounded by intelligence test scores. The differences were found in a variety of situations, with a variety of topics, in both the speech and writing of boys and girls. The subjects were all adolescents with just above average intelligence test scores. In general the results were consistent with Bernstein's views: there were grammatical differences in the utilization of simple, and especially complex, subordinations and the systems of the verbal group; there were differences in the lexical range of nouns, adjectives and adverbs; there were differences in socially directed tags, hesitations and code switching.

The Sociological Research Unit is extending these inquiries with particular reference to the language of primary school children, but also with a more general reference to their total educability. The initial goals were to describe variations in school performance and link these to variations in verbal behaviour. This pre-supposes the existence of a taxonomy of the grammatical, lexical and contextual features of the language. Halliday's Scale and Category Grammar has been the major system used (Halliday, McIntosh and Strevens, 1964). The second-stage goals were to link these variations to differences in parent-child interaction. In turn it was necessary to discover the constellations of attitudes and capacities which predisposed parents to adopt their particular child-rearing practices. These attitude clusters and capacities could then be located in the social structure and the sociological constraints determining them exposed. Parallel to the chain of influences through the familial system is that which can be traced through the educational system, through the peer group, the class teachers, head teacher and Local Education Authority and through the organizational features of the system.

Given the present state of data processing, it seems advisable to concentrate on a description of the sources of data and three main areas in which results are beginning to emerge:

1 social class differences in the mothers' reported behaviour and attitudes,
2 the language of primary school children and its differential association with social class, and
3 an attempt to change the expected life chances of a group of working class children by employing a special 'Use of Language' programme intended to switch the children from a 'restricted' to an 'elaborated' code.

Method for main samples

Nature of the data and procedures

Sample

The original sample comprised all two year Infant entrants to a 25% sample of the Local Education Authority schools in a predominantly working class London borough. About 350 five year old children in thirteen schools were involved. A year later six schools in a middle class area added a further 150 subjects. Data so far collected have come from and are about the children, their mothers, and teachers. Only data about children and mothers will be described, since the currently available results are restricted to these.

Maternal interview I

Almost all mothers of the children selected agreed to be interviewed, but not all mothers were approached. The 351 interviews used for most analyses were conducted about two months before the children started at primary school. Both closed and open-ended questions were asked. Roughly, the data can be broken into five sections:

1 Basic demographic data, age, size of family, type of housing, jobs and education of both parents, etc.
2 Knowledge of the educational system in general and primary schools in particular.
3 Attitudes to features of the educational system, including reports of behaviour relevant to the preparation of the child for school.
4 Attitudes to and reported behaviour concerning play, toys, reading, and children's questions.
5 Reported behaviour in discipline situations: what is done, what is said and explained to the child, and the reasons for the action taken.

Maternal interview II

This interview was conducted two years after the first, and comprised more detailed questions in the areas already examined. Among additional problems investigated were:

1 The perceived role of language as a vehicle for instruction in social and non-social skills.
2 Attitudes and behaviour to speech faults.
3 The structure of decision making in the family, particularly decisions affecting the child.
4 Definitions of anti-social behaviour and strategies for handling it.

Child data

So far data of three types have been collected:
1 *Standardized tests of intelligence and achievement.* The English Picture Vocabulary Test (Brimer and Dunn, 1962), the Crichton Vocabulary Scale (Raven, 1951), and the Coloured Progressive matrices (Raven, 1963) were each given within a month of the child's entry to Infant School. The Wechsler Intelligence Scale for Children (Wechsler, 1965) was given one year later. The children from the mainly working class borough were also given a standardized English attainment test after a further year.
2 *Teacher's ratings.* At the end of the first year, and half-way through the second year the teachers rated children in their class on a number of scales including cooperativeness, attentiveness, answering and questioning, brightness, and the likelihood of success in school.
3 *Speech samples.* Within three weeks of entering primary school each child performed a series of tasks

in a structured but informal interview, usually lasting half an hour. To initiate proceedings the child brought a painting or model to the interview room and talked about it. The child then constructed a model room with furniture and family figures and answered several questions about these. The other tasks comprised the narration of three stories about three sets of pictures, the description of objects and events in three postcard reproductions of paintings by Trotin, an open-ended story about what a child did in a free day, an explanation of how to play one of three games and the description and explanation of the behaviour of a toy elephant. It is difficult to see how one could select a representative sample of a child's speech, but it was hoped that the variety of the requirements of these tasks set would give a useful sample. The speech was recorded on tape. A similar sample was collected 20 months later. Other situations have been used for the collection of data from specially selected sub-samples of children, e.g. answers to 'wh' questions, perceptual and verbal discrimination tasks, paired associate learning.

Results

The results obtained so far can be reported under three headings. It is possible to report briefly on the sociological and social psychological explorations, socio-linguistic investigations, and some initial evaluations of the Language Programme.

Data from maternal interview I

The sociological and psychological data have so far been processed in three main ways:
1 The development of indices based upon the results of factor analyses. Such indices combine only scores which have known relationships with each other.
2 Initial contrasts of the knowledge, attitudes and reported behaviour of middle and working class mothers.
3 Preliminary examinations of associations between relevant maternal characteristics and the intelligence test scores of children.

The ultimate intention is to specify the antecedents of variations in the children's language, intelligence test scores and other behaviours in terms of the social psychological situation of the family, and to relate these variations in turn to sociological measures. Another way of expressing this, but giving a somewhat different meaning, would be to state that the intention is to elucidate 'social class' differences in terms of social psychological variables, at least as far as the learning of the children is concerned. The development of indices presupposes a mastery and completion of the coding of responses and the availability of suitable computational programmes and machinery. Neither was ready to hand, but initial processing nears completion and production runs are now imminent.

A 'Communication' index and an 'Attitude to Toy' index have already been shown to have strong relationships both backwards to social class and forwards to the intelligence test scores of the children. (Differences in 'toy ideology' are associated more strongly with non-verbal than verbal intelligence test scores, suggesting some types of learning experience which may be relevant to non-verbal test performance (Bernstein & Young, 1967).)

Attitudes of mothers

First runs have been made of social class differences on a variety of questions directed at knowledge, attitudes and reported behaviour. Among significant comparative differences found by Jean Jones (1966) are the following:
1 The middle class mother prepares herself and her child for his going to school. He is told about both active and passive segments of this role and about the similarities between home and school.
2 She is unlikely to fix a firm functional boundary between home and school, is satisfied with present possibilities for interaction with the school, and thinks she should support the teacher. If the child doesn't learn, she thinks that something can be done, that the school teacher or child is likely to be at fault and that the teacher is the most likely person to diagnose the trouble.
3 She has a favourable attitude to both basic skills and play and sees a proportionate amount of play as educationally important.
4 She sees toys as having exploratory and developmental functions. When she buys toys for a child, she reports that she takes the child's age and sex into account as well as the explorative and physical properties of the toy.
5 She is likely to read frequently and regularly to the child and to give various reasons for reading. She refers to its role as a sign of the affective mother-child bond, but also mentions its instrumental informative significance. Both middle class mothers and their children are much more likely to be members of a library.

These preliminary data suggest a host of further differences awaiting discovery. The problem, however, is not to find significant differences, but to locate distinct clusters of variables that may serve as major indices for descriptive and explanatory purposes. Modern techniques of factor analysis can be a potent aid in this endeavour and are proving informative in the areas of communication and control so far examined. It is hoped that factor analysis will eventually reduce the data to manageable proportions and help to suggest a pattern of possible causal links to explain the variability of the children's behaviour. The problem is made easier and harder by the high positive correlations among the scores. These high associations yield impressive general factors, but make the isolation of factors other than these difficult to achieve.

Reported behaviour of mothers

Discipline situations

The mothers' control procedures are providing interpretive problems partly because there are variations in the amount as well as type of control, but a summary statement, which does not do great injustice to the data, would posit that at one behavioural extreme is physical punishment and, at the other lie 'complex verbal appeals' to the child about the effects his behaviour has on both the behaviour and feelings of specified persons, such as himself and the mother. The implication is clear. At one extreme the child receives a minimal amount of information, mainly confined to a connection between the stimulus complex of the discipline situation and the punishment. At the other extreme the child is offered facts about the physical and social world and how these affect people; he is given information about points of view other than his own and the temporal dimension of his acts is extended. The data have been subjected to preliminary cross-breaks only, but it is apparent that simple physical punishment is more frequent in the working class and the more informative appeals in the middle class. It should be noted that the concern has been confined initially to restrictive controls, how the mother copes with problems. Techniques and reasons for rewarding have not been examined.

Answers to the child's questions

Brandis and Bernstein (Brandis & Henderson, 1970) report that middle class mothers are more likely to answer difficult questions and are prepared to chatter with the child in a greater variety of situations. Robinson and Rackstraw (1967) examined replies made by mothers who were asked to say how they would reply to two 'where from' and four 'why' questions supposedly posed by their child. Answers were classified in terms of the amount, accuracy, context and type of information made available. The children were grouped by sex, verbal IQ, social class and the 'Communication' index. Although IQ and sex had some relevance to the variety of answers, social class was the major differentiating variable. Relative to the working class, the middle class mothers were more likely to answer the questions, the information given was more accurate and there was more of it. The information was embedded in a less 'noisy' linguistic context, and when the modes of answers to the 'why' questions were categorized, the middle class mothers were found to be more likely to use arguments by analogy and a greater variety of purposive answers, while they were less likely to repeat the question as an answer or use simple appeals to the regularity of events.

Evaluation

The characteristics of the social class differences in maternal attitudes and reported behaviour do not constitute surprising discoveries, although some have unexpected emphases. That middle class mothers should apparently treat discipline situations as opportunities for verbally based instruction rather than problems for control might not have been expected. That some of the differences were so massive and so easily demonstrated even with relatively small samples of subjects and questions implies that the continuing experiences of middle and working class children add up to considerably different environments.

Two general features emerge with some clarity. The first is that relevant aspects of the sociological concept of social class can be broken down into differential patterns of interaction between mother and child, with the consequence that we are afforded a picture of how certain aspects of the life chances of children are transmitted. We also gain some insight into the powerful relevance of language to this mechanism. The middle class are not only oriented towards language as a major vehicle for the communication of information, but their command of language enables this communication to have a reasonable chance of success. The working class appear to use language primarily as one means of social control and the language they command would be ill-suited to other purposes. If we can distinguish between acts of informing and controlling, we can argue that our discipline situations were an inducement to move towards control, whereas our question/answer dialogue situations encouraged the mother to transmit information. However, working class mothers veer towards control in both cases, but middle class mothers move towards the communications of information and hence self-regulated control by the child.

Socio-linguistics: children's language

The results of the various linguistic analyses have not yet been co-ordinated and organized under appropriate linguistic categories and it is therefore easiest to report results by investigation. Selected sub-samples were used for all analyses, and although variables other than social class were examined, they will not be mentioned:

A. Grand grammatical analysis

The social class comparisons run across some 350 grammatical categories counted over the total speech sample of each child gave no pattern of significant differences.

B. Form class analysis (*Henderson*)

Two types of analysis were made of speech from a subset of the speech tasks. A token/type count was made of speech from the Picture story, the Trotin cards, and the Elephant. Middle class children used a wider range of nouns, adjectives, and verbs than working class children matched on intelligence test scores, sex and communication index (Brandis and Henderson, 1970). An analysis on the narrative Picture story and the descriptive Trotin cards showed that middle class children varied the proportion of form class tokens and types across tasks more than working class children (op. cit.)

C. Nominal group structure (*Hawkins*)

Without controls for any other possible sources of variation, analyses were made of the nominal groups used in the Picture stories and Trotin tasks. Middle class children used slightly fewer pronouns than working class children, but the working class used significantly more pronouns whose referents were not made verbally explicit. This was true of pronouns at head and modifier on both tasks. Other differences included the greater use of both epithets and rank-shifted clauses at head, epithets other than 'big' or 'little' at modifier, two or more ordinatives, and intensifiers before epithets.

D. Form and content of answers to questions

i) An analysis was made of answers to three questions, the main one being 'How do you play Hide and Seek?' Middle class children gave more precise and general answers, making fewer inappropriate assumptions about their listener's knowledge than working class children. They used more abstract linguistic structures and made clearer linguistic differentiations (Rackstraw and Robinson, 1967).

ii) In answer to 29 'wh' questions, middle class girls (aged 7) (analysis for boys not yet completed) differed from working class girls on several counts. For 'when' questions they were more likely to use an absolute rather than a relative time reference (e.g. 'on June 26th rather than last week'), and for 'why' questions they used fewer appeals to regularity and authority and more to categorization, cause and purpose. They gave answers which were more appropriate and complete, both grammatically and contextually (a closer correspondence with events). These differences are similar to those found for mothers (Robinson and Rackstraw, 1967).

Two extra analyses are worth a brief mention because they go beyond social class as a differentiating variable. In two investigations sub-samples of lower working class girls were divided into 'elaborated' and 'restricted' code users on the basis of the language they used in the speech sample. The linguistic criteria used to contrast the children were 1) Number of subordinate clauses. 2) Number of rankshifted clauses. 3) Number of adverbial groups. 4) Number of different verb tenses. These indices were generally consistent in their ordering of subjects ($W = 0.75$, $p < .001$), suggesting that it would be permissible to sum ranks across each index. In a 'Spot the Difference' experiment conducted eighteen months later, elaborated girls made fewer perceptual errors than restricted code girls and gave more accurate verbal descriptions of differences seen, with perceptual discrimination scores partialled out. A similar linguistic differentiation was made in the investigations into answers to 29 'wh' questions when the children were seven. Elaborated code girls differed from restricted code girls in the same direction as significant middle/working class differentiations on 13 out of 19 such differences (Sign test, $p = .048$).

Evaluation

An interesting methodological point is illustrated by the failure to find social class differences in grammar over the total speech sample in contrast to the success in finding differences for more detailed analyses in specific contexts. The suggestion is that it is more fruitful to perform a succession of particular analyses to facilitate the construction of the pattern of social class differences than to try to solve the problem with a sledgehammer, which may well obscure sets of contrastive differences.

The results found bear a remarkably good correspondence to those specified by Bernstein (1961) as being markers of 'restricted' and 'elaborated' codes, while the two last mentioned investigations imply the possibility of moving on from social class to a specification of more direct relationships between language and behaviour.

Evaluation of the language programme

Design of the investigation and description of the programme

The Language Programme was designed by the Unit psychologists D. M. and Georgina A. Gahagan, to make speech and language more salient in the lives of the children than it would otherwise have been, to improve and expand the range and type of grammatical and lexical facilities available to the children, to relate this usage to the external physical and social world and hence to equip the children with an increased awareness of new ways of describing and discussing this world. In terms of Bernstein's theory the aim could be summarized by saying that the objective was to orient and equip children, whose life chances would presage a 'restricted' code, with an 'elaborated' one. Factors which limited the scope of the programme were that its cost had to be minimal, when necessary it had to be adapted to over-crowded and materially inadequate classrooms, the time it could occupy had to avoid interference with normal work in basic skills, and it had to be executed by teachers who had received no exceptional training.

The programme was confined to twenty minutes a day, during which two or three tasks were utilized by the teachers. Most tasks had graduated degrees of complexity and difficulty to add interest and vary the demands upon the children. Initially the children played a passive role but eventually were responsible for thinking up, evaluating, and discussing the problems posed within the tasks. Only a few examples can be given to illustrate the content. The O'Grady game was expanded and elaborated. It was intended to enhance abilities to discriminate qualitative and quantitative physical and social differences and act upon them. To succeed, children had to analyse out their own attributes and those of relatives, friends and objects. At a later stage the children had to devise their own categories and discuss results. In an 'I-Spy game', specified new vocabulary was introduced. For 'The Surprise Box' the children had to describe and communicate to another child the nature of unseen objects. 'The Five Minute Story' (listened to on tape recorders) offered new vocabulary, exposed the child to increasingly complex syntax, and had 'Spot the Mistake' in it. Telephones were used for children to describe familiar objects to each other without mentioning the usual name. 'Question Time' and 'News Time' were made use of to develop vocabulary and syntax of questions and reports. 'Picture stories' were frequently used: children were given sets of pictures and had to discuss all possible features of the social and physical situation. Pictures were omitted and the order of presentation was altered, so that the children could develop an inferential and hypothetical approach to the stories. The teachers of the Language Programme children met fortnightly with the Unit psychologists to discuss the techniques and materials for the programme and the psychologists visited the classroom weekly to check that agreed procedures were being used.

The schools in the Language Programme study were a sub-set of the original 25% sample of those in the borough. Three groups of three were selected, matched on the IQ distribution of children leaving their attached Junior schools during the preceding three years. The programme ran in three schools (E1), a first control group had some intervention (C1), while a third group had none (C2). The intervention in C1 schools comprised fortnightly seminars with Dr. Bernstein during which problems of Infant School teaching were discussed, and various projects planned, carried out and evaluated. This was intended to offset the Hawthorne effect in E1. C2 was simply an additional control group.

Three means of evaluation of the Language Programme are to be pursued: 1) Comparisons in specific experiments intended to tap limited aspects of performance under controlled conditions, 2) comparisons on standarized tests, and 3) comparisons of the grammar and lexis of the children's speech to be made at periodic intervals.

Four experiments can be reported. Reports will concentrate on E1/C1 comparisons, although experiments normally contained additional variables such as IQ, sex, or code differences. The experiments were run when the programme had been in progress for at least four terms.

1 Evaluation with experiments

G. A. and D. M. Gahagan[2] have completed two investigations, both yielding encouraging results. The first was a paired-associate learning task in which the child has to respond with an appropriate response word, given a previously unassociated stimulus word. The list comprised eight pairs. Boys and girls aged between 6 years 9 months and 7 years 3 months were required to produce sentences linking the stimulus and response words of eight pairs of items presented pictorially, prior to learning the pairs by the method of anticipation. Children who had participated in the Language Programme (E1) produced more different verbs linking the stimulus and response items and took fewer trials to criterion than either of two groups of control children (C1 and C2). Verbal intelligence test scores (EPVT), obtained at the onset of the Language Programme, were not related to the number of different verbs produced, but were related to the learning measure. A significant negative correlation was found between trials to criterion and the number of different verbs produced. In a second experiment children were shown sets of four pictures arranged in a sequence. A fifth picture to complete or include in a specified gap in the story had to be chosen from four other pictures. E1 children of medium IQ (EPVT, 95–106) made more correct responses than comparable C1 children.

The third experiment 'Spot the difference' (Robinson and Creed 1968) also showed the relative superiority of E1 girls. Compared with C1, E1 girls made fewer errors of perceptual discrimination. They pointed to more differences and were more adept at describing the nature of differences they did notice. A second analysis of their total output of speech in this situation (Coulthard and Robinson, 1968) revealed several grammatical and lexical differences between the groups. In grammar, E1 girls included more nominal groups in clauses and more often used clauses to qualify a head (often a noun). Although they did not use more single modifiers, they were more likely to use two or more modifiers in a nominal group. C1 girls used simple rankshift more frequently, but the reverse held for complex rankshift. Lexical differences included a greater number of adjective types by E1 and a higher incidence of rare adjectives of colour. These results imply an increased facility for handling complex nominal groups and a greater variety of lexical units to insert in the grammatical structure.

In each case significant differences were obtained in directions consistent with the objective of orienting the experimental children towards the use of an elaborated code.

Answers to questions

Of the 19 significant differences found between middle and working class girls in their ways of answering 29 'wh' questions, 14 showed differences between E1 and

C1 girls in the same direction, 2 showed no difference and 3 were in the reverse direction. On a Sign Test this shows that the behaviour of the E1 girls was more similar than that of C1 girls to the middle class ($p = \cdot006$).

Standardized tests

Creed and Robinson attempted to analyse the special abilities and knowledge demanded by sub-tests of the WISC and were able to set up an expected pattern of differences between E1 and C1 children. The analysis was confounded by the nested factor of different schools, but it is noteworthy that pairs of girls (but not boys) matched for EPVT scores taken a year earlier did show significant differences in favour of E1 girls on the Vocabulary ($p < \cdot001$), Similarities ($p < \cdot001$) and Comprehension ($p < \cdot002$) sub-tests. Information, Arithmetic and the Non-verbal test showed no differences. This test was given after the programme had been running for two full terms.

Gahagan and Gahagan administered a standardized English Attainment Test after two years of the programme and found that E1 girls were making substantially higher scores than either of the control groups (C1 and C2).

Evaluation

The assessment of the efficacy of the Language Programme is still in bits and pieces, but several conclusions can be drawn. It does appear that such intervention can have significant effects upon the performance of children, and hence that such programmes might be a desirable addition to the curriculum of primary schools catering for linguistically disadvantaged children. One unexpected result was the apparent success with girls, but failure with boys. No solution of this mystery had yet been found: the materials and tasks do not seem to have been biased in favour of girls; the teachers do not report any bias in their behaviour; there is no evidence that boys differed from girls in intellectual capacity in such a way that the programme was beyond their abilities or beneath their needs. A single hint is given by the fact that on average the girls are rated by the teachers as more co-operative and attentive than the boys. One untested suggestion that normative sex roles may be relevant could be that while it is respectable and admirable for working class girls to be competent at language, such skills might be considered unmanly in boys, being perceived as incompatible with other positively valued attributes such as toughness, mechanical abilities, and physical prowess. If this is so, and it should not be difficult to test, primary school teachers have an awkward hurdle to jump before they can begin teaching. This result does raise with some force the point that any special intervention programmes must be geared to the particular values and capacities of the children towards whom they are directed.

Summary and conclusions

Although we are not yet in a position to integrate the assorted facts obtained, it does appear that Bernstein's theoretical framework is strongly supported by the evidence. Both mothers and children exhibit varieties of orientation to the world at large and language in particular that are a function of social class. For the working class mother language is one weapon in an armoury of control strategies: in discipline situations there is a preference for non-verbal strategies and abrupt commands, while questions from their children to obtain information are responded to with attempts to control, contain, or ignore them. This contrasts with the middle class mothers who convey more information in answer to questions, appear to encourage such curiosity, and who apparently treat discipline situations as opportunities for giving information. The one mother ignores and controls in both situations, the other emphasizes learning through language.

Even if all else were equal, it is not surprising that these differences are reflected in the language of the children. Relative to five year old working class children, their middle class peers have developed an elaborated linguistic structure for talking about objects and their attributes (nominal group) and they use a greater variety of lexical items to expound categories. Their speech differs from situation to situation and bears a closer correspondence to the non-linguistic world. They render their meanings verbally precise and unambiguous and make fewer illicit assumptions about the listeners' familiarity with their own world. The educational advantages to the middle class child have not been discussed, but they are clearly considerable. That schools could mount cheap easily-administered programmes to help offset this differential is implied by the positive results with the 'Use of Language' programmes.

(Some research difficulties encountered and their resolutions are given in Appendix A.)

Appendix A

The Sociological Research Unit has comprised an establishment of between six and fifteen workers. For most of its existence there were at least a dozen full-time research workers, with equal numbers of sociologists and linguists and slightly fewer psychologists. The organization was pyramidal in status, but there were fully open channels of communication. The largest single category of research workers were recent graduates.

The staff was supported by two full-time secretaries and a pool of transcribers who converted tape recordings to written transcripts. Local education authorities, teachers, parents and children were all co-operative and few administrative difficulties were encountered. It is worth mentioning that Professor Bernstein in particular and other members of staff endeavoured to tell all relevant authorities what research was being done and why. We have also reported the results back to these persons when and where possible.

As far as internal administration was concerned it may be most useful to list difficulties encountered or avoided and hope that our experience will be useful to other people:

1 It was important to develop a comprehensive cross-referenced filing system for the collection, storage, processing and retrieval of data. It is probably better to err on the side of excessive duplication and cross-referencing, especially where different people need to use the same information.

2 It would have been to our advantage if we had used a mobile laboratory to ensure the attainment of suitable and standard conditions of recording and testing. Schools differ in their resources and we had to spend many difficult hours trying to hear children's speech against a background of considerable noise.

3 We tried to organize each person's work in such a way that his time was divided between problems of general importance to the Unit and a small particular problem where individual initiative could be displayed. We found that research workers were not able to master this differentiation in a satisfactory way.

4 We found that undergraduate training was not adequate to our needs. Both sociologists and linguists were weak on methodology in the social sciences, particularly the translation of ideas into acceptable empirical investigations. Statistical thinking, descriptive and analytical statistics had not been given prominence in undergraduate courses. It became necessary to put on special courses to compensate for this.

Not all personnel appreciated the necessity of standard procedures for data collection (particularly interviewing) and data scoring (interscorer reliability).

5 The decision to transcribe speech was a wise one.

6 It is essential to time-cost all data collection and processing as early as possible and adopt feasible strategies.

7 The channels of communication among research workers in the country are woefully inadequate. People with similar problems pursue them in isolation from one another. This was particularly true on the computational side. We had to write special programmes for elementary statistical analyses—and still have to.

Notes

1 The research reported is financed by grants from the Department of Education and Science and the Ford Foundation to whom grateful acknowledgement is made. Its realization has depended upon the considerable co-operation given by Local Education Authorities, head teachers and teachers.

The work on children's answers to questions is currently supported by a grant from the Joseph Rowntree Memorial Trust, to whom similar acknowledgement is made.

2 Since published as *Talk Reform*, Routledge & Kegan Paul (1970).

References

Bernstein, B. (1961a). Social structure, language and learning. *Educ. Res.*, 3, 163–76.

Bernstein, B. (1961b). Social class and linguistic development: a theory of social learning, in A. H. Halsey, J. Floud and E. Anderson, eds., *Education, Economy and Society*. New York: Free Press.

Bernstein, B. and Young, D. (1967). Social class differences in conceptions of the uses of toys. *Sociology*, 1, 131–40, reprinted in B. Bernstein, ed., *Class, Codes and Control, Vol. 2*, London: Routledge & Kegan Paul 1972.

Brandis, W. and Henderson, D. (1970). *Social Class, Language and Communication*. London: Routledge & Kegan Paul.

Brimer, M. A. and Dunn, L. M. (1962). *The English Picture Vocabulary Tests*. London: National Foundation for Educational Research.

Coulthard, M. and Robinson, W. P. (1968). Nominal groups of 'elaborated' and 'restricted' code users. *Language and Speech*, 11, 234–50.

Halliday, M. A. K., McIntosh, A. and Strevens, P. (1964). *The Linguistic Sciences and Language Teaching*. London: Longmans.

Jones, Jean (1966). Social class and the under-fives. *New Society*, 221, 935–6.

Rackstraw, S. J. and Robinson, W. P. (1967). Social and psychological factors related to variability of answering behaviour in five year old children. *Language and Speech*, 10, 88–106.

Raven, J. C. (1951). *The Crichton Vocabulary Scale*. London: Lewis.

Raven, J. C. (1963). *The Coloured Progressive Matrices*. London: Lewis.

Robinson, W. P. and Creed C. D. (1968). Perceptual and verbal discriminations of 'elaborated' and 'restricted' code users. *Language and Speech*, 11, 182–93, reprinted in B. Bernstein, ed., *Class, Codes and Control, Vol. 2*. London: Routledge & Kegan Paul 1972.

Robinson, W. P. and Rackstraw, S. J. (1967). Variations in mothers' answers to children's questions as a function of social class, verbal intelligence test scores, and sex. *Sociology*, 1, 259–76.

14 A discussion of restricted and elaborated codes

Malcolm Coulthard

It is now eleven years since Bernstein (1958) first postulated two culturally determined kinds of language. The excitement and discussion aroused has been intense but of late the theory appears to have won complete acceptance. The purpose of this paper is to stimulate further discussion of the theory, its development and proof.

There has been no fundamental change in the theory since 1961, although later theoretical papers (1964, 1969a) have refined and extended it. Restricted and Elaborated codes arise in different social environments; the codes differ in their degree of structural predictability; the codes condition the way in which the speaker expresses himself and conceptualizes. This is a bald and very inadequate summary, but it will serve to begin a discussion.

The strength of the theory lies in the way it combines sociological, linguistic and psychological factors. It offers an intuitively acceptable explanation of some of the socio-cultural causes of under-achievement by working-class children reported in Crowther (1959) and Robbins (1963). This explanatory success obscures the fact that the exact relationship between the three factors is not suggested by the hypothesis. One would except a theory of the form

> Two distinct forms of language arise in two distinct social environments; these will be called Restricted and Elaborated codes. It is postulated that these codes will have the following syntactic and psychological features.

Instead Bernstein apparently divides language into two kinds, three times, using his sociological, linguistic and psychological definitions, and then gives each of the pairs the same names. He thus neatly sidesteps the problem of proving that a code originating in a certain social environment will have a certain grammatical structure and a certain cognitive effect—it

Source: *Educational Review* (1969), 22 (1), 38–50.

has these three features by definition. Papers such as 1958, 1959, 1961 assume the validity of the theory, and are more concerned with using it, to explain the failure of the working-class child at school and the difficulties of working-class psycho-analysis patients, or to discuss problems of 'reversibility of behaviour regulated by the implications of spoken language'.

As there is no basic differentiator of Restricted and Elaborated codes it follows that an experimental investigation could use any of the three definitions. Bernstein himself (1962a, 1962b) took, as Restricted code, the language spoken by working-class boys. Lawton (1965), following Bernstein (1958, 1962a), classifies language as Restricted or Elaborated according to whether it is used in Description or Abstraction sequences. Robinson and Creed (1968) used the structural predictability criterion to divide a group of working-class girls into Restricted and Elaborated code speakers. Although Lawton, and Robinson and Creed used one of the definitions from the theory to distinguish Restricted from Elaborate code speakers, their subjects do not also fit the sociological requisites—both Lawton's social classes are able to switch to an Elaborated code, while Robinson and Creed's Restricted and Elaborated code speakers are both from the same social class. Thus in both these cases speakers distinguished by one definition do not fit into the groups prescribed by another definition. Either these investigators have misinterpreted the theory or the three definitions are not always compatible.

Bernstein's own investigation began from the sociological definition, which suggests that this may be, in fact, the basic code distinguisher. A close reading of the various expositions of the theory is confusing. Bernstein makes frequent use of such expressions as 'could be, can be, may be, are thought to be, broadly speaking', which often introduce a tentativeness that he does not intend, while on the other hand he often asserts what has yet to be proved. For example

Children who have access to different speech systems or codes . . . may adopt quite different social and intellectual orientations (1969)

must be read as 'do adopt' in the light of the rest of the article, whereas

the characteristics of a public language are . . . (1961)

introduces a list of features which have never been empirically proved.

Bernstein combines this confusing mode of expression with a tendency to rephrase the definition of the codes for each article, and it is difficult to decide whether the resulting change in emphasis is intended or not:

the codes *are* functions of a particular form of social relationship (1962a)

the codes *are thought to be* functions of a particular form of social relationship (1926b)

Different forms of social relationship *may* generate quite different . . . linguistic codes (1964)

it is plausible to assume that . . . a social setting will generate a particular form of communication (1969a)

There are similar changes in both the structural and psychological definitions:

the codes *are* defined in terms of the probability of predicting (1962b)

the codes *can be* defined in terms of the probability of predicting (1962a)

the codes *will be* defined in terms of the relative ease or difficulty of predicting (1969a)

on a psychological level the codes *may be* distinguished by the extent to which each facilitates . . . or inhibits . . . the orientation to symbolize intent in a verbally explicit form (1962a)

it *is considered* that an Elaborated code facilitates the elaboration of intent (1962b)

[an Elaborated code] *will* facilitate the speaker in his attempt to put into words his purposes (1964)

The relative importance of the three factors appears to vary with each formulation—1962a stresses the sociological, 1962b the linguistic and 1964 the psychological definition—but nowhere is one definition stressed as the main one. Thus Lawton, and Robinson and Creed should have been quite safe using the other definitions. However, an examination of Bernstein's empirical papers throws new light on the problem. Although each is prefaced by the triple definition of the codes, the hypothesis they set out to prove suggests the primacy of the sociological definition, and could be phrased as follows:

there are critical social environments which cause

the growth of two distinct forms of language; it is postulated that (i) these codes differ in structural predictability, (ii) these codes affect the 'orientation to symbolize intent verbally'

Bernstein's papers 1962a and 1962b apparently proved these hypotheses, but, as the findings of Lawton and Robinson and Creed are at variance with the theory, it is necessary to examine the proof. The raw material for both papers is the tape recordings of five discussions of capital punishment—two between groups of public school boys, three between groups of messenger boys.

Bernstein (1962a) investigates the psychological definition of codes, which he presents in the introductory statement as differences in the 'orientation to symbolize intent in a verbally explicit form'. In the Results there is neither proof nor examples of the Elaborated code speakers succeeding in symbolizing intent verbally where Restricted code speakers fail. In fact there appears to be no attempt to measure this. Instead the paper is concerned with hesitation phenomena, which are used to provide

supporting evidence for the two codes and the different verbal planning orientations which are entailed.

'Verbal planning' occurs in none of the previous or subsequent definitions of the codes, and first appears when Bernstein is giving more information about the differences between the two codes. He says

The verbal planning function associated with [an Elaborated] code promotes a higher level of structural organization and lexical selection. The preparation and delivery of relatively explicit meaning is the major purpose of the code.

The linking, but unstated, assumption here is that an explicit meaning requires 'a high level of structural organization and lexical selection'. This, of course, raises the question of what 'explicit meaning' is. It is probably very similar to the 'elaboration of intent' (1962b), which in turn seems to mean raising the 'I above the We' (1969a). The reasoning is as follows: a Restricted code is one which enforces group solidarity; group solidarity produces 'a range of common assumptions' which will be expressed in frequently used, ready-formed phrases, ones with a high 'habit strength'; the use of ready formed phrases reduces the level of verbal planning, and therefore there is a link between the level of individuation and the level of verbal planning. But there is a weak link; there is no inherent reason why a group-held idea should not be expressed at a high level of verbal planning, or evidence that all individuated ideas are so expressed. Bernstein gives no examples of this repetitive use of stereotyped phrases and there seems no reason to reject Chomsky's assertion that the vast majority of utterances are newly formed for the occasion and unique.

Even if Bernstein's first assumption is correct, the

proof depends upon a second—namely that the level of verbal planning can be measured by hesitation phenomena. Bernstein quotes the work of Goldman-Eisler for support. In a summary of her work (1961) she says

> length of hesitation pauses has been shown to be a function of the predictability of the words following them

and also

> hesitation pauses are . . . distinguished from pauses placed between clauses for the purpose of rephrasing and emphasis by being much, and significantly, longer.

Thus the average pause per word for a given speaker will be almost entirely a function of his word selection hesitations, and can only be used to measure the amount of lexical 'information' in a passage. Bernstein is incorrect in using hesitations to assess the level of 'structural organization'.

The second part of Bernstein's proof is that because the middle class speak more slowly than the working class their level of verbal planning is higher. Given that 'verbal planning' is only taken to mean 'lexical selection', is this an acceptable proof? Goldman-Eisler (1961) showed that when a speaker switches from description to abstraction there is a marked slowing up in speech rate. She also observed that there are marked differences between individuals in their speech rate, and therefore did not claim that all abstraction speech is slower than all description. Indeed out of her nine subjects three produced abstraction sequences which were faster than the description sequences of four other subjects. She concludes in 1965

> it seems likely . . . that characteristic dispositions to pausing in speech could obscure any relationship that might exist between the quality of generalization and pause time.

It is thus not possible to compare the speech rate of one group of people with that of another and assume that differences are indicative of different 'levels of verbal planning'.

It is therefore suggested that this experiment suffers from two interpretative errors; firstly, hesitation phenomena are taken as indicative of 'structural organization'; secondly, speech rates are incorrectly assumed to be constant from individual to individual, varying only according to the quality of the content.

There are also problems about the treatment of the data. The groups for analysis were not the same as those in which the language samples were collected. As Bernstein explains,

> one subject each from group 1 and group 2 were exchanged, two subjects were shifted from group 4 to group 3 and one from group 3 was placed in group 4.

He does not report individual scores for his subjects, no doubt to save space, but one anomaly is that after the IQ averages for the five experimental groups have been presented, one member is removed from groups 4 and 5, because they 'failed to contribute a long utterance'. This must have affected the IQ means, but no alteration is made, and the results are interpreted in the light of the old IQ scores, even though the omission might conceivably have affected the validity of the comparisons.

Secondly, Bernstein (1962b) observes

> the nature of the distribution indicated that non-parametric tests of significance were more appropriate as these tests do not require that the data be normally distributed. [The test used is] a most useful alternative to the parametric 't' test when the researcher wishes to avoid the 't' test's assumptions

The sample used in 1962a is exactly the same, and thus it appears that the parametric tests of significance used were inappropriate. For this reason it is difficult to assess the value of the results reported in this paper.

Bernstein (1962b) is concerned with the linguistic definition of the theory. The results are inconclusive. Firstly, although the codes are defined in terms of structural predictability, no attempt is made to present the results in this form. The definition implies the ability to make statements of the form

> In a given sample of Restricted code one can expect 80%–90% of main clauses; subordinate clauses will be mainly temporal, with very few examples of causatives or concessives.

In other words predictability implies a series of norms for the codes. The anomaly is 'the definition of the codes in terms of predictability without their being tested by this criterion' (Lawton, 1968, p. 94). Instead the results are presented in the self-defining form: 'the middle class use more of X than do the working class.' These may be interesting facts but they say nothing about the codes *per se*.

Secondly Bernstein does not isolate many structural features. He discovers that a Restricted code has fewer subordinate clauses, fewer complex verb stems (though whether this is due to fewer complex tenses, fewer modals, or both, is impossible to say), fewer passives and more personal pronouns. As Lawton (1968, p. 96) observes,

> the differences in frequency between one social class and another on the various linguistic measures, although statistically significant, are not so great as to justify the term *'highly predictable'*.

Even if they were, four features do not seem enough to make predictions about the 'structural alternatives used to organize meaning'.

Thirdly, and more disturbing, is the stress Bernstein lays on the Elaborated code speakers using a greater number and variety of adverbs and adjectives. As the definition is a structural one, this fact is irrelevant, yet Bernstein uses it as part of his proof:

> the restriction on the use of adjectives, uncommon adjectives, uncommon adverbs, the simplicity of the verbal form, and the low proportion of subordinations supports the thesis that the working-class subjects relative to the middle class do not explicate intent verbally.

This statement raises doubts as to whether the definition of the codes has changed, but

> notice that the codes are not defined in terms of vocabulary or lexes (1969a)

confirms that lexical considerations are indeed irrelevant.

Fourthly, the language samples for 1962b are larger than those in 1962a. In 1962a all utterances of less than 40 syllables were omitted; in 1962b the speech sample

> excludes all words repeated, fragments, . . . sequences such as 'I mean' and 'I think' and terminal sequences such as 'isn't it', 'you know', 'ain't it', 'wouldn't he' etc.

As the experiment was designed to show that certain hesitation phenomena and certain grammatical structures are features of the same code and therefore co-occur, it is very odd that the speech samples are different. As the 1962b speech sample is larger, some of the under-40-syllable utterances omitted from 1962a must have been included. In 1962a the middle-class and working-class groups lost respectively 14·75% and 17·65% of the total words uttered, whereas in 1962b they only lost 9·3% and 9·4%. Thus the speech sample of the working-class group was increased by proportionately more than that of the middle-class group, and so contains proportionately more short, probably simple, utterances.

Finally, Bernstein's interpretation of the findings is

> the results of this study clearly indicate that the class groups are differently oriented in their structural selection and lexicon choices.

Do the figures in fact support such a conclusion? The use of the phrase 'differently oriented' implies that there are marked differences between the two codes and that the speakers fall into two discrete groups. This is patently not true. How, then is Bernstein able to claim significance for his figures? Probably because the Mann Whitney U test is not intended to support the conclusions he has drawn. Its function is to test whether group A performs significantly better *on average* than group B. For example, imagine an experiment to test the effect of training on performance in an IQ test. Two groups, A and B, are matched for IQ; then training is given to group B to improve their ability, and both groups are subsequently retested. The Mann Whitney U test would show whether the training given to group B had had a significant effect on

their performance. Even if it had there would still be people in group A who perform better than some in group B, but not as many. The test would not show that group B were now 'differently oriented' in their mental processes, but simply that *as a group, on average*, they perform better than A. Similar conclusions can be drawn about the speech of the middle- and working-class boys in this experiment. The figures suggest that the linguistic performance of the working-class boys, as a group, is depressed in relation to that of the middle-class boys; they certainly do not show two distinct groups 'differently oriented in their structural selections'.

Bernstein claims, for instance, that 'the working-class groups use a higher proportion of total personal pronouns'. He does not give individual figures, but, from the significance level, it is possible to guess at the scores. The result could have been achieved, at best, by *all* the working-class boys using fewer pronouns than 20% of the middle-class, and half the working-class using fewer than 30% of the middle-class; at worst three of the working-class might have used fewer pronouns than *any* of the middle-class. Such figures do not support the conclusions drawn.

Since 1962 Bernstein has produced no more evidence himself, and only quotes Lawton and Hawkins as later supporting evidence. Lawton (1964) is a replication of Bernstein's experiment, which

> must undoubtedly be regarded as confirming the evidence presented by Bernstein's work.

But it does no more than confirm the evidence; the criticism of the interpretation of the evidence above is still valid.

Hawkins (1969) is the most interesting and challenging empirical paper yet produced on Restricted and Elaborated codes. He begins from the finding of a computer-based investigation that the working class use more pronouns, the middle class more nouns. As the use of a pronoun can, in certain instances, convey 'exactly the same meaning more concisely',

> it was necessary to know how and where the pronouns or nouns were being used.

Hasan (1968) has shown that pronouns can be used either cohesively—when they refer to 'something already, or about to be, mentioned'—or exophorically —when they refer out to 'something in the environment of the speaker'. Hawkins points the significance of this distinction. Children who avoid exophoric reference 'can be understood outside the immediate context'; their speech 'can be interpreted on its own, without the pictures if necessary'; such a child 'makes no assumption that the listener can see the pictures in front of him'. He continues,

> if, then, we can show that the working-class children not only use more pronouns, but use more exophoric pronouns, than the middle-class, then we can show that they are using pronouns in a different kind of way for a different purpose.

It could be argued that, as the children were simply asked 'to look at some picture cards and tell the story', it is a little odd to classify them as to whether they assumed that the interviewer, who obviously could see the cards, could not. However, the conditions and instructions were the same for all the children, and there are some highly significant results, which 'substantiate the predictions derived from Bernstein's theory'. Do they in fact?

In this report, as in Bernstein 1962a, b, not all the data are presented. Nothing is said about the relative lengths of the speech samples from the two groups, and the differing uses of the two kinds of pronouns—cohesive and exophoric—are presented as raw scores not frequencies. Thus it is possible that the higher scores achieved by the working-class children are simply a function of the greater length of their speech samples, although this is unlikely.

Despite the stated intention to discover 'how and where the pronouns or nouns were being used' Hawkins presents the pronouns neither as a percentage of total nominal groups, of which they are just one instance, nor, more informatively, as a percentage of those nominal groups where a pronoun could have been used. Such a presentation could affect the figures considerably. The results for the 'descriptive speech' show that the middle class use fewer pronouns; however, it is the exophoric pronouns that Hawkins considers indicative, and the ratio of exophoric to cohesive is very similar for both groups—41·3% and 47·8%. These percentages are not sufficiently different to support a conclusion that the two groups 'are using pronouns in a different kind of way'.

Hawkins realizes the implications of suggesting that it is possible to divide speakers into two groups. To do so one must be able to separate all the members of one group from all of the other, on the important variables. The test he uses, the χ^2, does just this, but the significance levels are deceptive. To support a conclusion that the two groups are 'using pronouns in a different way' a minimum division would be 100 out of the 139 working-class do, and 100 out of the 124 middle-class do not, use exophoric pronouns, and even such a division would not be strong support for the existence of two differentiable codes. However a division as close as 75 middle-class and 64 working-class do not, and 49 middle-class and 75 working-class do use exophoric pronouns would give a significance level of ·03, which Hawkins considers 'statistically significant'. A division of 80 and 59 do and 44 and 80 do not would give a significance level far in excess of the ·004 which Hawkins achieves only once.

It is therefore argued that these figures do not support the division of the children into two groups, they simply demonstrate, once again, that on this particular variable the working class as a group performs worse than the middle class. It is a misinterpretation to use these figures to suggest that

the linguistic realization of universalistic modes of meaning is very different from the realization of particularistic orders of meaning. (Bernstein 1969b)

Since the empirical papers of 1962 Bernstein's theory has developed considerably, although there have been no attempts to test it in its new form. The first change occurs in 1964 when Bernstein observes

it is possible to distinguish two modes of an elaborated code. One mode facilitates relations between persons and the second facilitates relations between objects.

The inter-code differences have always been given a sociological explanation, but none is suggested for this intra-code distinction; no linguistic definition is offered, and the effect of using one or other of these Elaborated codes is not exemplified, beyond

it might have some relevance to the present problem of C. P. Snow's two cultures.

In 1969a Bernstein returns to this distinction.

Pluralistic societies are likely to produce strong orientations towards the person mode of an elaborated code, whereas monolithic societies are likely to strengthen the orientation towards the object mode.

No attempt is made to prove or even exemplify this person/object division, but it is extended to the Restricted code as well, producing four main codes.

The theory develops still further when Bernstein continues

object or person oriented codes can lead to the exploration of means or ends.

The difference between means and ends is not defined; there are again no linguistic correlates to help distinguish, for instance, between a Restricted code object (means) and a Restricted code object (ends). The reader is left to work out the distinction from a series of examples such as,

the code referents [of an Elaborated code object (means)] may be either relations between objects (future applied scientists?) *or*, . . . the status characteristics of persons (military, bureaucratic, occupational positions).

The theory now appears to have moved into a position where it is unprovable—no statement is made about the linguistic criteria, which were so important in the earlier formulations, and the sociological and psychological statements are highly speculative. The theory now has three binary divisions, producing eight codes, but there is no reason why it should stop here. The reader could soon be struggling to separate an Elaborated code object (means) non-striving managerial, from a Restricted code person (ends) upward-striving clerical.

There are still two large problems which are not

handled by the theory. Firstly, what is the process by which a Restricted code speaker can become an Elaborated code speaker? The comments on code changing in 1969a are confined to speculations about which variety of Elaborated code speakers of a given Restricted code might attain.

> individuals starting from restricted codes (person) will move towards elaborated codes (person) . . . they are likely to be restless in their search for belonging or they might accept some belief system which creates it for them. It is thought that many may become teachers, writers, community protest leaders.

Bernstein 1969b, concerned with compensatory education, says no more than that the task is 'the introduction of the child to the universalistic meanings of public forms of thought'.

The theory apparently contributes nothing to the incredibly difficult task of helping the Restricted code child. Not enough is known about the linguistic and psychological differences between the codes to allow a detailed teaching programme to be devised; but perhaps this is impossible, because the theory does not envisage degrees of restriction or elaboration, and so arguably there will be no way in which the teacher can measure progress, until the child suddenly crosses the threshold.

The second problem was raised by Lawton (1965). He found that the language of the boys he was testing varied according to context, and concluded,

> given the existence of Restricted and Elaborated codes it would now seem clear that objective linguistic measures of these codes *cannot* be considered as absolutes but will vary according to the situation. . . . In other words the figures quoted by Bernstein as indices of Restricted or Elaborated code in his papers should not be regarded as norms (in general) but only as norms in a discussion situation.

This is a frightening proposal; how many 'situations' must be postulated, and how can their boundaries be defined? Bernstein (1969a) is obviously troubled.

> It is clear that context is a major control upon syntactic and lexical selections, consequently it is not easy to give general linguistic criteria for the isolation of the codes . . . The definitions in the text would have *increasing relevance* to the extent that the speakers could freely determine for themselves the nature of the constraints upon their syntax and lexes.

In 1969b he says

> because a code is restricted . . . it does not mean that the children cannot produce at any time elaborated speech in particular contexts.

New facts have forced a gradual weakening of the linguistic definition and a lessening of its importance, until this contradiction suggests it will soon be rejected in its present form.

Bernstein's theory has provided a tremendous impetus for research in the last seven years. Now facts thrown up by this research, and difficulties encountered in using the theory to help Restricted code speakers with their language problems, suggest that a new formulation is necessary. Some account must be taken of the failure to divide speakers into two groups in the experiments and the simultaneous observation that within any group of speakers there is a wide range of ability.

It seems possible that codes will be abandoned as such and some more general idea of linguistic depression will be introduced to link a child's environment with the extent to which he falls below his potential linguistic ability. It is essential to demonstrate in considerable detail differences between actual and potential linguistic ability, before there can be any successful attempt to help the linguistically deprived child.

References

Bernstein, B. (1958). Some sociological determinants of perception. *B. J. Sociology*, 9, reprinted in B. Bernstein, *Class, Codes and Control, Vol. 1*. London: Routledge & Kegan Paul 1971.

Bernstein, B. (1959). A public language: some sociological determinants of linguistic form. *B. J. Sociology*, 10, reprinted in B. Bernstein, *Class, Codes and Control, Vol. 1*. London: Routledge & Kegan Paul 1971.

Bernstein, B. (1961). Social structure, language and learning. *Educ. Research*, 3.

Bernstein, B. (1962a). Linguistic codes, hesitation phenomena and intelligence. *Language and Speech*, 5, reprinted in B. Bernstein, *Class, Codes and Control, Vol. 1*. London: Routledge & Kegan Paul 1971.

Bernstein, B. (1962b). Social class, linguistic codes and grammatical elements. *Language and Speech*, 5, reprinted in B. Bernstein, *Class, Codes and Control, Vol. 1*.

London: Routledge & Kegan Paul 1971.

Bernstein, B. (1964). Elaborated and restricted codes: their origins and some consequences, in *Ethnography of Speech*, Monograph Issue of *American Anthropologist*, March 1964.

Bernstein, B. (1969a). A socio-linguistic approach to socialisation; with some references to educability, in D. Hymes and J. J. Gumperz, eds., *Directions in Socio-linguistics*. New York: Holt, Rinehart & Winston 1971, reprinted in B. Bernstein, *Class, Codes and Control, Vol. 1*. London: Routledge & Kegan Paul 1971.

Bernstein, B. (1969b). A critique of the concept 'Compensatory Education', in B. Bernstein, *Class, Codes and Control, Vol. 1*. London: Routledge & Kegan Paul 1971, reprinted as chapter 28 in this book, 'Education cannot compensate for society'.

Crowther. (1959). *15 to 18. Report to the Central Advisory Council for Education—England.* London: HMSO.

Goldman-Eisler, F. (1961). Hesitation and information in speech, in *Information Theory Fourth London Symposium,* ed. Cherry, C.

Goldman-Eisler, F. (1965). The common value of pausing time in spontaneous speech. *Quart. J. of Exp. Psych.,* **17.**

Hasan, R. (1968). Grammatical cohesion in spoken and written English, Part I (Nuffield Programme in Linguistics and English Teaching, Paper No. 7).

Hawkins, P. R. (1969). Social class, the nominal group and reference. *Language and Speech,* **11,** reprinted in B. Bernstein, ed., *Class, Codes and Control, Vol. 2.* London: Routledge & Kegan Paul 1972.

Lawton, D. (1964). Social class language differences in group discussions. *Language and Speech,* **7.**

Lawton, D. (1965). Social class language differences in individual interviews, mimeograph, Sociological Research Unit, University of London Institute of Education.

Lawton, D. (1968). *Social Class, Language and Education.* London: Routledge and Kegan Paul.

Robbins. (1963). *Higher Education. Report of the Committee on Higher Education.* London: HMSO.

Robinson, W. P. and Creed, C. D. (1968). Perceptual and verbal discriminations of 'elaborated' and 'restricted' code users. *Language and Speech,* **11.** reprinted in B. Bernstein, ed., *Class, Codes and Control, Vol. 2.* London: Routledge & Kegan Paul 1972.

15 Social class, language and socialization

Basil Bernstein

Introduction

It may be helpful to make explicit the theoretical origins of the thesis I have been developing over the past decade. Although, initially, the thesis appeared to be concerned with the problem of educability, this problem was embedded in and was stimulated by the wider question of the relationships between symbolic orders and social structure. The basic theoretical question, which dictated the approach to the initially narrow but important empirical problem, was concerned with the fundamental structure and changes in the structure of cultural transmission. Indeed, any detailed examination of what superficially may seem to be a string of somewhat repetitive papers, I think would show three things:

1 The gradual emergence of the dominance of the major theoretical problem from the local, empirical problem of the social antecedents of the educability of different groups of children.
2 Attempts to develop both the generality of the thesis and to develop increasing specificity at the contextual level.
3 Entailed in (2) were attempts to clarify both the logical and empirical status of the basic organizing concept, code. Unfortunately, until recently these attempts were more readily seen in the *planning* and *analysis* of the empirical research than available as formal statements.

Looking back, however, I think I would have created less misunderstanding if I had written about socio-linguistic codes rather than linguistic codes. Through using only the latter concept it gave the impression that I was reifying syntax and at the cost of semantics; or worse, suggesting that there was a one-to-one relation between meaning and a given syntax. Also, by defining the codes in a context free fashion, I robbed

Source: Basil Bernstein, *Class, Codes and Control, Vol. 1*, Routledge & Kegan Paul (1971), 170–89.

myself of properly understanding, at a theoretical level, their significance. *I should point out that nearly all the empirical planning was directed to trying to find out the code realizations in different contexts.*

The concept of socio-linguistic code points to the social structuring of meanings *and* to their diverse but *related* contextual linguistic realizations. A careful reading of the papers always shows the emphasis given to the form of the social relationship, that is to the structuring of relevant meanings. Indeed, role is defined as a complex coding activity controlling the creation and organization of specific meanings and the conditions for their transmission and reception. The general socio-linguistic thesis attempts to explore how symbolic systems are both realizations and regulators of the structure of social relationships. The particular symbolic system is that of speech *not* language.

It is pertinent, at this point, to make explicit earlier work in the social sciences which formed the implicit starting point of the thesis. It will then be seen, I hope, that the thesis is an integration of different streams of thought. The major starting points are Durkheim and Marx, and a small number of other thinkers have been drawn into the basic matrix. I shall very briefly, and so selectively, outline this matrix and some of the problems to which it gave rise.

Durkheim's work is a truly magnificent insight into the relationships between symbolic orders, social relationships and the structuring of experience. In a sense, if Marx turned Hegel on his head, then Durkheim attempted to turn Kant on his head. For in *Primitive Classification* and in *The Elementary Forms of the Religious Life*, Durkheim attempted to derive the basic categories of thought from the structuring of the social relation. It is beside the point as to his success. He raised the whole question of the relation between the classifications and frames of the symbolic order *and* the structuring of experience. In his study of different forms of social integration he pointed to the implicit, condensed, symbolic structure of mechanical solidarity and the more explicit and differentiated symbolic structures or organic solidarity. Cassirer, the early cultural anthropologists, and, in particular, Sapir (I was not aware of Von Humboldt until much later), sensitized me to the cultural properties of speech. Whorf, particularly where he refers to the fashions of speaking, frames of consistency, alerted me to the selective effect of the culture (acting through its patterning of social relationships) upon the *patterning* of grammar *together* with the pattern's semantic and thus cognitive significance. Whorf more than anyone, I think, opened up, at least for me, the question of the deep structure of linguistically regulated communication.

In all the above work I found two difficulties. If we grant the fundamental linkage of symbolic systems, social structure and the shaping of experience it is still unclear *how* such shaping takes place. The *processes* underlying the social structuring of experience are not explicit. The second difficulty is in dealing with the question of change of symbolic systems. Mead is of central importance in the solution of the first difficulty, the HOW. Mead outlined in general terms the relationships between role, reflexiveness and speech and in so doing provided the basis of the solution to the HOW. It is still the case that the Meadian solution does not allow us to deal with the problem of change. For the concept, which enables role to be related to a higher order concept, 'the generalized other', is, itself, not subject to systematic enquiry. Even if 'the generalized other' is placed within a Durkheimian framework, we are still left with the problem of change. Indeed, in Mead change is introduced only at the cost of the re-emergence of a traditional Western dichotomy in the concepts of the 'I' and the 'me'. The 'I' is both the indeterminate response to the 'me' and yet, at the same time, shapes it. The Meadian 'I' points to the voluntarism in the affairs of men, to the fundamental creativity of man, made possible by speech; a little before Chomsky.

Thus Meadian thought helps to solve the puzzle of the HOW but it does not help with the question of change in the structuring of experience; although both Mead implicitly and Durkheim explicitly pointed to the conditions which bring about pathological structuring of experience.

One major theory of the development of and change in symbolic structures is, of course, that of Marx. Although Marx is less concerned with the internal structure and the process of transmission of symbolic systems, he does give us a key to their institutionalization and change. The key is given in terms of the social significance of society's productive system and the power relationships to which the productive system gives rise. Further, access to, control over, orientation of and *change* in critical symbolic systems, according to the theory, is governed by power relationships as these are embodied in the class structure. It is not only capital, in the strict economic sense, which is subject to appropriation, manipulation and exploitation, but also *cultural* capital in the form of the symbolic systems through which man can extend and change the boundaries of his experience.

I am not putting forward a matrix of thought necessary for the study of the basic structure and change in the structure of cultural transmission, *only* the specific matrix which underlies my own approach. Essentially and briefly I have used Durkheim and Marx at the macro-level and Mead at the micro-level to realize a sociolinguistic thesis which could meet with a range of work in anthropology, linguistics, sociology and psychology.

I want first of all to make clear what I am not concerned with. Chomsky, in *Aspects of the Theory of Syntax*, neatly severs the study of the rule system of language from the study of the social rules which determine their contextual use. He does this by making a distinction between competence and performance. Competence refers to the child's tacit understanding of the rule system, performance relates to the essentially social use to which the rule system is put. Competence refers to man abstracted from contextual constraints. Performance refers to man in the grip of the contextual constraints which determine his speech acts. Competence refers to the Ideal, performance refers to the Fall. In this sense Chomsky's notion of competence is Platonic. Competence has its source in the very biology of man. There is no difference between men in terms of their access to the linguistic rule system. Here Chomsky like many other linguists before him, announces the communality of man; all men have equal access to the creative act which is language. On the other hand, performance is under the control of the social—performances are culturally specific acts, they refer to the choices which are made in specific speech encounters. Thus, according to Hymes, Chomsky indicates the tragedy of man, the potentiality of competence and the degeneration of performance.

Clearly, much is to be gained in rigour and explanatory power through the severing of the relationship between the formal properties of the grammar and the meanings which are realized in its use. But if we are to study speech, *la parole*, we are inevitably involved in a study of a rather different rule system; we are involved in a study of rules, formal and informal, which regulate the options we take up in various contexts in which we find ourselves. This second rule system is the cultural system. This raises immediately the question of the relationship between the linguistic rule system and the cultural system. Clearly, specific linguistic rule systems are part of the cultural system, but it has been argued that the linguistic rule system in various ways shapes the cultural system. This very briefly is the view of those who hold a narrow form of the linguistic relativity hypothesis. I do not intend to get involved in that particular quagmire. Instead, I shall take the view that the code which the linguist invents to explain the formal properties of the grammar is capable of generating any number of speech codes, and there is no reason for believing that any one language code is better than another in this respect. On this argument, language is a set of rules to which all speech codes must comply, but which speech codes are realized is a function of the culture acting through social relationships in specific contexts. Different speech forms or codes symbolize the form of the social relationship, regulate the nature of the speech encounters, and create for the speakers different orders of relevance and relation. The experience of the speakers is then transformed by what is made significant or relevant by the speech form. This is a sociological argument because the speech form is taken as a consequence of the form of the social relation or, put more generally, is a quality of a social structure. Let me qualify this immediately. Because the speech form is initially a function of a given social arrangement, it does not mean that the speech form does not in turn modify or even change that social structure which initially evolved the speech form. This formulation, indeed, invites the question: Under what conditions does a given speech form free itself sufficiently from its embodiment in the social structure so that the system of meanings it realizes points to alternative realities, alternative arrangements in the affairs of men? Here we become concerned immediately with the antecedents and consequences of the boundary maintaining principles of a culture or sub-culture. I am here suggesting a relationship between forms of boundary maintenance at the cultural level and forms of speech.

I am required to consider the relationship between language and socialization. It should be clear from these opening remarks that I am not concerned with language, but with speech, and concerned more specifically with the contextual constraints upon speech. Now what about socialization? I shall take the term to refer to the process whereby a child acquires a specific cultural identity, *and* to his responses to such an identity. Socialization refers to the process whereby the biological is transformed into a specific cultural being. It follows from this that the process of socialization is a complex process of control, whereby a particular moral, cognitive and affective awareness is evoked in the child and given a specific form and content. Socialization sensitizes the child to the various orderings of society as these are made substantive in the various roles he is expected to play. In a sense, then, socialization is a process for making people safe. The process acts selectively on the possibilities of man by creating through time a sense of the inevitability of a given social arrangement, and through limiting the areas of permitted change. The basic agencies of socialization in contemporary societies are the family, the peer group, school and work. It is through these agencies, and in particular through their relationship to each other, that the various orderings of society are made manifest.

Now it is quite clear that given this view of socialization it is necessary to limit the discussion. I shall limit our discussion to socialization within the family, but it should be obvious that the focusing and filtering of the child's experience within the family in a large measure is a microcosm of the macroscopic orderings of society. Our question now becomes: What are the sociological factors which affect linguistic performances within the family critical to the process of socialization?

Without a shadow of doubt the most formative influence upon the procedures of socialization, from a sociological viewpoint, is social class. The class structure influences work and educational roles and brings families into a special relationship with each other and deeply penetrates the structure of life experiences within the family. The class system has deeply marked the distribution of knowledge within society. It has given differential access to the sense that the world is permeable. It has sealed off communities from each other and had ranked these communities on a scale of invidious worth. We have three components, knowledge, possibility and invidious insulation. It would be a little naïve to believe that differences in knowledge, differences in the sense of the possible, combined with invidious insulation, rooted in differential *material* well-being, would not affect the forms of control and innovation in the socializing procedures of different social classes. I shall go on to argue that the deep structure of communication itself is affected, but not in any final or irrevocable way.

As an approach to my argument, let me glance at the social distribution of knowledge. We can see that the class system has affected the distribution of knowledge. Historically, and now, only a tiny percentage of the population has been socialized into knowledge at the level of the meta-languages of control and innovation, whereas the mass of the population has been socialized into knowledge at the level of context-tied operations.

A tiny percentage of the population has been given access to the principles of intellectual change, whereas the rest have been denied such access. This suggests that we might be able to distinguish between two orders of meaning. One we could call universalistic, the other particularistic. Universalistic meanings are those in which principles and operations are made linguistically explicit, whereas particularistic orders of meaning are meanings in which principles and operation are relatively linguistically implicit. If orders of meaning are universalistic, then the meanings are less tied to a given context. The meta-languages of public forms of thought as these apply to objects and persons realize meanings of a universalistic type. Where meanings have this characteristic then individuals have access to the grounds of their experience and can change the grounds of their experience. Where orders of meaning are particularistic, where principles are linguistically implicit, then such meanings are less context independent and *more* context bound, that is, tied to a local relationship and to a local social structure. Where the meaning system is particularistic, much of the meaning is embedded in the context and may be restricted to those who share a similar contextual history. Where meanings are universalistic, they are in principle available to all because the principles and operations have been made explicit, and so public.

I shall argue that forms of socialization orient the child towards speech codes which control access to relatively context-tied or relatively context-independent meanings. Thus I shall argue that elaborated codes orient their users towards universalistic meanings, whereas restricted codes orient, sensitize, their users to particularistic meanings: that the linguistic realization of the two orders are different, and so are the social relationships which realize them. Elaborated codes are less tied to a given or local structure and thus contain the potentiality of change in principles. In the case of elaborated codes the speech may be freed from its evoking social structure and it can take on an autonomy. A university is a place organized around talk. Restricted codes are more tied to a local social structure and have a reduced potential for change in principles. Where codes are elaborated, the socialized has more access to the grounds of his own socialization, and so can enter into a reflexive relationship to the social order he has taken over. Where codes are restricted, the socialized has less access to the grounds of his socialization, and this reflexiveness may be limited in range. *One of the effects of the class system is to limit access to elaborated codes.*

I shall go on to suggest that restricted codes have their basis in condensed symbols, whereas elaborated codes have their basis in articulated symbols; that restricted codes draw upon metaphor, whereas elaborated codes draw upon rationality; that these codes constrain the contextual use of language in critical socializing contexts and in this way regulate the orders of relevance and relation which the socialized takes over. From this point of view, change in habitual speech codes involves changes in the means by which object and person relationships are realized.

I want first to start with the notions of elaborated and restricted speech variants. A variant can be considered as the contextual constraints upon grammatical-lexical choices.

Sapir, Malinowski, Firth, Vygotsky and Luria have all pointed out from different points of view that the closer the identifications of speakers the greater the range of shared interests, the more probable that the speech will take a specific form. The range of syntactic alternatives is likely to be reduced and the lexis to be drawn from a narrow range. Thus, the form of these social relations is acting selectively on the meanings to be verbally realized. In these relationships the intent of the other person can be taken for granted as the speech is played out against a back-drop of common assumptions, common history, common interests. As a result, there is less need to raise meanings to the level of explicitness or elaboration. There is a reduced need to make explicit through syntactic choices the logical structure of the communication. Further, if the speaker wishes to individualize his communication, he is likely to do this by varying the expressive associates

of the speech. Under these conditions, the speech is likely to have a strong metaphoric element. In these situations the speaker may be more concerned with how something is said, when it is said; silence takes on a variety of meanings. Often in these encounters the speech cannot be understood apart from the context, and the context cannot be read by those who do not share the history of the relationships. Thus the form of the social relationship acts selectively in the meanings to be verbalized, which in turn affect the syntactic and lexical choices. The unspoken assumptions underlying the relationship are not available to those who are outside the relationship. For these are limited, and restricted to the speakers. The symbolic form of the communication is condensed, yet the specific cultural history of the relationship is alive in its form. We can say that the roles of the speakers are communalized roles. Thus, we can make a relationship between restricted social relationships based upon communalized roles and the verbal realization of their meaning. In the language of the earlier part of this paper, restricted social relationships based upon communalized roles evoke particularistic, that is, context-tied, meanings, realized through a restricted speech variant.

Imagine a husband and wife have just come out of the cinema, and are talking about the film: 'What do you think?' 'It had a lot to say' 'Yes, I thought so too—let's go to the Millers, there may be something going on there'. They arrive at the Millers, who ask about the film. An hour is spent in the complex, moral, political, aesthetic subtleties of the film and its place in the contemporary scene. Here we have an elaborated variant; the meanings now have to be made public to others who have not seen the film. The speech shows careful editing, at both the grammatical and lexical levels. It is no longer context-tied. The meanings are explicit, elaborated and individualized. Whilst expressive channels are clearly relevant, the burden of meaning inheres predominantly in the verbal channel. The experience of the listeners cannot be taken for granted. Thus each member of the group is on his own as he offers his interpretation. Elaborated variants of this kind involve the speakers in particular role relationships, and *if you cannot manage the role, you can't produce the appropriate speech.* For as the speaker proceeds to individualize his meanings, he is differentiated from others like a figure from its ground.

The roles receive less support from each other. There is a measure of isolation. *Difference* lies at the basis of the social relationship, and is made verbally active, whereas in the other context it is *consensus*. The insides of the speaker have become psychologically active through the verbal aspect of the communication. Various defensive strategies may be used to decrease potential vulnerability of self and to increase the vulnerability of others. The verbal aspect of the communication becomes a vehicle for the transmission of individuated symbols. The 'I' stands over the 'we'. Meanings which are discrete to the speaker must be offered so that they are intelligible to the listener.

Communalized roles have given way to individualized roles, condensed symbols to articulated symbols. Elaborated speech variants of this type realize universalistic meanings in the sense that they are less context-tied. Thus individualized roles are realized through elaborated speech variants which involve complex editing at the grammatical and lexical levels and which point to universalistic meanings.

Let me give another example. Consider the two following stories which Peter Hawkins, Assistant Research Officer in the Sociological Research Unit, University of London Institute of Education, constructed as a result of his analysis of the speech of middle-class and working-class five-year-old children. The children were given a series of four pictures which showed some boys playing football; in the second the ball goes through the window of a house; the third shows a woman looking out of the wondow and a man making an ominous gesture, and in the fourth the children are moving away.

Here are the two stories:

1 Three boys are playing football and one boy kicks the ball and it goes through the window the ball breaks the window and the boys are looking at it and a man comes out and shouts at them because they've broken the window so they run away and then that lady looks out of her window and she tells the boy off.
2 They're playing football and he kicks it and it goes through there it breaks the window and they're looking at it and he comes out and shouts at them because they've broken it so they run away and then she looks out and she tells them off.

With the first story the reader does not have to have the four pictures which were used as the basis for the story, whereas in the case of the second story the reader would require the initial pictures in order to make sense of the story. The first story is free of the context which generated it, whereas the second story is much more closely tied to its context. As a result the meanings of the second story are implicit, whereas the meanings of the first story are explicit. It is not that the working-class children do not have in their passive vocabulary the vocabulary used by the middle-class children. Nor is it the case that the children differ in their tacit understanding of the linguistic rule system. Rather, what we have here are differences in the use of language arising out of a specific context. One child makes explicit the meanings which he is realizing through language for the person he is telling the story to, whereas the second child does not to the same extent. The first child takes very little for granted, whereas the second child takes a great deal for granted. Thus for the first child the task was seen as a context in which his meanings were required to be made explicit, whereas the task for the second child was not seen as a task which required such explication of meaning. It would not be difficult to imagine a context where the first child

would produce speech rather like the second. What we are dealing with here are differences between the children in the way they realize in language-use apparently the same context. We could say that the speech of the first child generated universalistic meanings in the sense that the meanings are freed from the context and so understandable by all, whereas the speech of the second child generated particularistic meanings, in the sense that the meanings are closely tied to the context and would be fully understood by others only if they had access to the context which originally generated the speech.

It is again important to stress that the second child has access to a more differentiated noun phrase, but there is a restriction on its *use*. Geoffrey Turner, Linguist in the Sociological Research Unit, shows that working-class, five-year-old children in the same contexts examined by Hawkins, use fewer linguistic expressions of uncertainty when compared with the middle-class children. This does not mean that working-class children do *not* have access to such expressions, but that the eliciting speech context did not provoke them. Telling a story from pictures, talking about scenes on cards, *formally framed* contexts, do not encourage working-class children to consider the possibilities of alternate meanings and so there is a reduction in the linguistic expressions of uncertainty. Again, working-class children have access to a wide range of syntactic choices which involve the use of logical operators, 'because', 'but', 'either', 'or', 'only'. The constraints exist on the conditions for their *use*. Formally framed contexts used for eliciting context-independent universalistic meanings may evoke in the working-class child, relative to the middle-class child, restricted speech variants, because the working-class child has difficulty in managing the role relationships which such contexts require. This problem is further complicated when such contexts carry meanings very much removed from the child's cultural experience. In the same way we can show that there are constraints upon the middle-class child's use of language. Turner found that when middle-class children were asked to role-play in the picture story series, a higher percentage of these children, when compared with working-class children, initially refused. When the middle-class children were asked 'What is the man saying?' or linguistically equivalent questions, a relatively higher percentage said 'I don't know'. When this, question was followed by the hypothetical question 'What do you think the man might be saying?' they offered their interpretations. The working-class children role-played without difficulty. It seems then that middle-class children at five need to have a very precise instruction to *hypothesize in that particular* context. This may be because they are more concerned here with getting their answers right or correct. When the children were invited to tell a story about some doll-like figures (a little boy, a little girl, a sailor and a dog) the working-class children's stories were freer, longer and more imaginative than the stories of the middle-class children. The latter children's stories were tighter, constrained within a strong narrative frame. It was as if these children were dominated by what they took to be the *form* of a narrative and the content was secondary. This is an example of the concern of the middle-class child with the structure of the contextual frame. It may be worthwhile to amplify this further. A number of studies have shown that when working-class black children are asked to associate to a series of words, their responses show considerable diversity, both from the meaning and form-class of the stimulus word. Our analysis suggests this may be because the children for the following reasons are less constrained. The form-class of the stimulus word may have reduced associative significance and this would less constrain the selection of potential words *or* phrases. With such a weakening of the grammatical frame there is a greater range of alternatives as possible candidates for selection. Further, the closely controlled, middle-class, linguistic socialization of the young child may point the child towards both the grammatical significance of the stimulus word and towards a tight logical ordering of semantic space. Middle-class children may well have access to deep interpretative rules which regulate their linguistic responses in certain formalized contexts. The consequences may limit their imagination through the tightness of the frame which these interpretative rules create. It may even be that with *five*-year-old children, the middle-class child will innovate *more* with the arrangements of objects (i.e. bricks) than in his linguistic usage. His linguistic usage is under close supervision by adults. He has more *autonomy* in his play.

To return to our previous discussion, we can say, briefly, that as we move from communalized to individualized roles, so speech takes on an increasingly reflexive function. The unique selves of others become palpable through speech and enter into our own self; the grounds of our experience are made verbally explicit; the security of the condensed symbol is gone. It has been replaced by rationality. There is a change in the basis of our vulnerability.

So far, then, I have discussed certain types of speech variants and the role relationships which occasion them. I am now going to raise the generality of the discussion and focus upon the title of the paper. The socialization of the young in the family proceeds within a critical set of interrelated contexts. Analytically, we may distinguish four contexts.

1 The regulative context—these are authority relationships where the child is made aware of the rules of the moral order and their various backings.
2 The instructional context, where the child learns about the objective nature of objects and persons, and acquires skills of various kinds.
3 The imaginative or innovating context, where the child is encouraged to experiment and re-create his world on his own terms, and in his own way.
4 The interpersonal context, where the child is made

aware of affective states—his own, and others.

I am suggesting that the critical orderings of a culture or sub-culture are made substantive—are made palpable—through the forms of its linguistic realizations of these four contexts—initially in the family and kin.

Now if the linguistic realization of these four contexts involves the predominant use of restricted speech variants, I shall postulate that the deep structure of the communication is a restricted code having its basis in communalized roles, realizing context-dependent meanings, i.e. particularistic meaning orders. Clearly the specific grammatical and lexical choices will vary from one to another.

If the linguistic realization of these four contexts involves the predominant usage of elaborated speech variants, I shall postulate that the deep structure of the communication is an elaborated code having its basis in individualized roles realizing context-independent universalistic meanings.

In order to prevent misunderstanding an expansion of the text is here necessary. It is likely that where the code is restricted, the speech in the regulative context may well be limited to command and simple rule-announcing statements. The latter statements are not context-dependent in the sense previously given, for they announce general rules. We need to supplement the context-independent (universalistic) and context-dependent (particularistic) criteria with criteria which refer to the extent to which the speech in the regulative context varies in terms of its *contextual specificity*. If the speech is context-specific then the socializer cuts his meanings to the *specific* attributes/intentions of the socialized, the specific characteristics of the problem, the specific requirements of the context. Thus the general rule may be transmitted with degrees of *contextual specificity*. When this occurs the rule is individualized (fitted to the local circumstances) in the process of its transmission. Thus with code elaboration we should expect:

1 Some developed grounds for the rule
2 Some qualification of it in the light of the particular issue
3 Considerable *specificity* in terms of the socialized, the context and the issue.

This does *not* mean that there would be an *absence* of

Realization of the regulative context

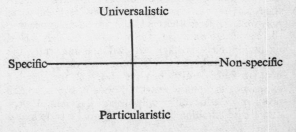

command statements. It is also likely that with code elaboration the socialized would be *given* opportunities (role options) to question.

Bernstein and Cook (1965) and Cook (1971) have developed a semantic coding grid which sets out with considerable delicacy a general category system which has been applied to a limited regulative context. G. Turner, linguist to the Sociological Research Unit, is attempting a linguistic realization of the same grid.

We can express the two sets of criteria diagrammatically. A limited application is given by Henderson (1970).

It may be necessary to utilize the two sets of criteria for *all* four socializing contexts.

If we look at the linguistic realization of the regulative context in greater detail we may be able to clear up another source of possible misunderstanding. In this context it is very likely that syntactic markers of the logical distribution of meaning will be extensively used.

> 'If you do that, then. . . .'
> 'Either you . . . or . . .'
> 'You can do that, but if . . .'
> 'You do that and you'll pay for it.'

Thus it is very likely that all young children may well in the *regulative* context have access to a range of syntactic markers which express the logical/hypothetical, irrespective of code restriction or elaboration. However, where the code is restricted it is expected that there will be reduced specificity in the sense outlined earlier. Further, the speech in the control situation is likely to be well organized in the sense that the sentences come as wholes. The child responds to the total *frame*. However, I would suggest that the informal *instructional* contexts within the family may well be limited in range and frequency. Thus the child, of course, would have access to, and so have *available*, the hypotheticals, conditionals, disjunctives etc., but these might be rarely used in *instructional* contexts. In the same way, as we have suggested earlier, all children have access to linguistic expressions of uncertainty but they may differ in the context in which they receive and realize such expressions.

I must emphasize that because the code is restricted it does not mean that speakers at no time will not use elaborated speech variants, only that the use of such variants will be infrequent in the socialization of the child in his family.

Now, all children have access to restricted codes and their various systems of condensed meaning, because the roles the code presupposes are universal. But there may well be selective access to elaborated codes because there is selective access to the role system which evokes its use. Society is likely to evaluate differently the experiences realized through these two codes. I cannot here go into details, but the different focusing of experience through a restricted code creates a major problem of educability only where the school produces discontinuity between its symbolic orders and those of the child. Our schools are not made for these children; why should the children respond? To ask the child to switch to an elaborated code which presupposes different role relationships and systems of meaning without a sensitive understanding of the required contexts may create for the child a bewildering and potentially damaging experience.

So far, then, I have sketched out a relationship between speech codes and socialization through the organization of roles through which the culture is made psychologically active in persons. I have indicated that access to the roles and thus to the codes is broadly related to social class. However, it is clearly the case that social class groups today are by no means homogeneous groups. Further, the division between elaborated and restricted codes is too simple. Finally, I have not indicated in any detail how these codes are evoked by families, and how the family types may shape their focus.

What I shall do now is to introduce a distinction between family types and their communication structures. These family types can be found empirically within each social class, although any one type may be rather more modal at any given historical period.

I shall distinguish between families according to the strength of their boundary maintaining procedures. Let me first give some idea of what I mean by boundary maintaining procedures. I shall first look at boundary maintenance as it is revealed in the symbolic ordering of space. Consider the lavatory. In one house, the room is pristine, bare and sharp, containing only the necessities for which the room is dedicated. In another there is a picture on the wall, in the third there are books, in the fourth all surfaces are covered with curious postcards. We have a continuum from a room celebrating the purity of categories to one celebrating the mixture of categories, from strong to weak boundary maintenance. Consider the kitchen. In one kitchen, shoes may not be placed on the table, nor the child's chamber pot—all objects and utensils have an assigned place. In another kitchen the boundaries separating the different classes of objects are weak. The symbolic ordering of space can give us indications of the relative strength of boundary maintaining procedures. Let us now look at the relationship between family members. Where boundary procedures are strong, the differentiation of members and the authority structure is based upon clear-cut, unambiguous definitions of the status of the member of the family. The boundaries between the statuses are strong and the social identities of the members very much a function of their age, sex and age-relation status. As a shorthand, we can characterize the family as *positional*.

On the other hand, where boundary procedures are weak or flexible, the differentiation between members and the authority relationships are less on the basis of position, because here the status boundaries are blurred. Where boundary procedures are weak, the differentiation between members is based more upon *differences between persons*. In such families the relationships become more egocentric and the unique attributes of family members are made more and more substantive in the communication structure. We will call these *person-centred* families. Such families do not reduce but increase the substantive expression of ambiguity and ambivalence. In person-centred families, the role system would be continuously evoking, accommodating and assimilating the different interests and attributes of its members. In such families, unlike positional families, the members would be making their roles rather than stepping into them. In a person-centred family, the child's developing self is differentiated by continuous adjustment to the verbally realized and elaborated intentions, qualifications and motives of others. The boundary between self and other is blurred. In positional families, the child takes over and responds to the formal pattern of obligation and privilege. It should be possible to see, without going into details, that the communication structures within these two types of family are somewhat differently focused. We might then expect that the reflexiveness induced by positional families is sensitized to the general attributes of persons, whereas the reflexiveness produced by person-centred families is more sensitive towards the particular aspects of persons. Think of the difference between Dartington Hall or Gordonstoun and public schools in England, or the difference between West Point and a progressive school in the USA. Thus, in person-centred families, the insides of the members are made public through the communication structure, and thus more of the person has been invaded and subject to control. Speech in such families is a major medium of control. In positional families, of course, speech is relevant but it symbolizes the boundaries given by the formal structure of the relationships. So far as the child is concerned, in positional families he attains a strong sense of social identity at the cost of autonomy; in person-centred families, the child attains a strong sense of autonomy but his social identity may be weak. Such ambiguity in the sense of identity, the lack of boundary, may move such children towards a radically closed value system.

If we now place these family types in the framework of the previous discussion, we can see that although the code may be elaborated, it may be differently focused according to the family type. Thus, we can have an elaborate code focusing upon persons or an elaborated code in a positional family may focus more on objects. We can expect the same with a restricted code. Normally, with code restriction we should expect a positional family; however, if it showed signs of being person-centred, then we might expect the children to be in a situation of potential code switch.

Where the code is elaborated, and focused by a person-centred family, then these children may well develop acute identity problems concerned with authenticity, with limiting responsibility—they may come to see language as phony, a system of counterfeit masking the absense of belief. They may move towards the restricted codes of the various peer group sub-cultures, or seek the condensed symbols of affective experience, or both.

One of the difficulties of this approach is to avoid implicit value judgments about the relative worth of speech systems and the cultures which they symbolize. Let it be said immediately that a restricted code gives access to a vast potential of meanings, of delicacy, subtlety and diversity of cultural forms, to a unique aesthetic the basis of which in condensed symbols may influence the form of the imagining. Yet, in complex industrialized societies its differently-focused experience may be disvalued and humiliated within schools, or seen, at best, to be irrelevant to the educational endeavour. For the schools are predicated upon an elaborated code and its system of social relationships. Although an elaborated code does not entail any specific value system, the value system of the middle class penetrates the texture of the very learning context itself.

Elaborated codes give access to alternative realities, yet they carry the potential of alienation, of feeling from thought, of self from other, of private belief *from role obligation.*

Finally I should like to consider briefly the sources of change of linguistic codes. The first major source of change I suggest is to be located in the division of labour. As the division of labour changes from simple to complex, then this changes the social and knowledge characteristics of occupational roles. In this process there is an extension of access, through education, to elaborated codes, but access is controlled by the class system. The focusing of the codes I have suggested is brought about by the boundary maintaining procedures within the family. However, we can generalize and say that the focusing of the codes is related to the boundary maintaining procedures as these affect the major socializing agencies—family, age group, education and work. We need, therefore, to consider together with the question of the degree and type of complexity of the division of labour, the value orientations of society which, it is hypothesized, affect the boundary maintaining procedures. It is the case that we can have societies with a similar complexity in their division of labour but which differ in their boundary maintaining procedures.

I suggest then that it is important to make a distinction between societies in terms of their boundary maintaining procedures if we are to deal with this question of the focusing of codes. One possible way of examining the relative strength of boundary maintenance is to consider the strength of the *constraints* upon the choice of values which legitimize authority/power relationships. Thus in societies where there is a weak constraint upon such legitimizing values, that is, where there is a variety of formally permitted legitimizing values, we might expect a marked shift towards person type control; whereas in societies with strong constraints upon legitimizing values, where there is a severe *restriction* upon the choice, we might expect a marked shift towards positional control.

I shall illustrate these relationships with reference to the family:

Division of labour	Constraints upon legitimising values (boundary maintenance)	
	Strong	Weak
Simple → Complex	↓	↓
↓ ↓	*Positional*	*Personal*
Speech codes	Working-class	Working-class
Restricted code		
↓		
Elaborated code	Middle-class	Middle-class

Thus the division of labour influences the availability of elaborated codes; the class system affects their distribution; the focusing of codes can be related to the boundary maintaining procedures, i.e. the value system. I must point out that this is only a coarse interpretative framework.

Conclusion

I have tried to show how the class system acts upon the deep structure of communication in the process of socialization. I refined the crudity of this analysis by showing how speech codes may be differently focused through family types. Finally, it is conceivable that there are general aspects of the analysis which might provide a starting point for the consideration of symbolic orders other than languages. I must point out that there is more to socialization than the forms of its linguistic realization.

References

Bernstein, B. (1970). Education cannot compensate for society. *New Society* no. 387, February. Reprinted here as chapter 28.

Bernstein, B. (1962). Family role systems, socialisation and communication, manuscript, Sociological Research Unit, University of London Institute of Education; also in A socio-linguistic approach to socialization. *Directions in Socio-linguistics*, Gumperz, J. J. and Hymes, D. (eds.) New York: Holt, Rinehart & Winston, reprinted in B. Bernstein (ed.), *Class, Codes and Control, Vol. 1*. London: Routledge & Kegan Paul 1971.

Bernstein, B. and Cook, J. (1965). Coding grid for maternal control, available from Department of Sociology, University of London Institute of Education.

Bernstein, B. and Henderson, D. (1969). Social class differences in the relevance of language to socialisation, *Sociology* 3, No. 1, reprinted in B. Bernstein (ed.), *Class, Codes and Control, Vol. 2*. London: Routledge & Kegan Paul 1972.

Bright, N. (ed.) (1966). *Sociolinguistics*. Mouton Press.

Carroll, J. B. (ed.) (1956). *Language, Thought and Reality: selected writings of Benjamin Lee Whorf*. New York: Wiley.

Cazden, C. B. (1969). Sub-cultural differences in child language: an interdisciplinary review. *Merrill-Palmer Quarterly* 12.

Chomsky, N. (1965). *Aspects of Linguistic Theory*. Cambridge M I T.

Cook, J. (1971). An enquiry into patterns of communication and control between mothers and their children in different social classes. Ph.D. Thesis, University of London. Published as *Social Control and Socialization*. London: Routledge & Kegan Paul 1972.

Coulthard, M. (1969). A discussion of restricted and elaborated codes. *Educ. Rev.* 22, No. 1.

Douglas, M. (1970). *Natural Symbols*. Barrie & Rockliff, The Cresset Press.

Fishman, J. A. (1960). A systematization of the Whorfian hypothesis. *Behavioral Science* 5.

Gumperz, J. J. and Hymes, D. (eds.) (1971). *Directions in Socio-linguistics*. New York: Holt, Rinehart & Winston.

Halliday, M. A. K. (1969). Relevant models of language. *Educ. Rev.* 22, No. 1.

Hawkins, P. R. (1969). Social class, the nominal group and reference. *Language and Speech* 12, No. 2.

Henderson, D. (1970). Contextual specificity, discretion and cognitive socialization: with special reference to language. *Sociology* 4, No. 3, reprinted in B. Bernstein (ed.), *Class, Codes and Control, Vol. 2*. London: Routledge & Kegan Paul 1972.

Hoijer, H. (ed.) (1954). Language in Culture. *American Anthropological Association Memoir* No. 79; also published by Univ. of Chicago Press.

Hymes, D. (1966). On communicative competence. Research Planning Conference on Language Development among Disadvantaged Children, Ferkauf Graduate School, Yeshiva University.

Hymes, D. (1967). Models of the interaction of language and social setting. *Journal of Social Issues* 23.

Labov, W. (1965). Stages in the acquisition of standard English, in Shuy, W. (ed.). *Social Dialects and Language Learning*. Champaign, Illinois: National Council of Teachers of English.

Labov, W. (1966). The social stratification of English in New York City, Washington D.C. Centre for Applied Linguistics.

Mandelbaum, D. (ed.) (1949). *Selected Writings of Edward Sapir*. Univ. of California Press.

Parsons, T. and Shils, E. A. (eds.) (1962). *Toward a General Theory of Action*. Harper Torchbooks (Chapter 1, especially).

Schatzman, L. and Strauss, A. L. (1955). Social class and modes of communication. *Am.J.Soc.* 60.

Turner, G. and Pickvance, R. E. (1971). Social class differences in the expression of uncertainty in five-year-old children. *Language and Speech*, reprinted in B. Bernstein (ed.). *Class, Codes and Control, Vol. 2*. London: Routledge & Kegan Paul 1972.

Williams, F. and Naremore, R. C. (1969). On the functional analysis of social class differences in modes of speech. *Speech Monographs* 36, No. 2.

Section IV Language in the classroom

The whole of this Reader is concerned with the role of language in education. Sometimes, as in Sections I and II, the theme is implicit, though the applications are not far to seek. In Section III the relevance of language differences in the educational context are quite clear, though even here the approach is often indirect. In Section IV, the theme becomes, for a while, quite explicit. The article by Barnes concentrates on oral language exchange and Rosen's paper rather more on written language. But both are concerned with that rather peculiar language situation, the classroom, a situation typically of unequal language exchange, both in type and in balance. And as Barnes himself points out, we need (and have not yet achieved) a comprehensive theory of language and learning in the classroom.

Barnes raises a number of issues. He is dissatisfied with current analyses of classroom language interaction because of their stress on overt language function at the expense of less obvious, but perhaps more important, levels of teacher behaviour. He sees the need to tease out those dimensions of situations, as he puts it, which affect children's performance, and to distinguish the pupil's interpretation of the classroom situation from the teacher's assumptions.

Barnes stresses the need for naturalistic studies in the classroom which are yet theoretically sound. We need to look at pupils' speech in lessons in the light of the demands made by teachers. And we need to examine the dimensions of teachers' classroom behaviour in relation to the appropriate dimensions of pupils' learning behaviour.

Rosen makes us aware of some of the important differences between the writer–reader relationship and the speaker–listener relationship in the educational process. Textbook language (spoken as well as written) has psychological as well as purely linguistic characteristics, and the language problems with which the reader of the textbook is confronted are not purely linguistic, but conceptual also.

Teachers have quite definite rules about what constitutes appropriate pupil language behaviour in the classroom. They ask questions and expect certain kinds of answers while rejecting others. These rules are determined both by the nature of the social situation and by the subject-matter and the teacher's approach to it. But the rules are virtually never made explicit, and are typically not clearly articulated even in the teacher's own mind. The child who (for many possible reasons) is not well attuned to the teacher's language rules, may have great difficulty in the classroom, as Barnes and Rosen both point out. But the bright child, who is quick to assimilate the teacher's language demands and has the competence to follow them, incurs a special danger—the empty verbalism behind which there is no real understanding. As Rosen points out tellingly 'few of us who have grown up in the system are free from some taint of this schooling'.

Asher Cashdan

16   Language and learning in the classroom

Douglas Barnes

Morton D. Waimon of Illinois State University pointed out in a recent article in this journal[1] that forty years' research in the United States into 'teacher effectiveness' had been generally fruitless. Such research failed because it looked for the permanent characteristics of an ideal teacher, as if a teacher's aims and behaviour never changed during a lesson, and as if all pupils responded best to the same teaching. The researchers were therefore unable to say anything to teachers which would help them improve their teaching.

Having thus dismissed earlier research into classroom behaviour, Dr Waimon turned to three more recent lines of research, those associated respectively with B. Othanel Smith, Arno Bellack, and Ned Flanders.[2] He pointed out that these studies have abandoned general statements about teachers in favour of the study of 'linguistic behaviour during teacher-pupil interaction'. Such studies of language in the classroom are based upon written transcriptions of tape-recordings made during lessons. By moving closer to the verbal give-and-take of lessons the researcher is more likely to be able to make statements which will be useful to teachers. 'Knowing what to observe about one's own teaching is the first step towards improving effectiveness.' So far one cannot but applaud.

It is when Dr Waimon goes on to demonstrate a method of analysis which he approves of—using methods very different from those of Bellack or Flanders—that one must dissent from his judgment. He quotes a short passage, but does not indicate whether it is constructed or comes from a real lesson. The teacher's statements have been analysed into large functional categories, such as gaining pupils' attention, disciplining pupils, making a statement about goals. The teacher's statements are also put into one of three categories derived from Thorndike: getting or maintaining readiness, helping pupils to emit an appropriate response, and rating pupil responses.

Source: *Journal of Curriculum Studies* (1971), 3 (1), 29–38.

It is hard to see how either of these crude forms of categorizing teachers' language will be of any more help to teachers than the earlier researches which were so justly dismissed. In effect, the researcher, in his eagerness to find categories which will allow him to quantify, moves away too soon from the language itself into generalities, before he has found what it is that the teacher can most usefully perceive about his language. (This could be argued against Flanders's methods too.) Language functions not only on the large scale of whole utterances and their overt and deliberate meanings, but simultaneously at various lower levels which sometimes carry quite other messages through the details of formal organization and intonation. It seems likely that pupils interpret not only the teacher's overt statements about what he wants, and how he values what they say and do, but also interprets signals carried at other levels. Thus it is not enough to analyse the teacher's language only at the so-called 'functional' level. Some writers have used the phrase 'the hidden curriculum'[3] (by analogy perhaps with Thelen's 'the hidden agenda'[4]) to refer to any classroom learning which goes on in spite of the teacher's conscious aims, perhaps determined by the personalities of teacher or pupils, by the teacher's unacknowledged assumptions about classroom control, and so on. For example, many teachers who include amongst their curricular aims that of teaching pupils to 'think critically' can be shown to be encouraging pupils in passive habits of learning which are far from critical.[5]

The kinds of information likely to escape from Dr Waimon's analysis can be illustrated by an extract from a transcript of an actual lesson. A teacher of Religious Education was asking eleven-year-old pupils to recapitulate information about life in New Testament Palestine.

T. How did they get the water from the well? . . . do you remember? . . . Yes?
P.1 They . . . ran the bucket down . . . er . . . and

it was fastened on to this bit of string and it (Here the words become inaudible for a phrase or two) . . . other end to the water.

T. You might do it that way . . . Where did they put the water . . . John?

P.2 In a big . . . er . . . pitcher.

T. Good . . . in a pitcher . . . which they carried on their . . .?

P.2 Heads.

T. Good.

In Dr Waimon's system this might be categorized as:

Recall question
Neutral rating (or Negative Rating)
More effort
Positive rating

And these would go to swell the number of items in each of these categories. But this would totally miss what is of interest to the teacher in this episode.

An intuitive description of this episode might run like this: the teacher wants a one-word answer 'pitcher', but his first pupil interprets his question as an invitation to describe a mechanical device, thus translating a request for simple recall of information into a request to generate a sequence of reasoning. The teacher, his attention mainly on his own intentions, receives the pupil's reasoning with a neutral form of words but an intonation which is firmly rejective, and this rejection is intensified by the warm tone of approval with which he greets the answer which gives him the words he wants. If such a rejection were to happen several times during a lesson it would be likely to signal to children that this teacher valued the recall of names more highly than the use of language to go through a sequence of reasoning. What is interesting here is not that it is a rejection, but that it is a rejection of one activity in favour of another.

Now there is nothing in this account which could be proved, nor will this precise situation ever occur again. But this is not to say that this kind of examination of classroom language is of no use. It is much more likely to be useful to teachers—that is, to help them to inspect their own teaching—than that represented by Dr Waimon's example. Moreover, the future development of objective research may necessitate the detailed examination of recordings and transcriptions to elicit from them those dimensions of situation which affect children's performance.

What has so far been argued against Dr Waimon's approach is that it is over-rationalistic. The example just given was intended to illustrate how easily the essential nature of an exchange can be lost in such an analysis. Another inadequacy of this approach is that in focusing upon the teacher's intentions, it totally ignores the pupils' contributions, and what lies behind them, that is, their interpretations of what the teacher says and does. (It is only fair to point out that this is not true of the work of Bellack and his associates.) The teacher's behaviour does not exist in a void,

but answers on the one hand to his curricular objectives and on the other to his perceptions of what his pupils are saying and doing. Part of good teaching lies in perceiving how the language used by pupils is contributing to or inhibiting their learning.

To call Dr Waimon's approach over-rationalistic is not to abdicate responsibility for what goes on in one's classroom. Indeed, to recognize the 'hidden curriculum', to perceive that pupils are learning to cope with the teacher's demands and with one another's as well as (or instead of) with the demands of the subject matter, is a step towards taking responsibility for one's part in this. Although the personal interactions of the classroom will probably never fall completely under the deliberate control of even the best teachers, we all wish to take as much responsibility as possible for what is learnt in our lessons. To do this teachers must become more aware of their classroom behaviour: at the same time as they are helped to be clear about curricular objectives, they should be helped to be more sharply perceptive of their own and their pupils' behaviour, and the relationship of this to their aims.

It is not enough to see the language of the classroom merely as the medium of classroom communication. Two other aspects of language are of importance to the teacher, and awareness of these must inform studies of classroom language. Language is so deeply embedded in many subjects of the secondary curriculum that it is sometimes difficult to separate learning the concepts and processes of a subject from learning to use language to represent and use these concepts and processes. The second aspect of language is potentially even more important: to put it succinctly language is a means of learning. The very act of verbalizing new knowledge often requires a re-organizing of the old and the new together.[6] For these reasons language in the classroom must be discussed in a wider context than that implied by Dr Waimon's interest in classroom interaction.

This paper is based upon the assumption that language is a major means of learning, and that the pupils' uses of language for learning are strongly influenced by the teacher's language, which prescribes to them their roles as learners. (The degree to which they accept this prescription depends upon the socio-linguistic expectations which they have built up during their past experience.) The mother tongue has an ambiguous status in the curriculum, because 'English' at once indicates a subject area, and a medium of learning and teaching. For this reason, it is not easy in secondary schools to apportion responsibility for the mother tongue. A slogan such as 'Every lesson is an English lesson' does nothing to specify to teachers, primary or secondary, what kind of responsibility for language is theirs. It tells them nothing about how their uses of language expand or limit the kinds of participation in learning open to their pupils. Thus, a study of the language of classroom interaction can be seen as a contribution to curricular theory in a second respect, in that it can help teachers other than

English specialists to define their responsibilities for their pupils' uses of language.

Any study of the uses of language for teaching and learning in classrooms is of more than theoretical interest. Teachers are only partly aware of their own uses of language, and still less aware of how and to what extent classroom language determines the kinds of involvement in learning which are open to their pupils. Nor are most teachers able to give a systematic account of which language activities best contribute to different kinds of learning, and this suggests that they may not be clearly perceptive of their pupils' uses of language. For example, most science teachers from time to time set their pupils practical work in small groups, but it is not easy to find any account of what kind of discussion will best help pupils to make explicit to themselves the principles exemplified in the practical work, nor of how the teacher can see to it that such discussion takes place. Similarly, some secondary schools are increasingly using 'packets' of materials accompanied by instructions addressed to pupils for work in the area of Humanities; there is need for theory about the effect of different verbal formulations of such instructions, about the contexts in which they are carried out, and about the teacher's role in such work.

There is an urgent need in educational discussion not only for a general theory of the part played by language in cognitive learning, but for special theories of language and learning in the classroom. This is not the place to discuss the debate about whether language enables or merely facilitates the growth of concepts; the importance of language in the classroom at secondary level cannot be denied.

Language as a means of learning has in the past been obscured by the stress laid on language as a means of teaching, and theoretical insights into language for learning have not yet made any strong impact upon classroom practice. Bruner[7] hints at the importance for learning of the difference between listener's choices and speaker's choices. By this he probably implies that a speaker, in order to express a logically connected sequence of ideas, has to select, organize, and relate them, at each point of choice selecting only one of a number of options. To do this he must operate more or less complex criteria, which he will not normally make explicit, or even be aware of. A listener, on the other hand, may be able to follow a speaker through a logically-connected sequence without being in the least aware of the many options not taken up, or of the criteria which informed the speaker's choices. He will only learn to operate these criteria when he himself becomes a speaker. Elsewhere Bruner emphasizes reciprocity in learning. By 'reciprocal learning' he refers to the way we learn in a dialogue: even while we are still talking we receive from our interlocutor information which enables us to reshape what we say while we are saying it. In reciprocal learning the learner in the very act of finding a verbal form for what he is learning receives promptings and modifications from the interlocutor's reactions and replies. Bruner argues that since the feedback occurs at the moment of choice such dialogue provides ideal circumstances for internalizing the interlocutor's criteria. Bruner is arguing for a greater emphasis upon spoken language in learning, and in doing so aligns himself with Vygotsky.[8] It is not clear, however, whether it is the demand to verbalize which is of primary importance, or whether a reciprocal dialogue with an adult is essential.

To emphasize that language is a major means of learning is not of course to deny that there are other means. Piaget and his followers hold that children learn to conceptualize first and that language comes in as a means of completing and representing such processes as classification and seriation.[9] Furth[10] suggests that deaf children develop non-linguistic means of conceptualizing. Nevertheless Piaget has never denied that language is essential to formal operations, when the adolescent's ability to set up hypothetical systems and to make his own thought-processes the object of attention requires a symbolic system which is 'creative',[11] in the sense that language is. Bruner has argued interestingly[12] that a child, having first organized experience through motor activities and visually, begins to learn a language and thereafter spends many years re-elaborating this experience of reality in ways made possible by the characteristics of the linguistic system. Whichever point of view one takes it is clear that learning to use language to think with is an essential part of most of the learning which goes on in both primary and secondary schools.

It has been suggested that the very act of verbalizing demands a reorganization of ideas which merits the name of learning. A moment's reflection, however, reminds us of occasions when we have used language not to accept but to avoid new perceptions. Thus we should ask under what conditions the act of putting something into words brings us into more full possession of it. All talking and writing is not equally fresh-minted: we vary in the extent to which we challenge ourselves to think (and feel) afresh. Indeed, Lawton[13] has shown that adolescents differ greatly one from another in this respect: one pupil may challenge himself to use language to think abstractly, while another may do so only in answer to a teacher's questions. Therefore it is not enough to tell teachers that their pupils' language is important; it is necessary to help them to understand how they can arrange discussion and writing in their classrooms so that their pupils benefit from them in the ways which they wish. Such advice—it is here argued—must be based upon a theory of learning which takes account of the socio-linguistic characteristics of classrooms.

A theory of language and classroom learning would have to take account of four aspects of classroom interaction, each partly depending on the previous one.

Pupils' expectations→ Context of situation→ Uses of language→ Learning

1. Pupils' expectations

The classroom behaviour of pupils is heavily influenced by the expectations which they bring to the lesson. These have been set up both by the pupil's experience of language outside the classroom, and by his particular experience of language in lessons. These two require separate treatment. It is well established that pupils' uses of language vary with social class; these differences seem related to those expectations about the possible functions of language established in the social milieu to which the child belongs. Thus children from working class homes are likely to perceive differently from middle class children the demands for linguistic performance made upon them in school, and any theory must take this into account.[14] There are of course many other variations in children's uses of language besides those which correlate with social class. These expectations are not immutable, and one value of a close study of language in the classroom would be to help teachers to plan more systematically to influence their pupils' habitual uses of language, not for communication only but for thinking and feeling. Pupils' expectations are partly determined by what has happened in similar lessons, and this is controlled by the teachers.

These expectations are determined by such matters as the usual reception given to pupils' speech and writing, including the amount of explicit correction they receive, by the teacher's relative emphasis upon what has been said or how it has been said, by the interest he shows in the pupil's contributions. If a teacher asks only questions which require pupils to give back what they have been taught this is likely to affect their learning behaviour in all his lessons. If a teacher corrects spelling errors in writing but never comments on its content, this is likely to affect the kind of writing he receives. That is, the pupil's perception of the demands made on him, and the kinds of behaviour open to him, is partly determined by expectations set in previous lessons.

2. Context of situation

The 'situation' in a lesson is not made of things but of meanings. These meanings arise as the pupils interpret the teacher's behaviour, one another's behaviour, and certain more objective matters (such as the size of the group) in the light of their expectations. Pupils' behaviour, including their language, is likely to be influenced by the way in which they perceive the subject matter and their role as learners of that subject, by the audience to which they are expected to address speech and writing, by the immediate task which they have been given (including how sharply it has been defined for them), by the presence or absence of non-verbal representations of the subject matter, by the relation of speech to any accompanying non-verbal activities, by the terms in which they are asked to speak or write, and so on. These aspects of the present situation are interpreted by pupils in the light of their expectations about how much participation in the lesson is expected of them, and of what kinds, about the relevance of their own existing knowledge drawn from outside, in the light, that is, of their expectations about their roles as learners in these lessons. Some secondary teachers abjure responsibility for the classroom contexts which they set up for their pupils' uses of language, and hold the English specialist responsible for all the linguistic behaviour of his pupils, even in contexts beyond his control.

3. Uses of language

The uses to which language is put by the pupils in any lesson depend not merely on language tasks explicitly required by the teacher, but upon each pupil's perception of the whole situation which provides a context for language use. (Many teachers seem to be unaware of this, and treat language as if it were a skill which can be learnt and then be available for use whatever the context of situation.) Psychological studies of the development of older children's language have in the past assumed that either spoken or written language behaviour can be usefully represented as a single ability without reference to context of situation. Context has either been held constant, or a variety of contexts have been treated as if homogeneous. There is an urgent need for studies of children's language which indicate those dimensions of situation which correlate with formal and other characteristics of the language used. Not enough is at present known about how various uses of language function as means of learning, nor about the extent to which these are determined by the pupil's perception of the context for that language.

4. Learning

A theoretical account of language and classroom learning could not stop short at classroom language, but would relate different uses of language to different learning outcomes. (Britton,[15] for example, discusses particular group conversations with and without the presence of a teacher and makes surmises about the kinds of learning which such conversations make possible.) To see the learning outcomes in terms of the results of pencil and paper tests, however, would not necessarily be appropriate: such tests carry their own rigorous context of situation, and this limits their use as a means of defining the outcomes of a range of different contexts. For example, there is reason to believe that children differ one from another in the extent to which their performance is determined by context. When pupils' performances on tests have served as dependent variables in correlational studies of classroom interaction this has seldom produced convincing results: here is a considerable methodological problem.

Such a theory lies at the intersection of a number of

academic disciplines. It is socio-linguistic in that it is concerned with the constraints upon pupils' language behaviour which arise from expectations brought from other social situations and from the characteristics of the classroom as a social setting. It lies within social psychology in that it is concerned with the manner in which certain social processes become transmuted into patterns of individual behaviour. It is necessarily evaluative rather than descriptive, since it must concern itself with making statements which might help teachers suit their means to their ends. In this context, however, it is most appropriate to note that this theory falls also into the field of curriculum theory. By beginning with the socio-linguistic constraints of the classroom, and moving from these to pupils' language and consequent learning, such a theory would invert the sequence which has become habitual in curriculum theory. A theory of language and classroom learning would begin with an analysis of some factors limiting pupils' performance in the classroom seen as a socio-linguistic context and then relate performance to kinds of learning. This sequence seems appropriate because classroom language, stemming from the language habits and assumptions of teacher and pupils, has a life of its own which is not entirely responsive to the immediate conscious intentions of the teacher.

Our understanding of how language acts as a means of classroom learning is so limited that naturalistic studies of classroom language at present provide insights quite out of proportion to their size. General descriptions of the language of lessons, uninformed by hypotheses about what dimensions of the language interaction are related to learning, are likely to be more time-consuming than fruitful. (This is to some degree true of the work of Bellack and his associates.) One value of naturalistic studies based upon the largely intuitive interpretation of language recorded in lessons is that they can provide the hypotheses for more systematic investigation. The present writer's study of twelve lessons taught during pupils' first term in secondary schools can be used to illustrate[16] the kinds of question raised by naturalistic studies of classroom language.

1. The pupils

Eleven-year-old pupils' contributions to twelve lessons in various secondary subjects showed these characteristics:

(a) On only eleven occasions did a pupil, by asking a question, or by offering a statement that was not a reply to the teacher, initiate a sequence of interaction.

(b) There were few occasions when pupils could be said to be 'thinking aloud', that is, re-organizing learning or solving a problem by verbalizing it. Most contributions from pupils were of one word or a little longer.

(c) On only two occasions was there exploration of the meaning of a word, though definitions of technical terms were asked for and given.

(d) Only in one lesson (physics) did pupils frequently mention out-of-school experience in order to relate it to new ideas being learnt.

In sum, the pupils were on the whole passive recipients of instruction, their role being mainly confined to indicating in short answers that they could rehearse what had previously been taught. Could these and other characteristics of their role behaviour as learners be shown to relate to characteristics of the teacher's role behaviour?

2. Teachers' demands on pupils

Study of teachers' questions proved informative.

(a) In many of the lessons (particularly in arts subjects) a majority of the teacher's questions asked for factual replies.

(b) Teachers hardly ever asked questions in order to get information which they did not possess: they used questions mainly to test recollection of what had already been taught previously.

(c) In some lessons pupils were asked to reason aloud: this often implied that they were to go over a sequence of thought given by the teacher. Teachers hardly ever followed a brief reply by requesting the pupil to expand it or make it more explicit. Teachers not infrequently interrupted pupils who did try to answer at length.

(d) Questions which asked pupils to refer to first-hand experience outside school were almost absent.

3. Teachers' use and awareness of language

(a) With one exception these teachers did not make much use in these lessons of the technical terminology of their subject specialism: when they did they usually seemed to be aware of doing so.

(b) The teachers tended to use technical terms as labels rather than as instruments of thought.

(c) All but one of the teachers used a great deal of what might be called 'text-book language', which, though not specific to the subject, referred to important concepts and processes. (For example: 'the position of . . . in relation to . . .') They seemed unaware that they used this language, or that it might provide difficulties of comprehension, or otherwise affect pupils' participation in the lesson.

(d) The language of one teacher was much more colloquial and less like written prose than that of the others. (The fact that this was accompanied by an unusually high level of pupil-participation suggests a topic for investigation.)

(e) Teachers varied in the explicitness with which they gave instructions to classes. (A similar variation in mothers' teaching styles to their small children has been usefully investigated.[17])

(f) Some teachers worked from non-verbal representations of subject-matter: diagrams, working models, pictures. It seems possible that in these cases language was used more by pupils and less by teachers, because the non-verbal media made the subject-matter open to public discussion. Success in explanation could be checked against public criteria provided by the model or diagram.

These notes will suggest that it would not be difficult to hypothesize relationships between dimensions of teachers' classroom behaviour and dimensions of pupils' learning behaviour, and that these hypotheses could form the basis for more objective studies. Some less obvious lines of enquiry include:

(a) The rate of questioning[18] which might be related to
    (i) a taxonomical analysis of questions
    (ii) the syntactical complexity of questions[19] and
    (iii) the length and complexity of pupils' replies.
(b) The extent to which pupils focus attention upon the given task or upon unintended signals from the teacher; this might be related to various dimensions of pupils' past experience and of the immediate context of situation. (Holt's unrigorous but perceptive books are suggestive here.[20])
(c) Teachers' linguistic styles,[21] which may relate to the level of pupil-participation, and especially to pupils' uses of language (i) for exploration as against providing expected answer, and (ii) for relating new knowledge to existing schemata.
(d) Syntactic and other characteristics of pupils' uses of language for learning, varying the context of situation, especially the presence and behaviour of the teacher.

This is not intended to suggest that the time for naturalistic studies is past. For example, it seems unlikely that (d) will be very valuable until informal studies of children's language have suggested significant dimensions of context of situation and ways of making them operational.

These suggestions, however, relate to only one aspect of language in the classroom, that is, to the effect of teachers' speech behaviour upon pupils' participation in learning. Other topics which would repay study include pupils' language in small group work, and variations in children's writing according to topic and context. But these possibilities cannot be developed here.

It would be absurd to suggest that an increased attention to classroom language will do miracles. Not only is there increasing evidence that teachers' non-verbal behaviour has an important influence on pupils' participation in lessons, but it is clearly possible that there are deeper levels of a child's personality which, by the time he first attends school, have already taken on an overall 'set' towards new experience. Notwithstanding Bernstein's work, it is not yet clear how far such personality patterns are available to change by new language experiences. In any case, pupils' lives outside school may be pushing them in quite other directions. It must also be admitted that some pupils do manage to learn passively from heavily directive teaching, perhaps entering into a silent dialogue with the lecturing teacher. Which pupils these are, and what previous experiences have lent them this ability, are also matters of interest.

Yet even when all these concessions have been made, the relationship between language and learning in the classroom remains a matter of great practical importance. If all teachers could learn to be as sensitive to language in the classroom as some already are, this might significantly raise the level of learning in all our schools.

Notes

1 M. D. Waimon. Judging the Effectiveness of Teaching, in *Journal of Curriculum Studies*, Vol. **1**, No. 3 (November 1969).

2 See A. A. Bellack et al., *The Language of the Classroom* (Teachers' College, Columbia 1966). Papers by Smith and by Flanders can be seen in B. J. Biddle and W. J. Ellena (eds.), *Contemporary Research on Teacher Effectiveness* (Holt, Rinehart and Winston 1964).

3 See the valuable discussion of this in Phillip W. Jackson, *Life in Classrooms* (Holt, Rinehart and Winston 1968).

4 H. A. Thelen, *Dynamics of Groups at Work* (University of Chicago Press 1954).

5 As in D. R. Gallo, Toward a more effective assessment of poetry teaching methods, in *Research in the Teaching of English*, **2**, 2 (1968).

6 See James Britton and Bernard Newsome, What is learnt in English Lessons?, in *Journal of Curriculum Studies*, **1**, 1 (November 1968).

7 J. S. Bruner, *On Knowing* (Harvard University Press 1962).

8 L. Vygotsky, *Thought and Language* (MIT 1962).

9 E.g. B. Inhelder and J. Piaget, *The Early Growth of Logic in the Child*, (London: Routledge & Kegan Paul 1964).

10 H. Furth, *Thinking without Language* (Free Press 1966).

11 Noam Chomsky, *Aspects of the Theory of Syntax* (MIT 1965).

12 Jerome S. Bruner et al., *Studies in Cognitive Growth* (New York: Wiley 1966).

13 D. Lawton, *Social Class, Language and Education* (London: Routledge & Kegan Paul 1968).

14 See Lawton (1968), op. cit.

15 James Britton, Talking to Learn, in D. Barnes, J. N. Britton and H. Rosen, *Language, the Learner and the School* (Penguin 1969).

16 D. Barnes, Language in the Secondary Classroom, in Barnes, Britton and Rosen (1969), op. cit.

17 R. D. Hess and V. C. Shipman, Early Experience and the Socialization of Cognitive Modes in Children in *Child Development*, **36**, 4 (1965).

18 J. Hoetker, Teacher questioning behaviour in nine Junior High School English classes, in *Research in the Teaching of English*, **2**, 2 (1968).

19 D. Scarbrough, The Language of the Primary Teacher, *English for Immigrants*, **2,** 1 (1968).
20 J. Holt, *How Children Fail* (Pitman 1964).
21 A study by M. A. Fitzpatrick of the effect of different language styles in lecturing is described in G. Kemelfield, Progress Report of the Schools Television Research Project—111, in *Educational Television International*, **3,** 2 (July 1969).

17 The language of textbooks

Harold Rosen

'Concepts and the language that infuses and implements them give power and strategy to cognitive activity.'[1] You are almost certainly having difficulty in making sense of that sentence. If you are not, you are fortunate and rare; if you are, then console yourself, your difficulty is useful. It should give you greater insight into the linguistic-intellectual bafflement which besets children in school, particularly in the secondary school and more particularly in 'subject' learning. Difficulties of this sort turn whole subjects into foggy mysteries and for many children the fog is so impenetrable that all higher levels of learning become unattainable. They permeate textbooks, are scattered indiscriminately throughout stodgy pages of dictated notes, and, less frequently, are part of the teacher's spoken instruction or exposition in the classroom.

Why does that opening quotation make us grope and fumble? First, it is a high-order abstraction, the components of which are themselves abstractions. It is language at the apex of a pyramid of experience, thought and verbalizing. All that was offered to you was this apex, but the vast range of human activities, details of which you could respond to with comfort and interest and which constitute the base of the pyramid, were hidden from you, as indeed were all the intervening tiers between base and apex. But there is more to it than that. The tone is highly formal, because the sentence avoids almost entirely that work-a-day language which we use to make contact with our fellows and which readily touches off responsive thought and experience. There are other difficulties to surmount. The sentence is highly compressed (three sets of yoked items, concepts-language, infuses-implements, power-strategy) and all the most important words are highly unpredictable. We could add, more subjectively, that the sentence in some ways seems bloodless, lifeless because it does not take its vitality from any particular situation; it has no context

Source: *Talking and Writing*, ed. J. N. Britton, Methuen (1967), 100–14.

of you and me and what we do. It provides no links with our personal world; any such links must be provided by us. It floats out there. It is a totally impersonal utterance as far away from spontaneous spoken utterance as the statutory provisions of the Education Act are from two boys having an argument in a school playground.

For all this, it is an utterance of great potential power.[2]

> . . . words like 'cause' and 'effect' do not refer to things in the way words like 'table' and 'chair' do (still less do they call up definite pictures in the mind), but they have distinctive and important meanings, and their use is a mark of the high degree of order and systematization imposed by us on the world we live in. In the same way the use of words like 'right' and 'wrong', 'duty', 'crime' (and many others subsumed under them: 'property', 'theft', 'punishment', 'reform', etc.), and of comparable words in other types of society presupposes a nexus of expected ways of behaviour . . .

Order and systematization; what rewards for mere words! What temptations!

Let's look at the problem another way. A pupil (fourth year in a secondary school) writes in his geography book:

> An erratic is quite an exciting result of glaciation as a large rock not geologically the same as its surroundings may be found perched incredibly precariously on smaller stones. This is an erratic.

His teacher has put a red ring round 'exciting' and written in the margin, 'No need to get excited. "Spectacular" a better word to use here.' Every need to get excited one would have thought; excitement about erratics cannot be so abundant that teachers can afford to dampen it. At least the teacher is showing some

119

concern for language, for the language of his subject, even if his concern is misplaced. How far has his concern taken him? Has he really worked out the nature of definition and what kind of difficulty the pupil, using his own language, had in attempting the task? What is 'better' about 'spectacular' and worse about 'exciting'? Perhaps he is pedagogically wrong and linguistically right. He knows, at least intuitively, that in *adult* scientific use 'exciting' would find no place in the definition of an erratic; this is his intuitive linguistic criterion. 'Exciting' brings to the definition personal, idiosyncratic, subjective aspects of an erratic which the recording scientist sets out to eliminate. An erratic is an erratic whether you get excited about it or not. To grasp fully what an erratic is you may indeed need to get excited about it, however mildly, but when you have learnt to distinguish between your excitement and the objective properties of the erratic, you have reached a stage when you know something about your own thinking. Thus there is also a psychological criterion of linguistic difficulty.

As the study of linguistics has developed it has increasingly drawn our attention away from older, and often obsessive, distinctions between kinds of language (correct—incorrect, good—bad, U—Non-U, etc.) and begun to develop new ones for us. They help us to analyse and understand the linguistic differences between different utterances. The concept of 'register' analyses language in three dimensions: *field of discourse* (what is the subject-matter?); *mode of discourse* (is it spoken or written?); *tenor of discourse* (what is the relationship between speaker and hearer, reader and writer? Or, 'how formal is the utterance?').[3] Thus we might say of a passage in a physics textbook that its field of discourse is physics, magnetism; its mode of discourse is written-scientific; and its tenor of discourse highly formal. Of course each of these categories can be refined and all three of them are interacting and inter-related.

How does this help us? First, when a pupil enters the field of discourse of most school subjects he is often called upon to express himself in the written mode before he has tried to order his experience in the mode in which he operates most easily, the spoken. A group of pupils on a field trip, in a museum, or working in a laboratory sharing impressions, jointly evolving conclusions, would use very different language from the language of their subject texbooks. It would also be different from the language they would use in a written record, however free they were to express this in their own way. In the written scientific mode boys and girls are often cut off from the non-language events to which they must refer (handling of substances and apparatus, living specimens, features of the landscape, buildings, museum exhibits, etc.). Thus their written language must carry the whole burden. Written-scientific language is, moreover, one very limited kind of English. How is the pupil to have access to experience of this mode? How is he to learn its distinctive features?

The tenor of this kind of discourse, i.e. highly formal, creates an even greater difficulty. The adult use of this tenor presumes, first, an enormous unknown audience about whom the only valid assumption is that they want access to the data and ideas without ambiguity and subjectivity and, secondly, a writer who wishes to make them available. This writer-reader relationship is the more sophisticated by virtue of its tenuousness. How unreal and remote this is for the ordinary pupil. It is even more unreal when one bears in mind that for him it is a mere pretence. He writes for no one; or for one person, who is not remote and unknown and who knows it all anyway.

An awareness of 'register' then can help us to see this special language learning problem more clearly and even give us some more clearly defined goals for language learning.[4]

Productive teaching is designed not to alter patterns already acquired but to add to his [the pupil's] resources; and to do so in such a way that he has the greatest range of the potentialities of the language available to him for appropriate use in all the varied situations in which he needs them.

What linguistics does not tell us, however, is what kind of difficulties school learners have in mastering this 'range of potentialities' and becoming sensitive to 'appropriate use'. Are some registers more difficult to learn to use than others? If so, why? Do we learn them in an order which relates to psychological and social development? Every teacher could give the beginnings of an answer to these questions but they are only beginnings, crude ones at that. We know that pupils will handle comfortably fiction narrative long before they can cope with historical-argument (if they ever do!). We need to fill out a detailed picture of this process. We need to know more about the process of transition to new and less accessible registers and their relationship to those already under control. Nor have the linguists got much further than distinguishing the *conventional* features of different registers. We would be just as interested to know in non-impressionistic terms what constitutes an effective use of a register. Thus for the linguist a good and a mediocre historical account may both be perfectly in register. What differentiates them? Not all registers are of equal educational importance, though which are the more important is a controversial issue (to some teachers the formalities of business letters obviously deserve high priority). All school subjects operate sub-languages which are encrusted with linguistic conventions, some of which still serve a useful purpose and some of which do not.[5]

The climate of more than half the continent is thus marked by the aridity and the high range of temperature experienced. The main sources of its rainfall are the Pacific and Indian Oceans, and therefore its rain-carrying winds are southerly and south-easterly. The near-approach of high land to these oceans limits the distribution of heavy rain to the peninsulas and islands of the south and south-east. Seasonally it is limited by the fact that such on-shore winds are experienced only in the summer season, hence giving rise to monsoonal rainfall.[5]

'Aridity', 'on-shore winds', 'monsoonal rainfall', even 'experienced', all seem to be valuable but what about 'near-approach of high land . . . limits the distribution . . .', 'seasonally it is limited by the fact that . . . hence giving rise to . . .'?

On the whole then we have a better apparatus for handling the linguistic aspects of textbook language than we have for the psychology of understanding and using it. We need a dimension which embraces both the linguistic and the psychological components. Until we know more about it let us call it the personal-imposed dimension. Most subject learning comes to be expressed almost entirely in impersonal language; this becomes more and more true as our pupils progress through the secondary school. In English lessons they will continue to use personal written language; they may also do so in history and geography, though in these subjects a sort of ill-defined journalism is often the accepted medium. In the sciences, however, and on many occasions in other lessons, impersonal language is the order of the day (even in music, or English!). When used effectively this language is weighty, detached, highly respected and fulfils the special needs it has been evolved to meet. But it is also a product of man's mature experience through centuries. It is the language of educated adults; for pupils it is hard and remote. For them to formulate even elementary concepts within this language requires lengthy linguistic and social experience and the opportunity to experiment with it freely. Two assumptions about this kind of language seem to be prevalent. First, it is thought many pupils will never be able to acquire it so that no special steps need to be taken to help them to do so. They should be trained in the 'practical' uses of language. Secondly, when pupils are thought to be suitable subjects for advanced learning, it is assumed that such difficulties as they encounter will be of some pure intellectual kind and that language will look after itself. The problem does not exist.[6]

Science textbooks are only exceptionally written in prose of the highest quality, and more often they are written in prose that may be described in contrary terms, yet the students who use these books do not in fact find them difficult to understand. They may be strange, because they deal with unfamiliar matters; they may be voluminous, making great demands on the memory; but they are not as obscure, even to the inexperienced reader, as the so-called average man is led to believe.

Yet this impersonal language is at the furthest pole from pupils' own spontaneous language, which leaves them free to use language in any way which satisfies their personal purposes, permitting them to leave upon it the stamp of their own subjective view of the world. Impersonal language requires them to eliminate their subjectivity or at least to cover its traces. The deepest personal involvement may precede or even accompany their exploration of the new areas of experience but they have to learn how to eliminate its voice.

This impersonal language, which needs differentiating still further, has two distinct qualities to which we have already drawn attention. First, it submits to certain language habits which are the product of a complex history. These are linguistic conventions which could well be looked at critically and, like any other conventions, they can be broken by anyone who has weighed their worth and found them to be stultifying and irksome.[7] Within these conventions, however, there is also language which has been perfected to embody rational thought, ultimately at its highest level. (Of course not all impersonal language is of this kind—'keep off the grass' for instance—but this is not the main object of our concern.) Little attempt has been made to study this dual quality of impersonal language; certainly teachers and textbook writers are not accustomed to looking at the language of their subjects from this point of view. There are times when they are more punctilious about the conventional rather than the linguistic-intellectual aspect of their subjects, as though one were to be more interested in the judge's wig than in justice.[8]

The mother tongue is acquired almost entirely through linguistic experience and activity. There cannot be many teachers of English who delude themselves that their pupils learn English solely or even mainly in English lessons. The home is a teacher; the environment is a teacher; so is other school learning. The home and environment extend the use of day-to-day 'natural' language and English derives strength from these spontaneous uses of language, providing the only occasions in which these uses can grow towards creative-imaginative writing and reading.

But school is the arena for other language learning. In other lessons there is the unique opportunity for access to new kinds of language. Here the pupil will be confronted with verbalized thought on a systematic and ordered basis. This will probably be his only chance, certainly his main chance, of acquiring the language and thought of impersonal observation and description, generalization and abstraction, theories, laws, the analysis of events remote in time or space, argument and speculation. The concepts which make all this possible are embodied in special languages and sub-languages. The more deeply a subject is penetrated and understood the further its language grows from the currency of everyday speech and from personal literature. In the effort to master it we lift our thinking towards it and as our thinking develops we use the language with greater confidence and purpose. Its potential is enormous and there are discoveries and fulfilments to be met in our struggles to master it.

Yet we know that many young people leave school afraid of this language, regarding it as alien and inaccessible; others mutter it like an incantation or sheltering behind it conceal their own ideas and doubts, hoping that the words themselves will work of their own accord. They cannot use this language flexibly, they are chained to its formulations. Some have so precarious a hold upon it that it slips away under stress. How can they be helped towards boldness and confidence and mastery? How can they be helped towards this language in such a way that it develops rather than retards their thinking?

A bridge needs to be built between personal, creative language and impersonal language. Children and young people should not be rushed into the use of the adult, mature language of a subject. Real learning means making knowledge personal, bringing to bear on it all of one's own experience that seems to be relevant. This is only possible when we express the new experience in our own language in our own way, taking over just so much of the new language of the subject as is right for us, trying it out and tasting it. The new language should be encountered in the most favourable circumstances, in lively books which have been produced by writers who have some kind of awareness of the problems we have been discussing.[9] M. Ilin discusses the candle flame in this way.[10]

> You only see the beams and nails and bricks when the house burns up. The same thing is true here: the water and coal are only visible when we make a small conflagration—light the candle.
>
> Very well. When the candle burns we get water and carbon. But what becomes of them? The water goes off in the form of steam. This is the steam which condensed on the spoon when we held it over the flame. But what becomes of the carbon? When the candle smokes the carbon goes off in the form of soot—tiny particles of carbon—and settles on the ceiling, walls and furniture of the room.
>
> But if the candle is burning well there is no soot, for the carbon is all burned up. Burned up? What do we mean by that? Now we have to begin at the beginning again. What becomes of the carbon when it burns up? One of two things: either it is lost, disappears entirely, or it is turned into some other substance which we simply don't see.
>
> Let's try to catch this ghost.

The creative-personal uses of language should not be seen as the exclusive affair of the English teacher inhabiting a shadowy and suspect world of 'self-expression'. New learning can and should be expressed in as personal a way as a young writer wants, side by side with his first efforts to move towards more impersonal treatment; this could well include poems and stories. The naked textbooks should always be supplemented with real documents and source material from real books, autobiographies, original works and novels. Any one class will contain pupils at very different stages of progress from the personal to the impersonal. If different ways of verbalizing new experience are left open to them they can cross the bridges when they are ready to cross them. We need to make it possible for all the pupil's hard won achievements of imagination and thinking, all those concepts he has already mastered, to help him forward to new concepts, and conversely for these new concepts to make living contact with his imagination and thought. Some indication of this process can be seen in these entries from the history book made by an eleven-year-old.

1 *Death of a Viking king*
King Rikki died at the break of day.
I am Thor his son
Today just before dusk
He will be pushed,
Pushed into the water,
In a burning ship.

The sun has just set
The people are gathering on the beach
A large Viking ship on rollers,
Waits,
Waits to be pushed into the sea
Priceless treasure is being loaded

On to the waiting ship,
Golden goblets
Plates, money,
Jewels, swords,
Shields and helmets,
Food and Drink
Suits of armour
And precious brocade
And then the body of the king
Is laid in the boat with greatest care
The oarsmen and servants start
Pushing it towards the sea.
It gathers speed,
And now a burning torch is thrown on board!
SPLASH!
The boat is in,
Burning
Sailing out to sea
Until at last a mass of flames
It sinks.

2 As Edward has spent much of his life in Normandy, Norman ways pleased him more than english ones. He had been brought up by monks and was himself in many ways a monk. In those days monks were often called 'Confessors'. Thus Edward's nickname came about as Edward the Confessor.

3 *Sutton Hoo treasure ship*
This is a helmet [a picture of it is pasted in the book] found in 500 pieces. It is made of iron covered bronze and then tin so that it looks white and shiny. However the eye brows and

moustache are bronze. The dragon's eyes are garnets (in between eyebrows).

Who writes textbooks? What is a good one? Perhaps we should consider first whether in our anxiety to leave behind the bad old days of elementary schools and the smatterings of knowledge which went with them we have not been too eager to see the glossy new textbook as a visible guarantee of real secondary education. In English lessons texts are beginning to replace textbooks and one historian has recently argued for the banishment of history textbooks from the history class.[11] The best textbooks in existence have to assume a kind of evenness of development in any group of users. Many seem to be written by people who have only read other textbooks; they may have been bigger and more difficult but they were textbooks none the less. The authors or compilers handle a grubby second-hand or umpteenth-hand language which they have accepted as part of 'the content' of the subject. They show little awareness of what pupils will make or fail to make of their language beyond some crude notions of easy and difficult vocabulary and shorter sentences.[12] Yet frequently it is in these books that pupils meet for the first time the written impersonal language of educated men.

Most school textbooks are written by teachers and an awareness of the language of their subject should be part of the equipment of all teachers. What kind of reality and personal meaning inheres in the concept 'revolution' for a class of fourteen-year-olds? Or in 'therefore', 'correlation', 'in direct proportion to'? How much is it convention and how much a necessity to say, 'let us assume'; 'limited the authority of the king'; 'ensure that seed dispersal takes place'? Clearly different subjects present different problems. The word 'power' will be used differently in geography, history, science and mathematics. The 'body' of the physics lesson is not the same as 'the body' of the biology lesson. The sciences can always be accompanied by observation, experiment and dicussion (are they?) but history and geography have to deal with second-hand experience. History handles difficult social concepts of politics. Geography sometimes deals with social institutions and sometimes scientific concepts of weather, geology and map-projections. We need to study more closely these language differences and how secondary pupils grapple with them.

Probably for all their shortcomings subject textbooks have for many pupils real value. However limited their use of impersonal language it is from the textbook that they learn it. Having said so much we can then recognize that textbooks also do harm. If more of them are to come flooding into our schools, and the market seems insatiable, we should take an unflinching look at them. Any history book will contain pages and sentences like this:

'Monasteries had formed part of English life in a very real sense.' What is a monastery? How does it 'form part of English life'? What 'English life'? What senses are there other than 'very real' senses? Can 'English life' of a past period take on meaning before many institutions like monasteries have been looked at concretely?

Language like this looks at children across a chasm. The worst way to bridge this chasm is to encourage children to take over whole chunks of it as a kind of jargon (examinations have been the great excuse). For fluent children, such as moderately successful grammar school pupils, this process is fatally easy. Probably few of us who have grown up in the system are free from some taint of this schooling. Instead of the new formulations representing hard-won victories of intellectual struggle or even partial victories, they are not even half-hearted skirmishes. Instead there is empty verbalism, sanctioned utterance and approved dogma; behind them is a void or a chaos. The personal view is made to seem irrelevant; it is outlawed. The conventions of this language are not taken over as are the conventions of other uses of language, at first experimentally and then with growing confidence, but unthinkingly, lock, stock and barrel. Language and experience have been torn asunder.

For other pupils, however, the gap between their own language and the textbook is so great that the textbook is mere noise. Their own language has not organized their thinking in such a way that they can be cognitively responsive in even a minimal sense. The textbook is alien both in its conventions and its strategies. The subject never begins to come through; it is another way of life. Though this is not a matter of language alone, language plays a big part. The willing bright pupil has sufficient language achievement behind him to enable him to mime the textbook though his hold may be precarious and over-dependent on verbatim memory. At least his morale will be high when he is confronted with new verbal experience. He has done it before; he will do it again. At the other extreme is the pupil who receives nothing but scrambled messages. He has failed to decode them in the past; he will fail again.

But most boys and girls do not drop neatly into these extreme categories. Many pupils are very ready for new uses of language and very responsive to them; they sense the adult status of an impersonal form of language and glimpse its power. The beginnings can be clearly seen in the primary school. It crops up in unexpected places, in the midst of personal writing for example.

. . . The copse we entered had a silver birch wood at one end and a drainage lake at the other. All over the land were channels draining the earth. The end of the lake nearest the wood was actually a reed bed. We set off in good spirits to erect the first net. After a short reconnoitre we placed it in a gap between a bramble bush and the end of the wood. This, my friend told me, was a good trap for titmice. This net up, we proceeded towards the lake and placed two nets at the reeded end.

Each net was sixty feet long and about ten feet high. They were supported at either end by a bamboo pole, which, when wanted to, pulled apart. We had to guy each pole because of the elastic pull of the net. The net itself, was of fine nylon mesh with four horizontal thick strands of elastic passing through the middle. The bird flew into the mesh, which stretched, and then dropped down behind one of the horizontal strands, thus falling into what may be termed a pocket. . . .

But they may not yet be ready to handle the whole apparatus of the fully developed language of a subject. Again and again young pupils are asked to deploy the language of objective argument when their own thinking has only reached the stage of committed assertion and passionate partisanship. Mostly we are in too great a hurry, rushing children not to the concept which is just ahead and therefore challenging, but to one which is well beyond their reach, outside the range of their thought and completely severed from their experience.

This discussion both implicitly and explicitly has pointed to some practical applications of an understanding of impersonal language. Let us bring some of them together.

The language of education is historically evolved and fashioned, embodying generations of endeavour to understand the universe and society. It remains inaccessible until the learner has made it interact with his own experience and past learning. The first way he achieves this is through social speech. We need to bring out into the light of day all the pupil's thinking and feeling about a subject. Whatever the final form of recording may be, however much it may be finally distilled into the bare impersonal item, it must begin as personal spontaneous language.[13]

Science is not an impersonal construction. It is no less, and no more, personal than other forms of communicated thought. This book is not less scientific because my manner is personal, and I make no apology for it. Science searches the common experience of people; and it is made by people, and it has their style.

Of course, there is talk and talk. 'What is the specific weight of mercury?' is very different from 'What were you trying to do?' 'How did you do it?' 'What did you find out?' And that is different from

spontaneous inquiry and observation. How often do genuine speculation and genuine argument enter into science lessons or geography or history? How much of the subterranean world of thought is brought to the surface?

The teacher's own talk plays a vital role. If he is only a glorified question-master and boiler-down of his own notes then his pupils will never catch sight of what happens to a subject when it becomes a real part of a person. They will never hear his doubts, nor his enthusiasm nor hear the biography of an idea in the life of an individual.

Do we need textbooks? What exactly for? How can we help pupils to use them? How should a first-form book differ from a fifth-form book? Can textbooks be made more like real books without sacrificing system and objectivity? A part of the answer must surely be that we must stop thinking in terms of one subject, one textbook, one year, one pupil.

We should attach much less importance to the linguistic conventions of our subjects and begin to sort out what these are. It is possible that our pupils will find fresher, livelier language than the dated and jaded jargon of the textbooks. Dictated notes and summaries should disappear for ever. Language cannot be used as a gift or a dole. What are notes for? A class can only know how it wants to make them when it knows what *use* it wants to make of them. In any case notes are cryptic and we probably use them too soon. Always the emphasis should be on the individual and the group shaping their own awareness in their own language without their being denied access to more mature formulations. Creative, personal interpretation should be provided for and welcomed. Space-fiction can be the free-est mode of speculation about astronomy, physics and society. Poetry is hospitable to all experience.

We need more patience. We are so anxious that each endeavour should be a perfect fragment of the finished product. In our anxiety that the little area of chemistry or history which we are examining should look like the real thing, like *bona fide* history or *bona fide* chemistry, paradoxically we make it unreal, much farther away from the real thing.

A serious concern with the language of the textbook, the language of a subject, is a proper and central concern for all teachers, for it involves the vital participants in most learning—words.

Notes

1 J. S. Bruner, Introduction to *Thought and Language* by L. S. Vygotsky. New York: Wiley 1962.
2 R. H. Robins, *General Linguistics: An Introductory Survey*.
3 For a fuller discussion of 'register' see Enkvist, Spencer and Gregory, *Linguistics and Style*, 86–91.
4 Halliday, McIntosh, Strevens, *The Linguistic Sciences and Language Teaching*. London: Longmans 1964, 241.
5 *Geography for Today*, Book III—written by a committee.
6 T. H. Savory, *The Language of Science*.

7 The change in the use of formal language by the Civil Service is a case in point. See Sir Ernest Gowers, *Plain Words*.
8 The word-by-word rote learning of laws, etc., is still very common. Is there only *one* way of expressing Boyle's Law? Compare the following versions:
(a) The volume of a given mass of gas at constant temperature is inversely proportional to the pressure to which it is subjected.
C. T. Smith, *Intermediate Physics*.

(b) The volume of a given mass of gas varies inversely as the pressure if the temperature remains constant.

W. Pearce, *School Physics.*

An interesting contrast is this lower level of abstraction.

(c) At the same temperature the rule is simple. By doubling the pressure, we halve the volume. By halving the pressure we double the volume. If we mean by matter what has mass, the amount of matter remains the same when we double or halve the space to contain it.

Lancelot Hogben, *Men, Missiles and Machines.*

9 A pioneer in this field is Amabel Williams-Ellis who for a long time has been aware of the need for using rich source material. See for example *Men Who Found-Out*, *Good Citizens*, etc.

10 M. Ilin, *100,000 Whys.*

11 Philip Abrams, 'History Without Textbooks', *Where?*; Autumn 1964.

12 There have been attempts to deal with the problem of 'readability' of textbooks but they do not deal with the problems raised here.

13 J. Bronowski, *The Common Sense of Science.*

Section V Language acquisition: language and thought

The acquisition of the ability to use language is one of the most impressive pieces of learning that an individual achieves in the course of his life. Possessing what seem in many ways to be rather limited cognitive abilities and having a very short attention and memory span, a child who is only just learning how to walk upright and feed himself, nevertheless begins to master the highly intricate and complex skill of language in a remarkably short period of time. What is even more striking is the way in which the child's attempts towards full grammatical speech display above all else a coherent, purposive and structured quality that leads one to view him as performing well at a task which linguists require many years of training to undertake: the construction of a syntactic and grammatical theory for a totally 'foreign' language. In addition, one must realize that the linguist is often able to talk about the language he is studying with its speakers; the child does not possess such a meta-language. Yet, none the less, each child quickly becomes a full and vocal member of the language community in which he lives, and is thus open to the linguistic transmission of cultural knowledge and all that that implies for maturation towards full adulthood and participation in society. Considering the importance and impressiveness of this process, it is surprising to note that it is only in the last ten years or so that much attention has been given by psychologists to the study of language learning in the child.

The conception and development of the revolutionary theories of transformational grammar is reflected in the growth of developmental psycholinguistics; indeed, the theoretical formulations of Noam Chomsky and his followers have supplied a framework within which many developmental studies have made valuable empirical observations. The general question with which most studies are concerned is this: How is it that a child, equipped at birth with no communication skills whatsoever, and only the most rudimentary verbal repertoire for expression, is able to acquire an ability as complex as language—and so reliably and regularly?

An adult who knows his language, possesses an elaborate set of rules which constitute its grammar. A child growing up in a community of adult speakers is faced with the task of constructing for himself a similar set of rules that will enable him both to understand and to speak the language that surrounds him. Chomsky argues persuasively that the general form of these grammatical rules may be common to all human languages and that the principles underlying the structure of language are so universally found that it is highly likely that these 'linguistic universals' are part of our genetic endowment. This approach argues against behaviourist assertions that it is possible to explain language acquisition as a process of imitation and selective reinforcement. Imitation is most certainly an observable and important factor, but Roger Brown and Ursula Bellugi show that not only does a child imitate his mother, often in so doing reducing her sentences by the omission of grammatical functors, but also that a mother characteristically imitates and expands her child's speech. In addition, children's speech is shown to possess striking regularities of construction, supporting the view that a child is progressively utilizing more complex grammatical forms: he is not only learning what to say, but also how to say it; that is, to construct his own sentences. To consider this linguistic interaction between mother and child as expressible in terms of selective reinforcement ignores the structural characteristics of the dialogue:

Adam	Mother
'Truck'	
'Put truck, Mommy'	'Put the truck where?'
'Put truck window'	'I think that one's too large to go in the window'

David McNeill shows that these regularities in children's speech suggest a great deal about the nature of cognitive growth in general, and that language may be only one aspect of a broader cognitive process, in which the acquisition of abilities in general conforms with the model of a transformational system, whereby abstract (or 'deep') cognitive structures may generate a virtually infinite range of complex behaviours (or 'surface' structures).

The interrelation between language and cognition has been the subject of much enquiry and experimental study, and the three papers on the topic that are presented in this section indicate three major positions in this controversial area. These readings have been chosen to illustrate both the differences in theory that result from isolating speech or language from each other and the added insight to be gained from a study of both competence and performance. Luria shows how a child's speech comes to be a potent means of controlling and organizing motor activity. The child who has not yet learned to speak is sensitive only to the here and now; he is under 'stimulus control', being directed in his actions by the impact of environmental stimulation. He is thus distracted by each novel stimulus as it appears, and is unable to maintain behaviour that is directed towards a specific goal in the face of this distraction. The child, when he acquires language, is enabled to represent and structure his action within the syntactic framework that language provides. This process of linguistic control is initially effective only in simple, non-conflict situations: for example, 'press when you see the red light, and don't press when you see the blue light' is utilized by the child of 2; 8 to 2; 10 only for its directive function. Re-written in terms of the function it serves for this age-group, the statement would read something like 'light-press'. It is only by the age of 4; 0 to 4; 6 that this restriction is overcome and the full semantic content of the contingency instruction is utilized by the child. It is at this stage, Luria suggests, that the child no longer needs to actually utter the control phrase: his speech for action has become internalized. This progressive internalization of cognitive functions through the medium of speech is paradigmatic of most Russian theory in this area.

Piaget, on the other hand, is more concerned with language, and Sinclair-de-Zwart suggests that in Piagetian theory the child's prelinguistic internalization of logical operations predates the acquisition of the linguistic forms for these operations. Thus, in Piaget's theory language is seen not as a precursor of cognition, but as relying upon the child having acquired the requisite cognitive structures non-verbally. Indeed, Piaget goes so far as to state that some of the child's logical operations are 'not expressible in ordinary, natural language'. So, for Piaget, speech is indicative of the progress of cognitive growth, reflecting but not determining the child's acquisition of such concepts as class, relation and conservation. These concepts are learned, not linguistically, but through the child operating on and manipulating his environment.

This section of the reader concludes with a paper by Bruner in which he presents a third genetic approach to cognitive growth that goes some way towards a synthesis of the positions of Luria and Piaget, by adopting a 'stage' theory of the development of representation:

Stage 1. Enactive: Adaptation at the motor level, moving, reaching, grasping, constructing 'action' sequences.

Stage 2. Iconic: The child responds to his environment in terms of percepts and concrete images. In general, one aspect of a situation dominates; for example, colour or shape.

Stage 3. Symbolic: The child is able to express general and abstract ideas in word and number. He has achieved conservation and can manipulate symbols; that is, talk and think, without recourse to actually performing such manipulations on the objects concerned.

Bruner believes that cognitive growth occurs not only from within, but also by the cultural transmisson of technologies, the main vehicle for this transmission being language. Thus, in the process of language acquisition and the development of thought, can be seen the evolutionary history of man.

John Oates

18 Language and the mind

Noam Chomsky

How does the mind work? To answer this question we must look at some of the work performed by the mind. One of its main functions is the acquisition of knowledge. The two major factors in acquisition of knowledge, perception and learning, have been the subject of study and speculation for centuries. It would not, I think, be misleading to characterize the major positions that have developed as outgrowths of classical rationalism and empiricism. The rationalist theories are marked by the importance they assign to *intrinsic* structures in mental operations—to central processes and organizing principles in perception, and to innate ideas and principles in learning. The empiricist approach, in contrast, has stressed the role of experience and control by environmental factors.

The classical empiricist view is that sensory images are transmitted to the brain as impressions. They remain as ideas that will be associated in various ways, depending on the fortuitous character of experience. In this view a language is merely a collection of words, phrases, and sentences, a habit system, acquired accidentally and extrinsically. In the formulation of Williard Quine, knowledge of a language (and, in fact, knowledge in general) can be represented as 'a fabric of sentences variously associated to one another and to nonverbal stimuli by the mechanism of conditioned response.' Acquisition of knowledge is only a matter of gradual construction of this fabric. When sensory experience is interpreted, the already established network may be activated in some fashion. In its essentials, this view has been predominant in modern behavioral science, and it has been accepted with little question by many philosophers as well.

The classical rationalist view is quite different. In this view the mind contains a system of 'common notions' that enable it to interpret the scattered and incoherent data of sense in terms of objects and their

Source: *Psychology Today*, February 1969, reprinted in *Child Language*, ed. A. Bar-Adon and W. F. Leopold, Prentice Hall, Inc. (1971), 425–33.

relations, cause and effect, whole and part, symmetry, gestalt properties, functions, and so on. Sensation, providing only fleeting and meaningless images, is degenerate and particular. Knowledge, much of it beyond immediate awareness, is rich in structure, involves universals, and is highly organized. The innate general principles that underlie and organize this knowledge, according to Leibniz, 'enter into our thoughts, of which they form the soul and the connection . . . although we do not at all think of them.'

This 'active' rationalist view of the acquisition of knowledge persisted through the romantic period in its essentials. With respect to language, it achieves its most illuminating expression in the profound investigations of Wilhelm von Humboldt. His theory of speech perception supposes a generative system of rules that underlies speech production as well as its interpretation. The system is generative in that it makes infinite use of finite means. He regards a language as a structure of forms and concepts based on a system of rules that determine their interrelations, arrangement, and organization. But these finite materials can be combined to make a never-ending product.

In the rationalist and romantic tradition of linguistic theory, the normal use of language is regarded as characteristically innovative. We construct sentences that are entirely new to us. There is no substantive notion of 'analogy' or 'generalization' that accounts for this creative aspect of language use. It is equally erroneous to describe language as a 'habit structure' or as a network of associated responses. The innovative element in normal use of language quickly exceeds the bounds of such marginal principles as analogy or generalization (under any substantive interpretation of these notions). It is important to emphasize this fact because the insight has been lost under the impact of the behaviorist assumptions that have dominated speculation and research in the twentieth century.

In Humboldt's view, acquisition of language is largely a matter of maturation of an innate language capacity. The maturation is guided by internal factors, by an innate 'form of language' that is sharpened, differentiated, and given its specific realization through experience. Language is thus a kind of latent structure in the human mind, developed and fixed by exposure to specific linguistic experience. Humboldt believes that all languages will be found to be very similar in their grammatical form, similar not on the surface but in their deeper inner structures. The innate organizing principles severely limit the class of possible languages, and these principles determine the properties of the language that is learned in the normal way.

The active and passive views of perception and learning have elaborated with varying degrees of clarity since the seventeenth century. These views can be confronted with empirical evidence in a variety of ways. Some recent work in psychology and neurophysiology is highly suggestive in this regard. There is evidence for the existence of central processes in perception, specifically for control over the functioning of sensory neurons by the brain-stem reticular system. Behavioral counterparts of this central control have been under investigation for several years. Furthermore, there is evidence for innate organization of the perceptual system of a highly specific sort at every level of biological organization. Studies of the visual system of the frog, the discovery of specialized cells responding to angle and motion in the lower cortical centers of cats and rabbits, and the somewhat comparable investigations of the auditory system of frogs—all are relevant to the classical questions of intrinsic structure mentioned earlier. These studies suggest that there are highly organized, innately determined perceptual systems that are adapted closely to the animal's 'life space' and that provide the basis for what we might call 'acquisition of knowledge.' Also relevant are certain behavioral studies of human infants, for example those showing the preference for faces over other complex stimuli.

These and other studies make it reasonable to inquire into the possibility that complex intellectual structures are determined narrowly by innate mental organization. What is perceived may be determined by mental processes of considerable depth. As far as language learning is concerned, it seems to me that a rather convincing argument can be made for the view that certain principles intrinsic to the mind provide invariant structures that are a precondition for linguistic experience. In the course of this article I would like to sketch some of the ways such conclusions might be clarified and firmly established.

There are several ways linguistic evidence can be used to reveal properties of human perception and learning. In this section we consider one research strategy that might take us nearer to this goal.

Let us say that in interpreting a certain physical stimulus a person constructs a 'percept.' This percept represents some of his conclusions (in general, unconscious) about the stimulus. To the extent that we can characterize such percepts, we can go on to investigate the mechanisms that relate stimulus and percept. Imagine a model of perception that takes stimuli as inputs and arrives at percepts as 'outputs.' The model might contain a system of beliefs, strategies for interpreting stimuli, and other factors, such as the organization of memory. We would then have a perceptual model that might be represented graphically as in Figure 1.

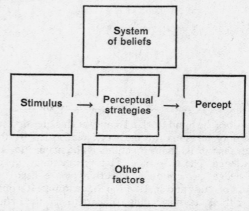

Figure 1 Each physical stimulus, after interpretation by the mental processes, will result in a percept.

Consider next the system of beliefs that is a component of the perceptual model. How was this acquired? To study this problem, we must investigate a second model, which takes certain data as input and gives as 'output' (again, internally represented) the system of beliefs operating in the perceptual model. This second model, a model of learning, would have its own intrinsic structure, as did the first. This structure might consist of conditions on the nature of the system of beliefs that can be acquired, of innate inductive strategies, and again, of other factors such as the organization of memory (see Figure 2).

Under further conditions, which are interesting but not relevant here, we can take these perceptual and learning models as theories of the acquisition of knowledge, rather than of belief. How then would the models apply to language? The input stimulus to the perceptual model is a speech signal, and the percept is a representation of the utterance that the hearer takes the signal to be and of the interpretation he assigns to it. We can think of the percept as the structural description of a linguistic expression which contains certain phonetic, semantic, and syntactic information. Most interesting is the syntactic information, which best can be discussed by examining a few typical cases.

The following three sentences seem to have the same syntactic structure.

(1) I told John to leave
(2) I expected John to leave
(3) I persuaded John to leave

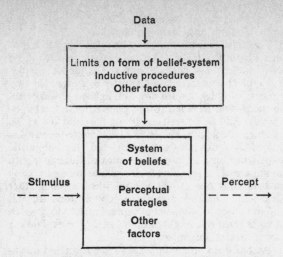

Data

Limits on form of belief-system
Inductive procedures
Other factors

System of beliefs

Stimulus → Perceptual strategies
Other factors → Percept

Figure 2 One's system of beliefs, a part of the perception model, is acquired from data as shown above.

Each contains the subject *I*, and the predicate of each consists of a verb (*told, expected, persuaded*), a noun phrase (*John*), and an embedded predicate phrase (*to leave*). This similarity is only superficial, however— a similarity in what we may call the 'surface structure' of these sentences, which differ in important ways when we consider them with somewhat greater care.

The differences can be seen when the sentences are paraphrased or subjected to certain grammatical operations, such as the conversion from active to passive forms. For example, in normal conversation the sentence 'I told John to leave' can be roughly paraphrased as:

(1a) What I told John was to leave

But the other two sentences cannot be paraphrased as:

(2a) *What I expected John was to leave

(3a) *What I persuaded John was to leave

Sentence (2) can be paraphrased as:

(2b) It was expected by me that John would leave

But the other two sentences cannot undergo a corresponding formal operation, yielding:

(1b) *It was told by me that John would leave

or

(3b) *It was persuaded by me that John would leave

Sentences (2) and (3) differ more subtly. In (3) *John* is the direct object of *persuade*, but in (2) *John* is not the direct object of *expect*. We can show this by using these verbs in slightly more complex sentences:

(4) I expected the doctor to examine John
(5) I persuaded the doctor to examine John

If we replace the embedded proposition *the doctor to examine John* with its passive form *John to be examined by the doctor*, the change to the passive does not, in itself, change the meaning. We can accept as paraphrases 'I expected the doctor to examine John' and

(4a) I expected John to be examined by the doctor

But we cannot accept as paraphrases 'I persuaded the doctor to examine John' and

(5a) I persuaded John to be examined by the doctor

The parts of these sentences differ in their grammatical functions. In 'I persuaded John to leave' *John* is both the object of *persuade* and the subject of *leave*. These facts must be represented in the percept since they are known, intuitively, to the hearer of the speech signal. No special training or instruction is necessary to enable the native speaker to understand these examples, to know which are 'wrong' and which 'right', although they may all be quite new to him. They are interpreted by the native speaker instantaneously and uniformly, in accordance with structural principles that are known tacitly, intuitively, and unconsciously.

These examples illustrate two significant points. First, the surface structure of a sentence, its organization into various phrases, may not reveal or immediately reflect its deep syntactic structure. The deep structure is not represented directly in the form of the speech signal; it is abstract. Second, the rules that determine deep and surface structure and their interrelation in particular cases must themselves be highly abstract. They are surely remote from consciousness, and in all likelihood they cannot be brought to consciousness.

A study of such examples, examples characteristic of all human languages that have been carefully studied, constitutes the first stage of the linguistic investigation outlined above, namely the study of the percept. The percept contains phonetic and semantic information related through the medium of syntactic structure. There are two aspects to this syntactic structure. It consists of a surface directly related to the phonetic form, and a deep structure that underlies the semantic interpretation. The deep structure is represented in the mind and rarely is indicated directly in the physical signal.

A language, then, involves a set of semantic-phonetic percepts, of sound-meaning correlations, the correlations being determined by the kind of intervening syntactic structure just illustrated. The English language correlates sound and meaning in one way, Japanese in another, and so on. But the general properties of percepts, their forms and mechanisms, are remarkably similar for all languages that have been carefully studied.

Returning to our models of perception and learning, we can now take up the problem of formulating the system of beliefs that is a central component in perceptual processes. In the case of language, the 'system of beliefs' would now be called the 'generative grammar,' the system of rules that specifies the sound-meaning correlation and generates the class of structural descriptions (percepts) that constitute the language in question. The generative grammar, then, represents the speaker-hearer's knowledge of his language. We can use the term *grammar of a language* ambiguously, as referring not only to the speaker's internalized, subconscious knowledge but to the professional linguist's representation of this internalized and intuitive system of rules as well.

How is this generative grammar acquired? Or, using our learning model, what is the internal structure of the device that could develop a generative grammar?

We can think of every normal human's internalized grammar as, in effect, a theory of his language. This theory provides a sound-meaning correlation for an infinite number of sentences. It provides an infinite set of structural descriptions; each contains a surface structure that determines phonetic form and a deep structure that determines semantic content.

In formal terms, then, we can describe the child's acquisition of language as a kind of theory construction. The child discovers the theory of his language with only small amounts of data from that language. Not only does his 'theory of the language' have an enormous predictive scope, but it also enables the child to reject a great deal of the very data on which the theory has been constructed. Normal speech consists, in large part, of fragments, false starts, blends, and other distortions of the underlying idealized forms. Nevertheless, as is evident from a study of the mature use of language, what the child learns is the underlying ideal theory. This is a remarkable fact. We must also bear in mind that the child constructs this ideal theory without explicit instruction, that he acquires this knowledge at a time when he is not capable of complex intellectual achievements in many other domains, and that this achievement is relatively independent of intelligence or the particular course of experience. These are facts that a theory of learning must face.

A scientist who approaches phenomena of this sort without prejudice or dogma would conclude that the acquired knowledge must be determined in a rather specific way by intrinsic properties of mental organization. He would then set himself the task of discovering the innate ideas and principles that make such acquisition of knowledge possible.

It is unimaginable that a highly specific, abstract, and tightly organized language comes by accident into the mind of every four-year-old child. If there were not an innate restriction on the form of grammar, then the child could employ innumerable theories to account for his linguistic experience, and no one system, or even small class of systems, would be found exclusively acceptable or even preferable. The child could not possibly acquire knowledge of a language. This restriction on the form of grammar is a precondition for linguistic experience, and it is surely the critical factor in determining the course and result of language learning. The child cannot know at birth which language he is going to learn. But he must 'know' that its grammar must be of a predetermined form that excludes many imaginable languages.

The child's task is to select the appropriate hypothesis from this restricted class. Having selected it, he can confirm his choice with the evidence further available to him. But neither the evidence nor any process of induction (in any well-defined sense) could in themselves have led to this choice. Once the hypothesis is sufficiently well confirmed the child knows the language defined by this hypothesis; consequently, his knowledge extends vastly beyond his linguistic experience, and he can reject much of this experience as imperfect, as resulting from the interaction of many factors, only one of which is the ideal grammar that determines a sound-meaning connection for an infinite class of linguistic expressions. Along such lines as these one might outline a theory to explain the acquisition of language.

As has been pointed out, both the form and meaning of a sentence are determined by syntactic structures that are not represented directly in the signal and that are related to the signal only at a distance, through a long sequence of interpretive rules. This property of abstractness in grammatical structure is of primary importance, and it is on this property that our inferences about mental processes are based. Let us examine this abstractness a little more closely.

Not many years ago, the process of sentence interpretation might have been described approximately along the following lines. A speech signal is received and segmented into successive units (overlapping at the borders). These units are analyzed in terms of their invariant phonetic properties and assigned to 'phonemes.' The sequence of phonemes, so constructed, is then segmented into minimal grammatically functioning units (morphemes and words). These are again categorized. Successive operations of segmentation and classification will lead to what I have called 'surface structure'—an analysis of a sentence into phrases, which can be represented as a proper bracketing of the sentence, with the bracketed units assigned to various categories, as in Figure 3. Each segment—phonetic, syntactic or semantic— would be identified in terms of certain invariant properties. This would be an exhaustive analysis of the structure of the sentence.

With such a conception of language structure, it made good sense to look forward hopefully to certain engineering applications of linguistics—for example, to voice-operated typewriters capable of segmenting an expression into its successive phonetic units and identifying these, so that speech could be converted to some form of phonetic writing in a mechanical way: to mechanical analysis of sentence structure by fairly straightforward and well-understood computational techniques; and perhaps even beyond to such projects as machine translation. But these hopes have by now been largely abandoned with the realization that this conception of grammatical structure is inadequate at every level, semantic, phonetic, and syntactic. Most important, at the level of syntactic organization, the surface structure indicates semantically significant relations only in extremely simple cases. In general, the deeper aspects of syntactic organization are representable by labeled bracketing, but of a very different sort from that seen in surface structure.

There is evidence of various sorts, both from phonetics and from experimental psychology, that labeled bracketing is an adequate representation of surface structure. It would go beyond the bounds of this paper to survey the phonetic evidence. A good deal of it is presented in a forthcoming book, *Sound Pattern of English*, by myself and Morris Halle. Similarly, very interesting experimental work by Jerry Fodor and his colleagues, based on earlier observations by D. E. Broadbent and Peter Ladefoged, has shown that the disruption of a speech signal (for example, by a superimposed click) tends to be perceived at the boundaries of phrases rather than at the point where the disruption actually occurred, and that in many cases the bracketing of surface structure can be read directly from the data on perceptual displacement. I think the evidence is rather good that labeled bracketing serves to represent the surface structure that is related to the perceived form of physical signals.

Deep structures are related to surface structures by a sequence of certain formal operations, operations now generally called 'grammatical transformations.' At the levels of sound, meaning, and syntax, the significant structural features of sentences are highly abstract. For this reason they cannot be recovered by elementary data-processing techniques. This fact lies behind the search for central processes in speech perception and the search for intrinsic, innate structure as the basis for language learning.

How can we represent deep structure? To answer this question we must consider the grammatical transformations that link surface structure to the underlying deep structure that is not always apparent.

Consider, for example, the operations of passivization and interrogation. In the sentences (1) John was examined by the doctor, and (2) did the doctor exa-mine John, both have a deep structure similar to paraphrase of Sentence 1, (3) the doctor examined John. The same network of grammatical relations determines the semantic interpretation in each case. Thus two of the grammatical transformations of English must be the operations of passivization and interrogation that form such surface structures as Sentences (1) and (2) from a deeper structure which in its essentials also underlies Sentence (3). Since the transformations ultimately produce surface structures, they must produce labeled bracketings (see Figure 3). But notice that these operations can apply in sequence: we can form the passive question 'was John examined by the doctor' by passivization followed by interrogation. Since the result of passivization is a labeled bracketing, it follows that the interrogative transformation operates on a labeled bracketing and forms a new labeled bracketing. Thus a transformation such as interrogation maps a labeled bracketing into a labeled bracketing.

By similar argument, we can show that all grammatical transformations are structure-dependent mappings of this sort and that the deep structures which underlie all sentences must themselves be labeled bracketings. Of course, the labeled bracketing that constitutes deep structure will in general be quite different from that representing the surface structure of a sentence. Our argument is somewhat oversimplified, but it is roughly correct. When made precise and fully accurate it strongly supports the view that deep structures, like surface structures, are formally to be taken as labeled bracketings, and that grammatical transformations are mappings of such structures onto other similar structures.

Recent studies have sought to explore the ways in which grammatical structure of the sort just described enters into mental operations. Much of this work has been based on a proposal formulated by George Miller as a first approximation, namely, that the amount of memory used to store a sentence should reflect the number of transformations used in deriving it. For example, H. B. Savin and E. Perchonock in-vestigated this assumption in the following way: they

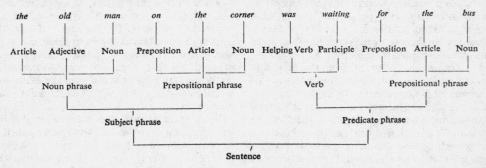

Figure 3 A type of sentence analysis now abandoned as inadequate at every level is this labeled bracketing which analyzes the sentence by successive division into larger units with each unit assigned to its own category.

presented to subjects a sentence followed by a sequence of unrelated words. They then determined the number of these unrelated words recalled when the subject attempted to repeat the sentence and the sequence of words. The more words recalled, the less memory used to store the sentence. The fewer words recalled, the more memory used to store the sentence. The results showed a remarkable correlation of amount of memory and number of transformations in certain simple cases. In fact, in their experimental material, shorter sentences with more transformations took up more 'space in memory' than longer sentences that involved fewer transformations.

Savin has extended this work and has shown that the effects of deep structure and surface structure can be differentiated by a similar technique. He considered paired sentences with approximately the same deep structure but with one of the pair being more complex in surface structure. He showed that, under the experimental conditions just described, the paired sentences were indistinguishable. But if the sequence of unrelated words precedes, rather than follows, the sentence being tested, then the more complex (in surface structure) of the pair is more difficult to repeat correctly than the simpler member. Savin's very plausible inference is that sentences are coded in memory in terms of deep structure. When the unrelated words precede the test sentence, these words use up a certain amount of short-term memory, and the sentence that is more complex in surface structure cannot be analyzed with the amount of memory remaining. But if the test sentence precedes the unrelated words, it is, once understood, stored in terms of deep structure, which is about the same in both cases. Therefore the same amount of memory remains, in the paired cases, for recall of the following words. This is a beautiful example of the way creative experimental studies can interweave with theoretical work in the study of language and of mental processes.

In speaking of mental processes we have returned to our original problem. We can now see why it is reasonable to maintain that the linguistic evidence supports an 'active' theory of acquisition of knowledge. The study of sentences and of speech perception, it seems to me, leads to a perceptual theory of a classical rationalist sort. Representative of this school, among others, were the seventeenth-century Cambridge Platonists, who developed the idea that our perception is guided by notions that originate from the mind and that provide the framework for the interpretation of sensory stimuli. It is not sufficient to suggest that this framework is a store of 'neural models' or 'schemata' which are in some manner applied to perception (as is postulated in some current theories of perception). We must go well beyond this assumption and return to the view of Wilhelm von Humboldt, who attributed to the mind a system of rules that generates such models and schemata under the stimulation of the senses. The system of rules itself determines the content of the percept that is formed.

We can offer more than this vague and metaphoric account. A generative grammar and an associated theory of speech perception provide a concrete example of the rules that operate and of the mental objects that they construct and manipulate. Physiology cannot yet explain the physical mechanisms that affect these abstract functions. But neither physiology nor psychology provides evidence that call this account into question or that suggests an alternative. As mentioned earlier, the most exciting current work in the physiology of perception shows that even the peripheral systems analyze stimuli into the complex properties of objects, and that central processes may significantly affect the information transmitted by the receptor organs.

The study of language, it seems to me, offers strong empirical evidence that empiricist theories of learning are quite inadequate. Serious efforts have been made in recent years to develop principles of induction, generalization, and data analysis that would account for knowledge of a language. These efforts have been a total failure. The methods and principles fail not for any superficial reason such as lack of time or data. They fail because they are intrinsically incapable of giving rise to the system of rules that underlies the normal use of language. What evidence is now available supports the view that all human languages share deep-seated properties of organization and structure. These properties—these linguistic universals—can be plausibly assumed to be an innate mental endowment rather than the result of learning. If this is true, then the study of language sheds light on certain long-standing issues in the theory of knowledge. Once again I see little reason to doubt that what is true of language is true of other forms of human knowledge as well.

There is one further question that might be raised at this point. How does the human mind come to have the innate properties that underlie acquisition of knowledge? Here linguistic evidence obviously provides no information at all. The process by which the human mind has achieved its present state of complexity and its particular form of innate organization are a complete mystery, as much of a mystery as the analogous questions that can be asked about the processes leading to the physical and mental organization of any other complex organism. It is perfectly safe to attribute this to evolution, so long as we bear in mind that there is no substance to this assertion—it amounts to nothing more than the belief that there is surely some naturalistic explanation for these phenomena.

There are, however, important aspects of the problem of language and mind that can be studied sensibly within the limitations of present understanding and technique. I think that, for the moment, the most productive investigations are those dealing with the nature of particular grammars and with the universal conditions met by all human languages. I have tried to suggest how one can move, in successive steps of increasing abstractness, from the study of percepts to the study of grammar and perceptual mechanisms, and from the study of grammar to the study of universal grammar and the mechanisms of learning.

In this area of convergence of linguistics, psychology, and philosophy, we can look forward to much exciting work in coming years.

19 Three processes in the child's acquisition of syntax

Roger Brown and Ursula Bellugi[1]

Some time in the second six months of life most children say a first intelligible word. A few months later most children are saying many words and some children go about the house all day long naming things (*table*, *doggie*, *ball*, etc.) and actions (*play*, *see*, *drop*, etc.) and an occasional quality (*blue*, *broke*, *bad*, etc.). At about 18 months children are likely to begin constructing two-word utterances; such a one, for instance, as *push car*.

A construction such as *push car* is not just two single-word utterances spoken in a certain order. As single-word utterances (they are sometimes called holophrases) both *push* and *car* would have primary stresses and terminal intonation contours. When they are two words programmed as a single utterance the primary stress would fall on *car* and so would the highest level of pitch. *Push* would be subordinated to *car* by a lesser stress and a lower pitch; the unity of the whole would appear in the absence of a terminal contour between words and the presence of such a contour at the end of the full sequence.

By the age of 36 months some children are so advanced in the construction process as to produce all the major varieties of English simple sentences up to a length of 10 or 11 words. For several years we have been studying the development of English syntax, of the sentence-constructing process, in children between 18 and 36 months of age. Most recently we have made a longitudinal study of a boy and girl whom we shall call Adam and Eve. We began work with Adam and Eve in October 1962 when Adam was 27 months old and Eve 18 months old. The two children were selected from some 30 whom we considered. They were selected primarily because their speech was exceptionally intelligible and because they talked a lot. We wanted to make it as easy as possible to transcribe accurately large quantities of child speech. Adam and Eve are the children of highly educated parents, the fathers were graduate students at Harvard and the

Source: *Harvard Educational Review* (1964), **34**, 133–51.

mothers are both college graduates. Both Adam and Eve were single children when we began the study. These facts must be remembered in generalizing the outcomes of the research.

Though Adam is 9 months older than Eve, his speech was only a little more advanced than hers in October 1962. The best single index of the level of speech development is the average length of utterance, and in October 1962 Adam's average was 1.84 morphemes and Eve's was 1.40 morphemes. The two children stayed fairly close together in the year that followed; in the records for the 38th week Adam's average was 3.55 and Eve's, 3.27. The processes we shall describe appeared in both children.

Every second week we visited each child for at least 2 hours and made a tape recording of everything said by the child as well as of everything said to the child. The mother was always present and most of the speech to the child is hers. Both mother and child became very much accustomed to our presence and learned to continue their usual routine with us as the observers.

One of us always made a written transcription, on the scene, of the speech of mother and child with notes about important actions and objects of attention. From this transcription and the tape a final transcription was made, and these transcriptions constitute the primary data of the study. For many purposes we require a 'distributional analysis' of the speech of the child. To this end the child's utterances in a given transcription were cross-classified and relisted under such headings as: '*A* + noun'; 'Noun + verb'; 'Verbs in the past'; 'Utterances containing the pronoun *it*', and so forth. The categorized utterances expose the syntactic regularities of the child's speech.

Each week we met as a research seminar, with other students of the psychology of language, to discuss the state of the construction process in one or the other of the two children as of that date. In these discussions small experiments were often suggested, experiments that had to be done within a few days if they were to be informative. At one time, for instance, we were uncertain whether Adam understood the semantic difference between putting a noun in subject position and putting it in object position. Consequently one of us paid an extra visit to Adam equipped with some toys. 'Adam,' we said, 'show us the duck pushing the boat.' And when he had done so: 'Now show us the boat pushing the duck.'

Another week we noticed that Adam sometimes pluralized nouns when they should have been pluralized and sometimes did not. We wondered whether he could make grammatical judgments about the plural, whether he could distinguish a correct form from an incorrect form. 'Adam,' we asked, 'which is right, "two shoes" or "two shoe"?' His answer on that occasion, produced with explosive enthusiasm, was: 'Pop goes the weasel!' The two-year-old child does not make a perfectly docile experimental subject.

The dialogue between mother and child does not read like a transcribed dialogue between two adults. Table 1 offers a sample section from an early transcribed record. It has some interesting properties. The conversation is, in the first place, very much in the here and now. From the child there is no speech of the sort that Bloomfield called 'displaced,' speech about other times and other places. Adam's utterances in the early months were largely a coding of contemporaneous events and impulses. The mother's speech differs from the speech that adults use to one another in many ways. Her sentences are short and simple; for the most part they are the kinds of sentences that Adam will produce a year later.

Table 1 A section from Adam's first record

Adam	Mother
See truck, Mommy.	
See truck,	
	Did you see the truck?
No I see truck.	
	No, you didn't see it?
	There goes one.
There go one.	
	Yes, there goes one.
See a truck.	
See truck, Mommy.	
See, truck.	
Truck.	
Put truck, Mommy.	
	Put the truck where?
Put truck window.	
	I think that one's too large to go in the window.

Perhaps because they are short, the sentences of the mother are perfectly grammatical. The sentences adults use to one another, perhaps because they are longer and more complex, are very often not grammatical, not well formed. Here for instance is a rather

representative example produced at a conference of psychologists and linguists: 'As far as I know, no one yet has done the in a way obvious now and interesting problem of doing a in a sense a structural frequency study of the alternative syntactical in a given language, say, like English, the alternative possible structures, and how what their hierarchical probability of occurrence structure is' (Maclay and Osgood, 1959). It seems unlikely that a child could learn the patterns of English syntax from such speech. His introduction to English ordinarily comes in the form of a simplified, repetitive, and idealized dialect. It may be that such an introduction is necessary for the acquisition of syntax to be possible, but we do not know that.

In the course of the brief interchange of Table 1, Adam imitates his mother in saying: 'There go one' immediately after she says 'There goes one.' The imitation is not perfect; Adam omits the inflection on the verb. His imitation is a reduction in that it omits something from the original. This kind of imitation with reduction is extremely common in the records of Adam and Eve, and it is the first process we shall discuss.

Imitation and reduction

Table 2 presents some model sentences spoken by the mothers, together with the imitations produced by Adam and Eve. These utterances were selected from hundreds in the records to illustrate some general propositions. The first thing to notice is that the imitations preserve the word order of the model sentences. To be sure, words in the model are often missing from the imitation, but the words preserved are in the order of the original. This is a fact that is so familiar and somehow reasonable that we did not at once recognize it as an empirical outcome, rather than as a natural necessity. But of course it is not a necessity; the outcome could have been otherwise. For example, words could have been said back in the reverse of their original order, the most recent first. The preservation of order suggests that the model sentence is processed by the child as a total construction rather than as a list of words.

Table 2 Some imitations produced by Adam and Eve

Model utterance	Child's imitation
Tank car	*Tank car*
Wait a minute	*Wait a minute*
Daddy's brief case	*Daddy brief case*
Fraser will be unhappy	*Fraser unhappy*
He's going out	*He go out*
That's an old time train	*Old time train*
It's not the same dog as Pepper	*Dog Pepper*
No, you can't write on Mr Cromer's shoe	*Write Cromer shoe*

In English the order of words in a sentence is an

important grammatical signal. Order is used to distinguish among subject, direct object, and indirect object, and it is one of the marks of imperative and interrogative constructions. The fact that the child's first sentences preserve the word order of their models accounts in part for the ability of an adult to 'understand' these sentences and so to feel that he is in communication with the child. It is conceivable that the child 'intends' the meanings coded by his word orders and that, when he preserves the order of an adult sentence, he does so because he wants to say what the order says. It is also possible that he preserves word order just because his brain works that way and that he has no comprehension of the semantic contrasts involved. In some languages word order is not an important grammatical signal. In Latin, for instance, 'Agricola amat puellam' has the same meaning as 'Puellam amat agricola' and subject-object relations are signalled by case endings. We would be interested to know whether children who are exposed to languages that do not utilize word order as a major syntactic signal preserve order as reliably as do children exposed to English.

The second thing to notice in Table 2 is that, when the models increase in length, there is not a corresponding increase in the imitation. The imitations stay in the range of 2 to 4 morphemes, which was the range characteristic of the children at this time. The children were operating under some constraint of length or span. This is not a limitation of vocabulary; the children knew hundreds of words. Neither is it a constraint of immediate memory. We infer this from the fact that the average length of utterances produced spontaneously, where immediate memory is not involved, is about the same as the average length of utterances produced as immediate imitations. The constraint is a limitation on the length of utterance the children are able to program or plan.[2] This kind of narrow-span limitation in children is characteristic of most or all of their intellectual operations. The limitation grows less restrictive with age, as a consequence, probably, of both neurological growth and practice, but of course it is never lifted altogether.

A constraint on length compels the imitating child to omit some words or morphemes from the mother's longer sentences. Which forms are retained and which omitted? The selection is not random but highly systematic. Forms retained in the examples of Table 2 include: *Daddy*, *Fraser*, *Pepper*, and *Cromer*; *tank car, minute, brief case, train, dog*, and *shoe*; *wait, go*, and *write*; *unhappy* and *old time*. For the most part they are nouns, verbs, and adjectives, though there are exceptions, as witness the initial pronoun *He* and the preposition *out* and the indefinite article *a*. Forms omitted in the samples of Table 2 include: the possessive inflection -*'s*, the modal auxiliary *will*, the contraction of the auxiliary verb *is*, the progressive inflection -*ing*, the preposition *on*, the articles *the* and *an*, and the modal auxiliary *can*. It is possible to make a general characterization of the forms likely to be retained that distinguishes them as a total class from the forms likely to be omitted.

Forms likely to be retained are nouns and verbs and, less often, adjectives, and these are the three large and 'open' parts of speech in English. The number of forms in any one of these parts of speech is extremely large and always growing. Words belonging to these classes are sometimes called 'contentives' because they have semantic content. Forms likely to be omitted are inflections, auxiliary verbs, articles, prepositions, and conjunctions. These forms belong to syntactic classes that are small and closed. Any one class has few members, and new members are not readily added. The omitted forms are the ones that linguists sometimes call 'functors', their grammatical *functions* being more obvious than their semantic content.

Why should young children omit functors and retain contentives? There is more than one plausible answer. Nouns, verbs, and adjectives are words that make reference. One can conceive of teaching the meanings of these words by speaking them, one at a time, and pointing at things or actions or qualities. And of course parents do exactly that. These are the kinds of words that children have been encouraged to practice speaking one at a time. The child arrives at the age of sentence construction with a stock of well-practiced nouns, verbs, and adjectives. It is not likely then that this prior practice causes him to retain the contentives from model sentences too long to be reproduced in full, that the child imitates those forms in speech he hears that are already well developed in him as individual habits? There is probably some truth in this explanation but it is not the only determinant since children will often select for retention contentives that are relatively unfamiliar to them.

We adults sometimes operate under a constraint on length, and the curious fact is that the English we produce in these circumstances bears a formal resemblance to the English produced by two-year-old children. When words cost money there is a premium on brevity or, to put it otherwise, a constraint on length. The result is 'telegraphic' English, and telegraphic English is an English of nouns, verbs, and adjectives. One does not send a cable reading: 'My car has broken down and I have lost my wallet; send money to me at the American Express in Paris' but rather 'Car broken down; wallet lost; send money American Express Paris.' The telegram omits *my, has, and, I, have, my, to, me, at, the, in*. All of these are functors. We make the same kind of telegraphic reduction when time or fatigue constrains us to be brief, as witness any set of notes taken at a fast-moving lecture.

A telegraphic transformation of English generally communicates very well. It does so because it retains the high-information words and drops the low-information words. We are here using 'information' in the sense of the mathematical theory of communication. The information carried by a word is inversely related to the chances of guessing it from context. From a given string of content words, missing functors can often be guessed, but the message, 'my has and I have my to me at the in', will not serve to get money to Paris. Perhaps children are able to make a communication analysis of adult speech and so adapt in an optimal way to their limitation of span. There is, however, another way in which the adaptive outcome might be achieved.

If you say aloud the model sentences of Table 2 you will find that you place the heavier stresses, the primary and secondary stresses in the sentences, on contentives rather than on functors. In fact the heavier stresses fall, for the most part, on the words the child retains. We first realized that this was the case when we found that, in the transcribing of the tapes, the words of the mother that we could hear most clearly were usually the words that the child reproduced. We had trouble hearing the weakly stressed functors and, of course, the child usually failed to reproduce them. Differential stress may then be the cause of the child's differential retention. The outcome is a maximally informative reduction, but the cause of this outcome need not be the making of an information analysis. The outcome may be an incidental consequence of the fact that English is a well-designed language that places its heavier stresses where they are needed, on contentives that cannot easily be guessed from context.

We are fairly sure that differential stress is one of the determinants of the child's telegraphic productions. For one thing, stress will also account for the way in which children reproduce polysyllabic words when the total is too much for them. Adam, for instance, gave us *'pression* for *expression* and Eve gave us *'raff* for *giraffe*; the more heavily-stressed syllables were the ones retained. In addition, we have tried the effect of placing heavy stresses on functors that do not ordinarily receive such stresses. To Adam we said: 'You say what I say' and then, speaking in a normal way at first: 'The doggie will bite.' Adam gave back: 'Doggie bite.' Then we stressed the auxiliary: 'The doggie *will* bite,' and after a few trials Adam made attempts at reproducing that auxiliary. A science fiction experiment comes to mind. If there were parents who stressed functors rather than contentives, would they have children whose speech was a kind of 'reciprocal telegraphic', made up of articles, prepositions, conjunctions, auxiliaries, and the like? Such children would be out of touch with the community as real children are not.

It may be that all the factors we have mentioned play some part in determining the child's selective imitations: the reference-making function of contentives, the fact that they are practiced as single words, the fact that they cannot be guessed from context, and the heavy stresses they receive. There are also other possible factors; for example, the left-to-right, earlier-to-later position of words in a sentence, but these make too long a story to tell here (Brown and Fraser, 1963). Whatever the causes, the first utterances produced as imitations of adult sentences are highly systematic reductions of their models. Furthermore, the telegraphic properties of these imitations appear also in the child's spontaneously produced utterances. When his speech is not modeled on an immediately prior adult sentence, it observes the same limitation on length and the same predilection for contentives as when it is modeled on an immediately prior sentence.

Imitation with expansion

In the course of the brief conversation set down in Table 1, Adam's mother at one point imitates Adam. The boy says: 'There go one' and mother responds: 'Yes, there goes one.' She does not exactly reproduce the model sentence of the child but instead adds something to it or expands it. What she adds is a functor, the inflection for third person, to the verb, the very form that Adam had omitted when he imitated his mother.

One of the first things we noticed when we began to study child speech several years ago was the frequency with which adults imitated children. Indeed they seemed to imitate more often than did the children themselves. We later came to realize that adult imitations are seldom exact reproductions; they are usually expansions. The mothers of Adam and Eve responded to the speech of their children with expansions about 30% of the time. We did it ourselves when we talked with the children. Indeed we found it very difficult to withhold expansions. A reduced or incomplete English sentence seems to constrain the English-speaking adult to expand it into the nearest properly formed complete sentence. Table 3 lists a few sample expansions from the hundreds in the records.

The first thing worthy of attention in the expansions of Table 3 is the fact that the words spoken by the mother preserve the order of the words in the child's sentences. To be sure, words and inflections are added, but they are fitted in before, and after, and between the words the child used; they are not generally permitted to disturb the order of the child's words. It is as if these latter were taken as constants by the mother, constants to which some sentence had to be fitted. She acts as if she were assuming that the

Table 3 Expansions of child speech produced by mothers

Child	Mother
Baby highchair	*Baby is in the highchair*
Mommy eggnog	*Mommy had her eggnog*
Eve lunch	*Eve is having lunch*
Mommy sandwich	*Mommy'll have a sandwich*
Sat wall	*He sat on the wall*
Throw Daddy	*Throw it to Daddy*
Pick glove	*Pick the glove up*

child means everything he says, all the words and also their order, but as if he might also mean more than he says. From the mother's point of view an expansion is a kind of communication check; it says in effect: 'Is this what you mean?'

The second thing to notice about Table 3 is the character of the forms added to the child's utterances. They include the auxiliaries *is* and *will*; the prepositions *in*, *on*, *to*, and *up*; the verb forms *is*, *have*, *had*, and *having*; the articles *a* and *the*; and the pronouns *her*, *he*, and *it*. For the most part, the words added are functors, and functors are of course the words that the child omits in his reductions.

The interaction between mother and child, is, much of the time, a cycle of reductions and expansions. There are two transformations involved. The reduction transformation has an almost completely specifiable and so mechanical character. One could program a machine to do it with the following instructions: 'Retain contentives (or stressed forms) in the order given up to some limit of length.' The expansion accomplished by Adam's mother when she added the third-person inflection to the verb and said, 'There goes one,' is also a completely specifiable transformation. The instructions would read: 'Retain the forms given in the order given and supply obligatory grammatical forms.' To be sure this mother-machine would have to be supplied with the obligatory rules of English grammar, but that could be done. However, the sentence 'There goes one' is atypical in that it only adds a compulsory and redundant inflection. The expansions of Table 3 all add forms that are not grammatically compulsory or redundant and these expansions cannot be mechanically generated by grammatical rules alone.

In Table 3 the upper four utterances produced by the child are all of the same grammatical type; all four consist of a proper noun followed by a common noun. However, the four are expanded in quite different ways. In particular, the form of the verb changes: it is first in the simple present tense; second in the simple past; third in the present progressive; and last in the simple future. All of these are perfectly grammatical but they are different. The second set of child utterances is formally uniform in that each one consists of a verb followed by a noun. The expansions are again all grammatical but quite unlike, especially with regard to the preposition supplied. In general, then, there are radical changes in the mother's expansions when there are no changes in the formal character of the utterances expanded. It follows that the expansions cannot be produced simply by making grammatically compulsory additions to the child's utterances.

How does a mother decide on the correct expansion of one of her child's utterances? Consider the utterance 'Eve lunch.' So far as grammar is concerned this utterance could be appropriately expanded in any one of a number of ways: 'Eve is having lunch'; 'Eve had lunch'; 'Eve will have lunch'; 'Eve's lunch', and so forth. On the occasion when Eve produced the utterance, however, one expansion seemed more appropriate than any other. It was then the noon hour, Eve was sitting at the table with a plate of food before her and her spoon and fingers were busy. In these circumstances 'Eve lunch' had to mean 'Eve is having lunch.' A little later when the plate had been stacked in the sink and Eve was getting down from her chair the utterance 'Eve lunch' would have suggested the expansion 'Eve has had her lunch.' Most expansions are responsive not only to the child's words but also to the circumstances attending their utterance.

What kind of instructions will generate the mother's expansions? The following are approximately correct: 'Retain the words given in the order given, and add those functors that will result in a well-formed simple sentence that is appropriate to the circumstances.' These are not instructions that any machine could follow. A machine could act on the instructions only if it were provided with detailed specifications for judging appropriateness, and no such specifications can, at present, be written. They exist, however, in implicit form in the brains of mothers and in the brains of all English-speaking adults, and so judgments of appropriateness can be made by such adults.

The expansion encodes aspects of reality that are not coded by the child's telegraphic utterance. Functors have meaning, but it is meaning that accrues to them in context rather than isolation. The meanings that are added by functors seem to be nothing less than the basic terms in which we construe reality: the time of an action, whether it is ongoing or completed, whether it is presently relevant or not; the concept of possession, and such relational concepts as are coded by *in*, *on*, *up*, *down*, and the like; the difference between a particular instance of a class ('Has anybody seen the paper?') and any instance of a class ('Has anybody seen *a* paper?'); the difference between extended substances given shape and size by an 'accidental' container (*sand*, *water*, *syrup*, etc.) and countable 'things' having a characteristic, fixed shape and size (*a cup*, *a man*, *a tree*, etc.). It seems to us that a mother, in expanding speech, may be teaching more than grammar; she may be teaching something like a world view.

As yet it has not been demonstrated that expansions are *necessary* for the learning of either grammar or a construction of reality. It has not even been demonstrated that expansions contribute to such learning. All we know is that some parents do expand and their children do learn. It is perfectly possible, however, that children can and do learn simply from hearing their parents or others make well-formed sentences in connection with various nonverbal circumstances. It may not be necessary or even helpful for these sentences to be expansions of utterances of the child. Only experiments contrasting expansion training with simple exposure to English will settle the matter. We hope to do such experiments.

There are, of course, reasons for expecting the expansion transformation to be an effective tutorial technique. By adding something to the words the child has just produced one confirms his response insofar as it is appropriate. In addition one takes him somewhat beyond that response but not greatly beyond it. One encodes additional meanings at a moment when he is most likely to be attending to the cues that can teach that meaning.

Induction of the latent structure

Adam, in the course of the conversation with his mother set down in Table 1, produced one utterance for which no adult is likely ever to have provided an exact model: 'No I see truck.' His mother elects to expand it as 'No, you didn't see it' and this expansion suggests that the child might have created the utterance by reducing an adult model containing the form *didn't*. However, the mother's expansion in this case does some violence to Adam's original version. He did not say *no* as his mother said it, with primary stress and final contour; Adam's *no*, had secondary stress and no final contour. It is not easy to imagine an adult model for this utterance. It seems more likely that the utterance was created by Adam as part of a continuing effort to discover the general rules for constructing English negatives.

In Table 4 are listed some utterances produced by Adam or Eve for which it is difficult to imagine any

Table 4 Utterances not likely to be imitations

My Cromer suitcase	You naughty are
Two foot	Why it can't turn off?
A bags	Put it on
A scissor	Cowboy did fighting me
A this truck	Put a gas on

adult model. It is unlikely that any adult said any of these to Adam or Eve, since they are very simple utterances and yet definitely ungrammatical. In addition, it is difficult, by adding functors alone, to build any of them up to simple grammatical sentences. Consequently it does not seem likely that these utterances are reductions of adult originals. It is more likely that they are mistakes which externalize the child's search for the regularities of English syntax.

We have long realized that the occurrence of certain kinds of errors on the level of morphology (or word construction) reveals the child's effort to induce regularities from speech. So long as a child speaks correctly, or at any rate so long as he speaks as correctly as the adults he hears, there is no way to tell whether he is simply repeating what he has heard or whether he is actually constructing. However, when he says something like 'I digged a hole,' we can often be sure that he is constructing. We can be sure, because it is unlikely that he could have heard *digged* from anyone and because we can see how, in processing words he has heard, he might have come by *digged*. It looks like an overgeneralization of the regular past inflection. The inductive operations of the child's mind

are externalized in such a creation. Overgeneralizations on the level of syntax (or sentence construction) are more difficult to identify because there are so many ways of adding functors so as to build up conceivable models. But this is difficult to do for the example of Table 4 and for several hundred other utterances in our records.

The processes of imitation and expansion are not sufficient to account for the degree of linguistic competence that children regularly acquire. These processes alone cannot teach more than the sum total of sentences that speakers of English have either modeled for a child to imitate or built up from a child's reductions. However, a child's linguistic competence extends far beyond this sum total of sentences. All children are able to understand and construct sentences they have never heard but which are nevertheless well formed, i.e., well formed in terms of general rules that are implicit in the sentences the child has heard. Somehow, then, every child processes the speech to which he is exposed so as to induce from it a latent structure. This latent rule structure is so general that a child can spin out its implications all his life long. It is both semantic and syntactic. The discovery of latent structure is the greatest of the processes involved in language acquisition and the most difficult to understand. We will provide an example of how the analysis can proceed by discussing the evolution in child speech of noun phrases.

A noun phrase in adult English includes a noun, but also more than a noun. One variety consists of a noun with assorted modifiers: *The girl*; *The pretty girl*; *That pretty girl*; *My girl*, and so forth. All of these are constructions that have the same syntactic privileges as do nouns alone. A noun phrase can be used in isolation to name or request something; it can be used in sentences in subject position, or in object position, or in predicate nominative position; all these are slots that a noun alone can also fill. A larger construction having the same syntactic privileges as its 'head' word is called, in linguistics, an 'endocentric' construction, and noun phrases are endocentric constructions.

For both Adam and Eve, in the early records, noun phrases usually occur as total, independent utterances rather than as components of sentences. Table 5 presents an assortment of such utterances. Each one consists of some sort of modifier, just one, preceding a noun. The modifiers or, as they are sometimes called, the 'pivot' words are a much smaller class than the noun class. Three students of child speech (Braine, 1963; Miller and Ervin, 1964; and Brown and Fraser, 1963) have independently discovered that this kind of construction is extremely common when children first begin to combine words.

It is possible to generalize the cases of Table 5 into a simple, implicit rule. The rule symbolized in Table 5 reads: 'In order to form a noun phrase of this type, select first one word from the small class of modifiers and select, second, one word from the large class of

Table 5 Noun phrases in isolation and rule for generating noun phrases at time 1

A coat	More coffee
A celery[a]	More nut[a]
A Becky[a]	Two sock[a]
A hands[a]	Two shoes
The top	Two tinker toy[a]
My Mommy	Big boot
My stool	Poor man
That Adam	Little top
That knee	Dirty knee

$$NP \rightarrow M + N$$

M→*a, big, dirty, little, more, my, poor, that, the, two.*
N→*Adam, Becky, boot, coat, coffee, knee, man, Mommy, nut, sock, stool, tinker toy, top* and very many others.

[a]Ungrammatical for an adult.

nouns.' This is a 'generative' rule, by which we mean that it is a program that would actually serve to build constructions of the type in question. It is offered as a model of the mental mechanism by which Adam and Eve generated such utterances. Furthermore, judging from our work with other children and from the reports of Braine and of Ervin and Miller, the model describes a mechanism present in many children when their average utterance is approximately two morphemes long.

We have found that even in our earliest records the M+N construction is sometimes used as a component of larger constructions. For instance, Eve said: 'Fix a Lassie' and 'Turn the page' and 'A horsie stuck' and Adam even said: 'Adam wear a shirt.' There are, at first, only a handful of these larger constructions, but there are very many constructions in which single nouns occur in subject or in object position.

Let us look again at the utterances of Table 5 and the rule generalizing them. The class M does not correspond with any syntactic class of adult English. In the class M are articles, a possessive pronoun, a cardinal number, a demonstrative adjective or pronoun, a quantifier, and some descriptive adjectives—a mixed bag indeed. For adult English these words cannot belong to the same syntactic class because they have very different privileges of occurrence in sentences. For the children the words do seem to function as one class that has the common privilege of occurrence before nouns.

If the initial words of the utterances in Table 5 are treated as one class M, then many utterances are generated which an adult speaker would judge to be ungrammatical. Consider the indefinite article *a*. Adults use it only to modify common count nouns in the singular such as *coat, dog, cup,* and so forth. We would not say *a celery,* or *a cereal,* or *a dirt,* since *celery, cereal,* and *dirt* are mass nouns. We would not say *a Becky* or *a Jimmy,* since *Becky* and *Jimmy* are proper nouns. We would not say *a hands* or *a shoes,* since *hands* and *shoes* are plural nouns. Adam and Eve

did, at first, form ungrammatical combinations such as these.

The numeral *two* we use only with count nouns in the plural. We would not say *two sock* since *sock* is singular, not *two water* since *water* is a mass noun. The word *more* we use before count nouns in the plural (*more nuts*) or before mass nouns in the singular (*more coffee*). Adam and Eve made a number of combinations involving *two* or *more* that we would not make.

Given the initially very undiscriminating use of words in the class M, it follows that one dimension of development must be a progressive differentiation of privileges, which means the division of M into smaller classes. There must also be subdivision of the noun class (N) for the reason that the privileges of occurrence of various kinds of modifiers must be described in terms of such subvarieties of N as the common noun and proper noun, the count noun and mass noun. There must eventually emerge a distinction between nouns singular and nouns plural, since this distinction figures in the privileges of occurrence of the several sorts of modifiers.

Sixteen weeks after our first records from Adam and Eve (Time 2), the differentiation had begun. By this time there were distributional reasons for separating out articles from demonstrative pronouns, and both of these from the residual class of modifiers. Some of the evidence for this conclusion appears in Table 6. In

Table 6 Subdivision of the modifier class

a. Privileges peculiar to articles

Obtained	Not obtained
A blue flower	Blue a flower
A nice nap	Nice a nap
A your car	Your a car
A my pencil	My a pencil

b. Privileges peculiar to demonstrative pronouns

Obtained	Not obtained
That a horse	A that horse
That a blue flower	A that blue flower
	Blue a that flower

general, one syntactic class is distinguished from another when the members of one class have combinational privileges not enjoyed by the members of the other. Consider, for example, the reasons for distinguishing articles (Art) from modifiers in general (M). Both articles and modifiers appeared in front of nouns in two-word utterances. However, in three-word utterances that were made up from the total pool of words and that had a noun in final position, the privileges of *a* and *the* were different from the privileges of all other modifiers. The articles occurred in initial position followed by a member of class M other than an article. No other modifier occurred in this first position; notice the 'Not obtained' examples of Table 6a. If the children had produced utterances like those not obtained (for example, *blue a flower,* or *your a car*), there would have been no difference in the privileges of occurrence of articles and modifiers and therefore no reason to separate out articles.

The record of Adam is especially instructive at this point. He created such notably ungrammatical combinations as 'a your car' and 'a my pencil.' It is very unlikely that adults provided models for these combinations. They argue strongly that Adam regarded all the words in the residual M class as syntactic equivalents and so generated these very odd utterances in which possessive pronouns appear where descriptive adjectives would be more acceptable.

Table 6b also presents some of the evidence for distinguishing demonstrative pronouns (Dem) from articles and modifiers. The pronouns occurred first and ahead of articles in three-and-four-word utterances—a position that neither articles nor modifiers ever filled. The sentences with demonstrative pronouns are recognizable as reductions that omit the copular verb *is*. Such sentences are not noun phrases in adult English, and ultimately they will not function as noun phrases in the speech of the children, but for the present they are not distinguishable distributionally from noun phrases.

Recall now the generative formula of Table 5 which constructs noun phrases by simply placing a modifier (M) before a noun (N). The differentiation of privileges illustrated in Table 6, and the syntactic classes this evidence motivates us to create, complicate the formula for generating noun phrases. In Table 7 we have written a single general formula for producing all noun phrases [NP → (Dem) + (Art) + (M) + N] and also the numerous more specific rules which are summarized by the general formula.

By the time of the 13th transcription, 26 weeks after we began our study, privileges of occurrence were much more finely differentiated, and consequently syntactic classes were more numerous. From the distributional evidence we judged that Adam had made five classes of his original class M: articles, descriptive adjectives, possessive pronouns, demonstrative pronouns, and a residual class of modifiers.

Table 7 Rules for generating noun phrases at time 2

$$NP^1 \to Dem + Art + M + N$$
$$NP^2 \to Art + M + N$$
$$NP^3 \to Dem + M + N$$
$$NP^4 \to Art + N$$
$$NP^5 \to M + N$$
$$NP^6 \to Dem + N \qquad NP \to (Dem)^a + (Art) + (M) + N$$

[a]Class within parentheses is optional.

The generative rules of Table 7 had become inadequate; there were no longer, for instance, any combinations like 'a your car.' Eve had the same set, except that she used two residual classes of modifiers. In addition, nouns had begun to subdivide for both children. The usage of proper nouns had become clearly distinct from the usage of count nouns. For Eve the evidence justified separating count nouns from mass nouns, but for Adam it still did not. Both children by this time were frequently pluralizing nouns, but as yet their syntactic control of the singular-plural distinction was imperfect.

In summary, one major aspect of the development of general structure in child speech is a progressive differentiation in the usage of words and therefore a progressive differentiation of syntactic classes. At the same time, however, there is an integrative process at work. From the first, an occasional noun phrase occurred as a component of some larger construction. At first these noun phrases were just two words long, and the range of positions in which they could occur was small. With time the noun phrases grew longer, were more frequently used, and were used in a greater range of positions. The noun-phrase structure as a whole, in all the permissible combinations of modifiers and nouns, was assuming the combinational privileges enjoyed by nouns in isolation.

In Table 8 are set down some of the sentence positions in which both nouns and noun phrases occurred in the speech of Adam and Eve.

Table 8 Some privileges of the noun phrase

Noun positions	Noun-phrase positions
That (*flower*)	*That* (*a blue flower*)
Where (*ball*) *go?*	*Where* (*the puzzle*) *go?*
Adam write (*penguin*)	*Doggie eat* (*the breakfast*)
(*Horsie*) *stop*	(*A horsie*) *crying*
Put (*hat*) *on*	*Put* (*the red hat*) *on*

It is the close match between the positions of nouns alone and of nouns with modifiers in the speech of Adam and Eve that justifies us in calling the longer constructions noun phrases. These longer constructions are, as they should be, endocentric; the head word alone has the same syntactic privileges as the head word with its modifiers. The continuing absence, in noun-phrase positions, of whole constructions of the type, 'That a blue flower,' signals the fact that these constructions are telegraphic versions of predicate nominative sentences, with the verb form *is* omitted. Examples of the kind of construction not obtained are: 'That (that a blue flower),' or 'Where (that a blue flower)?'

For adults the noun phrase is a subwhole of the sentence, what linguists call an 'immediate constituent'. The noun phrase has a kind of psychological unity. There are signs that the noun phrase was also an immediate constituent for Adam and Eve. Consider the sentence with the separable verb *put on*. The noun phrase in 'Put the red hat on' is, as a whole, fitted in between the verb and the particle, even as is the noun alone in 'Put hat on.' What is more, however, the location of pauses in the longer sentence on several occasions suggested the psychological organization, 'Put . . . the red hat . . . on,' rather than 'Put the red . . . hat on,' or 'Put the . . . red hat on.' In addition to this evidence, the use of pronouns suggests that the noun phrase is a psychological unit.

The unity of noun phrases in adult English is evidenced, in the first place, by the syntactic equivalence between such phrases and nouns alone. It is evidenced, in the second place, by the fact that pronouns are able to substitute for total noun phrases. In our immediately preceding sentence the pronoun 'It' stands for the rather involved construction: 'The unity of noun phrases in adult English'. The words called 'pronouns' in English would more aptly be called 'pro-noun-phrases' since it is the phrase rather than the noun that they usually replace. One does not replace 'unity' with 'it' and say 'The *it* of noun phrases in adult English.' In the speech of Adam and Eve, too, the pronoun came to function as a replacement for the noun phrase. Some of the clearer cases appear in Table 9.

Adam characteristically externalizes more of his learning than does Eve and his record is especially instructive in connection with the learning of pronouns. In his first eight records, taken during the first 16 weeks of the study, Adam quite often produced sentences containing both the pronoun and the noun or noun phrase that the pronoun should have replaced. One can see here the equivalence in process of establishment. First the substitute is produced and then, as if in explication, the form or forms that will eventually be replaced by the substitute. Adam spoke out his pronoun antecedents as chronological consequents. This is additional evidence of the unity of the noun phrase, since the noun phrases *my ladder* and *cowboy boot* are linked with *it* in Adam's speech in just the same way as the nouns *ladder* and *ball*.

We have described three processes involved in the child's acquisition of syntax. It is clear that the last of these, the induction of latent structure, is by far the most complex. It looks as if this last process will put a serious strain on any learning theory thus far conceived by psychology. The very intricate simultaneous differentiation and integration that constitutes the evolution of the noun phrase is more reminiscent of the biological development of an embryo than it is of the acquisition of a conditioned reflex.

Table 9 Pronouns replacing nouns or noun phrases, and pronouns produced together with nouns or noun phrases

Noun phrases replaced by pronouns	Pronouns and noun phrases in same utterances
Hit ball	*Mommy get it ladder*
Get it	*Mommy get it my ladder*
Ball go?	*Saw it ball*
Go get it	*Miss it garage*
Made it	*I miss it cowboy boot*
Made a ship	*I Adam drive that*
Fix a tricycle	*I Adam drive*
Fix it	*I Adam don't*

Notes

1 This investigation was supported by Public Health Service Research Grant MH-7088 from the National Institute of Mental Health.

We are grateful for intellectual stimulation and light-hearted companionship to Jean Berko Gleason, Samuel Anderson, Colin Fraser, David McNeill, and Daniel Slobin.
2 See Brown and Fraser (1963) for additional evidence of the constraint on sentence length.

References

Braine, M. D. S. (1963). The ontogeny of English phrase structure: The first phase. *Language* 39, 1–13.

Brown, R., and Fraser, C. (1963). The acquisition of syntax, In C. N. Cofer and Barbara S. Musgrave (eds.), *Verbal behavior and learning*. New York: McGraw-Hill.

Maclay, H., and Osgood, C. E. (1959). Hesitation phenomena in spontaneous English speech. *Word* 15, 19–44.

Miller, W., and Ervin, S. (1964). The development of grammar in child language, in U. Bellugi and R. Brown (eds.), The acquisition of language. *Child Developm. Monogr.* 29, 9–34.

20 The creation of language
D. McNeill

At the age of about one, a normal child, not impaired by hearing loss or speech impediment, will begin to say words. By one-and-a-half to two years, he will begin to form simple two- and three-word sentences. By four years, he will have mastered very nearly the entire complex and abstract structure of the English language. In slightly more than two years, therefore, children acquire full knowledge of the grammatical system of their native tongue. This stunning intellectual achievement is routinely performed by every pre-school child, but what is known about the process underlying it? The process is, as the title of this article implies, one of invention. On the basis of fundamental biological characteristics (of which only slight understanding is presently available), each generation creates language anew.

In order to understand the creation of language, one must understand something of what is created. The structure of language is not obvious to introspection, as any who have suffered through elementary school courses in 'grammar' will attest. However, the appropriate portrayal of language is a linguistic description, not an elementary school 'grammar'. The grammars of modern linguistics aim to describe the linguistic *knowledge* possessed by fluent speakers of a language —their linguistic 'competence', as the MIT linguist Noam Chomsky calls it. A recent article by John C. Marshall introduced readers to some aspects of these grammars (see 'The language of man', *Discovery*, October, 1964) so the nature of linguistic competence will be treated only briefly here.

Let us think about a single sentence. By so restricting our attention, we eliminate discourse, dialogue, and the exchange of ideas, all of which are important questions for understanding the development of language. In return we shall gain relative simplicity without losing an accurate vision of linguistic knowledge. A sentence consists of words arranged in a particular order, but it is much more than this. In addition, a sentence has structure; the words fall together in certain definite ways. As an example, take the sentence, *the professor berated the student*. It contains two major constituents (*the professor*) and (*berated the student*); the second of these, moreover, is itself made up of constituents, (*berated*) and (*the student*). The entire sentence, therefore, possesses a hierarchical structure in which some constituents contain others. This pattern can be represented by means of a tree-diagram in which lower-order constituents branch downward from higher-order ones. This much linguistic notation fulfils a fairly obvious purpose. Less obvious but equally important is the fact that sentences also possess a 'deep' or 'underlying' structure.

The importance of deep structure derives from its intimate involvement with our ability to extract meaning from sentences. Consider, for example, the similarities and differences between the two sentences, *John is easy to please* and *John is eager to please*. Superficially, these sentences are constructed in the same way, but the sentences clearly differ profoundly. In the first *John* is the object of the verb, whereas in the second *John* is the subject of the sentence. Every English speaker automatically understands this difference and yet it is not represented in the surface form of the two sentences. Instead, the two sentences differ in deep structure.

Grammatical relations, such as subject and object, are carried by structures *not* directly apparent in the surface form of sentences. We know something of 'abstract' linguistic features, aspects of sentences that lie behind their manifest form. The deep structure of sentences carries such abstract knowledge. Deep structures must, accordingly, be different from the corresponding surface structures, and even the simplest sentence has an underlying structure that differs in some respect from its manifest form. The problem for a theory of language acquisition is to explain the development of such abstractions.

Source: *Discovery* (1966), **27** (7), 34–8, reprinted in *Language*, ed. R. C. Oldfield and J. C. Marshall, Penguin (1968), 21–31.

A key linguistic concept is the notion of a grammatical transformation. A transformation is a rule of grammar that relates deep structures to surface structures. Our intuitions about sentences include abstract knowledge precisely because we have learned to use a transformational grammar. Without rules of transformation, all linguistic knowledge would have to be manifest in the surface form of sentences, and a sentence like *John is easy to please* would be impossible. The acquisition of transformations then, is importantly involved in the acquisition of language.

Acquiring a universal grammar

Let us think, not about children for the moment, but about an abstract 'Language Acquisition Device', which we shall call LAD for short (alternatively, a 'Language Acquisition System', or LAS—the feminine form). LAD receives a *corpus* of speech, which is a set of utterances, some grammatical, some not. The corpus may be large but it is not unlimited in size. It contains, let us say, the number of utterances ordinarily overheard by a two-year-old child. Upon receipt of this corpus, LAD creates a *grammatical system*. This, in turn, may be regarded as LAD's theory about the regularities that appear in the corpus of speech. As with any theory, LAD's grammatical system will allow predictions of future observations—predictions of which utterances will be grammatical sentences. It will also allow LAD to distinguish the aspects of utterances that are unimportant from the aspects that are grammatically significant.

LAD creates a grammar by passing the evidence contained in the corpus through some kind of internal structure. The sequence can be represented by a simple flow diagram:

corpus of speech ⟶ | LAD | ⟶ grammatical system

If we understand LAD's internal structure, we would understand how LAD invents a grammar. The problem is not unlike those exercises given to engineering students in which they must infer the internal wiring of a 'black box' from its various input-output relations. LAD is our 'black box'. Its input is a corpus of speech: its output is a grammatical system. Just as an engineering student, we need a theory of its internal structure.

One hint about LAD's internal structure arises from the fact that it must be able to acquire any natural language. We do not want LAD to find Bantu easier than, say, English, or Russian, or Japanese. Whatever is contained in LAD, therefore, must be universally applicable, so our theory of LAD will be (in part) a theory of linguistic universals. One way to portray some of the internal structure of LAD is to portray the structure common to all languages. This conclusion yields an important insight into the acquisition of language.

For notice that the problem of understanding LAD is exactly like the problem of understanding real children. Like LAD, children are exposed to a corpus of speech, and like LAD they develop grammatical competence on the basis of this corpus. Moreover, in the case of both LAD and children some kind of internal structure converts a corpus of speech into a grammatical system. Since the same corpus is input and the same grammatical system is output, LAD and children must have the same internal structure. LAD's internal structure therefore corresponds to the fundamental human capacity for language.

The abstract grammatical relations of subject-predicate and verb-object are linguistically universal. If they reflect a fundamental capacity for language, then children must impose these abstract relations on their earliest speech. The grammatical relations must appear early because a capacity for language *is* the reason (we suppose) that children acquire language quickly. The problem now is to find evidence on behalf of this hypothesis.

Two kinds may be mentioned. One comes from a small American child observed by Roger Brown, the other from a small Japanese child whom I have observed. We shall take up the American child first, a boy Brown calls Adam.

When Adam was two years old, he produced large numbers of word combinations. These were sentences in Adam's grammar. Two-word combinations were most common, three-word combinations somewhat less so, and four-word combinations were very rare. These sentences were the first that Brown recorded, and probably were among the first that Adam ever produced. A small sample is given below:

> Two boot
> Hear tractor
> See truck, mommy
> Adam make tower
> A gas

Roger Brown and his colleague Colin Fraser (1963) have called these sentences 'telegraphic', aptly capturing their abbreviated quality. Analysing many hundreds of such sentences, Brown and a second colleague, Ursula Bellugi (1964), concluded that Adam possessed three different grammatical classes, two of which resembled classes of adult English. There were nouns (*boot, tractor, truck, mommy, Adam, tower, gas*), verbs (*hear, see, make*), and a third class of 'modifiers' (*two* and *a* in the sentences above, plus adjectives, plus the words *this, that, other* and *'nother*). Adam's class of modifiers thus comprised several adult classes, but even his noun and verb classes failed to observe certain adult distinctions—for example, the difference between count (*boot*) and mass (*gas*) nouns.

Looking at Adam's sentences, an adult feels intuitively that they honour the basic grammatical relations of subject-predicate and verb-object. *Hear tractor* appears to be a verb and an object. *Adam make tower* appears to be a subject and a predicate, and the predicate in turn appears to be a verb and object. And so on. These intuitions are quite compelling, but of course they might also be quite wrong. Adam may not have intended these sentences in the way we interpret them. We need another means of examining Adam's speech that does not depend on our understanding of what he wanted to say.

One approach is based on the following calculations. With three grammatical classes, there are $(3)^2 = 9$ different two-word combinations, and $(3)^3 = 27$ different three-word combinations. If Adam were combining words at random, we should expect to find all (or nearly all) these nine and twenty-seven different combinations. However, they do not all honour the basic grammatical relations. Only four of the two-word combinations directly express one or another grammatical relation, and only eight of the three-word combinations do so. If Adam were attempting to use the basic grammatical relations from the first, he would restrict himself to these admissible patterns. That is exactly what he did. In eight hours of recorded speech, involving some 400 sentences, there were examples of every admissible combination but no examples of inadmissible ones.

It is not obvious that this should be the case on *a priori* grounds. Parental speech presents many examples of inadmissible combinations of Adam's grammatical classes. Take, for example, the combination, verb-verb-modifier. Because of the double verb, it does not express a grammatical relation, and sentences of this type—for example, *come eat this*—did not appear in Adam's early speech. But *come and eat this* is surely a common sentence-type in adult speech. It did not serve as a model for Adam because the adult sentence contains several transformations not yet part of Adam's grammatical competence. Lacking the appropriate transformations, there was no way for Adam to express the basic grammatical relations, so the sentence type did not appear.

Adam's restriction of the variety of sentence-types is one kind of evidence that children include abstract relations in their earliest speech. A second kind of evidence comes from a child acquiring a radically different language, Japanese.

Unlike English, Japanese is a postpositional language. Very roughly, postpositions correspond to English prepositions, but not all postpositions can be translated into prepositions, and conversely. Among the postpositions without an equivalent in English are two, *wa* and *ga*, that indicate the grammatical subject of sentences. According to the linguist S.-Y. Kuroda, *wa* and *ga* are carried into the surface structure by transformations that operate on the deep structure. In order for a child to acquire these transformations, therefore, the abstract relation of 'subject' must already be available. If it were not, a child would not be able to use *wa* or *ga* appropriately.

The child whose speech I have observed is a little girl living in Tokyo, who hears only Japanese and, at the time of writing, is two years old. In the interest of maintaining the tradition begun by Brown, I shall call her Izanami, after the goddess of Japanese mythology who helped create the world.

Izanami's sentences at this time are all two-, three-, and occasionally four-words long. She is, therefore, at the same stage as Adam, still within the earliest phase of grammatical development. In eight hours of recorded speech, there were one hundred occurrences of *ga*, but only six occurrences of *wa*. All Izanami's uses of *ga* were appropriate, and she rarely omitted the postposition when it was needed. Clearly Izanami can express the basic grammatical relation of 'subject' by means of the *ga*-transformation. Her earliest speech contains an abstract feature, as it must if a linguistic universal reflects an aspect of the fundamental capacity for language.

But what of *wa*? It is quite clear that Izanami does not know how to use it. Since she has the relation of 'subject' available to her, something must be blocking the *wa*-transformation itself. In parental speech, *wa* and *ga* appear in the same places, after the subject, so parental speech cannot explain the absence of *wa* from Izanami's grammar. Moreover, *wa* is used by Izanami's mother twice as often as *ga*, which if anything would favour the acquisition of *wa*. The explanation of *wa*'s absence seems to be the different uses to which *wa* and *ga* are put by Japanese grammar. Although both mark the subject of a sentence, their semantic implications are very different, and children do appear to be sensitive only to those embodied in *ga*.

The postposition *wa* is required whenever the predicate of a sentence is something attributed to the subject. It is the postposition for permanent conditions, the semantic significance of which is often translated in English by the expression 'as for . . .'; *as for this, it is a flower*, or *as for cats, they eat goldfish*. In such cases, the sentence presents an unchanging and 'inherent' connexion between the subject and the predicate.

The postposition *ga*, in contrast, is required whenever the subject of a sentence is merely linked to the predicate, the two standing in an *equal* and *temporary* relation. It is the postposition for momentary description, as in *a man is standing on the corner* or *the cat ate the goldfish*. In such cases, the sentence presents a fortuitious 'non-inherent' connexion between the subject and the predicate.

Therefore, children apparently attempt to express momentary description when employing the abstract relation of 'subject', not permanent connexions. This is a surprising result for several reasons.

One of the examples calling for *wa* above is a definition. In Japanese it would be, roughly, *this-wa is a flower*. We can be certain that Izanami understands sentences of this type in her mother's speech. They are the only way in which she receives new information and new vocabulary. Yet, *wa* does not appear in Izanami's grammar. Related to the use of *wa* in definitions is its use in describing stable relationships. One would say to a recalcitrant child, *people-wa eat their supper*. It is often assumed that children first develop grammar in an effort to *name* stable relationships in the physical world. Izanamı belies this hypothesis. In fact, on Izanamı's evidence, naming and grammatical development have nothing whatsoever to do with each other. All instances of appellation require *wa* in Japanese. Because Izanami, just as all children, names objects a great deal, her postposition would have to be *wa*, not *ga*, if there were a connexion between the acquisition of names and the acquisition of grammar. In fact, however, they are entirely independent.

Children exposed to English and children exposed to Japanese both include abstract grammatical relations in their earliest speech. To these children may be added a third child exposed to Russian. According to Dan I. Slobin (1966), here too, abstract grammatical relations appear in early speech. In spite of radical differences in the conditions of learning, therefore, children are found to do similar things. They do so because of their shared inborn capacity for language.

Acquiring a particular grammar

Our account of language acquisition is not yet complete. Ultimately, children do different things when the conditions of learning are different. Exposure to English does not lead to competence in Japanese! What has been left out of account is the acquisition of transformations. In considering this aspect of development, we shall see something of how a child brings his capacity for language into contact with the speech of his local community.

The general idea of a transformation is an instance of what Chomsky calls a 'formal' universal of language. Transformations appear in all languages, but the *particular* transformations of each language are peculiar to that language. Aside from sound, in fact, transformations are the main source of linguistic uniqueness.

How do children acquire transformations? Unfortunately, there is no definite answer. However, one view is that the process takes place in the same manner as scientific inference. On the basis of their capacity for language, children formulate hypotheses about regularities observed in parental speech. Each hypothesis is evaluated against further evidence, such as additional parental speech and parental reactions to a child's own speech. In pursuing this empirical programme, children may even perform linguistic experiments, the equivalent in most respects of the experiments conducted in scientific laboratories.

The experimental aspect is perhaps the most interesting, for it involves a symbiotic exchange between a child and his parent. Roger Brown (1964) has called attention to a common phenomenon in parent-child dialogues. Very often parents imitate children, and in so doing, enlarge a child's sentence into completely well-formed English. If a child says *doggie bite*, a parent may reply, *yes, he is biting*, adding the auxiliary verb, *is*, and the progressive inflection, *-ing*. Both additions exemplify details of English transformations, and do so within the context of the child's own speech. Brown calls this process 'expansion'. He finds that parents expand approximately 30 per cent of what two-year-old children say.

Expansions provide a natural experiment for a child. Suppose a child does say *doggie bite*. There are many possible expansions. In addition to *yes, he is biting*, an adult might say *he bit, he will bite, his biting* . . . and probably more. Each expansion holds constant the elements preserved in the child's sentence while varying a particular transformation, just as a real experiment holds some factors constant while varying others. Moreover, the observations in a real experiment are relevant to the hypothesis under test and the same is true in expansion. Suppose that context indicates to the parent that the child is talking about an event going on at the moment. The only possible expansion would then be *yes, he is biting*. If the child were in fact talking about this event as it occurred, and if he were looking for some way to express this idea, the expansion would provide relevant information.

There is one respect in which expansions and real experiments differ. An experimenter has some control over his observations, but a child does not. The child above may have meant that this dog always bites, in which event the expansion *yes, he is biting* would have provided mis-information. It is unlikely that this happens often. Presumably, one reason that adults do not expand more than 30 per cent of the time is that 70 per cent of the contexts are not clear, and so offer no guidance as to what a child means. Parents play safe with this powerful tool of science.

A capacity for language would contain a great deal more than the matters discussed in this article—the basic grammatical relations and the general idea of a transformation. It would certainly include, in addition, an ability to construct a dictionary of some kind as well as certain rules for using it. There are also universal phonetic principles, such as the stock of 'distinctive features' into which all speech sounds may be resolved, which probably correspond to a part of the capacity for language. There are probably universal principles whereby linguistic knowledge is converted into actual speaking or listening, although very little is known about this at the present time. (It is significant, nonetheless, that all children speak fluently, no matter how primitive their grammars may be.) All these things, plus still others not yet imagined, may make up the capacity for language, and may, therefore, contribute to the astonishing speed with which children acquire their native tongue.

However, the possibility is worth considering that very little of this is, in fact, a capacity for *language*. Much of what I have discussed may actually be the linguistic manifestation of a very general, though still inborn, cognitive capacity—cognition is the process by which the mind gets knowledge. If this is true, then the study of how language is acquired may provide insight into the very basis of mental life. For if the capacity for language is a special case of more general cognitive capacity, it would follow that the latter must have all the universal properties of the former. In short, the appropriate theory of mind may be a transformational system in which a vast range of complex ideas is converted into a much smaller range of abstract cognitive structures, just as a true grammar converts an infinite range of sentences into a limited number of abstract deep structures. Needless to say, the exploration of this possibility has only begun.

The basis for the rapid acquisition of language

Nonetheless, if for the moment we accept this view, the creation of language can be considered in a larger sense, speculating on an aspect of the evolution of language. Our speculations may shed some light on the basis of children's ability to acquire language in a very short period of time. The argument will be that language has come to mirror cognition through a long period of evolution which consisted of the addition of specific transformations—the rules that distinguish one language from another. The primaeval grammar may have been mainly free of transformations, just as systems of animal communication are free of transformations. It may have been a system in which the features now contained in the deep structure of sentences were very nearly all located in the surface structure. As such, it would have been very different from the cognitive system of primitive language users.

Moreover, if primaeval grammar was mostly free of transformation, it would need to have been very complex in order to have communicated a wide range of information. Without transformations to relate a large variety of surface structures to a limited number of abstract structures, all the different surface types must have been understood directly instead of indirectly through deep structures. A grammar of that degree of complexity would have taken many years to acquire. The suggestion, therefore, is this: specific transformations evolved in order to make acquisition of grammar possible at earlier ages. The pressure for evolution would have arisen from the need to·express great conceptual variety through economic means. The

consequence of evolution would have been a vast reduction in the complexity of language without loss of expressive power. In the end, the conceptual and linguistic systems would have been brought into alignment by making language abstract at precisely those points where cognition is abstract.

The innovators of such evolutionary change could only have been children attempting to acquire language. Adults had nothing to do with it. Language slowly became transformational because an occasional child reformulated the speech received from adults by inventing a transformation. This, of course, is what contemporary children do, too—invent transformations. The process of invention would be the same for children of the remote past as for children of today. The difference is that a contemporary child is presented with sentences that reflect the presence of transformations whereas a child of antiquity was not. But if the basic intellectual abilities of children in antiquity were roughly the same as now, this very fact —that transformed sentences signal the presence of transformations—explains how each innovation in the evolution of language could have been passed on to the next generation. The process of evolution would have been the process of language acquisition. Each new transformation would have slightly changed the corpus of speech that the innovator, now mature, presented to his progeny. His progeny then could have acquired the transformation in the usual manner, just as do contemporary children, and so language would have advanced.

The direction of evolution, according to the account just given, must have been toward simplicity. It was not toward complexity, as most theories of linguistic evolution have it. According to the present view, language changed from an extremely complex system, largely free of transformations and taking many years to acquire, to a much simpler system, rich in transformations and taking only a few years to acquire. Thus, the presence of transformations in contemporary language allows children to develop language with the great speed that they do. Indeed, transformations may have evolved precisely in order to enable every child as young as two to acquire a language—an achievement so commonplace that few people ever stop to question this remarkable act of creation.

References

Brown, R., and Bellugi, U. (1964). Three processes in the child's acquisition of syntax, *Harvard Educational Review* (1964) 34, 133–51; in Lenneberg, E. H. (ed.), *New directions in the study of language*. MIT Press, 131–61, reprinted here as chapter 19.

Brown, R., and Fraser, C. (1963). The acquisition of syntax, in Cofer, C. N., and Musgrave, B. S. (eds.), *Verbal behaviour and learning*. McGraw-Hill, 158–209.

Slobin, D. I. (1966). The acquisition of Russian as a native language, in Smith, F., and Miller, G. A. (eds.), *The genesis of language*. MIT Press, 129–48.

21 Development of the directive function of speech in early childhood

A. R. Luria

Along with the semantic and syntactic functions of speech, it is necessary to distinguish also its pragmatic or directive function. In the development of behavior this function manifests itself in the fact that a word gives rise to new temporary connexions in the brain and directs the system of activity of the child that has mastered it.

It was a full quarter of a century ago that the eminent Soviet psychologist, L. S. Vygotskij, pointed out the role played by the words of adults in the development of the child's mental processes and formulated his well-known thesis that what the child at first does with the help, and on the instructions, of the adult, he later begins to do by himself, supporting himself with his own speech; that speech as a form of communication with adults later becomes a means of organizing the child's own behavior, and that the function which was previously divided between two people later becomes an internal function of human behavior (Vygotskij, 1934, 1956). In the twenty-five years that have elapsed since Vygotskij's death the problem of the role of the word in the organization of mental life has been the subject of numerous Soviet investigations (Rozengardt, 1948; Ljublinskaja, 1955; Luria, 1955, 1956a, 1958; Kol'cova, 1958; and many others).

There arises, however, the question of how this pragmatic, directive function of the word is formed, and how its formation relates to the formation of the significative or generalizing functions of the word. A brief review of the pertinent experiments forms the topic of the present communication.

I

A child at the beginning of its second year of life is already in command of a considerable number of words. He understands such expressions as *cup*, *cat*, *fish*, *horse*, and can without difficulty hand someone the

object if it is mentioned. But is the pragmatic, directive function of speech at this stage as effective as its significative, nominative function? Can the cited word always direct the child's activity with full effectiveness?

An answer to this question is suggested by the experiments which we have carried out in collaboration with A. G. Poljakova.

Before a child aged 1; 2 to 1; 4, we placed some object, e.g., a toy *fish*, and asked him to hand it to us; the child did this without particular difficulty. We then asked him, in the same situation, to hand us the *cat*. The child at first looked at us in disbelief, then began to look around until he found the object which had been named. It would seem that the adult word fully determined the child's action.

Let us, however, repeat this experiment in a somewhat more complicated situation. Let us place before the child two objects: a toy *fish* at some distance from it, and half way toward the fish a brightly colored toy *cat*. If in this situation we ask a child of 1; 0 to 1; 2 to hand us the *fish*, his behavior will be different. The uttered word will evoke in him an orientational reaction, and his glance will be fixed on the fish; but his hand, stretched out toward the fish, will stop half way, turn toward the cat, and instead of giving us the fish that was requested, the child will grasp the *cat* and offer it to the experimenter. The directive function of the word will be maintained only up to the moment when it comes into conflict with the conditions of the external situation. While the word easily directs behavior in a situation that lacks conflict, it loses its directive role if the immediate orientational reaction is evoked by a more closely located, or brighter, or more interesting object.

It is only at the age of 1; 4 to 1; 6 that this phenomenon disappears and the selective effect of words is maintained even in conditions in which the components of the situation conflict with it.

We can easily disturb the directive function of the

Source: The directive function of speech in development and dissolution, part I, *Word* (1959), 15 (3), 341–52.

word in still another way. It is known that the word physiologically excites a certain system of connexions in the cortex. In the normal, mature nervous system these connexions possess considerable mobility and easily replace each other. As has been shown in many investigations (see Luria, 1956b, 1958; Homskaja, 1958), the mobility of the connexions evoked by the word (or, as I. P. Pavlov called it, by the second signal system of reality), is even greater than the mobility of connexions evoked by immediate signals.

However, the mobility of nervous processes in a very small child is still quite inadequate, and connexions evoked by the word possess a considerable inertia at the early stages of development. Taking this inadequacy of the mobility of connexions in the early stages of development as a premise, we can measure the effectiveness of the directive function of the word.

We place before a child of 1;0 to 1;2 two toys: a fish and a horse, this time placing them at the same distance and giving them dimensions and colors that are equally attractive. We ask the child to give us the *fish*: he does this easily. We repeat this experiment three or four times, and the effect remains the same. In exactly the same tone of voice, we now utter a different instruction and ask the child to hand us the *horse*. Despite the fact that the meaning of this word is well known to the child, the inertia of the connexions evoked by the first word is so great that in many cases the child again offers the experimenter the fish. The directive function of the changed verbal instructions is here vitiated by the inertia of the connexion that has been established.[1]

The loss of the directive function of a word whose meaning is well known can also be observed in an experiment involving actions designated by verbs. If we give a child of 1;2 to 1;4 a stick on which rings are placed and we instruct him, 'Put on the ring', he does this easily. With equal ease he will, in another situation, execute the instruction, 'Take off the ring'. However, if the child has several times *put on* a ring and is holding the next ring in his hands, the instruction '*Take off* the ring' loses its directive meaning and begins to function non-specifically, merely accelerating the activity of *putting on* the ring onto the stick (Poljakova's and Ljamina's experiment).

The directive role of the word at an early age is maintained only if the word does not conflict with the inert connexions which arose at an earlier instruction or which began with the child's own activity.

II

Experimental research can do more than ascertain the bare fact that the directive role of words is not fully effective at an early age. Such research can also *measure* the relative effectiveness of verbal signals as compared to the directive role of immediate, visual signals. In order to make this comparison as vivid as possible, we pass on to some experiments with somewhat older children—aged from 1;4 to 1;6 on the one hand, and from 1;8 to 2;0 on the other hand.

Let us first establish how effective the orienting (attention-directing) and directive role of a visual signal and its trace can be at this stage. We place before a child two inverted objects, a cup and a tumbler of non-transparent plastic. As the child watches, we hide a coin under the cup, which is placed to the left, and we ask the child to 'find' it. For a child of 1;4 to 1;6, this constitutes an interesting and meaningful task, which he solves without difficulty. We repeat this experiment three or four times, each time holding the coin under the cup within sight of the child. The solution will invariably be successful. Now, without interrupting the experiment, we change its conditions and hide the coin not under the cup on the left, but under the tumbler on the right. A certain proportion of children of the younger group will follow not the changed visual signal (more precisely, its trace), but the *influence of the inert motor stereotype*, and will put out their hands toward the cup on the left, carrying out the habitual movement reinforced in the previous experiment; only then will they turn to the tumbler under which the coin is hidden.

Let us now weaken the influence of the visual signal. We repeat the first experiment, but impose a short, ten-second delay between the hiding of the coin under the cup and the execution of the movement. This forces the child to act according to the *traces* of the visual signal whose effectiveness we are considering. The majority of children in the younger group successfully execute this task; only a few, the very youngest, cease to subordinate their actions to the visual instruction and begin to grasp both objects, losing track of the task of finding the coin that is hidden under one of them.

However, we again modify the conditions and after repeating the experiment three of four times with the cup and the ten-second delay we hide the coin under the tumbler located on the right, all within sight of the child. The picture now changes substantially. The ten-second delay turns out to be sufficient for the visual signal to yield its place to the decisive influence of the reinforced motor habit. The overwhelming majority of children now repeat the movement directed toward the cup on the left, ceasing to be directed by the image of the coin hidden under the tumbler on the right.

This orienting, directive influence of the visual signal is maintained better among children of the older group (1;8 to 2;0). Even when the execution of the movement is delayed, they solve the task well, directing their search to the object under which they saw the coin being hidden. This means that the orienting, directive role of the visual image becomes so effective at the end of the second year of life that the child submits to it completely, and successfully overcomes the inertia of the motor connexions which have arisen.

A completely different picture appears in those cases where we replace the immediate, visual signals by verbal ones. For this purpose we again place before the child the two above-mentioned objects, a cup and a tumbler, but this time unseen by the child, we slip the coin under the left-hand cup. In order to orient, i.e., to direct the actions of the child, we now draw upon a word rather than a visual image. We tell the child: 'The coin is under the cup . . . Find the coin!' This instruction attunes the child completely and the game continues, but its results turn out to be profoundly different. While the trace of an immediate visual impression caused all children of the younger group to reach with assurance for the cup under which they saw the coin being hidden, the verbal instruction turns out to be wholly insufficient for this directive role: a considerable proportion of the children of this age lose track of the task and begin to grasp *both* objects before them. When we repeated the experiment with a ten-second delay in the execution of the action, this loss of directed activity among the children of the younger group was almost universal.

We then returned to the experiments with the immediate (non-delayed) execution of the action. When we reinforced the required reaction by repeating the instructions several times, 'The coin is under the cup . . . Find the coin!', the children of the younger group turned out to be capable of executing it in an organized way: the word achieved the required directive function, and the children reached for the object named. However, if we altered the verbal instruction and, without changing the intonation, said, 'Now the coin is under the tumbler . . . Find it!', only an insignificant proportion of the children changed their movements, while the great majority repeated their previous movement. When a ten-second delay was imposed on the execution of the task, all the children of the younger group failed to let their action follow the changed verbal instruction; they continued to execute the stereotyped movement that had been reinforced in the previous experiment and, as before, turned to the cup on the left.

The children of the older group (1;8 to 2 years), who solved these tasks with uniform success when the directive role was played by a visual signal (in experiments with delayed as well as with immediate execution), turned out to lag behind when they had to execute the task according to verbal instructions. They did carry out both tasks well if they were allowed to make the necessary movement immediately; then they would turn to the cup after the instruction 'The coin is under the cup . . . Find the coin!' and to the tumbler if the instruction was 'The coin is under the tumbler . . . Find the coin!' However, it was enough to delay the execution of the instructions by ten seconds for this orienting, directive role of the verbal instruction to be insufficiently effective. After three repetitions of the experiment with the instruction 'The coin is under the cup . . . Find the coin!' the transition to another command—'The coin is under the tumbler . . . Find the coin!'—deprived the verbal instruction of its directive role, and the child continued inertly to execute the former habitual movement. In these cases the kinesthetic stereotype which had been worked out earlier overcame the insufficiently established effect of the word.

A comparative analysis of the orienting or directive functions of visual and verbal signals allows us to see how late the directive role of the word is formed in early childhood.

III

While the directive function of straightforward, 'deictic' speech is already formed around the age of two, the kind of speech that involves more complicated preliminary connexions—connexions which precede the action and organize it in advance—acquires a regulative function considerably later, and its development occupies the entire third and partly the fourth year of life.

This time let us turn to a child with a more complicated, involved instruction. 'When the light flashes, you will press the ball (rubber bulb)' or ' . . . you will raise your hand'. Such a verbal instruction, formulated this time in a syntactically complex, 'conditional' *sentence*, does not require any immediate realization of an action. It must close a preliminary verbal connexion, giving to the appearance of a stimulus ('light') a conditional meaning of the signal for action ('you will press the ball'). The directive role is played here not by a separate word, but by a relation, a synthesis of words entering into a sentence; instead of an immediate, 'triggering' role it acquires a preliminary, conditional, 'pre-triggering' function.

It has been shown experimentally (Jakovleva, 1958; Tikhomirov, 1958) that the possibility of establishing such a pre-triggering system of connexions on the basis of speech—not to speak of the possibility of subordinating further conditional reactions to it—is something unattainable for a child of two to two and a half years, and sometimes even for a three-year-old child.

The younger children of this group (1;10 to 2 years) appear unable to realize that synthesis of separate elements which is required by the instruction formulated in the sentence. Each individual word contained in the sentence evokes in the child an immediate orienting reaction, and as soon as he hears the beginning of the sentence, 'When the light flashes . . .', the child begins to look for the light with its eyes; when he hears the end of the sentence—'. . . you will press the ball'—he immediately presses the device in his hand. At this stage the separate words have already acquired an effective triggering function, but the creation, by means of words, of a preliminary pre-triggering system of connexions, which requires the inhibition of immediate reactions and their separation into individual fragments, turns out to be unattainable. This is why the actual presentation of a light signal—the flash of light—does not at this stage lead to a conditioned movement, and evokes only an immediate orienting reaction: the child begins simply to inspect the light, which has not yet become for him a conditional signal for the pressing of the ball.

It would, however, be incorrect to believe that the formation of this more complex form of directive speech—the closing of conditional, pre-triggering connexions—depends entirely on the ability to relate words which comprise a sentence, i.e., to do the work of synthesizing the elements of a sentence into a single system. Even when a child, some time later, is able to do this synthesizing work and begins to 'understand' the meaning of the whole sentence well, the effective directive role of the sentence can still remain absent for a long time.

Let us adduce the experiments which demonstrate this interesting fact.

We present a child at the end of the third year of his life (2;8 to 2;10) with an instruction of this kind, and we see a picture which differs basically from the one that we have just described. A child at this age will as a rule make the required connexion without particular difficulty, and when the light flashes he will press the ball; however, he will be unable to stop the movements which have been triggered by speech and he will very soon begin to press the ball regardless of the signal, continuing involuntarily to repeat the previous movements. Even the repetition of the instruction or the reinforcement of the inhibitory link which is hidden in it—even the request to 'Press *only* when the light flashes' and '*Not to press* when there is no light'—all this turns out to be powerless to stop the motor excitation that has begun; on the contrary, this excitation is sometimes even *reinforced* by the inhibitory instruction, which in the given case turns out still to lack its inhibitory meaning and continues to act *non-specifically*, only strengthening the dominant motor response.

While speech at this time has already acquired an effective connexion-closing triggering function, it has thus not yet acquired an affective inhibitory role.

This weakness of the inhibitory function of speech, as was shown by the observations of Tikhomirov (1958), can be seen most vividly by means of special experiments. Let us complicate the instruction described above and present it to a child of three to three and a half years. We will ask it to *press* the ball every time a *red* light goes on, and *not to press it* when a *blue* light goes on; in other words, we will place the child in circumstances in which speech requires a complex *selective* reaction—positive with respect to one signal (red) and inhibitory with respect to another (blue). We let the child repeat the instruction and we are persuaded that all the information included in the sentence has reached him and is retained. Does this mean that it also possesses an effective directive role?

The experiment shows that this practical correspondence between the semantic meaning of the sentence and its directive role does not appear for a long time. Having understood the meaning of the instruction and repeating it correctly, the child is practically unable to execute it: the excitation provoked by the signal turns out to be so considerable and diffuse that after only a few attempts the blue signal, too, begins to evoke in the child impulsive motor responses. At first he attempts to control them but later, as his excitement grows while the directive function of the inhibitory verbal instruction weakens, he begins to perform the movements without any restraint.

In clashing with the inert excitation evoked by a positive signal, the inhibitory link in the verbal instruction is crushed. At first the child retains the entire instruction, but though he repeats it correctly, he is nevertheless unable to subordinate his actions to it. It is not uncommon for the inert excitation evoked by the positive part of the instruction to become so overwhelming that, under the influence of his own impulsive reaction, the child loses the inhibitory link contained in the verbal signal and begins to assure the experimenter that the instruction required him to press the ball in response to both signals presented to him.

Thus the insufficient mobility of the child's neurodynamics at first destroys the directive role of the verbal instruction, and later distorts the entire system of links contained in it.

IV

The question now arises: Can we reinforce the regulating function of verbal connexions, and if so, how can this be done most effectively? The solution of this question may bring us closer to the description of certain mechanisms of the directive function of speech.

The experiments carried out by Paramonova (1956) showed that there are very simple means for heightening the directive influence of speech when the effect of the traces of a verbal instruction turn out to be insufficient.

Let us carry out an experiment of the kind already described with a three-year-old child. We ask him to press a ball in response to every *red* signal and to refrain from pressing it in response to every *blue* one. We introduce only one change into this experiment: we accompany each flash of the red light with the direct command 'Press!' and every flash of the blue lamp with a similar command, 'Don't press!' If such plainly directed speech is introduced, it allows the child quickly to work out a fairly effective system of selective reactions. What could not be attained through *preliminary* connexions evoked by a verbal instruction turns out to be easily attainable if we draw upon the *immediate* influence of verbal commands. In direct speech, the directive function has been fairly effectively established; its influence is therefore capable of concentrating the course of nervous processes and of producing a differentiated habit.

In the experiments just described we drew upon the

directive function of verbal commands in order to make more precise the influence of verbal instructions and to secure the organized course of the child's motor responses. Could we not, however, for this purpose draw upon the *child's own speech* and have it support the traces of the verbal instruction, which weaken relatively fast? After all, as L. S. Vygotskij has already shown, the function which at first is distributed between two people can easily turn into an internal psychological system, and what a child today does with help, he will tomorrow be able to do on his own. The investigation of the *directive possibilities of the child's own speech* can uncover a new and essential side of his linguistic development.

We repeat the experiment described, but introduce some substantial changes. In order to make it easier for the child to carry out his task correctly, we ask him *to give himself supplementary verbal commands*, accompanying each appearance of a red signal with the word 'Press!', and the appearance of each blue signal with the words 'Don't press!' Will this utilization of the child's own commands reinforce the action of the verbal instruction and strengthen its directive role?

The experiment shows that it is not so simple to obtain a directive influence from the child's own speech, and that over the first years of life the directive role of the child's own speech undergoes a complex course of development.

Let us begin with children of two to two and a half years and simplify our experiment for this purpose. We ask the child to respond to each flash of the red light by pressing the ball; but in order to remove those excessive movements which, as we have indicated above, are not subject to the control of an inhibitory instruction, we ask the child to accompany each motor reaction with the word 'Press!' (or even with something easier to pronounce, such as 'Now!' to, which we assign the meaning of a self-command). The experiments of S. V. Jakovleva (1958) have shown that the active speech of a child at this age is so insufficiently developed, and the underlying neurodynamics so inert, that the child of two to two and a half years of age still finds difficulty in coordinating his verbal commands with the signal and frequently begins to utter excessive, stereotyped commands. It is significant that even if the child succeeds and begins to say 'Press!' (or 'Now!') only when the signal appears, his entire energy is diverted to the utterance of this word, and the motor reaction which is supposed to be associated with it becomes extinct. The child at this age cannot yet create a *system* of neural processes that includes both verbal and motor links, and the word does not play any directive role.

As O. K. Tikhomirov's experiments (1958) showed, it is only at three years of age that the neurodynamics which underlie the speech processes are sufficiently mobile for the child to time his own verbal command with the signal and for the command to exert a directive influence on the motor response as it becomes a mobile link in a unified system with it. While the child is unable to control his excessive, diffuse pressings of the ball according to the preliminary instruction, he easily achieves this control when he begins to give himself the commands 'Press!' and 'Don't press!' In concentrating the diffuse excitation, the child's own verbal responses, functioning on a feedback principle, here acquire their directive function.

However, is this directive function of the child's own speech full-fledged? Control experiments have answered this question in the negative and have permitted us to see more deeply into the mechanisms of the early forms of the directive function of speech.

Let us return again to the more complicated experiment described above. We present a child of three to three and a half years with the instruction to press a ball every time a red light flashes and to refrain from pressing it when there is a blue flash, but we give him the possibility of accompanying each red signal with his affirmative command 'Press!' and every blue signal with his own inhibitory command, 'Don't press!' Does the directive role of the child's *inhibitory* verbal response have the same, full value as his *positive* verbal response?

The experiments which have been conducted for this purpose have disclosed some very substantial peculiarities of the regulating effect of the child's own speech. The verbal responses 'Press' and 'Don't press' turn out to have a complex structure. Physiologically they are, first of all, motor responses of the speech apparatus and are thus always connected with the positive phase of an innervation. But in virtue of their *meanings* they are systems of connexions which, in the former case, have a positive, and in the latter case, an inhibitory signal value. Which side of the child's own speech—the motor ('impulsive') or semantic ('selective') side—here influences the motor processes and acquires the directive role?

The experiments of O. K. Tikhomirov yield an answer to this question. A child of three to three and a half years easily responds to each light signal with the required word, but in uttering the command 'Don't press' in response to the blue signal, he not only fails to restrain his motor responses, but *presses the ball even harder*. Consequently, the child's own verbal reaction 'Don't press' exerts its influence not in its semantic aspect, i.e., not by the selective connexions which are behind it, but by its immediate 'impulsive' impact. This is why the directive influence of a child's own speech at this stage still has a non-selective, non-specific character.

At least one more year must pass before the directive role goes over to the selective system of semantic connexions which are behind the word, and—as Tikhomirov has observed—it is only at the age of four to four and a half years that the verbal response 'Don't press' actually acquires the inhibitory effect specific to speech.

However, for this stage of development one circumstance is typical: as soon as the directive role passes to the semantic aspect of speech and that aspect becomes dominant, external speech becomes superfluous. The directive role is taken over by those inner connexions which lie behind the word, and they now begin to display their selective effect in directing the further motor responses of the child.

The development of the pragmatic, directive aspect of speech constitutes a new chapter in psychology and psycholinguistics. It still has almost no facts to operate with that are derived from systematic investigation. However, by establishing the fact that by no means all the information carried by speech *ipso facto* acquires a directive value in determining human behavior, and by investigating the formation patterns of this directive role of speech, this chapter has already opened important new vistas for the scientific investigation of the organization of human behavior.

Note

1 In a number of cases such an experiment may not give the desired results. This happens when the dominant role in the child's behavior continues to be played by the *immediate orientational response to objects*. In such cases the child will alternately hand the experimenter now this object, now the other, and the directive function of speech will fail to be exercised from the start.

References

Homskaja, E. D. (1958). An investigation of the influence of speech responses on motor responses in children with cerebroasthenia (in Russian), in Luria (1958), 131–259.

Jakovleva, S. V. (1958). Conditions of formation of the simplest types of voluntary movement in children of pre-school age (in Russian) in Luria (1958), 47–71.

Kol'cova, M. M. (1958). *O formirovanii vysšej nervnoj dejatel'nosti rebënka* [On the formation of the child's higher neural activity]. Leningrad.

Ljublinskaja, A. A. (1955). *Rol' jazyka v umstvennom rezvitii rebënka* [The role of language in the mental development of the child] (= Leningradskij Pedagogičeskij Institut im. Gercena, *Učenye zapiski*, **112**).

Luria, A. R. (1955). The role of the word in the formation of temporary connexions in man (in Russian), *Voprosy psikhologii*, **1**, 73–86.

Luria, A. R. (1956a). On the directive role of speech in the formation of voluntary movements (in Russian), *Žurnal vysšej nervnoj dejatel'nosti*, **6**, no. 5, 645–62.

Luria, A. R., ed. (1956b, 1958). *Problemy vysšej dejatel'nosti rebënka* [Problems of the higher neural activity of the child], I and II. Moscow.

Luria, A. R., and F. Ia. Yudovich (1958). *Reč'i razvitie psikhičeskikh processov rebënka*. Moscow. English version: *Speech and the development of mental processes in the child*. London: Penguin 1959.

Paramonova, N. P. (1956). On the formation of interactions between the two signal systems in the normal child (in Russian) in Luria (1956b), 18–83.

Rozengardt-Pupko, T. L. (1948). *Reč'i razvitie vosprijatija v rannem detstve* [Speech and the development of perception in early childhood]. Moscow.

Tikhomirov, O. K. (1958). On the formation of voluntary movements in children of pre-school age (in Russian) in Luria (1958), 72–130.

Vygotskij, L. S. (1934). *Myšlenie i reč'* [Thought and Language]. Moscow.

Vygotskij, L. S. (1956). *Izbrannye psikhologičeskie issledovanija* [Selected Psychological Studies]. Moscow.

22 Developmental psycholinguistics
H. Sinclair-de-Zwart

One of the questions a Genevan psycholinguist who works with Jean Piaget hears often is: how does language figure in Piaget's theory? Does his theory of cognitive development provide a framework for the acquisition of language? Does he have an epistemology of language? It is difficult to answer these questions in a straightforward manner; the more so, since the few articles Piaget himself has written on language are almost uniquely concerned with the problem of language as a factor in development, and may seem to be written almost reluctantly (one of them starts off 'il aurait fallu me poser cette question à une epoque ou. . . .') (1963); his very early work, *Le langage et la pensée chez l'enfant* (1923) concerns far more 'la pensée' than 'le langage'. On the other hand, it is quite wrong to assert, as many authors do, that Piaget leaves language completely outside his considerations, and that, in fact, his experiments may lose some of their meaning because of this refusal to consider language as a separate, important variable.

To live with, or rather in, Piaget's theories for a number of years may have curious effects on a psycholinguist: from an initial irritation at the rather offhand manner in which language is dealt with in many of Piaget's works and in much of his experimentation, one reaches the conviction that spread over a number of works, Piaget has in fact provided the bases for a general theory of both language-acquisition and of the role of language as a factor of development. However this may be, the following is an attempt to explain and elaborate Piaget's views on language. These views will be presented in two contexts: language viewed as a factor in cognitive development, and as a possible theory of language-acquisition.

Source: excerpt from H. Sinclair-de-Zwart, Developmental psycholinguistics, *Studies in Cognitive Development* ed. D. Elkind and J. Flavell, Oxford University Press (1969), 315–25, reprinted in *Language and Thinking* ed. Parveen Adams, Penguin (1972), 366–76.

Piaget's conception of the role of language in cognitive development

In several articles Piaget has been most explicit on this relationship between language and intellectual operations. The two main points that recur in his writings on the subject are the following:

1 The sources of intellectual operations are not to be found in language, but in the preverbal, sensorimotor period where a system of schemes is elaborated that prefigures certain aspects of the structures of classes and relations, and elementary forms of conservation and operative reversibility. In fact, the acquisition of the permanency of objects (elaborated between 6 and 18 months) constitutes a first 'invariant'. The search for an object which has disappeared is conducted in function of its successive localizations: these localizations depend on the constitution of an elementary *groupe de déplacements*, in which detours (associativity) and returns (reversibility) are coordinated.

2 The formation of representational thought is contemporaneous with the acquisition of language; both belong to a more general process, that of the constitution of the symbolic function in general. This symbolic function has several aspects; different kinds of behaviors, all appearing at about the same time in development, indicate its beginnings. The first verbal utterances are intimately linked to, and contemporaneous with, symbolic play, deferred imitation, and mental images as interiorized imitations.

The first point is elaborated in many works by Piaget and his co-workers (Inhelder in particular). Intellectual operations are actions that have become interiorized and reversible, but they are still actions. The coordination and decentrations of sensorimotor activity are not limited to this first period of life, but are found, in a different form, at work in the constitution of operational intelligence as well. And, as Piaget frequently remarks (1963, p.72), they are also found in linguistic acts. This may account for a partial isomorphism between language and logic. It is important to bear in mind that already in the sensorimotor period object-permanency is a general acquisition. It would be a contradiction in terms to speak of one specific operation, since an operation is always part of a structured whole, of a system of operations; but in the same way, object-permanency is not to be understood as the permanency of one or of some objects (a toy, the baby's bottle) but of objects in general. Similarly, the *groupe de déplacements* does not mean that the baby can make one specific detour, or return to his starting point in one particular case: these first prefigurations of associativity and reversibility are, again, general. Thought has its roots in action; at the end of the sensorimotor period, and before the appearance of language or of the symbolic function in general, the baby has overcome his initial perceptive and motor egocentrism by a series of decentrations and co-ordinations. The construction of operations demands a new series of decentrations; not only from the momentary, present perceptive centration, but also from the totality of the actions of the subject.

As regards the second point, Piaget has devoted a whole work to *La formation du symbole chez l'enfant* (1946). This important work cannot be summarized in a few pages, but the main concepts bearing on the role of language in the development of thought may be expressed as follows.

At the end of the sensorimotor period the first decentrations appear in the child's dealings with his *hic-et-nunc* (here and now) environment; action-schemata appear that permit the child to attain his practical aims, which are limited to the immediate present and to the manipulation of concrete objects within his reach. These spatio-temporal restrictions will slowly disappear with the development of thought. Moreover, the activity of the baby is directed toward success in his manipulations (from the cognitive point of view) and toward personal satisfaction (from the affective point of view). Later on, his activity takes on another dimension: cognitively, immediate success will no longer be the sole aim, but he will search for explanations and will reflect on his own actions; affectively, he will seek not only satisfaction, but also communication; he will want to tell other people about his discoveries, that now become *knowledge of* objects and events rather than *reactions to* objects and events.

One might be tempted to regard language, in the sense of learning to speak one's mother tongue through contact with the persons in one's environment, as the sole or main instrument that causes this transformation. Piaget, however, shows clearly that language is only a symptom and not the source of this change. Retracing the development step by step through careful observation of his own children, he demonstrates that language, despite the fact that later on it becomes most pervasive and takes on the guise of an autonomous capacity, is only part of the symbolic function. The symbolic function can be defined essentially as the capacity to represent reality through the intermediary of signifiers that are distinct from what they signify. The important term in this definition is the word *distinct*. In fact, around six months of age the baby already is capable of treating a partial perceptive datum as an indication of the presence of the whole; even if only a bit of the object is visible, it indicates the presence of the object. But such signals are directly linked to the objects, or are part of the object, whereas distinct signifiers imply a differentiation between signifier and signified, *introduced by the subject himself*. Signals (like the tracks an animal leaves in the snow, or the smell of food, or visible bits of partially hidden objects) are temporally and spatially restricted; the most distinct signifiers (words, algebraic symbols, and such) are free from such restrictions. Using a slightly different terminology, the linguist Bally said that the signal is a signifier only for whoever interprets it; and that a sign (distinct signifier) is a 'voluntary act', and also meaningful for whoever uses it.

The child who pushes a small shell along the edge of a box saying 'meow' knows full well that the shell is not a cat and the edge of the box is not a fence. And even if for the child the words 'meow' or 'cat' are at first somehow inherent in the animal, they are signifiers, and certainly not the animal itself. Piaget introduces a dichotomy in the distinct signifiers themselves:

1 Symbols, which like the shell have a link of resemblance with the object or event.
2 Signs (words), which are arbitrary.

Symbols, moreover, are usually personal; every child invents them in his play, whereas signs are social. Finally, we may add, symbols are mostly isolated, though within the context of symbolic play they may be loosely associated; signs on the other hand form systems.

According to Piaget, this capacity to represent reality by distinct signifiers has its roots in imitation, which starts very early in the sensorimotor period (around six months of age) and which already constitutes some sort of representation by action. At the end of the sensorimotor period imitation becomes possible in the absence of the model, and evolves from a direct sensorimotor model to gesticulative evocation. First one sees action-schemes appear out of their proper context as representations (for instance, pretending to be asleep); then these representations become detached from the activity of the subject (for instance, putting a doll to sleep). Slowly these deferred imitations become interiorized, and constitute sketchy images, which the child can already use to anticipate future acts. Piaget gives several examples of these action-imitations that announce interiorization: when L. tries to open a box of matches (which is not quite shut), she first manipulates it, but without result; then she stops acting, seems to reflect on the problem and opens and shuts her mouth, several times in succession: she uses a motor-signifier to represent the problem and to find a way of solving it. After this short period of 'reflection' she pushes her finger into the small opening and pulls to open the box completely.

A wealth of such observations throws light on the development of the symbolizing capacity, which has many different aspects that are at first inextricably linked in observable behavior. Small children pass extremely swiftly from what looks like pure imitation to symbolic play and to acts of practical intelligence accompanied by words (or onomatopoaeia), but at first these different aspects cannot even be distinguished. Language as seen by Piaget is thus part of a much larger complex of processes that go on during the second year of life; it has the same roots, and in the beginning the same function as symbolic play, deferred imitation, and mental images; it does not appear 'from nothing' (nor simply from early, prelinguistic vocalizations) but partakes of the entire cognitive development in this crucial period. It is, of course, just as closely linked to affective development; but this aspect of the question has been frequently dealt with by other authors, and the aim of this paper is restricted to the relationship between language and intellectual operations.

In summary, Piaget considers language not to be a sufficient condition for the constitution of intellectual operations, and he has said so, explicitly, in several articles (1954, 1961, 1962, 1963, 1965, Piaget and Inhelder, 1966). As to the question of whether language (in the sense of the normal acquisition of natural language by the young child) is, if not a sufficient, all the same a necessary condition for the constitution of operations, Piaget leaves the question open as regards the operations of formal logic. He notes (1963, p.58) however, that these operations go beyond language, in the sense that neither the lattice of possible combinations nor the group of four transformations is as such present in language; they cannot even be expressed in ordinary, natural language. As regards concrete operations, Piaget considers language (again, in the limited sense) not even a necessary condition for their constitution, though he has not explicitly said so. However, he does state:

> the sensorimotor schemata seem to be of a fundamental importance from their very first beginnings; these schemes continue to develop and structure thought, even verbal thought, as action progresses, up till the constitution of logico-mathematical operations, which are the authentic end-product of coordinated action-logic, when the latter can be interiorized and combined into group structures (1965).

Moreover, as regards concrete operations, Piaget quotes experiments with deaf-mute children, which clearly seem to point to the fact that the symbolic function is an obvious necessity for the constitution

of these operations, but that the normal acquisition of a natural language is not. A brief summary of experimental data pertaining to the relationship between language and thought can be given and two different kinds of experiments can be distinguished.

1   The comparison of the reactions of normal children to Piaget-type tests with those of deaf-mute children on the one hand, and blind children on the other. The deaf-mutes have intact sensorimotor schemes, but have not acquired spoken language (or are only at the beginning of an 'oral' education), whereas the blind are in the inverse situation. Studies of deaf children have been made by Oléron (1957) and Furth (1966) among others. Their results concur fundamentally, and indicate that deaf children acquire the elementary logical operations with only a slight retardation as compared to normal children. The same stages of development are found as the ones established by Piaget on a normal population. Both Oléron and Furth point out some differences in the reactions of their deaf subjects (particularly in the conservation of liquids). In the case of the conservation of liquids, however, certain difficulties in the presentation of the tests may account for these differences (e.g. in the pouring of liquids, the distinction between the quantity of liquid and the volume of the container is difficult to convey).

Furth notes an interesting difference in the comparative performance of deaf and hearing on 'logical symbol discovery' versus 'symbol use' tasks. While the deaf are inferior to the hearing on the former, they show equal ability on the use of logical symbols in a structured task. Furth points to several factors that could explain the results: among others, a different approach on the part of the deaf towards problems that call for invention, which may be due to a general lack of social contact. Oléron finds that seriation-tests are only very slightly retarded; that spatial operations are normal, and that classifications possess the same general structures and appear at the same age as with normals, but seem slightly less mobile or flexible (when classificatory criteria have to be changed). Here again, the cause may be more due to a general lack of social exchange and stimulation than to operational retardation.

These results with deaf children are all the more striking when it is considered that the same tests are only solved by blind children, on the average, four years later than by normal. The sensorial deficit of the blind has retarded the constitution of sensorimotor schemes and inhibited their co-ordination. The verbal acquisitions cannot compensate for this retardation, and action-learning is necessary before blind children reach an operational level comparable to that of the normal and the deaf (Hatwell, 1960).

2   A second group of experiments, directly bearing on the relationship between language and intellectual operations has been carried out in Geneva by Inhelder in collaboration with the author. These experiments

have been described in detail elsewhere (Sinclair-de-Zwart, 1967), and in this paper we shall do no more than briefly indicate their technique and summarize the results. Our aims were twofold: (a) to see whether the profound modification that occurs in the child's thinking with the constitution of the first concrete operations is paralleled by a linguistic development; (b) if the answer to (a) were in the affirmative, to determine whether a child who still lacks a certain concept or operation would show operatory progress after having undergone verbal training aiming to make him acquire expressions used by children who already possess the concept in question.

Consequently, we first chose some Piagetian tasks (conservation of liquids and seriation) that call for understanding and using certain expressions (quantitative and dimensional terms and comparatives). We explored the child's verbal capacities in this domain by first asking him to describe simple situations (which do not touch upon conservation or seriation problems: e.g. we present the child with two dolls, to one of whom we give four big marbles and to the other two small marbles, and we ask: 'Is this fair? Are both dolls happy? Why not?' Or we ask him to tell us the difference between two pencils, e.g. a short thick one and a long thin one). After this exploration of the child's use of certain expressions, we studied his comprehension, by asking him to execute orders couched in 'adult' but simple terms (e.g. 'give more plasticine to the boy than to the girl'; 'find a pencil that is shorter but thicker than this one').

After dividing our subjects into three groups according to their results on the Piagetian conservation task (total absence of conservation, intermediary stage, and conservation present), we compared their answers in the verbal task. The results can be summarized as follows:

(a) No difference was found among the three groups in the comprehension tasks; in fact, almost all subjects executed all orders correctly; only a very few young children (four years old) had some difficulties in questions of the type: 'Find a pencil that is longer but thinner.'
(b) Striking differences were found between the two extreme groups (no conservation at all and conservation acquired) as regards the description tasks.

Of the children with conservation, 70 per cent used comparatives (without adjectives) for the description of different quantities of plasticine, and 100 per cent did so for the description of different numbers of marbles: *le garçon a plus que la fille* (the boy has more than the girl).

Of children without conservation, 90 per cent used absolute terms (in contrast to comparatives): *le garçon a beaucoup, la fille a peu* (the boy has a lot, the girl has a little).

An interesting point was that 20 per cent already used comparatives for discrete units (marbles) whereas they did not do so for continuous quantities (plasticine); and the conservation of discrete units is acquired before that of continuous quantities.

Of the children with conservation, 100 per cent used different terms for different dimensions, using two couples of opposites (e.g. *grand/petit, gros/mince,* big/little, fat/thin).

Of children without conservation, 75 per cent used undifferentiated terms for the two dimensions, i.e. they would use at least one word to indicate two dimensions: e.g. *gros* (fat) for long and for thick, or *petit* (small) for short and for thin.

Of children with conservation, 80 per cent described two objects differing in two dimensions in two sentences, coordinating the two dimensions: *ce crayon est (plus) long mais (plus) mince, l'autre est court mais gros* (this pencil is long(er) but thin(ner), the other is short but thick).

Of children without conservation, 90 per cent either described only the one dimension, or used four separate sentences, dealing first with length, and then with thickness: *ce crayon est long, l'autre est court, ce crayon* (the first one again) *est mince, l'autre est gros.* (Percentages are approximate; slight variations occurred in different groups of items and with different materials, not described here.)

In a second series of experiments we tried to teach children without conservation the expressions used by children with conservation: comparative terms, differentiated terms and co-ordinated description of a difference in two dimensions. After this verbal training we again tested their operational level in the conservation task. The results of these experiments were as follows:

It was easy (in the sense that only a small number of repetitions were necessary) to teach the children without conservation the use of differentiated terms; it was more difficult (and about a quarter of the subjects did not succeed) to teach them to use the comparatives *plus* and *moins* in our situations; it was still more difficult to teach them the co-ordinated structure *long et (mais) mince, court et (mais) gros.*

Even for children who succeeded in learning to use these expressions, operational progress was rare (10 per cent of our subjects acquired conservation).

On the other hand, more than half the children who made no clear operational progress, changed their answers in the post-test. Instead of simply using the level of the liquid to decide that there was more to drink in one of the glasses, they now noticed and described the co-varying dimensions (higher level, narrower glass); they sometimes explained that the liquid goes up higher in a narrower glass, but this did not lead them to the compensation argument and conservation.

From the first series of experiments we drew the following conclusions:
1 A distinction must be made between lexical acquisition and the acquisition of syntactical structures, the latter being more closely linked to operational level

than the former. The operator-like words (e.g. more, less, as much as, none) form a class apart whose correct use is also very closely linked to operational progress. The other lexical items (e.g. long, short, thin, thick, high, low) are far less closely linked to operativity.

2 Operational structuring and linguistic structuring or rather linguistic restructuring thus parallel each other. The lexical items are already being used or at least easily learned at a pre-operational level; the co-ordinated structures and operator-like words are correctly 'understood' in simple situations; but the latter are only precisely and regularly used with the advent of the first operational structures. Moreover, the difficulties encountered by the child in the use of these expressions seem to be the same as those he encounters in the development of the operations themselves: lack of decentration and incapacity to co-ordinate.

3 Verbal training leads subjects without conservation to direct their attention to pertinent aspects of the problem (co-variance of the dimensions), but it does not

ipso facto bring about the acquisition of operations. An additional experiment may be briefly mentioned: in interrogating a group of severely retarded children (ages 8 to 15, IQs 50 or below) we found that when we used the description patterns of children with conservation for simple orders (*donne plus à la poupée-fille, moins au garçon*), the retarded children were incapable of reacting consistently; but if we used the descriptive terms of our normal nonconservational group (e.g. *donne beaucoup à la fille, et peu au garçon*) their reactions were both correct and consistent. This result illustrated the psychological 'reality' of the different descriptive patterns used by normal children.

A second group of experiments dealt with seriation and its verbal aspects, and yielded comparable results.

These Genevan results, together with the results of the research on deaf and blind children mentioned earlier, confirm Piaget's view on the role of language in the constitution of intellectual operations: language is not the source of logic, but is on the contrary structured by logic.

References

Furth, H. C. (1966). *Thinking Without Language: the Psychological Implications of Deafness.* Free Press, New York.

Hatwell, Y. (1960). *Privation Sensorielle et Intelligence.* Presses Univers, Paris.

Oléron, P. (1957). *Recherches sur le Développement Mental des Sourdsmuets.* Centre National de Recherche Scientifique, Paris.

Piaget, J. (1923). *Le Langage et la Pensée chez L'Enfant.* Neuchâtel et Paris (trs. as *The Language and Thought of the Child,* Routledge & Kegan Paul 1959).

Piaget, J. (1946). *La Formation du Symbole chez L'Enfant,* Delachaux & Niestlé (trs. as *Play, Dreams and Imitation in Childhood,* Routledge & Kegan Paul 1962).

Piaget, J. (1954). Le Langage et la pensée du point de vue genetique; in G. Revensz (ed.), *Thinking and Speaking, A Symposium,* North Holland, Amsterdam.

Piaget, J. (1961). The language and thought of the child, in T. Shipley (ed.), *Classics in Psychology,* Philos. Lib., New York.

Paiget, J. (1962). *Comments on Vygotsky's Critical Remarks,* MIT Press.

Paiget, J. (1963). Langage et opérations intellectuelles, in *Problèmes de Psycholinguistique,* Symposium de l'association de psychologie scientifique de langue française. Neuchâtel, Presses Univers, Paris.

Piaget, J. (1965). Langage et pensée, tome 15, *La Reçue du Praticien,* 17, 2253–4.

Piaget, J., and Inhelder, B. (1966). *La Psychologie de L'Enfant,* Presses Univers, Paris ('Que sais-je?' series) (trs. as *The Psychology of the Child,* Routledge & Kegan Paul 1969).

Sinclair-de-Zwart, H. (1967). *Acquisition du Langage et Développement de la Pensée.*

23 The course of cognitive growth

Jerome S. Bruner

I shall take the view in what follows that the development of human intellectual functioning from infancy to such perfection as it may reach is shaped by a series of technological advances in the use of mind. Growth depends upon the mastery of techniques and cannot be understood without reference to such mastery. These techniques are not, in the main, inventions of the individuals who are 'growing up'; they are, rather, skills transmitted with varying efficiency and success by the culture—language being a prime example. Cognitive growth, then, is in a major way from the outside in as well as from the inside out.

Two matters will concern us. The first has to do with the techniques or technologies that aid growing human beings to represent in a manageable way the recurrent features of the complex environments in which they live. It is fruitful, I think, to distinguish three systems of processing information by which human beings construct models of their world: through action, through imagery, and through language. A second concern is with integration, the means whereby acts are organized into higher order ensembles, making possible the use of larger and larger units of information for the solution of particular problems.

Let me first elucidate these two theoretical matters, and then turn to an examination of the research upon which they are based, much of it from the Center for Cognitive Studies at Harvard.

On the occasion of the One Hundredth Anniversary of the publication of Darwin's *The Origin of Species*, Washburn and Howell (1960) presented a paper at the Chicago Centennial celebration containing the following passage:

> It would now appear . . . that the large size of the brain of certain hominids was a relatively late development and that the brain evolved due to

Source: *American Psychologist* (1964), **19**, 1–15, reprinted in *Research in Psychology*, ed. B. L. Kintz and J. L. Brunig, Scott, Foresman and Co. (1970), 289–96.

new selection pressures after *bipedalism and consequent upon the use of tools. The tool-using, ground-living, hunting way of life created the large human brain rather than a large-brained man discovering certain new ways of life. [We] believe this conclusion is the most important result of the recent fossil hominid discoveries and is one which carries far-reaching implications for the interpretation of human behavior and its origins. . . . The important point is that size of brain, insofar as it can be measured by cranial capacity, has increased some threefold subsequent to the use and manufacture of implements. . . . The uniqueness of modern man is seen as the result of a technical-social life which tripled the size of the brain, reduced the face, and modified many other structures of the body* (p. 49 f.).

This implies that the principal change in man over a long period of years—perhaps 500,000—has been alloplastic rather than autoplastic. That is to say, he has changed by linking himself with new, external implementation systems rather than by any conspicuous change in morphology. . . . The implement systems seem to have been of three general kinds—*amplifiers of human motor capacities* ranging from the cutting tool through the lever and wheel to the wide variety of modern devices; *amplifiers of sensory capacities* that include primitive devices such as smoke signaling and modern ones such as magnification and radar sensing, but also likely to include such 'software' as those conventionalized perceptual shortcuts that can be applied to the redundant sensory environment; and finally *amplifiers of human ratiocinative capacities* of infinite variety ranging from language systems to myth and theory and explanation. All of these forms of amplification are in major or minor degree conventionalized and transmitted by the culture, the last of them probably the most since ratiocinative amplifiers involve symbol systems governed by rules that must, for effective use, be shared.

Any implement system, to be effective, must produce an appropriate internal counterpart, an appropriate skill necessary for organizing sensorimotor acts, for organizing percepts, and for organizing our thoughts in a way that matches them to the requirements of implement systems. These internal skills, represented genetically as capacities, are slowly selected in evolution. In the deepest sense, then, man can be described as a species that has become specialized by the use of technological implements. His selection and survival have depended upon a morphology and set of capacities that could be linked with the alloplastic devices that have made his later evolution possible. We move, perceive, and think in a fashion that depends upon techniques rather than upon wired-in arrangements in our nervous system.

Where representation of the environment is concerned, it too depends upon techniques that are learned—and these are precisely the techniques that serve to amplify our motor acts, our perceptions, and our ratiocinative activities. We know and respond to recurrent regularities in our environment by skilled and patterned acts, by conventionalized spatio-qualitative imagery and selective perceptual organization, and through linguistic encoding which, as so many writers have remarked, places a selective lattice between us and the physical environment. In short, the capacities that have been shaped by our evolution as tool-users are the ones that we rely upon in the primary task of representation—the nature of which we shall consider in more detail directly.

As for integration, it is a truism that there are very few single or simple adults' acts that cannot be performed by a young child. In short, any more highly skilled activity can be decomposed into simpler components, each of which can be carried out by a less skilled operator. What higher skills require is that the component operations be combined. Maturation consists of an orchestration of these components into an integrated sequence. The 'distractability', so-called, of much early behavior may reflect each act's lack of imbeddedness. ... These integrated plans, in turn, reflect the routines and subroutines that one learns in the course of mastering the patterned nature of a social environment. So that integration, too, depends upon patterns that come from the outside in. ...

If we are to benefit from contact with recurrent regularities in the environment, we must represent them in some manner. To dismiss this problem as 'mere memory' is to misunderstand it. For the most important thing about memory is not storage of past experience, but rather the retrieval of what is relevant in some usable form. This depends upon how past experience is coded and processed so that it may indeed be relevant and usable in the present when needed. The end product of such a system of coding and processing is what we may speak of as a representation.

I shall call the three modes of representation mentioned earlier enactive representation, iconic representation, and symbolic representation. Their appearance in the life of the child is in that order, each depending upon the previous one for its development, yet all of them remaining more or less intact throughout life—barring such early accidents as blindness or deafness or cortical injury. By enactive representation I mean a mode of representing past events through appropriate motor response. We cannot, for example, give an adequate description of familiar sidewalks or floors over which we habitually walk, nor do we have much of an image of what they are like. Yet we get about them without tripping or even looking much. Such segments of our environment—bicycle riding, tying knots, aspects of driving—get represented in our muscles, so to speak. Iconic representation summarizes events by the selective organization of percepts and of images, by the spatial, temporal, and qualitative structures of the perceptual field and their transformed images. Images 'stand for' perceptual events in the close but conventionally selective way that a picture stands for the object pictured. Finally, a symbol system represents things by design features that include remoteness and arbitrariness. A word neither points directly to its referent here and now, nor does it resemble it as a picture. The lexeme 'Philadelphia' looks no more like the city so designated than does a nonsense syllable. The other property of language that is crucial is its productiveness in combination, far beyond what can be done with images or acts. 'Philadelphia is a lavender sachet in Grandmother's linen closet,' or $(x+2)^2 = x^2+4x+4 = x(x+4)+4$.

An example or two of enactive representation underlines its importance in infancy and in disturbed functioning, while illustrating its limitations. Piaget (1954) provides us with an observation from the closing weeks of the first year of life. The child is playing with a rattle in his crib. The rattle drops over the side. The child moves his clenched hand before his face, opens it, looks for the rattle. Not finding it there, he moves his hand, closed again, back to the edge of the crib, shakes it with movements like those he uses in shaking the rattle. Thereupon he moves his closed hand back toward his face, opens it, and looks. Again no rattle; and so he tries again. In several months, the child has benefited from experience to the degree that the rattle and action become separated. Whereas earlier he would not show signs of missing the rattle when it was removed unless he has begun reaching for it, now he cries and searches when the rattle is presented for a moment and hidden by a cover. He no longer repeats a movement to restore the rattle. In place of representation by action alone—where 'existence' is defined by the compass of present action—it is now defined by an image that persists autonomously.

A second example is provided by the results of injury to the occipital and temporal cortex in man. A patient is presented with a hard-boiled egg intact in its shell, and asked what it is. Holding it in his hand, he is embarrassed, for he cannot name it. He makes a motion as if to throw it and halts himself. Then he brings it to his mouth as if to bite it and stops before he gets there. He brings it to his ear and shakes it gently. He is puzzled. The experimenter takes the egg from him and cracks it on the table, handing it back. The patient then begins to peel the egg and announces what it is. He cannot identify objects without reference to the action he directs toward them.

The disadvantages of such a system are illustrated by Emerson's (1931) experiment in which children are told to place a ring on a board with seven rows and six columns of pegs, copying the position of a ring put on an identical board by the experimenter. Children ranging from three to twelve were examined in this experiment. ... The child's board could be placed in various positions relative to the experimenter's: right next to it, 90 degrees rotated away from it, 180 degrees rotated, placed face to face with it so that the child has to turn full around to make his placement, etc. The older the child, the better his performance. But the younger children could do about as well as the oldest so long as they did not have to change their own position vis-à-vis the experimenter's board in order to make a match on their own board. The more they had to turn, the more difficult the task. They were clearly depending upon their bodily orientation toward the experimenter's board to guide them. When this orientation is disturbed by having to turn, they lose the position on the board. Older children succeed even when they must turn, either by the use of imagery that is invariant across bodily displacements, or, later, by specifying column and row of the experimenter's ring and carrying the symbolized self-instruction back to their own board. It is a limited world, the world of enactive representation.

We know little about the conditions necessary for the growth of imagery and iconic representation, or to what extent parental or environmental intervention affects it during the earliest years. In ordinary adult learning a certain amount of motoric skill and practice seems to be a necessary precondition for the development of a simultaneous image to represent the sequence of acts involved. If an adult subject is made to choose a path through a complex bank of toggle switches, he does not form an image of the path, according to Mandler (1962), until he has mastered and over-practiced the task by successive manipulation. Then, finally, he reports that an image of the path has developed and that he is now using it rather than groping his way through.

Our main concern in what follows is not with the growth of iconic representation, but with the transition from it to symbolic representation. For it is in the development of symbolic representation that one finds, perhaps, the greatest thicket of psychological problems. The puzzle begins when the child first achieves the use of productive grammar, usually late in the second year of life. Toward the end of the second year, the child is master of the single-word, agrammatical utterance, the so-called holophrase. In the months following, there occurs a profound change in the use of language. Two classes of words appear—a pivot class and an open class—and the child launches forth on his career in combinatorial talking and, perhaps, thinking. Whereas before, lexemes like *allgone* and *mummy* and *sticky* and *bye-bye* were used singly, now, for example, *allgone* becomes a pivot word and is used in combination. Mother washes jam off the child's hands; he says *allgone sticky*. In the next days, if his speech is carefully followed (Braine, 1963), it will be apparent that he is trying out the limits of the pivot combinations, and one will even find constructions that have an extraordinary capacity for representing complex sequences—like *allgone bye-bye* after a visitor has departed. A recent and ingenious observation by Weir (1962) on her 2½-year-old son, recording his speech musings after he was in bed with lights out, indicates that at this stage there is a great deal of metalinguistic combinatorial play with words in which the child is exploring the limits of grammatical productiveness.

In effect, language provides a means, not only for representing experience, but also for transforming it. As Chomsky (1957) and Miller (1962) have both made clear in the last few years, the transformational rules of grammar provide a syntactic means of reworking the 'realities' one has encountered. Not only, if you will, did the dog bite the man, but the man was bitten by the dog, and perhaps the man was not bitten by the dog or was the man not bitten by the dog. The range of reworking that is made possible even by the three transformations of the passive, the negative, and the query is very striking indeed. Or the ordering device whereby the comparative mode makes it possible to connect what is *heavy* and what is *light* into the ordinal array of *heavy* and *less heavy* is again striking. Or, to take a final example, there is the discrimination that is made possible by the growth of attribute language such that the global dimension *big* and *little* can now be decomposed into *tall* and *short* on the one hand and *fat* and *skinny* on the other.

Once the child has succeeded in internalizing language as a cognitive instrument, it becomes possible for him to represent and systematically transform the regularities of experience with far greater flexibility and power than before. Interestingly enough, it is the recent Russian literature, particularly Vygotsky's (1962) book on language and thought, and the work of his disciple, Luria (1961), and his students that has highlighted these phenomena by calling attention to the so-called second-signal system which replaces classical conditioning with an internalized linguistic system for shaping and transforming experience itself.

If all these matters were not of such complexity and human import, I would apologize for taking so much time in speculation. We turn now to some new experiments designed to shed some light on the nature of representation and particularly upon the transition from its iconic to its symbolic form.

Let me begin with an experiment by Bruner and Kenney (1966) on the manner in which children between five and seven handle a double classification matrix. The materials of the experiment are nine plastic glasses, arranged so that they vary in 3 degrees of diameter and 3 degrees of height. They are set before the child initially on a 3 × 3 grid marked on a large piece of cardboard. To acquaint the child with the matrix, we first remove one, then two, and then three glasses from the matrix, asking the child to replace them. We also ask the children to describe how the glasses in the columns and rows are alike and how they differ. Then the glasses are scrambled and we ask the child to make something like what was there before by placing the glasses on the same grid that was used when the task was introduced. Now we scramble the glasses once more, but this time we place the glass that was formerly in the southwest corner of the grid in the southeast corner (it is the shortest, thinnest glass) and ask the child if he can make something like what was there before, leaving the one glass where we have just put it. That is the experiment.

The results can be quickly told. To begin with, there is no difference between ages 5, 6, and 7 either in terms of ability to replace glasses taken from the matrix or in building a matrix once it has been scrambled (but without the transposed glass). Virtually all the children succeed. Interestingly enough, *all* the children rebuild the matrix to match the original, almost as if they were copying what was there before. The only difference is that the older children are quicker.

Now compare the performance of the three ages in constructing the matrix with a single member transposed. Most of the seven-year-olds succeed in the transposed task, but hardly any of the youngest children. The youngest children seem to be dominated by an image of the original matrix. They try to put the transposed glass 'back where it belongs,' to rotate the cardboard so that 'it will be like before,' and sometimes they will start placing a few glasses neighboring the transposed glass correctly only to revert to the original arrangement. In several instances, five- or six-year-olds will simply try to reconstitute the old matrix, building right over the transposed glass. The seven-year-old, on the other hand, is more likely to pause, to treat the transposition as a problem, to talk to himself about 'where this should go.' The relation of place and size is for him a problem that requires reckoning, not simply copying.

Now consider the language children use for describing the dimensions of the matrix. Recall that the children were asked how glasses in a row and in a column were alike and how they differed. Children answered in three distinctive linguistic modes. One was *dimensional*, singling out two ends of an attribute— for example, 'That one is higher, and that one is

shorter.' A second was *global* in nature. Of glasses differing only in height the child says, 'That one is bigger and that one is little.' The same words could be used equally well for diameter or for nearly any other magnitude. Finally, there was *confounded* usage: 'That one is tall and that one is little,' where a dimensional term is used for one end of the continuum and a global term for the other. The children who used confounded descriptions had the most difficulty with the transposed matrix. Lumping all ages together, the children who use confounded descriptions were twice as likely to fail on the transposition task as those who used either dimensional or global terms. *But the language the children used had no relation whatsoever to their performance in reproducing the first untransposed matrix.* Inhelder and Sinclair in a personal communication also report that confounded language of this kind is associated with failure on conservation tasks in children of the same age, a subject to which we shall turn shortly.

The findings of this experiment suggest two things. First, that children who use iconic representation are more highly sensitized to the spatial-qualitative organization of experience and less to the ordering principles governing such organization. They can recognize and reproduce, but cannot produce new structures based on rule. And second, there is a suspicion that the language they bring to bear on the task is insufficient as a tool for ordering. If these notions are correct, then certain things should follow. For one thing, *improvement* in language should aid this type of problem solving. This remains to be investigated. But it is also reasonable to suppose that *activation* of language habits that the child has already mastered might improve performance as well—a hypothesis already suggested by the findings of Luria's students. Now, activation can be achieved by two means: One is by having the child 'say' the description of something before him that he must deal with symbolically. The other is to take advantage of the remoteness of reference that is a feature of language and have the child 'say' his description in the absence of the things to be described. In this way, there would be less likelihood of a perceptual-iconic representation becoming dominant and inhibiting the operation of symbolic processes. An experiment by Françoise Frank (1966) illustrates this later approach—the effects of saying before seeing.

Piaget and Inhelder have shown that if children between ages four and seven are presented two identical beakers which they judge equally full of water, they will no longer consider the water equal if the contents of one of the beakers is now poured into a beaker that is either wider or thinner than the original. If the second beaker is thinner, they will say it has more to drink, because the water is higher; if the second beaker is wider, they will say it has less because the water is lower. Comparable results can be obtained by pouring the contents of one glass into several smaller beakers. In Geneva terms, the child is not yet able to conserve liquid volume across transformations in its appearance. Consider how this behavior can be altered.

Françoise Frank first did the classic conservation tests to determine which children exhibited conservation and which did not. Her subjects were 4, 5, 6, and 7 years old. She then went on to other procedures, among which was the following. Two standard beakers are partly filled so that the child judges them to contain equal amounts of water. A wider beaker of the same height is introduced and the three beakers are now, except for their tops, hidden by a screen. The experimenter pours from a standard beaker into the wider beaker. The child, without seeing the water, is asked which has more to drink, or do they have the same amount, the standard or the wider beaker. In comparison with the unscreened pre-test, there is a striking increase in correct equality judgments. Correct responses jump from 0 per cent to 50 per cent among the 4s, from 20 per cent to 90 per cent among the 5s, and from 50 per cent to 100 per cent among the 6s. With the screen present, most children justify their correct judgment by noting that 'It's the same water,' or 'You only poured it.'

Now the screen is removed. All the four-year-olds change their minds. The perceptual display overwhelms them and they decide that the wider beaker has less water. But virtually all of the five-year-olds stick to their judgment, often invoking the difference between appearance and reality—'It looks like more to drink, but it is only the same because it is the same water and it was only poured from there to there,' to quote one typical five-year-old. And all of the 6s and all the 7s stick to their judgment. Now, some minutes later, Frank does a post-test on the children using a tall thin beaker along with the standard ones, and no screen, of course. The 4s are unaffected by their prior experience: None of them is able to grasp the idea of invariant quantity in the new task. With the 5s, instead of 20 per cent showing conservation, as in the pre-test, 70 per cent do. With both 6s and 7s, conservation increases from 50 per cent to 90 per cent. I should mention that control groups doing just a pre-test and post-test show no significant improvement in performance.

A related experiment of Nair's (1963) explores the arguments children use when they solve a conservation task correctly and when they do not. Her subjects were all five-year-olds. She transferred water from one rectangular clear plastic tank to another that was both longer and wider than the first. Ordinarily, a five-year-old will say there is less water in the second tank. The water is, of course, lower in the second tank. She had a toy duck swimming in the first container, and when the water was poured into the new container, she told the child that 'The duck was taking his water with him.'

Three kinds of arguments were set forth by the children to support their judgments. One is perceptual —having to do with the height, width, or apparent 'bigness' of the water. A second type has to do with action: The duck took the water along, or the water was only poured. A third one, 'transformational' argument, invokes the reversibility principle: If you poured the water back into the first container, it would look the same again.[1] Of the children who thought the water was not equal in amount after pouring, 15 per cent used nonperceptual arguments to justify their judgment. Of those who recognized the equality of the water, two-thirds used nonperceptual arguments. It is plain that if a child is to succeed in the conservation task, he must have some internalized verbal formula that shields him from the overpowering appearance of the visual displays much as in the Frank experiment. The explanations of the children who lacked conservation suggest how strongly oriented they were to the visual appearance of the displays they had to deal with.

My major concern has been to examine afresh the nature of intellectual growth. The account has surely done violence to the richness of the subject. It seems to me that growth depends upon the emergence of two forms of competence. Children, as they grow, must acquire ways of representing the recurrent regularities in their environment, and they must transcend the momentary by developing ways of linking past to present to future—representation and integration. I have suggested that we can conceive of growth in both of these domains as the emergence of new technologies for the unlocking and amplification of human intellectual powers. Like the growth of technology, the growth of intellect is not smoothly monotonic. Rather, it moves forward in spurts as innovations are adopted. Most of the innovations are transmitted to the child in some prototypic form by agents of the culture: ways of responding, ways of looking and imaging, and, most important, ways of translating what one has encountered into language.

I have relied heavily in this account on the successive emergence of action, image, and word as the vehicles of representation, a reliance based both upon our observations and upon modern readings of man's alloplastic evolution. Our attention has been directed largely to the transition between iconic and symbolic representation.

In children between four and twelve language comes to play an increasingly powerful role as an implement of knowing. Through simple experiments, I have tried to show how language shapes, augments, and even supercedes the child's earlier modes of processing information. Translation of experience into symbolic form, with its attendant means of achieving remote reference, transformation, and combination, opens up realms of intellectual possibility that are orders of magnitude beyond the most powerful image-forming system.

Once language becomes a medium for the translation of experience, there is a progressive release from immediacy. For language, as we have commented, has the new and powerful features of remoteness and arbitrariness: it permits productive, combinatorial operations in the *absence* of what is represented. With this achievement, the child can delay gratification by virtue of representing to himself what lies beyond the present, what other possibilities exist beyond the clue that is under his nose. The child may be *ready* for delay of gratification, but he is no more able to bring if off than somebody ready to build a house, save that he has not yet heard of tools.

As for how language becomes internalized as a program for ordering experience, I join those who despair for an answer. My speculation, for whatever it is worth, is that the process of internalization depends upon interaction with others, upon the need to develop corresponding categories and transformations for communal action. It is the need for cognitive coin that can be exchanged with those on whom we depend. What Roger Brown (1958) has called the Original Word Game ends up by being the Human Thinking Game.

If I have seemed to underemphasize the importance of inner capacities—for example, the capacity *for* language or *for* imagery—it is because I believe that this part of the story is given by the nature of man's evolution. What is significant about the growth of mind in the child is to what degree it depends not upon capacity but upon the unlocking of capacity by techniques that come from exposure to the specialized environment of a culture. Romantic clichés, like 'the veneer of culture' or 'natural man,' are as misleading if not as damaging as the view that the course of human development can be viewed independently of the educational process we arrange to make that development possible.

Note

1 Not one of the forty children who participated in this experiment used the compensation argument—that though the water was lower it was correspondingly wider and was, therefore, the same amount of water. This type of reasoning by compensation is said by Piaget and Inhelder (1962) to be the basis of conservation.

References

Braine, M. D. (1963). On learning the grammatical order of words. *Psychological Review* 70, 323–48.

Brown, R. *Words and things*. (1958). New York: Free Press.

Bruner, J. S. & Kenney, H. (1966). The development of the concepts of order and proportion in children. In J. S. Bruner, *Studies in cognitive growth*. New York: Wiley.

Chomsky, N. (1957). *Syntactic structures*. The Hague: Mouton.

Emerson, L. L. (1931). The effect of bodily orientation upon the young child's memory for position of objects, *Child Development* 2, 125–42.

Luria, A. R. (1961). *The role of speech in the regulation of normal and abnormal behavior*. New York: Liveright.

Mandler, G. (1962). From association to structure. *Psychological Review* 69, 415–27.

Miller, G. A. (1962). Some psychological studies of grammar. *American Psychologist* 17, 748–62.

Nair, P. (1963). An experiment in conservation, in Center for Cognitive Studies, *Annual Report*, Cambridge, Mass.

Piaget, J. (1955). *The Child's Construction of Reality*, trs. Margaret Cook. London: Routledge & Kegan Paul.

Piaget, J. & Inhelder, B. (1962). *Le développement des quantités physiques chez l'enfant*. (2nd rev. ed.) Neuchâtel, Switzerland: Delachaux & Niestlé.

Vygotsky, L. S. (1962). *Thought and language*, ed. & trans. by Eugenia Hanfmann & Gertrude Vakar. New York: Wiley.

Washburn, S. L. & Howell, F. C. (1960). Human evolution and culture, in S. Tax, *The evolution of man*, vol. 2. University of Chicago Press.

Weir, R. H. *Language in the crib*. (1962). The Hague: Mouton.

Section VI Language deprivation and educational disadvantage?

A substantial minority of British schoolchildren underfunction in the educational system. After ten or more years of school attendance their attainments are low. They are hostile to school and remain in the system only as long as they are compelled to do so. They are the disadvantaged children in our culture. They (or their parents) come from a wide variety of social and ethnic backgrounds, but most of them are still the indigenous British poor. Their accents, and their language also, differ in significant respects from those approved by the school and displayed 'naturally' by the children of the middle class. Many of them are the *restricted code* speakers of Section III.

Such children are at a distinct disadvantage in the school system. This disadvantage is commonly thought to have its origins in the language deprivation the children suffer at home in the pre-school years (and afterwards). But as we shall see, the concepts of deprivation and disadvantage are both complex and controversial. What is fairly clear is that the schools do relatively little to help, particularly in the language area. Even where the school is both sensitive to the problem and willing to help, it is far from evident exactly what should be done or how.

Stimulated by the Plowden Report, with its concept of the Educational Priority Area, many British educationists have looked to the American work on Compensatory Education to suggest ideas that might help. In school they have considered both 'enrichment' programmes, where attempts are made to supply the child with a whole range of assorted language and concrete experiences he is considered to have missed, and highly structured, often individually tailored, tutorial programmes which aim to remedy specific 'deficiencies'. Community-based programmes have concentrated rather on effecting changes in the child's social environment, focusing in particular on the home and mother.

At the same time, some educationists are becoming uneasily aware that the psychological analysis upon which their remedial programmes are based may not be an adequate one. And it is the sociologist who has largely created this awareness. For the psychological perspective tends to operate within an accepted socio-educational structure and focuses accordingly on the child's difficulties in conforming and learning within the mainstream culture. The sociologist questions more radically the whole notion of a social structure which can produce the concept of a deprived culture—something which exists (even in theory) only in the context of an accepted set of mainstream cultural values. In other words, the 'cultural inferiority' model with which the educationist operates may be producing the very difficulties it claims to pinpoint for remediation. There are a number of possibilities which need examining: perhaps the 'poor' culture does in fact have the educational skills with which we are concerned, but does not exploit them in the educational setting provided. Perhaps the performances asked for in the traditional intelligence and achievement tests tap surface language styles and tricks, but do not reach down to the basic cognitive skills which underly them and which constitute the real foundation of educational and social skills.

Much of the American work has been carried out with Negro populations in the United States. It would be dangerous to make facile generalizations from their situation to that of the poor in Britain. But we do need to ask ourselves how far the differences in language behaviour we observe in our population reflect differences in adequacy as opposed to acceptable (and equivalent) variation.

The articles selected for this section span this range of views. The Hess and Shipman paper reports a classic study of Negro mothers from different social backgrounds in conversation with their four-year-old children in a laboratory setting. They found considerable differences in how mothers operate both as teachers and as agents in the socialization process, and suggest that these differences are critical for the child's linguistic, cognitive and social development and for his educational prospects.

Marion Blank argues for the acceptance not of a global deficiency, but of a specific (yet far-reaching) deficit, in that she sees the child as lacking a 'symbolic system for thinking'. She argues against the general enrichment programme in favour of a quite specifically structured one-to-one tutorial programme. In the article reprinted here, Blank and Solomon discuss the detailed implementation of this programme and provide a full contrastive analysis of the operation of the tutorial programme as against the behaviour of a competent teacher operating within the framework of the conventional enrichment approach.

In the first of the sociological readings, Baratz and Baratz argue against both the social pathology and the genetic inferiority models in this field. They point out that these are not exhaustive alternatives and that the cultural difference hypothesis may be more powerful than either. The Labov article analyses Negro language from a similar standpoint to the Baratzes. Labov sets out to show that language differences can be specified and shown to be of equal value. Negro children are not lacking in language, nor need their language be less effective than that of the white middle class. He demonstrates that lower class language can handle logical and abstract argument effectively. Moreover, middle class language can often itself be shown to consist of the mere ritual manipulation of high status language indicators to conceal the lack of any precise or penetrating thought. It should be noted that not all the descriptions of Bernstein's work in this paper would meet with the agreement of Bernstein himself. For Bernstein's own work see the readings on pages 102–10 and 213–18.

The section closes with a paper by Bernstein in which he re-examines the basis of Compensatory Education. Bernstein stresses the need to provide an 'adequate education environment' in general, rather than trying to compensate for something that is lacking. He suggests that we should stop thinking in terms of compensation but consider instead the educational environment itself. And like Labov and the Baratzes he emphasizes the need to consider the child's own existing culture rather than regarding him as a 'deficit system' that needs to be filled out.

Asher Cashdan and Geoffrey Esland

24 Early experience and the socialization of cognitive modes in children

Robert D. Hess and Virginia C. Shipman

This paper deals with the question: what is cultural deprivation and how does it act to shape and depress the resources of the human mind? The arguments presented are: first, that the behavior which leads to social, educational, and economic poverty is socialized in early childhood; second, that the central quality involved in the effects of cultural deprivation is a lack of cognitive meaning in the mother-child communication system; and third, that the growth of cognitive processes is fostered in family control systems which offer and permit a wide range of alternatives of action and thought and that such growth is constricted by systems of control, which offer predetermined solutions and few alternatives for consideration and choice.

The research group was composed of 160 Negro mothers and their 4-year-old children selected from four different social status levels.

The data are presented to show social status differences among the four groups with respect to cognitive functioning and linguistic codes and to offer examples of relations between maternal and child behavior that are congruent with the general lines of argument laid out.

The problem

One of the questions arising from the contemporary concern with the education of culturally disadvantaged children is how we should conceptualize the effects of such deprivation upon the cognitive faculties of the child. The outcome is well known: children from deprived backgrounds score well below middle-class children on standard individual and group measures of intelligence (a gap that increases with age); they come to school without the skills necessary for coping with first grade curricula; their language development, both written and spoken, is relatively poor; auditory and visual discrimination skills are not well developed; in scholastic achievement they are retarded an average of 2 years by grade 6 and almost 3 years by grade 8;

Source: *Child Development* (1965), **36** (3), 869–86.

they are more likely to drop out of school before completing a secondary education; and even when they have adequate ability are less likely to go to college (Deutsch, 1963; Deutsch & Brown, 1964; Eells, Davis, Havighurst, Herriels, & Tyler 1951; John, 1963; Kennedy, Van de Riet, & White, 1963; Lesser, 1964).

For many years the central theoretical issues in this field dealt with the origin of these effects, argued in terms of the relative contribution of genetic as compared with environmental factors. Current interest in the effects of cultural deprivation ignores this classic debate; the more basic problem is to understand how cultural experience is translated into cognitive behavior and academic achievement (Bernstein, 1961; Hess, 1964).

The focus of concern is no longer upon the question of whether social and cultural disadvantage depress academic ability, but has shifted to a study of the mechanisms of exchange that mediate between the individual and his environment. The thrust of research and theory is toward conceptualizing social class as a discrete array of experiences and patterns of experience that can be examined in relation to the effects they have upon the emerging cognitive equipment of the young child. In short, the question this paper presents is this: what *is* cultural deprivation, and how does it act to shape and depress the resources of the human mind?

The arguments we wish to present here are these: first, that the behavior which leads to social, educational, and economic poverty is socialized in early childhood —that is, it is learned; second, that the central quality involved in the effects of cultural deprivation is a lack of cognitive meaning in the mother-child communication system; and, third, that the growth of cognitive processes is fostered in family control systems which offer and permit a wide range of alternatives of action and thought and that such growth is constricted by systems of control which offer predetermined solutions and few alternatives for consideration and choice.

In this paper we will argue that the structure of the social system and the structure of the family shape communication and language and that language shapes thought and cognitive styles of problem-solving. In the deprived-family context this means that the nature of the control system which relates parent to child restricts the number and kind of alternatives for action and thought that are opened to the child; such constriction precludes a tendency for the child to reflect, to consider and choose among alternatives for speech and action. It develops modes for dealing with stimuli and with problems which are impulsive rather than reflective, which deal with the immediate rather than the future, and which are disconnected rather than sequential.

This position draws from the work of Basil Bernstein (1961) of the University of London. In his view, language structures and conditions what the child learns and how he learns, setting limits within which future learning may take place. He identifies two forms of communication codes or styles of verbal behavior: *restricted* and *elaborated*. Restricted codes are stereotyped, limited, and condensed, lacking in specificity and the exactness needed for precise conceptualization and differentiation. Sentences are short, simple, often unfinished; there is little use of subordinate clauses for elaborating the content of the sentence; it is a language of implicit meaning, easily understood and commonly shared. It is the language form often used in impersonal situations when the intent is to promote solidarity or reduce tension. Restricted codes are nonspecific clichés, statements, or observations about events made in general terms that will be readily understood. The basic quality of this mode is to limit the range and detail of concept and information involved.

Elaborated codes, however, are those in which communication is individualized and the message is specific to a particular situation, topic, and person. It is more particular, more differentiated, and more precise. It permits expression of a wider and more complex range of thought, tending toward discrimination among cognitive and affective content.

The effects of early experience with these codes are not only upon the communication modes and cognitive structure—they also establish potential patterns of relation with the external world. It is one of the dynamic features of Bernstein's work that he views language as social behavior. As such, language is used by participants of a social network to elaborate and express social and other interpersonal relations and, in turn, is shaped and determined by these relations.

The interlacing of social interaction and language is illustrated by the distinction between two types of family control. One is oriented toward control by *status* appeal or ascribed role norms. The second is oriented toward *persons*. Families differ in the degree to which they utilize each of these types of regulatory appeal. In status- (position-) oriented families, behavior tends to be regulated in terms of role expectations. There is little opportunity for the unique characteristics of the child to influence the decision-making process or the interaction between parent and child. In these families, the internal or personal states of the children are not influential as a basis for decision. Norms of behavior are stressed with such imperatives as, 'You must do this because I say so,' or 'Girls don't act like that,' or other statements which rely on the status of the participants or a behavior norm for justification (Bernstein, 1964).

In the family, as in other social structures, control is exercised in part through status appeals. The feature that distinguishes among families is the extent to which the status-based control maneuvers are modified by orientation toward persons. In a person-oriented appeal system, the unique characteristics of the child modify status demands and are taken into account in interaction. The decisions of this type of family are individualized and less frequently related to status or role ascriptions. Behavior is justified in terms of feelings, preference, personal and unique reactions, and subjective states. This philosophy not only permits but demands an elaborated linguistic code and a wide range of linguistic and behavioral alternatives in interpersonal interaction. Status-oriented families may be regulated by less individuated commands, messages, and responses. Indeed, by its nature, the status-oriented family will rely more heavily on a restricted code. The verbal exchange is inherent in the structure—regulates it and is regulated by it.

These distinctions may be clarified by two examples of mother-child communication using these two types of codes. Assume that the emotional climate of two homes is approximately the same; the significant difference between them is in style of communication employed. A child is playing noisily in the kitchen with an assortment of pots and pans when the telephone rings. In one home the mother says, 'Be quiet,' or 'Shut up,' or issues any one of several other short, peremptory commands. In the other home the mother says, 'Would you keep quiet a minute? I want to talk on the phone.' The question our study poses is this: what inner response is elicited in the child, what is the effect upon his developing cognitive network of concepts and meaning in each of these situations? In one instance the child is asked for a simple mental response. He is asked to attend to an uncomplicated message and to make a conditioned response (to comply); he is not called upon to reflect or to make mental discriminations. In the other example the child is required to follow two or three ideas. He is asked to think of his behavior in relation to its effect upon another person. He must relate his behavior to a time dimension; he must perform a more complicated task to follow the communication of his mother in that his relationship to her is mediated in part through concepts and shared ideas; his mind is stimulated or exercised (in an elementary fashion) by a more elaborate and complex verbal communication initiated by the mother. As objects of these two divergent communication styles, repeated in various ways, in similar situations and circumstances during the preschool years, these two imaginary children would be expected to develop significantly different verbal facility and cognitive equipment by the time they enter the public-school system.

A person-oriented family allows the child to achieve the behavior rules (role requirements) by presenting them in a specific context for the child and by emphasizing the consequences of alternative actions. Status-oriented families present the rules in an assigned manner, where compliance is the *only* rule-following possibility. In these situations the role of power in the interaction is more obvious, and, indeed, coercion and defiance are likely interactional possibilities. From another perspective, status-oriented families use a more rigid learning and teaching model in which compliance, rather than rationale, is stressed.

A central dimension through which we look at maternal behavior is to inquire what responses are elicited and permitted by styles of communication and interaction. There are two axes of the child's behavior in which we have a particular interest. One of these is represented by an *assertive, initiatory* approach to learning, as contrasted with a *passive, compliant* mode of engagement; the other deals with the tendency to reach solutions impulsively or hastily as distinguished from a tendency to *reflect*, to compare alternatives, and to choose among available options.

These styles of cognitive behavior are related, in our hypotheses, to the dimensions of maternal linguistic codes and types of family control systems. A status-oriented statement, for example, tends to offer a set of regulations and rules for conduct and interaction that is based on arbitary decisions rather than upon logical consequences which result from selection of one or another alternatives. Elaborated and person-oriented statements lend themselves more easily to styles of cognitive approach that involve reflection and reflective comparison. Status-oriented statements tend to be restrictive of thought. Take our simple example of the two children and the telephone. The verbal categoric command to 'Be quiet' cuts off thought and offers little opportunity to relate the information conveyed in the command to the context in which it occurred. The more elaborated message, 'Would you be quiet a minute? I want to talk on the phone' gives the child a rationale for relating his behavior to a wider set of considerations. In effect, he has been given a *why* for his mother's request and, by this example, possibly becomes more likely to *ask* why in another situation. It may be through this type of verbal interaction that the child learns to look for action sequences in his own and others' behavior. Perhaps through these more intent-oriented statements the child comes to see the world as others see it and learns to take the role of others in viewing himself and his actions. The child comes to see the world as a set of possibilities from which he can make a personal selection. He learns to role play with an element of personal flexibility, not by role-conforming rigidity.

Research plan

For our project a research group of 163 Negro mothers and their 4-year-old children was selected from four different social status levels: Group A came from college-educated professional, executive, and managerial occupational levels; Group B came from skilled blue-collar occupational levels, with not more than high-school education; Group C came from unskilled or semiskilled occupational levels, with predominantly elementary-school education; Group D from unskilled or semiskilled occupational levels, with fathers absent and families supported by public assistance.

These mothers were interviewed twice in their homes and brought to the university for testing and for an interaction session between mother and child in which the mother was taught three simple tasks by the staff member and then asked to teach these tasks to the child.

One of these tasks was to sort or group a number of plastic toys by color and by function; a second task was to sort eight blocks by two characteristics simultaneously; the third task required the mother and child to work together to copy five designs on a toy called an Etch-a-Sketch. A description of various aspects of the project and some preliminary results have been presented in several papers (Brophy, Hess, & Shipman, 1965; Jackson, Hess, & Shipman, 1965; Meyer, Shipman, & Hess, 1964; Olim, Hess, & Shipman, 1965; Shipman & Hess, 1965).

Results

The data in this paper are organized to show social-status differences among the four groups in the dimensions of behavior described above to indicate something of the maternal teaching styles that are emerging and to offer examples of relations between maternal and child behavior that are congruent with the general lines of argument we have laid out.

Social-status differences

Verbal codes: restricted versus elaborated. One of the most striking and obvious differences between the environments provided by the mothers of the research group was in their patterns of language use. In our testing sessions, the most obvious social-class variations were in the total amount of verbal output in response to questions and tasks asking for verbal response. For example, as Table 1 shows, mothers from the middle-class gave protocols that were consistently longer in language productivity than did mothers from the other three groups.

Taking three different types of questions that called

for free response on the part of the mothers and counting the number of lines of typescript of the protocols, the tally for middle-class mothers was approximately 82 contrasted with an average of roughly 49 for mothers from the three other groups.

Table 1 Mean number of typed lines in three data-gathering situations

	Upper middle N = 40	Upper lower N = 40	Lower lower N = 36	ADC N = 36
School situations	34·68	22·80	18·86	18·64
Mastery situations	28·45	18·70	15·94	17·75
CAT card	18·72	9·62	12·39	12·24
Total	81·85	51·12	47·19	48·63

These differences in verbal products indicate the extent to which the maternal environments of children in different social-class groups tend to be mediated by verbal cue and thus offer (or fail to offer) opportunities for labeling, for identifying objects and feelings and adult models who can demonstrate the usefulness of language as a tool for dealing with interpersonal interaction and for ordering stimuli in the environment.

In addition to this gross disparity in verbal output there were differences in the quality of language used by mothers in the various status groups. One approach to the analysis of language used by these mothers was an examination of their responses to the following task: They were shown the Lion Card of the Children's Apperception Test and asked to tell their child a story relating to the card. This card is a picture of a lion sitting on a chair holding a pipe in his hand. Beside him is a cane. In the corner is a mouse peering out of a hole. The lion appears to be deep in thought. These protocols were the source of language samples which were summarized in nine scales (Table 2), two of which we wish to describe here.

Table 2 Social status differences in language usage
(Scores are the means for each group)

	Social Status			
Scale	Upper middle N = 40	Upper lower N = 42	Lower lower N = 40	ADC N = 41
Mean sentence length(a)	11·39	8·74	9·66	8·23
Adjective range(b)	31·99	28·32	28·37	30·49
Adverb range(c)	11·14	9·40	8·70	8·20
Verb elaboration(d)	·59	·52	·47	·44
Complex verb preference(e)	63·25	59·12	50·85	51·73
Syntactic structure elaboration(f)	8·89	6·90	8·07	6·46
Stimulus utilization	5·82	4·81	4·87	5·36
Introduced content	3·75	2·62	2·45	2·34
Abstraction(g)	5·60	4·89	3·71	1·75

(a) Average number of words per sentence.
(b) Proportion of uncommon adjective types to total nouns, expressed as a percentage.
(c) Proportion of uncommon adverb types to total verbs, adjectives, and adverbs, expressed as a percentage.
(d) Average number of complex verb types per sentence.
(e) Proportion of complex verb types to all verb types, simple and complex.
(f) Average number of weighted complex syntactic structures per 100 words.
(g) Proportion of abstract nouns and verbs (excluding repetitions) to total nouns and verbs (excluding repetitions), expressed as a percentage.

The first scale dealt with the mother's tendency to use abstract words. The index derived was a propor-

tion of abstract noun and verb types to total number of noun and verb types. Words were defined as abstract when the name of the object is thought of apart from the cases in which it is actually realized. For example, in the sentence, 'The lion is an *animal,*' 'animal' is an abstract word. However in the sentence, 'This animal in the picture is sitting on his throne,' 'animal' is not an abstract noun.

In our research group, middle-class mothers achieved an abstraction score of 5·6; the score for skilled work levels was 4·9; the score for the unskilled group was 3·7; for recipients of Aid to Dependent Children (ADC), 1·8.

The second scale dealt with the mother's tendency to use complex syntactic structures such as coordinate and subordinate clauses, unusual infinitive phrases (e.g., 'To drive well, you must be alert'), infinitive clauses (e.g., 'What to do next was the lion's problem'), and participial phrases (e.g., 'Continuing the story, the lion . . .'). The index of structural elaboration derived was a proportion of these complex syntactic structures, weighted in accordance with their complexity and with the degree to which they are strung together to form still more complicated structures (e.g., clauses within clauses), to the total number of sentences.

In the research group, mothers from the middle class had a structure elaboration index of 8·89; the score for ADC mothers was 6·46. The use of complex grammatical forms and elaboration of these forms into complex clauses and sentences provides a highly elaborated code with which to manipulate the environment symbolically. This type of code encourages the child to recognize the possibilities and subtleties inherent in language not only for communication but also for carrying on high-level cognitive procedures.

Control systems: person versus status orientation.— Our data on the mothers' use of status- as contrasted with person-oriented statements comes from maternal responses to questions inquiring what the mother would do in order to deal with several different hypothetical situations at school in which the child had broken the rules of the school, had failed to achieve, or had been wronged by a teacher or classmate. The results of this tally are shown in Table 3.

As is clear from these means, the greatest differences between status groups is in the tendency to utilize person-oriented statements. These differences are even greater if seen as a ratio of person-to-status type responses.

The orientation of the mothers to these different types of control is seen not only in prohibitive or reparative situations but in their instructions to their children in preparing them for new experiences. The data on this point come from answers to the question: 'Suppose your child were starting school tomorrow for the first time. What would you tell him? How would you prepare him for school?'

One mother, who was person-oriented and used elaborated verbal codes, replied as follows:

Table 3 Person-oriented and status-oriented units on school situation protocols (mothers)

A. Mean number

Social class	Person-oriented		Status-oriented		P/S Ratio	N
Upper middle	9·52	(1–19)	7·50	(0–19)	1·27	40
Upper lower	6·20	(0–20)	7·32	(2–17)	0·85	40
Lower lower	4·66	(0–15)	7·34	(2–17)	0·63	35
ADC	3·59	(0–16)	8·15	(3–29)	0·44	34

B. Mean per cent

Social class	Person-oriented	Status-oriented	N
Upper middle	36·92	27·78	40
Upper lower	31·65	36·92	40
Lower lower	26·43	40·69	35
ADC	20·85	51·09	34

Table 4 Information mothers would give to child on his first day at school

Social Status	Imperative	Instructive	Support	Preparation	Other	N
			% of Total Statements			
Upper middle	14·9	8·7	30·2	8·6	37·6	39
Upper lower	48·2	4·6	13·8	3·8	29·6	41
Lower lower	44·4	1·7	13·1	1·2	39·6	36
ADC	46·6	3·3	17·1	1·3	31·8	37
			% of mothers using category			
Upper middle	48·7	38·5	76·9	33·3	87·2	...
Upper lower	85·4	17·1	39·0	19·5	70·7	...
Lower lower	75·0	5·6	36·1	8·3	77·8	...
ADC	86·5	16·2	43·2	8·1	86·5	...

'First of all, I would remind her that she was going to school to learn, that her teacher would take my place, and that she would be expected to follow instructions. Also that her time was to be spent mostly in the classroom with other children, and that any questions or any problems that she might have she could consult with her teacher for assistance.'

'Anything else?'

'No, anything else would probably be confusing for her at her particular age.'

In terms of promoting educability, what did this mother do in her response? First, she was informative; she presented the school situation as comparable to one already familiar to the child; second, she offered reassurance and support to help the child deal with anxiety; third, she described the school situation as one that involves a personal relationship between the child and the teacher; and, fourth, she presented the classroom situation as one in which the child was to learn.

A second mother responded as follows to this question:

'Well, John, it's time to go to school now. You must know how to behave. The first day at school you should be a good boy and should do just what the teacher tells you to do.'

In contrast to the first mother, what did this mother do? First, she defined the role of the child as passive and compliant; second, the central issues she presented were those dealing with authority and the institution, rather than with learning; third, the relationship and roles she portrayed were sketched in terms of status and role expectations rather than in personal terms; and, fourth, her message was general, restricted, and vague, lacking information about how to deal with the problems of school except by passive compliance.

A more detailed analysis of the mothers' responses to this question grouped their statements as *imperative* or *instructive* (Table 4). An imperative statement was defined as an unqualified injunction or command, such as, 'Mind the teacher and do what she tells you to do,' or 'The first thing you have to do is be on time,' or 'Be nice and do not fight.' An instructive statement offers information or commands which carry a rationale or justification for the rule to be observed. Examples: 'If you are tardy or if you stay away from school, your marks will go down'; or 'I would tell him about the importance of minding the teacher. The teacher

needs his full cooperation. She will have so many children that she won't be able to pamper any youngster.'

Status differences in concept utilization.—One of the measures of cognitive style used with both mothers and children in the research group was the *S*'s mode of classificatory behavior. For the adult version, (Kagan, Moss & Sigel, 1963) *S* is required to make 12 consecutive sorts of MAPS figures placed in a prearranged random order on a large cardboard. After each sort she was asked to give her reason for putting certain figures together. This task was intended to reveal her typical or preferred manner of grouping stimuli and the level of abstraction that she uses in perceiving and ordering objects in the environment. Responses fell into four categories: descriptive part-whole, descriptive global, relational-contextual, and categorical-inferential. A descriptive response is a direct reference to physical attributes present in the stimuli, such as size, shape, or posture. Examples: 'They're all children,' or 'They are all lying down' or, 'They are all men.' The subject may also choose to use only a part of the figure—'They both have hats on.' In a relational-contextual response, any one stimulus gets its meaning from a relation with other stimuli. Examples: 'Doctor and nurse,' or 'Wife is cooking dinner for her husband,' or 'This guy looks like he shot this other guy.' In categorical-inferential responses sorts are based on nonobservable characteristics of the stimulus for which each stimulus is an independent representative of the total class. Examples: 'All of these people work for a living' or 'These are all handicapped people.'

As may be seen in Table 5, relational responses were most frequently offered; categorical-inferential were next most common, and descriptive most infrequent. The distribution of responses of our status groups showed that the middle-class group was high

Table 5 Mean responses to adult Sigel Sorting Task (MAPS)

Category	Social status		
	Upper middle N = 40	Upper lower N = 42	Low N
Total descriptive	3·18	2·19	
Descriptive part-whole	1·65	1·33	
Descriptive global	1·52	0·86	
Relational-contextual	5·52	6·7	
Categorical-inferential	3·30	3	

on descriptive and categorical; low-status groups were higher on relational. The greater use of relational categories by the working-class mothers is especially significant. Response times for relational sorts are usually shorter, indicating less reflection and evaluating of alternative hypotheses. Such responses also indicate relatively low attention to external stimuli details (Kagan, 1964). Relational responses are often subjective, reflecting a tendency to relate objects to personal concerns in contrast with the descriptive and categorical responses which tend to be objective and detached, more general, and more abstract. Categorical responses, in particular, represent thought processes that are more orderly and complex in organizing stimuli, suggesting more efficient strategies of information processing.

The most striking finding from the data obtained from the children's Sigel Sorting Task was the decreasing use of the cognitive style dimensions and increasing nonverbal responses with decrease in social-status level. As may be seen in the tables showing children's performance on the Sigel Sorting Task (Tables 6 and 7), although most upper middle-class children and a majority of the upper lower-class children use relational and descriptive global responses, there is no extensive use of any of the other cognitive style dimensions by the two lower lower-class groups. In looking at particular categories one may note the relative absence of descriptive part-whole responses for other than the middle-class group and the large rise in nonverbal responses below the middle-class level. These results would seem to reflect the relatively undeveloped verbal and conceptual ability of children from homes with restricted range of verbal and conceptual content.

Relational and descriptive global responses have been considered the most immature and would be hypothesized to occur most frequently in pre-school children. Relational responses are often subjective, using idiosyncratic and irrelevant cues; descriptive global responses, often referring to sex and occupational roles, are somewhat more dependent upon experience. On the other hand, descriptive part-whole responses have been shown to increase with age and would be expected to be used less frequently. However, these descriptive part-whole responses, which are correlated with favorable prognostic signs for educability (such as attentiveness, control and learning ability), were almost totally absent from all but the upper middle-class group. Kagan (1964) has described two fundamental cognitive dispositions involved in producing such analytic concepts: the tendency to reflect over alternative solutions that are simultaneously available and the tendency to analyze a visual stimulus into component parts. Both behaviors require a delayed discrimination response. One may describe the impairment noted for culturally disadvantaged children as arising from differences in opportunities for developing these reflective attitudes.

The mothers' use of relational responses was sig-

Table 6 Children's responses to Sigel Sorting Task (means)

Category	Social status			
	Upper middle N = 40	Upper lower N = 42	Lower lower N = 39	ADC N = 41
Descriptive part-whole	2·25	0·71	0·20	0·34
Descriptive global	2·80	2·29	1·51	0·98
Relational-contextual	3·18	2·31	1·18	1·02
Categorical-inferential	2·02	1·36	1·18	0·61
Nonscorable verbal responses	5·75	6·31	6·64	7·24
Nonverbal	3·00	6·41	7·08	8·76
No sort	1·00	0·62	2·21	1·05

Table 7 Percentage of four-year-old children responding in each of the categories

Category	Social status			
	Upper middle N = 40	Upper lower N = 42	Lower lower N = 39	ADC N = 41
Descriptive part-whole	40·0	28·6	18·0	14·6
Descriptive global	70·0	54·8	53·8	31·7
Total descriptive	80·0	66·7	59·0	39·0
Relational-contextual	77·5	66·7	41·0	43·9
Categorical-inferential	52·5	45·2	30·8	24·4
Nonscorable verbal	85·0	88·1	92·3	85·4
Nonverbal	52·5	66·7	82·0	87·8
No sort	12·5	7·1	25·6	19·5

nificantly correlated with their children's use of nonscorable and nonverbal responses on the Sigel task and with poor performance on the 8-Block and Etch-a-Sketch tasks. The mothers' inability or disinclination to take an abstract attitude on the Sigel task was correlated with ineffectual teaching on the 8-Block task and inability to plan and control the Etch-a-Sketch situation. Since relational responses have been found (Kagan, Moss & Sigel, 1963) to be correlated with impulsivity, tendencies for nonverbal rather than verbal teaching, mother-domination, and limited sequencing and discrimination might be expected and would be predicted to result in limited categorizing ability and impaired verbal skills in the child.

Analysis of maternal teaching styles

These differences among the status groups and among mothers within the groups appear in slightly different form in the teaching sessions in which the mothers and children engaged. There were large differences among the status groups in the ability of the mothers to teach and the children to learn. This is illustrated by the performance scores on the sorting tasks.

Let us describe the interaction between the mother and child in one of the structured teaching situations. The wide range of individual differences in linguistic and interactional styles of these mothers may be illustrated by excerpts from recordings. The task of the mother is to teach the child how to group or sort a small number of toys.

The first mother outlines the task for the child, gives sufficient help and explanation to permit the child to proceed on her own. She says:

'All right, Susan, this board is the place where we put the little toys; first of all you're supposed to learn how to place them according to color. Can you do that? The things that are all the same colour you put in one section; in the second section you put another group of colors, and in the third section you put the last group of colors. Can you do that? Or would you like to see me do it first?'

Child: 'I want to do it.'

This mother has given explicit information about the task and what is expected of the child; she has offered support and help of various kinds; and she has made it clear that she impelled the child to perform.

A second mother's style offers less clarity and precision. She says in introducing the same task:

'Now, I'll take them all off the board; now you put them all back on the board. What are these?'

Child: 'A truck.'

'All right, just put them right here; put the other one right here; all right put the other one there.'

This mother must rely more on nonverbal communication in her commands; she does not define the task for the child; the child is not provided with ideas or information that she can grasp in attempting to solve the problem; neither is she told what to expect or what the task is, even in general terms.

A third mother is even less explicit. She introduces the task as follows:

'I've got some chairs and cars, do you want to play the game?' Child does not respond. Mother continues: 'O.K. What's this?'

Child: 'A wagon?'

Mother: 'Hm?'

Child: 'A wagon?'

Mother: 'This is not a wagon. What's this?'

The conversation continues with this sort of exchange for several pages. Here again, the child is not provided with the essential information he needs to solve or to understand the problem. There is clearly some impelling on the part of the mother for the child to perform, but the child has not been told what he is to do. There were marked social-class differences in the ability of the children to learn from their mothers in the teaching sessions.

Each teaching session was concluded with an assessment by a staff member of the extent to which the child had learned the concepts taught by the mother. His achievement was scored in two ways: first, the ability to correctly place or sort the objects and, second, the ability to verbalize the principle on which the sorting or grouping was made.

Children from middle-class homes were well above children from working-class homes in performance on these sorting tasks, particularly in offering verbal explanations as to the basis for making the sort (Tables 8 and 9). Over 60 per cent of middle-class children placed the objects correctly on all tasks; the performance of working-class children ranged as low as 29 per cent correct. Approximately 40 per cent of these middle-class children who were successful were able to verbalize the sorting principle; working-class children were less able to explain the sorting principle, ranging

Table 8 Differences among status groups in children's performance in teaching situations (Toy sort task)

Social status	Placed correctly (%)	Verbalized correctly (%)		N
A. Identify sort (cars, spoons, chairs):				
Upper middle	61·5	28·2	45·8[a]	39
Upper lower	65·0	20·0	30·8	40
Lower lower	68·4	29·0	42·3	38
ADC	66·7	30·8	46·2	39
B. Color sort (red, green, yellow):				
Upper middle	69·2	28·2	40·7[a]	39
Upper lower	67·5	15·0	22·2	40
Lower lower	57·9	13·2	22·7	38
ADC	33·3	5·1	15·4	39

[a] Per cent of those who placed object correctly.

Table 9 Differences among status groups in children's performance in teaching situations (8-block task)

Social status	Placed correctly %	One-dimension verbalized %		Both verbalized %		N
A. Short O:						
Upper middle	75·0	57·5	57·5[a]	25·0	33·3[a]	40
Upper lower	51·2	39·0	43·2	2·4	4·8	41
Lower lower	50·0	20·0	33·3	15·8	31·6	38
ADC	43·6	20·5	22·2	2·6	5·9	39
B. Tall X:						
Upper middle	60·0	62·5	64·1[a]	27·5	45·8[a]	40
Upper lower	48·8	39·0	42·1	17·1	35·0	41
Lower lower	34·2	23·7	26·5	7·9	23·1	38
ADC	28·2	18·0	20·0	0·0	0·0	39

[a] Per cent of those who placed object correctly.

downward from the middle-class level to one task on which no child was able to verbalize correctly the basis of his sorting behavior. These differences clearly paralleled the relative abilities and teaching skills of the mothers from differing social-status groups.

The difference among the four status levels was apparent not only on these sorting and verbal skills but also in the mother's ability to regulate her own behavior and her child's in performing tasks which require planning or care rather than verbal or conceptual skill. These differences were revealed by the mother-child performance on the Etch-a-Sketch task. An Etch-a-Sketch toy is a small, flat box with a screen on which lines can be drawn by a device within the box. The marker is controlled by two knobs: one for horizontal movement, one for vertical. The mother is assigned one knob, the child the other. The mother is shown several designs which are to be reproduced. Together they attempt to copy the design models. The mother decides when their product is a satisfactory copy of the original. The products are scored by measuring deviations from the original designs.

These sessions were recorded, and the nonverbal interaction was described by an observer. Some of the most relevant results were these: middle-class mothers and children performed better on the task (14·6 point than mothers and children from the other gro (9·2; 8·3; 9·5; [Table 10]). Mothers of the lower-status groups were relatively persistent ing more complete figures than the mi mothers; mothers from the middle class child's efforts more than did other mot' just as much criticism; the child's coop by the observer was as good or be groups as in middle-class pairs (T little difference between the groups in affection expressed to the child by the mother (Brophy *et al.* 1965).

Table 10 Performance on Etch-a-Sketch task (means)

	Social status			
	Upper middle N = 40	Upper lower N = 42	Lower lower N = 40	ADC N = 41
Total score (range 0–40)	14·6	9·2	8·3	9·5
Average number of attempts	12·7	17·2	12·2	15·1
Complete figures rejected	2·3	3·6	3·5	3·4
Child's total score	5·9	4·0	3·4	4·0
Child's contribution to total score (per cent)	40·4	43·5	41·0	42·1

Table 11[a] Mother-child interaction on Etch-a-Sketch task (means)

	Social status			
	Upper middle N = 40	Upper lower N = 41	Lower lower N = 39	ADC N = 39
Praises child	4·6	6·9	7·2	7·5
Criticizes child	6·4	5·5	6·4	5·9
Overall acceptance of child	2·2	3·2	3·4	3·6
Child's cooperation	5·6	5·3	4·5	5·1
Level of affection shown to child	4·8	5·4	5·2	5·8

[a] Ratings made by observer; low number indicates more of the quality rated.

In these data, as in other not presented here, the mothers of the four status groups differed relatively little, on the average, in the affective elements of their interaction with their children. The gross differences appeared in the verbal and cognitive environments that they presented.

Against this background I would like to return for a moment to the problem of the meaning, or perhaps more correctly, the lack of meaning in cultural deprivation. One of the features of the behavior of the working-class mothers and children is a tendency to act without taking sufficient time for reflection and planning. In a sense one might call this impulsive behavior—not by acting out unconscious or forbidden impulses, but in a type of activity in which a particular act seems not to be related to the act that preceded it or to its consequences. In this sense it lacks meaning; it is not sufficiently related to the context in which it occurs, to the motivations of the participants, or to the goals of the task. This behavior may be verbal or motor; it shows itself in several ways. On the Etch-a-Sketch task, for example, the mother may silently watch a child make an error and then punish him. Another mother will anticipate the error, will warn the child that he is about to reach a decision point; she will prepare him by verbal and nonverbal cues to be careful, to look ahead, and to avoid the mistake. He is encouraged to reflect, to anticipate the consequences of his action, and in this way to avoid error. A problem-solving approach requires reflection and the ability to weigh decisions, to choose among alternatives. The effect of restricted speech and of status orientation is to foreclose the need for reflective weighing of alternatives and consequences, the use of an elaborated code, with its orientation to persons and to consequences (including future), tends to produce cognitive styles more easily adapted to problem-solving and reflection.

The objective of our study is to discover how teaching styles of the mothers induce and shape learning styles and information-processing strategies in the children. The picture that is beginning to emerge is that the meaning of deprivation is a deprivation of meaning—a cognitive environment in which behavior is controlled by status rules rather than by attention to the individual characteristics of a specific situation and one in which behavior is not mediated by verbal cues or by teaching that relates events to one another and the present to the future. This environment produces a child who relates to authority rather than to rationale, who, although often compliant, is not reflective in his behavior, and for whom the consequences of an act are largely considered in terms of immediate punishment or reward rather than future effects and long-range goals.

When the data are more complete, a more detailed analysis of the findings will enable us to examine the effect of maternal cognitive environments in terms of individual mother-child transactions, rather than in the gross categories of social class. This analysis will not only help us to understand how social-class environment is mediated through the interaction between mother and child but will give more precise information about the effects of individual maternal environments on the cognitive growth of the young child.

Note

1 This research is supported by the Research Division of the Children's Bureau, Social Security Administration; Department of Health, Education, and Welfare; Ford Foundation for the Advancement of Learning; and grants-in-aid from the Social Science Research Committee of the Division of Social Sciences, University of Chicago. Project staff members who made specific contributions to the analysis of data are Jere Brophy, Dina Feitelson, Roberta Meyer, and Ellis Olim. Hess's address: Committee on Human Development, University of Chicago, Chicago, Ill. 60637.

References

Bernstein, B. (1961). Social class and linguistic development: a theory of social learning, in A. H. Halsey, Jean Floud, & C. A. Anderson (eds.), *Education, economy, and society*. New York: Free Press.

Bernstein, B. (1964). Family role systems, communication, and socialization. Paper presented at Conf. on Development of Cross-Cultural Res. on the Education of Children and Adolescents, University of Chicago, February.

Brophy, J., Hess, R. D., & Shipman, Virginia (1965). Effects of social class and level of aspiration on performance in a structured mother-child interaction. Paper presented at Biennial Meeting of Soc. Res. Child Develpm., Minneapolis, Minn. March.

Deutsch, M. (1963). The disadvantaged child and the learning process, in A. H. Passow (ed.), *Education in depressed areas.* New York: Columbia Univer. TC, 163–180.

Deutsch, M., & Brown, B. (1964). Social influences in Negro-white intelligence differences. *J. soc. Issues* **20** (2), 24–35.

Eells, K., Davis, Allison, Havighurst, R. J., Herrick, V. E., & Tyler, R. W. (1951). *Intelligence and cultural differences.* University of Chicago Press.

Hess, R. D. (1964). Educability and rehabilitation: the future of the welfare class. *Marr. fam. Log* **26**, 422–429.

Jackson, J. D., Hess, R. D., & Shipman, Virginia (1965). Communication styles in teachers: an experiment. Paper presented at Amer. Educ. and Res. Ass., Chicago, February.

John, Vera (1963). The intellectual development of slum children: some preliminary findings. *Amer. J. Orthopsychiat.* **33**, 813–22.

Kagan, J., Moss, H. A., & Sigel, I. E. (1963). Psychological significance of styles of conceptualization. *Monogr. Soc. Res. Child. Develpm.* **28**, 2.

Kagan, J. (1964). Information processing in the child: significance of analytic and reflective attitudes. *Psychol. Monogr.* **78**. 1 (Whole No. 578).

Kennedy, W. A., Van de Riet, V., & White, J. C. Jr. (1963). A normative sample of intelligence and achievement of Negro elementary school children in the southeastern United States. *Monogr. Soc. Res. Child Develpm.* **28**, 6.

Lesser, G. (1964). Mental abilities of children in different social and cultural groups. New York: Cooperative Research Project 1635.

Meyer, Roberta, Shipman, Virginia, & Hess, R. D. (1964). Family structure and social class in the socialization of curiosity in urban preschool children. Paper presented at APA meeting in Los Angeles, Calif. September.

Olim, E. G., Hess, R. D., & Shipman, Virginia (1965). Relationship between mothers' language styles and cognitive styles of urban preschool children. Paper presented at Biennial Meeting of Soc. Res. Child Develpm., Minneapolis, Minn., March.

Shipman, Virginia, & Hess, R. D. (1965). Social class and sex differences in the utilization of language and the consequences for cognitive development. Paper presented at Midwest. Psychol. Ass., Chicago, April.

25 How shall the disadvantaged child be taught?

Marion Blank and Frances Solomon[1]

A 1-to-1 tutorial language program is illustrated in a series of dialogues between a teacher and a 4-year-old socially disadvantaged child. The teaching is analyzed both according to the deficiencies of the child's thinking and the techniques designed to foster the abstract thinking necessary to overcome these deficiencies. This program is contrasted to teaching done by a person trained in the traditional nursery school philosophy.

An eclectic approach to the teaching of language is usual in most preschool programs for disadvantaged children. Since their language deficiencies are extensive, it is hoped that the presentation of a massive array of possibly fruitful techniques is bound to lead to learning. In contrast, the present authors (Blank, 1968; Blank & Solomon, 1968) have presented the hypothesis that the deprived child's verbal weakness is so overwhelming that it blinds one to his more subtle but basic deficiency. This deficiency is the lack of a symbolic system for thinking. In order to develop this system, language is essential—but not all language is equally useful. In particular, we outlined a series of techniques in which the child was taught to use language so as to organize thoughts, to reflect upon situations, to comprehend the meaning of events, and to choose among alternatives. For example, one technique required the child to develop simple cause-and-effect models; for example, if the room is too bright when he comes in, he might be asked, 'How can we make it darker in here?' These techniques are in direct contrast to methods focused mainly on enlarging vocabulary for description and communication.

We further postulated that this type of teaching could not be done in the group situation. In observing children, even in small group settings, we have found that they often 'tune out' when the teacher attempts to structure a lesson. Once that occurs, almost infinite teaching skill is required to re-engage the child's attention without losing the interest of the rest of the group. Therefore it was decided to conduct the teaching on the basis of short (15-minute), one-to-one sessions between the teacher and the child.

An exploratory program using these techniques was conducted with a group of 22 disadvantaged children ranging in age from 3 years 3 months to 4 years 7 months (Blank & Solomon, 1968). The children were divided into four groups, two tutored and two untutored, matched as closely as possible for age, sex, and Stanford-Binet IQ scores. In one tutored group, each of six children received individual teaching five times per week; in the second tutored group, six children received the same teaching three times per week. The tutoring involved taking the child for this short period from his classroom to a familiar room in the school. One untutored group of three children had daily individual sessions, but no attempt was made to tutor them. These children were exposed to the identical materials and were permitted to engage in any activity of their choice. This group was included to control for the possible role of individual attention alone in facilitating intellectual performance. Another untutored group of seven children remained in the regular nursery school program with no additional attention. After 3 months (approximately 12 and 7 hours of tutoring for the tutored groups, respectively) the mean IQ increases in groups tutored five and three times per week were 14·5 and 7·0 points, respectively; in the untutored groups the changes were 2·0 and 1·3 points.

Source: *Child Development* (1969), 40 (1), 47–61.

In order to demonstrate these techniques in actual use, this paper presents two sessions with one of the 4-year-old children from the study. The sessions cover a 3-month period so as to illustrate the growth in her capacity to handle and structure cognitive material. A third session between this child and a nursery school teacher not trained in these techniques is also included here. We recorded a number of such sessions with teachers from established nursery schools. This was done to investigate the possibility that teachers might spontaneously adopt this approach to abstract thinking if permitted the opportunity of working on a one-to-one basis.

The commentary accompanying the dialogue is directed towards diagnosing both the deficiences of the child's thinking and the success of the teacher's methods in overcoming these deficiencies. 'Success,' of course, is evaluated according to the rationale of our philosophy of teaching abstract thinking.

Session 1

Julie was a highly impulsive, voluble 4-year-old of Puerto Rican background. She was charming, but a will-o'-the-wisp. Many deficiencies obscured her latent brightness; chief among them was an attention span even shorter than that of her peers.

A teacher trained in the principles of the program is seen here conducting one of the first sessions with Julie. The dialogue reads slowly, but actually covered only 5 minutes of a 15-minute session.

After the child had been in the room for several minutes, the teacher introduced some drawing materials:

Dialogue	*Interpretation*
TEACHER: I'm going to draw a picture, and then you're going to make one just like it. I'll give you a paper. What color crayon would you like to use?	Teacher's statements are designed to: (1) Tune child in to intended activity; (2) Have her make a specific verbal choice which will determine her next action.
JULIE: Yellow. [Child chooses correctly, immediately starts drawing in usually impulsive manner.]	Had child's choice not been consistent with verbalization, teacher would have initiated interchange to correct child.
TEACHER: *Wait*. Don't draw anything yet.	Teacher attempts to delay impulsivity.
JULIE: [Halts and focuses.]	
TEACHER: [Draws a circle.] What did I draw?	Teacher was not concerned with label per se, but rather, with posing a question so as to keep the child's attention.
JULIE: A ball.	
TEACHER: Could you make that ball? Make one just like mine.	Using child's word, teacher utilizes imitation as a means of getting child to complete a simple task.
JULIE: [Succeeds.]	
TEACHER: Good, now, I'm going to make a line *across* the ball. Can you do that? [Teacher draws a line across the circle.]	Teacher is trying to integrate another concept into the work. Almost any elementary but relevant concept which would have increased the complexity of the situation would have been suitable (e.g., drawing another figure inside the circle).
JULIE: [Draws an incorrect line from top to bottom of a circle.]	Child has merely reponded to the word 'line.' She has not heeded the total direction.
TEACHER: No, you drew it from the top to the bottom. We want it to go across. [Teacher indicates desired direction.]	
JULIE: [Draws line independently and correctly.] Now I went across.	Child's appropriate verbalization indicates und standing.
TEACHER: Very good. You know, we can also call a ball a circle. Do you know what I'm going to do with this circle? I'm going to get a green crayon and I'm going to fill in the *bottom half* of my circle. Would you like to get a green crayon and do the same thing? Fill it in so it looks like mine.	Since understanding is apparent, teacher int (1) the consensually validated label of circle increases the complexity by the dual ide and *color*. To help child handle this inc plexity, teacher perseveres with imi same thing'). It would have been be

JULIE: I like this color. I like all colors. I like flowers, too. I got that kind of crayon. I like brown—it's dark. We could play in the dark and we be scared.

TEACHER: But we're working with the green.

teacher not used the phrase 'would you like . . .' since it lends itself to the child's using an automatic response of 'no.' Since choice was not at issue, a specific demand such as 'please get' could have been put forth.

This talk typifies the random associations of young children's thinking. Judgment is required to differentiate this from a creative use of spontaneous language.

Teacher evaluates child's monologue as rambling and refuses to be led by it. She attempts to refocus child so that the child can experience the opportunity of completing an assignment.

JULIE: [Continues drawing but keeps up rambling conversation.] I got my new clothes. I gotta lot of new clothes in my house.

TEACHER: Would you work a little faster on this bottom one?

Since rapid tempo for this child is pleasurable, teacher introduces it to aid the child in completing her work.

JULIE: [Completes task.]

TEACHER: Very good. Now, look what I'm going to do. I'm going to get a purple crayon. I'm going to make the top of my circle purple. Look how fast I do it. Can you do yours like this?

Tempo retained as a means of handling child's short attention span.

JULIE: Fast—right? [Completes task.]

Child responds well to incorporating tempo into task.

TEACHER: Show me the top of the circle.

Teacher maintains concept of directionality.

JULIE: [Accomplishes task.]

TEACHER: Show me the bottom of your circle.

Normally, opposites are not taught together. If child did not know 'top,' teacher would not go on to 'bottom.' Since the child knew, the teacher could attempt to introduce the opposite concept.

JULIE: [Does as she is asked.]

TEACHER: Very good, Julie. Turn your paper upside down. Now show me which is the top.

This action is designed as a first step in enabling the child to see that top is a relative concept.

JULIE: [Points to bottom.]

This response shows that the child's concept of top is tied to the specific place designated originally. This error is typical in the development of a concept from the specific to the general.

TEACHER: No, this is the top now. [Points to area.] The top is always the highest place. Everything has a a top. When you turned your paper upside down, this became the top. Show me the top of your head.

Direct answers are usually avoided since the aim of the teaching is self-discovery. However, most factual information cannot be arrived at independently; therefore, the teacher gives this information. Teacher now begins to offer many examples of the concept.

JULIE: [Gestures correctly.]

TEACHER: Show me the top of the chair.

JULIE: [Satisfies this demand.]

Child is responding appropriately to concept posed by teacher. Thus, even though her response is nonverbal, it reflects thinking.

TEACHER: Show me the top of my boots.

Teacher specifically uses a low object to demonstrate that objects close to ground also have a 'top.'

JULIE: [Points correctly.]

TEACHER: Now, show me the top of the paper.

JULIE: [Points correctly.]

TEACHER: Show me the top of your drawing.

JULIE: [Gestures correctly.] The top is up here.

Child's correct response does not mean that she has a secure grasp of the concept, but she is developing a glimmering of the idea.

The teacher then reviewed the activities up to this point by having the child describe what they had done in that session (e.g., drawing, circle, across, top, bottom, same, color, etc.). Aid was given to help the child recall any significant omissions, and *she was made to ascertain whether her answers were correct*. If, for instance, she said she had used the color red, she was asked to find the drawing and determine if red was, in fact, the color used. If the child was unable to answer a question, the teacher might offer alternatives such as, 'Did we draw a circle or a box?' Thus, assistance was given when needed, but the direct answer was rarely given. A basic precept of this study is that a self-discovered answer is most effective for the development of thinking.

This simple review of recent activities is a memory-strengthening task which is not to be confused with the aimless reporting elicted by questions such as, 'What did you do yesterday?' Any answers given by the child to a question like the latter cannot be verified by the teacher. As a result, she has no means of demonstrating to the child whether his verbalizations correspond to reality. Therefore, all questions requiring memory in our program were restricted to verifiable events. These principles were continued throughout the teaching and are evident in the session that follows.

Session 2

The following dialogue with Julie is from a session held 3 months later. After entering the room, the teacher says:

TEACHER: Do you remember what we did when you were here yesterday?

The type of recall expected by now from child extends over greater time spans but is still verifiable. By contrast, in the early session, recall was restricted to tasks in the immediate session.

JULIE: Yes.

TEACHER: What did we do?

JULIE: I don't know.

Despite her affirmative answer to the previous question, the automatic negative response follows.

TEACHER: Let's see if I can help you. Is there anything on this table that we worked with the last time? [A limited variety of materials is present.]

Teacher presents visual aid to prod memory.

JULIE: [Points to blackboard.]

Child's gesture is correct.

TEACHER: That's just pointing. Tell me what we did.

Although a gesture would have been acceptable in an earlier session, teacher now demands a description, since child is capable of responding in language.

JULIE: We did—we did a square.

Without being given any hints, the child correctly describes the object she drew.

TEACHER: Right. What did we do with the square?

JULIE: [Hesitates.]

The teacher is making the child recount the next step in the past sequence.

TEACHER: Think about it for a minute.

Teacher makes a judgment that child can answer and delays offering help.

JULIE: We took it off. [Child refers to erasing.]

The pause has offered the child a chance to reflect. Her impulsive first answer has been replaced h accurate memory.

TEACHER: Good. Now, what did we use to take it off?

Teacher is continuing to focus on interrelated se of past events.

JULIE: I don't know.

TEACHER: [Brings blackboard forward.] All right— what would you do if you had a square on here and

Since the child is encountering diff chooses a slightly easier level by off you wanted to get rid of it? How could you get it off?

JULIE: Maybe we could use paper.

TEACHER: Why could we use paper? What would it do?

JULIE: It could take it off. It could rub it off.

TEACHER: Fine. Now, remember what we did? We didn't use paper to take off the square. Do you remember what it was we *did* use?

JULIE: A sponge.

TEACHER: Very good. Would you get the sponge for me and wet it? Get a paper towel and wet that too. Wet them both.

JULIE: [Goes to sink in room and reaches, not for the requested items, but for the soap.]

TEACHER: [Follows child over to sink.] Do we need the soap?

JULIE: No. [Takes sponge and piece of paper toweling and starts to return to seat.]

TEACHER: Do you remember what I asked you to do with the paper and sponge?

JULIE: Uh huh. Wet them.

TEACHER: Fine. Then, do that.

JULIE: [Wets toweling and sponge.] They are full of water.

TEACHER: Do you need all that water?

JULIE: [Shakes head to indicate 'no.']

TEACHER: What could you do to get rid of the water that you don't need?'

JULIE: [Squeezes water from both sponge and paper.]

TEACHER: What did you do?

JULIE: The water comes out.

TEACHER: That's fine Julie. You really didn't need all that water. [They return to the table.] Now, I'd like you to draw something for me on the blackboard.

JULIE: What color?

TEACHER: What color would you like to use?

JULIE: Green [and selects green crayon].

---

which has several alternative answers (e.g., 'What could you use to get it off?'). The child is thereby no longer limited to the past, where only one answer (the thing that actually happened) is correct.

Child is more successful with this relaxation in demand.

Teacher's question is to make child aware of the relationship between the object and the action for which it can be used.

Child grasps this connection and expresses herself in clear language.

Child's answer is correct. The reduced complexity helped her recall the past sequence.

This chain of commands is to help the child practice retaining several elements at one time.

This behavior illustrates the easy distractibility of a young child.

Teacher attempts to give aid by focussing on problem at hand.

Child has executed one segment of complex command in selecting the correct objects.

Teacher is offering assistance to help child remember last part of command. This emphasis on memory is intentional, since once a child has a grasp of how to relate past to present events, he has made a major gain in thinking.

Spontaneously verbalizes observation.

Offers question to help child arrive at simple cause-and-effect relation.

Child's response is correct on action level.

Even when child acts appropriately, he may not understand the rationale for the action. Teacher's question was designed to elicit this awareness.

The specific color is not integral to completing the task. Therefore, here and whenever possible, teacher gives child the opportunity to exercise choice.

TEACHER: Green is fine. Draw some green lines for me.

As opposed to random grabbing, this action follows a specific direction.

JULIE: I'll make some big ones.

TEACHER: Okay. We can work with big ones. Oh! Those are very big lines. What will happen if you wipe the sponge on those lines?

Since child's wish is not in conflict with the goal of the lesson, the teacher incorporates it into the lesson. The question is designed to help the child predict future events.

JULIE: I don't know.

TEACHER: Think about it, Julie. If you put this sponge over your lines and wipe them, what will happen?

Even though teacher thought child could not predict the outcome, she posed this question to help child recognize that a significant event is about to occur.

JULIE: [Moves sponge over drawing.]

TEACHER: What's happening to the lines, Julie?

JULIE: [With surprise.] They're not there anymore!

By having been focused, child gets a flash of insight that an interesting process is occurring. By contrast, when given no direction, children frequently just accept common phenomena without understanding. For example, if teacher had merely said 'erase it', child would have done so without any recognition of the processes involved.

TEACHER: [Holds sponge down to prevent child from lifting it.] If I lift up the sponge, what color is going to be on the sponge?

Another question to help child predict future events.

JULIE: White

Child automatically responds to word 'color' by naming any color.

TEACHER: Why white?

Regardless of whether child's answer is correct or incorrect, teacher makes child justify response.

JULIE: Green.

TEACHER: Tell me why you said green? Why do you think it will be green?

This question is asked so that child begins to recognize that prediction is based on observation and must be justified.

JULIE: 'Cause I wipe it off.

The action she describes is one aspect of the cause-and-effect idea that teacher is trying to develop.

TEACHER: What did you wipe off?

This question is to bring in other aspects necessary for the completion of the cause-and-effect idea.

JULIE: The green color.

Achieves correct answer.

TEACHER: Let's see if you're right. [Lifts sponge.] Green! You're right. Very good.

Shows child that prediction was correct.

The discussion went on to consider issues such as the effects on the sponge of erasing different colors, what happens to the chalk after it is erased, how to get chalk out of a sponge, comparison of sponge and paper toweling as erasers, and so forth.

This lesson, which lasted 20 minutes, was conducted with interest and enthusiasm on the part of the child w' 3 months before could not maintain a set course for more than a few minutes.

The lesson that follows was given in the same week as Session 2. It was taught by one of the nursery teachers who had been invited to visit the program. The teacher was told to teach a cognitively orient that she deemed appropriate for this age child.

Session 3

On this particular day, there were boxes of small plants in the room which the children were to plant outside. As she entered, Julie immediately looked at these flowers. The teacher noticed this and said:

TEACHER: Have you seen the flowers?

JULIE: I saw a beautiful flower outside.

> Because the specific referent was not designated (i.e., the flowers in the room), child reacted only to the word 'flower'.

TEACHER: A beautiful flower? What color was it?

> Teacher is led away from her initial referent and poses an unverifiable question.

JULIE: I don't know. It's a beautiful flower.

> It is not possible to ascertain whether child's response is a superficial verbalization or an accurate description.

TEACHER: Did you put it in the ground?

> Teacher appears to assume that child's comments reflect true interest. Thus, rather than initiating productive dialogue, teacher has limited herself to a very confined area.

JULIE: I picked it up.

> This response is likely to be a simple rote association.

TEACHER: You picked it up? What kind was it?

> Teacher here poses another unverifiable question.

JULIE: I don't know.

TEACHER: Was it little and yellow? Maybe it was a dandelion? Did you plant the flower? Was it a seed and now it's a flower?

> Teacher's questions involve multiple concepts, including an understanding of plant metamorphosis. This example illustrates the paradox of many pre-school language programs, in which it is common to ask extremely complex questions couched in deceptively simple terms. Because of the apparent simplicity, it is often not deemed necessary to give the aids necessary for grasping what are, in fact, complex ideas.

JULIE: [Nods.]

TEACHER: Why don't you draw a picture of the flower and then we can see what color it is.

> Teacher assumes that child's poverty of language prohibits explanation and that if the verbal requirements are replaced through drawing, child's knowledge will be revealed. This may, in fact, be true. However, since child's drawing is not verifiable, teacher cannot determine its accuracy. Thus, dialogue with seeming conceptual content can often be aimless.

JULIE: I'd like to do any color flower.

TEACHER: I'd love to have a drawing of it.

> In keeping with her permissive orientation, teacher drops her original request and follows child's superficial comment. If child were moving toward a productive idea of her own, this permissive acceptance would prove valuable.

JULIE: I'm gonna make a beautiful flower.

TEACHER: Good.

JULIE: What's this? [The child is referring to the design from the table which comes through on her drawing.]

> Child is beginning to observe and question her surroundings.

TEACHER: That's the table cloth coming up; the pattern.

> Teacher answers directly. The information requested by child is not simply factual but could be deduced by child herself through proper questioning.

An interchange about flowers then continued on the assumption that the child, in fact, had something definite she wanted to draw. The teacher did attempt to stimulate the child's recall of the specific flower but for this purpose again used unverifiable questions. After the child had drawn several flowers, the teacher said:

TEACHER: Do you know how many flowers you have there now?

Teacher here is attempting to lead child away from narrowness of flowers per se and integrate it with another concept, that is, number.

JULIE: Three. I'm 5 years old.

Child's association of one number with another has an understandable basis. However, her spontaneous use of the same words for a variety of phenomena (age, objects, etc.) suggests that she does not have a clear understanding of the concept of number. Although one would not expect greater understanding in a young child, one must be aware that confusion exists.

TEACHER: You're 5 years old? Maybe you could make flowers for how old you are. Do you know how many more you would need?

Teacher assumes that child can make an equation between numbers in terms of years and numbers of objects.

JULIE: Five.

Child does not answer question but, rather, repeats her response to earlier question.

TEACHER: Five *altogether*. And how many do you have here?

Teacher makes attempt to dissect the problem for simplification. However, the complexity involved requires an almost endless dissection, for example, 'Five equals the number of years you are; each flower represents one year; the flowers do not equal the desired number of years; additional flowers must be drawn; you need to consider the number of flowers you have drawn relative to the desired number five, etc.' This fantastic complexity is far beyond child's ability to comprehend, but it is in effect what has been asked of her.

JULIE: I'll make one more. What kind of brown is this? It's a tree.

Child shows a primitive understanding that *more* is needed, but not specifically how much or why. Her leading back to color may be a combination of avoiding a difficult issue or another intrusion of an impulsive idea.

TEACHER: Oh, that's pretty, Julie. That's very, very, nice.

Topic of numbers has been discarded without any advance in child's knowledge.

JULIE: I bet it's time to wake up now.

Child is referring to the nap time of the rest of the nursery group.

TEACHER: What time do you get up?

Teacher has misinterpreted child's referent to mean the time she wakes up at home. This confusion is reasonable, and where teaching time is unlimited, it is of no special significance. In a language program with a highly restricted time element, however, it hampers the few opportunities available to teach a child how to interpret correctly other people's frames of reference.

JULIE: I get up five o'clock.

TEACHER: In the morning? [Incredulously.] Do you really wake up at five o'clock in the morning?

It is likely that child is perseverating the 'five' from earlier discussion.

JULIE: I do.

TEACHER: And what time do you come to school?

JULIE: I don't know what time—nighttime?

This dialogue again illustrates the type of [...] cation between a child and teacher w[...] mistaken for a conceptual discussion (*[...]*

TEACHER: No.

JULIE: I think so; I got a clock. I'm tired.

daytime, nighttime, etc.) Child's lack of awareness of the absurdity of being in nursery school at night indicates that she is in a discussion beyond her depth. In her effort to respond, child is led to rely on prattle alone.

Discussion

We believe that the first two dialogues illustrate the marked changes that occurred in this child after only 6 hours of tutoring. These 15-minute sessions took place three times a week over a 3-month period. Nine hours would have been the optimum during this time span, but absences reduced the total possible time allocated.

The changes in the behavior were corroborated by a rise of 12 points from 86 to 98 on the Standford-Binet Intelligence Test. Similar changes which were statistically significant occurred for the total group of 12 children tutored as Julie had been. Although Julie's rise was only 12 points, one child's IQ rose 28 points. These changes occurred across a wide behavioral range including control of impulsivity, increase of attention span, and greater enjoyment in learning.

Verbal skills alone were not an indication of Julie's growth (and may well not be a good indicator for other children). For example, as her hyperactive state became more controlled, her initial *rate* of verbalization declined. In place of her scattered language outpouring, she began to harness the language skills she possessed and use them in a relevant and directed manner. No measures exist for discerning this growth in quality versus quantity of verbalization in the young child, although such measures are sorely needed.

It may be argued that any one-to-one situation may bring about this type of change. However, when the same nursery school teacher met with a control group of three children on an individual but nonteaching basis, there was no significant change. A relationship with an involved and warm adult has often been suggested as the missing link to learning. We submit that such a relationship is fruitless from a cognitive view, unless the time is structured and directed toward a language for cognition.

The session with the visiting teacher was included to offer clues as to why the one-to-one situation fails to develop thinking skills. We recognize that the dialogue is shown to a disadvantage in that the teacher was new to the situation and not well known to the child. However, it is representative of the type of session we recorded by a number of cooperating nursery school teachers. In addition, we feel that this sequence epitomizes the traditionally child-centred and permissive Gestalt of nursery school philosophy (see review by Weikart, 1967). In this type of program, which is designed to meet the needs of the middle-class child, language and intellectual development are placed *last* in a list of desired attributes to be developed. Even when cognitive skills are taught, the philosophy of 'what does the child *want* to do' is the pervasive element.

This philosophy was clearly illustrated in the visiting lesson where the teacher severely limited the scope of the material by continuing to focus on casual comments of the child. Regardless of whether she mistook these remarks for real interest or whether she was guided by a consideration for a child's words, the teacher missed the opportunity to lead Julie toward developing the higher level concepts of which she was capable.

On the other hand, when the teacher did initiate material, she posed seemingly simple questions which, in reality, were of enormous complexity. Since the teacher did not have the techniques for analyzing where the child's difficulty lay, she assumed that the concepts involved were well beyond the child. The failure to recognize the complexity of her questions reinforces the philosophy that thinking cannot be accelerated but must merely wait until the child is 'ready.' The teacher thus abdicates her leadership in favor of the ephemeral concept of 'readiness.' Consequently, she sees her role as merely structuring the surroundings so as to set the stage for the spontaneous emergence of reasoning.

If this is the viewpoint of many nursery schools attended by middle-class children, the question arises as to how these children develop cognitive skills without special tutoring. It is generally assumed that they absorb them at home. However, if the middle-class teacher *avoids* fostering these skills, might not the middle-class parent similarly avoid this type of dialogue? Evidence indicates that, compared to the lower class, there is a much greater richness of verbal interchange between parent and child in the middle-class home (Freeburg & Payne, 1967). Thus, language is pervasive in these homes, and the child is exposed 'naturally' to language skills throughout the day. The middle-class person is not accustomed to being limited to a special time (i.e., 15-minute periods) focused upon these skills, nor to the necessity for having such focusing. When a relevant situation arises, the middle-class parent will encourage discussion with his children. Such situations arise 'normally' during the course of the day and are therefore taken for granted. However, such times rarely emerge during the course of the day of the lower-class child. These opportunities must be created for him. Consequently, the teaching situation may appear artificial and constricted, since the 15-minute period must be utilized with a maximum of efficiency in order to grasp every possible opportunity for cognitive growth.

Note

1 This research was supported by US Public Health Service grant K3-MH-10, 749. The authors wish to thank Miss E. Johnson and the staff of the Bronx River Day Care Center for their cooperation and participation in the research. Author Blank's address: Department of Psychiatry, Albert Einstein College of Medicine, 1300 Morris Park Avenue, Bronx, New York 10461.

References

Blank, M. (1968). A methodology for fostering abstract thinking in deprived children. Paper presented at Ontario Institute for Studies in Education conference on Problems in the Teaching of Young Children, Toronto, March.

Blank, M., & Solomon, F. (1968). A tutorial language program to develop abstract thinking in socially disadvantaged preschool children. *Child Development* **39**, 379–90.

Freeburg, N. E., & Payne, D. T. (1967). Parental influence on cognitive development in early childhood: a review. *Child Development* **38**, 65–87.

Weikart, D. P. (1967). Preschool programs: preliminary findings. *Journal of Special Education* **1**, 163–81.

26   Early childhood intervention: the social science base of institutional racism

Stephen S. Baratz and Joan C. Baratz[1]

To understand the present political and academic furore over the efficacy—and therefore the future—of such early-intervention programs as Head Start, it is necessary first to examine the basic concepts and assumptions upon which these programs are founded and then to determine whether existing data can support such an approach to the problem of educating children from black ghettoes.

This paper attempts (1) to present an overview of the interventionist literature with particular emphasis on the role of the social pathology model in interpreting the behavior of the ghetto mother, and (2) to illustrate how the predominant ethnocentric view of the Negro community by social science produces a distorted image of the life patterns of that community. The importance of this distortion is that, when converted into the rationale of social action programs, it is a subtle but pernicious example of institutional racism.

This paper is concerned with the goals of intervention programs that deal with altering the child's home environment, with improving his language and cognitive skills, and most particularly with changing the patterns of child-rearing within the Negro home. These goals are, at best, unrealistic in terms of current linguistic and anthropological data and, at worst, ethnocentric and racist. We do not question the legitimacy of early childhood programs when they are described solely as nursery school situations and are not based on the need for remediation or intervention; nor do we question such programs when they increase chances for the employment of economically deprived Negroes. Finally we do not question such programs when they are described as opportunities to screen youngsters for possible physical disorders, even though follow-up treatment of such diagnostic screening is often unavailable.

We wish to examine in more detail, however, the social pathology model of behavior and intelligence in Head Start[2] projects. We shall attempt to demon-

Source: *Harvard Educational Review* (1970), 40 (1), 29–50.

strate that the theoretical base of the deficit model employed by Head Start programs denies obvious strengths within the Negro community and may inadvertently advocate the annihilation of a cultural system which is barely considered or understood by most social scientists. Some thirty years ago, Melville Herskovits (1938–39) made the following insightful observation when talking about culturally related behavioral differences:

> [We need to recognize the existence of] . . . the historical background of the . . . behavioral differences . . . being studied and those factors which make for . . . their . . . existence, and perpetuation. When, for instance, one sees vast programs of Negro education undertaken without the slightest consideration given even to the possibility of some retention of African habits of thought and speech that might influence the Negroes' reception of the instruction thus offered—one cannot but ask how we hope to reach the desired objectives. When we are confronted with psychological studies of race relations made in utter ignorance of characteristic African patterns of motivation and behavior or with sociological analyses of Negro family life which make not the slightest attempt to take into account even the chance that the phenomenon being studied might in some way have been influenced by the carry-over of certain African traditions, we can but wonder about the value of such work. (Herskovits 1938–9 p. 121)

It is one of the main contentions of this paper that most, if not all, of the research on the Negro has sorely missed the implications of Herskovits' statement. Rather, research on the Negro has been guided by an ethnocentric liberal ideology which denies cultural differences and thus acts against the best interests of the people it wishes to understand and eventually help.

Socio-political ideology and studies of the Negro

Though it has seldom been recognized by investigators, it has been virtually impossible for social science to divorce itself from ideological considerations when discussing contemporary race relations. As Killian (1968) has pointed out with reference to the social science role after the 1954 Supreme Court Decision:

> Because of their professional judgment that the theories were valid and because of the egalitarian and humanitarian ethos of the social sciences, many sociologists, psychologists, and anthropologists played the dual role of scientist and ideologist with force and conviction. Without gainsaying the validity of the conclusions that segregation is psychologically harmful to its victims, it must be recognised that the typically skeptical, even querulous attitude of scientists toward each other's work was largely suspended in this case. (Killian, 1968, p. 54)

Social science research with Negro groups has been postulated on an idealized norm of 'American behavior' against which all behavior is measured. This norm is defined operationally in terms of the way white middle-class America is supposed to behave. The normative view coincides with current social ideology—the egalitarian principle—which asserts that all people are created equal under the law and must be treated as such from a moral and political point of view. The normative view, however, wrongly equates equality with sameness. The application of this mis-interpreted egalitarian principle to social science data has often left the investigator with the unwelcome task of describing Negro behavior not as it is, but rather as it deviates from the normative system defined by the white middle class. The postulation of such a norm in place of legitimate Negro values or life ways has gained ascendance because of the pervasive assump-tions (1) that to be different from whites is to be inferior and (2) that there is no such thing as Negro culture. Thus we find Glazer and Moynihan (1963) stating: 'The Negro is only an American and nothing else. He has no values and culture to guard and protect' (Glazer, N. and Moynihan, D., 1963).

Billingsley (1968) has taken sharp objection to the Glazer and Moynihan statement, pointing out:

> The implications of the Glazer-Moynihan view of the Negro experience is far-reaching. To say that a people have no culture is to say that they have no common history which has shaped and taught them. And to deny the history of a people is to deny their humanity. (Billingsley, 1968, p. 37)

However, the total denial of Negro culture is con-sonant with the melting-pot mythology and it stems from a very narrow conceptualization of culture by non-anthropologists (Baratz and Baratz, 1969). Social science has refused to look beyond the surface similarities between Negro and white behavior and, therefore, has dismissed the idea of subtle yet enduring differences. In the absence of an ethno-historical perspective, when differences appear in behavior, intelligence, or cognition, they are explained as evidence of genetic defects or as evidence of the nega-tive effects of slavery, poverty, and discrimination. Thus, the social scientist interprets differences in behavior as genetic pathology or as the alleged pathology of the environment; he therefore fails to understand the distortion of the Negro culture that his ethnocentric assumptions and measuring devices have created. The picture that emerges from such an interpretive schema may be seen as culturally biased and as a distortion of the Negro experience.

Liberals have eagerly seized upon the social pathol-ogy model as a replacement for the genetic inferiority model. But both the genetic model and the social pathology model postulate that something is wrong with the black American. For the traditional racists, that something is transmitted by the genetic code; for the ethnocentric social pathologists, that some-thing is transmitted by the family. The major difference between the genetic model and the social pathology model lies in the attribution of causality, *not* in the analysis of the behaviors observed as sick, pathological, deviant, or underdeveloped. An example of the marked similarity between the genetic and the social pathology perspectives can be found in the literature concerning language abilities of Negroes.

Language abilities of Negroes

Language proficiency is considered at length in both the social and the genetic pathology models. This con-cern is not accidental, but is the result of a basic assumption shared by both the social pathologists and the genetic racists that one's linguistic competence is a measure of one's intellectual capacity.

Thus we find Shaler (1890), who believed in the genetic inferiority of the Negro, writing:

> His inherited habits of mind, framed on a very limited language—where the terms were well tied together and where the thought found in the words a bridge of easy passage—gave him much trouble when he came to employ our speech where the words are like widely separated steppingstones which require nimble wits in those who use them. (Shaler, 1890, p. 23)

And later, Gonzales (1922) describes the language of the Carolina coastal Negroes called Gullahs in a similar manner:

> Slovenly and careless of speech, these Gullahs seized upon peasant English used by some of the early settlers and by the white servants of the wealthier colonists, wrapped their clumsy tongues about it as well as they could, and, enriched with certain expressive African words, it issued through their flat noses and thick lips as so

workable a form of speech that it was gradually adopted by other slaves and became in time the accepted Negro speech of the lower districts of South Carolina and Georgia. With characteristic laziness, these Gullah Negroes took short cuts to the ears of their auditors, using as few words as possible, sometimes making one gender serve for three, one tense for several, and totally disregarding singular and plural numbers. (Gonzales, 1922, p. 10)

Hunt (1968) provides a similar description, but from the social pathology perspective, when he writes of the parents of Negro children:

These parents themselves have often failed to utilize prepositional relationships with precision, and their syntax is confused. Thus, they serve as poor linguistic models for their young children. (Hunt, 1968, p. 31)

And Deutsch (1963), writing on the same subject, states:

In observations of lower-class homes, it appears that speech sequences seem to be temporally very limited and poorly structured syntactically. It is thus not surprising to find that a major focus of deficit in the children's language development is syntactical organization and subject continuity. (Deutsch, 1963, p. 174)

Green (1964) gives us another example of the deficit orientation of social pathology thinkers:

The very inadequate speech that is used in the home is also used in the neighborhood, in the play group, and in the classroom. Since these poor English patterns are reconstructed constantly by the associations that these young people have, the school has to play a strong role in bringing about a change in order that these young people can communicate more adequately in our society. (Green, 1964, p. 123)

Finally, Hurst (1965) categorizes the speech of many Negro college freshmen as:

. . . [involving] such specific oral aberrations as phonemic and sub-phonemic replacements, segmental phonemes, phonetic distortions, defective syntax, misarticulations, mispronunciations, limited or poor vocabulary, and faulty phonology. These variables exist most commonly in unsystematic, multifarious combinations.

Because of their ethnocentric bias, both the social pathologists and the genetic racists have wrongly presumed that linguistic competence is synonymous with the development of standard English and, thus, they incorrectly interpret the different, yet highly abstract and complex, non-standard vernacular used by Negroes as evidence of linguistic incompetence or

underdevelopment (Baratz, J., 1969). Both share the view that to speak any linguistic system other than standard English is to be deficient and inferior.

Since as early as 1859, when Müller (1859) wrote the *History of Ancient Sanskrit Literature*, the racist contention has been that languages (and their cognitive components) could be hierarchically ordered. Müller himself offered German as the 'best' language for conceptualization, but it will not surprise anyone to learn that at various times and according to various writers, the 'best' language has been the language of the particular person doing the thinking about the matter. Thus, the ethnocentrism of the social pathology model, which defines a difference as a deficit, forces the misguided egalitarian into testing a racist assumption that some languages are better than others.

The logic of intervention

It is important, then, to understand that the entire intervention model of Head Start rests on an assumption of linguistic and cognitive deficits which must be remedied if the child is to succeed in school. The current linguistic data, however, do not support the assumption of a linguistic deficit. The linguistic competence of black children has been well documented in a number of recent investigations (Stewart, 1968; Labov and Cohen, 1967; Labov, 1969; Dillard, 1969; Baratz, 1969; Wolfram, 1969). Many lower-class Negro children speak a well ordered, highly structured, but different, dialect from that of standard English. These children have developed a language. Thus one of the basic rationales for intervention, that of developing language and cognitive skills in 'defective' children, cannot be supported by the current linguistic data.

None the less, the first intervention programs assumed that the causes of a Negro child's failure in school could be counteracted in those months prior to his entrance into school. Data soon became available concerning the effects of Head Start, indicating that three months was not enough time for intervention to be effective (Wolff and Stein, 1967). The social pathologists reasoned that the supposedly progressive deleterious effects of the early environment of the Negro child were so great they could not be overcome in a few months. This argument provided the basis for the extension of Head Start to a full year before school—and by extension into intervention programs which begin earlier and earlier in the child's life and which eventually call for interference with existent family and child-rearing activities.

This expanding web of concern is consistent with the deficit model. Postulation of one deficit which is unsuccessfully dealt with by intervention programs then leads to the discovery of more basic and fundamental deficits. Remediation or enrichment gradually broadens its scope of concern from the fostering of language competence to a broad-based restructuring of the entire cultural system. The end result of this line of argument occurs when investigators such as

Deutsch and Deutsch (1968) postulate that 'some environments are better than others'.

With the recognition of failures and limitations within Head Start and like programs with a social pathology base, proponents of intervention call for earlier and earlier intervention in the child's life. This follows from an interlocking set of assumptions which they frequently make:

1 that, upon entering school, the Negro disadvantaged child is unable to learn in the standard educational environment;
2 that this inability to learn is due to inadequate mothering;
3 that the ghetto environment does not provide adequate sensory stimulation for cognitive growth.

The first premise is buttressed by the continued reports of failure of black children in our schools. Indeed, they do not benefit from the standard educational environment. (That does not, however, say anything about whether they are capable of learning generally.) The second premise is an extension of the earlier work on mothering of institutionalized children as reported by Spitz (1945), Goldfarb (1955), Rheingold (1956), and Skeels and Dye (1939). Much of this literature, however, is predicated on the total absence of a mother or mothering agent. Indeed, the Skeels follow-up study (1960) indicates that a moronic mother is better than no mother at all. The difficulty in extending this logic to the ghetto child is that *he has a mother*, and his behavior derives precisely from her presence rather than her absence.

Then too, the sensory stimulation assumption was an over-extension of the earlier work of Kretch *et al.* (1962), where animals were raised in cages with either considerable sensory stimulation or *none* at all. Again, the model was that of absence of stimulation rather than difference in type and presentation of stimulation.

The inadequate mother hypothesis

It is important to understand that the inadequate mother hypothesis rests essentially on the grounds that the mother's behavior produces deficit children. It was created to account for a deficit that in actuality does not exist—that is, that ghetto mothers produce linguistically and cognitively impaired children who cannot learn. Black children are neither linguistically impoverished nor cognitively underdeveloped. Although their language system is different and, therefore, presents a handicap to the child attempting to negotiate with the standard English-speaking mainstream, it is none the less a fully developed, highly structured system that is more than adequate for aiding in abstract thinking. French children attempting to speak standard English are at a linguistic disadvantage; they are not linguistically deficient. Speaking standard English is a linguistic disadvantage for the black youth on the streets of Harlem. A disadvantage created by a difference is not the same thing as a deficit!

In addition, before reviewing some of the notions of the inadequate mother hypothesis, it is necessary to stress that the data presented in that literature fail to show anything more than correlations between child-rearing behaviors and school achievement. As has been discussed elsewhere (Baratz, S., 1968), these correlations cannot be utilized as if they are statements of cause and effect. Although available data do indeed indicate that these culturally different Negro children are not being educated by the public school system, the data fail to show (1) that such children have been unable to learn to think and (2) that, because of specific child-rearing practices and parental attitudes, these children are not able (and, presumably, will never be able) to read, write, and cipher—the prime teaching responsibilities of the public school system.

Nevertheless, the inadequate mother hypothesis has proliferated in the literature of educational psychology. Of chief concern in this literature is the mother-child interaction patterns of lower-class Negroes. Despite the insistence that these patterns are the chief cause of the child's deficits, the supporting data consist almost entirely of either (1) responses to sociological survey-type questionnaires or (2) interaction situations contrived in educational laboratories. There is almost no anthropologically-oriented field work that offers a description of what actually does happen *in the home* wherein the deficit is alleged to arise.

One of the chief complaints leveled against the black mother is that she is not a teacher. Thus one finds programs such as Caldwell's (1968) which call for the 'professionalization of motherhood,' or Gordon's (1968) which attempts to teach the mother how to talk to her child and how to teach him to think.

The first assumption of such programs is that the ghetto mother does not provide her child with adequate social and sensory stimulation (Hunt, 1961). However, further research into the ghetto environment has revealed that it is far from a vacuum; in fact, there is so much sensory stimulation (at least in the eyes and ears of the middle-class researcher) that a contrary thesis was necessarily espoused which argues that the ghetto sensory stimulation is excessive and therefore causes the child to inwardly tune it all out, thus creating a vacuum for himself (Deutsch, C., 1968).

More recently, studies of social interaction suggest that the amount of social stimulation may be quantitatively similar for lower-class and middle-class children. Thus, the quantitative deficit explanation now appears, of necessity, to be evolving into a qualitative explanation; that is, the child receives as much or even more stimulation as does the middle-class child, but the researchers feel this stimulation is not as 'distinctive' for the lower-class child as it is for the middle-class child (Kagan, 1968). Of course, it is interesting to note here that, except for those environments where social and sensory deprivation are extremely severe or total, a condition which is certainly not characteristic of the ghetto environment, there is not evidence to suggest that the ghetto child is cognitively impaired by his mother's sensory social interactions with him.

It has further been suggested that the ghetto mother manages her home in such a manner that the child has difficulty developing a proper sense of time and space—i.e. the organization of the house is not ordered around regularly occurring mealtimes and is not ruled by the White Anglo-Saxon Protestant maxim 'everything in its place, and a place for everything.' To the middle-class observer, such a home appears to be disorganized and chaotic, while it is merely organized differently. Thus we have data which tell what the mother does not do, but we are missing the data which describe what she does do and explain how the household manages to stay intact. Again, there is no extant research that indicates that the development of a concept of time is either helped or hindered by a child's growing up in an environment where there are regularly occurring meal and bedtimes. There is, however, a considerable literature concerning cultural differences in the concept of time (Henry, 1965).

Further, it is continually asserted that the ghetto mother does not talk or read to her child, thus supposedly hindering his intellectual growth and language development. Despite the fact that no study has ever indicated the minimal amount of stimulation necessary for the child to learn language, and despite the fact that *the child has in fact developed language*, the ghetto mother is still accused of causing language retardation in her infant.

The mother's involvement in reading activities is also presumed to be extremely important to the child's development and future school success. The conclusions of many studies of the black ghetto home stress the absence of books and the fact that ghetto mothers rarely read to their children. Although the presence of books in the home may be quite indicative of middle-class life styles, and stories when read may very well give pleasure to all children, there appears to be no evidence which demonstrates that reading to children is essential for their learning to read, or that such reading will enhance their real language development. Although Irwin's (1960) landmark study indicates that children who are systematically read to babble more, it does not demonstrate that they are linguistically more proficient than those children who are not read to systematically.

A further factor in the mother's behavior which is continually blamed for deficits in the child is her lack of communication to him of the importance of school achievement. Although the literature presents a great many cases which illustrate that the lower-class mother verbalizes great achievement motivations concerning her children, these verbalizations are largely discredited in the eyes of some psychologists (Katz, 1968) who see little action—e.g., helping with homework, joining the PTA—underlying her statement of achievement motivation for her child. (Here, ironically, the supposedly non-verbal mother is now being penalized for her verbal behavior.) Indeed, her verbalizations tend to exhort the child to behave and achieve in class in relation to some assumed behavioral norm rather than to some educational reward; e.g., learn to read because the teacher says so, not because there are many things that one can learn from books (Hess, *et al.*, 1968). Nonetheless, there do not appear to be any data which show that preschool children resist learning, avoid schooling, or generally do not wish to achieve in the classroom; nor are there data to suggest that intrinsic motivations (learn for learning's sake) are effective for teaching reading, or that extrinsic ones (do it because I tell you) are not. In fact, the behaviorist literature tends to indicate that different sub-groups (i.e. lower-class versus middle-class) respond differently to various reinforcements (for instance, food versus praise).

The recent work of Hess, Shipman, Brophy, and Bear (1968) is sure to add considerable fuel to the inadequate mother hypothesis. Hess and his colleagues collected data on 163 black mothers and their four-year-old children. The mothers were divided into four groups: professional, skilled, unskilled-family intact, and unskilled-father absent. Social workers collected data in two extensive home interviews. Later, the mothers and children came to the university where IQ and other formal tests were administered. The mothers were also presented with theoretical situations and asked what they would do or say—e.g., what would you say to your child on his first day of school. In addition, the mothers were asked to teach their children a block-sorting task and to replicate a design on an etch-a-sketch box with their children. The Hess *et al.* data furnished a good deal of information concerning teaching styles of lower- and middle-class black women. These data, however, were undoubtedly influenced by the fact that the situations in which they were elicited (i.e., interviewing and a laboratory task) are much more typical of middle-class experiences. Nevertheless, many differences in maternal language and teaching styles appeared. It would be a mistake, however, to conclude that these differences in language and teaching style cause the child to be uneducable. What makes him appear 'uneducable' is his failure in an educational system that is insensitive to the culturally different linguistic and cognitive styles that he brings to the classroom setting. The school, therefore, fails to use the child's distinct cultural patterns as the vehicle for teaching new skills and additional cultural styles.

One of the major difficulties with the work of Hess *et al.* lies in their concept of 'educability.' Superficially this refers to those skills which every child potentially possesses but which presumably are not developed if the mother's behavior is 'restricted' and not similar to that of those middle-class mothers who produce children who succeed in school. Those skills which the child potentially possesses, however, are not defined by Hess *et al.* simply as language development, but rather more subtly as the use of standard English. Concept development is not seen as the development of language for thought (There are, of course, no languages that one cannot think in!) but rather, it is defined in terms of performance on standardized tasks or measures of verbal elaboration. Again, motivation is described not in terms of wanting to read, but rather in terms of books around the house and the use of the public library. 'Educability' then, is really defined as specific middle-class mainstream behaviors rather than as the possession of universal processes through which specific behaviors can be channeled. The lower-class mother is *a priori* defined as inadequate because she is not middle-class.

In their discussions of the mothers' language behavior, Hess *et al.* rely heavily on the concepts of Basil Bernstein, who describes two different communicative styles generally used by lower- and middle-class English children. That the language and teaching behaviors of lower-class Negro mothers are different from those of middle-class mothers is beyond question. That the different behavior leads to cognitive defects has yet to be demonstrated. Carroll (1964) has discussed the methodological issue of the relationship of language style to cognition. To say, that a particular language has a deleterious effect on cognitive performance, speakers of that language must be tested for cognitive ability on a non-linguistic task— such a task has yet to be developed or tested.

The Hess data, while providing considerable information on maternal behavior differences in lower- and middle-class black women, do not indicate that the children from lower-class homes are any less ready to learn than are the middle-class children, nor do they demonstrate that these children will be less able— especially if they are placed in a school that takes advantage of their experiences, as the present school curriculum does in certain crucial regards for the middle-class child. The Hess data do show, however, that the behaviors of the middle-class Negro mothers are more typically mainstream and that what these mothers teach their children is more typically within mainstream expectations; therefore, such children tend to perform better in a testing situation—and subsequently in a school situation—which requires mainstream behaviors and heuristic styles than do lower-class children, who have learned something else.

There is much to be learned about maternal teaching styles and how they can be used to help the child function better in interactions with the mainstream culture. Research has indicated how unlike the middle-class mother the lower-class mother is, but there is very little description of who the lower-class mother is and what she does.

The failure of intervention

Intervention programs postulated on the inadequacy of the mother or the lack of environmental stimulation (Shaefer, 1969; Gordon, 1968; Klaus and Gray, 1968) fail after an initial spurt in IQ scores. This appears to be an artifact of the methodology, for the first contact with mainstream educational patterns (an agent intervening in the home, a Head Start Program, kindergarten or first grade in the public school) appears automatically to cause an increase in IQ for these children. This artifact is clearly evidenced in the 'catch-up' phenomenon where non-Head Start children gain in IQ apparently as a result of exposure to a school environment. The additional observation, that increases in IQ of both Head Start *and* non-Head Start children decrease after second or third grade, is a further indication that early childhood intervention is not where the answer to the failure of children in public school lies.

Interventionists argue that what is needed are school-based programs (Project Follow-Through) which maintain the 'gains' of Head Start by changing the nature of the school environment. In effect, this argument is a specious one since it was the intervention program itself which was supposed to insure the child's success in the schools as they are presently constituted. For the early childhood interventionists then to turn around and say that the schools do not do their job in maintaining the increases which the school itself has generated in non-Head Start children (as well as the increases of Head Start children) is indeed to point to the crux of the matter: the failure lies in the schools, not the parents, to educate these children. This clearly indicates that critical intervention must be done, but on the procedures and materials used in the schools rather than on the children those schools service. Intervention which works to eliminate archaic and inappropriate procedures for teaching these children and which substitutes procedures and materials that are culturally relevant is critically needed. It is important to note here that such intervention procedures—e.g. the use of Negro dialect in the teaching of reading (Baratz and Baratz, 1969)— are not ends in themselves. The goal of such procedures is to have the children perform adequately on standardized achievement tests. It is the process, not the goals, of education that must be changed for these children. *The educational problems of lower-class culturally different Negro children, as of other groups of culturally different children, are not so much related to inappropriate educational goals as to inadequate means for meeting these goals.*

It is not, therefore, a particular program for early childhood intervention at a critical period which affects IQ scores. Rather it is the initial contact with mainstream middle-class behaviors that tends to raise temporarily the scores of young children. As the test items, however, begin to rely more and more heavily on the language style and usage of the middle-class, these culturally different dialect-speaking children tend to decrease in test performance. Unlike the behaviors which initially raise IQ scores and which the child learns simply from contact with the middle-class system, fluency in a new language style and usage must be taught formally and systematically for it to be mastered. Indeed, this failure to teach the mainstream language styles and usage by means of the child's already existing system may well explain why the initial test gains of these children are not maintained.

The early childhood programs, as well as public schools, fail in the long run because they define educability in terms of a child's ability to perform within an alien culture; yet they make no attempt to teach him systematically new cultural patterns so that the initial spurt in test scores can be maintained. Educability, for culturally different children, should be defined primarily as the ability to learn new cultural patterns within the experience base and the culture with which the child is already familiar. The initial test scores of culturally different children must not be misevaluated as evidence of 'educability,' but rather should be viewed as evidence of the degree to which the child is familiar with the mainstream system upon which the tests are based both in content and presentation.

Because of the misconception of educability and the misevaluation of the test data, interventionists and educators create programs that are designed (1) to destroy an already functionally adequate system of behavior because it is viewed as pathological and (2) to impose a system of behaviour without recognizing the existence of a functionally adequate system of behavior already in place. (Thus it is comparable to attempting to pour water into an already wine-filled pitcher.) Education for culturally different children should not attempt to destroy functionally viable processes of the sub-culture, but rather should use these processes to teach additional cultural forms. The goal of such education should be to produce a bicultural child who is capable of functioning both in his sub-culture and in the mainstream.

However, since Head Start has disregarded or attempted unknowingly to destroy that which is a viable cultural system, we should not have been surprised by its failure in attempting to 'correct' these behaviors. Head Start has failed because its goal is to correct a deficit that simply does not exist. The idea that the Negro child has a defective linguistic and conceptual system has been challenged by the findings of Stewart (1964, 1967, 1968, 1969), Baratz, J. (1969), Labov (1969), and by Lesser and his colleagues (1965, 1967), who point to the structurally coherent but different linguistic and cognitive systems of these children. Indeed, the deficit model of Head Start forces the interventionist closer and closer to the moment of conception and to the possibility of genetic determination of the behavior now attributed to a negative environment. This position is plaintively described by Caldwell (1968):

> Most of us in enrichment . . . efforts—no matter how much lip service we pay to the genetic potential of the child—are passionate believers in the plasticity of the human organism. We need desperately to believe that we are born equalizable.

> With any failure to demonstrate the effectiveness of compensatory experiences offered to children of any given age, one is entitled to conclude parsimoniously that perhaps the enrichment was not offered at the proper time. (Caldwell, 1968, p. 81)

Elsewhere Caldwell refers to what she calls the Inevitable Hypothesis which we interpret as backing up further and further (intervene at four, at three, at one, at three months) until we are face to face with the possibility of genetic differences between Negroes and whites which forever preclude the possibility of remediation or enrichment. We are in Caldwell's debt for such a passionate statement of the real issue at hand. All educators concerned with intervention of any kind and unaware of the culture (and the alternative conceptual framework it offers) respond at a gut level to the implications which the failure of early childhood programs has for the overtly racist genetic model. The frustration due to the failure of intervention programs proposed by the social pathologists could lead to three possible lines of responses from those watching and participating in the unfolding of events. They are:

1 an increased preoccupation with very early intervention, at birth or shortly thereafter, to offset the allegedly 'vicious' effects of the inadequate environment of the Negro child;
2 the complete rejection of the possibility of intervention effects unless the child is totally removed from his environment to be cared for and educated by specialists;
3 the total rejection of the environmentalist-egalitarian position in favor of a program of selective eugenics for those who seem to be totally unable to meet the demands of a technological environment—scientific racism:

Suffice it to say that recently we have seen an articulation of all three of these unfeasible positions.

The clearest line of thought currently evident comes from people such as Shaefer (1969a), Gordon (1968), and Caldwell (1967) advocating the introduction of specialists into the home who would not only provide the missing stimulation to the child, but also teach the mother how to raise her children properly. Thus, the new input is an intensive attempt to change totally the child's environment and the parent's child-rearing patterns.

But the fear is that even such a massive attempt will still fail to innoculate the child against failure in the schools. Recognizing this, Caldwell (1967) provides the model for intervention programs which take the child completely out of the home for short periods of time for the purpose of providing him with the experiences unavailable to him during his first three years of life. It is only a short distance from this position to Bettelheim's statement (*New York Times*, March 1969) advocating total removal of Negro children to kibbutz-like controlled environments in order to overcome the effects of the allegedly negative values and practices of the ghetto—in short, the annihilation of distinctive Afro-American cultural styles.

Finally, the appearance of the scholarly article recently published by Arthur Jensen (1969) in the *Harvard Educational Review* represents the attempt of a former social pathologist to deal with the failure of the intervention programs. He may find his position politically distasteful but, for a scientist who lacks a cross-cultural perspective and a historical frame of reference, it is the only way to maintain his scientific integrity. Like most scholars who come to advocate an unpopular thesis, Jensen has done his homework. His familiarity with the data indicates to him the futility of denying (1) that Negro children perform less well on intelligence tests than whites and (2) that Head Start has failed in its intent to produce permanent shifts in IQ which lead to success in the educational system. Since Jensen rejects the social pathology model but retains a concept that describes Negro behavior as defective, it is not at all surprising that he has no alternative other than a model of genetic inferiority.

However, like the social pathologists who had to create an explanation (i.e., inadequate mothering) for a non-existent deficit, Jensen is also called upon to explain the reasons for a relative theory of genetic inferiority in the American Negro. His argument, similar to those of earlier genetic racists, states that the Negroes who were brought over as slaves 'were selected for docility and strength and not mental ability, and that through selective mating the mental qualities present never had a chance to flourish' (Edson, 1969). Interestingly enough, this contention was decimated almost thirty years ago by Melville Herskovits (1941) in his book, *The Myth of the Negro Past*, in which he presents historical and anthropological data to reject the notion of selective enslavement and breeding. It is precisely the absence of a sophisticated knowledge and perspective of cultural continuity and cultural change which has forced both the social pathologists and the genetic pathologists to feel that they have dealt with 'culture' if they acknowledge that certain test items are 'culture-bound.' Such changes represent very surface knowledge of the concept of culture and, in particular, do not deal with subtle yet significant cultural differences. Many social scientists believe that they are dealing with the culture when they describe the physical and social environment of these children. One must not confuse a description of the environment in which a particular culture thrives for the culture itself.

Because historical and political factors have combined to deny the existence of a Negro culture (Baratz and Baratz, 1969), social scientists have found themselves having to choose between either a genetic deficit model or a deficit model built on an inadequate environment (the 'culture' of poverty). However, our view of the current status of research on the Negro in the United States indicates that we are on the brink of a major scientific revolution with respect to American studies of the Negro and the social action programs that derive from them. This revolution began with Herskovits and is being forwarded by the linguistic and anthropological studies of Stewart (1964–1969), Szwed (1969), Abrahams (1967), Hannerz (1969), and others. The basic assumption of this research is that the behavior of Negroes is not pathological, but can be explained within a coherent, structured, distinct, American-Negro culture which represents a synthesis of African culture in contact with American European culture from the time of slavery to the present day.

Since the pathology model of the language and thought of Negroes as it is used in intervention programs has been created by the superimposition of a standard English template on a non-standard dialect system, producing a view of that non-standard system as defective and deviant, then the data gathered in support of that pathology view must be totally re-evaluated and old conclusions dismissed, not solely because they are non-productive, but also because they are ethnocentric and distorted and do not recognize the cultural perspective. The great impact of the misuse of the egalitarian model on social science studies of the Negro must be re-examined.

As long as the social pathology and genetic models of Negro behavior remain the sole alternatives for theory construction and social action, our science and our society are doomed to the kind of cyclical (environment to genes) thinking presently evident in race relations research. Fortunately, at this critical point in our history, we do have a third model available, capable of explaining both the genetic and social pathology views with greater economy and capable of offering viable research and societal alternatives.

The major support for the assertion of a revolution in scientific thinking about the Negro comes from the discovery that the urban Negro has a consistent, though different, linguistic system. This discovery is an anomaly in that it could not have been predicted from the social pathology paradigm. This finding, if we can judge from the incredulity expressed about it by our colleagues, violates many of the perceptions and expectations about Negro behavior which are built into the assumptive base of the social pathology model. This assumptive base, it is argued, has restricted our phenomenological field to deviations from normative behavior rather than to descriptions of different normative configurations. In the present case, it would appear that the defect and difference models of Negro behavior cannot exist side by side without a growing awareness of the need for change and radical reconstruction of our modes of theorizing and conceptualizing about Negro behavior.

However, there may be resistance to adopting the cultural difference model which stems not only from the inherent methodologies of the social pathology theory, but also from the much more vague, and often unexpressed sociopolitical view of the particular investigator seeking to support his view of our current racial situation—views which are unarticulated and therefore unexamined. Thus, the resistance we anticipate may be intensified by the fear that talking about differences in Negro behavior may automatically produce in the social pathologist the postulation of genetic differences. This fear, so often expressed, is related to the real fact that the genetic model itself relied on behavioral differences as the basis for its conclusions about genetic determination. Three points can be made here to deal with this concern: (1) it has not and should not be the role of rational scholarly discourse to dismiss data and knowledge simply because it does not fit a particular ideological position extant at a particular moment in history; (2) differences, which indicate that learning has taken place, are not deficits; and (3) the view of the current social pathology position is in many ways prone to the same criticisms leveled at the genetic pathology model.

The current scientific crisis will resolve itself solely on the basis of scholarly research and not ideology or polemic. The basic assumptions of scholarly research must be examined and models tried out that offer more successful and economical explanations.

In summary, the social pathology model has led social science to establish programs to prevent deficits which are simply not there. The failure of intervention reflects the ethnocentrism of methodologies and theories which do not give credence to the cognitive and intellectual skills of the child. A research program on the same scale as that mounted to support the social pathology model must be launched in order to discover the different, but not pathological, forms of Negro behavior. Then and only then can programs be created that utilize the child's differences as a means of furthering his acculturation to the mainstream while maintaining his individual identity and cultural heritage.

Notes

1 This paper is based on a paper presented to the Society for research in Child Development, March, 1969, Santa Monica, California. The work of the first author was done while he was Executive Secretary, Center for Study of Metropolitan Problems, National Institute of Mental Health. The work of the second author is supported in part by funds from NIMH Grant MH16078.

2 We recognize that no two Head Start projects are exactly alike. Head Start is used here as a generic term for intervention programs designed for under-privileged pre-school children.

References

Abrahams, R. (1967). *Deep Down in the Jungle*, revised edition. Hatboro, Pa.: Folklore Associates.

Baratz, J. (1968). Language development in the economically disadvantaged child: A perspective. *ASHA*, March.

Baratz, J. (1969). Linguistic and cultural factors in teaching English to ghetto children. *Elementary English*, 46, 199–203.

Baratz, J. (1969). Language and cognitive assessment of Negro children: Assumptions and research needs. *ASHA*, March.

Baratz, J. and Shuy, R. (1969) (eds.). *Teaching Black Children To Read*. Washington, DC: Center for Applied Linguistics.

Baratz, S. and J. (1968). Negro ghetto children and urban education: A cultural solution, *Bulletin of the Minnesota Council for the Social Studies*, Fall, 1968, reprinted in *Social Education*, 33, 4, 401–4.

Baratz, S. and J. (1969). The social pathology model: Historical Bases for psychology's denial of the existence of Negro culture. APA Paper, Washington, DC.

Baratz, S. (1970). Social science research strategies for the Afro-American, in J. Szwed, (ed.), *Black America*. New York: Basic Books.

Bettelheim, B. (1969). Psychologist questions value of Head Start program. *New York Times*, March 17.

Billingsley, A. (1968). *Black Families in White America*. Englewood Cliffs, New Jersey: Prentice-Hall, Inc.

Caldwell, B. (1968). The fourth dimension in early childhood education, in R. Hess and R. Bear, (eds.), *Early Education: Current Theory, Research and Action*. Chicago: Aldine Publishing Co.

Caldwell, B. (1967). What is the optimal learning environment for the young child? *American Journal of Orthopsychiatry*, 37, 9–21.

Carroll, J. (1964). *Language and Thought*. Englewood Cliffs, New Jersey: Prentice-Hall.

Deutsch, C. (1964). Auditory discrimination and learning social factors. *Merrill-Palmer Quarterly*, 10, 277–96.

Deutsch, M. (1963). The disadvantaged child and the learning process, in Passow (ed.), *Education in Depressed Areas*. New York: Columbia University Teachers College.

Deutsch, C. and Deutsch, M. (1968). Theory of early childhood environment programs, in R. Hess and R. Bear, (eds.), *Early Education: Current Theory, Research and Action*. Chicago: Aldine Publishing Co.

Dillard, J. L. (in press). *Black English in the United States*. New York: Random House.

Dye, H. B. (1939). A study of the effects of differential stimulation on mentally retarded children. The Procedures of the American Association of the Mentally Deficient, Vol. 44, 114–36.

Edson, L. (1969). jensenism, n. The theory that IQ is largely determined by the genes. *New York Times*, August 31, 10ff.

Glazer, N. and Moynihan, D. (1963). *Beyond the Melting Pot*. Cambridge, Massachusetts: MIT Press and the Harvard University Press.

Goldfarb, W. (1955). Emotional and intellectual consequences of psychological deprivation in infancy: A re-evaluation, in P. H. Hoch and J. Zobin (eds.), *Psychopathology of Childhood*. New York: Grune and Stratton.

Gonzales, A. (1922). *The Black Border: Gullah Stories of the Carolina Coast*. South Carolina: The State Company.

Gordon, I. (1968). Research Report: Infant performance. Gainesville, Florida: Institute for Development of Human Resources, University of Florida.

Green, R. (1964). Dialect sampling and language values, in R. Shuy, (ed.), *Social Dialects and Language Learning*. Champaign, Ill.: NCTE, 120–3.

Hannerz, U. (1969). *Soulside Inquiries into Ghetto Children and Community*. Stockholm, Sweden: Almquist & Wiksele.

Henry, J. (1965). White people's time, colored people's time. *Transaction*, March-April.

Herskovits, M. (1938–9). The ancestry of the American Negro. *American Scholar*, reprinted in *The New World Negro*. Bloomington, Indiana University Press, 1966. 114–22.

Herskovits, M. (1941). *The Myth of the Negro Past*. New York: Harper and Brothers.

Hess, R., Shipman, V., Brophy, J. & Bear, R. (1968). *The Cognitive Environments of Urban Preschool Children*. The Graduate School of Education, University of Chicago.

Hunt, J. McV. (1961). *Intelligence and Experience*. New York: The Ronald Press Company.

Hunt, J. McV. (1968). Towards the prevention of incompetence, in J. W. Carter, (ed.), *Research Contributions from Psychology to Community Health*. New York: Behavioural Publications.

Hurst, C. G., Jr. (1965). *Psychological Correlates in Dialectolalia*, Washington, DC, Howard University: Communities Research Center.

Irwin, D. C. (1960). Infant speech: Effect of systematic reading of stories. *Journal of Speech and Hearing Research*, 3, 187–90.

Jensen, A. (1969). How much can we boost IQ and scholastic achievement? *Harvard Educational Review*, 39, 1–123.

Kagan, J. (1968). His struggle for identity, *Saturday Review*, December.

Katz, I. (1968). Research issue on evaluation of educational opportunity: Academic motivation, *Harvard Educational Review*, 38, 57–65.

Killian, L. M. (1968). *The Impossible Revolution?* New York: Random House.

Klaus, R. A. and Gray, S. W. (1968). The early training project for disadvantaged children: A report after five years. *Monograph, SRCD*, 33.

Kretch, D., Rosenzweig, M. & Bennet, E. L. (1962). Relations between brain chemistry and problem solving among rats raised in enriched and impoverished environments. *Journal of Comparative Physiological Psychology*, 55, 801–7.

Labov, W. (1969). The logic of nonstandard English, in J. Alatis, (ed.), *School of Languages and Linguistics Monograph Series, No. 22*. Georgetown University, 1–43, and reprinted in this volume as chapter 27.

Labov, W. and Cohen, P. (1967). Systematic relations of standard rules in grammar of Negro speakers. Project Literacy 7.

Lesser, G., Fifer, G. & Clark, D. H. (1965). Mental abilities of children from different social class and cultural groups. *Monograph of Society for Research in Child Development*, 30, 647.

Malone, C. A. (1967). Developmental deviations considered in the light of environmental forces, in Pavenstedt, E., (ed.), *The Drifters: Children of Disorganized Lower Class Families*. Boston: Little, Brown and Co.

Müller, F. M. (1859). *History of Ancient Sanskrit Literature, so far as it illustrates the primitive religion of the Brahmans*. London: Williams and Norgate.

Rheingold, H. (1956). The modification of social responsiveness in institutional babies, *Monograph of Society for Research and Child Development*, 21, (2), Serial No. 63.

Shaefer, E. (1969a). Tutoring the 'disadvantaged'. *The Washington Post*, February 9.

Shaefer, E. (1969b). Home tutoring, maternal behavior and intellectual development, APA Paper, Washington, DC.

Shaler, N. S. (1890). The nature of the Negro. *Arena*, 3, 23–35.

Skeels, H. (1960). Adult status of children with contrasting early life experiences. *Monograph Society for Research in Child Development*, 31, 3, 1–65.

Skeels, H. and Dye, H. (1939). A study of the effects of differential stimulation on mentally retarded children. *Proceeding of the American Association for Mental Deficiency*, 44, 114–136.

Spitz, R. (1945). Hospitalism: An inquiry into the genesis of psychiatric conditions in early childhood. *Psychoanalytic Study of the Child*, 1, 53–74.

Stewart, W. (1964). Urban Negro Speech: Sociolinguistic factors affecting English teaching, in R. Shuy, (ed.), *Social Dialects and Language Learning*, NTCE, Champaign, Ill.

Stewart, W. (1966). Social dialects, in E. Gordon, (ed.), *Research Planning Conference on Language Development in Disadvantaged Children*, Yeshiva University.

Stewart, W. (1967). Sociolinguistic factors in the history of American Negro dialects, *The Florida FL Reporter*, 5, 2, Spring.

Stewart, W. (1969a). Sociopolitical issues in the linguistic treatment of Negro dialect. *School of Languages and Linguistics Monograph Series, No. 22*. Georgetown University, 215–23.

Stewart, W. (1969b). Historical and structural bases for the recognition of Negro dialect. *School of Languages and Linguistics Monograph Series, No. 22*. Georgetown University, 239–47.

Stewart, W. (1968). Continuity and change in American Negro dialects, *The Florida FL Reporter*, Spring.

Stewart, W. (1969). On the use of Negro dialect in the teaching of reading, in J. Baratz and R. Shuy, (eds.), *Teaching Black Children To Read*. Washington, DC: Center for Applied Linguistics.

Stewart, W. (1969). Teaching black language: A forum lecture for Voice of America, Washington, DC, May.

Stodolsky, S. and Lesser, G. (1967). Learning patterns in the disadvantaged. *Harvard Educational Review*, 37, 546–93.

Szwed. J. (1969). Ethnohistory of the Afro-American in the United States, APA Paper, Washington, DC.

Szwed, J. (1970). *Black America*. New York: Basic Books.

Wolff, M. and Stein, A. (1967). Head Start six months later. *Phi Delta Kappan*, March. Reprinted in J. Frost, (ed.), *Early Childhood Education Rediscovered*. New York: Holt, Rinehart & Winston, Inc., 293–7.

Wolfram, W. (1969). *Sociolinguistic description of Detriot Negro speech*. Washington, DC.: Center for Applied Linguistics.

27 The logic of nonstandard English

W. Labov

In the past decade, a great deal of federally sponsored research has been devoted to the educational problems of children in ghetto schools. In order to account for the poor performance of children in these schools, educational psychologists have attempted to discover what kind of disadvantage or defect they are suffering from. The viewpoint which has been widely accepted, and used as the basis for large-scale intervention programs, is that the children show a cultural deficit as a result of an impoverished environment in their early years. Considerable attention has been given to language. In this area, the deficit theory appears as the concept of 'verbal deprivation': Negro children from the ghetto area receive little verbal stimulation, are said to hear very little well-formed language, and as a result are impoverished in their means of verbal expression: they cannot speak complete sentences, do not know the names of common objects, cannot form concepts or convey logical thoughts.

Unfortunately, these notions are based upon the work of educational psychologists who know very little about language and even less about Negro children. The concept of verbal deprivation has no basis in social reality: in fact, Negro children in the urban ghettos receive a great deal of verbal stimulation, hear more well-formed sentences than middle-class children, and participate fully in a highly verbal culture; they have the same basic vocabulary, possess the same capacity for conceptual learning, and use the same logic as anyone else who learns to speak and understand English.

The notion of 'verbal deprivation' is a part of the modern mythology of educational psychology, typical of the unfounded notions which tend to expand rapidly in our educational system. In past decades

Source: excerpts from W. Labov, The logic of nonstandard English, *Georgetown Monographs on Language and Linguistics* (1969), **22**, 1–22, 26–31, reprinted in *Language and Poverty* ed. Frederick Williams, Markham, Chicago (1970), 153–73, 178–84, 187.

linguists have been as guilty as others in promoting such intellectual fashions at the expense of both teachers and children. But the myth of verbal deprivation is particularly dangerous, because it diverts attention from real defects of our educational system to imaginary defects of the child; and as we shall see, it leads its sponsors inevitably to the hypothesis of the genetic inferiority of Negro children which it was originally designed to avoid.

The most useful service which linguists can perform today is to clear away the illusion of 'verbal deprivation' and provide a more adequate notion of the relations between standard and non-standard dialects. In the writings of many prominent educational psychologists, we find a very poor understanding of the nature of language. Children are treated as if they have no language of their own in the pre-school programs put forward by Bereiter and Engelmann (1966). The linguistic behavior of ghetto children in test situations is the principal evidence for their genetic inferiority in the view of Arthur Jensen (1969). In this paper, I will examine critically both of these approaches to the language and intelligence of the populations labelled 'verbally' and 'culturally deprived'.[1] I will attempt to explain how the myth of verbal deprivation has arisen, bringing to bear the methodological findings of sociolinguistic work, and some substantive facts about language which are known to all linguists. I will be particularly concerned with the relation between concept formation on the one hand, and dialect differences on the other, since it is in this area that the most dangerous misunderstandings are to be found.

Verbality

The general setting in which the deficit theory has arisen consists of a number of facts which are known to all of us: that Negro children in the central urban ghettos do badly on all school subjects, including arithmetic and reading. In reading, they average more than two years behind the national norm.[2] Furthermore, this lag is cumulative, so that they do worse comparatively in the fifth grade than in the first grade. Reports in the literature show that this bad performance is correlated most closely with socio-economic status. Segregated ethnic groups, however, seem to do worse than others: in particular, Indians, Mexican-Americans and Negro children. Our own work in New York City confirms the fact that most Negro children read very poorly; however, our studies in the speech community show that the situation is even worse than has been reported. If one separates the isolated and peripheral individuals from the members of the central peer groups, the peer group members show even worse reading records, and to all intents and purposes are not learning to read at all during the time they spend in school (Labov and Robins, 1969).

In speaking of children in the urban ghetto areas, the term 'lower-class' is frequently used as opposed to 'middle-class'. In the several sociolinguistic studies we have carried out, and in many parallel studies, it is useful to distinguish a 'lower-class' group from a 'working-class'. Lower-class families are typically female-based or 'matri-focal', with no father present to provide steady economic support, whereas for the working-class there is typically an intact nuclear family with the father holding a semi-skilled or un-skilled job. The educational problems of ghetto areas run across this important class distinction; there is no evidence, for example, that the father's presence or absence is closely correlated with educational achievement.[3] The peer groups we have studied in South Central Harlem, representing the basic vernacular culture, include members from both family types. The attack against 'cultural deprivation' in the ghetto is overtly directed at family structures typical of lower-class families, but the educational failure we have been discussing is characteristic of both working-class and lower-class children.

In the balance of this paper, I will therefore refer to children from urban ghetto areas, rather than 'lower-class' children: the population we are concerned with are those who participate fully in the vernacular culture of the street and who have been alienated from the school system.[4] We are obviously dealing with the effects of the caste system of American society—essentially a 'color marking' system. Everyone recognizes this. The question is, by what mechanism does the color bar prevent children from learning to read? One answer is the notion of 'cultural deprivation' put forward by Martin Deutsch and others: the Negro children are said to lack the favorable factors in their home environment which enable middle-class children to do well in school. (Deutsch *et al.*, 1967; Deutsch, Katz and Jensen, 1968.) These factors involve the development of various cognitive skills through verbal interaction with adults, including the ability to reason abstractly, speak fluently, and focus upon long-range goals. In their publications, these psychologists also recognize broader social factors.[5] However, the deficit theory does not focus upon the interaction of the Negro child with white society so much as on his failure to interact with his mother at home. In the literature we find very little direct observation of verbal interaction in the Negro home; most typically, the investigators ask the child if he has dinner with his parents, and if he engages in dinner-table conversation with them. He is also asked whether his family takes him on trips to museums and other cultural activities. This slender thread of evidence is used to explain and interpret the large body of tests carried out in the laboratory and in the school.

The most extreme view which proceeds from this orientation—and one that is now being widely accepted—is that lower-class Negro children have no language at all. The notion is first drawn from Basil Bernstein's writings that 'much of lower-class language consists of a kind of incidental "emotional" accompaniment to action here and now' (Jensen, 1968, p. 118). Bernstein's views are filtered through a strong bias against all forms of working-class behavior, so that middle-class language is seen as superior in every respect—as 'more abstract, and necessarily somewhat more flexible, detailed and subtle'. One can proceed through a range of such views until one comes to the practical program of Carl Bereiter, Siefried Engelmann and their associates (Bereiter *et al.*, 1966; Bereiter and Engelmann, 1966). Bereiter's program for an academically oriented preschool is based upon their premise that Negro children must have a language with which they can learn, and their empirical finding that these children come to school without such a language. In his work with four-year-old Negro children from Urbana, Bereiter reports that their communication was by gestures, 'single words', and 'a series of badly-connected words or phrases', such as *They mine* and *Me got juice*. He reports that Negro children could not ask questions, that 'without exaggerating ... these four-year-olds could make no statements of any kind'. Furthermore, when these children were asked 'Where is the book?', they did not know enough to look at the table where the book was lying in order to answer. Thus Bereiter concludes that the children's speech forms are nothing more than a series of emotional cries, and he decides to treat them 'as if the children had no language at all'. He identifies their speech with his interpretation of Bernstein's restricted code: 'the language of culturally deprived children ... is not merely an underdeveloped version of standard English, but is a basically non-logical mode of expressive behavior' (Bereiter *et al.*, 1966, p. 113). The basic program of his preschool is to teach them a new language devised by Engelmann, which consists of a limited series of questions and answers such as *Where is the squirrel? The squirrel is in the tree.* The children will not be punished if they use their vernacular speech on the playground, but they will not be allowed to use it in the schoolroom. If they should answer the question *Where is the squirrel?* with the illogical vernacular form *In the tree* they will be reprehended by various means and made to say, *The squirrel is in the tree.*

Linguists and psycholinguists who have worked with Negro children are apt to dismiss this view of their language as utter nonsense. Yet there is no reason to reject Bereiter's observations as spurious: they were certainly not made up: on the contrary, they give us a very clear view of the behavior of student and teacher which can be duplicated in any classroom. In our own work outside of the adult-dominated environments of school and home,[6] we do not observe Negro children behaving like this, but on many occasions we have been asked to help analyze the results of research into verbal deprivation in such test situations.

Here, for example, is a complete interview with a Negro boy, one of hundreds carried out in a New York City school. The boy enters a room where there is a large, friendly white interviewer, who puts on the table in front of him a block or a fire engine, and says 'Tell me everything you can about this'. (The interviewer's further remarks are in parentheses.)

[*12 seconds of silence*]
(What would you say it looks like?)
[*8 seconds of silence*]
A space ship.
(Hmmmm.)
[*13 seconds of silence*]
Like a je-et.
[*12 seconds of silence*]
Like a plane.
[*20 seconds of silence*]
(What color is it?)
Orange. [*2 seconds*] An' whi-ite. [*2 seconds*] An' green.
[*6 seconds of silence*]
(An' what could you use it for?)
[*8 seconds of silence*]
A je-et.
[*6 seconds of silence*]
(If you had two of them, what would you do with them?)
[*6 seconds of silence*]
Give one to somebody.
(Hmmmm. Who do you think would like to have it?)
[*10 seconds of silence*]
Cla-rence.
(Mm. Where do you think we could get another one of these?)
At the store.
(Oh ka-ay!)

We have here the same kind of defensive, monosyllabic behavior which is reported in Bereiter's work. What is the situation that produces it? The child is in an asymmetrical situation where anything he says can literally be held against him. He has learned a number of devices to *avoid* saying anything in this situation, and he works very hard to achieve this end. One may observe the intonation patterns which Negro children often use when they are asked a question to which

the answer is obvious. The answer may be read as 'Will this satisfy you?'

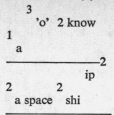

If one takes this interview as a measure of the verbal capacity of the child, it must be as his capacity to defend himself in a hostile and threatening situation. But unfortunately, thousands of such interviews are used as evidence of the child's total verbal capacity, or more simply his 'verbality'; it is argued that this lack of verbality *explains* his poor performance in school. Operation Headstart and other intervention programs have largely been based upon the 'deficit theory'—the notions that such interviews give us a measure of the child's verbal capacity and that the verbal stimulation which he has been missing can be supplied in a pre-school environment.

The verbal behavior which is shown by the child in the test situation quoted above is not the result of the ineptness of the interviewer. It is rather the result of regular sociolinguistic factors operating upon adult and child in this asymmetrical situation. In our work in urban ghetto areas, we have often encountered such behavior. Ordinarily we worked with boys 10–17 years old; and whenever we extended our approach downward to 8- or 9-year olds, we began to see the need for different techniques to explore the verbal capacity of the child. At one point we began a series of interviews with younger brothers of the 'Thunderbirds' in 1390 5th Avenue. Clarence Robins returned after an interview with 8-year-old Leon L., who showed the following minimal response to topics which arouse intense interest in other interviews with older boys.

CR: What if you saw somebody kickin' somebody else on the ground, or was using a stick, what would you do if you saw that?
LEON: Mmmm.
CR: If it was supposed to be a fair fight—
LEON: I don' know.
CR: You don' know? Would you do anything . . . huh? I can't hear you.
LEON: No.
CR: Did you ever see somebody got beat up real bad?
LEON: . . . Nope ? ? ?
CR: Well—uh—did you ever get into a fight with a guy?
LEON: Nope.
CR: That was bigger than you?
LEON: Nope.
CR: You never been in a fight?
LEON: Nope.
CR: Nobody ever pick on you?

LEON: Nope.

CR: Nobody ever hit you?

LEON: Nope.

CR: How come?

LEON: Ah 'on' know.

CP: Didn't you ever hit somebody?

LEON: Nope.

CR: [*incredulous*] You never hit nobody?

LEON: Mhm.

CR: Aww, ba-a-a-be, you ain't gonna tell me that.

It may be that Leon is here defending himself against accusations of wrong-doing, since Clarence knows that Leon has been in fights, that he has been taking pencils away from little boys, etc. But if we turn to a more neutral subject, we find the same pattern:

CR: You watch—you like to watch television? . . . Hey, Leon . . . you like to watch television? [*Leon nods*] What's your favorite program?

LEON: Uhhmmmm . . . I look at cartoons.

CR: Well, what's your favorite one? What's your favorite program?

LEON: Superman . . .

CR: Yeah? Did you see Superman—ah—yesterday, or day before yesterday: when's the last time you saw Superman?

LEON: Sa-aturday . . .

CR: You rem—you saw it Saturday? What was the story all about? You remember the story?

LEON: M-m.

CR: You don't remember the story of what—that you saw of Superman?

LEON: Nope.

CR: You don't remember what happened, huh?

LEON: Hm-m.

CR: I see—ah—what other stories do you like to watch on T.V.?

LEON: Mmmm ? ? ? . . . umm . . . [*glottalization*]

CR: Hmm? [*4 seconds*]

LEON: Hh?

CR: What's th' other stories that you like to watch?

LEON: ^{2}Mi - ighty^2 Mouse^2 . . .

CR: And what else?

LEON: Ummmm . . . ahm . . .

This nonverbal behavior occurs in a relatively *favorable* context for adult–child interaction; since the adult is a Negro man raised in Harlem, who knows this particular neighborhood and these boys very well. He is a skilled interviewer who has obtained a very high level of verbal response with techniques developed for a different age level, and he has an extraordinary advantage over most teachers or experimenters in these respects. But even his skills and personality are ineffective in breaking down the social constraints that prevail here.

When we reviewed the record of this interview with Leon, we decided to use it as a test of our own knowledge of the sociolinguistic factors which control speech. We made the following changes in the social

situation: in the next interview with Leon, Clarence

1 brought along a supply of potato chips, changing the 'interview' into something more in the nature of a party;

2 brought along Leon's best friend, 8-year-old Gregory;

3 reduced the height imbalance (when Clarence got down on the floor of Leon's room, he dropped from 6ft 2in. to 3ft 6in.);

4 introduced taboo words and taboo topics, and proved to Leon's surprise that one can say anything into our microphone without any fear of retaliation.

The result of these changes is a striking difference in the volume and style of speech.

CR: Is there anybody who says *your momma drink pee?*

{ LEON: [*rapidly and breathlessly*] Yee-ah!

{ GREG: Yup!

LEON: And your father eat doo-doo for breakfas'!

CR: Ohhh!! [*laughs*]

LEON: And they say *your father—your father eat doo-doo for dinner!*

GREG: When they sound on me, I say *CBM.*

CR: What that mean?

{ LEON: Congo-booger-snatch! [*laughs*]

{ GREG: Congo booger-snatcher! [*laughs*]

GREG: And sometimes I'll curse with *BB.*

CR: What that?

GREG: Black boy! [*Leon—crunching on potato chips*] Oh that's a *MBB.*

CR: MBB. What's that?

GREG: 'Merican Black Boy!

CR: Ohh . . .

GREG: Anyway, 'Mericans is same like white people, right?

LEON: And they talk about Allah.

CR: Oh yeah?

GREG: Yeah.

CR: What they say about Allah?

{ LEON: Allah—Allah is God.

{ GREG: Allah—

CR: And what else?

LEON: I don' know the res'.

GREG: Allah i—Allah is God, Allah is the only God, Allah—

LEON: Allah is the *son* of God.

GREG: But can he make magic?

LEON: Nope.

GREG: I know who can make magic.

CR: Who can?

LEON: The God, the *real* one.

CR: Who can make magic?

GREG: The son of po'—[CR: Hm?] I'm sayin' the po'k chop God! He only a po'k chop God!^{7} [*Leon chuckles*]

The 'nonverbal' Leon is now competing actively for the floor; Gregory and Leon talk to each other as much as they do to the interviewer.

One can make a more direct comparison of the two

interviews by examining the section on fighting. Leon persists in denying that he fights, but he can no longer use monosyllabic answers, and Gregory cuts through his façade in a way that Clarence Robins alone was unable to do.

CR: Now, you said you had this fight, but I wanted you to tell me about the fight that you had.
LEON: I ain't had no fight.
{GREG: Yes, you did!   He said Barry,
{CR: You said you had one! you had a fight with Butchie,
{GREG: An he say Garland . . . an' Michael.
{CR: an' Barry . . .
{LEON: I di'n'; you said that, Gregory!
{GREG: You did.
{LEON: You know you said that!
{GREG: You said Garland, remember that?
{GREG: You said Garland!   Yes you did!
{CR: You said Garland, that's right.
GREG: He said Mich—an' I say Michael.
{CR: Did you have a fight with Garland?
{LEON: Uh-uh.
CR: You had one, and he beat you up, too!
GREG: Yes he did!
LEON: No, I di—I never had a fight with Butch! . . .

The same pattern can be seen on other local topics, where the interviewer brings neighborhood gossip to bear on Leon and Gregory acts as a witness.

CR: . . . Hey Gregory! heard that around here . . . and I'm 'on' tell you who said it, too . . .
LEON: Who?
{CR: about you . . .
{LEON: Who?
{GREG: I'd say it!
CR: They said that—they say that the only person you play with is David Gilbert.
{LEON: Yee-ah! yee-ah! yee-ah! . . .
{GREG: That's who you play with!
{LEON: I 'on' play with him no more!
{GREG: Yes you do!
LEON: I 'on' play with him no more!
GREG: But remember, about me and Robbie?
LEON: So that's not—
GREG: and you went to Petey and Gilbert's house, 'member? *Ah haaah*!!
LEON: So that's—so—but I would—I had came back out, an' I ain't go to his house no more . . .

The observer must now draw a very different conclusion about the verbal capacity of Leon. The monosyllabic speaker who had nothing to say about anything and cannot remember what he did yesterday has disappeared. Instead, we have two boys who have so much to say they keep interrupting each other, who seem to have no difficulty in using the English language to express themselves. And we in turn obtain the volume of speech and the rich array of grammatical devices which we need for analyzing the structure of

nonstandard Negro English (NNE): negative concord [*I 'on' play with him no more*], the pluperfect [*had came back out*], negative perfect [*I ain't had*], the negative preterite [*I ain't go*], and so on.

One can now transfer this demonstration of the sociolinguistic control of speech to other test situations—including IQ and reading tests in school. It should be immediately apparent that none of the standard tests will come anywhere near measuring Leon's verbal capacity. On these tests he will show up as very much the monosyllabic, inept, ignorant, bumbling child of our first interview. The teacher has far less ability than Clarence Robins to elicit speech from this child; Clarence knows the community, the things that Leon has been doing, and the things that Leon would like to talk about. But the power relationships in a one-to-one confrontation between adult and child are too asymmetrical. This does not mean that some Negro children will not talk a great deal when alone with an adult, or that an adult cannot get close to any child. It means that the social situation is the most powerful determinant of verbal behavior and that an adult must enter into the right social relation with a child if he wants to find out what a child can do: this is just what many teachers cannot do.

The view of the Negro speech community which we obtain from our work in the ghetto areas is precisely the opposite from that reported by Deutsch, Engelmann and Bereiter. We see a child bathed in verbal stimulation from morning to night. We see many speech events which depend upon the competitive exhibition of verbal skills: sounding, singing, toasts, rifting, louding—a whole range of activities in which the individual gains status through his use of language.[8] We see the younger child trying to acquire these skills from older children—hanging around on the outskirts of the older peer groups, and imitating this behavior to the best of his ability. We see no connection between verbal skill at the speech events characteristic of the street culture and success in the schoolroom.

Verbosity

There are undoubtedly many verbal skills which children from ghetto areas must learn in order to do well in the school situation, and some of these are indeed characteristic of middle-class verbal behavior. Precision in spelling, practice in handling abstract symbols, the ability to state explicitly the meaning of words, and a richer knowledge of the Latinate vocabulary, may all be useful acquisitions. But is it true that *all* of the middle-class verbal habits are functional and desirable in the school situation? Before we impose middle-class verbal style upon children from other cultural groups, we should find out how much of this is useful for the main work of analyzing and generalizing, and how much is merely stylistic—or even dysfunctional. In high school and college middle-class children spontaneously complicate their syntax to the point that instructors despair of getting them to make their language simpler and clearer. In every learned journal one can find examples of jargon and empty elaboration—and complaints about it. Is the 'elaborated code' of Bernstein really so 'flexible, detailed and subtle' as some psychologists believe (Jensen, 1968, p. 119)? Isn't it also turgid, redundant, and empty? Is it not simply an elaborated *style*, rather than a superior code or system?[9]

Our work in the speech community makes it painfully obvious that in many ways working-class speakers are more effective narrators, reasoners and debators than many middle-class speakers who temporize, qualify, and lose their argument in a mass of irrelevant detail. Many academic writers try to rid themselves of that part of middle-class style that is empty pretension, and keep that part that is needed for precision. But the average middle-class speaker that we encounter makes no such effort; he is enmeshed in verbiage, the victim of sociolinguistic factors beyond his control.

I will not attempt to support this argument here with systematic quantitative evidence, although it is possible to develop measures which show how far middle-class speakers can wander from the point. I would like to contrast two speakers dealing with roughly the same topic—matters of belief. The first is Larry H., a 15-year-old core member of the Jets, being interviewed by John Lewis. Larry is one of the loudest and roughest members of the Jets, one who gives the least recognition to the conventional rules of politeness.[10] For most readers of this paper, first contact with Larry would produce some fairly negative reactions on both sides: it is probable that you would not *like* him any more than his teachers do. Larry causes trouble in and out of school; he was put back from the eleventh grade to the ninth, and has been threatened with further action by the school authorities.

JL: What happens to you after you die? Do you know?
LARRY: Yeah, I know.
JL: What?
LARRY: After they put you in the ground, your body turns into—ah—bones, an' shit.
JL: What happens to your spirit?
LARRY: Your spirit—soon as you die, your spirit leaves you.
JL: And where does the spirit go?
LARRY: Well, it all depends . . .
JL: On what?
LARRY: You know, like some people say if you're good an' shit, your spirit goin' t' heaven . . . 'n if you bad, your spirit goin' to hell. Well, bullshit! Your spirit goin' to hell anyway, good or bad.
JL: Why?
LARRY: Why? I'll tell you why. 'Cause you see, doesn' nobody really know that it's a God, y'know, 'cause I mean I have seen black gods, pink gods, white gods, all color gods, and don't nobody know it's really a God. An' when they be sayin' if you good, you goin' t' heaven, tha's bullshit, 'cause you ain't

goin' to no heaven, 'cause it ain't no heaven for you to go to.

Larry is a paradigmatic speaker of nonstandard Negro English (NNE) as opposed to standard English (SE). His grammar shows a high concentration of such characteristic NNE forms as negative inversion [*don't nobody know* . . .], negative concord [*you ain't goin' to no heaven* . . .], invariant *be* [*when they be sayin'* . . .], dummy *it* for SE *there* [*it ain't no heaven* . . .], optional copula deletion [*if you're good . . if you bad* . . .], and full forms of auxiliaries [*I have seen* . . .]. The only SE influence in this passage is the one case of *doesn't* instead of the invariant *don't* of NNE. Larry also provides a paradigmatic example of the rhetorical style of NNE: he can sum up a complex argument in a few words, and the full force of his opinions comes through without qualification or reservation. He is eminently quotable, and his interviews give us many concise statements of the NNE point of view. One can almost say that Larry *speaks* the NNE culture (see Labov, Cohen, Robins and Lewis, 1968, vol. 2, pp. 38, 71–3, 291–2).

It is the logical form of this passage which is of particular interest here. Larry presents a complex set of interdependent propositions which can be explicated by setting out the SE equivalents in linear order. The basic argument is to deny the twin propositions

(A) If you are good, (B) then your spirit will go to heaven.
(–A) If you are bad. (C) then your spirit will go to hell.

Larry denies (B), and asserts that *if* (A) *or* (–A), *then* (C). His argument may be outlined as follows:

(1) Everyone has a different idea of what God is like.
(2) Therefore nobody really knows that God exists.
(3) If there is a heaven, it was made by God.
(4) If God doesn't exist, he couldn't have made heaven.
(5) Therefore heaven does not exist.
(6) You can't go somewhere that doesn't exist.
(–B) Therefore you can't go to heaven.
(C) Therefore you are going to hell.

The argument is presented in the order: (C), because (2) because (1), therefore (2), therefore (–B) because (5) and (6). Part of the argument is implicit: the connection (2) therefore (–B) leaves unstated the connecting links (3) and (4), and in this interval Larry strengthens the propositions from the form (2) *Nobody knows if there is* . . . to (5) *There is no* . . . Otherwise, the case is presented explicitly as well as economically. The complex argument is summed up in Larry's last sentence, which shows formally the dependence of (–B) on (5) and (6):

An' when they be sayin' if you good, you goin' t' heaven,
[*The proposition, if* A, *then* B]
Tha's bullshit,
[*is absurd*]

'cause you ain't goin' to no heaven
[*because* −B]
'cause it ain't no heaven for you to go to.
[*because* (5) *and* (6)].

This hypothetical argument is not carried on at a high level of seriousness. It is a game played with ideas as counters, in which opponents use a wide variety of verbal devices to win. There is no personal commitment to any of these propositions, and no reluctance to strengthen one's argument by bending the rules of logic as in the (2–5) sequence. But if the opponent invokes the rule of logic, they hold. In John Lewis' interviews, he often makes this move, and the force of his argument is always acknowledged and countered within the rules of logic. In this case, he pointed out the fallacy that the argument (2–3–4–5–6) leads to (−C) as well as (−B), so it cannot be used to support Larry's assertion (C):

JL: Well, if there's no heaven, how could there be a hell?
LARRY: I mean—ye—eah. Well, let me tell you, it ain't no hell, 'cause this is hell right here, y'know!
JL: This is hell?
LARRY: Yeah, this is hell right here!

Larry's answer is quick, ingenious and decisive. The application of the (3–4–5) argument to hell is denied, since hell is here, and therefore conclusion (C) stands. These are not ready-made or preconceived opinions, but new propositions devised to win the logical argument in the game being played. The reader will note the speed and precision of Larry's mental operations. He does not wander, or insert meaningless verbiage. The only repetition is (2), placed before and after (1) in his original statement. It is often said that the nonstandard vernacular is not suited for dealing with abstract or hypothetical questions, but in fact speakers from the NNE community take great delight in exercising their wit and logic on the most improbable and problematical matters. Despite the fact that Larry H. does not believe in God, and has just denied all knowledge of him, John Lewis advances the following hypothetical question:

JL: . . . But, just say that there is a God, what color is he? White or black?
LARRY: Well, if it is a God . . . I wouldn' know what color, I couldn' say,—couldn' nobody say what color he is or really *would* be.
JL: But now, jus' suppose there was a God—
LARRY: Unless'n they say . . .
JL: No, I was jus' sayin' jus' suppose there is a God, would he be white or black?
LARRY: . . . He'd be white, man.
JL: Why?
LARRY: Why? I'll tell you why. 'Cause the average whitey out here got everything, you dig? And the nigger ain't got shit, y'know? Y'understan'? So—um—for—in order for *that* to happen, you know it ain't no black God that's doin' that bullshit.

No one can hear Larry's answer to this question without being convinced that they are in the presence of a skilled speaker with great 'verbal presence of mind', who can use the English language expertly for many purposes. Larry's answer to John Lewis is again a complex argument. The formulation is not SE, but it is clear and effective even for those not familiar with the vernacular. The nearest SE equivalent might be: 'So you know that God isn't black, because if he was, he wouldn't have arranged things like that.'

The reader will have noted that this analysis is being carried out in standard English, and the inevitable challenge is: why not write in NNE, then, or in your own nonstandard dialect? The fundamental reason is, of course, one of firmly fixed social conventions. All communities agree that SE is the 'proper' medium for formal writing and public communication. Furthermore, it seems likely that SE has an advantage over NNE in explicit analysis of surface forms, which is what we are doing here. We will return to this opposition between explicitness and logical statement in the section on grammaticality. First, however, it will be helpful to examine SE in its primary natural setting as the medium for informal spoken communication of middle-class speakers.

Let us now turn to the second speaker, an upper-middle-class, college educated Negro man being interviewed by Clarence Robins in our survey of adults in Central Harlem.

CR: Do you know of anything that someone can do, to have someone who has passed on visit him in a dream?
CHARLES M: Well, I even heard my parents say that there is such a thing as something in dreams some things like that, and sometimes dreams do come true. I have personally never had a dream come true. I've never dreamt that somebody was dying and they actually died, (Mhm) or that I was going to have ten dollars the next day and somehow I got ten dollars in my pocket. (Mhm). I don't particularly believe in that, I don't think it's true. I do feel, though, that there is such a thing as—ah—witchcraft. I do feel that in certain cultures there is such a thing as witchcraft, or some sort of *science* of witchcraft; I don't think that it's just a matter of believing hard enough that there is such a thing as witchcraft. I do believe that there is such a thing that a person can put himself in a state of *mind* (Mhm), or that—er—something could be given them to intoxicate them in a certain—to a certain frame of mind—that—that could actually be considered witchcraft.

Charles M. is obviously a 'good speaker' who strikes the listener as well-educated, intelligent and sincere. He is a likeable and attractive person—the kind of person that middle-class listeners rate very high on a scale of 'job suitability' and equally high as a potential friend.[11] His language is more moderate and tempered than Larry's; he makes every effort to qualify his opinions, and seems anxious to avoid any misstatements or over-statements. From these qualities emerges the primary characteristic of this passage—its *verbosity*. Words multiply, some modifying and qualifying, others repeating or padding the main argument. The first half of this extract is a response to the initial question on dreams, basically:

1 Some people say that dreams sometimes come true.
2 I have never had a dream come true.
3 Therefore I don't believe (1).

Some characteristic filler phrases appear here: *such a thing as, some things like that, particularly*. Two examples of dreams given after (2) are afterthoughts that might have been given after (1). Proposition (3) is stated twice for no obvious reason. Nevertheless, this much of Charles M's response is well-directed to the point of the question. He then volunteers a statement of his beliefs about witchcraft which shows the difficulty of middle-class speakers who (a) want to express a belief in something but (b) want to show themselves as judicious, rational and free from superstitions. The basic proposition can be stated simply in five words:

But I believe in witchcraft.

However, the idea is enlarged to exactly 100 words, and it is difficult to see what else is being said. In the following quotations, padding which can be removed without change in meaning is shown in brackets.

1 'I [do] feel, though, that there is [such a thing as] witchcraft.' *Feel* seems to be a euphemism for 'believe'.
2 '[I do feel that] in certain cultures [there is such a thing as witchcraft].' This repetition seems designed only to introduce the word *culture*, which lets us know that the speaker knows about anthropology. Does *certain cultures* mean 'not in ours' or 'not in all'?
3 '[or some sort of *science* of witchcraft.]' This addition seems to have no clear meaning at all. What is a 'science' of witchcraft as opposed to just plain witchcraft?[12] The main function is to introduce the word 'science', though it seems to have no connection to what follows.
4 'I don't think that it's just [a matter of] believing hard enough that [there is such a thing as] witchcraft.' The speaker argues that witchcraft is not merely a belief; there is more to it.
5 'I [do] believe that [there is such a thing that] a person can put himself in a state of *mind* . . . that [could actually be considered] witchcraft.' Is witchcraft as a state of mind different from the state of belief denied in (4)?
6 'or that something could be given them to intoxicate them [to a certain frame of mind] . . .' The third learned word, *intoxicate*, is introduced by this addition. The vacuity of this passage becomes more evident if we remove repetitions, fashionable words and stylistic decorations:

But I believe in witchcraft.
I don't think witchcraft is just a belief.

A person can put himself or be put in a state of mind that is witchcraft.

Without the extra verbiage and the OK words like *science, culture* and *intoxicate*, Charles M. appears as something less than a first-rate thinker. The initial impression of him as a good speaker is simply our long-conditioned reaction to middle-class verbosity: we know that people who use these stylistic devices are educated people, and we are inclined to credit them with saying something intelligent. Our reactions are accurate in one sense: Charles M. is more educated than Larry. But is he more rational, more logical, or more intelligent? Is he any better at thinking out a problem to its solution? Does he deal more easily with abstractions? There is no reason to think so. Charles M. succeeds in letting us know that he is educated, but in the end we do not know what he is trying to say, and neither does he.

In the previous section I have attempted to explain the origin of the myth that lower-class Negro children are nonverbal. The examples just given may help to account for the corresponding myth that middle-class language is in itself better suited for dealing with abstract, logically complex and hypothetical questions. These examples are intended to have a certain negative force. They are not controlled experiments: on the contrary, this and the preceding section are designed to convince the reader that the controlled experiments that have been offered in evidence are misleading. The only thing that is 'controlled' is the superficial form of the stimulus: all children are asked 'What do you think of capital punishment?' or 'Tell me everything you can about this.' But the speaker's interpretation of these requests, and the action he believes is appropriate in response is completely uncontrolled. One can view these test stimuli as requests for information, commands for action, as threats of punishment, or as meaningless sequences of words. They are probably intended as something altogether different: as requests for display;[13] but in any case the experimenter is normally unaware of the problem of interpretation. The methods of educational psychologists like Deutsch, Jensen and Bereiter follow the pattern designed for animal experiments where motivation is controlled by such simple methods as withholding food until a certain weight reduction is reached. With human subjects, it is absurd to believe that an identical 'stimulus' is obtained by asking everyone the 'same question'. Since the crucial intervening variables of interpretation and motivation are uncontrolled, most of the literature on verbal deprivation tells us nothing about the capacities of children. They are only the trappings of science: an approach which substitutes the formal procedures of the scientific method for the activity itself. With our present limited grasp of these problems, the best we can do to understand the verbal capacities of children is to study them within the cultural context in which they were developed.

It is not only the NNE vernacular which should be

studied in this way, but also the language of middle-class children. The explicitness and precision which we hope to gain from copying middle-class forms are often the product of the test situation, and limited to it. For example, it was stated in the first part of this paper that working-class children hear more well-formed sentences than middle-class children. This statement may seem extraordinary in the light of the current belief of many linguists that most people do not speak in well-formed sentences, and that their actual speech production or 'performance' is ungrammatical.[14] But those who have worked with any body of natural speech know that this is not the case. Our own studies of the 'Grammaticality of Every-day Speech' show that the great majority of utterances in all contexts are complete sentences, and most of the rest can be reduced to grammatical form by a small set of 'editing rules'.[15] The proportions of grammatical sentences vary with class backgrounds and styles. The highest percentage of well-formed sentences are found in casual speech, and working-class speakers use more well-formed sentences than middle-class speakers. The widespread myth that most speech is ungrammatical is no doubt based upon tapes made at learned conferences, where we obtain the maximum number of irreducibly ungrammatical sequences.

It is true that technical and scientific books are written in a style which is markedly 'middle-class'. But unfortunately, we often fail to achieve the explicitness and precision which we look for in such writing; and the speech of many middle-class people departs maximally from this target. All too often, 'standard English' is represented by a style that is simultaneously overparticular and vague. The accumulating flow of words buries rather than strikes the target. It is this verbosity which is most easily taught and most easily learned, so that words take the place of thought, and nothing can be found behind them.

When Bernstein described his 'elaborated code' in general terms, it emerges as a subtle and sophisticated mode of planning utterances, achieving structural variety, taking the other person's knowledge into account, and so on. But when it comes to describing the actual difference between middle-class and working-class speakers, we are presented with a proliferation of 'I think', of the passive, of modals and auxiliaries, of the first person pronoun, of uncommon words; these are the bench marks of hemming and hawing, backing and filling, that are used by Charles M., devices which often obscure whatever positive contribution education can make to our use of language. When we have discovered how much middle-class style is a matter of fashion and how much actually helps us express our ideas clearly, we will have done ourselves a great service; we will then be in a position to say what standard grammatical rules must be taught to non-standard speakers in the early grades.

Grammaticality

Let us now examine Bereiter's own data on the verbal behavior of the children he dealt with. The expressions *They mine* and *Me got juice* are cited as examples of a language which lacks the means for expressing logical relations—in this case characterized as 'a series of badly connected words'. (Bereiter, 1966, pp. 113 ff.) In the case of *They mine*, it is apparent that Bereiter confuses the notions of logic and explicitness. We know that there are many languages of the world which do not have a present copula, and which conjoin subject and predicate complement without a verb. Russian, Hungarian and Arabic may be foreign; but they are not by that same token illogical. In the case of non-standard Negro English we are not dealing with even this superficial grammatical difference, but rather with a low-level rule which carries contraction one step farther to delete single consonants representing the verbs *is*, *have*, or *will* (Labov, Cohen, Robins and Lewis, 1968, sect. 3.4). We have yet to find any children who do not sometimes use the full forms of *is* and *will*, even though they may frequently delete it. Our recent studies with Negro children four to seven years old indicate that they use the full form of the copula *is* more often than pre-adolescents 10 to 12 years old, or the adolescents 14 to 17 years old.[16]

Furthermore, the deletion of the *is* or *are* in non-standard Negro English is not the result of erratic or illogical behavior: it follows the same regular rules as standard English contraction. Wherever standard English can contract, Negro children use either the contracted form or (more commonly) the deleted zero form. Thus *They mine* corresponds to standard *They're mine*, not to the full form *They are mine*. On the other hand, no such deletion is possible in positions where standard English cannot contract: just as one cannot say *That's what they're* in standard English, *That's what they* is equally impossible in the vernacular we are considering. The internal constraints upon both of these rules show that we are dealing with a phonological process like contraction, sensitive to such phonetic conditions as whether or not the next word begins with a vowel or a consonant. The appropriate use of the deletion rule, like the contraction rule, requires a deep and intimate knowledge of English grammar and phonology. Such knowledge is not available for conscious inspection by native speakers: the rules we have recently worked out for standard contraction (Labov, Cohen, Robins and Lewis, 1968, sect. 3.4) have never appeared in any grammar, and are certainly not a part of the conscious knowledge of any standard English speakers. Nevertheless, the adult or child who uses these rules must have formed at some level of psychological organization clear concepts of 'tense marker', 'verb phrase', 'rule ordering', 'sentence embedding', 'pronoun', and many other grammatical categories which are essential parts of any logical system.

Bereiter's reaction to the sentence *Me got juice* is even more puzzling. If Bereiter believes that *Me got juice* is not a logical expression, it can only be that he interprets the use of the objective pronoun *me* as representing a difference in logical relationship to the verb: that the child is in fact saying that *the juice got him* rather than *he got the juice*! If on the other hand the child means 'I got juice', then this sentence form shows only that he has not learned the formal rules for the use of the subject form *I* and oblique form *me*. We have in fact encountered many children who do not have these formal rules in order at the ages of four, five, six or even eight.[17] It is extremely difficult to construct a minimal pair to show that the difference between *he* and *him*, or *she* and *her*, carries cognitive meaning. In almost every case, it is the context which tells us who is the agent and who is acted upon. We must then ask: what differences in cognitive, structural orientation are signalled by the fact that the child has not learned this formal rule? In the tests carried out by Jane Torrey it is evident that the children concerned do understand the difference in meaning between *she* and *her* when another person uses the forms; all that remains is that the children themselves do not use the two forms. Our knowledge of the cognitive correlates of grammatical differences is certainly in its infancy; for this is one of very many questions which we simply cannot answer. At the moment we do not know how to construct any kind of experiment which would lead to an answer; we do not even know what type of cognitive correlate we would be looking for.

Bereiter shows even more profound ignorance of the rules of discourse and of syntax when he rejects *In the tree* as an illogical, or badly-formed answer to *Where is the squirrel?* Such elliptical answers are of course used by everyone; they show the appropriate deletion of subject and main verb, leaving the locative which is questioned by *wh + there*. The reply *In the tree* demonstrates that the listener has been attentive to and apprehended the syntax of the speaker.[18] Whatever formal structure we wish to write for expressions such as *Yes* or *Home* or *In the tree*, it is obvious that they cannot be interpreted without knowing the structure of the question which preceded them, and that they presuppose an understanding of the syntax of the question. Thus if you ask me 'Where is the squirrel?' it is necessary for me to understand the process of *wh*-attachment, *wh*-attraction to the front of the sentence, and flip-flop of auxiliary and subject to produce this sentence from an underlying form which would otherwise have produced *The squirrel is there*. If the child had answered *The tree*, or *Squirrel the tree*, or *The in tree*, we would then assume that he did not understand the syntax of the full form, *The squirrel is in the tree*. Given the data that Bereiter presents, we cannot conclude that the child has no grammar, but only that the investigator does not understand the rules of grammar. It does not necessarily do any harm to use the full form *The squirrel is in the tree*, if one wants to make fully explicit the rules of grammar which the child has internalized. Much of logical analysis consists of making explicit just that kind of internalized rule. But it is hard to believe that any good can come from a program which begins with so many misconceptions about the input data. Bereiter and Engelmann believe that in teaching the child to say *The squirrel is in the tree* or *This is a box* and *This is not a box* they are teaching him an entirely new language, whereas in fact they are only teaching him to produce slightly different forms of the language he already has.

What's wrong with being wrong?

If there is a failure of logic involved here, it is surely in the approach of the verbal deprivation theorists, rather than in the mental abilities of the children concerned. We can isolate six distinct steps in the reasoning which has led to programs such as those of Deutsch, Bereiter and Engelmann:

1 The lower-class child's verbal response to a formal and threatening situation is used to demonstrate his lack of verbal capacity, or verbal deficit.
2 This verbal deficit is declared to be a major cause of the lower-class child's poor performance in school.
3 Since middle-class children do better in school, middle-class speech habits are seen to be necessary for learning.
4 Class and ethnic differences in grammatical form are equated with differences in the capacity for logical analysis.
5 Teaching the child to mimic certain formal speech patterns used by middle-class teachers is seen as teaching him to think logically.
6 Children who learn these formal speech patterns are then said to be thinking logically and it is predicted that they will do much better in reading and arithmetic in the years to follow.

In the previous sections of this paper, I have tried to show that these propositions are wrong, concentrating on (1), (4), and (5). Proposition (3) is the primary logical fallacy which illicitly identifies a form of speech as the *cause* of middle-class achievement in school. Proposition (6) is the one which is most easily shown to be wrong in fact, as we will note below.

However, it is not too naïve to ask, 'What is wrong with being wrong?' There is no competing educational theory which is being dismantled by this program; and there does not seem to be any great harm in having children repeat *This is not a box* for twenty minutes a day. We have already conceded that NNE children need help in analysing language into its surface components, and in being more explicit. But there are serious and damaging consequences of the verbal deprivation theory which may be considered under two headings: (1) the theoretical bias, and (2) the consequences of failure.

(1) It is widely recognized that the teacher's attitude towards the child is an important factor in his success or failure. The work of Rosenthal on 'self-fulfilling prophecies' shows that the progress of children in the early grades can be dramatically affected by a single

random labelling of certain children as 'intellectual bloomers' (Rosenthal and Jacobson, 1968). When the everyday language of Negro children is stigmatized as 'not a language at all' and 'not possessing the means for logical thought', the effect of such a labelling is repeated many times during each day of the school year. Every time that a child uses a form of NNE without the copula or with negative concord, he will be labelling himself for the teacher's benefit as 'illogical', as a 'nonceptual thinker'. Bereiter and Engelmann, Deutsch and Jensen are giving teachers a ready-made, theoretical basis for the prejudice they already feel against the lower-class Negro child and his language. When they hear him say *I don't want none* or *They mine*, they will be hearing through the bias provided by the verbal deprivation theory: not an English dialect different from theirs, but the primitive mentality of the savage mind.

But what if the teacher succeeds in training the child to use the new language consistently? The verbal deprivation theory holds that this will lead to a whole chain of successes in school, and that the child will be drawn away from the vernacular culture into the middle-class world. Undoubtedly this will happen with a few isolated individuals, just as it happens in every school system today, for a few children. But we are concerned not with the few but the many, and for the majority of Negro children the distance between them and the school is bound to widen under this approach.

Proponents of the deficit theory have a strange view of social organization outside of the classroom: they see the attraction of the peer group as a 'substitute' for success and gratification normally provided by the school. For example, Whiteman and Deutsch introduce their account of the deprivation hypothesis with an eye-witness account of a child who accidentally dropped his school notebook into a puddle of water and walked away without picking it up.

> A policeman who had been standing nearby walked over to the puddle and stared at the notebook with some degree of disbelief (Whiteman and Deutsch, 1968, pp. 86–7).

The child's alienation from school is explained as the result of his coming to school without the 'verbal, conceptual, attentional and learning skills requisite to school success'. The authors see the child as 'suffering from feelings of inferiority because he is failing; ... he withdraws or becomes hostile, finding gratification elsewhere, such as in his peer group.'

To view the peer group as a mere substitute for school shows an extraordinary lack of knowledge of adolescent culture. In our studies in South Central Harlem we have seen the reverse situation: the children who are rejected by the peer group are quite likely to succeed in school. In middle-class suburban areas, many children do fail in school because of their personal deficiencies; in ghetto areas, it is the healthy, vigorous popular child with normal intelligence who cannot read and fails all along the line. It is not necessary to document here the influence of the peer group upon the behavior of youth in our society; but we may note that somewhere between the time that children first learn to talk and puberty, their language is restructured to fit the rules used by their peer group. From a linguistic viewpoint, the peer group is certainly a more powerful influence than the family (Gans, 1962). Less directly, the pressures of peer group activity are also felt within the school. Many children, particularly those who are not doing well in school, show a sudden sharp down turn in the fourth and fifth grades, and children in the ghetto schools are no exception. It is at the same age, at nine or ten years old, that the influence of the vernacular peer group becomes predominant.[19] Instead of dealing with isolated individuals, the school is then dealing with children who are integrated into groups of their own, with rewards and value systems which oppose those of the school. Those who know the sociolinguistic situation cannot doubt that reaction against the Bereiter–Engelmann approach in later years will be even more violent on the part of the students involved, and that the rejection of the school system will be even more categorical.

The essential fallacy of the verbal deprivation theory lies in tracing the educational failure of the child to his personal deficiencies. At present, these deficiencies are said to be caused by his home environment. It is traditional to explain a child's failure in school by his inadequacy; but when failure reaches such massive proportions, it seems to us necessary to look at the social and cultural obstacles to learning, and the inability of the school to adjust to the social situation. Operation Headstart is designed to repair the child, rather than the school; to the extent that it is based upon this inverted logic, it is bound to fail.

(2) The second area in which the verbal deprivation theory is doing serious harm to our educational system is in the consequences of this failure, and the reaction to it. If Operation Headstart fails, the interpretations which we receive will be from the same educational psychologists who designed this program. The fault will be found not in the data, the theory, nor in the methods used, but rather in the children who have failed to respond to the opportunities offered to them. When Negro children fail to show the significant advance which the deprivation theory predicts, it will be further proof of the profound gulf which separates their mental processes from those of civilized, middle-class mankind.

A sense of the 'failure' of Operation Headstart is already in the air. Some prominent figures in the program are reacting to this situation by saying that intervention did not take place early enough. Bettye M. Caldwell notes that:

> ... the research literature of the last decade dealing with social-class differences has made abundantly clear that all parents are not qualified

to provide even the basic essentials of physical and psychological care to their children (Caldwell, 1967, p. 16).

The deficit theory now begins to focus on the 'long-standing patterns of parental deficit' which fill the literature. 'There is, perhaps unfortunately,' writes Caldwell, 'no literacy test for motherhood.' Failing such eugenic measures, she has proposed 'educationally oriented day care for culturally deprived children between six months and three years of age'. The children are returned home each evening to 'maintain primary emotional relationships with their own families', but during the day they are removed to 'hopefully prevent the deceleration in rate of development which seems to occur in many deprived children around the age of two to three years' (Caldwell, 1967, p. 17).

There are others who feel that even the best of the intervention programs, such as those of Bereiter and Engelmann, will not help the Negro child no matter when they are applied—that we are faced once again with the 'inevitable hypothesis' of the genetic inferiority of the Negro people. Many readers of this paper are undoubtedly familiar with the paper of Arthur Jensen in the *Harvard Educational Review* (1969) which received early and widespread publicity. Jensen begins with the following quotation from the United States Commission on Civil Rights as evidence of the failure of compensatory education.

> The fact remains, however, that none of the programs appear to have raised significantly the achievement of participating pupils, as a group, within the period evaluated by the Commission (p. 138).

Jensen believes that the verbal deprivation theorists with whom he had been associated—Deutsch, Whiteman, Katz, Bereiter—have been given every opportunity to prove their case—and have failed. This opinion is part of the argument which leads him to the overall conclusion that 'the preponderance of the evidence is ... less consistent with a strictly environmental hypothesis than with the genetic hypothesis'; that racism, or the belief in the genetic inferiority of Negroes, is a correct view in the light of the present evidence.

Jensen argues that the middle-class white population is differentiated from the working-class white and Negro population in the ability for 'cognitive or conceptual learning', which Jensen calls Level II intelligence as against mere 'associative learning' or Level I intelligence:

> certain neural structures must also be available for Level II abilities to develop, and these are conceived of as being different from the neural structures underlying Level I. The genetic factors involved in each of these types of ability are presumed to have become differentially distributed in the population as a function of social class, since Level II has been most important for

scholastic performance under the traditional methods of instruction.

Thus Jensen found that one group of middle-class children were helped by their concept-forming ability to recall twenty familiar objects that could be classified into four categories: animals, furniture, clothing, or foods. Lower-class Negro children did just as well as middle-class children with a miscellaneous set, but showed no improvement with objects that could be so categorized.

The research of the educational psychologists cited here is presented in formal and objective style, and is widely received as impartial scientific evidence. Jensen's paper has already been reported by Joseph Alsop and William F. Buckley Jr. as 'massive, apparently authoritative ...' (*NY Post* 3/20/69). It is not my intention to examine these materials in detail; but it is important to realize that we are dealing with special pleading by those who have a strong personal commitment. Jensen is concerned with class differences in cognitive style and verbal learning. His earlier papers incorporated the cultural deprivation theory which he now rejects as a basic explanation.[20] He classifies the Negro children who fail in school as 'slow-learners' and 'mentally-retarded', and urged that we find out how much their retardation is due to environmental factors and how much is due to 'more basic biological factors' (Jensen 1968, p. 167). His conviction that the problem must be located in the child leads him to accept and reprint some truly extraordinary data. To support the genetic hypothesis he cites the following table of Heber for the racial distribution of mental retardation.

Table 1 Estimated prevalence of children with IQs below 75

SES	White	Negro
1	0·5	3·1
2	0·8	14·5
3	2·1	22·8
4	3·1	37·8
5	7·8	42·9

This report, that almost half of lower-class Negro children are mentally retarded, could be accepted only by someone who has no knowledge of the children or the community. If he had wished to, Jensen could easily have checked this against the records of any school in any urban ghetto area. Taking IQ tests at their face value, there is no correspondence between these figures and the communities we know. For example, among 75 boys we worked with in Central Harlem who would fall into Heber's SES 4 or 5, there were only three with IQs below 75: one spoke very little English, one could barely see, and the third was emotionally disturbed. When the second was retested, he scored 91, and the third retested at 87.[21] There are of course hundreds of realistic reports available to

Jensen: he simply selected one which would strengthen his case for the genetic inferiority of Negro children, and deliberately deleted the information that this was a study of an area selected in advance because of its high incidence of mental retardation.[22]

The frequent use of tables and statistics by educational psychologists serves to give outside readers the impression that this field is a science, and that the opinions of the authors should be given the same attention and respect that we give to the conclusions of physicists or chemists. But careful examination of the input data will often show that there is no direct relationship between the conclusions and the evidence (in Jensen's case, between IQ tests in a specially selected district of Milwaukee and intelligence of lower-class Negro children). Furthermore, the operations performed upon the data frequently carry us very far from the common-sense experience which is our only safeguard against conclusions heavily weighted by the author's theory. As another example, we may take some of the evidence presented by Whiteman and Deutsch for the cultural deprivation hypothesis. The core of Martin Deutsch's environmental explanation of low school performance is the Deprivation Index—a numerical scale based on six dichotomized variables. One variable is 'The educational aspirational level of the parent for the child'. Most people would agree that a parent who did not care if a child finished high school would be a disadvantageous factor in the child's educational career. In dichotomizing this variable Deutsch was faced with the fact that the educational aspiration of Negro parents is in fact very high—higher than for the white population, as he shows in other papers.[23] In order to fit this data into Deprivation Index, he therefore set the cutting point for the deprived group as 'college or less'. (Whiteman

and Deutsch, 1968, p. 100.) Thus if a Negro child's father says that he wants his son to go all the way through college, the child will fall into the 'deprived' class on this variable. In order to receive the two points given to the 'less deprived' on the index, it would be necessary for the child's parent to insist on graduate school or medical school! This decision is never discussed by the authors: it simply stands as a *fait accompli* in the tables. Readers of this literature who are not committed to one point of view would be wise to look as carefully as possible at the original data which lie behind each statement, and check the conclusions against their own knowledge of the people and community being described.

No one can doubt that the inadequacy of Operation Headstart and of the verbal deprivation hypothesis has now become a crucial issue in our society.[24] The controversy which is beginning over Jensen's article will undoubtedly take as given that programs such as Bereiter and Engelmann's have tested and measured the verbal capacity of the ghetto child. The cultural sociolinguistic obstacles to this intervention program are not considered; and the argument proceeds upon the data provided by the large, friendly interviewers that we have seen at work in the extracts given above.

That educational psychology should be strongly influenced by a theory so false to the facts of language is unfortunate; but that children should be the victims of this ignorance is intolerable. It may seem that the fallacies of the verbal deprivation theory are so obvious that they are hardly worth exposing; I have tried to show that it is an important job for us to undertake. If linguists can contribute some of their available knowledge and energy towards this end, we will have done a great deal to justify the support that society has given to basic research in our field.

Notes

1 I am indebted to Rosalind Weiner of the Early Childhood Education group of Operation Headstart in New York City, and to Joan Baratz, of the Educational Development Corp., Washington DC, for pointing out to me the scope and seriousness of the educational issues involved here, and the ways in which the cultural deprivation theory has affected federal intervention programs in recent years.

2 A report of average reading comprehension scores in New York City was published in the *New York Times* on 3 December 1968. The schools attended by most of the peer group members we have studied showed the following scores:

School	Grade	Reading score	National norm
JHS 13	7	5·6	7·7
	9	7·6	9·7
JHS 120	7	5·6	7·7
	9	7·0	9·7
IS 88	6	5·3	6·7
	8	7·2	8·7

The average is then more than two full years behind grade in the ninth grade.

3 There are a number of studies reported recently which show no relation between school achievement and presence of a father in the nuclear family. Preliminary findings to this effect are cited from a study by Bernard Mackler of CUE in Thos. S. Langer and Stanley T. Michaels, *Life Stress and Mental Health* (New York: Free Press), Chapter 8, Jensen (1969) cites James Coleman's study *Equality of educational opportunity*, p. 506, and others to illustrate the same point.

4 The concept of 'nonstandard Negro English', and the vernacular culture in which it is embedded, is presented in detail in Labov, Cohen, Robins and Lewis (1968), sections 1, 2, 3 and 4.1. See Volume 2, section 4.3, for the linguistic traits which distinguish speakers who participate fully in the NNE culture from marginal and isolated individuals.

5 For example, in Deutsch, Katz and Jensen (1968) there is a section on 'Social and Psychological Perspectives' which includes a chapter by Proshansky and Newton on 'The Nature and Meaning of Negro Self-Identity' and one by Rosenthal and Jacobson on 'Self-Fulfilling Prophecies in the Classroom'.

6 The research cited here was carried out in South Central Harlem and other ghetto areas in 1965–1968 to describe

structural and functional differences between nonstandard Negro English and standard English of the classroom. It was supported by the Office of Education as Co-operative Research Projects 3091 and 3288. Detailed reports are given in Labov, Cohen and Robins (1965), Labov (1967) and Labov, Cohen, Robins and Lewis (1968).

7 The reference to the *pork chop God* condenses several concepts of black nationalism current in the Harlem community. A *pork chop* is a Negro who has not lost the traditional subservient ideology of the South, who has no knowledge of himself in Muslim terms, and the *pork chop God* would be the traditional God of Southern Baptists. He and his followers may be pork chops, but he still holds the power in Leon and Gregory's world.

8 For detailed accounts of these speech events, see Labov, Cohen, Robins and Lewis (1968, section 4.2).

9 The term *code* is central in Bernstein's description of the differences between working-class and middle-class styles of speech. The restrictions and elaborations of speech observed are labelled as 'codes' to indicate the principles governing selection from the range of possible English sentences. No rules or detailed description of the operation of such codes are provided as yet, so that this central concept remains to be specified.

10 A direct view of Larry's verbal style in a hostile encounter is given in Labov, Cohen, Robins and Lewis (1968), Vol. 2, pp. 39–43. Gray's Oral Reading Test was being given to a group of Jets on the steps of a brown-stone house in Harlem, and the landlord tried unsuccessfully to make the Jets move. Larry's verbal style in this encounter matches the reports he gives of himself in a number of narratives cited in section 4.8.

11 See Labov, Cohen, Robins and Lewis (1968), section 4.6, for a description of subjective reaction tests which utilize these evaluative dimensions.

12 Several middle-class readers of this passage have suggested that *science* here refers to some form of control as opposed to belief; the 'science of witchcraft' would then be a kind of engineering of mental states; other interpretations can of course be provided. The fact remains that no such subtleties of interpretation are needed to understand Larry's remarks.

13 The concept of a 'request for verbal display' is here drawn from Alan Blum's treatment of the therapeutic interview in The Sociology of Mental Illness, mimeographed (to appear in *For Thomas Szaz*).

14 In a number of presentations, Chomsky has asserted that the great majority of the sentences which a child hears are ungrammatical ('95 per cent'). In Chomsky (1965, p. 58), this notion is presented as one of the arguments in his general statement of the 'nativist' position: 'A consideration of the character of the grammar that is acquired, *the degenerate quality and narrowly limited extent of the available data* [my emphasis] the striking uniformity of the resulting grammars, and their independence of intelligence, motivation, and emotional state, over wide ranges of variation, leave little hope that much of the structure of the language can be learned . . .'

15 The editing rules are presented in Labov (1966).

16 From work on the grammars and comprehension of Negro children four to eight years old being carried out by Professor Jane Torrey of Connecticut College in extension of the research cited above in Labov, Cohen, Robins and Lewis (1968).

17 From the research of Jane Torrey cited in footnote 16.

18 The attention to the speaker's syntax required of the listener is analyzed in detail by Harvey Sacks in his unpublished 1968 lectures.

19 For the relationship between age and membership in peer groups, see Wilmott (1966).

20 In Deutsch, Katz and Jensen (1968), Jensen expounds the verbal deprivation theory in considerable detail. For example: 'During this "labelling" period . . . some very important social-class differences may exert their effects on verbal learning. Lower-class parents engage in relatively little of this naming or "labelling" play with their children . . . That words are discrete labels for things seems to be better known by the middle-class child entering first grade than by the lower-class child. Much of this knowledge is gained in the parent-child interaction, as when the parent looks at a picture book with the child . . .' (p. 119).

21 Heber's studies of 88 Negro mothers in Milwaukee are cited frequently throughout Jensen (1969). The estimates in this table are not given in relation to a particular Milwaukee sample, but for the general population. Heber's study was specifically designed to cover an area of Milwaukee which was known to contain a large concentration of retarded children, Negro and white, and he has stated that his findings were 'grossly misinterpreted' by Jensen (*Milwaukee Sentinel*, 11 June 1969).

22 The IQ scores given here are from group rather than individual tests and must therefore not be weighted heavily: the scores are from the Pintner-Cunningham test, usually given in the first grade in New York City schools in the 1950s.

23 Table 15.1 in Deutsch *et al.* (1967, p. 312, section C), shows that some degree of college training was desired by 96, 97 and 100 per cent of Negro parents in Class levels I, II and III respectively. The corresponding figures for whites were 79, 95 and 97 per cent. In an earlier version of this paper, this discussion could be interpreted as implying that Whiteman and Deutsch had used data in the same way as Jensen to rate the Negro group as low as possible. As they point out [personal communication], the inclusion of this item in the Deprivation Index had the opposite effect, and it could easily have been omitted if that had been their intention. They also argue that they had sound statistical grounds for dichotomizing as they did. The criticism which I intended to make is that there is something drastically wrong with operations which produce definitions of deprivation such as the one cited here. It should of course be noted that Whiteman and Deutsch have strongly opposed Jensen's genetic hypothesis and vigorously criticized his logic and data.

24 The negative report of the Westinghouse Learning Corporation and Ohio University on Operation Headstart was published in the *New York Times* (on 13 April 1969). This evidence for the failure of the program was widely publicized and it seems likely that the report's discouraging conclusions 'will be used by conservative Congressmen as a weapon against any kind of expenditure for disadvantaged' children, especially Negroes. The two hypotheses mentioned to account for this failure is that the impact of Headstart is lost through poor teaching later on, and more recently, that poor children have been so badly damaged in infancy by their lower-class environment that Headstart cannot make much difference. The third 'inevitable' hypothesis of Jensen is not reported here.

References

Bereiter, C. *et al.* (1966). An academically oriented pre-school for culturally deprived children, in F. M. Hechinger, (ed.), *Pre-School Education Today*. Doubleday, 105–37.

Bereiter, C. and Engelmann, S. (1966). *Teaching Disadvantaged Children in the Pre-School*. Prentice-Hall.

Caldwell, B. M. (1967). What is the optional learning environment for the young child?, *Amer. J. Orthopsychiatry*, vol. 37, no. 1, 8–21.

Chomsky, N. (1965). *Aspects of the Theory of Syntax*. MIT Press.

Deutsch, M. *et al.* (1967). *The Disadvantaged Child*. Basic Books.

Deutsch, M., Katz, I., and Jensen, A. R. (eds.) (1968). *Social Class, Race and Psychological Development*. Holt.

Gans, H. (1962). The peer group society, in *The Urban Villagers*, Free Press.

Jensen, A. (1968). Social class and verbal learning, in Deutsch, Katz and Jensen, *Social Class, Race and Psychological Development*. Holt.

Jensen, A. (1969). How much can we boost IQ and scholastic achievement? *Harvard Educational Review*, 39, 1.

Labov, W. (1966). On the grammaticality of everyday speech, Paper given at the annual meeting of the Linguistic Society of America, New York City, December.

Labov, W. (1967). Some sources of reading problems for Negro speakers of non-standard English, in A. Frazier, (ed.), *New Directions in Elementary English*. National Council of Teachers of English, 140–67. Reprinted in Joan C. Baratz and R. W. Shuy, (eds.) *Teaching Black Children to Read*. Washington DC, Center for Applied Linguistics, 29–67.

Labov, W., Cohen, P. and Robins, C. (1965). *A Preliminary Study of the Structure of English Used by Negro and Puerto Rican Speakers in New York City*. Final Report, Co-operative Research Project no. 3091. Office of Education, Washington DC.

Labov, W., Cohen, P., Robins, C. and Lewis, J. (1968). *A Study of the Non-Standard English of Negro and Puerto Rican Speakers in New York City*. Final Report, Co-operative Research Project no. 3288, Office of Education, Washington, DC, vols. 1 and 2.

Labov, W., and Robins, C. (1969). A note on the relation of reading failure to peer-group status in urban ghettos, *The Teachers' College Record*, vol. 70, 5.

Rosenthal, R., and Jacobson, L. (1968). Self-fulfilling prophecies in the classroom: teachers' expectations as unintended determinants of pupils' intellectual competence, in Deutsch, Katz and Jensen, *Social Class, Race and Psychological Development*. Holt.

Whiteman, M., and Deutsch, M. (1968). Social disadvantage as related to intellective and language development, in Deutsch, Katz and Jensen, *Social Class, Race and Psychological Development*. Holt.

Willmott, P. (1966). *Adolescent Boys of East London*. Routledge & Kegan Paul.

28 Education cannot compensate for society[1]

Basil Bernstein

The context in which children learn is usually a middle-class one. Should we try to coax them to that 'standard', or seek what is valid in their own lives?

Since the late 1950s there has been a steady out-pouring of papers and books in the United States which are concerned with the education of children of low social class whose *material* circumstances are inadequate, or with the education of black children of low social class whose *material* circumstances are chronically inadequate. A vast research and educational bureaucracy developed in the United States, which was financed by funds obtained from federal, state or private foundations. New educational categories were developed—'the culturally deprived', 'the linguistically deprived', 'the socially disadvantaged'; and the notion of 'compensatory education' was introduced as a means of changing the status of the children in these categories.

Compensatory education emerged in the form of massive pre-school programmes like Project Headstart (see Ruth Adam, *New Society*, 30 October 1969), large-scale research programmes such as those of Deutsch in the early 1960s and a plethora of small-scale 'intervention' or 'enrichment' programmes for pre-school children or children in the first years of compulsory education. Very few sociologists were involved in these studies, because education was a low-status area. On the whole they were carried out by psychologists.

The focus of these studies was on the child in the family and on the local classroom relationship between teacher and child. In the last two years one can detect a change in this focus. As a result of the movements towards integration and the opposed movement towards segregation (the latter a response to the wishes of the various Black Power groups), more studies are being made in the United States of the *school*. Robert Rosenthal's classic study, *Pygmalion in the Classroom*, drew attention to the critical importance of the teacher's expectations of the child.

In this country we have been aware of the educa-

Source: *New Society*, 26 February 1970, 344–7.

tional problem since the writings of Sir Cyril Burt before the war. His book, *The Backward Child*, is probably still the best study we have. After the war, a series of sociological surveys and public inquiries into education brought this educational problem into the arena of national debate, and so of social policy. Now in Wales there is a large research unit, financed by the Schools Council, concerned with compensatory education. Important research of a different kind is taking place in the University of Birmingham into the problems of the education of Commonwealth children. The Social Science Research Council and the Department of Education and Science have given £175,000 in part for the development of special pre-school programmes concerned to introduce children to compensatory education. There is also the whole educational priority area programme (described by Anne Corbett in 'Are educational priority areas working?', *New Society*, 13 November 1969).

One university department of education offers an advanced diploma in compensatory education. Colleges of education also offer special courses under the same title. So it might be worth a few lines to consider the assumptions underlying this work and the concepts which describe it, particularly as my own writings have sometimes been used (and more often abused) to highlight aspects of the general problems and dilemmas.

To begin with, I find the term, 'compensatory education', a curious one for a number of reasons. I do not understand how we can talk about offering compensatory education to children who in the first place have not, as yet, been offered an adequate education environment. The Newsom Report on secondary schools showed that 79 per cent of all secondary modern schools in slum and problem areas were materially grossly inadequate, and that the holding power of these schools over the teachers was horrifyingly low. The same report also showed very clearly the depression in the reading scores of these children, compared with the reading scores of children who were at school in areas which were neither problem nor slum. This does not conflict with the finding that, on average, for the country as a whole, there has been an improvement in children's reading ability. The Plowden Report on the primary schools was rather more coy about all the above points, but we have little reason to believe that the situation is very much better for primary schools in similar areas.

Thus we offer a large number of children, both at the primary and secondary levels, materially inadequate schools and a higher turnover of teaching staff; and we further expect a small group of dedicated teachers to cope. The strain on these teachers inevitably produces fatigue and illness and it is not uncommon to find, in any week, teachers having to deal with doubled-up classes of 80 children. And we wonder why the children display very early in their educational life a range of learning difficulties.

At the same time, the organization of schools creates delicate overt and covert streaming arrangements which neatly lower the expectations and motivations of both teachers and taught. A vicious spiral is set up, with an all too determinate outcome. It would seem, then, that we have failed to provide, on the scale required, an *initial* satisfactory educational environment.

The concept, 'compensatory education', serves to direct attention away from the internal organization and the educational context of the school, and focus our attention on the families and children. 'Compensatory education' implies that something is lacking in the family, and so in the child. As a result, the children are unable to benefit from schools.

It follows, then, that the school has to 'compensate' for the something which is missing in the family, and the children are looked at as deficit systems. If only the parents were interested in the goodies we offer, if only they were like middle-class parents, then we could do our job. Once the problem is seen even implicitly in this way, then it becomes appropriate to coin the terms 'cultural deprivation', 'linguistic deprivation', and so on. And then these labels do their own sad work.

If children are labelled 'culturally deprived', then it follows that the parents are inadequate; the spontaneous realizations of their culture, its images and symbolic representations, are of reduced value and significance. Teachers will have lower expectations of the children, which the children will undoubtedly fulfil. All that informs the child, that gives meaning and purpose to him outside of the school, ceases to be valid or accorded significance and opportunity for enhancement within the school. He has to orient towards a different structure of meaning, whether it is in the form of reading books (*Janet and John*), in the form of language use and dialect, or in the patterns of social relationships.

Alternatively the meaning structure of the school is explained to the parents and imposed on, rather than integrated within, the form and content of their world. A wedge is progressively driven between the child as a member of a family and community, and the child as a member of a school. Either way the child is expected, and his parents as well, to drop their social identity, their way of life and its symbolic representations, at the school gate. For, by definition, their culture is deprived, and the parents are inadequate in both the moral and the skill orders they transmit.

I do not mean by this that in these circumstances no satisfactory home-school relations can take place or do take place: I mean rather that the best thing is for the parents to be brought *within* the educational experience of the schoolchild by doing what they can do, and this with confidence. There are many ways in which parents can help the child in this learning, which are within the parents' spheres of competence. If this happens, then the parents can feel adequate and confident both in relation to the child and the school. This may mean that the contents of the learning in school should be drawn much more from the child's experience in his family and community.

So far I have criticized the use of the concept of 'compensatory education' because it distracts attention from the deficiencies in the school itself and focuses upon deficiences within the community, family and child. We can add to these criticisms a third.

This concept points to the overwhelming significance of the early years of the child's life in the shaping of his later development. Clearly there is much evidence to support this view and to support its implication that we should create an extensive nursery-school system. However, it would be foolhardy indeed to write off the post-seven-years-of-age educational experience as having little influence.

Minimally, what is required *initially* is to consider the whole age period up to the conclusion of the primary stages as a unity. This would require considering our approach, at any *one* age, in the context of the whole of the primary stage. This implies a systematic, rather than a piecemeal, approach. I am arguing here for taking as the unit, not a particular period in the life of the child—for example, three to five years, or five to seven years—but taking as the unit a stage of education: the primary stage. We should see all we do in terms of the sequencing of learning, the development of sensitivities within the context of the primary stage. In order to accomplish this, the present social and educational division between infant and junior stages must be weakened, as well as the insulation between primary and secondary stages. Otherwise gains at any one age, for the child, may well be vitiated by losses at a later age.

We should stop thinking in terms of 'compensatory education' but consider, instead, most seriously and systematically the conditions and contexts of the educational environment.

The very form our research takes tends to confirm the beliefs underlying the organization, transmission and evaluation of knowledge by the school. Research proceeds by assessing the criteria of attainment that schools hold, and then measures the competence of different social groups in reaching these criteria. We take one group of children, whom we know beforehand possess attributes favourable to school achievement; and a second group of children, whom we know beforehand lack these attributes. Then we evaluate one group in terms of what it *lacks* when compared with another. In this way research, unwittingly, underscores the notion of *deficit* and confirms the status quo of a given organization, transmission and, in particular, evaluation of knowledge. Research very rarely challenges or exposes the social assumptions underlying what counts as valid knowledge, or what counts as a valid realization of that knowledge. There are exceptions in the area of curriculum development; but, even here, the work often has no built-in attempt to evaluate the changes. This holds particularly for educational priority area 'feasibility' projects.

Finally, we do not face up to the basic question: what is the potential for change within educational institutions as they are presently constituted? A lot of activity does not necessarily mean *action*.

I have taken so much space discussing the new educational concepts and categories because, in a small way, the work I have been doing had inadvertently contributed towards their formulation. It might be, and has been said, that my research—through focusing upon the subculture and forms of family socialization—has also distracted attention from the conditions and contexts of learning in school. The focus on usage of language has sometimes led people to divorce the use of language from the substratum of cultural meanings which are initially responsible for the language use. The concept, 'restricted code', to describe working-class speech, has been equated with 'linguistic deprivation' or even with the 'non-verbal' child.

We can distinguish between uses of language which can be called 'context-bound' and uses of language which are less context-bound. Consider, for example, the two following stories which the linguist, Peter Hawkins, constructed as a result of his analysis of the speech of middle-class and working-class five-year-old children. The children were given a series of four pictures which told a story and they were invited to tell the story. The first picture shows some boys playing football; in the second the ball goes through the window of a house; the third shows a man making a threatening gesture; and in the fourth a woman looks out of a window and the children are moving away. Here are the two stories:

1 Three boys are playing football and one boy kicks the ball and it goes through the window the ball breaks the window and the boys are looking at it and a man comes out and shouts at them because they've broken the window so they run away and then that lady looks out of her window and she tells the boys off. (No. of nouns: 13. No. of pronouns: 6.)

2 They're playing football and he kicks it and it goes through there it breaks the window and they're looking at it and he comes out and shouts at them because they've broken it so they run away and then she looks out and she tells them off. (No. of nouns: 2. No. of pronouns: 14.)

With the first story, the reader does not have to have the four pictures which were used as the basis for the story, whereas in the case of the second story the reader would require the initial pictures in order to make sense of the story. The first story is free of the context which generated it, whereas the second story is much more closely tied to its context. As a result, the meanings of the second story are implicit, whereas the meanings of the first story are explicit.

It is not that the working-class children do not have, in their passive vocabulary, the vocabulary used by the middle-class children. Nor is it the case that the children differ in their tacit understanding of the linguistic rule system. Rather, what we have here are differences in the use of language arising out of a specific context. One child makes explicit the meanings which he is realizing through language for the person he is telling the story to, whereas the second child does not to the same extent.

The first child takes very little for granted, whereas the second child takes a great deal for granted. Thus, for the first child, the task was seen as a context in which his meanings were required *to be made* explicit, whereas the task for the second child was not seen as a task which required such explication of meaning. It would not be difficult to imagine a context where the first child would produce speech rather like the second.

What we are dealing with here are differences between the children in the way they realize, in language use, what is apparently the same context. We could say that the speech of the first child generated universalistic meanings, in the sense that the meanings are freed from the context and so understandable by all; whereas the speech of the second child generated particularistic meanings, in the sense that the meanings are closely tied to the context and would be only fully understood by others if they had access to the context which originally generated the speech. Thus universalistic meanings are less bound to a given context, whereas particularistic meanings are severely context-bound.

Let us take another example. One mother, when she controls her child, places a great emphasis on language, because she wishes to make explicit, and to elaborate for the child, certain rules and reasons for the rules *and* their consequences. In this way the child has access through language to the relationships between his particular act which evoked the mother's control, and certain general principles, reasons and consequences which serve to universalize the particular act.

Another mother places less emphasis on language when she controls her child and deals with only the particular act: she does not relate it to general principles and their reasoned basis and consequences.

Both children learn that there is something they are supposed, or not supposed, to do; but the first child has learned rather more than this. The grounds of the mother's acts have been made explicit and elaborated; whereas the grounds of the second mother's acts are implicit, they are unspoken.

Our research shows just this. The social classes differ in terms of the *contexts* which evoke certain linguistic realizations. Many mothers in the middle class (and it is important to add not all), relative to the working class (and again it is important to add not all by any means), place greater emphasis on the use of language in socializing the child into the moral order, in disciplining the child, in the communication and recognition of feeling. Here again we can say that the child is oriented towards universalistic meanings which transcend a given context, whereas the second child is oriented towards particularistic meanings which are closely tied to a given context and so do not transcend it. This does not mean that working-class mothers are non-verbal, only that they differ from the middle-class mothers in the *contexts* which evoke universalistic meanings. They are *not* linguistically deprived, neither are their children.

We can generalize from these two examples and say that certain groups of children, through the forms of their socialization, are oriented towards receiving and offering universalistic meanings in certain contexts, whereas other groups of children are oriented towards particularistic meanings. The linguistic realizations of universalistic orders of meaning are very different from the linguistic realizations of particularistic orders of meaning, and so are the forms of the social relation (for example, between mother and child) which generate these. We can say, then, that what is made available for learning, how it is made available, and the patterns of social relation, are also very different.

Now, when we consider the children in school, we can see that there is likely to be difficulty. For the school is necessarily concerned with the transmission and development of universalistic orders of meaning. The school is concerned with making explicit—and elaborating through language—principles and operations as these apply to objects (the science subjects) and persons (the arts subjects). One child, through his socialization, is already sensitive to the symbolic orders of the school, whereas the second child is much less sensitive to the universalistic orders of the school. The second child is oriented towards particularistic orders of meaning which are context-bound, in which principles and operations are implicit, and towards a form of language use through which such meanings are realized.

The school is necessarily trying to develop in the child orders of relevance and relation as these apply to persons and objects, which are not initially the ones he spontaneously moves towards. The problem of educability at one level, whether it is in Europe, the United States or newly developing societies, can be understood in terms of a confrontation between (a) the school's universalistic orders of meaning and the social relationships which generate them, and (b) the particularistic orders of meanings and the social relationships which generate them, which the child brings with him to the school. Orientations towards 'meta-languages' of control and innovation are not made available to these children as part of their initial socialization.

The school is attempting to transmit un-common-sense knowledge—i.e. public knowledge realized through various 'meta-languages'. This knowledge is what I have called universalistic. However, both implicitly and explicitly, schools transmit values and an attendant morality, which affect the contents and contexts of education. They do this by establishing criteria for acceptable pupil and staff conduct. These values and morals also affect the content of educational knowledge through the selection of books, texts and films, and through the examples and analogies used to assist access to public knowledge (universalistic meanings). Thus, the working-class child may be placed at a considerable disadvantage in relation to the *total* culture of the school. It is not made for him; he may not answer to it.

The universalistic functions of language—where meanings are less context-bound—point to an 'elaborated code'. The more particularistic functions point to a 'restricted code'. Because a code is restricted it does not mean that a child is non-verbal, nor is he in the technical sense linguistically deprived, for he possesses the same tacit understanding of the linguistic rule system as any child. It does not mean that the children cannot produce, at any time, elaborated speech variants in *particular* contexts.

It is critically important to distinguish between speech variants and a restricted code. A speech variant is a pattern of linguistic choices which is specific to a particular context—for example, when talking to children, a policeman giving evidence in a court, talking to friends whom one knows well, the rituals of cocktail parties, or train encounters. Because a code is restricted it does not mean that a speaker will not in some contexts, and under specific conditions, use a range of modifiers or subordinations, or whatever. But it does mean that where such choices are made they will be highly *context-specific*.

This 'concept code' refers to the transmission of the deep-meaning structure of a culture or sub-culture—the 'code' meaning structure.

'Codes', on this view, make substantive the culture or subculture by controlling the linguistic realizations of contexts critical to socialization. Building on the work of Professor Michael Halliday, one can distinguish four critical contexts:

1 The regulative contexts: these are the authority relations where the child is made aware of the molar order and its various backings.
2 The instructional contexts: here the child learns

about the objective nature of objects and acquires various skills.

3 The imaginative or innovating contexts: here the child is encouraged to experiment and re-create his world on his own terms and in his own way.

4 The interpersonal contexts: here the child is made aware of affective states—his own and others.

In practice these are interdependent, but the emphasis and contents will vary from one group to another. I suggest that the critical orderings of a culture or subculture are made substantive, are made palpable, through the way it realizes these four contexts linguistically—initially in the family. If these four contexts are realized through the predominant use of restricted speech variants with particularistic —i.e. relatively context-tied—meanings, then the deep structure of the communication is controlled by a restricted code. If these four contexts are realized predominantly through elaborated speech variants, with relatively context-independent—i.e. universalistic —meanings, then the deep structure of communication is controlled by an elaborated code. Because the code is restricted, it does not mean that the users *never* use elaborated speech variants. It only means that such variants will be used infrequently in the process of socializing the child in his family.

The 'concept code' makes a distinction similar to the distinction which linguists make between the 'surface' and 'deep' structure of the grammar. (See David Havano, *New Society*, 9 January 1969, and Ernest Gellner, 29 May 1969, on Noam Chomsky's work.) Sentences which look superficially different can be shown to be generated from the same rules.

The linguistic choices involved in a précis will be markedly different from the linguistic choices involved in a self-conscious poem. These in turn will be markedly different from the linguistic choices involved in an analysis of physical or moral principles: or different again from the linguistic realization of forms of control by a mother. But they may all, under certain conditions, reveal that speech codes—either restricted *or* elaborated—underlie them.

Now because the subculture or culture, through its forms of social integration, generates a restricted code, it does not mean that the resultant speech and meaning system is linguistically or culturally deprived, that the children have nothing to offer the school, that their imaginings are not significant. Nor does it mean that we have to teach the children formal grammar. Nor does it mean that we have to interfere with their dialect.

There is nothing, but nothing, in the dialect as such, which prevents a child from internalizing and learning to use universalistic meanings. But if the contexts of learning—for example, the reading of books—are not contexts which are triggers for the children's imaginings, are not triggers for the children's curiosity and explorations in his family and community, then the

child is not at home in the educational world. If the teacher has to say continuously, 'Say it again, dear; I didn't understand you', then in the end the child may say nothing. If the culture of the teacher is to become part of the consciousness of the child, then the culture of the child must first be in the consciousness of the teacher.

This may mean that the teacher must be able to understand the child's dialect, rather than deliberately attempting to change it. Much of the context of our schools is unwittingly drawn from aspects of the symbolic world of the middle class, and so when the child steps into school he is stepping into a symbolic system which does not provide for him a linkage with his life outside.

It is an accepted educational principle that we should work with what the child can offer; why don't we practise it? The introduction of the child to the universalistic meanings of public forms of thought is not 'compensatory education'; *it is education*. It is not making children middle class; how it is done, through the implicit values underlying the form and content of the educational environment, might.

We need to distinguish between the principles and operations that teachers transmit and develop in the children, and the contexts they create in order to do this. We should start knowing that the social experience the child already possesses is valid and significant, and that this social experience should be reflected back to him as being valid and significant. It can only be reflected back to him if it is part of the texture of the learning experience we create. If we spent as much time thinking through the implications of this as we do thinking about the implications of Piaget's development sequences, then it would be possible for schools to become exciting and challenging environments for parents, the children themselves and teachers.

We need to examine the social assumptions underlying the organization, distribution and evaluation of knowledge, for there is not one, and only one, answer. The power relationships created outside the school penetrate the organization, distribution and evaluation of knowledge through the social context. The definition of 'educability' is itself, at any one time, an attenuated consequence of these power relationships.

We must consider Robert Lynd's question: 'knowledge for what?' And the answer cannot be given only in terms of whether six-year-old children should be able to read, count and write. We do not know what a child is capable of, as we have as yet no theory which enables us to create sets of optimal learning environments; and even if such a theory existed, it is most unlikely that resources would be available to make it substantive on the scale required. It may well be that one of the tests of an educational system is that its outcomes are relatively unpredictable.

Notes

1 This article is a more spelled-out version of one which forms a chapter in *Education for Democracy*, ed. Colin Stoneman and David Rubinstein, Penguin Education Special (1970), 110–21.

References

Bernstein, Basil (1970). A sociolinguistic approach to socialization: with some reference to educability, in J. J. Gumperz and Dell Hymes (eds.), *Directions in Socio-linguistics*. New York: Holt, Rinehart & Winston, re-printed in B. Bernstein, (ed) *Class, Codes and Control, Vol. 1*. Routledge & Kegan Paul 1971.

Bernstein, Basil and Henderson, D. (1969). Social class differences in the relevance of language to socialization. *Sociology* 3 (1), reprinted in B. Bernstein, (ed.), *Class, Codes and Control, Vol. 2*. Routledge & Kegan Paul 1972.

Fantini, M. D. and Weinstein, G. (1968). *The Disadvantaged: Challenge to Education*. Harper & Row.

Halliday, M. A. K. (1969). Relevant models of language. *Educational Review* 22 (1).

Hawkins, P. R. (1969). Social class, the national group and reference. *Language and Speech* 12 (2).

Section VII Language and values

In this section we consider ways in which language functions in the framing of value judgments. The approach is primarily philosophical. The sorts of questions being asked are 'What are the characteristics of prescriptive language?', 'Can value judgments be said to be "true" or "false"?', 'What logically distinguishes appropriate criteria in the making of value judgments?'.

The field is vast, and could in principle range from judgments about food and wine ('Is there such a thing as "good" taste in food, or is what you like just "a matter of taste"?') to judgments about the use of language in Shakespeare ('For what literary reasons does he dwell on the concept of "nothingness" in *King Lear*?'); from judgments of efficiency ('This is a good screwdriver') to judgments of 'ultimate values' such as lovingness, truthfulness, honesty, or whatever.

We have chosen to illustrate *three* areas in which value judgments are commonly made: those of morality, politics and aesthetics. It would clearly be impossible in the space available to study *all* the linguistic implications of judgments in these areas, and we have in fact concentrated on illustrating the way in which *analysis of key concepts* can help towards throwing light on the significance of such language-use. The first reading consists of three short extracts from Hare's book *The Language of Morals*. In extract A, Hare introduces his general line of argument by indicating the inter-relationships between various forms of 'prescriptive language'—of which moral judgments form a sub-group. In extract B, he shows why he thinks it of *practical* importance to understand the nature of moral language. In extract C, he explores in more detail the use of the word 'good' in moral contexts, and considers the various criteria logically connected with the framing of moral and non-moral judgments.

In the second reading, Wollheim demonstrates that normative political language necessarily has 'moral' components: the use of the term 'democracy' has moral as well as historical connotations.

Barrett's paper is written at a more complex level philosophically, and is included in the Reader as an illustration of the sort of interest analytical philosophers have in the nature of aesthetic value judgments, and of the way in which they regard the study of *language* as being of central importance in the elucidation of problems related to an area in which value judgments are made.

Alan Harris

29 The language of morals

R. M. Hare

A. Prescriptive language and moral judgements

If we were to ask of a person 'What are his moral principles?' the way in which we could be most sure of a true answer would be by studying what he *did*. He might, to be sure, profess in his conversation all sorts of principles, which in his actions he completely disregarded; but it would be when, knowing all the relevant facts of a situation, he was faced with choices or decisions between alternative courses of action, between alternative answers to the question 'What shall I do?' that he would reveal in what principles of conduct he really believed. The reason why actions are in a peculiar way revelatory of moral principles is that the function of moral principles is to guide conduct. The language of morals is one sort of prescriptive language. And this is what makes ethics worth studying: for the question 'What shall I do?' is one that we cannot for long evade; the problems of conduct, though sometimes less diverting than crossword puzzles, *have to be solved* in a way that crossword puzzles do not. We cannot wait to see the solution in the next issue, because on the solution of the problems depends what happens in the next issue. Thus, in a world in which the problems of conduct become every day more complex and tormenting, there is a great need for an understanding of the language in which these problems are posed and answered. For confusion about our moral language leads, not merely to theoretical muddles, but to needless practical perplexities.

An old-fashioned, but still useful, way of studying anything is *per genus et differentiam*; if moral language belongs to the genus 'prescriptive language', we shall most easily understand its nature if we compare and contrast first of all prescriptive language with other sorts of language, and then moral language with other sorts of prescriptive language. I shall proceed from the simple to the more complex. I shall deal first

Source: R. M. Hare, *The Language of Morals*, Clarendon Press (1952), 1–3, 72–6, 137–50.

with the simplest form of prescriptive language, the ordinary imperative sentence. The logical behaviour of this type of sentence is of great interest to the student of moral language because, in spite of its comparative simplicity, it raises in an easily discernible form many of the problems which have beset ethical theory. Therefore, although it is no part of my purpose to 'reduce' moral language to imperatives, the study of imperatives is by far the best introduction to the study of ethics; and if the reader does not at once see the relevance to ethics of the earlier part of the discussion, I must ask him to be patient. Neglect of the principles enunciated here is the source of many of the most insidious confusions in ethics.

From singular imperatives I shall proceed to universal imperatives or principles. The discussion of these, and of how we come to adopt or reject them, will give me an opportunity of describing the processes of teaching and learning, and the logic of the language that we use for these purposes. Since one of the most important uses of moral language is in moral teaching, the relevance of this discussion to ethics will be obvious.

I shall then go on to discuss a kind of prescriptive language which is more nearly related to the language of morals than is the simple imperative. This is the language of non-moral value-judgements—all those sentences containing words like 'ought', 'right', and 'good' which are not moral judgements. I shall seek to establish that many of the features which have caused trouble to students of ethics are also displayed by these sorts of sentence—so much so that a proper understanding of them does much to elucidate the problems of ethics itself. I shall take the two most typical moral words 'good' and 'ought' in turn, and shall discuss first their non-moral uses, and then their moral ones; in each case I hope to show that these uses have many features in common. In conclusion I shall relate the logic of 'ought' and 'good', in both moral and non-moral contexts, to the logic of imperatives by constructing a logical model in which artificial concepts, which could to some extent do duty for the value-words of ordinary language, are defined in terms of a modified imperative mood. This model is not to be taken too seriously; it is intended only as a very rough schematization of the preceding discussion, which itself contains the substance of what I have to say.

Thus the classification of prescriptive language which I propose may be represented as follows:

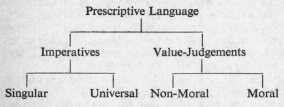

Prescriptive Language

Imperatives   Value-Judgements

Singular   Universal   Non-Moral   Moral

This classification is rough only; for example, it will be seen that the so-called 'universal imperatives' of ordinary language are not proper universals. Nor do I wish to suggest that the classification is exhaustive; there are, for example, many different kinds of singular imperatives, and of non-moral value-judgements; and there are other kinds of imperatives besides singular and universal. But the classification is good enough to begin with.

B. The practical importance of moral language

Let us consider a process that seems to occur quite often in history; it occurred in Greece during the fifth and fourth centuries, and it has occurred in our own time. Suppose that the people of a certain generation —I will call it the first generation—have got very settled principles, inherited from their fathers. Suppose that they have become so settled as to be second nature, so that generally speaking people act on the principles without thinking, and their power of making considered decisions of principle becomes atrophied. They act always by the book, and come to no harm, because the state of the world in their time remains much the same as that for which the principles were thought out. But their sons, the second generation, as they grow up, find that conditions have changed (e.g. through a protracted war or an industrial revolution), and that the principles in which they have been brought up are no longer adequate. Since, in their education, much stress has been laid on observing principles, and very little on making the decisions on which these principles are ultimately based, their morality has no roots, and becomes completely unstable. Books on 'The Whole Duty of Man' are no longer written or read. Often, when they do what it says in such books, they subsequently find cause to regret their decisions; and there are too many cases of this kind for any confidence in the old principles, as a body, to remain. No doubt there are among these old principles certain very general ones, which will remain acceptable unless human nature

and the state of the world undergo a most fundamental change; but the second generation, not having been brought up to make decisions of principle, but to do what it says in the book, will not, most of them, be able to make those crucial decisions which would determine which principles to keep, which to modify, and which to abandon. Some people, the Polemarchuses of the second generation, will have been so steeped in the old principles that they just follow them come what may; and these will on the whole be more fortunate than the others, for it is better to have some principles, even if they sometimes lead to decisions which we regret, than to be morally adrift. The bulk of the second generation, and still more perhaps of the third, will not know which of the principles to keep and which to reject; and so they will come more and more to live from day to day—not a bad thing, because it trains their powers of decision, but it is an unpleasant and dangerous state to be in. A few among them, the rebels, will shout from the house-tops that some or all of the old moral principles are worthless; some of these rebels will advocate new principles of their own; some will have nothing to offer. Though they increase the confusion, these rebels perform the useful function of making people decide between their rival principles; and if they not only advocate new principles, but sincerely try to live by them, they are conducting a moral experiment which may be of the utmost value to man (in which case they go down in history as great moral teachers), or may, on the other hand, prove disastrous both to them and to their disciples.

It may take several generations for this disease to play itself out. Morality regains its vigour when ordinary people have learnt afresh to decide for themselves what principles to live by, and more especially what principles to teach their children. Since the world, though subject to vast material changes, changes only very slowly in matters that are fundamental from the moral point of view, the principles which win the acceptance of the mass of people are not likely to differ enormously from those which their fathers came to distrust. The moral principles of Aristotle resemble those of Aeschylus more than they differ from them, and we ourselves shall perhaps come back to something recognizably like the morality of our grandfathers. But there will be some changes; some of the principles advocated by the rebels will have been adopted. That is how morality progresses— or retrogresses. The process is, as we shall see, reflected by very subtle changes in the uses of value-words; the impossibility of translating Aristotle's catalogue of virtues into modern English may serve as an example, and the disappearance without trace of the word 'righteous' may serve as another.

The question 'How shall I bring up my children?' which we have mentioned, is one to the logic of which, since ancient times, few philosophers have given much attention. A child's moral upbringing has an effect upon him which will remain largely untouched by anything that happens to him thereafter. If he has had a stable upbringing, whether on good principles or on bad ones, it will be extremely difficult for him to abandon those principles in later life—difficult but not impossible. They will have for him the force of an objective moral law; and his behaviour will seem to give much evidence in support of intuitionist ethical theories, provided that it is not compared with the behaviour of those who stick just as firmly to quite different principles. But nevertheless, unless our education has been so thorough as to transform us into automata, we can come to doubt or even reject these principles; that is what makes human beings, whose moral systems change, different from ants, whose 'moral system' does not. Therefore, even if for me the question 'What shall I do in such and such a situation?' is almost invariably answered without ambiguity by the moral intuition which my upbringing has given me, I may, if I ask myself 'How shall I bring up my children?' pause before giving an answer. It is here that the most fundamental moral decisions of all arise; and it is here, if only moral philosophers would pay attention to them, that the most characteristic uses of moral words are to be found. Shall I bring up my children *exactly* as I was brought up, so that they have the same intuitions about morals as I have? Or have circumstances altered, so that the moral character of the father will not provide a suitable equipment for the children? Perhaps I shall try to bring them up like their father, and shall fail; perhaps their new environment will be too strong for me, and they will come to repudiate my principles. Or I may have become so bewildered by the strange new world that, although I still act from force of habit on the principles that I have learnt, I simply do not know what principles to impart to my children, if, indeed, one in my condition can impart any settled principles at all. On all these questions, I have to make up my mind; only the most hide-bound father will try to bring up his children, without thinking, in exactly the way that he himself was brought up; and even he will usually fail disastrously.

Many of the dark places of ethics become clearer when we consider this dilemma in which parents are liable to find themselves. We have already noticed that, although principles have in the end to rest upon decisions of principle, decisions as such cannot be taught; only principles can be taught. It is the powerlessness of the parent to make for his son those many decisions of principle which the son during his future career will make, that gives moral language its characteristic shape. The only instrument which the parent possesses is moral education—the teaching of principles by example and precept, backed up by chastisement and other more up-to-date psychological methods. Shall he use these means, and to what extent? Certain generations of parents have had no doubts about this question. They have used them to the full; and the result has been to turn their children into good institutionists, able to cling to the rails, but bad at steering round corners. At other times parents—and

who shall blame them?—suffer from lack of confidence; they are not sure enough what they themselves think, to be ready to impart to their children a stable way of life. The children of such a generation are likely to grow up opportunists, well able to make individual decisions, but without the settled body of principles which is the most priceless heritage that any generation can leave to its successors. For, though principles are in the end built upon decisions of principle, the building is the work of many generations, and the man who has to start from the beginning is to be pitied; he will not be likely, unless he is a genius, to achieve many conclusions of importance, any more than the average boy, turned loose without instruction upon a desert island, or even in a laboratory, would be likely to make any of the major scientific discoveries.

The dilemma between these two extreme courses in education is plainly a false one. Why it is a false one is apparent, if we recall what was said earlier about the dynamic relation between decisions and principles. It is very like learning to drive. It would be foolish, in teaching someone to drive, to try to inculcate into him such fixed and comprehensive principles that he would never have to make an independent decision. It would be equally foolish to go to the other extreme and leave it to him to find his own way of driving. What we do, if we are sensible, is to give him a solid basis of principles, but at the same time ample opportunity of making the decisions upon which these principles are based, and by which they are modified, improved, adapted to changed circumstances, or even abandoned if they become entirely unsuited to a new environment. To teach only the principles, without giving the opportunity of subjecting them to the learner's own decisions of principle, is like teaching science exclusively from textbooks without entering a laboratory. On the other hand, to abandon one's child or one's driving-pupil to his own self-expression is like putting a boy into a laboratory and saying 'Get on with it'. The boy may enjoy himself or kill himself, but will probably not learn much science.

C. 'Good' in moral and non-moral contexts

There has been a disposition among philosophers to do one of two opposite things. The first is to suppose that all value-judgements whatever relate to the performance by an object of a function distinct from the object itself. The second is to suppose that, because there are some objects which are commended for their own sakes, and do not have an obvious function beyond their mere existence, to commend such an object is to do something quite different from commending an object which does have a function. It will help us to avoid doing either of these things if we avail ourselves of the general notions of 'virtue' and 'standard'

When we are dealing with objects which are evaluated solely in virtue of their performance of a function, the virtues of such objects will consist in those characteristics which either promote, or themselves constitute, the good performance of the function. The matter can be made clear by supposing that what we are judging is the *performance* of the object, not the object itself. Imagine that we are judging a fire-extinguisher. To do so we watch it being used to put out a fire, and then judge its performance. Certain characteristics of the performance count as virtues (e.g. putting out the fire quickly, causing little damage to property, emitting no dangerous fumes, small consumption of expensive chemicals, &c.). Note that certain of the expressions used in specifying the standard (e.g. 'damage' and 'dangerous') are themselves value-expressions; these indicate that the specification of the standard is not in itself complete, but includes 'cross-references' to standards for evaluating, respectively, the state of repair of property, and the effect of gases on the human body. It would be impossible to specify the standard completely without having for purposes of reference a specification of all the other standards to which it is necessary to refer. Aristotle[1] gives examples of such cross-references in which the standards are arranged hierarchically, the cross-references being all in the same direction. It does not seem obvious that they need be so arranged, though it would be tidy if they were.

Now what we must notice, for our present purposes, about the above list of virtues of the fire-extinguisher's performance, is that it is just a list of virtues, not differing logically from the list of virtues of a class of objects not having a function. Compare it, for example, with the list of virtues of a good bath. A good bath is good both instrumentally (in that it is conducive to cleanliness) and intrinsically (for we should not have nearly so many baths if our only purpose in having them were to become clean). Let us for the moment ignore the instrumental goodness of the bath, and concentrate on its intrinsic goodness. To be good intrinsically, a bath must be within a certain range of temperature, which must be maintained throughout its duration; the vessel must be above a certain minimum size, which varies with that of the bather; it must be of a certain shape; and it must be full of soft clean water, there must be soap above a certain degree of fineness (e.g. not containing abrasives or free caustics)—and the reader may add to the list according to his taste. In this specification I have tried to avoid cross-references to other standards, but I have not been entirely successful; e.g., 'clean water' means 'water in which there is no dirt', and what is to count as dirt is a matter for evaluation. Thus even where we are dealing with intrinsic goodness we cannot avoid cross-references, and therefore it is not the necessity for cross-references which makes goodness instrumental.

We notice that in both cases—the fire-extinguisher and the bath—we have a standard or list of virtues, and commend objects which possess these virtues. In the case of the fire-extinguisher we commend directly its performance, and the object only indirectly; in the case of the bath we might be said to commend the object directly. But this is really a distinction without a difference; are we to say that 'inducing heat in my skin' is a performance of the bath, or are we to say that 'being hot' is a quality of the bath? Similarly, one of the virtues required in a good pineapple is that it should be sweet; is its sweetness an intrinsic quality of the pineapple, or is it the disposition to produce certain desirable sensations in me? When we can answer such questions, we shall be able to draw a precise distinction between intrinsic and instrumental goodness.

It would, however, be a mistake to say that there is *no* difference between what we do when we commend a fire-extinguisher and what we do when we commend a sunset. We commend them for entirely different reasons, and in the case of the fire-extinguisher these reasons all refer to what it is intended to do. We saw above that if 'good' is followed by a functional word (e.g. the name of an instrument), this word itself gives us a partial specification of the virtues required; whereas in other cases this specification is absent. All that I am maintaining is that the logical apparatus of virtues and standards which I have been elaborating is sufficiently general to cover both instrumental and intrinsic goodness. And to see this is to make the first step towards seeing that it may be general enough to cover moral goodness too. To this question we must now turn.

Let us review some of the reasons that have led people to hold that the use of the word 'good' in moral contexts is totally different from its use in non-moral ones. The first reason is connected with the difference between intrinsic and instrumental good, and we have already dealt with it. The second reason is that the properties which make a man morally good are obviously different from those which make a chronometer good. It is therefore easy to think that the *meaning* of the word 'good' is different in the two cases. But this can now be seen to be a mistaken conclusion. The descriptive meaning is certainly different, as the descriptive meaning of 'good' in 'good apple' is different from its meaning in 'good cactus'; but the evaluative meaning is the same—in both cases we are commending. We are commending as a man, not as a chronometer. If we insisted on calling the meaning of 'good' different, because the virtues required in objects of different classes are different, we should end up with what Mr. Urmson calls 'a homonym with as many punning meanings as the situations it applied to.'[2]

The third reason is this: it is felt that somehow 'moral goodness' is more august, more important, and therefore deserves to have a logic all its own. This plea seldom comes out into the open; but it lies behind much of the argument, and in itself has something to recommend it. We do attach more importance to a man's being a good man than to a chronometer's being a good chronometer. We do not *blame* chronometers for being bad (though we do blame their makers). We get stirred up about moral goodness in a way that few people get stirred up about technical or other sorts of goodness. This is why many readers will have been irritated by my supposing that the behaviour of 'good' in 'good sewage effluent' can have any interest for the moral philosopher. We have to ask, therefore, why it is that we feel this way, and whether the fact that we do makes it necessary for us to give an entirely different account of the logic of 'good' in the two cases.

We get stirred up about the goodness of men because we are men. This means that the acceptance of a judgement, that such and such a man's act is good in circumstances of a certain sort, involves the acceptance of the judgement that it would be good, were we ourselves placed in similar circumstances, to do likewise. And since we might *be* placed in similar circumstances, we feel deeply about the question. We feel less deeply, it must be admitted, about the question, whether it was a bad act of Agamemnon to sacrifice Iphigenia, than about the question, whether it was a bad act of Mrs. Smith to travel on the railway without paying her fare; for we are not likely to be in Agamemnon's position, but most of us travel on railways. Acceptance of a moral judgement about Mrs. Smith's act is likely to have a closer bearing upon our future conduct than acceptance of one about Agamemnon's. But we never envisage ourselves turning into chronometers.

These observations are to a certain extent confirmed by the behaviour of technicians and artists. As Hesiod pointed out, these people do get stirred up about their respective non-moral goodnesses, in the way that ordinary people get stirred up about moral questions: 'Potters get angry with potters, and carpenters with carpenters, and beggars with beggars, and poets with poets.'[3] Commercial competition is not the only reason —for it is possible to compete without malice. When an architect, for example, says of another architect's house, with feeling, 'That is a thoroughly badly designed house', the reason for the feeling is that if he were to admit that the house was well designed, he would be admitting that in avoiding in his own work features like those of the design in question, he had been wrong; and this might mean altering his whole way of designing houses, which would be painful.

Further, we cannot get out of being men, as we can get out of being architects or out of making or using chronometers. Since this is so, there is no avoiding the (often painful) consequences of abiding by the moral judgements that we make. The architect who was forced to admit that a rival's house was better than anything he had ever produced or could produce, might be upset; but in the last resort he could become a barman instead. But if I admit that the life of St. Francis was morally better than mine, and really mean this as an evaluation, there is nothing for it but to try to be more like St. Francis, which is arduous. That is why most of our 'moral judgements' about the saints are merely conventional—we never intend them to be a guide in determining our own conduct.

Moreover, in the case of differences about morals it is very difficult, and, in cases where the effect on our own life is profound, impossible, to say 'It's all a matter of taste; let's agree to differ'; for to agree to differ is only possible when we can be sure that we shall not be forced to make choices which will radically affect the choices of other people. This is especially true where choices have to be made cooperatively; it must be pointed out, however, that though most moral choices are of this kind, this sort of situation is not peculiar to morals. The members of the Kon-Tiki expedition could not have agreed to differ about how to build their raft, and families sharing a kitchen cannot agree to differ about its organization. But although we can usually get out of building rafts or sharing kitchens, we cannot easily get out of living in societies with other people. Perhaps men living in complete isolation could agree to differ about morals. It would at any rate seem that communities not in close contact with one another could agree to differ about some moral questions without actual inconvenience. To say this, of course, is not necessarily to maintain any kind of moral relativism, for communities could agree to differ about whether the earth was round. To agree to differ is to say, in effect, 'We will differ about this question, but let us not be angry or fight about it'; and not to say 'we will differ, but let us not differ'; for the latter would be a logical impossibility. And so if two communities agreed to differ about, say, the moral desirability of legalized gambling in their respective territories, what would happen would be this; they would say 'We will continue to hold, one of us that it is wrong to legalize gambling, and the other that it is not wrong; but we will not get angry about each other's laws, or seek to interfere in each other's administration of them'. And the same thing might be done about other matters than gambling, provided that what each community did had slight effect outside its own borders. Such agreements will not work, however, if one community holds it to be a moral duty to prevent certain practices taking place wherever they occur.

Such a case is worth considering in order to contrast with it the more usual state of affairs; normally the moral judgements that we make, and hold to, deeply affect the lives of our neighbours; and this in itself is enough to explain the peculiar place that we assign to them. If we add to this the logical point, already mentioned, that moral judgements always have a possible bearing on our own conduct, in that we cannot in the fullest sense accept them without conforming to them, then no further explanation is needed of the special status of morals. This special status does not require a special logic to back it up; it results from the fact that we are using the ordinary apparatus of value-language in order to commend or condemn the most intimate actions of ourselves and those like us. We may add that the 'emotivity' of much moral utterance, which some have thought to be of the essence of evaluative language, is only a symptom— and a most unreliable one—of an evaluative use of words. Moral language is frequently emotive, simply because the situations in which it is typically used are situations about which we often feel deeply. One of the chief uses of the comparison which I have been drawing between moral and non-moral value-language is to make it clear that the essential logical features of value-words can be present where the emotions are not markedly involved.

It might be objected, that my account of the matter gives no means of distinguishing prudential judgements like 'It is never a good thing to volunteer for anything in the Army' from properly moral judgements like 'It is not good to break one's promises'. But the considerations given earlier enable us to distinguish satisfactorily between these two classes of judgement. It is clear from the context that in the second case we are commending within a different class of comparison, and requiring a different set of virtues. Sometimes we commend an act within the class of acts having an effect upon the agent's future happiness; sometimes we commend an act within the class of acts indicative of his moral character, that is to say, those acts which show whether or not he is a good man—and the class of comparison 'man' in this context is the class 'man to try to become like'. Which of these we are doing is always clear from the context, and there is nearly always a further verbal difference too, as in the example quoted. It must be admitted, however, that a great deal of research has still to be done on the different classes of comparison within which we commend people and acts.

When we use the word 'good' in order to commend morally, we are always directly or indirectly commending *people*. Even when we use the expression 'good act' or others like it, the reference is indirectly to human characters. This, as has often been pointed out, constitutes a difference between the words 'good' and 'right'. In speaking, therefore, of moral goodness, I shall speak only of the expression 'good man' and similar expressions. We have to consider whether in fact this expression has the same logical features as the non-moral uses of 'good' which we have been discussing, remembering that clearly 'man' in 'good man' is not normally a functional word, and never so when moral commendation is being given.

First, let us take that characteristic of 'good' which has been called its supervenience. Suppose that we say 'St. Francis was a good man'. It is logically impossible to say this and to maintain at the same time that there might have been another man placed in precisely the same circumstances as St. Francis, and who behaved in them in exactly the same way, but who differed from St. Francis in this respect only, that he was not a good man. I am supposing, of course, that the judgement is made in both cases upon the whole life of the subject, 'inner' and overt.

Next, the explanation of this logical impossibility does not lie in any form of naturalism; it is not the case that there is any conjunction C of descriptive characteristics such that to say that a man has C entails that he is morally good. For, if this were the case, we should be unable to commend any man for having those characteristics; we should only be able to say that he had them. Nevertheless, the judgement that a man is morally good is not logically independent of the judgement that he has certain other characteristics which we may call virtues or good-making characteristics; there is a relation between them, although it is not one of entailment or of identity of meaning.

Our previous discussion of non-moral goodness helps us to understand what the relation is. It is that a statement of the characteristics of the man (the minor or factual premiss) *together with* a specification of a standard for judging men morally (the major premiss), entails a moral judgement upon him. And moral standards have many of the features that we have found in other value-standards. 'Good', as used in morals, has a descriptive and an evaluative meaning, and the latter is primary. To know the descriptive meaning is to know by what standards the speaker is judging. Let us take a case where the standard is well known. If a parson says of a girl that she is a good girl, we can form a shrewd idea, of what description she is; we may expect her to go to church, for example. It is therefore easy to fall into the error of supposing that by calling her a good girl the parson means simply that she has these descriptive characteristics.

It is quite true that part of what the parson means is that the girl has these characteristics; but it is to be hoped that this is not all he means. He also means to commend her for having them; and part of his meaning is primary. The reason why we know, when a parson says a girl is good, what sort of girl she is, how she normally behaves, &c., is that parsons are usually consistent in the way they award commendation. It is through being used consistently by parsons for commending certain sorts of behaviour in girls that the word comes to have a descriptive force.

To this unkind parody may be added another. If two Indian Army majors of the old school had been talking about a new arrival in the Mess, and one of them had said 'He's an awfully good man', we could have guessed that the subaltern referred to played polo, stuck pigs with *élan*, and was not on familiar terms with educated Indians. The remark, therefore, would have conveyed information to one versed in the culture of British India. It would have been informative, because officers of the Indian Army were accustomed to award commendation or the reverse according to consistent standards. But it cannot have been informative in the beginning. The standard must have got established by some pioneer evaluators; when the Indian Army was young there was no established standard for the behaviour of subalterns. The standard became established by officers making commendatory judgements which were not statements of fact or informative in the least, to the effect that it was the mark of a good man, for example, to play polo. For these pioneers, the sentence 'Plunkett is a good man' did not in any way entail the sentence 'Plunkett plays polo' or vice versa. The former was an expression of commendation, the latter a statement of fact. But we may suppose that, after generations of officers had always commended people who played polo, it came to be assumed that, if an officer said that another officer was a good man, he must mean that, among other things, he played polo; and so the word 'good', as used by Indian Army officers, came to be, to this extent, descriptive, without in the least losing its primary evaluative meaning.

Of course, the evaluative meaning might get lost, or at least wear thin. It is of the essence of a standard to be stable; but the perpetual danger is that stability may harden to overrigidity and ossification. It is possible to lay too much stress on the descriptive force and too little on the evaluative; standards only remain current when those who make judgements in accordance with them are quite sure that, whatever else they may be doing, they are evaluating (i.e. really seeking to guide conduct). Suppose that the Indian Army comes to be unable to use the words 'good man' in any other way than descriptively, to mean 'man who plays polo, &c.'; they will then have fallen into a kind of naïve naturalism, and will be unable to commend subalterns for playing polo; and this means that they will not be able to hand on to new generations of officers their established standards. If a new subaltern has had, before his posting, the standards of a bank clerk with a timid interest in pink politics, those are the standards which he will continue to have; for his superior officers will have lost the linguistic means of teaching him any others. And even if the older officers are themselves using the word 'good' evaluatively, the extreme descriptive rigidity of their standards may lead the new subaltern to understand the word, as they use it, descriptively. This is how value-words get into inverted commas.

That the descriptive meaning of the word 'good' is in morals, as elsewhere, secondary to the evaluative, may be seen in the following example. Let us suppose that a missionary, armed with a grammar book, lands on a cannibal island. The vocabulary of his grammar book gives him the equivalent, in the cannibals' language, of the English word 'good'. Let us suppose that, by a queer coincidence, the word is 'good'. And let us suppose, also, that it really is the equivalent— that it is, as the *Oxford English Dictionary* puts it, 'the most general adjective of commendation' in their language. If the missionary has mastered his vocabulary, he can, *so long as he uses the word evaluatively and not descriptively*, communicate with them about morals quite happily. They know that when he uses the word he is commending the person or object that he applies it to. The only thing they will find odd is that he applies it to such unexpected people, people who are meek and gentle and do not collect large quantities of scalps; whereas they themselves are accustomed to commend people who are bold and burly and collect more scalps than the average. But they and the missionary are under no misapprehension about the

meaning, in the evaluative sense, of the word 'good'; it is the word one uses for commending. If they were under such a misapprehension, moral communication between them would be impossible.

We thus have a situation which would appear paradoxical to someone who thought that 'good' (either in English or in the cannibals' language) was a quality-word like 'red'. Even if the qualities in people which the missionary commended had nothing in common with the qualities which the cannibals commended, yet they would both know what the word 'good' meant. If 'good' were like 'red', this would be impossible; for then the cannibals' word and the English word would not be synonymous. If this were so, then when the missionary said that people who collected no scalps were good (English), and the cannibals said that people who collected a lot of scalps were good (cannibal), they would not be disagreeing, because in English (at any rate missionary English), 'good' would mean among other things 'doing no murder', whereas in the cannibals' language 'good' would mean something quite different, among other things 'productive of maximum scalps'. It is because in its primary evaluative meaning 'good' means neither of these things, but is in both languages the most general adjective of commendation, that the missionary can use it to teach the cannibals Christian morals.

Suppose, however, that the missionary's mission is successful. Then, the former cannibals will come to commend the same qualities in people as the missionary, and the words 'good man' will come to have a more or less common descriptive meaning. The danger will then be that the cannibals may, after a generation or two, think that that is the only sort of meaning they have. 'Good' will in that case mean for them, simply 'doing what it says in the Sermon on the Mount'; and they may come to forget that it is a word of commendation; they will not realize that opinions about moral goodness have a bearing on what they themselves are to *do*. Their standards will then be in mortal danger. A Communist, landing on the island to convert the people to *his* way of life, may even take advantage of the ossification of their standards. He may say 'All these "good" Christians— missionaries and colonial servants and the rest—are just deceiving you to their own profit'. This would be to use the word descriptively with a dash of irony; and he could not do this plausibly unless the standards of the Christians had become considerably ossified. Some of the ploys of Thrasymachus in the first book of Plato's *Republic* are very similar to this.

If the reader will turn back to extract B he will see that such vicissitudes of the word 'good' reflect accurately the sort of moral development there described. Moral principles or standards are first established; then they get too rigid, and the words used in referring to them become too dominantly descriptive; their evaluative force has to be painfully revived before the standards are out of danger. In the course of revival, the standards get adapted to changed circumstances; moral reform takes place, and its instrument is the evaluative use of value-language. The remedy, in fact, for moral stagnation and decay is to learn to use our value-language for the purpose for which it is designed; and this involves not merely a lesson in talking, but a lesson in doing that which we commend; for unless we are prepared to do this we are doing no more than pay lip-service to a conventional standard.

Notes

1 *Nichomachean Ethics*, 1. i. 2.
2 *Mind*, lix (1950), 161 (also in *Logic and Language*, ii, ed. Flew, 176).
3 *Works and Days*, 25.

30 Democracy

Richard Wollheim[1]

Contemporary discussions of Democracy may be brought under four rough headings: the *meaning* of Democracy, the *conditions* of Democracy, the *justification* of Democracy, and the *relation of Democracy to other political concepts and principles*.

1. The problem of the meaning of Democracy arises as soon as one considers with any degree of literalness the word itself: *democracy*, the 'rule of the people'. For contrast this with other similar words, such as *plutocracy* 'rule of the rich', and *theo-cracy*, the 'rule of the priests'.[2] Immediately two questions assert themselves. In the first place, how can the people rule in the way in which the rich or the priests clearly can? For surely there are too many of them for it to be a practical possibility. And secondly, if the people rule, who is there left to be ruled? (It is to be observed that in the classical world neither of these two questions arose with the force that they do for us. For in the first place, the City State was generally small enough to permit the people to participate directly in government. Secondly, to most classical thinkers the word 'demos' meant the people in the sense of 'the common people' or 'the ordinary man', or, more simply, 'the poor', not in the modern sense of 'the people as a whole', or 'every member of society': in consequence if the demos ruled, this left the rich and the noble to be ruled over.)

Two traditions of democratic thought can be identified by the way in which they treat this problem. One tradition, stemming ultimately from Rousseau, insists on taking this problem very literally and proposing to it a radical and peculiar solution. To begin with, all the members of society are said to possess two wills or selves: a 'true' or 'real' self, and an 'arbitrary' or 'fitful' self. All the true selves in any community are harmonious in their demands, whereas it is a mark of the arbitrary selves that they are discordant. In terms of this para-psychological assumption the two questions outlined above—or the 'paradox of self-govern-

Source: *Journal of the History of Ideas* (1958), **19** (2), 233–42.

ment', as a thinker of this school, Bernard Bosanquet called it—are readily solved. For to the first question, how can the people rule, being so many and so diverse?, the reply comes that it is their better selves that rule, and these selves, though naturally diverse, are necessarily harmonious. Secondly, to the question, who remains to be ruled if everyone rules?, the answer is given that though in a Democracy the ruled are certainly different from the rulers as much as they are in a plutocracy or in a theocracy, they are however different, not in being different people, but in being different parts of the same people—that is, the ruled are arbitrary or fitful selves of those whose real or true selves are the rulers.[3]

This tradition of thought, for all its metaphysical neatness, would appear to raise as many problems as it solves; and these further problems to be debarred of solution. For no empirical method is suggested whereby we can recognize or pick out the dictates of the true or real selves as opposed to those of the arbitrary selves. Indeed, when, as usually happens in this tradition of thought, the true self is further identified with moral self, it is clear that no such method could be provided without falling into the errors of ethical Naturalism. From all this one might well assume that this 'idealist' tradition of democratic thought would lead to a total and barren scepticism about democratic practice. In fact the result has been rather different. Idealist thinkers have been led to support the notion of a supreme legislator or leader who would be able to penetrate the surface of conflicting individual desires and intuit the underlying rational and harmonious will of the community. Such a conception has been called 'Totalitarian Democracy'.[4] If in Anglo-American political thought, little or no attention has ever been paid by 'idealist' thinkers to this very difficult problem of the practical interpretation of their theory, such self-denial, though saying something for their political wisdom, scarcely redounds to their intellectual credit.

A different answer to this problem is provided by a school of thought, more empiricist in outlook, which seeks to remove the so-called paradox at an earlier stage. On this view, though in a Democracy the people rule, they do not rule in the sense in which the rich might rule in a plutocracy or the priests in a theocracy; that is to say, they do not rule in the sense of holding in their own hands and wielding directly the supreme legislative and executive powers. They rule in a modified sense in that they exercise some control over the use of these powers. And in this sense of ruling, the argument continues, there can be no difficulty in seeing how the people, many of them though there may be, can rule. Equally on this view, there is no difficulty in seeing how the people can at once rule and be ruled. For the supreme legislative and executive powers, like any other external force or instrument, can be controlled *by* a group of people and yet also exercised *over* that group. This empiricist solution differs from the idealist solution above in that the paradox that is supposed to arise from the fact that the rulers and the ruled are in a Democracy identical, is disposed of, not by any dialectical legerdemain leading to a radical reinterpretation of political experience, but by an analysis which seeks to understand the concept of 'rule' or 'government' as it appears in the context of democratic thought, without in any way altering it.

However, it would be a mistake to assume that this empiricist view does not also give rise to further problems. For though it may answer the difficulties connected with the size or vastness of the ruling group in a Democracy, it still leaves unsettled those which arise or are alleged to arise out of its diversities and disharmonies. If the people do not agree upon how the supreme legislative and executive powers of the community are to be used—as they most likely will not—how can they control the use of these powers? Such difficulties certainly exist. It is, however, error to regard these as metaphysical or logical, rather than practical, difficulties. For there is no absurdity or inconsistency or self-contradiction in supposing the people to exert control over policy even when the policy pursued is not the taste of all. The only issue is whether the method employed for selecting policy by aggregating tastes is 'reasonable' or 'fair', and this issue is practical.

In Anglo-Saxon countries the usual method employed for ensuring popular control is that of representative institutions with a composition determined by specific electoral procedures, and these methods have over the years been found to satisfy the natural or intuitive demands of 'reasonableness' and 'fairness'. However, it needs to be emphasized that all these devices are no more than well-tried means of securing democratic control: none of them logically guarantees such control.

Though much of the criticism levelled at representative institutions is grossly exaggerated in that it assimilates the abuses of the system to its necessary concomitants, it does provide certain healthy reminders of how the system can go wrong. These may be brought under four headings:

(i) The society may be so sunk in apathy or swept away by hysteria that the majority vote is untypical of the considered ideas and desires of the majority of the society. To guard against apathy certain democratic countries have introduced compulsory voting (Australia, Belgium, Switzerland, etc.). In spite of the arguments that can be put forward in favor of this measure—most of which were raised in the debates in the Australian Parliament on its introduction in 1924—it has generally been regarded as 'undemocratic' in itself. Against mass hysteria no plausible constitutional safeguard has yet been proposed.

(ii) The society may be entirely reasonable and balanced in its voting habits, and yet, through some technical aspect of the electoral procedure, it may be impossible to arrive at a decision that can properly be said to represent the wishes of the majority. The limiting case which arises for any electoral procedure is where each of the alternatives voted upon attracts an equal number of voters, for then no decision whatsoever is forthcoming. A more difficult case is where a decision is forthcoming, but this clearly does not tally with what ordinarily or intuitively would be thought to be the majority will. It can be demonstrated that for every known 'reasonable' method of voting if the alternatives are three or more there is a situation in which this is bound to happen.[5] The only absolutely foolproof system is where every elector votes in turn on every pair of alternatives—a scarcely practical method.[6] (Proportional representation, often at this stage recommended as a panacea, merely transfers these difficulties from the electoral stage to the legislative stage.)

(iii) The society may know its own mind, express it unequivocally through the electoral procedure, and then the majority so established may enforce its policy with a complete disregard for the desires, interests or rights of the minority. Fears of the 'tyranny of the majority' were a constant theme in the nineteenth century, the great age of democratic thought. In the twentieth century, the great age of democratic practice, these fears have not on the whole been realized—though, significantly, where they have been, the reality has been on a scale far exceeding the worst envisaged. It would seem that the problem here is sociological rather than political, in that social conditioning is more likely to be an effective remedy than a system of constitutional checks and balances.

(iv) The majority may know its own mind, express it through the electoral mechanism, and the majority so constituted so far from tyrannizing over the minority, may fail even to exert rule over it. For power can fall into the hands of a minority within the majority. Some thinkers have indeed claimed that any machinery of majority rule is bound to put effective control into the hands of a minority. But this would seem to be exaggeration. Since the end of the last century, increasing attention has, however, been paid to the oligarchic tendencies implicit in democratic machinery: in particular, those relating to party organization and program construction.

Perhaps the most important single lesson to be learnt from these objections is that Democracy cannot be self-guaranteeing. It is exposed to risks, in the first place, from the mechanism that is devised to implement it, and secondly, from the other elements in society. It has been called justifiably, a 'calculated risk'.[7]

2. The question of the conditions of Democracy, i.e., what must exist for Democracy to exist, is one of the great problems of the age. Unfortunately, a great deal of contemporary discussion of it is bedevilled by an essential ambiguity in the nature of the question. It is often unclear whether the question is *logical*, i.e., what conditions must be satisfied for us to say correctly that Democracy exists, or *empirical*, i.e., what conditions must exist elsewhere in society for Democracy to come into existence and to survive.[8] Such ambiguity is common in theoretical arguments, but in this context there are two additional factors to account for its persistence. One is the absence of any developed sociology of politics; and the other is the extreme prestige attached to the word 'Democracy', so that writers tend to take over any concomitant of Democracy that they like and write about it as if it were part of Democracy.

In contemporary discussions of the conditions of Democracy, three issues have been singled out for particular attention:

(i) The connection between Democracy and Socialism. Those who assert that there is a real connection between the two may be divided into three groups:

First, there are the Marxists. These are sometimes taken to assert that Democracy is incomplete without socialism. This, however, is a misunderstanding of their true position. For what they wish to do is not so much to extend the concept of Democracy as to transpose it completely. Believing in what has been called the 'impotence of politics',[9] they are indifferent to constitutional and political organization, but at the same time want to secure the full prestige of this concept for their own preference in what they consider to be the truly important field—that of economic organization. It is significant that the use of the word 'Democracy' as a word of praise in Marxist thought dates from the time when it became a universally honorific word.

Secondly, there are the Democratic Socialists. Of these the Guild Socialists used to argue that a society could not truly be called 'democratic' unless all the institutions in it were themselves democratic. Amongst these institutions were to be numbered factories and other industrial plants, and the democratization of such institutions necessarily involves workers' control, i.e., Socialism.[10] Nowadays, most Socialists would prefer to use less *a priori* arguments. Some would use a pragmatic argument, namely that political Democracy cannot be truly safe without economic reorganization: and again others would prefer a moral argument to

the effect that there is an inconsistency in applying the principle of equality in the field of politics and denying it in the field of economics.

Thirdly, there are the conservatives who argue that Democracy is in its nature incompatible with Socialism. There are a number of arguments raised in current discussion to this effect: they are differentiated according to the feature of Democracy that they hold to be the ground of this incompatibility. Some have held this to be competition, others tolerance, others the existence of property. A recent argument that has attracted attention is that which maintains that Democracy requires freedom, freedom requires the Rule of Law, and Socialism in its advocacy of bureaucratic planning has to dispense with the Rule of Law.[11] Against this it has been urged in the first place, that the Rule of Law guarantees security, not freedom; and secondly, that even if economic planning does contract freedom in some directions, it extends it in others and the overall effect may well be an increase rather than a diminution.[12]

(ii) The connection between Democracy and the belief in Democracy. Since John Stuart Mill who claimed (ironically enough) that Democracy was not suitable for 'Malays and Bedouins', it has been generally conceded by even the most fervent democrats that there are some conditions that a population must satisfy for it to be fit for Democracy. However, despite the practical urgency of this problem with the break-up of the old colonial empires, our knowledge of what these conditions are has not increased. On one condition—which to some appears to have a certain intuitive obviousness—controversy has been bitter: viz., the belief in, or acceptance of, Democracy. Now if this condition is taken as applying to society as a whole it is obviously true, perhaps logically so. But it does not follow from this that it is therefore true of every single member of a society. Society to be democratic must believe in Democracy; but how many members it can successfully contain who do not themselves believe in Democracy, is a question incapable of any *a priori* answer. It depends on the restraints that these dissidents are prepared to put upon their own behavior, on the moral or spiritual authority that they wield over others, and on the extent to which their behavior can be neutralized by other factors in society (free speech, the press, education, etc.).

(iii) The connection between Democracy and Constitutionalism. It would be common ground to nearly all supporters of Democracy that there are certain laws or regulations that ought not to be passed even if the greater part or indeed the whole of the people favor them. To some it has seemed desirable to inscribe these 'moral limitations' of Democracy in a charter or Constitution. Some English thinkers have gloried in the fact that liberties enjoyed in Great Britain are to be found not in any Constitution but in the accumulated precedents of common law.[13] It would seem, however, that though this may well be something to be grateful for, it is not a matter for pride, and it is perfectly natural that other, and in particular younger, Democracies should prefer to express their ideals in a more systematic if necessarily more 'artificial' fashion.

However, the issue somewhat changes when the Constitution is regarded not merely as a systematic statement of the liberties recognized in society but as a method of guaranteeing them. In such cases the Constitution is accompanied by some mechanism for enforcing provisions like that of judicial review. To certain thinkers this has seemed the obvious requirement of Democracy; by others it has been regarded as inequitable, incompetent, and unnecessary. It is inequitable because it tries to limit the power of the living majority by means of 'the dead hand' of the past: it is incompetent because the only cases where it is likely to arise are just those where the Constitution itself will require 'interpretation'; and it is unnecessary because a society that is likely to accept the findings of such a mechanism is unlikely seriously to offend against the spirit of its Constitution. These strictures are sometimes supported by a historical examination of the record of actual mechanisms, e.g., the history of 'judicial review' in the US as an instrument of Democracy.[14]

3. There are in circulation in Anglo-Saxon thought a number of arguments, all purporting to justify Democracy. These arguments vary greatly in acceptability according to the number and validity of the principles they invoke, the truth of the factual assumptions they make use of, and the relevance of the kind of Democracy for which they argue to the kind that we experience.

(i) To exercise rule or to enjoy any form of political authority is a kind of moral education. On egalitarian grounds the opportunity for such self-improvement should be extended to as many as possible. In Democracy it is extended to all: therefore Democracy is the best of all forms of government. This argument, which is originally to be found in Aristotle (*Pol.* III. 1277b), may have had some application within the confines of the Polis, but applied to the conditions of the modern world it seems hopelessly unrealistic. Significantly enough, it is the characteristic argument of a kind of Liberalism which is or was peculiarly associated with a classical education.

(ii) The second argument is that true opinion on political and moral matters is the privilege of the common man. Accordingly, power in a community should reside with him: and this it does only in a Democracy. Hence the superiority of Democracy. As we have seen, this argument is central to the Greek conception of Democracy. In modern thought it has received reinforcement from a certain sentimental theory of the goodness of human nature uncorrupted by wealth, luxury and education. In contrast to this, Democracy has come in for much criticism based on the so-called discovery of man's 'irrationality' by modern psychology. Much of this criticism is con-

fused, and, if it proves anything, proves not so much the weakness of Democracy as the weakness of this particular argument for it.

(iii) A more materialistic version of the preceding argument makes the ordinary man the best judge not of what is right for the community but of his own interests. In consequence, if the people are allowed to control the government, then the interests of the people will be dominant. Democracy is identified with popular control, and therefore vindicated. This argument is the argument of the Utilitarians, supported in their case by a thoroughgoing psychological egoism. It also has been subjected to a great deal of empirical criticism. Recent sociology has, for instance, cast doubt on the classical notions of class by bringing out what has been called (perhaps misleadingly) the 'subjective' element in class determination. Nevertheless the argument has considerable weight.

(iv) A further retreat from the positions maintained in the two previous arguments leads to the completely sceptical argument for Democracy. According to this argument, it is impossible for anyone to discover what is the right course of action for the community, or where the true interests of its inhabitants reside. From this it follows that everyone in the community should be allowed to do what he wants to do as far as is socially possible. The only society in which this can happen is the one in which everyone has some control in the government: therefore Democracy is favored. As a variant of this argument, it may be maintained that even if one can discover what is ideally the right course of action to pursue, it would be wrong to insist on it unless everyone in the community recognized its rightness. Accordingly in practice one must adopt a sceptical attitude towards government and allow people to have the laws, institutions, etc., that they want: hence Democracy.

It seems to be certainly the case that scepticism does involve Democracy—even if the link is not as rigorous or as formal as some would believe. It does not follow from this, though—as certain critics of Democracy would have us believe—that Democracy involves scepticism.

(v) At the opposite end of the scale it is maintained that everyone has a natural right to control government and that this right is recognized only in Democracy: therefore Democracy is the best form of government. This argument has been subjected to two lines of criticism, both of which are misguided. The first is that the conception of 'a natural right' is metaphysical. Now natural rights are capable of, and often receive, a metaphysical interpretation, but this is not necessary. To say that something is a natural right may merely be a way of saying that it is an ultimate value. Secondly, it has been urged that it is absurd to allow that everyone has a natural right to exercise control over government when in fact not everyone can do so. But this argument assumes that the right in question is, in the terminology of jurisprudence, 'a right proper' (i.e., correlative to duty) whereas it seems more natural to assume that it is a liberty or privilege.[15]

(vi) Finally, it may be maintained that it is irrelevant whether Democracy does in fact maximize welfare, safeguard rights, accord with natural law, etc., for the fact is that under modern conditions it is the only working possibility. No member of an emancipated industrial society will put up with political tutelage. He insists on having a fair chance of influencing the government in accordance with his own desires and ideas; and by a 'fair' chance he means a chance 'as good as the next man's.' This argument was succinctly summarized in the nineteenth century by the conservative James Fitz-James Stephen who said that in Democracy we count heads to avoid breaking them; and it remains to-day one of the best arguments in favor of Democracy on account of its extreme economy.

4. The relation of the concept of Democracy to other notions such as Equality, Liberty, etc., falls outside the scope of this article.

Notes

1 This article was prepared in co-operation with the project of a 'Dictionary of Fundamental Terms of Philosophy and Political Thought' sponsored by the International Council for Philosophy and Humanistic Studies and planned and carried out with the assistance of UNESCO.

2 G. A. Paul, Democracy, *Chambers Encyclopaedia*, 4 (1944), 430–1.

3 Bernard Bosanquet, *The Philosophical Theory of the State* (London 1899).

4 J. L. Talmon, *The Origins of Totalitarian Democracy* (London 1952).

5 E. J. Nanson, Methods of Election, *Transactions and Proceedings of the Royal Society of Victoria*, 19 (1883), 197–240; Kenneth Arrow, *Social Choices and Individual Values* (New York 1951).

6 Robert A. Dahl, *A Preface to Democratic Theory* (Chicago 1956).

7 Robert A. Dahl and Charles Lindblom, *Politics, Economics and Welfare* (New York 1953).

8 Joseph A. Schumpeter, *Capitalism, Socialism and Democracy* (New York 1947).

9 Karl R. Popper, *The Open Society and Its Enemies* (London 1945).

10 G. D. H. Cole, *Guild Socialism Re-Stated* (London 1920).

11 F. A. von Hayek, *The Road to Serfdom* (London 1944).

12 Hans Kelsen, Democracy and Socialism, *Conference on Jurisprudence and Politics* (Chicago 1954), 63–87.

13 A. V. Dicey, *Introduction to the Study of the Law of the Constitution* (London 1885).

14 Henry S. Commager, *Majority Rule and Minority Rights* (New York–London 1943).

15 Richard Wollheim and Isaiah Berlin, Equality, *Proceedings of the Aristotelian Society*, 30 (1956), 281–326.

31 Are 'bad works of art' works of art?

C. Barrett

I

Some years ago I came across the following question thrown out almost casually in the course of discussion: How many of us, it was asked, want to call a 'bad work of art' a 'work of art'?[1] The question was clearly rhetorical; the author quite obviously did not consider that anyone in his right mind would suggest that a bad work of art was a work of art. This struck me as rather odd. Surely there can be good and bad works of art, just as there can be good and bad apples or good and bad men. An apple does not cease to be an apple just because it is bad, unless, perhaps, it has become thoroughly rotten; but the gardener who says: 'The Coxes are bad this year' does not mean that they have grown rotten on the trees, much less that they are not apples at all. Moreover, if so-called bad works of art are not works of art, what are they? You may not think highly of the works in the Royal Academy Summer Exhibition but they are not totally dissimilar to some works in Bond Street next door which are highly regarded.

However, there are certain terms which do not readily admit of the epithet 'bad' (or 'good' for that matter). It is odd to speak of a 'bad saint' (though it is conceivable that a saint who did not answer one's petitions might be so described). It is also somewhat odd to speak of a 'bad gentleman' (unless in the now obsolete sense of a member of the landed gentry). Such terms have goodness built into them, so to speak. They are honorific terms. To qualify them with the epithet 'bad' is to be guilty of a contradiction: to take with one hand what one gives with the other.

Is the term 'work of art' like that? Is it an honorific term, used exclusively honorifically, so that to speak of a bad work of art is to involve oneself in a contradiction?

We undoubtedly use the term 'work of art' honori-

fically. 'You wouldn't call *that* a work of art, would you?' more briefly: 'But is it art?' are common expressions. On the other hand, we also use 'work of art' in what seems to be a non-honorific or neutral sense. We speak in a non-committal way of works of art being auctioned at Sotheby's or of the National Gallery housing works of art or of thefts of works of art, but this does not commit us to saying that all these works are works of art in the honorific sense.[2]

Indeed, so far from it being obvious that 'work of art' is an exclusively honorific term, it is almost a commonplace among philosophers today that 'work of art' admits of a neutral as well as an honorific use. John Kemp writes:[3]

> I am using both 'artist' and 'work of art' in a neutral sense, so as to include ... bad and indifferent paintings, poems, etc. as well as good ones; I am not using them in an honorific sense, although they are frequently, and quite properly, so used.

And Morris Weitz implies the distinction when he says:[4]

> Thus, if one chooses to employ 'Art' evaluatively, as many do, so that 'This is a work of art and not (aesthetically) good' makes no sense, he uses 'Art' in such a way that he refuses to *call* anything a work of art unless it embodies his criterion of excellence.

Henry Khatchadourian makes the same point when he says:[5]

> 'work of art', with emphasis on 'art' is also used as a value term, as equivalent to '*good* work (of art)'

The most uncompromising statement of the opposite view (the view implied in the rhetorical question with which this paper started) was made by Collingwood in his *Principles of Art*:[6]

Source: *Philosophy and the Arts*, Royal Institute of Philosophy Lectures, 6, 1971/2, London: Macmillan.

The definition of any given kind of thing is also the definition of a good thing of that kind: for a thing that is good in its kind is only a thing which possesses the attributes of that kind.

This is a more sweeping claim, too sweeping to be discussed here. It seems possible to maintain that the definition of *certain* kinds of things is honorific without having to maintain that the definition of *every* kind of thing is honorific. The question which we are concerned with is the limited one: is the term which we apply to the kind of thing we call a 'work of art' exclusively honorific?

In the face of common and philosophical usage it would seem a piece of arbitrary verbal legislation to suggest that there is only an honorific use of the term 'work of art'. Common usage, however, is not conclusive. The fact that we may appear to use a term neutrally as well as honorifically is not proof that we in fact do so. We speak of 'bad coins'. A bad coin is one which for some reason or another cannot be accepted as coin-of-the-realm or legal tender. To call a coin 'bad' may simply be another way of saying that it is not coin-of-the-realm. Because we use the term 'bad', it does not follow that there is a neutral sense of 'coin-of-the-realm' which admits of good and bad. In the same way, it might be argued, the term 'bad work of art' in common usage may be interpreted as meaning false, seeming or putative work of art; something which is not really a work of art at all.

But our use of the phrase 'bad work of art' is varied. Some works so described may indeed be false or putative. Works which we also describe as *kitsch* or *schmaltz* (the Germans seem either more prolific in producing this sort of thing or more perceptive in detecting it) are obvious candidates for this category. But not all bad art is pseudo art. Moreover, when we say of a particular work of art—the Leonardo cartoon, perhaps—'now that is a work of art', we do not imply that the other works in the National Gallery are not works of art. This, however, might be taken care of by saying that our use of 'work of art' allows for two tiers or degrees of honorificity. To call something a 'work of art' at all is to honour it, but further honour can be conferred by use of italics or a certain tone of voice. C. S. Lewis's tutor used to say of some of his ideas that they had risen to the dignity of error—that is, above the level of gibberish—and required only to be refuted.

Yet even if common usage can be taken care of in this way, philosophical usage will not succumb so easily. To establish the thesis that 'work of art' is exclusively honorific, it must be shown either that the so-called neutral use is in reality crypto-honorific or that any attempt to define 'works of art' neutrally leads inevitably to some absurdity. In spite of my initial doubts and hesitations, I believe that such an attack on the neutralist position can succeed. In other words, a neutral definition of 'work of art' which is truly neutral, i.e. is not crypto-honorific, is inevitably driven to absurdity.

II

This can be demonstrated by beginning with the definitions of those who confidently assume that a neutral definition can be given. In every case some honorific or positive evaluative term or terms are included in the definition. But before discussing specific cases, I must determine more specifically what I mean by an honorific term. I consider a term (or the use of a term) to be honorific if, among its defining characteristics, there is one or more which commits the user to a favourable judgment of it, as a member of its kind, on pain of contradiction. Thus to say of a Stakhanovite that he is work-shy is contradictory, since calling him a Stakhanovite commits one to saying that he is a good worker. Similarly, to say of a gentleman that he is dishonourable, ungallant to women, etc., is self-contradictory, since such a bounder is no gentleman. The case of 'works of art' is slightly different, since it has already been suggested that its honorificity is two tiered; one can say: 'Now that is what I call a *work of art*.' Nevertheless, there are certain works which are not just bad works but not works of art in any sense, and no neutral criterion will differentiate them from dull, mediocre, inept, pretentious or downright bad works of art.[7]

It would be impossible, and unnecessary, to examine all attempted definitions of 'work of art' in order to show that they are crypto-honorific; one will suffice to demonstrate the way in which honorific terms get included in so-called neutral definitions. Morris Weitz provides the following instance of what he cautiously describes as 'criteria of recognition' of a work of art:[8]

> when we describe something as a work of art, we do so under the conditions of there being present some sort of artifact, made by human skill, ingenuity and imagination, which embodies in its sensuous, public medium—stone, wood, sounds, words—certain distinguishable elements and relations.

Although he denies that a set of necessary or sufficient conditions for describing something as a 'work of art' can be forthcoming, it is hard to see how we could withhold that description from something which fulfilled all Weitz's conditions. However, that is not the point at issue. The question is: is this a neutral definition? Clearly it is not. We may have neutral tests for deciding what is an artifact or what is a sensuous, public medium, and, possibly, though this is more doubtful, whether human skill has been used; but when it comes to such things as ingenuity and, still more, imagination we are committed to passing a favourable judgment on the work. The work may be faulted on certain counts, but if it displays ingenuity and imagination (as these terms are ordinarily understood when applied to the arts), it cannot be utterly trite and banal; a host of pejorative epithets are ruled out.

Every other definition which I have come across,

with one exception, which I shall come to later, contains honorific terms. I now wish to show that this is necessarily the case. One reason in support of this is that if a neutral definition of work of art could be devised then certain sections of the community would long ago have devised it. I am referring chiefly to officers of the Inland Revenue and Customs and Excise. Brancusi's *Bird in Flight* was refused entry into the United States as a work of art on the grounds that it bore no resemblance to a bird. 'What hunter', one official asked, 'would want to shoot a bird like that?' An expert had to be called in to assure the officials that, despite appearances, it was indeed a work of art. It is said that William Scott managed to get his semi-abstract pictures admitted into Ireland duty-free on the grounds that they were unfinished works of art—hardly even begun, as the customsman remarked. At the opposite extreme, it is reported that at an exhibition in the Hayward Gallery, where pieces of dyed hessian and piles of sand were on show, the cleaners were reluctant to remove some polythene sacks of rubbish for fear that they might have been part of the exhibition.

It might be objected that the reason for these mistakes, if they were mistakes, was that the term 'work of art' is open-textured or open-ended, not that it necessarily involves favourable evaluation. That it is open-textured in some sense of that word I don't deny. New forms of art such as abstract and semi-abstract art, and whatever one may wish to call Barry Flanagan's dyed hessian and piles of sand, call for continual revision of our criteria for calling something a work of art. But the decision to include such objects within the category of works of art is not a purely intellectual one as was the decision to regard $\sqrt{-1}$ as a number, albeit an imaginary number. That is, it is not based solely on the similarity between such works and accepted paintings and sculpture, because it is precisely this similarity which is denied. It is only where people are persuaded that the qualities which they admire in accepted works of art are present also in these *outré* works that the latter are accepted as works of art. What makes things difficult for customs officials and cleaners is that the term 'work of art' fluctuates with the fluctuations of taste. Until a neutral account of value judgments can be given, that is, until it can be shown that some set of qualities non-evaluatively described, imply a value judgment, no neutral definition of 'work of art' will be forthcoming. I have reason to believe, however—though it would require another paper to argue the case—that such an event is not likely to take place in our lifetime.

The same point can be made by adapting an example offered by Professor Kennick. Let us imagine a storekeeper being sent into a warehouse and asked to bring out the works of art stored there. What is he likely to do? Unless he is an exceptional storekeeper he will probably bring out all the paintings, statues, tapestries and ornaments. He will probably leave behind the posters. He may be puzzled by the photo-

graphs but will probably leave them behind, too. He may also be puzzled by the furniture, glass, ceramics, needlework, cutlery, etc., but will probably be guided by two principles: if it is (1) old or (2) ornamented, bringing it out; otherwise leaving it behind. The garden roller, the Swedish or Japanese functional crockery, cutlery and furniture, and the moleskin trousers will be left behind. (I might add, in parentheses, to simplify matters, that there are no works of literature, no scores or gramophone records, no films, etc. in the warehouse; only works of the visual arts.) It is also probable that Claus Oldenberg's outsize tube of toothpaste, Jim Dine's washbasin, Yves Klein's monochrome painting and Tinguely's auto-destructive machine will be left behind. On the other hand, the storekeeper might well bring out the china ducks (including Donald Duck) and the garden gnomes. (An advanced critic might have brought out the moleskin trousers and left the Raphael.)

I agree with Kennick that none of the existing definitions of 'work of art' would have helped the storekeeper, but this is not because these definitions are more obscure than what they define, but because the use of the term 'work of art' calls for an exercise of aesthetic judgment which we do not usually expect of storekeepers, customs officials and cleaners.[9]

At this point I should like to introduce a distinction which might make a neutral definition of 'work of art' possible, a distinction between what I shall call the *assertive* and the *acquiescent* use of the term 'work of art'. By the *assertive* use of 'work of art' I have in mind a *claim* made by the speaker that some work is or is not a work of art. The clearest expression of this use would take the form: 'Now *that* is what I call a work of *art*' or 'It simply is *not art*, whatever else it is.' The claim can also be made by exhibiting or giving serious critical attention to or by rejecting or pointedly neglecting a work. I take it that this is roughly what Professor Gallie has in mind when he calls 'work of art' an essentially contested concept.[10] On the other hand, one is using the term *acquiescently* when one makes no special claim that a work is or is not a work of art, but simply goes along with accepted usage in so far as this can be ascertained. This is presumably the way in which the term is used by government officials, particularly officers of the Inland Revenue and Customs and Excise, by cleaners, storekeepers and so on. But it may also be used in this way by those who have a very definite idea of what is and what is not a work of art. They acquiesce out of courtesy so as not to give offence or arouse acrimony.

The acquiescent use obviously does not commit the user to a favourable judgment. One may agree to call something a work of art even if one would not so describe it oneself. Hence, it is not honorific. Thus the way is open for a neutral definition. But what form would such a definition take? Clearly it would be unsatisfactory to define a work of art as anything which is *regarded* as a work of art, since the definition would contain that which is to be defined. But for 'work of art' one might substitute 'any work of aesthetic interest, attitude or regard'. Yet even assuming that some meaning can be given to this formula,[11] it would not be entirely satisfactory, since everything can be regarded aesthetically, but not everything is a work of art. But if one adds some such modification as 'anything which is considered to have aesthetic value and is offered as an object to be regarded aesthetically' this difficulty could be partially overcome.[10] The puzzlement of the customs officials faced with Brancusi's *Bird in Flight* and of the cleaners at the Hayward Gallery could thus be explained, not as an aberrant aesthetic judgment, but as being due to ignorance of the fact that the former was rated highly and offered as an object to be regarded aesthetically and the sacks of rubbish were not.

But such a definition would run into some serious difficulties.

First, it seems plausible to argue that when Mozart was composing his Jupiter Symphony or Shakespeare was writing *Hamlet* what they had in their minds were works of art, and they would still have been works of art even if they had never been committed to paper. Oscar Wilde told his publishers that he had completed *Lady Windermere's Fan* even though he had not written a word of it. The notion of a private work of art (*de facto* not *de jure* private) cannot arbitrarily be ruled out.

There are a number of ways of evading this difficulty. The most sensible seems to be to regard this as a limiting case. The artist who is merely contemplating a work of art in his mind is at least offering it to himself, and what he is offering to himself is in principle public, i.e. were he to commit it to paper, canvas, etc. it could be offered in the fullest sense.

A second objection can be put like this. There are in our museums and art galleries a number of objects—medieval or cycladic statues, negro masks, drinking vessels, etc.—which until recently were not regarded aesthetically but now are. According to the definition given above they were not works of art; they have only recently become so. This gives rise to the objection: either they were always works of art or they are not works of art now. Merely offering something for aesthetic consideration cannot make it into a work of art if it was not one already. Something cannot wait to become a work of art until it is offered for aesthetic consideration. It seems more plausible to say that we have recognized that it was a work of art all the time than to say that, by displaying it in a museum, we have made it into a work of art. Moreover, recognizing it as a work of art can only mean appreciating its aesthetic value. Thus one has to fall back on the honorific sense of 'work of art'.

In reply to this it may be said that such objects were potential works of art but objects with a non-aesthetic function. They become works of art when they are given a new status or function by being placed in a museum. A madonna in a museum has (temporarily) ceased to be a cult object, and a cycladic mother-goddess, which had long ceased to be a cult object, acquires a new role on being placed in the museum in the context of other objects with high aesthetic value and not merely of antiquarian interest. Of course, whoever placed them there and called them works of art presumably has a high regard for them and would have used the term 'work of art' honorifically. But someone else might acquiesce in calling them works of art without sharing this high regard.

There is a third, more serious objection. However acquiescent a person may be, there comes a time when his tolerance reaches a limit. At what point this limit is reached will vary with his taste and cultural background. Few connoisseurs would agree to call china ducks or garden gnomes works of art; the plain man in the street is reluctant to admit that a good deal of what is nowadays exhibited in fashionable galleries is art. This lack of tolerance might be defended, in the case of the gnomes at least, on the grounds that people who like such things have a sentimental or other interest in them, not an aesthetic interest. This is a questionable move at best. What if it could be shown that their interest is genuinely aesthetic and that they regard these things highly? Either such objects have to be accepted as works of art—which is bordering on the absurd—or they have to be excluded from the class of work of art. Since their exclusion would be based on judgment of their aesthetic value, the term 'work of art' would then be used honorifically.[11]

This problem was posed in a slightly different form by Marcel Duchamp's ready-mades. When Duchamp exhibited an inverted bicycle-wheel, a coal-shovel, a moustached print of the *Mona Lisa*, an inverted urinal, etc. he stated specifically that 'The choice was based on a reaction of *visual indifference* with a total absence of good or bad taste.' In other words, he did not value the works highly; nor did he choose them because they were positively ugly, as garden gnomes may be; they were, as he said, aesthetically indifferent, neither of high nor low aesthetic value. Now according to the neutral acquiescent definition these could not be works of art, because they were not rated highly. Duchamp's own attitude was ambiguous. As Hans Richter reports in one place: 'These works . . . are not works of art but of non-art' but in another place he says:[12]

He declared that these ready-mades became works of art as soon as he said they were . . . When he 'chose' this or that object . . . it was lifted from the limbo of unregarded objects into the living world of works of art: *looking at it made it into art*!

It is possible to alter the neutral acquiescent definition to include among works of art anything that anyone exhibits as an object to be looked at or declares to be a work of art. But this move leads to two absurdities: that of saying that an object not worth looking at is an object to be looked at, and secondly that anything is a work of art if anyone declares it to be one. On the other hand to rule out works which no one thinks highly of is to make the value judgment that these are not worth being called works of art even acquiescently.[13]

So whichever way one turns in an attempt to formulate a neutral definition of work of art one is forced to choose between some absurdity or other, or introduce some crypto-honorific element.

III

This brings us back to the initial question whether, if 'work of art' is used in an exclusively honorific sense, it makes sense to speak of bad works of art.

The answer to this depends on whether one uses a single fixed criterion or set of criteria or different interrelated criteria.

If there is one fixed quality or set of qualities, the possession of which constitutes something a work of art, then to say that a work has this quality or set of qualities and is aesthetically bad seems contradictory. It may be bad in some other respect—technically, morally, socially,—but not as a work of art. I have in mind there such qualities as being inspired, imaginative, expressive, formally significant, creative—whatever these may mean. Bad works of art according to this criterion are uninspired, unimaginative, inexpressive, non-significant, uncreative, etc. But they are not merely bad; they are strictly speaking, not works of art.

But if, instead of a fixed quality or set of qualities, one is operating with different sets, is it still contradictory to speak of a 'bad work of art'? Let us imagine, to quote Helen Knight's example, that the term 'tennis player' were used honorifically but that someone would qualify as a tennis player even if his (or her) style was bad but his match-winning ability was good (he won matches), or if he had a perfect style, played all the strokes perfectly, but, for reasons of temperament, seldom got beyond the first round at Wimbledon. Would it be contradictory to say that these two players were 'tennis players' (in the honorific sense—they both, after all, made Wimbledon), but they were bad because one did not play tennis as it should be played and the other could not win a championship? It seems to me that it would not. From one point of view each is good enough to qualify as a tennis player; from another point of view, they are not good enough—a *really* good player would both play well and win matches.

Might not the same be true of works of art? Take a painter like Blake, a composer like Tchaikovsky, a poet like Kipling or a playwright like Barrie. One might want to say that their works were bad for technical reasons or on account of their sentimentality, jingoism or coyness, yet for other reasons—vision, technical brilliance, insight—one might still want to call them works of art. They pass a certain test, they rise above a certain standard, and yet on other counts they fail. They have risen above mediocrity, trash, pastiche and general ineptitude—and yet have a sufficient number of defects to be called bad. (Even if the phrase 'bad work of art' sounds odd, there is nothing linguistically odd about saying of something that it is a work of art but bad.)

Now it might be objected that even if this were so, such works are not bad *as works of art*. Moreover, insofar as they are works of art they are good; so they are both good and bad works of art. As to the first part of the objection, it may indeed be the case that a work of art is called bad for a reason which is not relevant to it as a work of art. A march, which is otherwise an excellent piece of music, may be bad as a march because it is not easy to march to—the beat is not sufficiently clearly stressed. But if the reason for calling a work bad belongs to the class of considerations which would be accepted as relevant to calling a work good as a work of art, then (assuming that the reason is valid) the work is bad as a work of art. If structural organization, vividness, freshness, psychological insight, elegance, are reasons for calling a work good as a work of art (or calling it a 'work of art'), then the absence of these may count as reasons for calling it bad as a work of art.

As for the second part of the objection, I do not see any problem about accepting the fact that a work may be both good and bad as a work of art. The alternative is to say that only those works which are without any aesthetic defect whatsoever are works of art. But surely this is going too far. Is there any work which reaches this standard? I can think of none. (It is arguable that to be without any notable aesthetic defect would itself be an aesthetic defect.)

These objections take a curate's egg view of the value of works of art. It is as though one can hive off the good—the true works of art—and ignore the rest. 'Brahms's symphonies are works of art *in spite of* lamentable lapses into sentimentality.' But I don't think this view can be sustained. For someone who regarded the symphonies of Brahms as turgid, pompous, academic and mawkish—defects which he considered more serious than lack of invention or thinness—and yet who recognized their other artistic merits, it would not be possible to ignore the defects and concentrate on the merits, since the meritorious elements are, alas, used in the service of the defective or inextricably bound up with them. All he can say is: 'Pity about Brahms. Such a waste of talent. If only he could have forgotten about Beethoven and Auntie Flo.' Perhaps of a bad work of art (in the honorific sense) it can be said: 'There but for this defect or that goes a great work' and this is a great deal more than can be said of works which would not even qualify as bad works of art.

Two points remain to be made. If it makes sense to speak of a bad work of art, it is still possible to speak of certain works which one particularly admires in a doubly honorific sense. Thus to say of 'The Stag at Bay', for example, 'That is what I call a work of *art*', is not to say that Michaelangelo's 'Creation of Adam' is to be excluded from the august company of works of art, but merely to proclaim the superlative merits of Landseer's masterpiece.

The second point is that if 'bad work of art' should be expurged from the language, so should 'good work of art' since it would be redundant. I have tried to show that 'bad work of art' is not necessarily self-contradictory, even though 'work of art' is used honorifically. A good work of art would then be a work whose merits outweighed its defects, or one whose merits were of an outstanding order; a work of which we might say: 'Now *that* is what I call a work of *art*'.

Notes

1 Sonia Greger, Presentational Theories Need Unpacking, *British Journal of Aesthetics*, 9, 2, 159.

2 There is also the neutral sense which is more or less synonymous with 'visual art' or what the French call an *objet d'art*. We are not concerned with this here.

3 J. Kemp, The Work of Art and the Artist's Intentions, *British Journal of Aesthetics*, 4, 2, 147. Cf. R. F. Racy, The Aesthetic Experience, ibid. 9, 4: 'The point which one wishes to make is that good art and bad art all come under the classification of art, just as good machines and bad machines are all machines', 350.

4 M. Weitz, The Role of Theory in Aesthetics, *Journal of Aesthetics and Art Criticism*, 15, 34.

5 H. Khatchadourian, Art Names and Aesthetic Judgments, *Philosophy*, 36, 31n.

6 E. G. Collingwood, *The Principles of Art*, Oxford 1938, 280.

7 There are various necessary conditions for something being a work of art: it must be man-made or at least chosen and displayed, it must be proposed for aesthetic enjoyment, etc. But if these alone were accepted we would have to admit that every parlour mantlepiece, shrine and grave was a work of art, since they are intended as, and believed to be, objects of aesthetic delight. I am assuming that they would not be called works of art, much less bad works of art. If I am wrong in this, then my whole thesis falls to the ground.

8 M. Weitz, op. cit., 32.

9 Citing the difficulties of the Customs or Inland Revenue is only partially frivolous. Practical legal tests often give an edge to philosophical discussion. In this instance philosophical discussion might have practical fruit. For administrative convenience it has been decided, for instance, that 'multiples' shall be subject to tax on the grounds that they are commercial products (which is true). Yet not only are they original works of art (they are not copies or even prints) but they are by eminent artists, such as Vasarely, Le Parc, Soto (all of whom have won international prizes). (The fear is, presumably, that the manufacturers of garden shears will claim that their products are works of art too.)

10 W. B. Gallie, Essentially Contested Concepts, *Proceedings of the Aristotelian Society*, 1955–6, 167–8.

11 It is not within the scope of this paper to determine the meaning of the terms 'aesthetic interest' or (below) 'aesthetic value'. In the discussion which followed this paper, Miss Ruby Meager, the chairman, suggested that one could say that 'what accredited and paid critics regard as works of art are works of art' and this would be an acquiescent, neutral definition of 'work of art'. I agree. But the trouble is that accredited and paid critics do not agree among themselves, and if they did, it would still be open to a budding critic to disagree with their verdict (description) and win support for his views.

12 H. Richter, *Dada*, London 1965, 52 and 88–9.

13 I do not wish to deny that certain things can be declared *not* to be works of art by applying neutral criteria, e.g. that they are not man-made or not made with the intention of giving aesthetic pleasure or whatever. The point is that these conditions are not sufficient to guarantee that the thing in question *is* a work of art.

Section VIII Language and literature

The language function of which literature is a part is present in *all* people—we all at times take part in every one of these activities: narrative, monologue, dialogue, speaking, writing and reading. When we read novels and poems, magazines and newspapers and take part in conversations, we are using language to fit the external world into our own world. From a very early age the story is a powerful vehicle through which we channel and come to terms with feelings. 'Once upon a time . . .' or 'The Brangwens had lived for generations on the Marsh Farm . . .' signal a mode of expression in which statements of an affective nature are going to be organized so that the writer and the reader may make a detached evaluation of experience.

Harding's article explores the extent to which the process of reading a novel (a sophisticated construct) is essentially similar to that of the day-dream or a conversation with a neighbour. The spectator at a play, or the reader of a novel, is offered representations of events about which he is able to make detached evaluative responses which modify and confirm his existing values. The symbolic representation of experience, whether in children's play or our own gossip, is of the same order as that of the novel, the poem or the song; all of these modes enable the on-looker to contemplate the possibilities and consequences of the experience portrayed: 'In literature . . . the author invites his audience to share in an exploration, and extension and refinement of his and their common interests; and as a corollary, to refine and modify their value judgments'. This article raises fundamental questions about literature, and our response to literature, posing the possibility that our taste in gossip and in films may be the same kind of thing as our taste in literature.

The role of the onlooker is further explored in Britton's article. Here he re-names the role as 'spectator' and places it in a wider analysis of language functions. Of particular concern in our discussion of the language of literature is his description of the 'poetic' function of language. Here he extends Harding's account by introducing the notion of the formal organization involved in literature: 'the formal design created by a complex of emotions dynamically related'. While there *is* a continuity between gossip and literature, there is also a distinction. 'The poetic utterance is a construct or artifact, a verbal object'; gossip fulfils an immediate and expressive function: 'expressive language is loosely structured, free to fluctuate'. However, both enable us to stand back and review the possibilities of experience.

An analysis of secondary school children's writing in all aspects of the curriculum has led to the article's map of language functions. The exploration of the role of the spectator raises fundamentally the importance of literature in a man's life. If we accept this, we may then focus our attention on the educational purpose of spectator role activities, particularly those which value an individual's own experience in his own language. We need to recognize a continuum which runs from the free fluctuation and loose construction of expressive language to fully-structured poetic utterance, and acknowledge the status of our own, and children's, responses and utterances along this continuum.

Elizabeth Grugeon

32 The role of the onlooker

D. W. Harding

The novel reader or playgoer who knows well enough that he at least is not indulging in escape, that he is not passive, that he enjoys no vicarious satisfaction, may sometimes find himself wondering what, more positively, he is doing. He is not passive, but is he active in quite the same way as the man digging a ditch or the scientist bringing facts into order? He makes a full imaginative response to a fiction, but this somehow is not escaping from reality—although, on the other hand, he doesn't fall into the error of thinking about the characters of plays or novels as real people. He concerns himself instead, as we know, with the total pattern they contribute to. But is this pattern the same kind of pattern as he might find in an abstract painting or a piece of music?

These confusions and doubts are of course perversely naïve, but the uncertainty they point to is not entirely sham, at least in my own mind. And although they raise questions whose detail and comprehensiveness alike take them beyond the range of an article, I want to attempt a naïve and explicit statement of one idea that touches them all: that of the part played by the spectator or reader. What is the nature of his response? What mode of activity is he engaged in? Or, to put it differently, with what other modes of activity do we tacitly contrast his response?

To answer this question, I suggest, we need to distinguish four modes of activity. The first is what would universally be recognized as 'activity': 'actually doing things', or, for the sake of a distinguishing term, an operative response. Next comes the intellectual comprehension of things and events around us, a response which stops at comprehension and involves no attempt to control or modify what is comprehended. The third mode of activity consists in looking at things or listening to them, not in order to use them or to understand them intellectually, but simply for the sake of experiencing them and organizing them at the level of perception. The fourth mode of response is

Source: *Scrutiny* (1937), 6 (3), 247–58.

that of detached evaluation, and it is in this that the role of the spectator typically consists.

These diversions must be examined in some detail. But first it should be observed that they possess no value implications. Within each mode of activity may be found pursuits of every degree of complexity, skill and value, from the trivial occupations of idle moments to the most significant undertakings we are capable of. And for a preliminary description it seems most convenient to identify them under their trivial forms, as they appear when we are more or less idling, but always with the implication that the more highly developed and complex forms of activity fall into the same broad divisions.

At the level of idling there may first be observed a wide range of pursuits in which we are, as we say, actually 'doing' something, as distinct from thinking or watching, talking or imagining. It may be throwing stones, collecting shells, dismembering flies, paddling, playing patience, whittling at a bit of wood, rubbing a tiki smoother and smoother, smoking and drinking. In all these we are controlling some feature of our surroundings: we maintain it or modify it according as it does or does not meet our desires or the impulses of the moment. Or, of course, we may only be seeking to control it or wishing helplessly that we could, but in this case our concern with the environment is basically the same. For the sake of a name we may speak of this as the operative relationship to objects or events. It is the most familiar and the best understood.

Secondly, amongst the occupations of idleness there occurs a whole class of which the only satisfaction is 'getting to understand things'; exploring places, finding out how toys work, watching birds to discover their habits, and so forth. Here it may be convenient to follow such writers as Spranger and refer to these as 'theoretical' pursuits, using the term to describe every kind of activity in which comprehension is aimed at for its own sake. It goes without saying that in all activity, including the operative, some effort of comprehension is bound to occur; but it usually occurs as a means to the satisfaction of some other desire. In the theoretical relationship to events, the effort of understanding and systematizing our experience is made for the direct satisfaction which that gives, as an end in itself. At one level of complexity we call it 'idle curiosity', at another, 'devotion to science', and it comprises, of course, an immense part of human activity.

The third sort of idle pastime is just to watch things or listen to them—a stretch of landscape, say, or birds flying, or the rhythm made by the wheels of a train— and to do this without attempting any intellectual comprehension but simply enjoying the experience at the perceptual level. This is rather rare among the relaxations. For what usually happens is that people look, not at the pattern of a countryside, but at an impressive 'view' or a peaceful 'view', rich in emotional associations; and this, as I hope to show, is the fourth kind of relationship, the evaluative. The purely perceptual contemplation to be considered for the moment may occur, for instance, if, when we see waves breaking, we watch them until we have grasped as a perceptual whole the broad rhythm of their approaching, climbing, breaking and washing back, and can then see each new wave as slightly varying the pattern without destroying it. It occurs whenever we attend to the visual design of a picture or building or the auditory pattern of a piece of music. It need hardly be said that the perceptual pattern of a work of art is closely associated, and may seem to fuse, with other aspects, with its representational significance and its direct emotional effect. But our interest in pattern, whether in art or elsewhere, remains distinguishable as the effort simply to extend and refine our perceptual experience and to unify it into increasingly complex or subtle wholes, always at the level of perception.

Here, as with all these distinctions, it would be absurd to suggest that any one kind of relationship to events was likely to occur in isolation. We are constantly 'doing something' to objects in order the better to enjoy looking at them; as we do when we add some leaves to a bunch of flowers to break up the masses and vary the colour. And at more complex levels the painter or musician, in so far as his concern is with perceptual patterns, spends his time in operative activity—'doing'—in order to produce something to contemplate perceptually, something to look at or listen to. In most activity we must of course expect a continuous fusion of operative response, intellectual comprehension, perceptual enjoyment, and the fourth —the evaluative—form of response. Yet though they are no more than aspects or phases of a complex whole, one or other generally predominates and gives the total activity certain characteristics that ordinary discussion naturally attempts to distinguish.

Both the second and third of these modes of response—comprehension and perceptual contemplation —may be regarded as a form of looking on, but the typical spectator is far more commonly engaged in an evaluative response. This is the fourth mode of activity which has to be distinguished. At a street accident the spectators are thrilled or horrified, pitying, or perhaps ironic; they may judge one or other of the participants to have been at fault, they may reflect on the stupidities of modern transport. In all this they remain, as we say, 'detached'. But though they make no direct operative response they still assess the event in the light of all the interests, desires, sentiments and ideals that they can relate it to; and they feel it to be noteworthy, commonplace, agreeable or disagreeable, tragic, funny, contemptible, heroic—to mention a few of the cruder responses. The theoretical viewpoint, the effort at intellectual comprehension, is inextricably involved; but once value judgments have been made the spectator's relationship to the event has gone beyond mere comprehension. The same may be said of looking at crops and cattle and appreciating the prosperity of a countryside, enjoying the peacefulness of a river, being impressed by the power and ingenuity of a machine, experiencing mixed feelings at seeing a stoat kill a rabbit, wondering at the coolness of steeplejacks, and so on over an enormous range of everyday experience. It is in this detached, non-operative evaluation that the spectator's role most commonly consists.

Evaluation or assessment of our situation is going on in some form every moment of our lives; even in sleep it continues, and we shift about to get more comfortable, or wake up altogether if disturbances around us seem to require it. But in such circumstances we are not regarded as spectators, for the assessment is in direct preparation for an operative response. Similarly the typical role of spectator is not found in situations where we wish to participate and are unable to. The thwarting of an operative response gives rise to such experiences as grief, envy, helpless fury, resignation, rebellious disappointment, or remorse. These emotions arise on occasions when our evaluation is clearly preparatory to action but the action is either unsuccessful or has to be inhibited. We are in the physical position of the spectator without having his detachment. And in everyday speech we are then said not to be 'merely looking on' but to be 'looking on helplessly'.

Nor is the typical spectator the man who neglects to make an operative response that is expected of him, the man whom we accuse of 'looking on indifferently'. The type of spectator with whom a study of leisure pursuits is concerned neither tries unsuccessfully nor neglects an obligation to participate in what is going on. What, then, is the nature of the bond between the onlooker and the event? And—the corollary of this question—in what sense is the onlooker detached? These questions must be answered before the role of the onlooker can be understood. And for the sake of simplicity I wish first to consider only the onlooker who watches actual events, watches events for what they are and not for what they portray, and to leave till later the spectator at a play or the reader of a novel who is offered representations of events.

In the first place a scene may secure the onlooker's interest because it discloses or makes more vivid to him certain of the possibilities of his surroundings, possibilities which, although not directly involving him at the moment, must yet affect his expectations. Our hopes and anxieties for ourselves and other people very largely depend upon what we have learnt, as spectators, of the possibilities that surround us. Our interest in these possibilities extends beyond the desire to comprehend them intellectually. They are relevant to our other desires and values; we not only comprehend them, we are glad or sorry about them on account of the significance they have for ourselves, for our friends or perhaps for people in general.

But besides this it may safely be said that no event would secure our attention as spectators unless we were bound by some sentiment or ideal, however slight and weak, to the people or things which were directly involved. One factor governing the strength of our concern, therefore, will be the intensity of the sentiment that binds us to the participant; and just as the strength of our sentiments and ideals varies by imperceptible degrees so does the extent of our detachment or involvement when looking on at an event. The adversities and the good fortune of a very close friend may affect the spectator even more than they would have done if they had happened to himself; those of a slight acquaintance or a stranger make him somewhat concerned or rather pleased. The slight bond between him and the stranger consists in the liking and sympathy he has for the stranger perhaps as a human being, as a fellow-countryman, as a foreign visitor, as a child, as an old person, as one in misfortune, or as a member of a social class or of a sex, and so on through the innumerable categories represented in the organization of our sentiments and ideals.

The intensity of the attitudes evoked in us as spectators therefore depends on two things: the strength of the sentiment that binds us to the participant, and the importance of the event in the light of our own values. From this fact there spring subtle differences between, for instance, seeing a stranger badly injured and seeing a very close friend suffering from toothache; the intensity of our disturbance may be just about the same in the two cases, but the difference between the distresses occasioned by each is perfectly— sometimes disturbingly—evident to us. So too news of the rescue of national idols, lost explorers or airmen, may give us about the same degree of relief or elation as we get from hearing that an acquaintance has passed an examination. Peculiarities of temperament and character and habits of mind will also affect the question of the onlooker's degree of detachment, but apart from that it will depend on the seriousness of the event and the strength of the sentiments or ideals binding the spectator to the participant.

Detached evaluative responses, though less intense, tend to be more widely comprehensive than the evaluation which precedes participation. One views the event in a more distant perspective and relates it to a more extensive system of information, beliefs and values. And this detached evaluative response undoubtedly possesses the utmost importance in building up, confirming and modifying all but the very simplest of our values. It is as onlookers from a distance that we can most readily endure the penetration of general principles among our sentiments. Broadly humane sentiments towards negroes, for instance, are more easily met with in England and Holland than in South Africa or the Old South of the United States. Similarly the first contingents of exiles and refugees, whether Belgians, German Jews or Basques, are welcomed more eagerly than later arrivals, for the latter are no longer merely representatives of distressed humanity but people who are now known to possess displeasing habits and peculiar traits of personality. The event we look on at from a distance affects us, but it is set in a wider context than the urgencies of participating relationships usually permit us to call up around events. And for this reason, if we could obliterate the effects on a man of all the occasions when he was 'merely a spectator' it would be profoundly to alter his character and outlook.

The greater the social saturation of our environment the more strongly and extensively will our personality be influenced by the scenes we look on at. But the social environment is not essential to their effect. In a completely non-human environment we may still be influenced by what we see of animal life and natural forces. It may be birds feeding their young, the sea undermining cliffs, hares at the mating season, ivy smothering a tree—scenes like this affect the observer's future expectations, they establish his belief of what is 'the kind of thing that does happen' and even of what is natural and what isn't. Their importance may therefore be enormous even when there is a minimum of social preparation for interpreting them.

In an environment which is highly saturated socially, where dandelions are weeds and sunflowers plants, where dogs are fed and rabbits eaten, or where a heather-covered hillside looks just like a picture and a snowfall makes everything seem Christmassy, there our experience as spectators will have even greater effectiveness in our cultural moulding. Everything we look on at is tacitly and unintentionally treated as an object lesson by our fellow-spectators; speech and gesture, smiles, nudges, clucks, tuts and glances are constantly at work to sanction or correct the feelings we have as spectators. (Needless to say, our fellow-onlookers' influence need not be only positive—it may be largely inverse if we tend towards indocility and negativism.) Reciprocally, of course, we are sanctioning and challenging our fellows. And when we are not in the physical presence of others their moulds are still shaping our behaviour even if only by suggesting what we can do now that we're alone for once.

This, then, is one direction in which our experience

as spectators gains significance from the social saturation of our environment. Equally important are the processes that may take place when the events which we watch involve other human beings and a social relationship is established between them and the onlooker. As soon as the participant becomes aware, however faintly and however tacitly, of the attitude of the observer to him, the social process of reciprocal sanctioning or challenging has begun. It may be the faintest of attitudes, friendly or hostile, respectful or wondering, it may be the merest trace of sympathy, amusement, pity, but once it has occurred and been detected, whether openly admitted or not, the participant and the onlooker are influencing each other; either confirming or challenging the values that each has expressed in his behaviour or attitude.

This process is greatly intensified when the relationship has been openly admitted and some people are fulfilling the explicit role of spectator before others who perform to them; when we have passed, that is, from the state of idly watching men repairing roads, people gathering in crowds, marrying, fighting, dancing, burying, and playing games for their own amusement, and have accepted the invitation to form part of an audience for jugglers, acrobats, professional footballers, or speedway riders. When this point has been reached we may speak of display entertainment: a social situation, that is, which comprises not only display but the intention of display, and implies an audience which has come expecting to be interested and which offers some degree of approbation or disapproval.

In this way our attitude as spectators, although not directly operative, does come to have an effect on what is done and what is valued in our social group. The members of an appreciative audience are in effect assuring the performer and one another that what he is doing is worth doing; a view that he, of course, equally implies by having undertaken the performance. This sanctioning effect is more significant in other forms of entertainment still to be discussed, but even in display entertainment it is obviously effective as a means of reinforcing certain of the community's values. Gate money, newspaper descriptions, and supporters' clubs are the footballer's assurance from his community, and its members' reiteration to each other, that what he does is a good thing to do.

The role of the spectator cannot be at all fully understood until some attention has been given to the further range of possibility opened up when we pass from direct experience of our surroundings to that represented symbolically. The vast importance of representation for operative and theoretical activities is obvious; achievements that would be impossible without language, mathematical symbols and notations of every kind are an essential part of our civilization.

In perceptual contemplation, it goes without saying, there is little representation; in that mode of response we are concerned exclusively with the appearance of things, not with what they stand for. One of the few clear exceptions is found in the representation of depth in a picture; the perceptual pattern may be formed in three dimensions, and to grasp it even at the perceptual level we must have seen certain of the lines and shapes as representing a third dimension. A further exception perhaps occurs, though this is more doubtful, if the perceptual design ever depends upon represented movement; El Greco's 'Laocoon' is possibly an instance. In general we should have to say that representation is important in this mode of response only when the conceptual meaning of the material in some way affects our perception of it.

It is in the spectator's detached evaluative relationship to experience that the vastly increased scope achieved by representation most concerns us. We commonly think of such representation as the means by which one person communicates with another, but first it must be observed that the representation of experience may be entirely private, as in day-dreaming and solitary make-believe play. Here we represent possibilities to ourselves, usually pleasant or in some way satisfying possibilities, our evaluation of them going on simultaneously with—being in fact indistinguishable from—our representation of them. What we represent may be actual experiences from our own past, things that have happened to others but which we now transfer to ourselves, or merely possibilities of experience.

In this connection a word must be said about fairy tales and other fantasies that assume physically impossible happenings. Whether these are communicated to others or remain private their significance for our present purpose remains the same: the physical impossibility as such is not what we are most interested in; it is merely the least laborious and most vivid means of representing some quite possible piece of human experience. Everyone has a bit of luck from time to time: the three miraculous wishes provide a dramatic compression of that possibility and allow the consequences to be discussed. Anyone might be down-trodden and finally be given a helping hand and succeed in turning the tables; a fairy godmother is a vivid way of saying how delightful that would be. We may use Coleridge's phrase, perhaps, and say that the fairy tale involves a 'willing suspension of disbelief', but here, I think, the phrase means simply that we are acquiescing in a recognized technique of communication about the possibilities of life—the familiar 'suppose' technique of children's conversation. In the works of Hans Andersen this presentation and discussion of possibilities in human experience is always evident (and sometimes obtrusive); in the older traditional tales it may be less insistent and a little overshadowed at times by a simpler interest in wonders (which is not the same as an acceptance of the impossible). But it is probably never absent, even if to find it we have to go to psycho-analysis for a less obvious interpretation of the manifest story.

To return to day-dreaming and play, it must be noted that every degree of abandonment to the recalled or invented situation may occur. We may at times, as it were, give it no more than a sceptical glance, perhaps contrasting it immediately with our present situation; we may allow it to develop great vividness and yet remain only onlookers, never letting our real surroundings be far beyond the margins of attention and always being able at the least necessity to switch back to where we really are; or it may reach the extreme vividness, obliterating everything else, that the night dream possesses, and then, whether as day-dreamers or madmen, we have abandoned the role of onlooker and given ourselves up to hallucinated participation.

When we stop representing the possibilities of experience privately and begin to communicate them, two important features of social life arise. The first, occurring mostly among children, is co-operative make-believe play. The second is gossip.

In the former all who take part have combined in themselves the roles of both entertainer and audience: they are representing possibilities of experience—for instance of being teachers and children, hosts and guests, tradesmen and customers—and simultaneously in their role of audience, they are evaluating them. Make-believe play is a co-operative day-dreaming, and all that has been said concerning the gradual approach to hallucinated participation in day-dreaming applies here too. Especially it should be noted that in most make-believe play nothing approximating closely to hallucination ever does occur—the child too easily switches back from being a teacher or a mother and becomes a child playing a game of make-believe.

This is not to overlook the fact that some roles are preferred and competed for; it is more thrilling to contemplate the possibility that *I* am the teacher or mother than merely that someone is, or that you are. Here the term 'vicarious satisfaction' offers itself temptingly. I believe (though it is a difficult point, on which opinion naturally wavers) that we should reserve this term for hallucinated participation, and that hallucinated participation does not necessarily or usually occur in make-believe play. But this point is the nucleus of rather far-reaching psychological problems, and in an article of this length it must be neglected.

Gossip is the second method through which the possibilities of experience—reported or imagined—may be communicated and evaluated. Here the roles of entertainer and audience have been differentiated, and we can observe a faint approach towards formal entertainment (especially when a social group extrudes a recognized raconteur or wit). Gossip still differs from formal entertainment, however, in two ways. For one thing the roles of entertainer and audience are passed backwards and forwards from one person to another. And, further, the audience's attitude—of agreement, emphatic or qualified, or of disagreement—may be expressed directly and promptly to the speaker. But the essential fact in gossip as in entertainment is that the speaker who raises a topic is

presenting what he takes to be an interesting situation—actual or possible—in what he regards as an appropriate light. He expects his hearers to agree on the interest of the situation and the fittingness of his attitude, whether it be the hushed fascination with which he talks of cancer or his truculent satisfaction at the nation's increased armaments.

The playwright, the novelist, the song-writer and the film-producing team are all doing the same thing as the gossip, however innocent they may be of witting propagandist intentions. Each invites his audience to agree that the experience he portrays is possible and interesting, and that his attitude to it, implicit in his portrayal, is fitting. In the less developed levels of entertainment the process is chiefly one of reinforcing commonplace values in a trivially varied array of situations. In the representational arts, most obviously in literature, the author invites his audience to share in an exploration, an extension and refinement, of his and their common interests; and, as a corollary, to refine or modify their value judgments. (What he regards as a development, of course, they may consider retrograde.) If this development of interest and refinement of judgment occur at all in entertainment they occur so gradually, and with such careful consolidation of each change, as never to demand any great degree of plasticity in opinion or feeling from the audience. If any serious degree of exploration does find its way into an entertainment programme it is commonly claimed as 'art' by those who like it and decried as highbrow or immoral by the rest.

Where do these considerations lead? They answer no question, but they perhaps suggest a different formulation of some and draw attention to others that are neglected. They discourage attempts at oversimple statements of the difference between 'art' and 'entertainment', since they make it less certain that the arts or even the entertainments form a homogeneous category of quite the kind they are sometimes supposed to. They invite a rather more considered statement of the notions behind the terms active and passive in such contexts as this. And they suggest that the ideas of vicarious satisfaction and escape may deserve closer scrutiny.

This view of the onlooker's mode of activity also raises general questions of criticism. Are the same standards applicable in criticizing achievements in all four modes of activity—could the moralist, the philosopher or scientist, the critic of abstract design, the critic of literature and representational art all adopt the same guiding principles of criticism? If not, where do the differences lie? And to come nearer to literary criticism, is our taste in gossip the same kind of thing, or not, as our taste in films and trivial fiction? And is this latter continuous, or not, with our taste in literature? Few of these questions can be answered by yes or no, and an extended examination of them leads one into the area where abstract concepts go over into the concrete details from which they draw whatever life they may have.

33 What's the use? A schematic account of language functions

James Britton

A preliminary note

We shall be concerned in this article with the functions of extended discourse—a text or a piece of extended speech (not excluding dialogue). Thus, the notion of an overall function, a function that dominates in a hierarchy of functions, must be kept in mind.

We shall be concerned with 'typical function': necessarily so if we are to face up to the distressing facts that a speaker may have hidden and devious intentions in making himself heard; that he may fail to do what he intended; that the effect of an utterance may differ for each member of an audience; and that an utterance may set up a chain of consequences with no determinable cut-off point.

Our salvation lies in the notion of 'context' as Lyons has interpreted it:

> I consider that the idea of context as 'universe of discourse' (in Urban's sense) should be incorporated in any linguistic theory of meaning. Under this head I include the conventions and pre-suppositions maintained by 'the mutual acknowledgement of communicating subjects' in the particular type of linguistic behaviour (telling a story, philosophizing, buying and selling, praying, writing a novel, etc.) . . . (Lyons, 1963, pp. 83–84).

Thus 'the conventions and presuppositions maintained by the mutual acknowledgement of communicating subjects' provide a mature speaker or writer with a repertoire of known choices of function within our culture, and enable a mature listener or reader to recognize which choice has been made.

The rules of the game operate within 'the mutual acknowledgement of communicating subjects' and are therefore open to change. If advertisers, for example, insist on writing what seem to be fragments of

Source: *Educational Review* (1971), **23** (3), 205–19.

autobiography for the purpose of selling tours, additional rules come to be written in.

Some of the things we say suggest that we may use words to support more general ways of classifying or representing experience: more general and perhaps more elementary ways. Thus (as has often been noticed) we speak of 'sinking into despair' and 'rising to the height of our ambitions'; we 'fall into disfavour' and 'rise to an occasion', and we call education 'a ladder'. It seems likely that some general spatial sense of height and depth constitutes a non-verbal mode of classifying, and that this underlies the habits of speech by which the things we aspire to or strive for are located 'up above', while the things we shun or are at the mercy of are located 'down below'. (When we speak of 'the height of folly' or 'the height of the ridiculous', we are probably mocking some instance by giving it, so to speak, a prize—a booby prize.)

Certainly language, as a way of representing the world, is inextricably interwoven with other forms of representation. My example was trivial, but the statement is crucial, and takes us on to an even more important hypothesis, that what distinguishes man from the other animals is not language *per se*, but the whole process of representation.

It is the process of representation that makes a man's view of the world (if we interpret behaviour aright) so vastly different from that of the other animals who live in it with him. Indeed, to speak of an animal's 'view of the world' at all is probably misleading; whereas man's every response to the environment is likely to be mediated by his total view of the world as he knows it. By symbolizing, by representing to himself the world as he experiences it, man creates, if Cassirer is right, a retrospect which by projection gives him also a prospect (Cassirer, 1946, p. 38). In the human world, the here-and-now is set in a rich context, a world constructed of experiences derived from elsewhere and other times. In such a world, what goes away may be expected to come back, 'out of sight' does not mean 'out of mind', change need not be kaleidoscopic, and very little that happens to us will be wholly unforeseen.

I have laboured the point because I want to suggest that it is typically human to be insistently preoccupied with this world representation, this retrospect and prospect a man constructs for himself. It is of immense importance to him, I believe. It is his true theatre of operations since all he does is done in the light of it; his hopes for the future depend upon its efficacy; and above all his sense of who he is and what it is worth for him to be alive in the world derive from it. We might even say that he is more preoccupied with it than he is with the moment by moment interaction with environment that constitutes his immediate experience. A man's consciousness, in fact, is like the little dog with the brass band: it is for ever running ahead, or dropping back, or trotting alongside, while the procession of actual events moves steadily on.

Our world representation may owe its vividness to sense images and the symbols (however we think of them) that mark emotional categories: for its *organization* it relies very largely upon language. As we talk about events—present, past or imagined—we shape them in the light of, and incorporate them into, the body of our experience, the total. We may of course fail in our attempt to adjust the corpus and digest the new event: life does sometimes make irreconcilable demands upon all of us. To preserve the order, harmony, unity of our represented world we may ignore the recalcitrant event (or aspect of events); or we may, over a period of time, continue the effort to come to terms with it. Those who too readily ignore disturbing aspects of experience are destined to operate in the actual world by means of a represented world that grows less and less like it: and so the fool has his paradise.

The expressive function

If human consciousness is like the little dog with the brass band we may expect to find its volatile nature revealed in a man's expressive speech. Being more or less intimate, unrehearsed, such speech is free to follow the shifting focus of attention, clothing a speaker's preoccupations the more faithfully because it is committed to no other task, meets no demands but his own, takes for granted a listener's readiness to be interested both in the speaker and his message.

Expressive speech is language close to the speaker: what engages his attention is freely verbalized, and as he presents his view of things, his loaded commentary upon the world, so he also presents himself. Thus, it is above all in expressive speech that we get to know one another, each offering his unique identity and (at our best) offering and accepting both what is common and what differentiates us.

Secondly, it is in expressive speech that we are likely to rehearse the growing points of our formulation and analysis of experience. Thus we may suppose that all the important products and projects that have affected human society are likely to have been given their first draft in talk between the originator and someone who was sufficiently 'in the picture' to hear and consider utterances not yet ready for a wider hearing. Such a listener would ideally concern himself first with the speaker and his thinking, those mental processes that lie behind the utterance; though, having 'understood', he might take account also of the forms of the utterance itself and assist in its modification to suit a wider audience.

But of course our use of expressive speech is not limited to the original and far-reaching. It is our principal means of exchanging opinions, attitudes, beliefs in face-to-face situations. As such, I would judge it to be a far more important instrument for influencing each other and affecting public opinion and social action than any sermon, political speech, pamphlet, manifesto or other public utterance.

'Expressive' is one of the three principal language functions in the scheme I want to outline. It is a scheme that was worked out in the course of classifying some two thousand pieces of written work, in all school subjects, produced by boys and girls of eleven to eighteen, though its application is not confined to the written language. In order to explain the remaining terms, I need to refer back to the general theory with which I began.

The roles of participant and spectator

Once we suppose that man operates in the actual world by means of his representation of it, we can see for him an alternative mode of behaviour: he may operate *upon the representation itself* without seeking any direct effect in the actual world. We may in fact see in this formulation a way of describing a great deal of his spontaneous image-making. (Susanne Langer calls man 'a proliferator of images' and postulates a new need not recognized in the other animals, a 'need of symbolization'.) (Langer, 1960, p. 41.) These two kinds of behaviour seem to me essentially and interestingly different. (For a fuller discussion see Chapter II in my *Language and Learning*.) 'Operating in the actual world' I want to call 'being in the role of participant': 'operating directly upon the represented world' (improvising upon past experience, for example, or supplying gaps in our picture by drawing upon other people's experiences—but both taken up out of concern for our world picture and not as a means to some end in the actual here-and-now)—this I want to call 'being in the role of spectator'. Contrast Othello telling the story of his life to Desdemona and her father (where all three are in the role of spectator) with a beggar telling a hardluck story to enhance his appeal, or a historian reading a novel, or any other narrative, in order to check on a point of historical fact (each of them, in pursuing his own current ends through the agency of the narrative being in the role of participant).

To be in the role of spectator is to be concerned with events not now taking place (past events or imagined events), and to be concerned with them *per se* (as an interruption to or a holiday from the march of actual events) and *not as a means to some ongoing transaction with the actual.*

Suppose I recount an interesting experience to a friend—for his entertainment and my own pleasure in doing so. I shall continue to breathe, stand up, sit down, drink maybe, or eat, attend occasionally to what is going on around me—offer him another drink, move nearer the fire if I am cold, answer a child's question, and so on. But mentally I am 'living in the past'—these other things are seen as unattended background to, or interruptions of, what I am principally concerned to do; which is to rehearse in mind an experience that is not now going on, but has been experienced in the past.

What I feel as background or interruption to my spectator role activity is likely to be similarly felt by my listener. In other words, in sharing this past experience with him I induce him also to take up the spectator role. But it is an experience I had, he did not. It follows that I may similarly take up the role of spectator of experiences *I* have never had—and that, I suggest, is what I do when I read a novel or watch a film, or when I enter into possible future experiences in my day-dreaming.

When we use language to get something done, we are all in the role of participants—participants in a very general sense in the world's affairs: and, as we have suggested, this must be taken to include the use of language to recount or recreate real or imagined experience in order to inform, or teach, or make plans, or solicit help, or achieve any other practical outcome.

We must note finally that taking up the spectator role does not indicate any lack of involvement in the experiences being recounted: we do indeed 'participate' in the story or the fiction or the dream, but since the events that involve us are distinct from ongoing events, and not subordinated to ongoing events as means to end, this participation does not put us in the role of participant.

The three main categories

The two roles of participant and spectator are thus seen to represent two different relationships between what is being *said* (or written or thought) and what is being *done*, and to cover between them all uses of language. We see our three main function categories, Transactional, Expressive and Poetic, related to the two roles as follows:

Participant role		Spectator role
TRANSACTIONAL————EXPRESSIVE————POETIC		

When the demands made of a participant (in the world's affairs) are at a maximum, we have called the function 'transactional', a term that will need no explaining. Where the use of language in spectator role achieves its fullest satisfactions, we have called the function 'poetic', a term meant to include any example of the verbal arts. The expressive function straddles the participant/spectator distinction, but the dividing line at this mid-point is a shadowy one, and expressive language, as we have seen, is loosely structured, free to fluctuate. Thus, to modify an earlier example, if I recount the story of my recent holiday for your entertainment (and to enjoy it myself in retrospect), the talk is likely to be expressive, in the spectator role. If as you listen you become interested in the place I am describing as a possible holiday trip for yourself, you may ask for information about it— switching to participant role, but probably staying in the expressive. If, however, you pursue this line of enquiry and begin seriously to plan your holiday, your questions, directing my answers, may have the effect of shifting us both into transactional speech. A less likely alternative: if you were to become so interested in my account *as narrative*, and if under your encouragement I warmed to my task of constructing a story (and had the talent to do so), my language might move from the expressive to the poetic function. Finally (lest it appear that the expressive function operates only as a stage *en route* to something else) if as you listen to my talk we warm *to each other*, we may begin to exchange experiences, opinions, evaluations, and—now in spectator role, now in participant—intensify the reciprocal processes of exploring the other and revealing the self that constitute the expressive function of conversational utterance.

The poetic function

D. W. Harding long ago laid the foundations of the theory that associates literature with the role of spectator (Harding, 1937). He saw gossip and the novel as two instances of 'imaginary spectatorship in a social setting', and suggested that in each a *detached evaluative response* to the possibilities of experience was being offered by the speaker (writer) and invited of the listener (reader). 'The result', he said, 'is a vast extension of the range of possible human experience that can be offered socially for contemplation and assessment.' Though as participants we evaluate a situation in order to operate within it, as spectators we are able to relate events more amply to a broader spectrum of values. 'Detached and distanced evaluation is sometimes sharper for avoiding the blurrings and bufferings that participant action brings, and the spectator often sees the event in a broader context than the participant can tolerate. To obliterate the effects on a man of the occasions on which he was only an onlooker would be profoundly to change his outlook and values' (Harding, 1962, p. 136).

To put this point very simply: freed of a participant's need to *act* (to interact socially, to keep his end up, to turn events to his own advantage etc.), a spectator is able to attend more fully and more exclusively to the evaluative processes. I want now to add a new point within the same framework: freed of the necessity for action, a spectator is able to attend more fully to the utterance *as utterance*—that is to say, to its forms of language and to formal features of whatever the language portrays: the pattern of events in a narrative; the configuration of an idea or a theory; and, above all, the pattern of feelings evoked— the rise and fall of emotional tension, the succession of love, hate, anger, fear, relief, pity that may attend his response to the experiences portrayed. I say 'above all' because I believe Harding's view of the detached evaluative response may be enhanced by recognizing that the effect of feeling upon a participant has this marked difference from its effect upon a spectator. As we participate in events, feeling seems to operate primarily as a spur to action: we might even say that it discharges itself in action. As spectators, we hold it to savour it; and as we read on (or listen, or speak, or write), to savour not simply an emotion but the formal design created by a complex of emotions dynamically related.

If gossip and the novel are linked as exemplars of language in the spectator role, they are differentiated in the degree to which they realize the opportunities for formal organization. In our terms, most gossip will be expressive in function (as will be also the loosely autobiographical written narratives of the English lesson): the novel, the play, the poem, on the other hand, take on the poetic function in so far as they achieve the necessary degree of formal organization, formal unity. (What is the necessary degree will be an arbitrary decision related to the purpose of making an analysis.)

For the poetic utterance is a construct or artifact, a verbal object. To exaggerate the matter, as many poets and critics have done, its function is not *to say* but *to be*: or—more commodiously—where other utterances have *meaning*, a poetic utterance has *import*. This is a matter we shall return to in a moment.

The transactional function

Transactional language has two main sub-divisions which we have labelled, familiarly enough, *informative* and *conative*. The informative covers both the giving and the seeking of information; the full range of what is meant by 'information' takes us into considerable complications in the way of sub-categories. The conative is quite straightforward in theory since we have chosen to define it narrowly, but applying the distinctions in practice presents difficulties. For language to qualify as conative in function, the speaker's intention to change his listener's behaviour, opinions or attitudes must be deliberate and recognizable— recognizable, that is, to an observer, even where it is so disguised as to deceive a victim to whom it is addressed.

Transactional and poetic contrasted

Before describing further sub-categories of the transactional, let us attempt to clarify some of the major issues, first by briefly contrasting the two poles of the system, transactional and poetic language.

TRANSACTIONAL (Participant role)	POETIC (Spectator role)
The utterance is an immediate means to an end outside itself.	The utterance is an immediate end in itself, and not a means. i.e. it is a verbal artifact, a construct.
The form it takes, the way it is organized, is dictated primarily by the desire to achieve that end efficiently.	The arrangement *is* the construct, i.e. the way items are formally disposed is an inseparable part of the meaning of the utterance.
Attention to the forms of the language is incidental to understanding, and will often be minimal.	Attention to the forms of the language is an essential part of a listener's (reader's) response.
The speaker (writer) is concerned in his utterance to enmesh with his listener's relevant knowledge, experience, interests: and the listener is at liberty to contextualize what he finds relevant, selectively. This 'piecemeal contextualization' we take to be a part of the conventions governing transactional language.	The speaker (writer) is concerned to create relations internal to the utterance, and achieve a unity, a construct that is discrete from actuality. Thus he resists piecemeal contextualization; i.e. the conventions holding between speaker and listener in poetic language call for 'global contextualization'.

Contextualization of the poetic

The difference in mode of contextualization (the manner in which we relate what is in the utterance to what we know, think, feel already) is a crucial one. As we read a poetic text we must of course draw at all points upon our own experience in order to interpret what is on the page; but, if we are responding according to the conventions governing poetic language, our principle of selection and organization of this material will be one of subordination to every clue the text can offer us. This process, then, might be thought of as the converse of 'piecemeal contextualization'—in fact the converse of contextualization itself. When we have completed the structuring of the raw material of our own experience in obedience to the demands of the text—having as it were recreated the construct as a unity—we may then go on to relate its total import to our own experience as a whole, our general views and beliefs on the issues involved.

It is in this way that the artist with a message gets

his message across. A work that invites piecemeal contextualization must forgo the formal coherence and unity of the poetic construct: its message may be forceful, but it is not poetically conveyed: we should classify it as 'transactional'. On the other hand, the first thing to record about the poetic work is to classify it as 'poetic': however, we may then go on and allot it to a second category in accordance with the function that seems appropriate to its 'global contextualization'. We might for example call *1984* or *Catch 22* 'Poetic (Conative)'; C. P. Snow's *The New Men* or Patrick White's *The Tree of Man*, 'Poetic (Informative)'; and perhaps Lowry's *Under the Volcano* and Joyce's *Ulysses*, 'Poetic (Expressive)'. That the scheme should make room for such judgments is more important than that we should agree in making them—mercifully. And for the vast majority of works of literature all we shall need to say, or want to say, will probably be said in classifying them as 'Poetic'.

As far as satire is concerned, our claim that the poetic function should rank as primary is perhaps somewhat encouraged by the consideration that most of the satires that continue to be read concern themselves with causes which, if not lost, are at least won.

Sub-categories of the informative

Of the many possible ways of subdividing informative uses of language, we have chosen one based on James Moffett's analysis of the relation between a speaker and his topic: between the 'I' and the 'it', where 'I', 'you' and 'it' represent the three components of a communication situation (Moffett, 1968). He calls his analysis 'an abstractive scale', and sees it as operating in close interconnexion with a 'rhetorical scale' representing the range of relations between the 'I' and the 'you'. He marks off four positions on his abstractive scale, moving from the least to the most abstract, from the 'codification of our world that most nearly reflects the structure of that world to codification that more and more resembles the structure of the mind' (Moffett, 1968, p. 9). Here, more or less in the form that he gives them, are his four categories:

1 Recording: the drama of what is happening.
  Chronologic of perceptual selectivity.
  (e.g. an on the spot recording of what is happening before the guillotine.)
2 Reporting: the narrative of what happened.
  Chronologic of memory selectivity.
  (e.g. an eye-witness account of what happened one day during the French Revolution.)
3 Generalizing: the exposition of what happens.
  (e.g. a historical generalization about the Reign of Terror.)
4 Theorizing: the argumentation of what will, may, happen.
  Tautologic of transformation.
  (e.g. a political scientist's theory about revolutions.)
                (Moffett, 1968, pp. 34, 35 and 47.)

Having acknowledged a substantial debt (which will become obvious), I shall leave Moffett's account in bare outline and go into greater detail in explaining the modified form of scale we have used to subdivide our informative category.

But first to make a more general point: Moffett in fact applies his scale to all forms of discourse: we have used it where it seemed focal, where it systematized observed differences between utterances that seemed important. The relation between a speaker and his topic is likely to be crucial in the informative category, which is after all the category Jakobson called 'the referential function' and which he defined as 'focus upon the topic' (see Sebeok, 1960, p. 357). The scale might be applied to expressive discourse, but would not add a great deal of information, or to conative discourse, but somewhat irrelevantly. To apply it to poetic discourse would, I suspect, be to introduce an alien concept (and our notion of global contextualization will suggest reasons).

Basing our requirements on the data to be classified —the two thousand scripts collected from secondary schools—we finally introduced three transitional categories, making seven out of Moffett's four.
(i) *Record*. The speaker records what is going on *here and now*, and/or describes what is to be observed here and now. (Compare what is often called 'running commentary'.) The principle of organization is chronological or 'spatial' (qualitative, descriptive).

We have made the assumption that the prerequisite classifying processes are no more demanding if one says, 'The policeman's coat is blue with silver buttons' than if one says, 'The policeman is shouting and waving his baton': i.e. that *describing* is not *per se* a generalizing activity and thus related to the analogic in a way *narrating* is not.
(ii) *Report*. The speaker reports what went on or what was to be observed on a particular occasion at a particular place. The principle of organization is, again, chronological/spatial. Note that the speaker, since he takes up a retrospective stance, has a basis of selection not available to the speaker of *record*.

Some historical statements are in this category since they deal with directly observable events: e.g. 'In May 1836 an exploring expedition led by the surveyor-general attacked a party of aborigines killing seven and wounding four.' But more commonly, historical statements are generalizations based upon scattered observations and observations over a period of time: e.g. 'The record of relations between the settlers and the natives was an unhappy one.' Such statements, in themselves, are *analogic* (Category (v)). However, isolated sentences of either type are likely to be embedded in a text that contains both types: classification will in any case be in accordance with what seems to be dominant, and in this particular case a balance of analogic statements with related statements of report is likely to be characteristic of the best analogic discourse.

(iii) *Generalized narrative or descriptive information.* The speaker reports what goes on (or used to go on) habitually, or what might be, or have been, habitually observed over a series of occasions in a series of places. E.g. What we do on Sundays; what coffee-houses were like; how we get our water supply. Classes of events or of 'appearances' are organized on a chronological/spatial principle. This category thus marks the first step towards generalization, away from the particularity of report.

We include in this sub-category a great deal of everyday informational discourse, discourse in which the speaker generalizes from a number of observable events or procedures or concrete situations (e.g. recipes, practical hints, descriptions of simple processes or procedures).

(iv) *Analogic, low-level of generalization.* An arrangement of loosely related and low-level general statements: a concatenation or agglomeration of such statements, for example about the industries of Scotland or the effects of the Thirty Years War. The principle of organization, is, however, classificatory rather than chronological/spatial.

(v) *Analogic.* This, rather than (iii) or (iv), is Moffett's 'generalizing' category. Here generalizations are made and are related hierarchically or logically: i.e. the principle or organization is again classificatory, but more rigorously so than in (iv).

A great deal of scientific and historical discourse will come into this category, but it will include any attempt to relate statements on the basis of their respective levels of generality, from whatever areas of experience they may be drawn. E.g. 'The differences are large and variable. Taking an objective view of my parents as the adults I know best, an obvious difference is that I am at school learning, whereas they have left school and work. This means that they bring home the money and I do not. I am dependent on them and responsible to them.'

(vi) *Speculative* (*Analogic/tautologic*). This is another transitional category that seemed to be required since a great deal of open-ended speculation arises when a speaker makes, as it were, horizontal moves in his thinking—framing general hypotheses on the basis of general propositions—and yet does not reach conclusions which would provide a genuinely theoretical analysis.

(vii) *Tautologic* (*Moffett's 'theorizing'*). Here the systematic combining of abstract propositions leads to new conclusions, which form a further extension of the system or theory. The basis of organization is, in a strict sense, *theoretical*.

Though its claim to belong to this category can hardly be sustained on the evidence of one sentence, we judged the school-boy's piece from which this was taken to qualify for inclusion: 'The social life of man is characterized not by virtue of his being a tool-using animal but by virtue of his being a language-generating animal.'

At this point I imagine a reader might be tempted by a common common-sense to ask with me a low-level question: What then becomes of these high-level abstractions? Do they reverberate for ever in a perpetual tautology? And I suppose our answer should be along these lines: that we give them intellectual assent in so far as (1) we accept as valid the steps in thinking by which they were arrived at and (2) they support or strengthen important ideas or beliefs we already hold; and perhaps (3) they modify some lesser beliefs or replace them with ones that fit better into the total edifice: then presumably at some points in the whole network there will be tests applied which show whether the system works in practice, whether it provides reliable guidelines to choice at the level of behaviour.

What is important is to realize, as Moffett points out, that the more abstract processes derive from *and remain dependent on* those at lower levels. Thus, the series of categories from (i) to (vii) has clear developmental implications: to say this, however, is to broach an important aspect of our study which this article cannot attempt to deal with.

Sub-categories of the conative

We distinguish two sub-categories of the conative, *regulative* and *persuasive*. The regulative represents a direct exercise of influence, and it aims more often at affecting action or behaviour than at changing attitudes, opinions or beliefs. It covers on the one hand simple requests such as 'Pass the mustard', and on the other, rules and instructions issued to those obliged to obey them, and recommendations that carry the weight of authority or the force of a speaker's wishes.

It should be noted that recipe books, and a great many other varieties of technological discourse, may use a conative form, but since their function is informative they are classified in the informative categories.

In ordinarily polite society a request to pass the mustard is not expected to be refused: the regulative utterance is enough. In authority situations those giving the instructions speak in the expectation that they will be obeyed. Persuasive language, the second sub-division of the conative, is employed where no such expectation of compliance operates: usually because it is inappropriate, but sometimes in cases where the expectation has met disappointment, or the speaker has chosen not to invoke it although he might have done. Here the speaker's will is, as it were, diverted into an effort to *work upon* the listener in support of the course of action he recommends, or (more typically perhaps) the opinion, attitude, belief he is putting forward. Thus it is one strategy of persuasive language to foresee and counter possible objections, bringing the weight of logical argument to bear; it is another strategy to work upon a listener's feelings, employing perhaps the wiles of classical rhetoric, whether recognized as such or not.

What's the use?

So there it is—the outline of a scheme in progress (an appendix gives the category numbering). If it seems to us rather tenuous at times we take heart from the thought that we shall understand it much better when we have completed a study of the two thousand scripts and have applied it also to a four-year follow-up study of the school-work of about a hundred eleven-year-olds and a hundred fourteen-year-olds.

We believe it may offer one approach to the consideration of 'language across the curriculum'—an undertaking that must call into question some very general matters concerning teachers' objectives, as well as some very particular ones regarding the diverse linguistic demands made on children as they move from one lesson to another in the day's programme.

Of the general matters, it is the interrelationships of the main categories that interest us most—as well as the *interrelatedness* of the various linguistic demands and achievements. We would hope, for instance, that expressive language may be increasingly seen to play a key role in all learning (even the most subject-oriented)

as well as in learning to use language; and that the educational value of spectator role activities may come to be better understood and more convincingly argued. We see such activities indeed as reflecting a concern for 'the compleat man': for it is the corpus of an individual's experience that makes him the person he is; that generates the pluses and minuses of his fluctuating verdict on the world, his fluctuating acceptance of the human condition, his fluctuating faith in himself. And spectator role activities, across the whole range from expressive to poetic utterance, represent a concern for this corpus.

Appendix

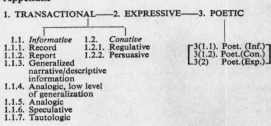

References

Britton, James (1970). *Language and Learning*. London: Allen Lane The Penguin Press.

Cassirer, Ernst (1946). (transl. Susanne K. Langer). *Language and Myth*. New York: Dover Publications.

Harding, D. W. (1937). The role of the onlooker, in *Scrutiny*, **6** (3), 247–58. Cambridge: Deighton Bell, reprinted here as chapter 32.

Harding, D. W. (1962). Psychological Processes in the Reading of Fiction, in *British Journal of Aesthetics*, II (2), 133–47. London: Thames & Hudson.

Langer, Susanne K. (1960). *Philosophy in a New Key* (3rd edition). Cambridge, Mass.: Harvard University Press.

Lyons, John (1963). *Structural Semantics*. Oxford: Blackwell.

Moffet, James (1968). *Teaching the Universe of Discourse*. Boston: Houghton, Mifflin & Co.

Sebeok, Thomas A. (ed.) (1960). *Style in Language*. New York: Wiley, for Jakobson, Roman, Linguistics and Poetics.

Acknowledgments

Acknowledgments are due to my colleagues in the Schools Council Writing Research Project: Miss Nancy Martin, Dr. Harold Rosen, Messrs. Tony Burgess, Dennis Griffiths, Alex McLeod and Bernard Newsome.

Set books for the Open University
Language and Learning course

Title	Author	Date	Publisher
Language in Education (Course Reader)	Cashdan, A. and Grugeon, E. (eds.)	1972	Routledge & Kegan Paul/ The Open University Press
Language, the Learner and the School	Barnes, D. *et al.*	1969	Penguin
Language and Learning	Britton, J. N.	1970	Allen Lane The Penguin Press
Freedom and Reason	Hare, R. M.	1963	Oxford University Press
Social Class, Language and Education	Lawton, D.	1968	Routledge & Kegan Paul
Speech and the Development of Mental Processes in the Child	Luria, A. R. and Yudovich, F. Ia.	1971	Penguin
Chomsky	Lyons, J.	1970	Fontana
Psycholinguistics	Slobin, D. I.	1971	Scott, Foresman

Index